INTERNAL AUDITING

INTERNAL AUDITING
Principles and Techniques

Richard L. Ratliff, Ph.D., CIA
University of Otago, New Zealand

Wanda A. Wallace, Ph.D., CIA, CPA, CMA
Texas A&M University

James K. Loebbecke, CPA
University of Utah

William G. McFarland, CPA
The Church of Jesus Christ of Latter-day Saints

The Institute of Internal Auditors
Altamonte Springs, Florida

ISBN 0-89413-167-2
Library of Congress Catalog Card Number: 87-61536

86399 6/88w
90011 1/90w
91017 2/91w
92137 9/92w
93184 10/93w
95305 2/95w

Foreword

The Institute of Internal Auditors has a primary responsibility to research, disseminate, and promote knowledge and information concerning internal auditing including internal control and related subjects. The benefits of this work are not limited to the 30,000 practitioners worldwide who are members of The IIA. As a student of internal auditing today, you are the practitioner of tomorrow, and it is critically important that you receive a solid foundation in the fundamentals of the profession. That's why, nearly five years ago, we commissioned *Internal Auditing: Principles and Techniques.*

The major focus of this book is risk, for risk is the primary consideration in determining what is audited and how audits are performed. In view of recent developments including rampant exposures of fraud and financial mismanagement, internal controls and risk assessment are more important than ever in the practice of internal auditing.

For those who are about to enter the profession of internal auditing, as well as those who are already practicing, a complete understanding of the risk-driven audit process is absolutely essential. *Internal Auditing: Principles and Techniques* is designed to provide that knowledge, as well as a complete overview of audit skills, applications, standards, and more.

When The Institute of Internal Auditors was founded in 1941, we chose "Progress Through Sharing" as our motto. This book has certainly put that motto into practice. We feel it is our responsibility to share knowledge with our colleagues as well as those who are on the brink of entering our increasingly important profession. We hope that you will benefit from this knowledge.

On behalf of The Institute of Internal Auditors, I would like to express our appreciation to the authors, Richard L. Ratliff, Ph.D., CIA; Wanda A. Wallace, Ph.D., CIA, CPA, CMA; James K. Loebbecke, CPA; and William G. McFarland, CPA, for their enthusiasm and perserverance with this project. Their contributions will surely lead you, the students of today and the practitioners of tomorrow, to a greater appreciation of the theory and applications of internal auditing.

Ronald L. Bell, CIA
Chairman of the Board
The Institute of Internal Auditors
1987-88

Preface

Students of internal auditing deserve a solid foundation in its theory and applications. This textbook, almost five years in the making, has been written with this primary focus in mind. The increase in the number of colleges and universities offering internal auditing courses, and the scarcity of teaching materials, prompted The Institute of Internal Auditors (IIA) to produce a textbook suitable for these courses and adaptable to a variety of teaching methods and course demands.

We have assumed that readers have completed a set of introductory business and economics courses, including microeconomics, basic financial and management accounting, marketing, management, corporate finance, computerized management information systems, and statistics. For this reason, we assume that most students studying this text are at least college juniors. The text may be used for upper-level undergraduate or masters-level courses.

The fundamental thesis of the text is that internal auditing is risk-driven. Risk is the primary consideration in determining what is audited and how audits are performed. The text discusses in detail a generalized audit process designed to provide the flexible structure necessary to allow risk to drive the process.

We have tried to keep faith with both the letter and the spirit of The Institute of Internal Auditors' official pronouncements, in the belief that these pronouncements have set a high standard for professional performance. We have also tried to provide room for adaptation to individual organizations.

The manuscript has undergone extensive review by college faculty members, internal auditing practitioners, and students. Much of the material has been presented to various professional seminars for discussion and evaluation. We believe that this material represents a reasonable consensus of what internal auditing is, but perhaps more importantly, an ideal of what it can be.

The text is divided into four major sections and includes three appendices. Section I introduces internal auditing, professional standards, and some basic concepts, including internal control systems and audit evidence. This section provides an important foundation for information included later in the text. Section II presents a detailed discussion of the general audit process and its management. Section III discusses three technical areas and skills that are important to internal auditors — human relations, sampling, and quantitative methods. Section IV discusses specific types of audit applications, including general operational, performance, compliance, financial, electronic data processing (EDP), and fraud auditing.

Appendix I outlines typical internal controls and sources of audit evidence for a few representative systems common to most organizations. These systems include marketing and sales, accounts and notes receivable, purchasing and receiving, inventory management, personnel and payroll, production and cost accounting, and facilities and equipment. Internal control systems for cash receipts and disbursements and for EDP systems are discussed in Chapters 16 and 17, respectively.

Appendix II reproduces The IIA's *Professional Standards Bulletins* for easy reference.

Appendix III includes individual case materials, each requiring approximately 12 to 25 hours to complete. These cases are designed as term projects. Most instructors are likely to assign between one and three of these cases in any one course of study. The five cases are provided to offer a selection that will be suitable to varying course needs.

We doubt that any one internal auditing course will cover all of the material presented in the text. Because of the varying course needs, we expect instructors to choose from the materials in order to best achieve their individual course objectives.

One course outline that has proven effective for an introductory upper-level undergraduate course covers Sections I and II, with one assigned case study from Appendix III. Where a second course is taught, Sections III and IV would be appropriate, with the remaining cases. Of course, additional readings from current periodicals also may be helpful. The text is designed as a self-contained unit and no additional materials are required, except as desired by the instructor.

We wish to thank the many college faculty members, internal auditing professionals, and students who have aided immensely in the preparation of this textbook. We especially wish to thank the late Leon Radde, CIA, CPA, former chairman of the board of The Institute of Internal Auditors, whose patient encouragement and high expectations were most valuable. We also wish to thank John Dattola, director of professional development for The Institute of Internal Auditors, and Karen Brogan, IIA editor, who orchestrated the book's production. We appreciate the valuable feedback provided by our review committee, including Dr. Glenn E. Sumners, John J. Fernandes, Dr. Thomas A. Gavin, Joe P. Marusak, and Chris P. Neck. Many students have spent hours studying the preliminary drafts of the text and the problems, and have provided invaluable feedback on how the material could be improved. We hope we have responded to their suggestions effectively. Finally, we appreciate the long hours spent by our typists, especially Dolores A. Donohoo, who devoted many evenings and weekends to preparing several drafts of the manuscript.

While we recognize the important contributions made by so many others, we also realize that we bear the responsibility for any shortcomings contained in this text, and we hope that there are few. May you thoroughly enjoy your study of internal auditing, and may it be an exciting, profitable adventure.

Richard L. Ratliff
Wanda A. Wallace
James K. Loebbecke
William G. McFarland

About the Authors

Richard L. Ratliff, Ph.D., CIA, is an associate professor of accounting at the University of Otago in Dunedin, New Zealand. He is a Certified Internal Auditor and former audit director for the Church of Jesus Christ of Latter-day Saints. Dr. Ratliff has led numerous seminars for The Institute of Internal Auditors and has published articles on auditing, finance, business, and education in professional and scholastic journals. He holds a doctorate from the University of North Carolina at Chapel Hill and has taught internal auditing for several years.

Wanda A. Wallace, Ph.D., CIA, CPA, CMA, is the Deborah D. Shelton Systems Professor of Accounting at Texas A&M University. She is a past recipient of the Wildman Gold Medal awarded to the most significant literary contribution to the advancement of public accounting over a three-year period by the American Accounting Association (AAA) and Deloitte Haskins & Sells. She has also won two AWSCPA Literary Awards. Dr. Wallace has authored seven books and over 60 articles in such journals as the *Accounting Review, Journal of Accounting Research, CPA Journal,* and the *Harvard Business Review.* She was awarded a Certificate of Distinguished Performance on the Certified Management Accounting Examination and the Highest Achievement Award (Gold Medal) on the international Certified Internal Auditor Examination. Dr. Wallace is a member of a joint task force of the AICPA and Canadian Institute of Chartered Accountants which is drafting practical guidance on applying the *Statement on Auditing Standards No. 9.* She is extremely active in the academic profession, screening applicants for Fulbright Scholar awards and serving on the editoral boards of five national journals. Dr. Wallace served on the 1982–1984 board of regents of The Institute of Internal Auditors.

James K. Loebbecke, CPA, is professor of accounting at the University of Utah Graduate School of Business and a former audit partner with Touche Ross & Co. He has served on the Auditing Standards Board of the American Institute of Certified Public Accountants and is a member of the American Accounting Association. He is the recipient of the 1987 Wildman Medal and the University of Utah School of Accounting's 1985–1986 Outstanding Teaching Award. Mr. Loebbecke is the co-author of several books and monographs on accounting- and auditing-related subjects and is a frequent contributor to major publications in the field.

William G. McFarland, CPA, is the Managing Director of Auditing for the worldwide activities of The Church of Jesus Christ of Latter-day Saints. Mr. McFarland previously held positions as audit executive and parter-in-charge, respectively, with the Salt Lake City and Spokane offices of Ernst & Whinney, where he was active in the firm's recruiting and staff-training programs. In recent years he has served on the Boards of Advisors of the

Schools of Accounting at Brigham Young University and the University of Utah, and as a member of the Dean's Advisory Council of the College of Business at Utah State University. Mr. McFarland is a graduate of Utah State University and is a member of The Institute of Internal Auditors, the American Institute of Certified Public Accountants, and the Utah Association of Certified Public Accountants.

Contents

SECTION I: INTRODUCTORY MATERIALS AND CONCEPTS

SECTION IV: TYPES OF AUDIT APPLICATIONS

APPENDICES

List of Exhibits

11 Follow-Up Reviews and Audit Evaluation

12 Internal Auditing Management

13 Human Relations

14 Sampling

15 Quantitative Methods for Auditors

SECTION I

INTRODUCTORY MATERIALS AND CONCEPTS

1 Introduction and Conceptual Foundation

Internal auditing is one of the most exciting, challenging, and dynamic professional opportunities available today. The profession is responding to a growing demand from top echelons of corporations, governments, and not-for-profit organizations. Managements of these organizations are seeking objective information about organizational activities, especially control over those activities. Consequently, internal auditors generally work "in the trenches" of key operations, often have the attention of top-level decision-makers, provide important information for management, and enjoy excellent pay and career opportunities.

Interestingly, most business and accounting students, as well as the general public, know very little about internal auditing. Internal auditors typically do not attract the public spotlight because of the relatively low profile usually required for the work. However, the high level of professional expertise required and the critical nature of their responsibilities place internal auditors in integral positions within many of the world's leading institutions.

This first chapter is intended to acquaint you with the field and to provide an introduction to the rest of the textbook, which covers a broad array of topics important to the study and practice of internal auditing. This chapter includes the following sections:

- An audit scenario.
- A brief background.
- The need for a conceptual foundation.
- Conceptual overview.
- Management responsibility.

The authors appreciate the helpful suggestions provided by Lewis F. Davidson and Rodney J. Redding on the material in this chapter concerning the relationship between risk and internal auditing.

3

- The internal auditing function.
- The internal auditing organization.
- Practical considerations.
- Careers in auditing.

An Audit Scenario

The following scenario describes an internal audit project performed for a large international construction company.

Management at the headquarters in Dallas noticed that construction costs per square foot of certain buildings had increased markedly and unexpectedly in recent months and requested an audit. Two auditors were assigned to audit the purchasing function for one of the company's South American offices.

The auditors interviewed the management in Dallas to clarify the nature and extent of the concerns. They studied available cost reports and more general economic data in search of possible clues to the problem. They examined previous audit reports, trying to determine if such a problem had been discovered by previous auditors. The auditors telephoned company management in South America for its assessment of the situation.

From this preliminary study, the auditors learned that no unusual or unexpected inflationary change had occurred in the local economy or in the local currency/U.S. dollar exchange rate. While a similar problem of unexpected cost increases had occurred two years earlier, it was attributed to locally high inflation and was short-lived. Local management blamed the current increased costs upon a dramatic increase in workload and inadequate staff needed to manage the increased load. They said that the heavier workload made adequate supervision of the work impossible; consequently, several projects had required extensive rework, and purchases were more difficult to control. Management was subcontracting and supervising the work instead of using contractors for the projects.

The management at headquarters said that the local office had been working at under capacity and that only recently had enough work been contracted to make operations there profitable. They felt that costs were not being carefully controlled.

The auditors decided that a trip to the local office in South America would help resolve the problem. They inspected several building projects, studied the local policies and procedures manuals, interviewed local management and construction supervisors, flowcharted the purchasing process, examined accounting records, and contacted several suppliers for information. The auditors discovered three problems:

1. The purchasing manager felt heavily pressured to supply materials, equipment, and subcontracted work on time, and recently stopped negotiating prices or seeking bids for major purchases. The purchasing manager began accepting first offers, which significantly increased the company's costs.
2. The auditors discovered a dozen large purchases for which the company had made double payments, due to payment of subsequent invoices sent by suppliers after the first invoice already had been paid.
3. A bug in a new computerized accounting system assigned triple the correct amount of overhead costs to projects.

While the last problem did not actually increase costs, it distorted the reported cost figures. The first two problems did affect costs.

The auditors met with local management in South America to discuss their findings. After returning to Dallas, they met with management at headquarters and prepared a written report of the audit. Appropriate changes were made at the local office in South America, and although total costs increased because of more projects, the cost per square foot decreased to an acceptable amount.

This scenario illustrates one of many possible examples of internal auditing. Not all internal audits involve international operations; two auditors are not necessarily standard; many audit techniques are available to choose from; and not all problems are so easily solved. Also, internal auditors for different organizations may have somewhat different responsibilities.

The example does, however, offer some perspective as to the nature of internal auditing work, the extensive involvement with management, and the variety of internal auditing challenges.

Brief Background to Internal Auditing

While internal auditing has been performed for centuries, it has come to be recognized as a modern profession only during the past approximately 40 years. In 1941, The Institute of Internal Auditors was founded in New York City when 25 internal auditors agreed upon the need for an organization to help them share their common concerns and interests. Prior to that time these internal auditors met only on an informal basis with limited contact with others who had similar positions. They discovered that even though they were working in different businesses and industries, they had some remarkable commonalities, suggesting the need for a more formal, ongoing relationship.

Some changes have occurred since those early years, but The IIA has continued to serve as the principal vehicle for promoting the profession. IIA headquarters has since been moved to Altamonte Springs, Florida. The IIA has grown to more than 30,000 members, serves as the profession's standards-making entity, and administers a certification program for internal auditors. The IIA also conducts conferences worldwide as well as continuing education seminars and programs. Largely through the efforts of The IIA, the profession of internal auditing has acquired the respect and trust of both government and industry in providing an internal, objective review and evaluation of organizational activities.

Molding Forces

In an effort to comply with the Foreign Corrupt Practices Act passed into law by Congress in 1977, corporate managers have looked to internal auditors on an ever-growing scale. Applicable to publicly and privately held U.S. firms and to foreign companies filing statements with the Securities and Exchange Commission (SEC) of the U.S. government, the Act prohibits the practice of offering bribes to officials of foreign countries for favorable treatment. The Act also requires companies that report to the SEC to keep reasonably complete and accurate accounting records, and to maintain adequate internal controls to ensure that transactions are properly authorized, that financial statements are properly prepared, and that assets are safeguarded. The Act also was passed to help prevent secret slush funds and bribery. The Act provides that if firms fail to meet its provisions, they may be subject to fines; in addition, corporate managers are individually subject to uninsurable fines and to jail sentences.

Although the use of internal auditors is not specified by the law, such use provides management with a convenient, effective means of trying to meet the law's requirements.

The federal government also employs a strong internal auditing function that is managed by the Comptroller General of the United States — the General Accounting Office (GAO). The GAO sets its own standards of auditor performance through the Comptroller Generals's office.

Business management and government are but two of many forces that have influenced the profession's development. Other examples also help illustrate these different forces.

The increasingly thorough and sophisticated procedures required for external audits have been driving up audit costs for years. Management and CPA firms have searched for suitable ways to reduce these costs and still maintain adequate audit coverage and quality. Internal auditors, often hired from CPA firms, have been used as a partial answer to this search for cost-reduction measures.

The New York Stock Exchange (NYSE), the SEC, and the American Institute of Certified Public Accountants (AICPA) have led a concerted effort to persuade corporations to establish audit committees comprising independent members of the boards of directors. Ideally, members of these audit committees do not have management duties within the corporations. They are called "outside directors." Such audit committees have been appointed for the nation's largest corporations.

The responsibilities of these committees generally include the selection of the companies' public accountants (external auditors) and the review of internal auditing performance. They usually supervise the selection of internal auditing department directors and review the time and expense budgets for internal auditing departments prior to each budget period.

The argument for audit committees states that outside directors can preserve a higher degree of freedom from management influence (called "independence") for the two auditing functions than normally exists when operating management is solely in charge of those functions. Most of the profession's leaders believe that such independence helps preserve objectivity and freedom from distorted audit results.

Management's need for objective, quality information extends beyond purely financial information. The combination of internal auditors' competence and independence and the highly integrative nature of operations has prompted an evolution toward a more comprehensive internal audit function, including the examination of administration, operations, accounting, and financial management.

Several different types of internal audits may be conducted that reflect this broad, comprehensive perspective:

- Audits of accounting records.
- Audits of operations, projects, or programs.
- Audits of organizational performance.
- Audits of computerized information systems.

The Need for a Conceptual Foundation

The practice of internal auditing in a growing number of different organizations and industries has prompted concern among the profession's leaders and spokesmen for the development of a body of governing principles. Internal auditors are responsible to managements who define the nature and the extent of internal auditing duties in their respective organizations. "Management" in this case includes operating management and the board of directors. A good conceptual foundation can assist management and professional auditors in evaluating the appropriateness of assigned responsibilities.

Standards for Practice

A general conceptual framework cannot provide the detailed guidance required to practice internal auditing. Standards for practice help form a bridge between theory and specific audit procedures. Standards written without a clear, formalized conceptual basis are little more than arbitrary rules. Eventually they are likely to prove to be inconsistent. On the other hand, standards are likely to improve the auditing process when they rest upon a sound conceptual basis. This chapter describes a conceptual overview of internal auditing, and Chapter 2 discusses the application of these principles in formalized standards adopted by The IIA.

Performance Evaluation and Comparisons

We have mentioned that different internal auditing practices may exist in different organizations. A conceptual foundation offers a structure in which to study and understand these differences. It also offers a reference by which to measure the quality of internal auditing departments. Such a reference helps management to evaluate the performance of internal auditing departments, and it helps compare the performance of internal auditing departments in different organizations. These evaluations and comparisons are made in the normal evolution of individual internal auditing functions and of the profession as a whole.

Conceptual Overview

Exhibit 1-1 illustrates a conceptual overview of internal auditing. Consideration begins with management, which has the responsibility for planning, organizing, and directing the organization's activities. This responsibility may be viewed as control over those activities. Internal auditing emerges from this management control function. Further, it may be characterized by its primary objective, the dominant factor driving its various activities, and its relationships to other functions in and affiliated with the organization.

The primary objective of internal auditing is to provide an appraisal of the organization's controls to facilitate management. The relative risk of various activities is the single most critical factor in directing the internal auditing function. Relative independence from other functions provides internal auditors with the objectivity and the status necessary to effectively fulfill their responsibilities. The following sections expand these basic propositions to provide a more thorough conceptual overview.

```
┌─────────────────────────────────────────────────────────────┐
│                         Exhibit 1-1                           │
│          Conceptual Overview of Internal Auditing            │
│                                                               │
│      ┌─────────────────────────────────────────────┐         │
│      │           MANAGEMENT CONTROL                 │         │
│      └─────────────────────────────────────────────┘         │
│                           │                                   │
│      ┌─────────────────────────────────────────────┐         │
│      │            INTERNAL AUDITING                 │         │
│      │  •  Primary Objective: Appraisal of Controls │         │
│      │  •  Primary Determinant of Activities: Relative Risk │ │
│      │  •  Means of Fulfilling Responsibilities: Independence │
│      └─────────────────────────────────────────────┘         │
└─────────────────────────────────────────────────────────────┘
```

Management Responsibility and Control

The basic precepts of internal auditing rest on an understanding of organizational management, which has three basic responsibilities. It plans, organizes, and directs the activities of the organization in order to achieve organizational objectives and goals.

Planning involves establishing objectives and goals and charting a preferred method of utilizing resources and functional components intended to achieve those objectives and goals. Resources include manpower, facilities and equipment, materials, and money. Components typically include organizational functions such as marketing, production, and accounting.

Objectives here represent broad, general statements of what management intends to accomplish. Goals represent specific, measurable targets along the path to accomplishing objectives. As an example, suppose a company has the objective of acquiring the largest share of the medicated shampoo market in the western United States. It might establish goals of 6 percent of the market by the end of the first year, 12 percent by the end of the second year, and 22 percent by the end of the third year of its drive.

Organizing means gathering the required people, facilities, materials, and funds and arranging them within the functional components, subject to a framework of policies, plans, and standards, in such a way that the objectives and goals can be achieved.

Directing means authorizing, instructing, and monitoring performance, and periodically comparing actual to planned performance. Directing also includes documenting (1) the exercise of authority, (2) compliance with policies, procedures, and standards, (3) the supervision, observation, and testing of activities, and (4) the performance of planned activities.

Categories of Management Responsibility

The responsibilities of management may be considered within the structure of three categories — strategic, tactical, and operational. All three levels require planning, organizing, and directing activities. The differences among the three levels primarily involve differences in breadth of concern and time frame. Typical *strategic* issues might include the following:

1. The nature of the business to be conducted by the organization.
2. The market at which the organization will aim its sales of products or services.
3. The image that the organization hopes to acquire and maintain.

Typical *tactical* issues might include:

1. The extent to which the management information system is computerized.
2. Timing policies for shipments of goods to customers.
3. Product distribution methods.
4. Recruitment of new managers.

Typical *operational* issues might include:

1. Materials needed for a production cycle.
2. Specific personnel assignments.
3. Production quotas.

Strategic management focuses on the broadest, the most global, and the longest-term issues. Tactical management focuses on how to accomplish overall strategy. Tactical management's interests are medium range and more focused on specific organizational components. Operational management's interests are specific day-to-day tasks required to get the work done.

It may appear that top managers are responsible only for strategic management, middle managers only for tactical management, and lower-level managers only for operational management. In reality, while each layer of management may focus primarily on these respective responsibilities, activities are so heavily integrated and coordinated that each layer of management plays some role at all three levels — strategic, tactical, and operational.

In very small organizations all management functions are performed by a single person. As organizations become larger, however, the total management function requires more people. At that point, more structure may be imposed upon the organization. Activities within the structure are subject to established policies, standards, and procedures, which can be thought of as a pervasive network of system controls, generally called *internal controls.* These controls are employed to maintain effective control over activities and operations. "Control" implies a general condition, while "controls" are methods used to achieve the condition.

Control Objectives   All management activities may be viewed within the context of control systems, the objectives of which are:

1. The reliability and the integrity of information.
2. Compliance with policies, plans, procedures, laws, and regulations.
3. The safeguarding of assets.
4. The economical and efficient use of resources.
5. The accomplishment of established objectives and goals for operations and programs. (See General Standard 300, *Standards for the Professional Practice of Internal Auditing* , IIA, 1978.)

The better the management, the more effectively the five basic control objectives are likely to be achieved.

The Internal Auditing Function   The increased complexity in larger organizations gives rise to the need for a management device to monitor the control system itself. Management seeks assurance that the control systems are functioning satisfactorily. If controls are inadequate and not operating properly, then regardless of how well management has planned, the organization may be in danger.

Management is responsible for the organization's internal control, and increasingly utilizes internal auditors to monitor the performance of the organization's control systems. The auditors serve as a feedback mechanism for the management function.

But what should the governing principles be in the development of the internal auditing function? The following discussion outlines some of these principles that constitute the conceptual basis for establishing an internal auditing function. Although this initial discussion is somewhat idealistic, later sections discuss some "real-world" considerations that often modify the applications of these principles.

Nature of Auditing Responsibility

Given that internal auditing is limited primarily to the control system, what is the nature of its responsibility within that sphere of activity? There are four possibilities:

1. Formulation of controls.
2. Implementation of controls.
3. Testing operational compliance with controls.
4. Evaluation of controls.

Exhibit 1-2 outlines areas of management that typically are responsible for these four activities. Administrative and operational management traditionally formulate the control system. Operational management implements controls and tests compliance of operations with prescribed controls on a day-to-day basis. Internal auditing tests that compliance. Administrative and operational management continually evaluate the control system, searching for possible improvements. Internal auditing also evaluates the adequacy and effectiveness of the control system, but generally more systematically and more thoroughly than management does.

Exhibit 1-2
Nature of Audit Responsibility

POSSIBLE RESPONSIBILITIES FOR CONTROLS	AREA OF MANAGEMENT PRIMARILY CONCERNED
Formulation of Controls	Administrative Management Operational Management
Implementation of Controls	Operational Management
Testing Compliance with Controls	Internal Auditing Operational Management
Evaluation of Controls	Internal Auditing Administrative Management Operational Management

An illustration may help point out the differences among the four responsibilities for controls — formulation, implementation, compliance tests, and evaluation. The financial vice president and the controller's office are likely to develop the policies and procedures for paying a company's debts. This work constitutes the formulation of that part of the financial control system.

The controller's office trains and supervises employees who are expected to follow the policies and procedures. The training and supervision constitute the implementation of the controls.

The controller, with the help of various assistant controllers and clerks, monitors the activities of the accounts payable department on a daily basis. The internal auditing department periodically examines whether the policies and procedures are being followed. These efforts represent tests of compliance.

Finally, the vice president and the controller generally reconsider policies as problems arise and during budgeting and performance reviews. The internal auditors also review the policies and procedures to determine if they are well-designed and if they actually facilitate prompt payment of debts, in the right amounts, for items representing legitimate claims on the company. These latter functions constitute the evaluation of the controls.

The formulation and implementation of controls are part of management's decision-making and operating functions. If internal auditing were to become involved in either of these activities, the ability of the auditor to objectively test and evaluate those controls would be jeopardized. It is difficult to maintain an unbiased, objective attitude in a critical examination of one's own work. Consequently, these logical limits restrict the internal auditing function to (1) testing compliance with prescribed internal controls and (2) evaluating those controls, although the evaluation may occur in the design, the implementation, or the operational stages.

Two Dimensions for the Evaluation of Control Systems   Internal auditors evaluate two dimensions of the control system — the design and the effectiveness. A well-designed control system is one that gives adequate assurance that the organization's objectives will be achieved at a reasonable cost. An effective control system is one that accomplishes what it was designed to do.

A poorly designed system may be effective only because the people involved are able to make it work. On the other hand, a well-designed system may be ineffective if the people trying to make it work do not understand it. It is the auditor's job to evaluate both aspects.

Evaluation of controls may be made at the formulation stage as well as at the post-implementation stage. Auditors are sometimes called upon to review proposed controls before implementation. Often, if there are problems, it is more economical to discover them early.

The Extent of Auditing Responsibility

In order to understand the extent of the auditors' responsibility, it helps to understand, at least conceptually, the ways that organizations may be controlled. Examples of the various internal means of control may be illustrated as follows:

1. Management style.
2. Organizational objectives.
3. Policies.
4. Standards.
5. Procedures.

These examples represent different degrees of detail in the control system, and they are essentially hierarchical in nature. Procedures are the most detailed means of control. Management style, a less precise concept, represents the other end of the control spectrum.

Each successive level of control is likely to evolve from the previous level. From a particular management style, organizational objectives will be developed, followed by policies, standards of performance, and finally, detailed operational procedures. Such a top-down process helps to ensure consistency from one level to the next.

The Auditor's Concern. Because of the highly integrative nature of controls, internal auditors often examine all levels and means of internal control. However, upper-level line managers and executive management traditionally have assumed responsibility for the evaluation of organizational performance in terms of objectives and management style.

Performance evaluation is a part of the control system. But rather than making the evaluation, internal auditors are responsible for determining whether the methods of evaluation are appropriate. These methods may be expressed in the form of policies, standards, and procedures. Management makes performance evaluation decisions. Internal auditors evaluate the decision process, generally stopping short of evaluating an individual manager's performance.

Levels of Authority. Earlier in this chapter, we mentioned three different categories of management concerns — strategic, tactical, and operational. The approach to internal auditing outlined in this chapter leads to the development of an internal auditing function with authority to examine controls at all levels of activity, as illustrated in Exhibit 1-3.

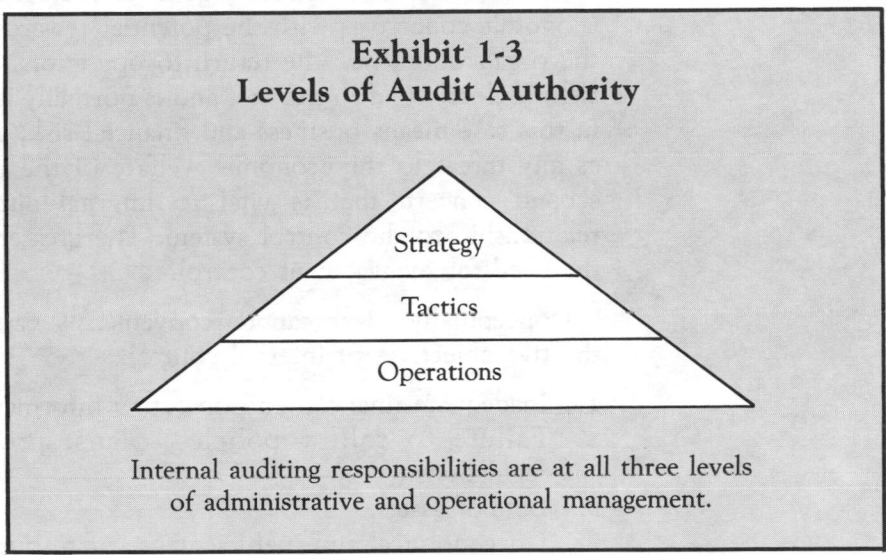

**Exhibit 1-3
Levels of Audit Authority**

Strategy

Tactics

Operations

Internal auditing responsibilities are at all three levels
of administrative and operational management.

All five internal control objectives may occur at all levels of organizational activity. Internal auditors are concerned with all of these control objectives. Consequently, they may examine all levels of management and operational control.

The Concept of Direction — What and When to Audit

Auditors must answer three questions: What should they audit? When should they audit it? For what purpose do they audit? First, the auditors should audit that part of the control system that produces the most benefit for the costs incurred. The costs include the audit staff's time and related expenses, such as travel. The benefits accrue from significant findings that improve control over key aspects of business operations. More importantly, benefits accrue from finding trouble spots and avoiding would-be losses.

There also is a benefit from the "threat value" of an audit. Even when there are no deficiencies found during an audit, the fact that members of the organization know that their activities are likely to be audited periodically often motivates improved performance and better internal control.

In many cases the relative costs of conducting audits of various operations are not significantly different. Consequently, the main factor governing the allocation of internal audit resources is the risk of failing to achieve one or more of the internal control objectives.

How Risk Influences Audit Direction. Management's first economic concern is with the potential rewards that are available to the organization, i.e., the return to operations. The second concern, risk, is closely tied to the first and is normally just as important. Risk in this case means business and financial risk, and it may be defined as any threat to the economic welfare of the organization. It is this second concern that is vital to internal auditors because of its relationship to the control system. The greater the risk, the greater the need for management control.

Conceptually, risks can be conveniently categorized according to the five objectives of internal control:

1. Inadequate financial and operating information.
2. Failure to follow policies, plans, procedures, laws, and regulations.
3. Loss of assets.
4. Uneconomical and inefficient use of resources.
5. Failure to achieve objectives and goals.

Some risks are extremely difficult, even impossible, to control, but management usually can buy insurance to minimize possible losses. In other cases, management simply may require a higher economic return as compensation for assuming increased uninsurable risk.

In general, then, management seeks to minimize risks by (1) increasing system controls, (2) insuring possible losses, and (3) seeking greater returns when greater risks are assumed.

In determining when to audit, internal auditors assess not only the type of risk, but more importantly, how much risk is present. They might screen the entire organization, assess the relative risks associated with the various activities, and rank the activities in order of their relative levels of risk. Activities of greater risk are then examined first.

Two key factors enter into the auditor's ranking of risks. First, how much potential loss is present? Second, what is the probability of a loss actually occurring? The level of risk is a combination of these two factors. Of course, risk may also be considered from the positive side. Rather than considering only potential losses, internal auditors also consider potential payoffs with their associated probabilities; i.e., a lost potential payoff is similar in nature to a loss actually incurred, and the relative risk of such a loss should be considered.

Risk Measurement   The monetary measurement of risk may be virtually impossible to determine. For example, the amount exposed to loss in planning a new product for sale may be impossible to quantify with precision. Often there are methods of making reasonable estimates, but exactness is more difficult. Likewise, the exact probability that a loss will occur is impossible to calculate with currently available methods, although later chapters discuss some methods that are useful in quantifying risks.

Consequently, any estimate of risk is just that — an estimate. Any initial estimate of risk for a particular area is subject to limited information. The initial estimate of risk is merely a "first pass" at ranking the possible activities to be audited. It is unlikely that the auditors' first assessment of risk will remain entirely consistent with later assessments. As more information is made available, reassessments and comparisons of risk will be needed.

Even with these qualifications, initial estimates of risk can be useful. The exercise of identifying key risk areas has value, since management may not know what types of risk are present for various activities. In addition, the evaluation and comparison of the relative magnitude of the operation's risks, however subjective, can offer valuable guidance in planning the auditing process.

Consider, for example, three areas of risk and their estimated potential losses. In the first case, assume that there is an estimated $6 million in inventory that could be stolen. In the second case, assume that a potential loss of sales due to poor product quality has been estimated to be $10 million. In the third case, assume that an estimated $25 million in loans could be lost to the company if there were poor payment practices on previous loans.

If we were to judge risks based only upon the amounts of the potential losses, the first concern to internal auditors would be debt management, followed by product quality control, and finally, inventory management.

Suppose the internal auditors have reviewed the probability of loss in each case. They believe that the probability of inventory being stolen is as much as 75 percent, meaning that three out of every four of the inventory items are likely to be taken illegally, without payment. They believe that the probability of loss of sales due to poor product quality is perhaps 40 percent. Further, they estimate that the probability of a loss of new loans is very low (no more than 1 percent) because of an excellent payment record on past loans and the company's strong financial statements. Exhibit 1-4 illustrates the combined effect of the estimated potential losses and their respective probabilities of occurrence on risk.

Exhibit 1-4
Risk Assessment Chart

ORIGIN OF RISK	TYPE OF RISK	EPA[1]	EPL[2]	ER[3]
Theft of Inventory	Loss of Assets	$ 6,000,000	High: .75	$4,500,000
Loss of Sales Due to Poor Quality of Product	Noncompliance with Set Standards	$10,000,000	Medium: .40	$4,000,000
Loss of New Funds from Lenders Due to Poor Payment Practices	Inefficient Operations	$25,000,000	Very Low: .01	$ 250,000

[1]EPA means estimated potential amount.
[2]EPL means estimated probability of loss.
[3]ER means estimated risk. (EPA times EPL equals ER.)

The formulation of risk may be expressed mathematically as:

$$R = pr(E)$$

where R is the risk, E is the amount of exposure (i.e., the potential loss expressed in monetary units), and pr is the probability of loss due to the ineffectiveness of the control system.

Although the loss of new funds is potentially higher than losses in the other two areas, the very low probability of that loss reduces the risk significantly. In fact, the order of the risk estimates reverses when the probabilities are considered.

The factor that most affects the probabilities is internal control. Good controls reduce the probability of loss and, therefore, risk. Poor controls increase the probability of loss.

Organizational Relationships That Influence the Audit Function

The discussion so far has strong implications for how the internal auditing function interacts with other groups related to the organization. These groups include, among others, administrative and operational management, the board of directors, and external auditors.

Management vis-à-vis Internal Auditing. The term "management" here is meant to designate the operating executives of an organization rather than the board of directors. In order to maintain objectivity, internal auditing must remain independent of operations and the decision-making processes of the organization, and should remain independent of undue influence by management.

We already have addressed the need to remain independent of the decision-making process, but the need to remain independent of undue management influence warrants further explanation. The auditor's objectivity could be jeopardized by any perceived or real intimidation by management personnel who might be affected by audit findings. Should these personnel be in positions to influence the internal auditor's compensation, promotion, or tenure, the auditor might be unwilling to be critical of them, despite the appropriateness of such criticism. Also, if the auditor has a psychological affiliation with management (i.e., he or she feels like a "member of the management team"), then the auditor's independence, and therefore objectivity, can be at risk.

An important question arises as a result of this need for independence from management and decision-making. Who are the constituents of internal auditing?

Traditionally, managers have been the primary constituents, with external auditors and, more recently, boards of directors as secondary constituents. The approach described in this chapter promotes boards of directors as primary constituents of internal auditing, along with executive, middle, and operational management.

Conceptually, internal auditing should not report administratively to management. Internal auditing may retain a reporting responsibility to management, but it may better maintain its primary responsibility to a higher authority, such as the board of directors. Theoretically, this arrangement permits operating management to work through the board of directors to have internal auditors examine matters of concern.

Top executives frequently sit on boards of directors and are often in control of those boards. In such cases it makes little difference whether the internal auditors report to the board or to executive management, since the two are effectively the same. When there are some outside directors, auditor independence is easier to establish and maintain.

Boards of Directors — A Governing Force. A board of directors of an organization bears the final responsibility of management. While members of boards may be called by various names — "directors," "trustees," "commissioners," etc. — their functions are about the same. Although the nomenclature is not always clear, corporations generally have directors, government bodies have commissioners, and not-for-profit organizations have trustees. Sometimes not-for-profit organizations call their board members "governors."

This level of management sets the broad purposes of operations, and those purposes guide how control systems should be designed and monitored. The separate, yet congruent, roles of differing management levels create "cause and effect" forces within the organization, which in turn create needs for "checks and balances." These natural forces create a need for the independence of internal auditing from operational management, since any management lower than the board level may act contrary to system objectives.

For example, research studies have strongly suggested that individual managers often behave in ways that will secure their own personal interests rather than promote the ultimate welfare of the entire organization. Consequently, the managers' long-term horizons may be much shorter than the board's.

Suppose a plant manager perceives that his chances of advancement are enhanced if production costs are minimized. If the manager cuts costs at the expense of product quality, the firm's sales eventually could be adversely affected. The manager's "ultimate" objective was advancement. The board's objective was probably something more like market share growth. The two objectives are not necessarily consistent.

Also, a manager may want to avoid risks that might jeopardize his or her own position in the organization if the results were to turn out badly. In contrast, board members might prefer taking some risks when the potential payoffs are high enough to compensate for the risks.

This problem of maintaining goal congruence among different levels of management has long plagued organizations. It also has occupied the interests of researchers in both management and accounting. The control system should foster goal congruence. Independent internal auditors can evaluate goal congruence among different levels of the organization more objectively than internal auditors who are not independent of management.

Audit Committee — A Linkage with the Board. The advent of audit committees comprising outside directors as members to oversee the audit function further enhances the internal auditor's independence from management. The stronger the tie between the audit committee and the internal auditing function, the greater the likelihood of independence and resultant objectivity in audit examinations and reports. The audit committee should at least be responsible for supervising the hiring, promotion, and compensation of the head of the auditing department. Overseeing the development of the internal auditing function is a major responsibility of the audit committee; auditing policies, standards, and procedures should also be approved by the committee.

Exhibit 1-5 illustrates the ideal differentiation between internal auditing's administrative and reporting responsibilities. Notice the direct administrative link between internal auditing and the board of directors through the audit committee.

In this illustration, there are four levels of management instead of the three outlined earlier in the chapter. That is because the strategic management function is performed primarily by two organizational bodies — the board of directors and executive management. The relationship of internal auditing to these two bodies is easier to illustrate by separating them in the diagram.

This arrangement maximizes the usefulness of internal auditing by making auditing information available to all members of the organization who need it, while at the same time preserving the objectivity of that information.

External Auditors vis-à-vis Internal Auditors. "External auditing" refers to audits of financial statements performed by CPA firms. The primary purpose of these audits is to attest to the integrity of the financial statements. The board of directors contracts with a CPA firm to perform this work. Because the CPA firm is a business organization separate from the organization whose financial statements are being audited, the auditors performing these audits often are called "independent auditors."

"Internal auditing" refers to audit work performed by a staff of professional auditors who are employees of the organization being audited. Although internal auditors maintain a degree of independence from the activities they audit in order to preserve their

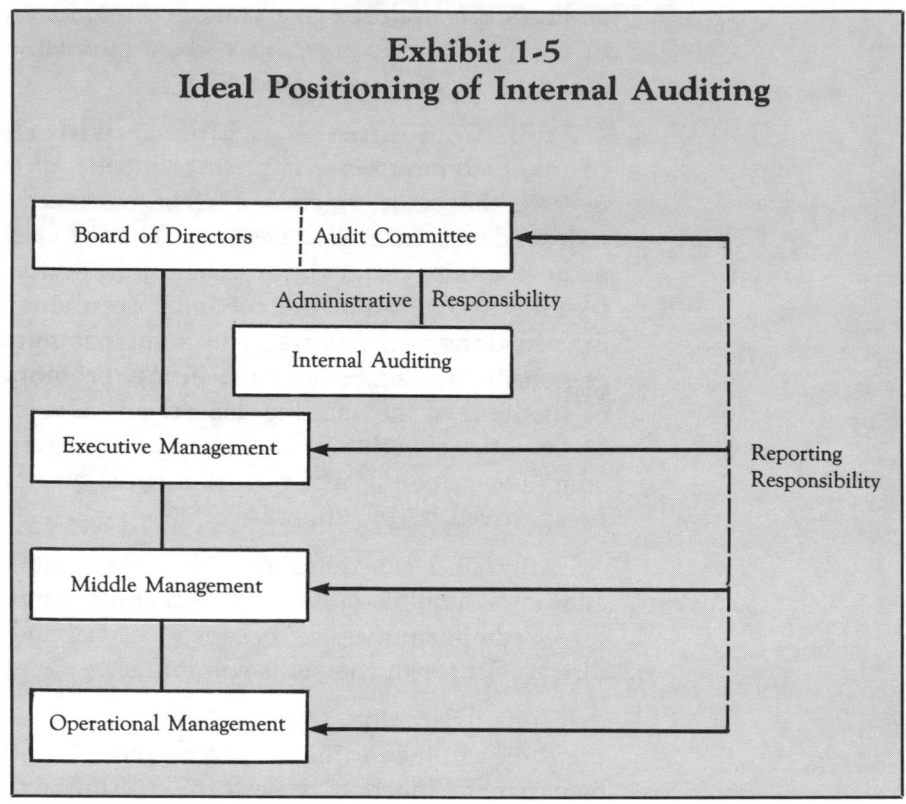

Exhibit 1-5
Ideal Positioning of Internal Auditing

objectivity, the term "independent auditors" is reserved for external auditors. The range of internal auditing activities is extremely broad, extending throughout the organization into every aspect of operations and involving all levels of authority. The external audit, however, focuses primarily upon the financial accounting system and those organizational activities which can have a direct material effect upon the financial statements.

It may be convenient to think of internal auditing activities as falling into two broad categories: (1) a part of internal control and (2) assistance in the audit of an organization's financial statements. The primary emphasis in this book is upon internal auditing as a part of internal control.

The second category of responsibility relates to requests in many companies for internal auditors to assist in the external audit of an organization's financial statements. This external audit is only tangentially interested in the internal control system as a basis for reliance upon the accounting system for a fair presentation of the financial statements.

The AICPA *Statement on Auditing Standards No. 9* specifies that external auditors must base their justification for any reliance they place upon work done by internal auditors for the purpose of external financial auditing upon two criteria: (1) the internal auditors' competence and (2) their objectivity. The level of internal auditing responsibility described in this chapter requires competent individuals who are skilled in auditing techniques and who have a broad perspective of controls. Such individuals would be competent to assist in the external financial audit of the organization. In addition, the internal auditing function, as described, enhances internal auditors' objectivity by preserving their independence from operations and administration.

The internal auditors do not direct the external audit of a company's financial statements. Any financial statements submitted to the SEC under the Securities Act of 1934 must be audited by independent outside auditors. The role of the internal auditors in this setting is to assist the external auditors.

Internal auditors can eliminate the need for some, perhaps much, of the work that might otherwise be done by the external auditors. Examples of this are the use of internal auditing evaluations of cash controls, receivables, payables, and other financial activities. Because the early phases of the external audit include an evaluation of the internal financial control system, the work done by internal auditors to test that control system is valuable to external auditors.

Often, the costs of the external audit can be greatly reduced if the outside auditor can use the work that has already been done by internal auditors. In order to place reliance on such work, the external auditors review and test the work performed.

Although internal auditors may be asked to assist in the external audit, some of them resist such assignments because they believe they have higher priorities.

The Internal Auditing Organization

Typically, internal auditing departments comprise relatively few skilled professionals when compared to most other departments. In some organizations there may be only one internal auditor. Other internal auditing departments may employ more than 100 auditors. In many organizations, experience in internal auditing is so highly valued that any employee on a management track is encouraged to spend a tour of duty in the internal auditing department.

The typical internal auditing department has four levels of professional auditors, as illustrated in Exhibit 1-6.

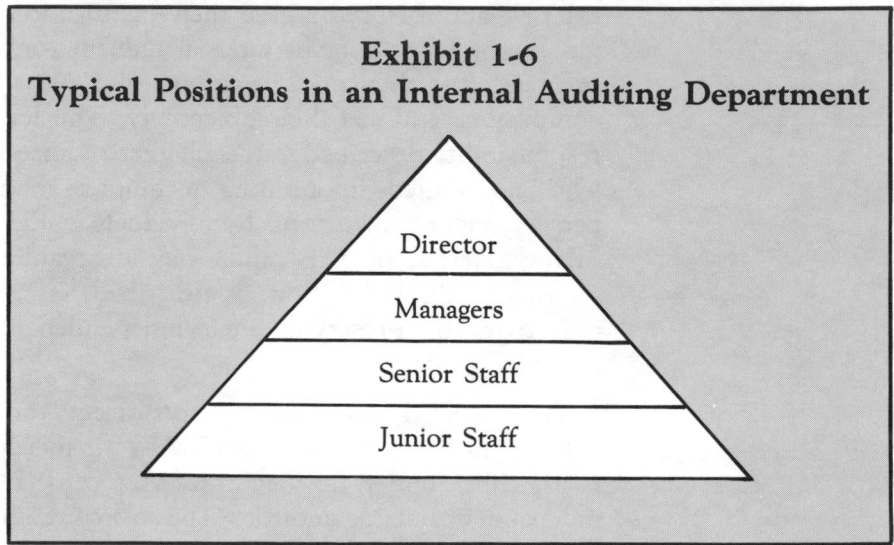

Exhibit 1-6
Typical Positions in an Internal Auditing Department

Director

Managers

Senior Staff

Junior Staff

The *director* of internal auditing has responsibility for the overall internal auditing function. This person gives overall direction to the department, establishes a planning process, provides auditing policies and procedures, manages departmental personnel, coordinates audit work with external auditors, and establishes an audit quality assurance program. The director also interfaces with the audit committee.

An internal auditing *manager* typically runs individual audits, including planning and coordinating the audit work. Managers usually have extensive auditing and supervisory experience.

Senior staff auditors supervise aspects of the audit work and perform much of the actual detail work. Senior auditors usually have at least three years of auditing experience.

Junior staff auditors usually do the less complex and more routine work. They are beginning professionals, or sometimes are fulfilling management training requirements for other departments.

People with a variety of backgrounds become internal auditors. Many become staff auditors immediately upon graduation from colleges or universities. The most typical academic majors are business and accounting. Others enter internal auditing as a career change. Frequently, organizations hire CPAs from public firms.

For example, the internal auditing department for one major corporation employs the following people: an engineer and former president of a subsidiary company of a large corporation; four former controllers; two former college professors; three attorneys; three former partners with large public accounting firms; numerous other CPAs formerly with public accounting firms; a former Internal Revenue Service administrator; a former FBI agent; a linguist; several computer specialists; and recent college graduates with degrees in accounting/auditing. Although the experience of employees in this department may not be typical, the example indicates the varied backgrounds of persons entering the internal auditing profession.

Practical Considerations Affecting Internal Auditing

Previous sections outlined principles for the development of the ideal internal auditing function in ideal circumstances. This section discusses how practical considerations often can have important effects upon what internal auditing departments do. Four such practical considerations involve ad hoc audits, multiple roles assumed by internal auditing departments, the audit committee, and geographically dispersed organizations.

Each organization applies the principles to meet its own needs, in light of some very real circumstances that may affect how auditing is practiced.

Ad Hoc Audits

Situations arise in almost any organization that will require auditors to leave a planned program and perform previously unplanned work.

Suppose, for example, that internal auditors for a manufacturer are examining supplier contracts when executives find an error in the calculation of interest on bonds payable. Suppose the error has occurred consistently over the past six months and requires an immediate, large payment of cash to bondholders, including additional interest charges. If inadequate controls have made the risk of future misstatements and payments sufficiently high, the auditors may postpone their present audit and immediately begin an examination of the internal controls over long-term payables. Upon completion of this study, the auditors may go back to their previous schedule.

Notwithstanding the justifiable periodic interruptions that temporarily affect the primary thrust of the auditing function, the entity is more likely to maximize its internal auditing department's cost effectiveness by following the general strategy of planning audits according to a schedule of relative risks. Even the decision to perform ad hoc audits would better be made in terms of risk.

Multiple Roles

While the internal auditing function may be well defined conceptually, internal auditing departments often are called upon to perform tasks outside that function. The practical choice of where to restrict the activities of the internal auditing department depends upon several factors. These factors include the array of skills possessed by the organization's auditors, the skills of its managers and demands placed upon them, the complexity of the organization, and the immediate needs of the organization.

Sometimes internal auditors may be in a better position to perform particular tasks than anyone else in the organization. They cross functional lines in their normal audit activities. Their training in broad control systems gives them an integrated perspective of the organization and its different components. Their time demands also may be more flexible.

Consequently, some internal auditing departments may become involved in the evaluation of management and operational performance. In fact, specific auditing methods have been developed for these more difficult evaluations, which often are described as "management audits" and "performance audits."

Similarly, because of practical considerations, internal auditing departments also may become involved in planning and even in the design of operational procedures, especially where those procedures become part of the control system.

Exhibit 1-7 illustrates the question, "What roles should the internal auditing department assume in the organization?" As a department becomes more involved in operational and administrative decision-making, there is a cost. To the extent that internal auditors accept decision-making authority outside the auditing function of internal controls, their independence is jeopardized, and very likely their objectivity as well.

But the question of role is not as simple as it may seem. Nor is the answer. Most internal auditing departments will likely, at some time, be assigned tasks outside their auditing function. It is not that internal auditors should not perform these duties. Rather, when they do, they (and management) must recognize the nature of the differences in the duties in order to perform them in a way that minimizes conflict with the primary responsibilities of the internal auditing function.

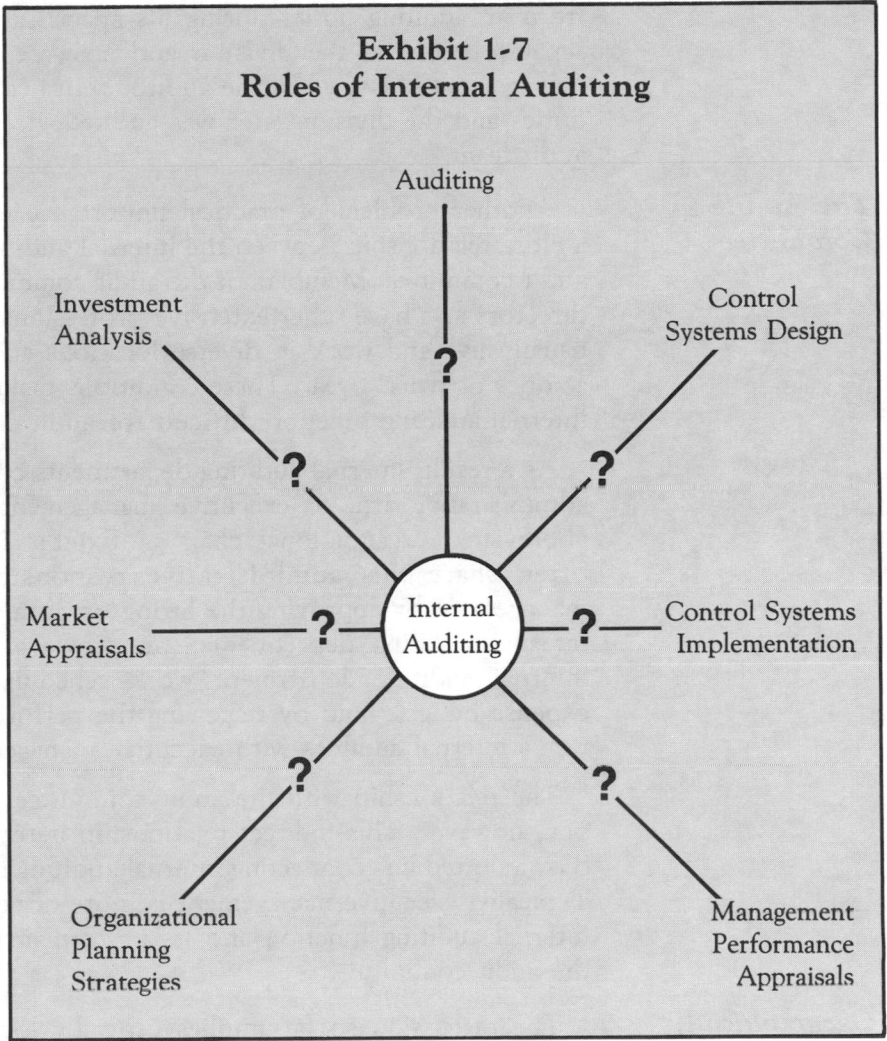

Exhibit 1-7
Roles of Internal Auditing

For example, one large corporate auditing department employed several specialists in computerized information systems. When one division of the corporation needed a new management information system (MIS), executive management requested that one of those auditors be assigned to direct the entire development, installation, and testing of the new MIS.

It was determined that the internal auditor was indeed the most qualified employee to direct the project. To preserve the integrity of the internal auditing function, however, that auditor was released from all auditing duties during his special assignment. He set up a separate office at the division and answered directly to divisional management. Also, when the auditor returned to his regular auditing duties and the division later was audited, he was excluded from the audit team.

The Audit Committee

Another problem of practical importance lies in how to establish a close relationship between the internal auditing department and the audit committee. Members of the audit committee are usually outside directors and have other extensive professional responsibilities. They usually live and work in diverse locations and meet as infrequently as once or twice a year. These conditions make administration of the internal auditing function difficult for audit committees.

As a result, internal auditing departments commonly are under the administrative arm of executive management, as illustrated in the abbreviated organizational chart in Exhibit 1-8. Audit committees often share this administrative responsibility with executive management by approving the hiring or dismissal of the directors of internal auditing departments; by previewing and approving the internal auditing department work schedules, staffing plans, and expense budgets; and by reviewing the performance of the organization's internal auditors with executive managers.

The relationship with the audit committee typically is an indirect one, however. This indirect relationship is represented in Exhibit 1-8 by a dotted line connecting internal auditing to the audit committee. Typically, executive management is more directly responsible for the internal auditing function and its performance in consultation with the audit committee.

Geographically Dispersed Organizations

The discussion so far implies centrally located management and internal auditing functions in organizations. Many large organizations, however, have widely dispersed subsidiaries and divisions in various locations around the country or the world. Consequently, because of the great need for internal auditing services at different locations and the cost considerations for providing those services, the internal auditing function may be decentralized as well, so that each subsidiary and division has its own auditors.

In such cases where different internal auditing units are spread geographically, they sometimes may be directed more easily by local executive management than by a centrally located auditing administration or an audit committee of the board. When this type of organization occurs, central auditors may be given the authority to examine any part of the organization.

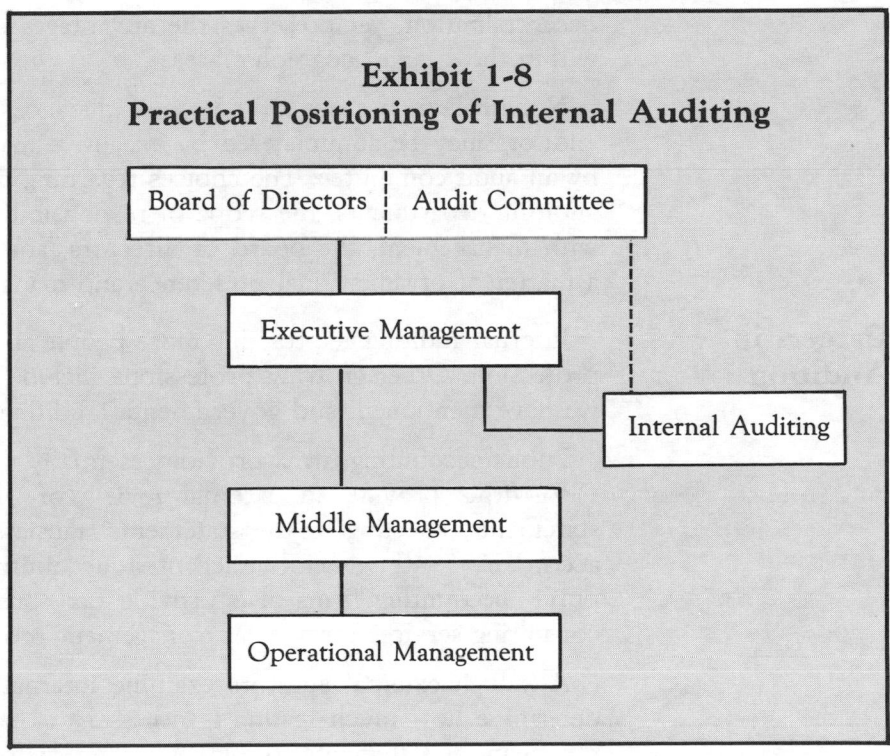

Exhibit 1-8
Practical Positioning of Internal Auditing

These auditors typically are assigned the largest, the most difficult, and the most critical audits in terms of the entire organization. The auditors for the specific subsidiaries and divisions have more restricted authority and are limited to the local subunits.

Other larger organizations, however, even though they are widely dispersed, maintain only a centralized auditing function. These organizations tend to favor the increased independence, objectivity, and coordination of audit activities afforded by centralization.

Some large international companies have a few auditing units centrally located in major geographical areas of their operations. For example, suppose the auditing function of one organization is divided among three offices located in three area headquarters — Houston, Tokyo, and London. The auditors in Houston are responsible for all North American and South American operations, the auditors in Tokyo for all Asian operations, and the auditors in London for all European operations. This arrangement offers the advantages of some decentralization, yet preserves the advantages of centralized auditing within these large geographic areas.

Nonetheless, because of time and distance constraints, deployed auditors may be administered by executive management rather than by an audit committee. The choices regarding the number of internal auditing departments, the scope of responsibilities, and relationships with management, the board of directors, and external auditors are a matter of organizational preference and management style.

Careers in Auditing

Internal auditing is attracting more people and is becoming a major profession. Other growing professions include public accounting, as we have mentioned, and governmental auditing.

Public accounting firms provide essentially three types of services. CPA firms provide an external review of organizations' financial statements, attesting to the statements' fairness and presentation in accordance with generally accepted accounting principles. These public accounting firms also provide tax consultation services and consulting services for special management problems.

Although external auditors examine internal controls in order to determine how much testing is necessary to express an opinion on the financial statements, the CPA's concern focuses primarily upon financial accounting controls. The internal auditor is concerned with the entire internal control system — management controls, operational controls, controls for the protection of assets, and accounting controls.

The American Institute of Certified Public Accountants (AICPA) is the national standards-making body for the practice of public accounting.

The profession of public accounting has grown remarkably since the passage of the Securities Act of 1934, which requires all companies whose stocks are traded publicly to undergo "independent" (i.e., external) audits of their financial statements. Since the SEC oversees the practices of accounting and reporting for publicly traded corporations, the AICPA has developed a close, although sometimes controversial, working relationship with the SEC. State laws govern the certification and licensing practices for CPAs.

The practice of internal auditing is not as closely monitored and controlled by law as is external auditing. Although the Foreign Corrupt Practices Act of 1977 has stimulated the growth of internal auditing, there are no legal requirements for corporate internal auditors.

Governmental auditors, at all levels, are required by law to audit government-related activities. Some governmental auditing positions (such as the state auditor in many states) are elective offices, and others are political appointments. Most government auditors, however, are recruited or hired like private-sector employees. They are not politically linked, but act as an administrative arm of government.

Many professional governmental auditors are employed by the Inspector General's Office and the General Accounting Office of the federal government. While governmental auditing offers a separate career path from corporate internal auditing, these auditors essentially perform an internal auditing function for the government.

QUESTIONS

1. What is The Institute of Internal Auditors? Discuss briefly its history and current functions.
2. What are some indications of the recognition given to internal auditing by other organizations?
3. What dominant forces outside the profession have exerted significant influence on the development of the growth and practice of internal auditing? How?
4. What is the ideal relationship among (a) a conceptual framework for internal auditing, (b) The IIA's internal auditing standards, and (c) specific procedures for conducting audits?
5. Explain the three primary responsibilities of management. How does internal auditing relate to each of these management responsibilities?
6. This chapter discusses risk as the single most important factor in the development of the internal auditing function. Explain.
7. What is the mathematical formulation for risk given in the chapter? Explain the effect of the two variables, E and Pr, upon risk.
8. What is the nature of the internal auditing department's function within an organization?
9. What is the difference between evaluating and suggesting internal controls at the design stage and actually designing the control system for management? Why is the distinction important?
10. What is the extent of the internal auditing responsibility as described in the chapter? Explain any limitations.
11. What is the auditor's responsibility with respect to the performance evaluation process?
12. Compare and contrast the independence and the objectivity of internal and external auditors.
13. What authority does the internal auditing function have over the executive level of management? Over other levels? Why?
14. Explain the relationships between internal auditing and (a) executive management, (b) the board of directors, and (c) external auditors, respectively.
15. What practical considerations affect how internal auditing actually is practiced? Briefly, how does each type of consideration affect an organization's internal auditing function?
16. Identify and describe the four levels of professional auditors typically found in modern organizations.
17. What is the ideal background from which to enter internal auditing?
18. How does internal auditing compare to external auditing performed by public accounting firms?
19. What is the standards-making body for public accounting firms?
20. What different types of governmental auditing positions are there? How does governmental auditing compare to internal auditing?

EXERCISES

E-1

The StarComp Corporation has grown rapidly in the last five years. In fact, recent sales figures showed the company to be the fifth-largest personal computer producer in the country. Last year, the company purchased a chain of retail electronics stores through which to market StarComp products and other household electronic appliances, games, etc. The controller of the company has suggested the establishment of an internal auditing department, and an executive committee is meeting to determine the best way to implement the proposal. The company's president or chief executive officer (CEO), the vice president of production, the controller, and the vice president of finance are discussing the most appropriate administrative level to which the new department director should report. Suggestions have included (1) the CEO, (2) the vice president of finance, (3) the controller, and (4) the audit committee of the board of directors.

Required:

a. What advantages and/or disadvantages would there be in placing the director of internal auditing under any one of the four proposed levels of management? Discuss each of the four proposals.
b. Of these four suggestions, which one do you think would be the best selection? Why?

E-2

The director of internal auditing in a large food company recently said that it is the primary job of internal auditing to identify all reasonable, foreseeable risk areas in the organization and to review those areas.

Required:

What do you think of this statement? Explain.

E-3

The following activities are performed as part of the internal control system for the loan department of a large bank:

1. Verification of the existence of loan collateral by a physical inspection of the pledged property and by documentation confirming ownership.
2. Confirmation of loan balances with banking customers. (The auditee mails the "confirmations" to outside parties. They are requested to verify the information in writing and return the verification to the auditors.)
3. Preparation of an aging of loan balances.
4. Directing a loan officer to obtain updated credit reports from customers who are delinquent in their payments on large notes.
5. Deciding upon the information required for loan applications.
6. Approval and denial of loan applications.
7. Designing a computer filing system for notes held by the bank.
8. Evaluation of the adequacy of the billing procedures designed to maximize the number of prompt payments by loan customers.

Required:

a. Determine whether each of the activities would best be classified as (1) a design of controls, (2) an implementation of controls, (3) a test of compliance with controls, or (4) an evaluation of controls.
b. Which of the activities are appropriate for the internal auditing function?

E-4

The internal auditing director recently sent some internal control guidelines to the director of the EDP department. The EDP department was designing a new production costing and inventory control system and requested some control guidelines from the internal auditing department. The director of EDP made the following statement to one of his colleagues in the department: "The auditors are going to be looking at our new system sooner or later, anyway. We may as well build the controls into the program now, so we won't have to make major changes later."

Required:

a. Does providing such control guidelines jeopardize the internal auditor's independence and/or objectivity? Why?
b. Suppose the EDP director actually sent the finished program to the internal auditors to study for internal control weaknesses and to recommend changes for improved control of production costs and savings. If this were done before implementation of the system, and the EDP department incorporated the recommended changes into the program, what effect would this situation have upon the internal auditors' independence and objectivity in future audits of the EDP department?

E-5

The CEO of a firm telephoned the director of internal auditing and began the conversation something like this: "Ed, I have come to have a great deal of confidence in your judgment because of the work I have seen come out of your department. You obviously understand the direction that this company is moving in and how to get there. We are having an executive committee meeting next Monday to decide if we should open a new plant in our eastern market area and close down the one that has given us so many problems up north. I would like for you to be at that meeting."

Required:

a. How might the director of internal auditing reply, remaining consistent with the principles outlined in this chapter?
b. Realistically, how do you think the director of internal auditing should react?

E-6

You are the director of internal auditing at a university. Recently you met with the manager of data processing and expressed the desire to establish a more effective interface between the two departments.

The manager of data processing subsequently requested your views and help on a new computerized accounts payable system being developed. The manager recommended that the internal auditing department assume line responsibility for auditing all suppliers' invoices prior to each one's payment.

The manager also requested that the internal auditing department make suggestions during the development of the system, assist in its installation, and approve the completed system after making a final review.

Required:

State how you would respond to the data processing manager and give the reason why you would accept or reject each of the following:

a. The recommendation that your department be responsible for the preaudit of suppliers' invoices.
b. The request that you make suggestions during the development of the system.
c. The request that you assist in the installation of the system and approve the system after making a final review.

(CIA Exam Adapted)

E-7

The internal auditors for a transportation company investigated four areas of that company. These areas were:

1. Collections of accounts receivable.
2. Purchase of fuel from wholesale suppliers for the company's fleet of trucks.
3. Sale of used trucks at auctions.
4. Purchase of advertising in the mass media.

The auditors determined that the total exposure to loss in accounts receivable was $7.8 million, the total exposure to loss in the purchase of fuel was $36 million, possible losses from sales of used trucks were estimated to be $3 million, and possible losses in the purchase of advertising were estimated to be $2 million during the year. In each case the figure is based upon the estimated possible annual loss. After a brief evaluation of internal controls, the auditors estimated that control over receivable collections was excellent, over fuel purchases — excellent, over the sale of used trucks — good, and over purchases of advertising — extremely poor.

Required:

a. How would you rank the risks of the four areas, based only upon the amount of exposure to loss?
b. Using the following probabilities associated with the quality of internal control, how do your rankings change, if at all? Why?

Internal Control	*Probability of Loss*
Excellent	.02
Very Good	.15
Good	.25
Average	.50
Fair	.75
Poor	.85
Extremely Poor	.98

c. Name at least one possible way that the losses could occur in each of the four areas.

E-8

The internal auditing department recently completed two audits, and the director of internal auditing is puzzled about what to recommend to management in the audit reports. The first audit was of a construction project in the downtown area of a large city. A significant part of the audit was aimed at evaluating the control procedures designed to protect pedestrian and automobile traffic near the construction site from accidental injury or damage. The auditors determined that the project managers had taken all reasonable precautions, but that significant risks still existed, that someone could get hurt, and that the company might suffer significant costs in damages.

In the second audit, the auditors found that control procedures were operating adequately in the management of the company's investments portfolio, but that the portfolio still was operating at a very low profit level.

Required:

Since the auditors had found that the internal control procedures were satisfactory, what might the director of internal auditing recommend to management that might help them better manage the risks in each of the two operations?

E-9

The director of the marketing department stormed into the internal auditing department, threw his copy of an audit report onto the audit manager's desk, and yelled, "How I manage my department is my own business. I don't need any of your little auditors running down to my department and telling everyone else that I am authoritarian or anything else with my employees. How do you think this report will make me look to the board of directors? Besides, you auditors are supposed to be looking after the money, aren't you? Just stay out of marketing. What do you know about marketing, anyway?"

The company's CEO had asked the internal auditors to investigate the costs for training personnel in the marketing department. Top management felt that the costs might be excessive. The auditors discovered that the cost per employee actually had decreased during the last five years, but that the turnover in the department had tripled during that same period, causing the overall costs to increase substantially.

The director of marketing had been employed in that position for six years. In their report, the auditors noted that although the control over the costs of individual training appeared satisfactory, a number of the employees in the marketing department had complained about the marketing director's management style. They said he was very authoritarian, and almost all of the employees who had resigned mentioned in their exit interviews that he had driven them to it. The auditors examined exit interview forms for many of the employees who had left the company, and discovered that the primary reason given for leaving was the manager's style. Also, the auditors noticed that the number of employees who had been fired had doubled during the past five years over the previous five years. In addition to adding personnel to keep up with the growth of the company, replacements had to be hired to fill the vacant positions. The auditors pointed out that the costs had increased because of the high number of marketing employees continuously being trained.

Required:

How could the audit manager justify to the director of the marketing department what the auditors had done, especially since auditors typically are not responsible for the performance evaluations of managers?

E-10

The board of directors of Crystal, Inc. has decided to change the administrative structure of its management organization in order to accomplish several objectives related to internal auditing:

1. The board wants to expand the scope of the auditors' responsibility to include a broader range of operations.
2. The board wants to increase the degree of auditor independence from operational and administrative management.
3. The board wants to expand the auditing department and recruit highly qualified auditors who would be capable of being promoted to top executive positions in the company as its operations grow into new markets.
4. The board wants to have more direct access to the internal auditing department in order to pursue specific questions that might otherwise not be investigated.
5. The board wants audit reports to go to all management levels where the information might be relevant.
6. The board wants the internal auditors to be able to assist with the external audit, which is conducted by an outside CPA firm, in order to decrease the cost of that audit.

Currently, the internal auditing department is under the administrative arm of the corporate controller's office and is responsible almost exclusively for audits of the internal financial control system. In the past, all of the internal auditors were hired from local CPA firms. Under the current system the audit reports go directly to the controller, his or her supervisor, and the corporate vice president of finance. A summary report is given annually to the board of directors regarding the internal auditing activities of the previous accounting period.

Required:

a. Diagram the current administrative and reporting relationships between the internal auditing department and the various levels of management in the company.

b. Propose a new administrative and reporting structure for the internal auditing function that would help achieve the objectives set by the board of directors. Diagram this structure.

c. Explain how your proposed structure would help achieve the different objectives.

E-11

A new computerized inventory system has been installed in the warehousing division of an industrial engine and machine manufacturer. The warehousing manager has complained loudly in recent weeks that the new system is costing the company upwards of $500,000 a month in sales due to goods that are "lost" because of errors in the system. The EDP department insists that the system is well designed and that tests have shown it to be operating almost perfectly. EDP personnel say that the problem must be in the warehousing department itself. The vice president of operations has called the director of internal auditing for help. The plea included something like, "The internal auditors are our only hope for resolving this problem. Help!"

Required:

a. Does such a task violate the principles of the internal auditing function outlined in the chapter?

b. Should the internal auditing department get involved? Why or why not?

PROBLEMS

P-1

Rocky's Chicken Huts, Inc. is a growing, publicly owned chain of fast food outlets. Patrick McBride, president of the chain, has decided that the company is large enough to establish an internal auditing department. He has been told by the company's public accountants that the company needs internal auditors and that other similar organizations have rather extensive internal auditing operations. Mr. McBride is interviewing various people for the position of director of internal auditing for the company, and you are one of three candidates he has selected as the most promising. He has decided to make his selection based upon how each of the three candidates proposes to develop the internal auditing function in the company.

Required:

Write a concise but comprehensive outline of the principles you would use to develop the internal auditing function for Rocky's Chicken Huts, Inc. In your outline, include the general principles for directing the audit function through the organization, the nature of the auditing responsibility, the extent of that responsibility, the level of authority given internal auditing, and the nature of the relationships between the internal auditing function and other functions related to the company.

P-2

Modern Industries, Inc. employs a corporate auditing department with a professional staff of 16 auditors. The director of the auditing department is a retired FBI agent who worked for five years with a public accounting firm before joining the FBI. The director makes it a practice of hiring only CPAs who have experience in financial auditing with public accounting firms. The director of auditing reports directly to the president of Modern Industries, who established the department in 1978 in order to guard against violations of the Foreign Corrupt Practices Act.

The president has given the director of auditing explicit instructions to accomplish two objectives for the department: (1) guard against irregularities in the financial internal control of the company and (2) assist the external auditors in order to decrease the company's fees to the firm's public accountants.

The audit director has consistently maintained that in order to do his job correctly, the department must restrict itself to testing the financial record-keeping system's compliance with formally established internal control procedures, standards, and policies. He maintains that it is operational management's job to evaluate the controls and to design and implement them. He says that the company might want to hire the CPA firm's management services staff to design a financial internal control system for the company.

The director of internal auditing runs what he calls a "tight ship." The male auditors are expected to wear only dark suits with white shirts and dark, conservative ties. The women are instructed to wear equally conservative suits with skirts. Each auditor attends an annual conference on fraud detection, and on the walls of every office in the department is an 8" by 10" photograph of what the director calls the department mascot — Hector, a large Doberman pinscher. Every auditor is issued a thick notebook and is instructed to carry it in the inside pocket of his or her suit jacket. When anything suspicious is observed in the financial operations of the firm, the auditor is required to write down the observation in the notebook and, later, to enter it in a departmental log. These observed irregularities are checked by a team of two auditors within a maximum of ten days. Regular audits are conducted on a random basis to enhance the surprise factor. All of the auditing reports are delivered directly to the president of the company, who reviews them with the director of internal auditing. Recommendations for changes are made by the president through the operational chain of command, so that the supervisors within the departments where the changes are to take place will be the ones to institute them. The director of auditing recommended this plan of implementing changes in order to preserve the company auditors' objectivity and independence of operations.

Required:

a. Evaluate the internal auditing function in Modern Industries, Inc. based upon the principles contained in this chapter. Explain your evaluations.
b. What changes, if any, would you make in the function? Explain what you would hope to accomplish with each recommended change.

2 Professionalism in Internal Auditing

Professionalism in any endeavor connotes status and credibility. The economic community has come to expect a high degree of professionalism from internal auditors. This expectation arises from what is becoming a tradition of excellence in the profession. Many internal auditors and their managers have made significant efforts to set and maintain high standards for the profession and to establish internal auditing as a key management function in the successful operation of their organizations.

Professionalism in internal auditing may be considered at three levels:

1. The profession in general.
2. Internal auditing departments.
3. Individual practitioners.

At its broadest level, The Institute of Internal Auditors (IIA) and the United States General Accounting Office (GAO) have led the way in promoting professionalism for the practice of internal auditing. At the same time, organizations requrie a high degree of professionalism from their internal auditing departments. Consequently, people who go into internal auditing must maintain high personal standards of conduct and performance in order to meet the expectations of the profession in general and the demands of specific organizations.

This chapter will help you understand the importance of each of these three levels in the development and maintenance of professionalism in internal auditing.

Actions by The Institute of Internal Auditors   The IIA has taken four important steps in promoting a high degree of professionalism among internal auditors and their departments in organizations around the world. The Institute has adopted:

1. A *Statement of Responsibilities of Internal Auditing*.
2. *Standards for the Professional Practice of Internal Auditing*.
3. A *Code of Ethics* for internal auditors.
4. A program of auditor certification.

Each of these actions was taken in an effort to encourage the best possible performance of the internal auditing function by competent individuals of high integrity, using sound principles.

Unlike similar actions taken by the American Institute of Certified Public Accountants (AICPA), these steps are not legally binding upon professional internal auditors. Federal and state laws uphold the licensing and the practice of public accounting and support AICPA actions. Some states have enacted laws adopting The IIA's *Standards* for their state auditors, but the provisions are restricted to governmental auditors for those states.

The guidance offered by The IIA represents strong professional encouragement. Consequently, The IIA has been forced to use various methods of persuasion and education to establish and maintain a state of the art for internal auditing that will adequately serve the demands being made on the profession. As a result of these efforts, many companies have formally adopted The IIA's *Standards* and the *Code of Ethics* as company policy.

The following discussion outlines each of the four steps taken by The Institute to promote professionalism among internal auditors, their departments, and individual practitioners.

Statement of Responsibilities

The *Statement of Responsibilities of Internal Auditing* has been changed several times since it was first drafted in 1947. Its overall purpose remains unchanged, however, and that is to establish a set of guidelines defining the proper role and responsibilities of the internal auditing function within organizations. This document, shown in Exhibit 2-1, presents a more concise, practical statement than the conceptual discussion given in the previous chapter. The *Statement* serves as a general foundation upon which to establish charters for internal auditing departments, and formally outlines their role and authority in their respective organizations.

This *Statement* covers four topics:

1. The nature of the internal auditing function.
2. The objective and scope of internal auditing.
3. The responsibility and authority given the internal auditing function.
4. The independence of the function.

Exhibit 2-1
Statement of Responsibilities of Internal Auditing

The purpose of this statement is to provide in summary form a general understanding of the role and responsibilities of internal auditing. For more specific guidance, readers should refer to the *Standards for the Professional Practice of Internal Auditing.*

NATURE

Internal auditing is an independent appraisal activity established within an organization as a service to the organization. It is a control which functions by examining and evaluating the adequacy and effectiveness of other controls.

OBJECTIVE AND SCOPE

The objective of internal auditing is to assist members of the organization in the effective discharge of their responsibilities. To this end, internal auditing furnishes them with analyses, appraisals, recommendations, counsel, and information concerning the activities reviewed. The audit objective includes promoting effective control at reasonable cost.

The scope of internal auditing encompasses the examination and evaluation of the adequacy and effectiveness of the organization's system of internal control and the quality of performance in carrying out assigned responsibilities. The scope of internal auditing includes:

- Reviewing the reliability and integrity of financial and operating information and the means used to identify, measure, classify, and report such information.
- Reviewing the systems established to ensure compliance with those policies, plans, procedures, laws, and regulations which could have a significant impact on operations and reports, and determining whether the organization is in compliance.
- Reviewing the means of safeguarding assets and, as appropriate, verifying the existence of such assets.
- Appraising the economy and efficiency with which resources are employed.
- Reviewing operations or programs to ascertain whether results are consistent with established objectives and goals and whether the operations or programs are being carried out as planned.

RESPONSIBILITY AND AUTHORITY

Internal auditing functions under the policies established by management and the board. The purpose, authority and responsibility of the internal auditing department should be defined in a formal written document (charter), approved by management, and accepted by the board. The charter should make clear the purposes of the internal auditing department, specify the unrestricted scope of its work, and declare that auditors are to have no authority or responsibility for the activities they audit.

The responsibility of internal auditing is to serve the organization in a manner that is consistent with the *Standards for the Professional Practice of Internal Auditing* and with professional standards of conduct such as the *Code of Ethics* of The Institute of Internal Auditors, Inc. This responsibility includes coordinating internal audit activities with others so as to best achieve the audit objectives and the objectives of the organization.

INDEPENDENCE

Internal auditors should be independent of the activities they audit. Internal auditors are independent when they can carry out their work freely and objectively. Independence permits internal auditors to render the impartial and unbiased judgments essential to the proper conduct of audits. It is achieved through organizational status and objectivity.

Organizational status should be sufficient to assure a broad range of audit coverage, and adequate consideration of and effective action on audit findings and recommendations.

Objectivity requires that internal auditors have an independent mental attitude, and an honest belief in their work product. Drafting procedures, designing, installing, and operating systems are not audit functions. Performing such activities is presumed to impair audit objectivity.

The *Statement of Responsibilities of Internal Auditors* was originally issued by The Institute of Internal Auditors in 1947. The current *Statement*, revised in 1981, embodies the concepts previously established and includes such changes as are deemed advisable in light of the present status of the profession.

Let's examine the provisions related to each of the four topics.

Nature of Internal Auditing. The *Statement of Responsibilities of Internal Auditing* states the nature of internal auditing as follows:

> Internal auditing is an independent appraisal activity established within an organization as a service to the organization. It is a control which functions by examining and evaluating the adequacy and effectiveness of other controls.

This provision is consistent with our previous discussion of the conceptual nature of the internal auditing function, which we presented as a part of the control function of management. The activity of internal auditing is described as an "independent appraisal." The nature of that appraisal is described as an examination and evaluation of (1) the adequacy (i.e., the design), and (2) the operational effectiveness of the control system. The parameters of the internal auditing function would include tests of the control system to determine if it is operating as it was designed to. Although an evaluation of controls is appropriate, the parameters of internal auditing responsibilities do not include either the design or the implementation of controls.

As an illustration of this *Statement,* it would be appropriate for the internal auditors of an organization to test whether the personnel department is complying with a prescribed procedure to contact previous employers of job applicants, to evaluate whether the procedure is designed to acquire the desired information, and even whether the procedure is necessary as an effective control device. The *Statement* does not suggest that the internal auditors should design the procedure and be responsible for implementing or for managing it.

Notice that independence is specified as a necessary condition for the establishment of the internal auditing function within an organization. This aspect of the function is so important that the fourth section of the *Statement of Responsibilities of Internal Auditing* addresses that issue solely.

Objective and Scope. The *Statement* of the objective and scope of the internal auditing function reads as follows:

> The objective of internal auditing is to assist members of the organization in the effective discharge of their responsibilities. To this end, internal auditing furnishes them with analysis, appraisals, recommendations, counsel, and information concerning the activities reviewed. The audit objective includes promoting effective control at reasonable cost.
>
> The scope of internal auditing encompasses the examination and evaluation of the adequacy and effectiveness of the organization's system of internal control and the quality of performance in carrying out assigned responsibilities. The scope of internal auditing includes:

- Reviewing the reliability and the integrity of financial and operating information and the means used to identify, measure, classify, and report such information.
- Reviewing the systems established to ensure compliance with those policies, plans, procedures, laws, and regulations which could have a significant impact on operations and reports, and determining whether the organization is in compliance.
- Reviewing the means of safeguarding assets and, as appropriate, verifying the existence of such assets.
- Appraising the economy and efficiency with which resources are employed.
- Reviewing operations or programs to ascertain whether results are consistent with established objectives and goals and whether the operations or programs are being carried out as planned.

These paragraphs provide a kind of "target" for internal auditing activities. The target is described in terms of an overall objective, the range of internal auditing activity, and the areas and functions of the organization where internal auditing takes place. The objective is broad, providing for general help to various members of the organization and aiming specifically at their success in meeting their assigned responsibilities. The "help" may take any of several forms, as outlined in the *Statement,* and should be directed to two key concerns. First, internal auditing should be concerned with effective control. Second, internal auditing should aim at cost-effective control. Some control measures may cost more than they are worth, and therefore could be counterproductive.

The scope of internal auditing, according to the *Statement,* has two dimensions: (1) *what* internal auditors do and (2) *where* they do it. What internal auditors do is examine and evaluate. What they examine and evaluate is the organization's system of internal controls, the quality of various functions, and employees' performance related to specifically assigned responsibilities.

The responsibility that internal auditing assumes for performance, however, is somewhat restricted and qualified. In the case of examining and evaluating performance, the internal auditing department restricts the scope of its coverage to specific responsibilities that are assigned to individuals or to their respective units within the organization. The internal auditing department examines and evaluates performance to compare the actual performance with plans, specified activities, standards, objectives, policies, and goals. That type of performance review is really a review of controls, since plans, specified activities, standards, objectives, policies, and goals are a part of the control system. On the other hand, this review is used as a part of the more general management performance evaluation, which remains the prerogative of the management function.

Internal auditing reports are used in that process, but the responsibility of internal auditing does not necessarily extend into the "softer" evaluations for which there may not be specified criteria with which to compare actual performance. This particular aspect of internal auditing responsibility involves a delicate differentiation between auditing and management appraisal. The key to fulfilling this responsibility successfully is to remain objective and independent of any part of the decision process, which is the sole domain of administrative and operational management.

On the occasions when auditors are required to examine areas that do not have formal, specified performance criteria, they may be forced to compare actual performance to industry averages or standards, or to performance of similar organizations. It is important for the auditors to seek out measurable criteria — those specifying a quantifiable measure — and to leave the decision on what to do about deviations from those criteria up to management. Of course, auditors often are requested to make recommendations. In performing audits, those measurements taken from external sources, and any comparisons with them, should be scrutinized carefully, because the organization may not bear the same characteristics as the organizations for which the external measurements were computed. Often the stated goals and objectives of top management are helpful to the auditor in making such comparisons.

The *Statement* also says that internal auditors should scrutinize the control over the organization's assets. This scrutiny helps management protect the organization's property from losses due to fire, theft, improper use, and exposure to natural elements.

The *Statement* goes on to include an appraisal by internal auditors of how well the organization's resources are being managed. At this point, the prescribed scope of the internal auditing function appears to include a more general appraisal of management's performance than is prescribed earlier in the *Statement.* By evaluating the economy and the efficiency of the use of the organization's resources, the internal auditing function is, in fact, appraising management itself, since management is responsible for the use of those resources.

This in itself is not contradictory to theory, but such a general evaluation may not show comparisons of actual performance with prescribed standards, because standards of efficiency and economical operations may not be available. The evaluation may, in fact, be more of a judgment call.

Where operating standards are available, there is no conflict. Many internal auditing departments restrict their appraisal of efficiency to an evaluation in terms of documented operating standards. The *Standards for the Professional Practice of Internal Auditing* even suggests such a restriction. Actual practice in many other internal auditing departments includes a more general evaluation. Notice that such an appraisal does not include the authority to decide what to do about any inefficiencies or uneconomical use of resources.

As organizations have become larger, management has had an increasingly difficult task of monitoring operations, and has been forced to focus on higher-level concerns, sometimes at the expense of the detailed operations. Since the primary concern of management is the effectiveness of operations, most of the effort has been concentrated there. Yet management hesitates to neglect efficiency, because efficiency is important to performance, and if it deteriorates, effectiveness also may be threatened. Consequently, internal auditors often are called upon to examine the efficiency of operations as well as the effectiveness of controls.

Responsibility and Authority. The Responsibility and Authority section of the *Statement* is as follows:

> Internal auditing functions under the policies established by management and the board. The purpose, authority, and responsibility of the internal auditing department should be defined in a formal written document (charter), approved by management, and accepted by the board. The charter should make clear the purposes of the internal auditing department, specify the unrestricted scope of its work, and declare that auditors are to have no authority or responsibility for the activities they audit.
>
> The responsibility of internal auditing is to serve the organization in a manner that is consistent with the *Standards for the Professional Practice of Internal Auditing* and with professional standards of conduct such as the *Code of Ethics* of The Institute of Internal Auditors. This responsibility includes coordinating internal audit activities with others so as to best achieve the audit objectives and the objectives of the organization.

By being subject to policies established only by management, the internal auditing function jeopardizes its independence of management and, consequently, its all-important objectivity. Notice, however, that the first sentence prescribes that the board also should participate in policy-setting for the internal auditing function.

The rest of the first paragraph goes on to prescribe specific remedies for the danger posed by establishing an internal auditing function under management direction. First, the *Statement* indicates that the board of directors should review and approve internal auditing policies.

Second, a formal charter should be drafted documenting the boundaries of the internal auditing function. It should (a) establish the internal auditing department within the organization, (b) define its status and the scope of internal auditing authority and responsibility, (c) authorize access to records, personnel, and property needed to conduct the audit, and (d) prescribe its various relationships to other units within the organization and to those outside the organization. Outsiders include clients or customers, suppliers, subsidiaries, owners, and external auditors or other contracted service organizations.

The charter should be approved by both management and the board of directors. Board approval helps protect an organization's auditors against capricious policy changes by management.

Third, the *Statement* specifies an unrestricted scope of internal auditing work. By including this provision in the charter, internal auditing will have the authority it needs to monitor the controls of the total system without interference from management.

Finally, the *Statement* provides that auditors have no authority over, or responsibility for, the activities they audit; this serves to strengthen their independence and objectivity. Management, searching for know-how and minimal interruptions of normal routines, might try to persuade the internal auditors to take on operational responsibilities along with their auditing work. Provisions in the charter help protect the independence of auditors.

The second paragraph of this Responsibility and Authority section specifies, by reference, the standards for professional performance and conduct. The *Statement* references the *Standards for the Professional Practice of Internal Auditing* and the *Code of Ethics* of The Institute of Internal Auditors, both of which are discussed in this chapter.

The last sentence of this section indicates that while internal auditors may enjoy a high degree of responsibility and authority within the organization, they must not impose demands upon the organization that would unnecessarily inconvenience others or interrupt or interfere with their activities. After all, an overall responsibility of the internal auditing function is to assist the organization and those working in it to fulfill their responsibilities. This consideration requires cooperation and coordination of the internal auditing function with other organizational activities, except in rare circumstances when to do so would jeopardize what are considered to be more important audit objectives. Some situations, for example, may necessitate the element of surprise, which logically would interrupt the natural workflow of the operations under review.

Independence. In addition to the previous references to the need for auditor independence, this section describes the nature of independence, the reason for its importance, and two conditions required to protect it. The section reads as follows:

> Internal auditors should be independent of the activities they audit. Internal auditors are independent when they can carry out their work freely and objectively. Independence permits internal auditors to render the impartial and unbiased judgments essential

to the proper conduct of audits. It is achieved through organizational status and objectivity.

Organizational status should be sufficient to assure a broad range of audit coverage, and adequate consideration of and effective action on audit findings and recommendations.

Objectivity requires that internal auditors have an independent mental attitude and an honest belief in their work product. Drafting procedures, designing, installing, and operating systems are not audit functions. Performing such activities is presumed to impair audit objectivity.

The nature of auditor independence is described in the first paragraph as the ability to "carry out their [the auditors'] work freely and objectively." In this case "freely" means without outside interference from management or others in the organization. "Objectively" means to have a mental and an emotional detachment from the part of the organization being audited.

The reason independence is so important is that it "permits internal auditors to render . . . impartial and unbiased judgments . . . ." The auditor's effectiveness and, therefore, his or her value to the organization is dependent upon those judgments.

The conditions necessary to protect independence are (1) organizational status and (2) auditor objectivity. The *Statement* indicates that the auditors' status should be such that they are taken seriously throughout the organization. What this normally means is that the more respect management gives the auditing function, the higher the regard others have for it and, consequently, the greater the attention given to audit findings and recommendations. This status is most easily achieved by placing internal auditing at a high level within the organizational hierarchy.

Auditor objectivity results from mental discipline. To encourage an objective attitude, the *Statement* excludes auditor involvement from all operations in any decision-making capacity, except to render judgments on systems designed and implemented to control operations.

The provisions in the *Statement of Responsibilities of Internal Auditing* outline a prescribed role for the internal auditing function and introduce the need for more detailed standards of professional practice and behavior for internal auditors. In essence, this *Statement* establishes a setting for the internal auditing function. The more detailed standards state clearly the criteria governing how internal auditing should be performed.

Standards of Practice

The *Standards for the Professional Practice of Internal Auditing* was published by The IIA in 1978. The introduction to the *Standards* reiterates many of the provisions in the *Statement of Responsibilities of Internal Auditing.* In contrast to the rather large set of codified standards for the public accounting profession, the main body of the *Standards* is written concisely in less than 20 pages. The *Standards* is divided into five general sections and covers the various aspects of auditing within an organization:

1. Independence.
2. Professional Proficiency.
3. Scope of Work.
4. Performance of Audit Work.
5. Management of the Internal Auditing Department.

The standards outlined in these sections have proven to be reasonably comprehensive and applicable in a variety of settings — private and public corporations, government, and not-for-profit organizations.

Although the *Standards* is the official IIA pronouncement on how internal auditing ought to be practiced, The IIA has adopted a new plan for amending the *Standards* when important general questions arise that the current document does not answer adequately. On such occasions, The IIA issues *Statements on Internal Auditing Standards (SIAS).* These statements represent extensions and interpretations of the standards set forth in the original 1978 document and are not considered changes.

Six *SIAS*s have been accepted by The IIA: "Control: Concepts and Responsibilities" (1983), "Communicating Results" (1983), "Deterrence, Detection, Investigation, and Reporting of Fraud" (1985), "Quality Assurance" (1986), "Internal Auditors' Relationships with Independent Outside Auditors" (1987), and "Audit Working Papers" (1988). We cover each of these topics in later chapters and reproduce the additional standards in those chapters.

In 1981, The Institute began publishing *Professional Standards Bulletins* in *The Internal Auditor,* the journal of The Institute of Internal Auditors, to address questions of general interest. Specific bulletins are referenced throughout this text where applicable, and all of the bulletins current at the time of printing are reproduced in Appendix II at the end of the book.

Every student of internal auditing should know and understand the *Standards for the Professional Practice of Internal Auditing.* Because of its importance and relative brevity, we have reproduced the

Standards in its entirety below. You will notice that parts of the *Standards* are quite similar to the *Statement of Responsibilities,* with additional provisions defining methods and criteria for establishing an appropriate internal auditing function within the organization. Later chapters discuss individual standards in more detail as they relate to specific topics.

Standards for the Professional Practice of Internal Auditing
INTRODUCTION

Internal auditing is an independent appraisal function established within an organization to examine and evaluate its activities as a service to the organization. The objective of internal auditing is to assist members of the organization in the effective discharge of their responsibilities. To this end, internal auditing furnishes them with analyses, appraisals, recommendations, counsel, and information concerning the activities reviewed.

The members of the organization assisted by internal auditing include those in management and the board of directors. Internal auditors owe a responsibility to both, providing them with information about the adequacy and effectiveness of the organization's system of internal control and the quality of performance. The information furnished to each may differ in format and detail, depending upon the requirements and requests of management and the board.

The internal auditing department is an integral part of the organization and functions under the policies established by management and the board. The statement of purpose, authority, and responsibility (charter) for the internal auditing department, approved by management and accepted by the board, should be consistent with the *Standards for the Professional Practice of Internal Auditing.*

This charter should make clear the purposes of the internal auditing department, specify the unrestricted scope its work, and declare that auditors are to have no authority or responsibility for the activities they audit.

Throughout the world internal auditing is performed in diverse environments and within organizations that vary in purpose, size, and structure. In addition, the laws and customs within various countries differ from one another. These differences may affect the practice of internal auditing in each environment. The implementation of these *Standards,* therefore, will be governed by the environment in which the internal auditing department carries out its assigned responsibilities. But compliance with the concepts enunciated by these *Standards* is essential before the responsibilities of internal auditors can be met.

"Independence," as used in these *Standards,* requires clarification. Internal auditors must be independent of the activities they audit. Such independence permits internal auditors to perform their work freely and objectively. Without independence, the desired results of internal auditing cannot be realized.

In setting these *Standards,* the following developments were considered:

1. Boards of directors are being held increasingly accountable for the adequacy and effectiveness of their organizations' systems of internal control and quality of performance.
2. Members of management are demonstrating increased acceptance of internal auditing as a means of supplying objective analyses, appraisals, recommendations, counsel, and information on the organization's controls and performance.
3. External auditors are using the results of internal audits to complement their own work where the internal auditors have provided suitable evidence of independence and adequate, professional audit work.

In light of such developments, the purposes of these *Standards* are to:

1. Impart an understanding of the role and responsibilities of internal auditing to all levels of management, boards of directors, public bodies, external auditors, and related professional organizations.
2. Establish the basis for the guidance and measurement of internal auditing performance.
3. Improve the practice of internal auditing.

The *Standards* differentiate among the varied responsibilities of the organization, the internal auditing department, the director of internal auditing, and internal auditors.

The five general *Standards* are expressed in italicized statements in upper case. Following each of these general *Standards* are specific standards expressed in italicized statements in lower case. Accompanying each specific standard are guidelines describing suitable means of meeting that standard. The *Standards* encompass:

1. The independence of the internal auditing department from the activities audited and the objectivity of internal auditors.

2. The proficiency of internal auditors and the professional care they should exercise.
3. The scope of internal auditing work.
4. The performance of internal auditing assignments.
5. The management of the internal auditing department.

The *Standards* and the accompanying guidelines employ three terms which have been given specific meanings. These are as follows:

The term *board* includes boards of directors, audit committees of such boards, heads of agencies or legislative bodies to whom internal auditors report, boards of governors or trustees of nonprofit organizations, and any other designated governing bodies of organizations.

The terms *director of internal auditing* and *director* identify the top position in an internal auditing department.

The term *internal auditing department* includes any unit or activity within an organization which performs internal auditing functions.

100 INDEPENDENCE
INTERNAL AUDITORS SHOULD BE INDEPENDENT OF THE ACTIVITIES THEY AUDIT.

.01 Internal auditors are independent when they can carry out their work freely and objectively. Independence permits internal auditors to render the impartial and unbiased judgments essential to the proper conduct of audits. It is achieved through organizational status and objectivity.

110 Organizational Status
The organizational status of the internal auditing department should be sufficient to permit the accomplishment of its audit responsibilities.

.01 Internal auditors should have the support of management and of the board of directors so that they can gain the cooperation of auditees and perform their work free from interference.

  .1 The director of the internal auditing department should be responsible to an individual in the organization with sufficient authority to promote independence and to ensure broad audit coverage, adequate consideration of audit reports, and appropriate action on audit recommendations.

  .2 The director should have direct communication with the board. Regular communication with the board helps assure independence and provides a means for the board and the director to keep each other informed on matters of mutual interest.

.3   Independence is enhanced when the board concurs in the appointment or removal of the director of the internal auditing department.

.4   The purpose, authority, and responsibility of the internal auditing department should be defined in a formal written document (charter). The director should seek approval of the charter by management as well as acceptance by the board. The charter should (a) establish the department's position within the organization; (b) authorize access to records, personnel, and physical properties relevant to the performance of audits; and (c) define the scope of internal auditing activities.

.5   The director of internal auditing should submit annually to management for approval and to the board for its information a summary of the department's audit work schedule, staffing plan, and financial budget. The director should also submit all significant interim changes for approval and information. Audit work schedules, staffing plans, and financial budgets should inform management and the board of the scope of internal auditing work and of any limitations placed on that scope.

.6   The director of internal auditing should submit activity reports to management and to the board annually or more frequently as necessary. Activity reports should highlight significant audit findings and recommendations and should inform management and the board of any significant deviations from approved audit work schedules, staffing plans, and financial budgets, and the reasons for them.

120   Objectivity
Internal auditors should be objective in performing audits.

.01   Objectivity is an independent mental attitude which internal auditors should maintain in performing audits. Internal auditors are not to subordinate their judgment on audit matters to that of others.

.02   Objectivity requires internal auditors to perform audits in such a manner that they have an honest belief in their work product and that no significant quality compromises are made. Internal auditors are not to be placed in situations in which they feel unable to make objective professional judgments.

.1   Staff assignments should be made so that potential and actual conflicts of interest and bias are avoided. The director should periodically obtain from the audit staff information concerning potential conflicts of interest and bias.

.2   Internal auditors should report to the director any situations in which a conflict of interest or bias is present or may reasonably be inferred. The director should then reassign such auditors.

.3   Staff assignments of internal auditors should be rotated periodically whenever it is practicable to do so.

.4   Internal auditors should not assume operating responsibilities. But if on occasion management directs internal auditors to perform nonaudit work, it should be understood that they are not functioning as internal auditors. Moreover, objectivity is presumed to be impaired when internal auditors audit any activity for which they had authority or responsibility. This impairment should be considered when reporting audit results.

.5   Persons transferred to or temporarily engaged by the internal auditing department should not be assigned to audit those activities they previously performed until a reasonable period of time has elapsed. Such assignments are presumed to impair objectivity and should be considered when supervising the audit work and reporting audit results.

.6   The results of internal auditing work should be reviewed before the related audit report is released to provide reasonable assurance that the work was performed objectively.

.03   The internal auditor's objectivity is not adversely affected when the auditor recommends standards of control for systems or reviews procedures before they are implemented. Designing, installing, and operating systems are not audit functions. Also, the drafting of procedures for systems is not an audit function. Performing such activities is presumed to impair audit objectivity.

200   PROFESSIONAL PROFICIENCY
INTERNAL AUDITS SHOULD BE PERFORMED WITH PROFICIENCY AND DUE PROFESSIONAL CARE.

.01   Professional proficiency is the responsibility of the internal auditing department and each internal auditor. The department should assign to each audit those persons who collectively possess the necessary knowledge, skills, and disciplines to conduct the audit properly.

THE INTERNAL AUDITING DEPARTMENT

210   Staffing

The internal auditing department should provide assurance that the technical proficiency and educational background of internal auditors are appropriate for the audits to be performed.

.01   The director of internal auditing should establish suitable criteria of education and experience for filling internal auditing positions, giving due consideration to scope of work and level of responsibility.

.02   Reasonable assurance should be obtained as to each prospective auditor's qualifications and proficiency.

220   Knowledge, Skills, and Disciplines

The internal auditing department should possess or should obtain the knowledge, skills, and disciplines needed to carry out its audit responsibilities.

.01   The internal auditing staff should collectively possess the knowledge and skills essential to the practice of the profession within the organization. These attributes include proficiency in applying internal auditing standards, procedures, and techniques.

.02   The internal auditing department should have employees or use consultants who are qualified in such disciplines as accounting, economics, finance, statistics, electronic data processing, engineering, taxation, and law as needed to meet audit responsibilities. Each member of the department, however, need not be qualified in all of these disciplines.

230   Supervision

The internal auditing department should provide assurance that internal audits are properly supervised.

.01   The director of internal auditing is responsible for providing appropriate audit supervision. Supervision is a continuing process, beginning with planning and ending with the conclusion of the audit assignment.

.02   Supervision includes:

.1   Providing suitable instructions to subordinates at the outset of the audit and approving the audit program.

.2   Seeing that the approved audit program is carried out unless deviations are both justified and authorized.

.3   Determining that audit working papers adequately support the audit findings, conclusions, and reports.

.4   Making sure that audit reports are accurate, objective, clear, concise, constructive, and timely.

.5   Determining that audit objectives are being met.

.03   Appropriate evidence of supervision should be documented and retained.

.04   The extent of supervision required will depend on the proficiency of the internal auditors and the difficulty of the audit assignment.

.05   All internal auditing assignments, whether performed by or for the internal auditing department, remain the responsibility of its director.

THE INTERNAL AUDITOR

240   Compliance with Standards of Conduct

Internal auditors should comply with professional standards of conduct.

.01   The *Code of Ethics* of The Institute of Internal Auditors sets forth standards of conduct and provides a basis for enforcement among its members. The *Code* calls for high standards of honesty, objectivity, diligence, and loyalty to which internal auditors should conform.

250   Knowledge, Skills, and Disciplines

Internal auditors should possess the knowledge, skills, and disciplines essential to the performance of internal audits.

.01   Each internal auditor should possess certain knowledge and skills as follows:

.1   Proficiency in applying internal auditing standards, procedures, and techniques is required in performing internal audits. Proficiency means the ability to apply knowledge to situations likely to be encountered and to deal with them without extensive recourse to technical research and assistance.

.2   Proficiency in accounting principles and techniques is required of auditors who work extensively with financial records and reports.

.3   An understanding of management principles is required to recognize and evaluate the materiality and significance of deviations from good business practice. An understanding means the ability to apply broad knowledge to situations likely to be encountered, to recognize significant deviations, and to be able to carry out the research necessary to arrive at reasonable solutions.

.4   An appreciation is required of the fundamentals of such subjects as accounting, economics, commercial law, taxation, finance, quantitative methods, and computerized information systems. An appreciation means the ability to recognize the existence of problems or potential problems and to determine the further research to be undertaken or the assistance to be obtained.

260   Human Relations and Communications

Internal auditors should be skilled in dealing with people and in communicating effectively.

.01   Internal auditors should understand human relations and maintain satisfactory relationships with auditees.

.02   Internal auditors should be skilled in oral and written communications so that they can clearly and effectively convey such matters as audit objectives, evaluations, conclusions, and recommendations.

270   Continuing Education

Internal auditors should maintain their technical competence through continuing education.

.01   Internal auditors are responsible for continuing their education in order to maintain their proficiency. They should keep informed about improvements and current developments in internal auditing standards, procedures, and techniques. Continuing education may be obtained through membership and participation in professional societies; attendance at conferences, seminars, college courses, and in-house training programs; and participation in research projects.

280   Due Professional Care

Internal auditors should exercise due professional care in performing internal audits.

.01   Due professional care calls for the application of the care and skill expected of a reasonably prudent and competent internal auditor in the same or similar circumstances. Professional care should, therefore, be appropriate to the complexities of the audit being performed. In exercising due professional care, internal auditors should be alert to the possibility of intentional wrongdoing, errors and omissions, inefficiency, waste, ineffectiveness, and conflicts of interest. They should also be alert to those conditions and activities where irregularities are most likely to occur. In addition, they should identify inadequate controls and recommend improvements to promote compliance with acceptable procedures and practices.

.02   Due care implies reasonable care and competence, not infallibility or extraordinary performance. Due care requires the auditor to conduct examinations and verifications to a reasonable extent, but does not require detailed audits of all transactions. Accordingly, the internal auditor cannot give absolute assurance that noncompliance or irregularities do not exist. Nevertheless, the possibility of material irregularities or noncompliance should be considered whenever the internal auditor undertakes an internal auditing assignment.

.03   When an internal auditor suspects wrongdoing, the appropriate authorities within the organization should be informed. The internal auditor may recommend whatever investigation is considered necessary in the circumstances. Thereafter, the auditor should follow up to see that the internal auditing department's responsibilities have been met.

.04   Exercising due professional care means using reasonable audit skill and judgment in performing the audit. To this end, the internal auditor should consider:

.1   The extent of audit work needed to achieve audit objectives.

.2   The relative materiality or significance of matters to which audit procedures are applied.

.3   The adequacy and the effectiveness of internal controls.

.4   The cost of auditing in relation to potential benefits.

.05   Due professional care includes evaluating established operating standards and determining whether those standards are acceptable and are being met. When such standards are vague, authoritative interpretations should be sought. If internal auditors are required to interpret or select operating standards, they should seek agreement with auditees as to the standards needed to measure operating performance.

300   SCOPE OF WORK

THE SCOPE OF THE INTERNAL AUDIT SHOULD EN-COMPASS THE EXAMINATION AND EVALUATION OF THE ADEQUACY AND EFFECTIVENESS OF THE OR-GANIZATION'S SYSTEM OF INTERNAL CONTROL AND THE QUALITY OF PERFORMANCE IN CARRYING OUT ASSIGNED RESPONSIBILITIES.

.01   The scope of internal auditing work, as specified in this standard, encompasses what audit work should be performed. It is recognized, however, that management and the board of directors provide general direction as to the scope of work and the activities to be audited.

.02   The purpose of the review for adequacy of the system of internal control is to ascertain whether the system established provides reasonable assurance that the organization's objectives and goals will be met efficiently and economically.

.03   The purpose of the review for effectiveness of the system of internal control is to ascertain whether the system is functioning as intended.

.04   The purpose of the review for quality of performance is to ascertain whether the organization's objectives and goals have been achieved.

.05   The primary objectives of internal control are to ensure:
  .1   The reliability and integrity of information.
  .2   Compliance with policies, plans, procedures, laws, and regulations.
  .3   The safeguarding of assets.
  .4   The economical and efficient use of resources.
  .5   The accomplishment of established objectives and goals for operations or programs.

310   Reliability and Integrity of Information

Internal auditors should review the reliability and integrity of financial and operating information and the means used to identify, measure, classify, and report such information.

.01   Information systems provide data for decision making, control, and compliance with external requirements. Therefore, internal auditors should examine information systems and, as appropriate, ascertain whether:
  .1   Financial and operating records and reports contain accurate, reliable, timely, complete, and useful information.
  .2   Controls over record keeping and reporting are adequate and effective.

320   Compliance with Policies, Plans, Procedures, Laws, and Regulations

Internal auditors should review the systems established to ensure compliance with those policies, plans, procedures, laws, and regulations which could have a significant impact on operations and reports, and should determine whether the organization is in compliance.

.01   Management is responsible for establishing the systems designed to ensure compliance with such requirements as policies, plans, procedures, and applicable laws and regulations. Internal auditors are responsible for determining whether the systems are adequate and effective and whether the activities audited are complying with the appropriate requirements.

330   Safeguarding of Assets

Internal auditors should review the means of safeguarding assets and, as appropriate, verify the existence of such assets.

.01   Internal auditors should review the means used to safeguard assets from various types of losses such as those resulting from theft, fire, improper or illegal activities, and exposure to the elements.

.02   Internal auditors, when verifying the existence of assets, should use appropriate audit procedures.

340   Economical and Efficient Use of Resources

Internal auditors should appraise the economy and efficiency with which resources are employed.

.01   Management is responsible for setting operating standards to measure an activity's economical and efficient use of resources. Internal auditors are responsible for determining whether:

.1   Operating standards have been established for measuring economy and efficiency.

.2   Established operating standards are understood and are being met.

.3   Deviations from operating standards are identified, analyzed, and communicated to those responsible for corrective action.

.4   Corrective action has been taken.

.02   Audits related to the economical and efficient use of resources should identify such conditions as:

.1   Underutilized facilities.

.2   Nonproductive work.

.3   Procedures which are not cost justified.

.4   Overstaffing or understaffing.

350   Accomplishment of Established Objectives and Goals for Operations and Programs[1]

Internal auditors should review operations or programs to ascertain whether results are consistent with established objectives and goals and whether the operations or programs are being carried out as planned.

---

[1]"Operations" are defined as ongoing activities, such as production. "Programs" are defined as primarily single-purpose activities, such as volunteer recruitment.

.01 Management is responsible for establishing operating or program objectives and goals, developing and implementing control procedures, and accomplishing desired operating or program results. Internal auditors should ascertain whether such objectives and goals conform with those of the organization and whether they are being met.

.02 Internal auditors can provide assistance to managers who are developing objectives, goals, and systems by determining whether the underlying assumptions are appropriate; whether accurate, current, and relevant information is being used; and whether suitable controls have been incorporated into the operations or programs.

400 PERFORMANCE OF AUDIT WORK
AUDIT WORK SHOULD INCLUDE PLANNING THE AUDIT, EXAMINING AND EVALUATING INFORMA-TION, COMMUNICATING RESULTS, AND FOLLOWING UP.

.01 The internal auditor is responsible for planning and conducting the audit assignment, subject to supervisory review and approval.

410 Planning the Audit
Internal auditors should plan each audit.

.01 Planning should be documented and should include:

.1 Establishing audit objectives and scope of work.

.2 Obtaining background information about the activities to be audited.

.3 Determining the resources necessary to perform the audit.

.4 Communicating with all who need to know about the audit.

.5 Performing, as appropriate, an on-site survey to become familiar with the activities and controls to be audited, to identify areas for audit emphasis, and to invite auditee comments and suggestions.

.6 Writing the audit program.

.7 Determining how, when, and to whom audit results will be communicated.

.8 Obtaining approval of the audit work plan.

420 Examining and Evaluating Information
Internal auditors should collect, analyze, interpret, and document information to support audit results.

.01 The process of examining and evaluating information is as follows:

.1   Information should be collected on all matters related to the audit objectives and scope of work.

.2   Information should be sufficient, competent, relevant, and useful to provide a sound basis for audit findings and recommendations.

Sufficient information is factual, adequate, and convincing so that a prudent, informed person would reach the same conclusions as the auditor.

Competent information is reliable and the best attainable through the use of appropriate audit techniques.

Relevant information supports audit findings and recommendations and is consistent with the objectives for the audit.

Useful information helps the organization meet its goals.

.3   Audit procedures, including the testing and sampling techniques employed, should be selected in advance, where practicable, and expanded or altered if circumstances warrant.

.4   The process of collecting, analyzing, interpreting, and documenting information should be supervised to provide reasonable assurance that the auditor's objectivity is maintained and that audit goals are met.

.5   Working papers that document the audit should be prepared by the auditor and reviewed by management of the internal auditing department. These papers should record the information obtained and the analyses made and should support the bases for the findings and recommendations to be reported.

430   Communicating Results

Internal auditors should report the results of their audit work.

.01   A signed, written report should be issued after the audit examination is completed. Interim reports may be written or oral and may be transmitted formally or informally.

.02   The internal auditor should discuss conclusions and recommendations at appropriate levels of management before issuing final written reports.

.03   Reports should be objective, clear, concise, constructive, and timely.

.04   Reports should present the purpose, scope, and results of the audit; and, where appropriate, reports should contain an expression of the auditor's opinion.

.05   Reports may include recommendations for potential improvements and acknowledge satisfactory performance and corrective action.

.06   The auditee's views about audit conclusions or recommendations may be included in the audit report.

.07   The director of internal auditing or designee should review and approve the final audit report before issuance and should decide to whom the report will be distributed.

440   Following Up

Internal auditors should follow up to ascertain that appropriate action is taken on reported audit findings.

.01   Internal auditing should determine that corrective action was taken and is achieving the desired results, or that management or the board has assumed the risk of not taking corrective action on reported findings.

500   MANAGEMENT OF THE INTERNAL AUDITING DEPARTMENT

THE DIRECTOR OF INTERNAL AUDITING SHOULD PROPERLY MANAGE THE INTERNAL AUDITING DEPARTMENT.

.01   The director of internal auditing is responsible for properly managing the department so that:

.1   Audit work fulfills the general purposes and responsibilities approved by management and accepted by the board.

.2   Resources of the internal auditing department are efficiently and effectively employed.

.3   Audit work conforms to the *Standards for the Professional Practice of Internal Auditing.*

510   Purpose, Authority, and Responsibility

The director of internal auditing should have a statement of purpose, authority, and responsibility for the internal auditing department.

.01   The director of internal auditing is responsible for seeking the approval of management and the acceptance by the board of a formal written document (charter) for the internal auditing department.

520   Planning

The director of internal auditing should establish plans to carry out the responsibilities of the internal auditing department.

.01   These plans should be consistent with the internal auditing department's charter and with the goals of the organization.

.02   The planning process involves establishing:

.1 Goals.

.2 Audit work schedules.

.3 Staffing plans and financial budgets.

.4 Activity reports.

.03 The goals of the internal auditing department should be capable of being accomplished within specified operating plans and budgets and, to the extent possible, should be measurable. They should be accompanied by measurement criteria and targeted dates of accomplishment.

.04 Audit work schedules should include (a) what activities are to be audited; (b) when they will be audited; and (c) the estimated time required, taking into account the scope of the audit work planned and the nature and extent of audit work performed by others. Matters to be considered in establishing audit work schedule priorities should include (a) the date and results of the last audit; (b) financial exposure; (c) potential loss and risk; (d) requests by management; (e) major changes in operations, programs, systems, and controls; (f) opportunities to achieve operating benefits; and (g) changes to and capabilities of the audit staff. The work schedules should be sufficiently flexible to cover unanticipated demands on the internal auditing department.

.05 Staffing plans and financial budgets, including the number of auditors and the knowledge, skills, and disciplines required to perform their work, should be determined from audit work schedules, administrative activities, education and training requirements, and audit research and development efforts.

.06 Activity reports should be submitted periodically to management and to the board. These reports should compare (a) performance with the department's goals and audit work schedules and (b) expenditures with financial budgets. They should explain the reason for major variances and indicate any action taken or needed.

530   Policies and Procedures

The director of internal auditing should provide written policies and procedures to guide the audit staff.

.01 The form and content of written policies and procedures should be appropriate to the size and structure of the internal auditing department and the complexity of its work. Formal administrative and technical audit manuals may not be needed by all internal auditing departments. A small internal auditing department may be managed informally. Its audit staff may be directed and controlled through daily, close supervision and written memoranda. In a large internal auditing department, more formal and comprehensive policies and procedures are essential to guide the audit staff in the consistent compliance with the department's standards of performance.

540   Personnel Management and Development

The director of internal auditing should establish a program for selecting and developing the human resources of the internal auditing department.

.01   The program should provide for:

.1   Developing written job descriptions for each level of the audit staff.

.2   Selecting qualified and competent individuals.

.3   Training and providing continuing educational opportunities for each internal auditor.

.4   Appraising each internal auditor's performance at least annually.

.5   Providing counsel to internal auditors on their performance and professional development.

550   External Auditors

The director of internal auditing should coordinate internal and external audit efforts.

.01   The internal and external audit work should be coordinated to ensure adequate audit coverage and to minimize duplicate efforts.

.02   Coordination of audit efforts involves:

.1   Periodic meetings to discuss matters of mutual interest.

.2   Access to each other's audit programs and working papers.

.3   Exchange of audit reports and management letters.

.4   Common understanding of audit techniques, methods, and terminology.

560   Quality Assurance

The director of internal auditing should establish and maintain a quality assurance program to evaluate the operations of the internal auditing department.

.01   The purpose of this program is to provide reasonable assurance that audit work conforms with these *Standards,* the internal auditing department's charter, and other applicable standards. A quality assurance program should include the following elements:

.1   Supervision.

.2   Internal reviews.

.3   External reviews.

.02 Supervision of the work of the internal auditors should be carried out continually to assure conformance with internal auditing standards, departmental policies, and audit programs.

.03 Internal reviews should be performed periodically by members of the internal auditing staff to appraise the quality of the audit work performed. These reviews should be performed in the same manner as any other internal audit.

.04 External reviews of the internal auditing department should be performed to appraise the quality of the department's operations. These reviews should be performed by qualified persons who are independent of the organization and who do not have either a real or an apparent conflict of interest. Such reviews should be conducted at least once every three years. On completion of the review, a formal, written report should be issued. The report should express an opinion as to the department's compliance with the *Standards for the Professional Practice of Internal Auditing* and, as appropriate, should include recommendations for improvement.

Code of Ethics

Both the *Statement of Responsibilities of Internal Auditing* and the *Standards for the Professional Practice of Internal Auditing* state the necessity of internal auditors in meeting appropriate standards of conduct. The Responsibility and Authority section of the *Statement of Responsibilities of Internal Auditing* states that internal auditing should "serve the organization in a manner that is consistent with . . . professional standards of conduct such as the *Code of Ethics* of The Institute of Internal Auditors." Guideline 240.01 of the *Standards for the Professional Practice of Internal Auditing* states that "internal auditors should comply with professional standards of conduct," and it specifies The IIA's *Code of Ethics* as the appropriate basis of evaluation.

Actually, there are two formulations of The Institute's *Code of Ethics:* one for the general membership of The Institute and one for Certified Internal Auditors (CIAs), who have passed a certification examination and meet certain professional experience requirements. While the introductory statements of these two documents differ somewhat, the articles outlining the code of conduct are identical (with the exception of the eighth and final article of the general membership's code, which has been eliminated from the CIA code). A more significant difference between the two is a statement in the CIA *Code of Ethics* which states that a violation of the *Code* is grounds for removal of the auditor's certification.

Because the articles are identical, however, with the one exception, we will limit our discussion of the *Code* to the presentation given for the general membership of The Institute, which was adopted in 1968.

The *Code* specifies three reasons for a formal statement of standards by The IIA to guide the professional conduct of internal auditors:

1. The members of The Institute of Internal Auditors represent the profession of internal auditing.
2. Managements rely on the profession of internal auditing.
3. Members of The Institute must maintain high standards of conduct, honor, and character in order to carry out proper and meaningful internal auditing practice.

The *Code* goes on to state that internal auditors have "a responsibility to conduct themselves so that their good faith and integrity should not be open to question." So stating, the *Code* then dictates eight articles outlining what The Institute considers to be the standards of proper professional conduct for internal auditors:

ARTICLE I

Members shall have an obligation to exercise honesty, objectivity, and diligence in the performance of their duties and responsibilities.

This article identifies three personal characteristics that form the foundation upon which the other articles rest. Without honesty, members of the profession cannot be entrusted with the responsibilities and the authority necessary to perform the internal auditing function adequately.

We already have discussed the importance of objectivity. An auditor also must be diligent when performing his or her work. A lack of diligence can, and probably will, increase the chance of errors, oversights, and misinterpretations, all of which will jeopardize the auditor's credibility and value to the organization.

ARTICLE II

Members, in holding the trust of their employers, shall exhibit loyalty in all matters pertaining to the affairs of the employer or to whomever they may be rendering a service. However, members shall not knowingly be a party to any illegal or improper activity.

In contrast to the external auditor, the internal auditor assumes an advocacy position with respect to the organization. Questions arise, however: Who is the "employer"? Does it mean the inanimate corporate entity? Does it mean management? If so, which management? (There are different levels and divisions of management responsibility.) Or is it the individual who hired the auditor?

Other questions arise regarding the term "loyalty." What does it mean for an internal auditor to be loyal? Can loyalty manifest itself in different forms in different relationships? If so, could an internal auditor have conflicting loyalties due to the numerous parties representing his or her employer and others for whom a service may be rendered? How should such conflicts be resolved?

These are difficult questions and have not yet been definitively answered. Basically, however, this article states that internal auditors have an ethical responsibility to honor the trusts placed in them by their constituents — (a) people in the organization to whom they answer administratively and (b) those others whom they serve who might not have direct administrative responsibility for the auditors. Internal auditors have an ethical responsibility to do their part to see that these groups are successful in fulfilling their respective duties and responsibilities. Any act that violates that trust, except in cases of illegal or improper activities, violates the spirit of this article.

Suppose, for example, that during an audit of accounts payable the auditors discovered that one of the organization's major suppliers was not offering discounts for early payment, despite the fact that the supplier was offering discounts to other companies on similar purchases. The control system may have been functioning properly, no illegal activity was going on, and no accounting errors were caused by the practice. However, loyalty (and the goal of efficiency) should persuade the auditors to report this information to management.

In other situations of potential conflicts of interest, the auditor's loyalty should lie with his or her employer. For example, such an occasion might occur if an auditor had close personal friends working in a division being audited, and it was discovered that the friends were involved in some potential wrongdoing. The auditor would be confronted with the choice of protecting the friends or objectively including the facts of the case in the audit report. This article dictates that the auditor should remain objective and should include the information in the report.

As a related example, some internal auditing departments even have policies forbidding their auditors to fraternize with auditees. Such policies are designed to avoid the development of the close personal bonds which might compromise the auditors' objectivity.

Certainly, auditors should be independent of management's decision process and of the activities they audit. They also should be objective in their judgments. But they must remember that they should be loyal to their employer's interests.

ARTICLE III

Members shall refrain from entering into any activity which may be in conflict with the interest of their employers or which would prejudice their ability to carry out objectively their duties and responsibilities.

As with the previous article, the emphasis here is on the internal auditor's relationship with the employer and his or her responsibility for the employer's interests. There may be occasions when an auditor faces circumstances where there may be two or more choices, one or more of which conflict with the employer's welfare. In these cases, the auditor has an ethical responsibility to act in the employer's best interest without prejudicing his or her objectivity.

An example of a potential conflict of interest would be if the internal auditor invested in an insurance agency and was responsible for commenting on the adequacy of insurance coverage, which may be handled by that same agency. Under the circumstances, the auditor's objectivity could be questioned. In any situation where the auditor is emotionally torn between alternatives, he or she should decide in favor of the employer's interests, and still retain the objectivity necessary for fulfilling the audit responsibilities. By following generally accepted auditing methods and procedures, the auditor is better able to avoid compromising his or her objectivity.

ARTICLE IV

Members shall not accept a fee or a gift from an employee, a client, a customer, or a business associate of their employer without the knowledge and consent of their senior management.

In contrast to the other articles, which prescribe general principles of conduct, this article identifies a specific situation which might jeopardize the auditor's objectivity and which might conflict with the employer's interests. Certainly, by accepting personal fees or gifts, the auditor's ability to maintain a professionally objective attitude might reasonably be questioned. In such situations, it is better to avoid even the appearance of compromise. *Professional Standards Bulletin 84-5* specifies that such avoidance is advisable regardless of whether the offer comes from a current auditee or from an employee or area not being audited. Plus, according to this bulletin, "internal auditors should report the offer of all material fees or gifts immediately to their immediate supervisors." On the other hand, small promotional items, such as pens or calendars that are available to the general public and are of minimal value, are not likely to hinder the internal auditor's professional judgment.

There may be occasions when a gift, even of substantial value, may be appropriate. In these cases, the knowledge and consent of senior management likely will protect the auditor against an otherwise compromising situation.

ARTICLE V

Members shall be prudent in the use of information acquired in the course of their duties. They shall not use confidential information for any personal gain nor in a manner which would be detrimental to the welfare of their employers.

In the course of their work, auditors learn a great deal about their organizations and the people working there. Some information can be potentially valuable to various other people and organizations, especially to competitive organizations. During recent years, the theft and sale of trade secrets, sometimes called "corporate espionage," has become an increasingly serious problem for many companies. Indeed, it is an international problem. The internal auditor is ethically bound to keep confidential information confidential.

Even when it is appropriate to communicate potentially sensitive information, internal auditors should do so in a prudent manner, and divulge it only to those who really have a right and a need to know. For example, internal auditors often are privy to information of major importance to the careers of individuals within the organization. Regardless of whether the information is positive or negative, the auditors should report the information only to responsible parties who need it for effective decision-making regarding the organization's performance. The information should not be bandied about as a mere conversation piece. At other times, information may have critical legal implications. Again, only those decision-makers who rightfully need the information should get it.

ARTICLE VI

Members, in expressing an opinion, shall use all reasonable care to obtain sufficient factual evidence to warrant such expression. In their reporting, members shall reveal such material facts known to them which, if not revealed, could either distort the report of the results of operations under review or conceal unlawful practice.

The first part of this article states that auditors should not render an opinion without adequate information to justify the opinion. The second part stipulates that if auditors have information that would be material to management's judgment, they are ethically responsible for reporting the information. With regard to the first provision, unsubstantiated claims can seriously endanger the organization. The primary danger is that the conclusions and claims might be wrong, thereby prompting decisions and actions that otherwise would be unwarranted. Sometimes it is difficult to understand a situation clearly even when all of the available information is known; when significant evidence has been either ignored or overlooked, it is even more difficult. It is a matter of professional propriety for the auditor to develop a strong, convincing argument for his or her opinions. Such arguments are possible only with adequate factual evidence, which requires direct support, not merely hearsay.

But what about occasions when the evidence is not sufficient for a final conclusion and a report is to be issued? There are times when the auditors, for various reasons, simply cannot gather conclusive evidence. Sometimes only by waiting for a final outcome can the answers to some questions be known with certainty. A good example is a particular marketing strategy which in the beginning may violate numerous control measures, but because of a manager's hunch is adopted anyway. The auditors can only point out the observed control violations and the potential risks.

At other times auditors may even suspect wrongdoing, but have not gathered enough evidence to confirm their suspicions. It is not unusual for auditors to turn their cases over to the company's security department, which then will further investigate any suspected wrongdoing. Not all firms employ such security persons, however. In those instances, the investigation is done by the internal auditors, external auditors, legal counsel, trained investigators, or even law enforcement agencies. The selection of who performs the investigation depends upon the seriousness of the suspected wrongdoing and the strength of the evidence suggesting such wrongdoing.

Where evidence is not conclusive, the auditors must be careful not to state any strong, final conclusions that are not supported by sufficient factual evidence. Conclusions may be only as strong as the evidence. Additional information on evidence and its effect upon the audit process is included in Chapter 4.

With regard to the second part of this article, given that it is the auditor's responsibility to assist management in its control function, the clearer and the more accurate the audit reports are, the more help the auditor will be. Distorting or concealing any relevant facts represents disloyalty to the employer and violates other articles of the *Code.* Generally, when such a case of concealment or distortion occurs, it results from a conflict of interest.

For example, when an internal auditor discovered a sizable fraud in a medical service clinic, a party to the fraud approached the auditor in an effort to persuade him to ignore the evidence in the final report if the money was returned and the records were corrected. The auditor knew the party well and later admitted to a momentary conflict with his employer's interests. Fortunately, however, his better judgment prevailed, and he included all of the facts in his report, as he had discovered them.

ARTICLE VII

Members shall continually strive for improvement in the proficiency and effectiveness of their service.

Other professions have similar provisions in their codes of ethics prescribing professional development. Indeed, such a principle seems basic to our way of life, in that we all seem to be striving for personal improvement.

The professions often appear to make a relatively organized effort. Generally, this results from a rapidly changing state of the art. Various schools and seminars offer opportunities for ongoing professional development. Some organizations offer their own professional development courses. The Institute of Internal Auditors has an active international seminar program to assist internal auditors in fulfilling their responsibilities in this area.

ARTICLE VIII

Members shall abide by the bylaws and uphold the objectives of The Institute of Internal Auditors. In the practice of their profession, they shall be ever mindful of their obligation to maintain the high standard of competence, morality, and dignity which The Institute of Internal Auditors and its members have established.

Like the first article, this one outlines the personal characteristics and commitment required to uphold the stature necessary for the successful practice of internal auditing as a profession that functions within the highest levels of organizational leadership. As their standard, internal auditors are instructed to use The Institute and its members. A standard of competence is outlined in the *Standards for the Professional Practice of Internal Auditing.* A standard of morality is outlined by the other articles in the *Code of Ethics,* and with this article, it also includes the consensus attitudes held by members of The Institute. These, because of the basic composition of the profession, represent relatively conservative, traditional moral values. A standard of dignity has been established by The Institute through its various activities, publications, professional development seminars, and relationships with other groups in the government and business communities.

Auditor Certification

In 1974, The Institute of Internal Auditors began to certify internal auditors who qualified under one of two sets of criteria. The first set applied only to auditors who, at that time, had practiced auditing in a decision-making capacity and who agreed to honor The Institute's *Code of Ethics.* These first auditors were certified under what is called a "grandfather clause."

The second set of criteria has applied to all auditors certified since then. These criteria include holding a baccalaureate degree from an accredited college-level institution, two years of appropriate experience, subscription to the *Code of Ethics,* and passage of a four-part examination. The examination includes sections on (1) the theory and practice of internal auditing (in two parts), (2) management, quantitative methods, and information systems, and (3) accounting, finance, and economics.

This certification program promotes a standard of excellence for the profession among those who call themselves professional internal auditors. Certification is not required to practice internal auditing, however, and many internal auditors practice without certification. On the other hand, the program has established a recognized standard for the profession, and tests a common body of knowledge agreed to be necessary for the internal auditing professional. Some people believe that all practicing internal auditors should be certified.

Actions by the U.S. General Accounting Office

More than a decade ago, the General Accounting Office (GAO) of the U.S. government recognized the need for auditing standards prescribed for federal auditors. In 1972, the GAO issued *Standards for Audit of Governmental Organizations, Programs, Activities, and Functions,* which has become better known as "the yellow book."

This document, printed by the U.S. Government Printing Office, outlines specific standards for three kinds of audits: (1) financial and compliance audits, (2) economy and efficiency audits, and (3) program results audits. These three types of audits are described in "the yellow book" as follows:

> Financial and compliance — determines (a) whether the financial statements of an audited entity present fairly the financial position and the results of financial operations in accordance with generally accepted accounting principles and (b) whether the entity has complied with laws and regulations that may have a material effect upon the financial statements.

Economy and efficiency — determines (a) whether the entity is managing and utilizing its resources (such as personnel, property, space) economically and efficiently, (b) the causes of inefficiencies or uneconomical practices, and (c) whether the entity has complied with laws and regulations concerning matters of economy and efficiency.

Program results — determines (a) whether the desired results or benefits established by the legislature or other authorizing body are being achieved and (b) whether the agency has considered alternatives that might yield desired results at a lower cost.

The financial and compliance audits are important to federal auditors because public accounting firms typically do not audit U.S. government financial statements. Consequently, government auditors fulfill this function.

Notice, however, that the broad nature of the overall auditing function goes far beyond the auditing of financial statements and includes the examination of ongoing operations and programs. This broad perspective is quite in harmony with internal auditing in the private sector. In fact, the "yellow book" states that The IIA's standards, as reprinted in this chapter, are compatible with those established by the GAO for governmental auditors.

A distinctive feature of the GAO standards is that they subscribe to the AICPA standards for external audits and integrate them into the U.S. government audit function.

Because of the compatibility of The IIA's and the GAO's standards and the wide applicability of The IIA's standards, references to internal auditing standards in this textbook are made with respect to those established and published by The IIA. We believe that students who may eventually practice auditing for the federal government will discover that the principles outlined in this text may be applied in that setting, as well as in other government and private-sector settings.

Actions by Internal Auditing Departments

Several measures can be taken within individual internal auditing departments to promote professionalism. The *Standards for the Professional Practice of Internal Auditing* outlines and discusses three important ways: (1) proper staffing, (2) acquisition of necessary knowledge, skills, and disciplines, and (3) proper supervision of audit work. Four related measures include the following:

1. Establishing appropriate specific charter provisions.
2. Adhering to professional standards.
3. Maintaining a core of professional auditors.
4. Establishing appropriate training opportunities.

Let's briefly examine each of these four measures:

Charters

The *Standards* states that charters should be written and approved by management and the board of directors, and should outline the purpose, authority, and responsibility of the internal auditing department within the organization. The specific provisions, however, are left largely to the organizations themselves. These specific provisions should include the following topics:

1. Establishment of the internal auditing function.
2. The goal or objective of the auditing function.
3. The authority granted to the department.
4. The scope of work authorized for the internal auditing department.
5. The organizational status of the department.
6. Acceptable standards of performance for the department.
7. The department's administrative and reporting relationships.
8. Responsibility for following up on audit findings.
9. Approval of the charter by executive management and the audit committee.

A careful drafting of this document can promote and help maintain a high level of expectation for the professional integrity and performance within the department. It also can promote the status of the internal auditing function.

Professional Standards

The standards established by The IIA represent only strong encouragement. They are, however, the most widely accepted body of standards for the profession. They are a commonly held measure of excellence for internal auditors, and by accepting these standards, internal auditing departments can promote and sustain a high degree of professionalism within their respective organizations. While the GAO has published "the yellow book," comprising a similar set of standards for the practice of auditing for the U.S. government, the *Standards for the Professional Practice of Internal Auditing* published by The IIA is recognized internationally by auditors of commercial, governmental, and not-for-profit organizations. The voluntary acceptance of The IIA's standards by internal auditing departments promotes a uniformly high quality of practice within the profession.

Professional Auditors

It is the practice in many companies to use the internal auditing department as a management training school, where trainees work as auditors for anywhere from six months to three years, and then are transferred to middle management positions elsewhere in the organizations. Sometimes the auditing staff can be composed almost totally of these "transient" auditors. Such a practice can jeopardize the quality and the professionalism of the audit function itself.

There are several advantages to using the internal auditing department as a means of training prospective managers. They can gain a global, integrated perspective of the overall organization by participating in a variety of audits. This variety provides them with a good introduction to the detailed operations of individual functions and activities. The trainees also get to know many key personnel in the organization and can compare managers and operations. They all benefit the internal auditing department by bringing a fresh look to audited operations. When they graduate into management positions, they are likely to understand internal control and the audit role better, and to help expedite audits of their operations.

Because of the disadvantages, however, it is a wise practice among better internal auditing departments to keep a core of highly competent professional auditors within the department. The proportion of management trainees should be kept small enough to enable the department to fulfill its duties with well-trained, well-supervised staff members who understand the audit function and can work effectively and efficiently. Although others may assist in the work, the department should maintain a core of professionals.

Training

Professional development, as an important responsibility of the internal auditor, can be encouraged by sponsoring in-house training programs or by sending staff members to appropriate outside training programs. Individual consulting firms, The American Management Association, CPA firms, and The Institute of Internal Auditors conduct a variety of seminars designed to help internal auditors keep abreast of developments within the profession and to expand and sharpen their individual skills.

Individual Appearance and Conduct

The *Standards for the Professional Practice of Internal Auditing* details six areas where individual auditors can develop their professionalism. They are (1) compliance with the *Code of Ethics* of The Institute, (2) acquisition of the knowledge, skills, and disciplines essential for the performance of internal audits, (3) development of human relations and communications skills, (4) continuance of their education during their careers, (5) the exercise of due professional care in performing their duties, and (6) by qualifying as a Certified Internal Auditor or a Certified Public Accountant, the auditor demonstrates a commonly recognized measure of professionalism.

These six steps represent ways that the individual can exercise professionalism in auditing. There is yet another area of importance. Although not a usual part of the university curriculum, professional appearance and personal conduct are recognized to be important by most successful business people. These two dimensions of professionalism in auditing are vital to the success of the individual auditor and, in most cases, to the success of the internal auditing department. Every internal auditor should be well versed in appropriate personal behavior in the office, at social gatherings, and at meals. They should have an appropriate wardrobe and a neat, well-organized work environment. They should have impeccable telephone manners.

While instruction in these and other aspects of personal etiquette is not an objective of this chapter, we strongly encourage students to study and acquire the personal traits of a professional business person. These traits will be important for advancement within the organization.

QUESTIONS

1. Briefly, what responsibilities have The Institute of Internal Auditors (IIA), internal auditing departments, and individual practitioners assumed in the development of professionalism in internal auditing?
2. What specific steps has The IIA taken to promote professionalism?
3. What authority does The IIA have in the enforcement of its standards and *Code of Ethics?* Explain.
4. Explain briefly each of the provisions in the *Statement of Responsibilities of Internal Auditing.*
5. What are the five General Standards contained in the *Standards for the Professional Practice of Internal Auditing?*
6. The introduction to the *Standards for the Professional Practice of Internal Auditing* states that it is the objective of internal auditing "to assist members of the organization in the effective discharge of their responsibilities." Who are the members assisted by internal auditing? What is the nature of the responsibility owed to those members?
7. Identify six specific things that can be done, according to Guideline 110.01 in the *Standards,* to help the internal auditing department acquire organizational status in order to accomplish its audit responsibilities.
8. Identify six ways that internal auditors can help to minimize their chances of being placed in situations in which they feel unable to make objective professional judgments.
9. What is the director of internal auditing's responsibility for audit supervision?
10. An auditor's preparation is divided into three levels of knowledge, skills, and disciplines. The highest level is proficiency, followed by understanding and, finally, appreciation. What does it mean to have proficiency? An understanding? An appreciation?
11. What does it mean for an auditor to exercise "due professional care"?
12. What are the primary objectives of internal control, according to the *Standards for the Professional Practice of Internal Auditing?*
13. Distinguish between management's responsibility and the responsibility of internal auditing with respect to the economical and efficient use of resources. What practical difficulties arise for the auditors?
14. What is the auditor's responsibility for planning the audit, for examining and evaluating information, for communicating results, and for following up?
15. What are the three goals and responsibilities of the director of internal auditing with respect to managing the auditing department?
16. What three key elements should be present in an effective quality assurance program for an internal auditing department?
17. What is "the yellow book"? Discuss its provisions and significance.
18. What are the eight articles of the *Code of Ethics* of The Institute of Internal Auditors? What is the difference between the *Code of Ethics* for the general membership of The IIA and that for Certified Internal Auditors?
19. What measures, other than those outlined in the *Standards,* can be taken by internal auditing departments to promote and maintain professionalism?

20. Identify seven ways that the individual internal auditor can increase his or her own professionalism.

EXERCISES

E-1

Maxwell Corporation is establishing a new internal auditing department and has hired Fred Johnson as the director of the new department. Mr. Johnson has set the establishment of a charter for the department as his top priority. In a meeting with the corporate general manager, Mr. Johnson outlined specific provisions that he felt were important and should be included in the charter. Four of them were:

- The director of internal auditing reports administratively to the corporate general manager, although the audit committee of the board of directors must approve the hiring or firing of the director of internal auditing.
- Corporate management must provide the internal auditing department with access to all corporate documents necessary for the completion of its audits.
- The internal auditing department, at the request of the company's external auditors and with the approval of the director of internal auditing, may assist in the gathering of information and performance of audit tests for the annual audit of the company's financial statements. All judgments and opinions resulting from that audit, however, are the sole responsibility of the external auditors.
- The internal auditing department, under the supervision of the director of internal auditing, shall have the responsibility to develop standards of control for EDP operations.

Required:

Comment on the appropriateness of each of the four proposed provisions.

E-2

Internal auditors for a bank were conducting a review of the bank's loan department. In the course of this review, an auditor noticed that one loan officer approved several loans based upon unusually old credit reports on the persons making loan applications. The auditor became concerned and directed the loan officer to obtain updated credit reports on all future loan applications before approving any of them. The auditor reported this directive with his other findings.

Required:

Was the auditor's action appropriate? Cite a specific reference in the *Standards for the Professional Practice of Internal Auditing* to support your answer.

E-3

The IIA's *Code of Ethics* states that internal auditors should not enter into any activity which would "be in conflict with the interest of their employers." An internal auditor for State Life Insurance Company belonged to a fraternal organization and was appointed to work on a committee to investigate and recommend a group life insurance policy for the members of the organization.

Required:

Was the auditor's work on this committee in violation of the *Code of Ethics?* Explain your answer.

E-4

Hal Beard, director of the electronic data processing operations of Wingfield Industries Corporation, and Jerry Goldstein, director of internal auditing for the company, were assigned to sit together at a formal dinner held on the evening following the annual golf day for the management and staff of headquarters. About midway through the meal, people at surrounding tables heard an intense argument break out between the two. Finally, Hal stood up and shouted at Jerry, "Your auditors had better not stick their noses into my department. Setting standards of control for our system designs is my business. You auditors stay out of it. Besides, if your guys start telling us about our standards, that would violate your own standard of objectivity which you seem to hold so dear." With that comment, Hal stormed from the room, leaving his meal half eaten.

Required:

Is the internal auditor's objectivity compromised by recommending standards of control in the EDP department in the design of its systems? Why or why not?

E-5

The board of directors of Middle West Company is considering the administrative reorganization of the company's management structure. The company's controller previously had been an internal auditor and had expressed his preference that the internal auditing department be placed under his jurisdiction because, as he said, "Internal auditing really is an accounting function, anyway."

Required:

Evaluate the controller's statement, with specific reference to the *Standards for the Professional Practice of Internal Auditing.*

E-6

The following is a list of four possible internal auditing responsibilities:

1. Reviewing the reliability and the integrity of divisional financial reports.
2. Determining compliance with applicable laws and regulations.
3. Ascertaining whether operating goals and objectives are being achieved.
4. Reviewing the economy and the efficiency with which resources are employed.

Required:

Evaluate each of the four responsibilities in terms of the scope of responsibilities that would be properly assigned to the internal auditing function.

(CIA Exam Adapted)

E-7

The charter of a utility company's internal auditing department includes a provision that the company's board of directors approve the appointment or dismissal of the director of internal auditing.

Required:
a. What objective do you think the company has in including this provision in its charter for the internal auditing department? Cite specifically the *Standards for the Professional Practice of Internal Auditing.*
b. Name three other measures that may be taken to help achieve the same objective.

E-8

Clyde Sweeney, a recent recruit from a local CPA firm, was hired as an internal auditor for Chickadee Bakeries, Inc., a chain of retail bakeries in the Midwest. During Mr. Sweeney's first meeting with Marvin Parker, the director of internal auditing, a question arose about the concept of professional proficiency. Mr. Parker suggested that Mr. Sweeney study professional proficiency carefully, as it applies to internal auditors and their departments. When Mr. Sweeney began to study the *Standards for the Professional Practice of Internal Auditing,* he discovered that proficiency standards are divided into those that apply to the internal auditing department and those that apply to the individual auditor.

Required:
a. List the professional proficiency standards that apply to the department.
b. List the professional proficiency standards for individual auditors.
c. Explain why it is desirable for Mr. Sweeney to understand both lists.

E-9

Daniel Townsend recently was assigned to work on an audit of the Valleyview production plant of a large manufacturing company. He just came to work in the internal auditing department three months ago. He had been an assistant to the Valleyview production plant superintendent for the previous four years.

Required:
a. What professional standard of practice appears to be violated in this scenario?
b. Explain the potential dangers that this standard is designed to avoid.
c. Do you see any possible advantages in having Mr. Townsend involved in the audit? Explain.

E-10

The vice president of operations for a utilities company sought out the lead auditor of a team working in a nearby plant. The vice president had recommended that one of the young managers at the plant be assigned to internal auditing for a year to get a broader perspective of the firm. Such an assignment would serve as preparation for the greater management responsibilities expected for the young manager in the future. The vice president had spoken with the young man that morning and discovered that he had not been assigned to the audit of the plant where he used to work. The vice president asked the lead auditor why the young man had not been included, especially since he was so familiar with the plant's operations and could save the other auditors a great deal of time (and, consequently, money) in understanding the operations and performing the audit.

Required:

Explain conceptually why the young manager might be left off the audit team. Do you agree with that decision?

E-11

A group of new internal auditors from different organizations met at a seminar held in a large city in New England. One of the topics of discussion was the relevance of a single set of standards for the practice of internal auditing. Some of the participants wondered, since internal auditing is so different from organization to organization, what purpose, if any, a single set of performance standards might serve. The seminar leader suggested that the participants examine the adopted *Standards for the Professional Practice of Internal Auditing* for some clues.

Required:

a. What purposes are the adopted standards designed to serve? (See the introduction to the *Standards.*)

b. Do you agree that a single set of standards might be inadequate for internal auditing in general, especially since internal auditing activities do differ among organizations? Explain.

E-12

Following are five statements regarding the internal auditing function within organizations:

1. Internal auditors should report any situations in which a conflict of interest or bias is present or may be reasonably inferred to the director of internal auditing.
2. External reviews of the internal auditing department should be performed to appraise the quality of the department's operations.
3. The purpose, authority, and responsibility of the internal auditing department should be defined in a formal written document.
4. Suitable criteria of education and experience for filling internal auditing positions should be established.
5. Internal reviews of the internal auditing department should be performed by members of its staff to appraise the quality of the audit work.

Required:

a. Identify the section of either the *Code of Ethics* or the *Standards for the Professional Practice of Internal Auditing* that would most likely apply to each of the statements above.

b. Discuss each statement in terms of its consistency with the respective provisions of the *Code of Ethics* or the *Standards*.

(CIA Exam Adapted)

E-13

Suppose you have been appointed to be a member of a three-person external review team to evaluate the internal auditing department of a medium-sized chain of retail department stores in the Southwest. One of the team's directives is to evaluate whether the department exercises due professional care in its work. In fact, the president of the company, when giving the charge to your team, specified that he wanted to be sure that the "auditing department's procedures would provide management with the assurance that all of the company's transactions are recorded and reported correctly, and that all of the company policies are being followed — no ifs, ands, or buts about it."

He also wants assurance that the auditors will use appropriate procedures that will provide "absolute certainty" of their results.

Required:
a. What do you think of the president's charge?
b. Using the provisions in the *Standards for the Professional Practice of Internal Auditing* regarding due professional care as your guide, how would you modify this charge, if at all?

E-14

In the course of an audit of the vehicle maintenance department at the regional headquarters of a large car and truck rental firm, the auditors found out in an interview with the shop manager that a vice president of the firm, who lived locally, regularly brought his personal car to be maintained by the shop. The auditors included this information from the interview in their report. The auditors concluded from the interview that appropriate controls were not operating in this situation and should be established as soon as possible.

Required:
a. Evaluate the information given to the auditors in terms of its sufficiency, completeness, relevance, and usefulness.
b. Comment on how you would have proceeded, following the interview, if you were the internal auditor.

E-15

William J. Jones is an audit supervisor for Belthorp Industries. During an audit of the plant's facilities, which are located on the shoreline of the Bountiful River, he discovered that a thick, foul-smelling sludge was being pumped from the plant into the river. The trees and plant life surrounding the entry point appeared sick and sparse.

Mr. Jones knew that there was a state law forbidding the direct deposit of industrial sludge into the state's waterways without proper treatment, and he also knew that this particular sludge probably was doing considerable harm to the fish and animal life downstream.

Required:

a. Identify the appropriate provisions of the *Code of Ethics* and the *Standards* that would help him decide what he should do.

b. What are his responsibilities in this situation?

E-16

A large computer manufacturing and sales firm has a management training program for its junior managers. A major part of this program includes an 18-month tour of duty in the internal auditing department. Top management has stated that a tour of duty in internal auditing will do more than any other experience to give these young managers an organizational perspective. Because of a slowdown in the economy, the firm has decreased the size of its permanent audit staff, but has maintained the flow of management trainees through the department. The president of the company says that this practice will cut expenses and still provide an excellent training program for young executives.

Required:

What are some possible dangers of such a practice? Specify dangers to the overall organization, the auditing department, and individuals involved in the program (both auditors and trainees).

PROBLEMS
P-1

A company markets a diverse line of light and heavy products in both domestic and world markets. The company retains export/import brokers to perform its sales function in certain areas of the world. The internal audit department has performed an audit of the export division of the company, with emphasis primarily on the transactions involving the brokers. The audit team is completing its audit report and has submitted its working papers and preliminary draft report to the audit supervisor.

Following are selected items from the auditor's working papers:

1. The manager of the export division has assured us that he has full confidence in his brokers and that there is no need to extend the audit into the brokers' records. He assures us that the errors we noted were oversights that will be corrected. On the basis of his assurance, we are satisfied that our company's interests are properly protected.

2. The errors that we noted in our limited test of calculations of special allowances, discounts, and commissions all appear to have occurred in our billing department. We have recommended that this department's internal operations be completely reviewed.

3. Certain transfers of funds, such as commissions, between the company and the brokers appear to be somewhat unusual. However, the export manager assures us that these

transfers are in accordance with company and legal requirements and that it is not necessary to pursue the question further.

4. Certain types of expenses and commissions were not fully documented, but the export manager is satisfied that this is because of the special nature of the transactions and the customers involved. He has assured us that these cases have been fully approved.

5. Insurance, traffic, collection, and banking arrangements all appear to be processed on the approval of the export manager. They all appear to be reasonable.

6. We are of the opinion that none of the above is worthy of specific mention in the final report. These matters will be included in the group of miscellaneous minor items being considered by the export manager.

Required:
Assume the role of the audit supervisor:

a. For each of the six situations described above, state the principle in the *Code of Ethics* which applies.

b. State what action you would take in each of the six situations in order to satisfy the requirement(s) set forth by the *Code of Ethics*.

(CIA Exam Adapted)

P-2
You are the director of internal auditing at a university. Recently, you met with the manager of administrative data processing and expressed the desire to establish a more effective interface between the two departments.

Subsequently, the manager of data processing requested your views and help on a new computerized accounts payable system being developed. The manager recommended that internal auditing assume line responsibility for auditing suppliers' invoices prior to payment.

The manager also requested that internal auditing make suggestions during the development of the system, assist in its installation, and approve the completed system after making a final review.

Required:
Evaluate the requests made by the manager of data processing in the three areas:

1. The recommendation that your department be responsible for the preaudit of suppliers' invoices.

2. The request that you make suggestions during the development of the system.

3. The request that you assist in the installation of the system and approve the system after making a final review.

(CIA Exam Adapted)

P-3
The director of internal auditing for a marketing organization received the following memorandum from the controller:

During the last audit of my department, the internal auditors on several occasions told the accountants and accounting clerks what they should do in carrying out their respective accounting tasks along with how and when they should do them. Some of my accounting supervisors were told that certain adjusting entries should be made to correct prior period errors and to adjust the carrying values of certain assets.

I realize that the internal auditing staff is very knowledgeable about accounting principles, accounting systems, and the activities within my department. Some of the auditors used to work in this department, and others are experienced accountants with various professional credentials.

There is no question that the auditors' directions helped my department solve some of its problems and did, in fact, correct some significant deficiencies in the company's financial statements. Nevertheless, I strongly believe that the auditors went beyond their authority while performing this audit.

Required:

a. In terms of the *Statement of Responsibilities of Internal Auditing,* discuss the internal auditors' actions described above.

b. Identify three problems which may arise if the issue of authority is not resolved.

(CIA Exam Adapted)

P-4

You are the director of internal auditing for Black Company. A disgruntled Grey Company employee informed you that certain sales people who work for Grey have been giving kickbacks to your company's director of purchasing in order to secure additional business. The informer believes that these kickbacks were paid in cash and that they averaged about $5,000 per year for the past three years, or about 5 percent of Black's annual purchases from Grey Company. Black's director of purchasing is one of your longtime business friends. When you inform him of what you have learned, he readily admits that he accepted kickbacks from Grey. He pleads with you to overlook his mistake and to not report it to Black's management because:

1. His family would suffer if it became known.
2. He accepted the money to pay for large medical bills for one of his children.
3. The amount he had accepted from Grey Company was a very insignificant percentage of his total purchasing volume.
4. Your company had not incurred any losses because the prices paid to Grey were competitive.
5. He stressed his 20-year record of efficient and dedicated service with Black Company.
6. You and he are well aware that it is company policy to immediately discharge anyone who accepts kickbacks.

Required:

a. Give the substance of two articles from the *Code of Ethics* that relate to the situation above.

b. Give the substance of four specific standards from the *Standards for the Professional Practice of Internal Auditing* that apply to the situation above.
c. Summarize briefly three actions that the director of internal auditing should take.

(CIA Exam Adapted)

P-5

The director of internal auditing has established the practice of an internal auditors' meeting, called an "opening conference," with the branch manager at the beginning of each audit. The purpose of this meeting is to discuss the general audit approach, the planned areas of audit coverage, and the expected duration of the audit.

During a recent opening conference, a branch manager told the auditors that the timing of the audit was "all wrong" and that all approvals for interviewing personnel must be obtained through his office. The senior auditor resented the attitude of the branch manager and said so. Feeling there was no alternative to these conditions, the auditors agreed among themselves to interpret strictly a company policy of minimizing disruptions to normal branch operations during an audit. Therefore, they made it a point not to meet with the branch manager to discuss the audit findings until the exit conference.

At the exit conference, all areas of agreement and disagreement between the internal auditors and the branch manager were discussed and documented. However, in order to emphasize the branch manager's uncooperative attitude, the final internal audit report included only the findings and recommendations with which the branch manager disagreed.

Required:

a. Describe one departure from each of the scope, objectivity, and reporting portions of the *Standards for the Professional Practice of Internal Auditing* in the situation above.
b. Explain at least two adverse effects for each of the departures given above.

(CIA Exam Adapted)

3 Control of Internal Systems

The key function of internal auditing is monitoring the control system of an organization. In this chapter we discuss management objectives, internal control objectives, types of internal controls, methods of internal control, and related matters. The purpose is to provide a sound understanding of internal control concepts in order to better understand the internal auditing function and process, which are discussed in detail in other chapters. An appendix to this chapter contains a copy of the first *Statement on Internal Auditing Standards (SIAS),* titled "Control: Concepts and Responsibilities," which summarizes many of the concepts discussed in this chapter.

The management control process is expected to ensure that an organization is working toward its stated objectives and that required resources to achieve such goals are available when needed. This is accomplished by defining and communicating corporate objectives and programs, by motivating the organization toward the achievement of those goals, and by providing standards against which the organization's progress can be appraised.

Role of Management Objectives

The overall purposes of an organization are translated by management into operating objectives. To ensure that those objectives are met, management sets plans and establishes control over the execution of the plans.

How Operating Objectives Relate to Control

Operating objectives direct the day-to-day activities which, in turn, are controlled by internal control systems. Unfortunately, operating objectives sometimes conflict. For example, joint operating objectives are likely to be the adequate safeguarding of assets and the efficient production of goods. Consider new materials and how they might be requisitioned. Effective safeguarding procedures require some type of formal requisition to be filled out for the storekeeper, even though some delay may occur as requisitioners wait for the paperwork to be completed. Employees may point out that a far more efficient means of filling raw material needs would be for all employees to "take what's needed," with no requirement that time-consuming paperwork be completed. In fact, some employees who choose to maximize efficiency over safeguarding objectives may work to discover some means of circumventing the formal requisition process.

By understanding such a tendency by employees, the entity can design controls that are as compatible with operating objectives as possible. To continue the example: rather than permitting backlogs in the storekeeper function, management can assign two or more storekeepers so that the waiting time for requisitioning materials is minimized. In this manner, incentives to circumvent controls are decreased and the entity can concurrently meet its safeguarding and efficiency objectives. Of course, before implementing the control, management must weigh its cost compared to the expected benefit. The second storekeeper adds several thousands of dollars in cost to the operation. This cost should be less than any expected losses from lost goods and production inefficiencies without the control.

The rank ordering, or prioritization, of objectives directs the development of controls. For example, if a key objective is to get billings out within a day of shipment, it may be impossible to test the mathematical accuracy of every billing. In such a setting, the ramifications of not meeting the operating objective must be balanced against the risks resulting from mathematical inaccuracies in billings. The result may be the establishment of control procedures whereby only those shipments exceeding a specified dollar amount are subjected to mathematical accuracy tests.

The Influence of Particular Objectives upon the Design of Controls and the Role of Internal Auditing

The design of controls, as well as the role of an internal auditing function which is assigned oversight responsibility for the control system, is greatly influenced by the specific set of goals which management is striving to achieve. For example, rapid growth of an entity poses a risk that controls will be lost over decentralized operations run by growing numbers of inexperienced employees. The need for the centralization of key controls, the monitoring of decentralized operations, and formal hiring and training procedures becomes apparent in such a setting. On the other hand, suppose that the entity's size is stable, turnover is low, and operations are centralized. In this case, the importance of field visits by internal auditors, formal training programs, or too centralized a set of controls within the organization is diminished.

A specific contrast in operating objectives can be useful in demonstrating the extent to which controls, operations, and internal auditors must be coordinated. Assume that one entity wishes to expand its customer base to increase the volume of sales. In so doing, management accepts the inevitability of incurring greater amounts of bad debt expense, as well as greater interest costs associated with the extension of more credit.

The volume of anticipated sales makes credit checks on 100 percent of the customer base impractical. In fact, management's key goal is to offer credit to all, but to cut its losses when collection problems arise. This means that the control system must be designed to include a continuous monitoring system whereby aging schedules for receivables are prepared to detect past-due receivables. Those accounts are then flagged so as not to receive additional credit. Internal auditors, in turn, have an oversight role to not merely check compliance with set procedures, but to assess the effectiveness with which ongoing monitoring is performed. For example, are agings prepared on a sufficiently timely basis? Are "old" accounts identified in a reasonable fashion? Is the communication link to the sales department sufficiently expedient to avoid undue credit risk exposure?

The management of another entity might, for example, want to maintain its current customer base, but reduce the cost of carrying receivables, including the amount of bad debts. Credit policies then would be tightened, as would controls over the extension of credit. In this setting, controls would be "front-end," credit checks would be required before credit could be granted, and terms which deter delayed payment would be offered — for example, offers of cash discounts to encourage prompt payment, or the levying of late payment charges. The internal auditor would focus more on compliance with set control procedures, which act as a filtering device to avoid subsequent losses from poor credit-granting policies. This does not mean that the internal auditor ignores other signs of effectiveness within the credit department; it merely shows a more compliance-oriented audit within a reasonably structured control environment.

Internal auditors can assume highly diverse roles due to varying management objectives. For example, in an expanding firm, the internal auditors are likely to be requested to advise management regarding control design. In an entity that is converting to an EDP system, the internal auditor may be requested to critique planned control designs. In a stable company, the internal audit function may be thought of as a "thermostat" over the control system, overseeing its operation within some reasonable range. Cost savings may be expected to accrue regularly through increased operational auditing activities.

In contrast, for a new company that is perhaps not even undergoing an external audit yet, the internal auditors may assume more of a financial auditing orientation, providing assurance as to the reasonableness of output generated by the accounting system. In a highly regulated environment, internal auditors may be asked to do more compliance-oriented engagements to help detect trouble spots on a timely basis.

Cost/Benefit Considerations in Setting Management and Control Objectives

Up to this point, numerous cost/benefit considerations have been discussed. The completion of credit checks on 100 percent of an expanding customer base was presumed to be too costly. Similarly, the risk arising from the decentralization of controls when newly hired employees are handling the expanded operations was judged to be excessive. The importance of considering efficiency implications when determining whether one storekeeper of materials is adequate for effective control over raw material requisitions was cited, with an emphasis on the adverse incentive effects of inefficient control procedures.

No management or control objective should be set without considering the cost/benefit picture which would result from trying to achieve such an objective. A management objective of producing its product line in the "least possible time" or a control objective of "never permitting override" of a control procedure would be incompatible with the long-range effectiveness of any entity's operations.

"Least amount of time" would imply no controls; they are time consuming without being a direct contributor to completing the produced goods.

Procedures for override allow management to adapt a system that is established with routine transactions to the occasional nonroutine transaction that merits an alternative processing approach. It is usually unrealistic to not allow for override.

By considering cost/benefit dimensions, the objectives can be tailored to a practical and useful form; i.e., achievable and compatible with both operating and control-related goals. For example, it is apparent that controls are, in part, responsible for smooth operations, just as operating objectives drive the design of controls. If the extreme operating objective of "least time" to produce were pursued, the implied loss of controls could result in stockouts or excessive inventory balances and uncertainty as to total production cost levels.

For a summary of the typical types of trade-offs discussed in cost/benefit analyses of control systems, examine Exhibit 3-1. Obviously, each general dimension must be translated to dollars and cents in a specific control context if insights are to be gained. For example, if a certain control is expected to be 90 percent effective in deterring pilferage but will require one hour of an employee's time each week, does this control make sense? If the exposure to pilferage is $50,000 per year, the employee's time (one hour per week) costs out at $10 per hour. If a supervisor's time (15 minutes per week) is $20 per hour, the total costs convert to: ($10 times 52 weeks) plus (one-quarter hour times $20 times 52 weeks) equals $520 plus $260, which equals $780 — clearly below the exposure level. Assuming there are no other costs, the decision should be to install that particular control.

The Traditional Distinction Between Administrative and Accounting Controls

In evaluating controls, the auditor may find it useful to apply a traditional distinction between different types of controls: administrative vs. accounting. Administrative control focuses on operations without any direct link to accounting records. A commonly cited administrative control is the requirement that salespeople submit reports on how many customer visits they make over certain periods. Although this is a very effective control over the operating goals of providing adequate customer service and striving for increased sales, it results in no direct control effects on reported accounting numbers. Of course, the term "direct" is important. By looking at historical relationships between the number of customer visits and the total sales level, a "reasonableness" test evolves. Also, a "spillover" effect can be observed by looking at the controls in all segments of operations. The more accountability that is demanded in nonfinancial areas, the more positive the attitudes are likely to be with respect to control requirements of the accounting-financial information system.

While administrative controls are directed to overall operations, accounting controls are concerned with the integrity and accuracy of the accounting system and all financial reports being generated. The following desired attributes of any accounting information system are of concern:

1. Completeness — are all transactions reflected in or captured by the accounting system?
2. Validity — arc only valid transactions recorded?
3. Authorization — are all transactions properly authorized for inclusion in operations and in the accounting records?
4. Accuracy — are reported numbers accurate representations of the economic transactions that have occurred?

Exhibit 3-1
Cost/Benefit Dimensions of Control Evaluation

TYPICAL COSTS	TYPICAL BENEFITS
Control compliance is likely to require time that would otherwise be spent on operating responsibilities.	Improved accountability; more effective safeguarding of assets.
Controls often require documentation that has a related cost process.	Better control over resources used in production.
The authorization process in a control system involves several management layers and demands substantial time of top management.	Compliance with policies and procedures is more likely to occur with built-in checks and balances.
At times, controls are in direct conflict with operating goals; for example, telephone orders may be most efficient, yet control requirements may demand that written orders be placed when the dollar amount exceeds a set limit.	Avoids preoccupation with efficiency through production of various effectiveness measures.

Any controls that directly influence these attributes of the accounting information system are referred to as accounting controls.

Financial audits tend to emphasize accounting controls, while operational audits tend to emphasize administrative controls that are more focused upon management's operating objectives. However, certain controls from each classification are likely to be relevant to any given audit activity.

Objectives of Internal Control

In Chapter 1, we listed five general objectives of internal control. In this section, we will discuss each control objective in more detail.

Reliability and Integrity of Information

Information systems have become increasingly important as organizations have become larger and more complex. The information systems themselves have become increasingly sophisticated.

Typically, information systems are divided into two aspects: (1) financial accounting and (2) operating information systems. The accounting information system generates the organization's financial statements and, typically, a variety of budgets and cost reports for managers. The operating information system typically gathers information relating to various aspects of operations and generates reports on levels of activity, functional responsibilities, and so forth. The objective of internal control to maintain reliability and integrity in the information system is important for the decision-making processes of management.

For example, suppose the marketing department issued a report to management showing a rapid growth in sales in a particular region. Such information may cause management to increase promotional activities, build facilities, hire various types of employees, and increase inventories to support this expansion of regional activity. If, however, the information is erroneous and sales have not increased in the amounts indicated, substantial misapplications of the organization's resources could result.

Compliance with Policies, Plans, Procedures, Laws, and Regulations

Perhaps the most typical methods used by management to maintain internal control are the establishment of policies, plans, and procedures. Laws and regulations are imposed upon the organization from the outside. The purpose of these control devices is to ensure a planned, systematic, and orderly operation. Failure to comply with these controls jeopardizes the coordinated efforts which such controls promote. In addition to determining compliance with these controls, internal auditors also review and evaluate the adequacy of policies, plans, and procedures.

Safeguarding of Assets

Typically, the most visible controls are designed and implemented to protect the organization's assets. These controls include such things as locks on doors, security guards, computer passwords, vaults, fences, and joint responsibility for certain valuable assets.

Economy and Efficiency of Operations

A fundamental concept in economics is that of "scarce resources." The idea is simply that there is a limited supply of resources to satisfy all of our wants. The principle applies to organizational management and its desire for the company to perform with as little waste as possible and at an optimum trade-off of costs and benefits. If facilities are underutilized, if work is non-productive, if certain procedures are not cost-justified, and if there is either overstaffing or understaffing, then the organization will suffer. Operating standards provide a convenient measure of economy and efficiency. Usually the most visible evidence of the effects of uneconomical or inefficient operations will be reflected in the organization's financial statements. Such evidence may not always be readily apparent, however, and internal auditors, as well as others, should be constantly alert for improvements in this area.

Accomplishment of Organizational Objectives and Goals for Operations and Programs

Certainly, if an organization fails to achieve its objectives and goals, how well it does anything else really does not matter. The focus of all controls and all organizational activities should be on the accomplishment of objectives and goals. Internal auditors play an especially important role in this area because of their broad perspective of the overall organization and its internal control systems. By examining and evaluating the internal control systems, internal auditors are in a position to assess the overall directions in which the organization is moving.

For example, suppose that the internal auditors for a large corporation discover that one division is attempting to introduce a series of revolutionary new household products designed to create an image of dynamic innovation. Suppose that corporate management, with the guidance of the board of directors, has established a policy to maintain a conservative, stable image in order to develop long-term customer trust and loyalty. Headquarters has consciously decided to pursue the introduction of new products at a relatively slow pace with little public fanfare. In this case, the auditors are in a position to point out the inconsistencies in the organization's operations and the apparent conflict in corporate development.

Types of Internal Controls

Internal control systems comprise five types of internal controls which we will discuss in this section. They may be described as preventive, detective, corrective, directive, and compensating controls.

Preventive Controls

Preventive controls are intended to prevent errors from occurring. For that reason, they are "before-the-fact" or "a priori" controls that could trigger an obstacle that prevents the processing of a particular transaction. Credit checks, use of an approved vendor listing, and guards at exit points are intended to prevent sales to unworthy credit risks, prevent the use of unacceptable suppliers, and prevent the removal of assets, respectively.

Some people maintain that preventive controls are superior and less costly than detective controls since they prevent losses and therefore reduce certain risks. However, no preventive control can be expected to be foolproof or even to be complied with 100 percent of the time. Therefore, preventive controls may be ineffective on occasion unless an entity recognizes the dependence of preventive controls upon detective controls as a follow-up check.

Detective Controls   As the name suggests, detective controls are intended to detect errors after they have occurred. Reconciliation of bank statements is a key detective control over cash. Assume that an entity required two check-signers on all disbursements over $10,000. However, since one of the two check-signers was out of town and the disbursement was considered to be urgent, the preventive control was overridden. The bank did not question the single check-signer, despite the fact that the checks have preprinted messages indicating that two signatures are required for amounts in excess of $10,000. During the reconciliation process, the $10,000 check was discovered. This detective control prompted investigation. A third authorized check-signer was designated so that controls would not be circumvented in the future merely because someone was out of town. In addition, a written reminder was sent to the key banks with which the entity transacted business, emphasizing that no check in excess of $10,000 was to be processed unless there were dual signatures (as indicated on the face of the check).

Now, imagine the potential effect of having no detective control in such a setting. Anytime one of the two check-signers was absent, the system could be overridden. Risk exposure would increase substantially. One check-signer could become aware of this common "overriding of controls" and could abuse controls by authorizing the processing of inappropriate transactions during the other's absence. The control atmosphere could deteriorate, encouraging the override of control procedures whenever they became inconvenient. The worst effect of a situation where there are no detective controls is that the entity may be unaware of the problem or its scope. A substantial amount of money could be lost before anyone discovered it, which reduces the chances of recovering the loss.

The point, of course, is that in the absence of a perfect, practical preventive control system, monitoring devices in the form of detective controls are essential components of a well-designed control system. Detective controls may be cheaper to apply than preventive controls in certain settings because transactions can be tested. Exhibit 3-2 contains examples of both preventive and detective controls.

Corrective Controls   Corrective controls correct the problems identified by detective controls. For example, a computer on a routine edit may be able to detect unauthorized vendor codings, but then go on to read the vendor's name, match that name to a master file of approved vendors, select the appropriate vendor coding, and correct the original record. The editing check adapts to the setting; if the coding is authorized, it merely proceeds through the transaction file.

Exhibit 3-2
Examples of Preventive and Detective Controls

PREVENTIVE	DETECTIVE
Require two check-signers on all large disbursements.	Prepare a bank reconciliation.
Require the use of an Authorized Vendors list.	Reconcile vendors' statements to recorded payables.
Reconcile invoices to receiving reports before authorizing payment.	Count physical inventory, being alert to the need for obsolescence reserves.
Check mathematical accuracy of invoices before payment.	Observe payroll distribution on a test basis.

The term "corrective controls" is sometimes applied to controls over correcting entries. For example, assume the computer could not find the vendor's name on the master file. In other words, an error was made not just on the vendor coding, but an unauthorized vendor also had been selected as a supplier. An exception report would be generated to report errors that could not be corrected automatically.

At this point, some employee will have responsibility for investigating the purchase order. The situation may call for a change in the invoice to another supplier or an approval process to add the original supplier to the approved vendor listing. It is imperative that corrective actions are well controlled. Otherwise, purchase orders might be altered in a manner that is detrimental to operations (for example, substitution of "dissimilar" products could occur), or the authorized vendor listing might become spurious due to the ease with which it could be altered. Many entities require "corrected transactions" to be processed in the same way as original transactions, as such an approach is believed to be more effective in controlling the recording process. A "supplementary" set of alternative controls, applied on an irregular basis, is thought to be more susceptible to breakdown than would be the case for routine processing controls.

Directive Controls   Directive controls are designed to produce positive results, while the focus of preventive, detective, and corrective controls is upon the prevention, detection, and correction of negative results. Often management will direct certain activities. For example, a manager of a construction firm might instruct the firm's various project managers to hire local workers as often as possible. This policy might be intended to create a more favorable image for the company in the various communities where it is operating.

Some people view directive controls as preventive controls because, when good things happen, bad things are *prevented* from happening. We recognize the close relationship between the two, but because *Statement on Internal Auditing Standards No. 1* (quoted in the appendix to this chapter) lists directive controls separately, and because there is a slight difference in the focus of each, we also consider them separately.

Compensating Controls   At times, what appears to be a weakness in control is not really a problem, due to the presence of compensating controls. As the name suggests, such controls can compensate for shortcomings elsewhere. A bank reconciliation process, performed by a party who is independent of the disbursements- or receipts-related routine duties, can compensate for a number of flaws in the controls that are typically established over these types of transactions. Similarly, owner-manager supervision often can compensate for a lack of segregated duties in smaller organizations.

The logic of such controls is evident. Their design represents a fail-safe approach to limiting risk exposure. This exposure must be analyzed in the context of what could happen, given particular system shortcomings.

When considering compensating controls, the preventive versus the detective characteristics of controls assumes added importance. For what is the control compensating? Is it a means of precluding loss and misstatement or a means of detecting losses and misstatements? It is clear that the latter does not substitute for the former, and yet the capability of detective controls compensating for otherwise material weaknesses cannot be denied. The key to this situation is how timely that detection is and what magnitude of loss or misstatement is possible within that time frame.

As with all dimensions of control evaluation, the appropriateness of the design of compensating controls can only be determined through cost/benefit analysis. The potential losses accruing from not having such compensating controls must be balanced against expenditures for designing and maintaining these controls. In this type of evaluation, it is important to recognize that a single control may be a direct control over transaction A and a compensating control over transaction B at the same time. Therefore, benefits must be analyzed in a manner that reflects the wide variety of positive effects of particular controls beyond their primary control objective.

Summary

Organizations use all five of these types of controls. The controls are balanced in such a way that positive actions are encouraged and negative results are discouraged. When the results are bad, they may be detected and corrected. And where some controls are missing, other controls may compensate for any negative effects that might otherwise occur. The decisions on how to establish the appropriate mix of these different types of controls are based upon the relative cost/benefit trade-offs among the various alternative combinations that might be considered. In the final analysis, organizations develop their internal control systems in order to achieve the five objectives of internal control.

Methods of Internal Control

The five internal control objectives and the five types of internal controls lead to a set of specific control methods that may be categorized as follows:

1. Organization controls.
2. Operational controls.
3. Controls for personnel management.
4. Review controls.
5. Facilities and equipment.

Organization Controls

Organization controls establish the framework within which the company conducts its various activities. These controls range from the very general to the specific — outlining responsibilities, lines of authority, and specific job requirements. There are four types of organization controls. We will discuss each one in turn.

Purpose, Authority, and Responsibility. Organizations establish overall guidance for their various divisions and departments with statements of purpose, authority, and responsibility. These statements outline the function to be performed, the authorized range of activities, and specific responsibilities within the organization, including reporting responsibilities.

For example, according to the introduction to the *Standards,* the internal auditing department is responsible for providing an independent examination and evaluation of the organization's activities to assist management and the board of directors in fulfilling their responsibilities. The internal auditing department should have the authority to examine all organizational activities and have unrestricted access to the organization's personnel, records, facilities, and other assets. The internal auditing department has the responsibility to perform its functions in accordance with the *Standards for the Professional Practice of Internal Auditing* as established by The IIA. Typically, other departments and divisions of organizations also have statements of purpose, authority, and responsibility.

Organizational Structure. Management organizes resources into various components, such as financial management, production, marketing, engineering, shipping and receiving, and research and development. These divisions of responsibility establish a structure within which the overall missions of the organization may be accomplished. Such structure not only identifies the individual components, but also may delineate the operational and informational interrelationships among the various structural components. The most common method of setting forth organizational structure is through the organization chart.

Decision Authority. The next level of organizational detail is established by outlining the key decisions for which the various organizational components are responsible. For example, it is likely that the controller of an organization will determine the appropriate financial controls and accounting principles to be employed in the organization's accounting operations. And a production manager will be responsible for determining the most appropriate means of fulfilling production commitments.

Job Descriptions (Including Segregation of Related Duties). The most detailed level of organizational controls is demonstrated in written job descriptions. Organizations typically outline in some detail the specific requirements of each job in the organization, including specific responsibilities; reporting relationships; and job qualifications, including training and experience.

One of the principal risks in most large organizations is the potential loss resulting from a single employee, or a small group of employees acting together, who can control a transaction from beginning to end, which includes having direct access to and control over the assets and the accounting for these assets. The recording of activities or transactions in an organization should be separate from the actual management and custody of assets. For example, suppose a single employee could order products from suppliers, receive the shipment of those products, record the order and receipt of the goods in the accounting records, and write the check in payment of the goods. The danger here should be obvious: this employee could manipulate the system in a variety of ways for his or her own benefit and to the detriment of the organization.

Operational Controls

Operational controls dictate the manner in which the organization performs its various activities and conducts its affairs. We will discuss seven methods of operational control.

Planning. The first operational control in any organization is planning. Effective planning is basic to the success of any enterprise and ranges from the very general to extremely detailed. In all cases, however, organizations should document their plans, whether it be in the form of minutes of meetings where plans are formulated, or formally written and approved plans of operations. Organizations usually formulate long-range plans for periods of from five to 10 years, medium-range plans from between one and five years, and short-range plans for less than a year. Of course, the specific time frames differ among organizations, but the general use of long-range, medium-range, and short-range plans is common.

Budgeting. Almost all organizations formulate their plans into financial and activity budgets, usually at least on an annual basis. These budgets generally are formulated for the overall organization and are broken down into separate budgets for different organizational components. Budgets may range from only a few pages to hundreds of pages for large organizations. These budgets provide a detailed outline of anticipated financial and operational activity for the periods covered. Such budgets provide effective control and allocation of an organization's resources.

Accounting and Information Systems. The accounting and information system of an organization systematically tracks and documents summary reports of the organization's various activities. The periodic reports generated by these systems provide management and others with important information related to their respective areas of responsibility. Without such information, decision-makers would be greatly limited in their knowledge of organizational performance. Accounting and information systems permeate the entire organization and, ideally, reflect an integrated image of the organization's various activities. Many specific internal controls govern the operation of these important systems.

Documentation. A fundamental practice of internal control is to document, usually in writing, the organization's various activities.

Important basic documentation includes such things as purchase orders, work orders, receiving slips, check stubs, remittance advices, customer billings, requisitions, and reconciliations of bank accounts and general ledger accounts. In fact, one of the most sizeable problems facing any organization is the management and storage of the mountains of documents related to its activities.

Authorization. Authorization or approval should be required before any business is conducted on behalf of the organization. Even when employees are given specific authority to make decisions, review procedures frequently are required to ensure that abuses are avoided. Authorization can be "blanket" or specific in nature. For example, blanket authorization can be given to a purchasing agent to make purchases up to $1,000. Additional approval by a supervisor may be required for purchases in excess of $1,000. In most cases, the exercise of specific authorization, including the review of authorized decisions, should be documented for the protection of both the organization and the person making the decision.

Policies and Procedures. Established policies and procedures provide the guidance that is necessary for most organizational activities. Policies and procedures help ensure consistent performance at a required level of quality. Without adequate policies and procedures, an organization is subject to performance that is inconsistent, unpredictable, and unreliable. Usually, policies and procedures should be written down in a convenient format and made available to members of the organization according to their various responsibilities. The absence of appropriate policies and procedures, or noncompliance with such policies and procedures, usually indicates a lack of adequate internal control.

Orderliness. The orderliness of records, work areas, storage areas, and processes is important to any operation. Clutter and disorder breed confusion, lost items, and inefficiency.

Personnel Controls   In addition to outlining job responsibilities in an organization, there are three controls that help ensure suitable performance by employees.

Recruiting and Selection of Suitable Personnel. Organizations generally establish qualification guidelines for personnel in different positions. Such personnel are then recruited, screened, and hired. The personnel qualifications are met whenever possible. Typical qualifications might include educational requirements, work experience, professional certifications, conformance with a professional code of ethics, and a willingness to conform to an organizational code of ethics, including the avoidance of conflicts of interest. Excellent organizational structure, lines of authority, and job descriptions, while important, do not substitute for good employees. Personnel who are unsuitable to perform their assigned tasks can threaten even the best-designed organization.

Orientation, Training, and Development. Even though an organization may hire well-qualified individuals, those employees require an orientation and, usually, ongoing training and development in order to improve their abilities and to advance within the organization. Job orientation should be given immediately upon employment. Training and development may include in-house classes, self-study programs, attendance at appropriate seminars and conferences, on-the-job training, and courses conducted outside the organization. Most organizations recognize the importance of training and development to the overall success of the enterprise. As a result, they typically either provide the orientation and the training and development opportunities, or pay for it if it must be conducted outside the organization.

Supervision. Almost all employees require some degree of supervision. Supervisory responsibilities include specific job instructions, observation of the work process, and examination of the work product. The amount of supervision may vary, of course, depending upon the abilities of the individual employee and the complexity of work tasks.

Periodic Review

Three kinds of periodic review help organizations assess the progress and performance of their employees, operations, and programs.

Review of Individual Employees. Most organizations provide a performance review of individual employees at least annually. Typically, these reviews are conducted by the employee's supervisor and include a survey of the employee's past performance, specific areas that need improvement, and plans or goals that will help the employee to improve.

Internal Review of Operations and Programs. Periodic reviews are conducted by the management of specific operations and programs to determine the efficiency and effectiveness with which those activities are being conducted. The frequency of these reviews varies with the operations under review. Ongoing, relatively unchanging operations generally require less frequent review, while temporary programs and operations experiencing rapid and dynamic change generally require more frequent review. Internal auditors also provide internal reviews of the organization's control systems.

External Reviews. Public accounting firms perform reviews of organizations' internal accounting controls and financial statements. In many organizations, government regulators and industrial review teams also perform periodic reviews. These reviews by outside parties generally focus upon a relatively narrow aspect of an organization's operations. Public accountants, for example, focus their attention upon financial statements. A city's fire inspectors focus their attention upon fire safety. The federal government may send a team of evaluators to examine a particular program being conducted by the organization under federal contract.

Facilities and Equipment

Organizations use a variety of physical facilities and equipment in their operations. Suitable facilities and equipment help build effective and efficient operations and help protect the organization's assets. Unsuitable facilities and equipment jeopardize both the operations and the assets. Facilities include buildings, fences, parking lots, reservoirs, etc. Equipment includes machinery, tools, computers, and computer software. Considerations regarding suitable facilities and equipment include such things as design, repair, maintenance, and cleanliness.

Control Points

Another concept that is important in understanding internal controls is control points. A control point is a point in a process where an error or irregularity is likely to occur, creating a need for control. For example, a purchasing department may require a purchasing supervisor to review all of the purchase orders for accuracy and completeness before sending them to the company's suppliers. This review represents a control point. Any operation is likely to have several key control points. A variety of preventive, detective, corrective, and directive controls may be employed at various points within a system to help ensure that the organization's internal control objectives are being met.

Threats to Internal Control

While there are many possible threats to effective internal control, four important threats deserve specific mention. These are management override, conflicts of interest, access to assets, and substance over form.

Management Override

A key threat to any control system is management override. A well-designed control system, if set aside at management's discretion, can be equivalent to no controls in terms of risk. As suggested earlier, circumstances can arise in which management override is justified. However, the control environment can be maintained if such an override is effectively monitored and limited to those settings in which the override is a practical necessity. For example, employees could be required to fill out a form whenever they are requested to override a major established control procedure. This form would document who requested the override, when it was requested, the nature of the override, and the transaction involved. The overriding of controls should be generally discouraged, and the important role for the described form should be clearly understood by employees.

To minimize the risk of management override, a documentation system for such overrides should be established as discussed above, and training should emphasize that failure to follow such documentation procedures may even result in the loss of one's job. Employees should be made aware of sensitive transactions and of the entity's related policies, including its code of ethics.

Access to Assets

The best way to safeguard assets is to control access to them. This control over access ranges from requiring identification badges in order to gain admittance to the premises to utilizing passwords to protect data files from unauthorized viewing or alteration. In other words, several levels of access controls should be built into an entity's operations, and only those who require access should be granted it.

Some access to assets occurs indirectly via poor control over blank forms. For example, someone might remove blank checks, write unauthorized checks, and remove assets from the company in spite of never really having had direct access to cash. A similar yet far more subtle situation is the lack of control over blank purchase orders. These blank forms could be inappropriately processed in order to authorize delivery to individuals or locations outside the entity's physical operations. Controlled access means control over assets as well as control over the methods of authorizing the acquisition or transfer of assets.

Information is a key asset over which access controls must be established. Not only should data files and programs only be accessible to those requiring such information (with an emphasis on avoiding conflicts of interest), but formal distribution lists for reporting purposes should be developed. This authorized list of who gets access to what information is essential to an effective control environment. Similarly, those who are authorized to change data bases, create input, or otherwise alter information flow should be specified, controlled in number to the extent that is practical, and viewed as having access to a key asset of the enterprise.

Substance over Form

Often controls can appear to be well designed and still lack substance. For example, two check-signers may be required for expenditures over $1,000. However, unless both signers review the supporting documents for the transaction, the approval process lacks substance. Similarly, competitive bidding may be required, but if bids are only solicited from the same three suppliers every time, in spite of the availability of alternative suppliers, the purpose of the bidding procedure is defeated.

A blatant example of form prevailing over substance is the claim by a purchasing department that purchases exceeding a set dollar amount had the necessary approvals, when actually they had circumvented the control by breaking large orders into smaller purchases of an amount not "requiring" special approval.

Substantive control is most likely to prevail when an effective information system is present that provides feedback to each employee and clearly communicates prescribed policies.

Conflicts of
Interest

Employee conflicts of interest pose a threat to organizations. When an employee's loyalties are divided there is the distinct risk that he or she will choose a course of action detrimental to the organization's welfare. For example, suppose the purchasing agent for a manufacturing company has a financial interest in one of the company's potential suppliers. The employee's personal income depends not only upon his or her performance within the organization, but also may be augmented by profits from the other business. When faced with the decision of which supplier to use, this potential conflict of interest could persuade the employee to disregard established criteria for vendor selection and to favor the one in which he or she has a financial interest.

Nepotism also poses serious conflicts of interest. That is the reason some large organizations have strict policies against the employment of more than one member of the same family.

Conflicts of interest may arise in many forms. Any time an employee is faced with dual loyalties regarding his or her work responsibilities, there is a conflict of interest. Many companies review potential conflicts of interest with their employees and require them to sign statements disclosing their potential conflicts of interest. Internal auditors must remain alert to such circumstances.

Often, entities periodically require signed declarations of potential conflicts of interest and compliance with established codes of ethics. Since dealings in certain sensitive transactions are punishable by personal fines against management (such as those prescribed in the Foreign Corrupt Practices Act), simple information flow as to this personal risk to employees can be an effective deterrent to their involvement in such transactions.

Developing a Control Environment

Each organization develops its own control environment, i.e., the application of its own sets of internal control systems to meet its needs and attitudes. Some of these control environments establish more effective control than others. Internal auditors can assist top management in establishing an effective control environment. In particular, management should explain effective segregation of duties and include detailed examples of incompatible duty assignments. Such examples are provided in Exhibit 3-3. The importance of training employees to understand their control responsibilities should be emphasized. Not only must employees learn how to perform their control duties, but they also must understand the role of such duties and the operating ramifications of superficial compliance. The most effective means of communicating the importance of control responsibilities is by integrating such duties into the entity's performance evaluation system.

Rather than stressing the "policing" or "bothersome" nature of controls and auditors' activities, the constructive role of controls, as well as the monitoring of controls, should be emphasized. The likelihood of cost savings, the employees' ability to be more effective in executing job responsibilities, and the objectivity of performance assessments generated by a well-controlled information system are all positive aspects of controls.

An example of a personal benefit of controls is provided by a purchasing agent's comment that he never wanted to negotiate a big contract alone — he always wanted a "witness." He felt this would effectively preclude unwarranted suspicions by others that he might have taken some sort of kickback as he negotiated an acceptable price. False accusations by potential suppliers who were not selected could be avoided or at least defended through two-man negotiation sessions (established in large part to meet the entity's control obectives).

When the constructive role of controls is emphasized, employees can be encouraged to voluntarily comply with designed controls and to participate in the future development and enhancement of those controls.

Designing General and Specific Controls

General controls relate to the control environment and are distinct from the concept of specific controls that are typically directed at detailed procedures and activities. The classic example of the difference between general and specific controls is shown by the segregation of duties. For example, controls over purchases may be effective because they require competitive bids, the use of authorized vendors, the recomputation of mathematical accuracy, and the tie-

Exhibit 3-3
Examples of Incompatible Duty Assignments

JOB RESPONSIBILITIES	POSSIBLE RAMIFICATION
Receipt of cash collections and maintenance of accounting records for accounts receivable.	Could extract cash and adjust the books via an accounts receivable write-off or may "lap" accounts receivable (i.e., extract payments from customer No. 1, give customer No. 2 credit for No. 1's payment, give customer No. 3 credit for No. 2's payment, etc., keeping some customers' payments for personal use).
Authorization of purchase orders and control over receiving dock.	Could authorize expenditure for personal assets, taking possession at the receiving dock; then fail to generate documentation typically forwarded to accounting, or misrepresent details on such documentation.
Authorization of loans and approval of adjusting journal entries.	Could cover up poor loan decisions by authorizing write-offs or reclassifications.
Approval authority over cash disbursements and responsibility for initiating and approving purchase orders.	Could authorize purchases from a bogus supplier, pay for these purchases, and thereby abscond with cash assets.

in to receiving reports. However, if the duties of purchasing are not effectively segregated from cash disbursements and the custody of assets, the general control environment can virtually eliminate, or at least offset, the potential effectiveness of such specific controls. In this case, the segregation of duties would be a general control because of the general effect it has on operations, whereas requiring competitive bids is specific to a particular activity.

The importance of general controls in permitting specific controls to operate effectively is even clearer in an EDP environment. Assume that general controls are not established over program changes. This would mean that at any one time it would be impossible to clearly determine which version of the computer programs was in use. No matter which specific controls are set over EDP, it is not possible to develop effective controls in the absence of key general controls.

Risk Assessment

The design of controls should be driven by risk assessments. Wherever risk exposure exists in the form of a potential loss of assets or misstatements of accounting or management information, controls should be established to limit that risk. The greater the risk, the more extensive the control that is warranted. Risk encompasses the total dollars in assets that are exposed to loss, as well as the probability of such loss occurring.

Selecting Transactional Controls

Controls should be designed to ensure that every transaction is documented, that bogus transactions are not input on the system, and that all valid exchanges are recorded accurately. The types of controls selected will in large part depend on the quantity and the nature of the transactions. For example, specialized forms that are prenumbered and are required to complete certain types of transactions make a great deal of sense when a large quantity of similar transactions is being processed. Multipurpose forms that are less formal, but subject to similar numerical control, may be preferable for a smaller entity.

Tying General Controls to Specific Controls

Every general control can be viewed as having related specific controls that actually establish and monitor internal control. A general control over cash disbursements requires specific authorization, completeness, and accuracy controls to lead to accurate recorded balances. Without certain general controls, as has already been suggested, some specific controls become useless. Therefore, a system designer needs to concurrently consider potential risk, stated risk, and actual risk exposure when selecting which specific controls are warranted.

Planned Redundancy

A one-to-one relationship between control procedures and control objectives is not necessarily optimal. Often more than one procedure is instituted per control, which reflects planned redundancy in the control system. This is considered beneficial since control procedures can break down due to fatigue, human error, and similar circumstances. By establishing redundant controls, a backup control exists in case some event or oversight precludes the effectiveness of the first control check.

Cost/Benefit
Considerations

Control design should be directed by cost/benefit considerations. The consequences of not having controls should be weighed against the cost of establishing and implementing various configurations of controls. Those controls should be implemented to the extent that they are cost-justifiable. In analyzing costs, it is essential that both direct and indirect costs are considered. For example, the misrepresentation of financial statements may have consequences for management's ability to make decisions, and may also have liability ramifications. Both possible consequences need to be evaluated within the cost/benefit analysis of which controls to implement that are directed to the accuracy of accounting numbers.

Inherent Limitations of Internal Control

There is no such thing as a perfect control system. All controls are subject to certain inherent limitations. These include the element of human error which encompasses the misunderstanding of control responsibilities, carelessness in executing those duties, the effects of fatigue or stress, and the tendency at times to let judgment or familiarity supersede instructions to the contrary in overriding established controls. No matter how well a control system is designed, it is subject to deterioration or nonapplicability over time — particularly due to changes in operations intended to be monitored by established controls.

Describing Internal Control Systems

One way to understand specific internal control systems is to describe them. For example, suppose the internal auditors for a city are examining the maintenance system for vehicles in the city's motor pool. To conduct the audit, the internal auditors must understand the operations involved, the maintenance procedures, and the specific controls employed in those procedures.

There are three methods commonly used to describe such a system with its controls: (1) narrative descriptions, (2) flowcharts, and (3) internal control questionnaires (ICQs).

Narrative
Descriptions

Narrative descriptions detail the operations step by step, usually in paragraph or outline form. Exhibit 3-4 gives an example of a narrative description for the city's motor-pool maintenance procedures.

Exhibit 3-4
Motor-Pool Maintenance Procedures

The city's motor pool comprises two departments: (1) the fleet's management department and (2) the fleet's maintenance department. The former is located beside the city offices on Cedar Road. The fleet manager and his two assistants work at this location. There is also an open parking lot with spaces for 30 vehicles: 10 trucks and 20 cars. The fleet currently includes eight trucks and 16 cars.

The fleet's maintenance department is housed one block away in the city garage on Pine Street. Maintenance employees include a manager, three mechanics, and two assistant mechanics.

A step-by-step outline of motor-pool maintenance procedures includes the following:

1. The fleet manager inspects the vehicles daily for needed maintenance:
   a.   Logs miles.
   b.   Checks drivers' reports from previous day.
   c.   Examines tire and body condition.
2. The fleet manager checks a regular maintenance schedule for each vehicle to determine regular maintenance work to be performed.
3. The fleet manager fills out a work order in duplicate for all maintenance work to be done that day, including regular maintenance and any special work on vehicles. He files one copy.
4. The vehicles are then taken to the fleet's maintenance shop with the duplicate work order.
5. The maintenance manager reviews the work order and examines the vehicles, evaluating the work to be done.
6. The maintenance manager assigns the work to be distributed among the mechanics and their helpers, determining priorities of the work. Vehicles requiring major engine or body work may be subcontracted to a local garage or body shop. The maintenance manager signs the work order authorizing the subcontracted work.
7. Each mechanic or mechanic's helper performs the assigned work and checks the vehicle for other needed services. As the mechanics or their helpers observe what they believe are needed maintenance procedures not included on the work order, they notify the maintenance manager, who may add the

> additional work to the work order if he agrees that it needs to be done.
>
> 8. When the work is completed, both in the maintenance department and the subcontracted work, the maintenance manager inspects each vehicle and sends it back to the motor pool with the signed work orders indicating that all procedures were completed.
> 9. The motor-pool manager records the date, the work performed, and the mileage for each vehicle returned from the maintenance department in a log book, and sends the signed work orders to the accounting offices.
> 10. The garage and the body shops where subcontracted work is performed send invoices to the city's accounting offices where the invoices are compared with the work orders sent from the motor-pool manager before payment.

Flowcharts

To prepare a flowchart for any set of procedures, it is important to understand the two types and the components and symbols used in each. The first type of flowchart often is called a horizontal or systems flowchart. It shows the different departments or functions involved in a process horizontally across the top. In our example these departments would be the motor-pool management department, the motor-pool maintenance department, the subcontracting garage and body shops, and the accounting department. Exhibit 3-5 illustrates the different symbols typically used in the horizontal or systems flowchart. Using these symbols, a flowchart can be constructed for the motor-pool maintenance procedures. See Exhibit 3-7.

The controls employed in these maintenance procedures are of particular interest. The flowchart identifies specific control points in the system (see the small numbered circles).

The second type is a vertical flowchart. It is particularly useful in outlining step-by-step processes, but does not necessarily show the system components as clearly as the horizontal flowchart. Symbols typically used in vertical flowcharts are illustrated in Exhibit 3-6. A vertical flowchart for motor-pool maintenance procedures is shown in Exhibit 3-8.

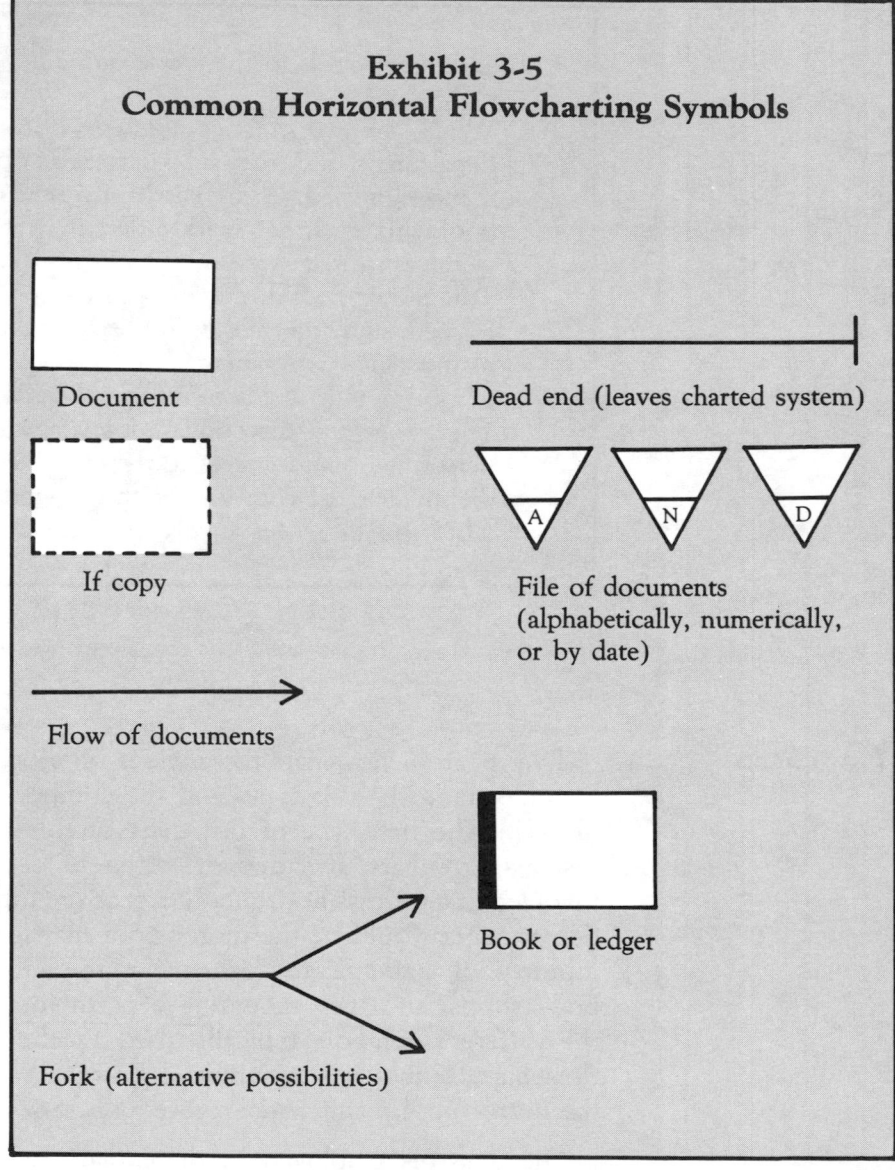

Exhibit 3-5
Common Horizontal Flowcharting Symbols

Document

If copy

Flow of documents

Fork (alternative possibilities)

Dead end (leaves charted system)

File of documents
(alphabetically, numerically,
or by date)

Book or ledger

Exhibit 3-6
Common Vertical Flowcharting Symbols

Process Symbol — any processing function; defined operation causing a change in value, form, or location of information. Example: a billing clerk prepares a sales invoice.

Document — paper documents and reports of all types. Example: a sales invoice.

Off-line Storage — off-line storage of documents, records, and EDP files. Example: a duplicate sales invoice is filed in numerical order.

Transmittal Tape — a proof or adding machine tape used for control purposes. Example: an adding machine tape of sales invoices.

Input/Output Symbol — used to indicate information entering or leaving a system. Example: a receipt of order from a customer.

Decision — used to indicate that a decision is made requiring different actions for "yes/no" answers. Example: is customer's credit satisfactory?

Annotation — the addition of descriptive comments or explanatory notes as clarification. Example: a billing clerk checks credit before preparing an invoice.

Directional Flow Lines — the direction of processing or data flow.

Connector — exit to or entry from another part of a chart; keyed in by using numbers or letters. Example: a document transfer from one department into another department.

Source: Alvin A. Arens and James K. Loebbecke, _Auditing: An Integrated Approach,_ Third Edition, 1984, p. 145. Adapted with permission of Prentice-Hall, Inc., Englewood Cliffs, New Jersey.

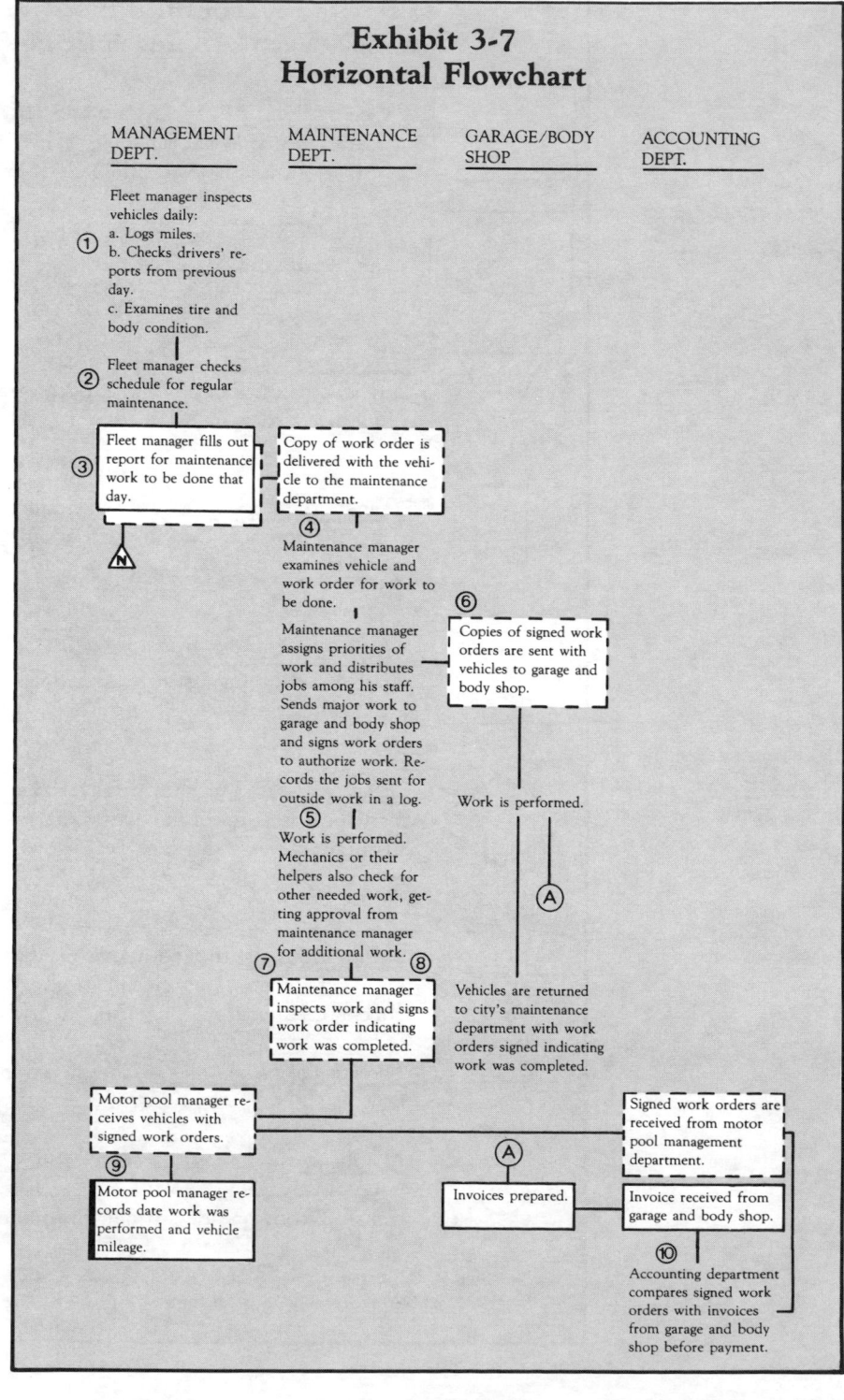

Exhibit 3-7
Horizontal Flowchart

MANAGEMENT DEPT.	MAINTENANCE DEPT.	GARAGE/BODY SHOP	ACCOUNTING DEPT.

① Fleet manager inspects vehicles daily:
a. Logs miles.
b. Checks drivers' reports from previous day.
c. Examines tire and body condition.

② Fleet manager checks schedule for regular maintenance.

③ Fleet manager fills out report for maintenance work to be done that day.

Copy of work order is delivered with the vehicle to the maintenance department.

④ Maintenance manager examines vehicle and work order for work to be done.

Maintenance manager assigns priorities of work and distributes jobs among his staff. Sends major work to garage and body shop and signs work orders to authorize work. Records the jobs sent for outside work in a log.

⑥ Copies of signed work orders are sent with vehicles to garage and body shop.

Work is performed.

⑤ Work is performed. Mechanics or their helpers also check for other needed work, getting approval from maintenance manager for additional work.

Ⓐ

⑦ ⑧ Maintenance manager inspects work and signs work order indicating work was completed.

Vehicles are returned to city's maintenance department with work orders signed indicating work was completed.

Motor pool manager receives vehicles with signed work orders.

Signed work orders are received from motor pool management department.

⑨ Motor pool manager records date work was performed and vehicle mileage.

Ⓐ Invoices prepared.

Invoice received from garage and body shop.

⑩ Accounting department compares signed work orders with invoices from garage and body shop before payment.

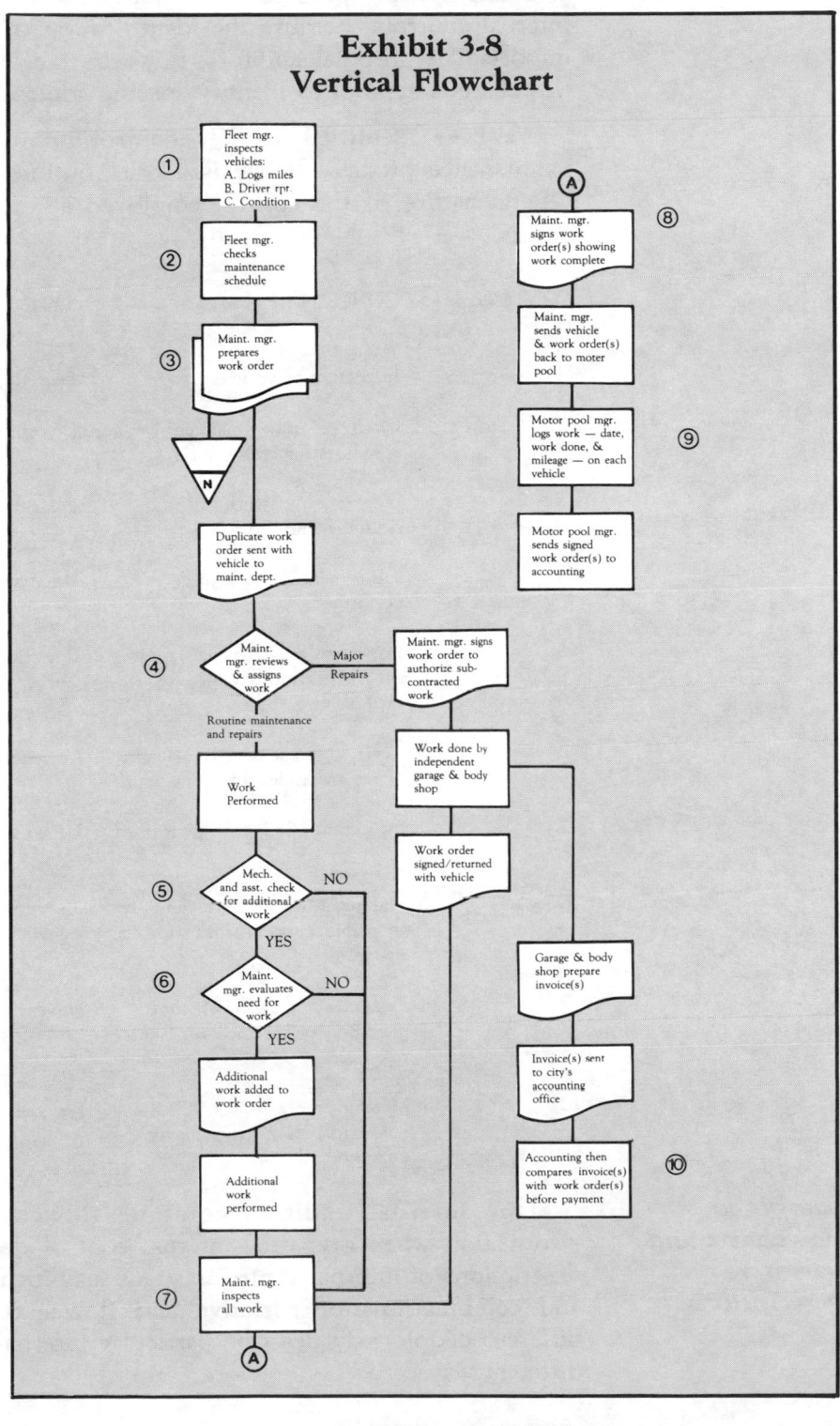

Exhibit 3-8
Vertical Flowchart

Usually people preparing flowcharts do not specifically pinpoint internal controls. Because the identification of control points is so important to internal auditors, however, we have included in both flowcharts a symbol to identify specific control points.

We have identified 10 key control points in the motor-pool maintenance process. Below is a brief outline of the type and the general nature of the control employed at each of the 10 control points.

CONTROL POINT	CONTROL	TYPE	GENERAL METHOD
1	Inspection of vehicles	Detective	Procedure
2	Check of routine maintenance schedules for each vehicle	Detective	Procedure
3	Preparation of work order to document needed work	Preventive	Documentation
4	Assignment of work to be performed	Directive	Procedure
5	Inspection by mechanic's assistant for previously undetected maintenance needs	Detective, Corrective	Procedure
6	Review by maintenance manager of recommended additional work	Corrective	Supervisory Control
7	Inspection of all work performed	Detective	Supervisory Control
8	Maintenance manager assumes responsibility for all work with his signature	Preventive	Documentation
9	Documentation of work completed on each vehicle for future reference	Preventive	Documentation
10	Matching work orders with invoices to prevent payment for unauthorized work	Preventive	Accounting Procedure

Combined Flowcharts and Narrative Descriptions

Many internal auditors combine flowcharts with narrative information when preparing internal control descriptions. Different descriptions of internal control systems may include varying amounts and combinations of narrative and flowchart components. And different people may describe particular internal control systems in different ways.

While we have illustrated the typical symbols used in horizontal flowcharts and those used in vertical flowcharts, some people may use selected vertical flowcharting symbols in horizontal flowcharts, or vice versa. Because of the variety of preferences in the selection of flowcharting symbols, it is helpful to include a legend that defines the specific symbols chosen for a given flowchart.

There are other preferences among people preparing descriptions of internal control systems. One person may prepare a totally narrative description. Another person also may prepare a totally narrative description, but in a different form. The same is true for two people preparing flowcharts for internal control systems. One flowchart may be different from another. Still other people may combine flowcharting and narrative techniques in various ways to produce somewhat different descriptions. There may not be one best way to describe any internal control system, and preferences are subjective. The primary consideration in any description, however, is clarity. The person preparing the description has an obligation to accurately reflect the operations with any applicable controls so that they may be easily and clearly understood, not only by the preparer, but by others who may be examining these documents.

Internal Control Questionnaires (ICQs)

In the early stages of an audit, internal auditors frequently interview auditee personnel and ask a series of questions about the auditee's internal control systems. Auditors commonly use prepared, structured questionnaires in these interviews. The questionnaires may be quite detailed and may contain many questions pertaining to the auditee's control environment, the specific control methods employed, a comparison with prescribed controls, and the achievement of internal control objectives. The questions are usually asked in such a way that the auditee can answer in a yes/no or short-answer format to help expedite the interview.

Once the internal control questionnaire (ICQ) is complete, the internal auditor has a profile of the design and effectiveness of the auditee's internal control systems. The disadvantages of ICQs are that (a) they require considerable time to administer, (b) usually the auditee can anticipate the preferred response to each question and sometimes may not be truthful or may not give adequate consideration to the question, and (c) ICQs are often difficult and time-consuming to prepare. Despite these shortcomings, however, ICQs provide valuable audit information. The discussion on ICQs in Chapter 8 is more extensive and includes illustrations.

Appendix

STATEMENT ON INTERNAL AUDITING STANDARDS NO. 1
Control: Concepts and Responsibilities

Foreword

The Institute of Internal Auditors issued its *Standards for the Professional Practice of Internal Auditing* in 1978 "to serve the entire profession in all types of businesses, in various levels of government, and in all other organizations where internal auditors are found . . . to represent the practice of internal auditing as it should be . . . ." Experience and success have demonstrated the credibility of the basic principles promoted in the *Standards.*

The *Standards* states that internal auditing is to assist members of the organization in the effective discharge of their responsibilities by providing them with information regarding control. However, differences of opinion have existed regarding the nature of control and the roles of the participants in its establishment, maintenance, and evaluation.

This statement provides guidance on these issues by focusing on guidelines 300.02 and 300.03 and providing three additional guidelines.

Summary

This statement provides guidance to internal auditors on the nature of control and the roles of the participants in its establishment, maintenance, and evaluation. Major conclusions include:

- A control is any action taken by management to enhance the likelihood that established objectives and goals will be achieved.
- Control results from management's planning, organizing, and directing.
- The many variants of the term control (for example, administrative control, management control, internal control) can be incorporated within the generic term.
- The overall system of control is conceptual in nature. It is the integrated collection of systems used by an organization to achieve its objectives and goals.
- Management plans, organizes, and directs in such a fashion as to provide reasonable assurance that established objectives and goals will be achieved.
- Internal auditing examines and evaluates the planning, organizing, and directing processes to determine whether reasonable assurance exists that objectives and goals will be achieved. All systems, processes, operations, functions, and activities within the organization are subject to internal auditing's evaluations. Such evaluations, in the aggregrate, provide information to appraise the overall system of control.

Background

Controls were defined early in the evolutionary process of organizational management as mechanisms or practices used to prevent or detect unauthorized activity. The purpose of controls was later expanded to include the concept of getting things done. Current usage leans toward any effort made to enhance the probability of accomplishing objectives.

Examples of "controls" abound. A partial list relating to protection of cash highlights the diversity of opinions: a safe, a locked safe, a requirement to lock cash in a safe, a procedure directing the storage of cash in a locked safe, restricted access to a safe and its contents, assignment of responsibility for protecting cash, authorizing cash disbursements, a record of cash disbursements and receipts, and unannounced cash counts. This diversity should not be construed as indicating a problem; in fact, the opposite may very well be true. All of these may be regarded as controls, depending on circumstances and the specific activity being reviewed.

As illustrated above, control is used as a noun, a verb, and an adjective; the term is used to describe a physical device, a method of performing an activity, a step in a process, a means to an end, and an end in itself.

Differences of opinion exist regarding the term "system of internal control." This term was used in a 1949 American Institute of Certified Public Accountants study titled *Internal Control — Elements of a Coordinated System and Its Importance to Management and the Independent Public Accountants.* From the external auditor's viewpoint, the importance of the system of internal control was "to establish a basis for reliance thereon in determining the nature, extent, and timing of audit tests to be applied in the examination of the financial statement." Since then, the term has been used by auditors to describe the set of controls within a specific system, operation, or department; it has also been used in the context of the organization's system of internal control.

It is clear that management and internal auditors are interested both in specific controls within specific systems and in overall control. It is generally agreed that their scope of interest (and responsibilities) extends beyond that of external auditors. To clearly delineate the difference between the broader control concerns of management and internal auditors and the narrower control concerns of external auditors, the broader concept of control will hereafter be referred to as the "overall system of control."

Differences of opinion exist regarding the specific nature of management's role in the establishment, maintenance, and evaluation of control. For example, it is commonly stated that management plans, organizes, directs, and controls. Thus, at least conceptually, controlling has been viewed as a separate activity. However, specific actions taken by management to enhance the likelihood that objectives and goals will be achieved, such as the setting of standards, the monitoring for compliance to those standards, and the related feedback to those in a position to take corrective action, are ongoing and fully integrated

---

Note: As used in this statement, the term "management" includes anyone in an organization with responsibilities for setting and/or achieving objectives.

with planning, organizing, and directing activities. Therefore, controlling can be viewed as a part of planning, organizing, and directing rather than as a separate activity.

There is also diversity of opinion as to how much of the management process is subject to internal auditing's review. Since such diversity of opinion regarding the nature of control and roles played by the participants may cause or contribute to less than optimum performance by internal auditors, the following concepts were formulated to serve the profession. These concepts guide the interpretations contained in the remainder of this statement:

- Management plans, organizes, and directs in such a manner as to provide reasonable assurance that established objectives and goals will be achieved.
- Internal auditors examine and evaluate the planning, organizing, and directing processes to determine whether reasonable assurance exists that objectives and goals will be achieved. Thus, all systems, processes, operations, functions, and activities within the organization are subject to internal auditing's evaluations.
- External auditors evaluate "internal accounting control" within the parameters stated in their Generally Accepted Auditing Standards.
- Audit committees have guidance and oversight responsibilities related to internal and external auditing's performance.
- Boards of directors have guidance and oversight responsibilities related to subordinate management's performance.

Interpretations of Existing Guidelines
Guideline 300.02

Guideline 300.02 states the purpose of the review for adequacy of the system of internal control is to ascertain whether the system established provides reasonable assurance that the organization's objectives and goals will be met efficiently and economically.

.1 Objectives are the broadest statements of what the organization chooses to accomplish. The establishment of objectives precedes the selection of goals and the design, implementation, and maintenance of systems whose purpose is to meet the organization's objectives and goals.

.2 Goals are specific objectives of specific systems and may be otherwise referred to as operating or program objectives or goals, operating standards, performance levels, targets, or expected results. Goals should be identified for each system. They should be clearly defined, measurable, attainable, and consistent with established broader objectives; and they should explicitly recognize the risks associated with not achieving those objectives.

.3 A system (process, operation, function, or activity) is an arrangement, a set, or a collection of concepts, parts, activities, and/or people that are connected or interrelated to achieve objectives and goals. (This definition applies to both manual and automated systems.) A system may also be a collection of subsystems operating together for a common objective or goal.

.4 Adequate control is present if management has planned and organized (designed) in a manner which provides reasonable assurance that the organization's objectives and goals will be achieved efficiently and economically. The system-design process begins with the establishment of objectives and goals. This is followed by connecting or interrelating concepts, parts, activities, and/or people in such a manner as to operate together to achieve the established objectives and goals. If system design is properly performed, planned activities should be executed as designed and expected results should be attained.

.5 Reasonable assurance is provided when cost-effective actions are taken to restrict deviations to a tolerable level. This implies, for example, that material errors and improper or illegal acts will be prevented or detected and corrected within a timely period by employees in the normal course of performing their assigned duties. The cost-benefit relationship is considered by management during the design of systems. The potential loss associated with any exposure or risk is weighed against the cost to control it.

.6 Efficient performance accomplishes objectives and goals in an accurate and timely fashion with minimal use of resources.

.7 Economical performance accomplishes objectives and goals at a cost commensurate with the risk. The term efficient incorporates the concept of economical performance.

Guideline 300.03

Guideline 300.03 states the purpose of the review for effectiveness of the system of internal control is to ascertain whether the system is functioning as intended.

.1 Effective control is present when management directs systems in such a manner as to provide reasonable assurance that the organization's objectives and goals will be achieved.

.2 Directing involves — in addition to accomplishing objectives and planned activities — authorizing and monitoring performance, periodically comparing actual with planned performance, and documenting these activities to provide additional assurance that systems operate as planned.

.2.1 Authorizing includes initiating or granting permission to perform activities or transactions. Authorization implies that the authorizing authority has verified and validated that the activity or transaction conforms with established policies and procedures.

.2.2 Monitoring encompasses supervising, observing, and testing activities and appropriately reporting to responsible individuals. Monitoring provides an ongoing verification of progress toward achievement of objectives and goals.

.2.3 Periodic comparison of actual to planned performance enhances the likelihood that activities occur as planned.

.2.4 Documenting provides evidence of the exercise of authority and responsibility; compliance with policies, procedures, and standards of performance; supervising, observing, and testing activities; and verification of planned performance.

New Guidelines

Guideline 300.06 — Concepts of Control

Guideline 300.06: A control is any action taken by management to enhance the likelihood that established objectives and goals will be achieved. Management plans, organizes, and directs the performance of sufficient actions to provide reasonable assurance that objectives and goals will be achieved. Thus, control is the result of proper planning, organizing, and directing by management.

.1 Controls may be preventive (to deter undesirable events from occurring), detective (to detect and correct undesirable events which have occurred), or directive (to cause or encourage a desirable event to occur).

.2 All variants of the term control (administrative control, internal accounting control, internal control, management control, operational control, output control, preventive control, etc.) can be incorporated within the generic term. These variants differ primarily in terms of the objectives to be achieved. Since these variants are useful in describing specific control applications, participants in the control process should be familiar with the terms as well as their applications. However, the methodology followed by internal auditing in evaluating such controls is consistent for all of the variants.

.3 The variant "internal control" came into general use to distinguish controls within an organization from those existing externally to the organization (such as laws). Since internal auditors operate within an organization and, among other responsibilities, evaluate management's response to external stimuli (such as laws), no such distinction between internal and external controls is necessary. Also, from the organization's viewpoint, internal controls are all activities which attempt to ensure the accomplishment of the organization's objectives and goals. For the purpose of this statement, internal control is considered synonymous with control within the organization.

.4 The overall system of control is conceptual in nature. It is the integrated collection of controlled systems used by an organization to achieve its objectives and goals.

Guideline 300.07 — Management Responsibilities

Guideline 300.07: Management plans, organizes, and directs in such a fashion as to provide reasonable assurance that established objectives and goals will be achieved.

.1 Planning and organizing involve the establishment of objectives and goals and the use of such tools as organization charts, flowcharts, procedures, records, and reports to establish the flow of data and the responsibilities of individuals for performing activities, establishing information trails, and setting standards of performance.

.2 Directing involves certain activities to provide additional assurance that systems operate as planned. These activities include authorizing and monitoring performance, periodically comparing actual with planned performance, and appropriately documenting these activities.

.3 Management ensures that its objectives and goals remain appropriate and that its systems remain current. Therefore, management periodically reviews its objectives and goals and modifies its systems to accommodate changes in internal and external conditions.

.4 Management establishes and maintains an environment that fosters control.

Guideline 300.08 — Internal Auditing Responsibilities

Guideline 300.08: Internal auditing examines and evaluates the planning, organizing, and directing processes to determine whether reasonable assurance exists that objectives and goals will be achieved. Such evaluations, in the aggregate, provide information to appraise the overall system of control.

.1 All systems, processes, operations, functions, and activities within the organization are subject to internal auditing's evaluations.

.2 Internal auditing's evaluations should encompass whether reasonable assurance exists that:

    a. objectives and goals have been established;

    b. authorizing, monitoring, and periodic comparison activities have been planned, performed, and documented as necessary to attain objectives and goals; and

    c. planned results have been achieved (objectives and goals have been accomplished).

.3 Internal auditing performs evaluations at specific points in time but should be alert to actual or potential changes in conditions which affect the ability to provide assurance from a forward-looking perspective. In those cases, internal auditing should address the risk that performance may deteriorate.

QUESTIONS

1. How should operating objectives influence control design? How should the cost/benefit issues affect control design?
2. Distinguish between administrative and accounting controls.
3. Outline the five control objectives.
4. Discuss the five types of internal controls and give an example of each one.
5. How do preventive controls differ from detective controls? Are they mutually exclusive, redundant, or complementary? Provide three examples to support your response.
6. List the methods of internal controls by category.
7. What is meant by management override? Should it be prohibited? How should its occurrence be monitored?
8. Explain why periodic comparison of assets and liabilities to recorded assets and liabilities is deemed to be an important control procedure.
9. What types of duties should be segregated, and why?
10. Distinguish between general and specific controls. How do they tend to interact?
11. Describe the effects of risk assessment on control design. Is redundancy in a control system ever justifiable based on risk assessments? Explain your response and provide two examples to demonstrate your point.
12. Discuss major threats to internal controls.
13. An owner-manager of a medium-sized business was overheard by an internal auditor to claim, "My company's control system cannot be beaten." What information should the internal audit department provide to that owner-manager?
14. What three methods often are used to describe internal control systems?
15. What are the advantages and the disadvantages of narrative descriptions of internal control systems?
16. What are two common types of flowcharting techniques?
17. What distinguishes horizontal flowcharts from vertical flowcharts?
18. Illustrate and define typical symbols for horizontal flowcharts and for vertical flowcharts.
19. What is an easy way to identify control points when preparing flowcharts? What are control points?
20. What is an ICQ?

EXERCISES
E-1
The internal control function of internal auditors has been viewed as being equivalent to the diagnosis responsibilities of a medical doctor. The diagnostic-treatment process is a combination detection/isolation/predictive process as depicted in the flowchart on the following page.

Required:
Describe how this flowchart relates to internal auditors' control activities and how a medical diagnostician's role differs from the internal auditor's.

Source: Leo L. Pipino, "The Internal Auditor as Diagnostician in an EDP Environment," *The Internal Auditor*, February 1978, p. 85.

E-2
You have been asked to appraise the adequacy of control over the purchase and use of direct and indirect materials and supplies. In order to appraise the adequacy of the control over this item, you ask the following questions:

1. Are quotations, based on uniform specifications, received from several qualified supply sources for all major commodities?
2. Are the quantities that are received independently verified by someone outside the purchasing and accounting departments?
3. Is quality inspection performed by someone outside the purchasing department?
4. Are the facilities for and the control over the storing and issuance of materials adequate?
5. Does the cost of loss of materials in yields conform to reasonable standards?
6. Are yields of scrap and by-products controlled?
7. Is the grading and inspection of products produced independent of the operating, sales, and billing responsibilities?
8. Is the internal control over payment of accounts payable invoices for materials and services good?

Required:
Explain why each of the questions is relevant to evaluating control. Tie each item to key control concepts and describe the ramifications of a "no" response to each item.

Adapted from W. A. Walker, "Internal Audit Procedures for Controlling Costs," *Journal of Accountancy*, May 1950, p. 383.

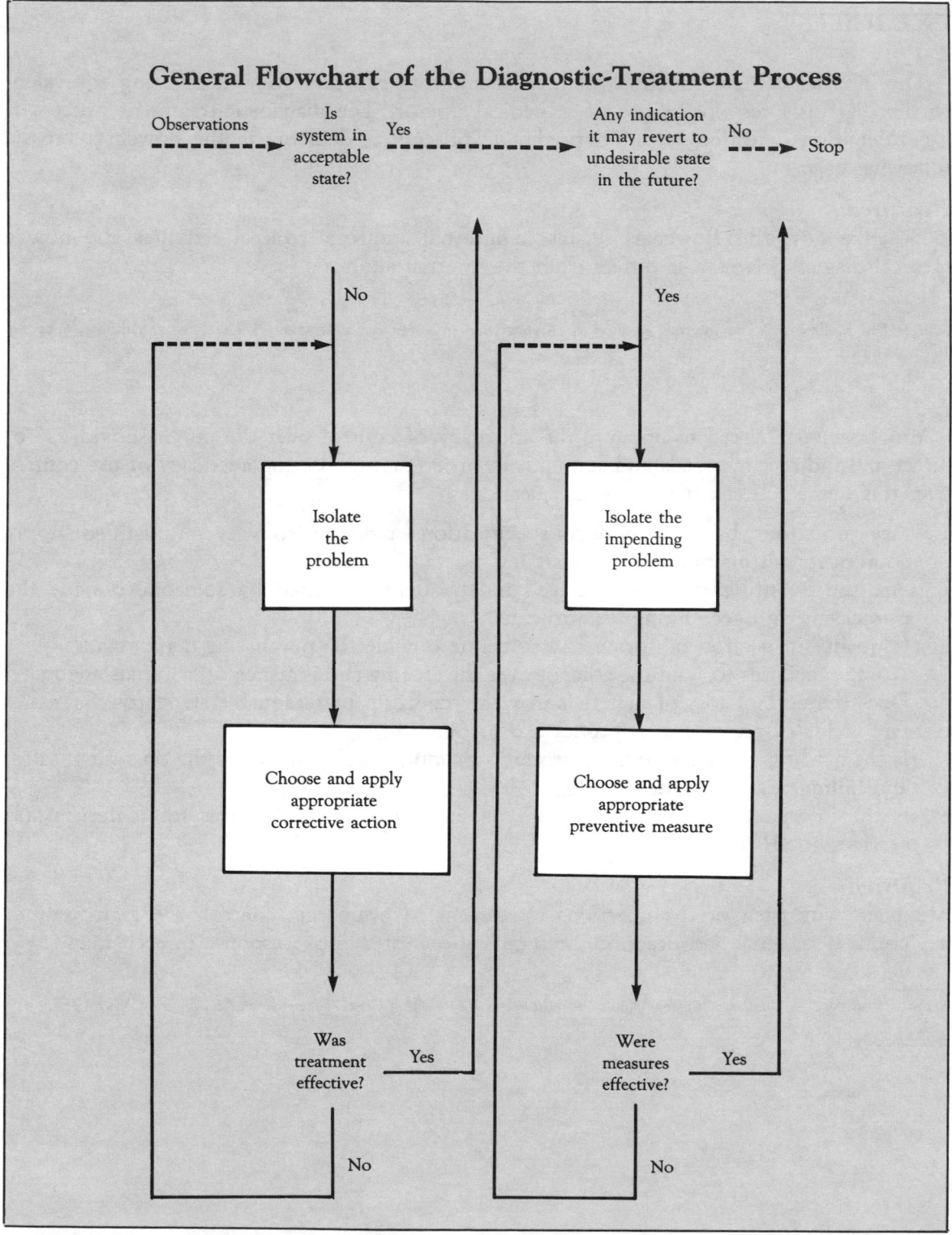

General Flowchart of the Diagnostic-Treatment Process

E-3

Two internal auditors were casually discussing their role within the organization. One of them declared, "Our primary role is to protect; our secondary role is to maximize profits." The other queried, "How do you separate these activities?"

Required:

Comment on the two auditors' perspectives and how the profession tends to address the roles being described.

E-4

The attention of many accountants was directed to internal controls by newspaper reports of a certain major case of fraud that happened in a company quite a few months ago. A considerable sum was extracted by the cashier, who prepared checks for legitimate suppliers and supported them by canceled invoices, purchase requisitions, and purchase orders, and then forged the names of those authorized to approve these documents. He also placed the receiving department stamp on the purchase order and inserted information to indicate that the material had been received. The checks and the supporting documents were entered by members of the accounting department in the voucher distribution record and charged to inventory. The cashier then presented these checks, with all supporting documents, for signature and countersignature by company executives. The checks were returned to the cashier who was supposed to mail them. Instead, the checks were torn up and the supporting documents went to their respective files. The cashier then proceeded to prepare other checks under fictitious company names. These checks were made out in different amounts, but aggregated to the same total. The checks, with all of the forged supporting documents, then were presented to the executives for signature and returned to the cashier, who tore up the supporting documents and took over the checks himself. All of the checks were returned directly to the cashier who prepared the bank reconciliation.

What can we learn from such a case? At first glance we might get upset and start reviewing our own procedures to install all of the internal checks and controls of which we had ever heard. In connection with accounts payable, we might see to it that:

1. Purchase requisitions are properly prepared by the departments using the goods or services with the authority to purchase.
2. Proper bidding procedures and approvals are set up, and that all invoices flow through the purchasing department for approval on prices and terms.
3. Copies of the purchase orders are furnished to personnel at the receiving docks, giving them the authority to receive goods and to check quantity and quality.
4. Invoices entered for payment are properly approved for prices, terms, distribution, and receipt of material.
5. Checks are presented to both the signer and the countersigner with all of the supporting documents attached.

But all of these things were done in the case mentioned. Many of the "trimmings" of internal control were present, but the heart of internal control was absent. It is, of course, recognized that the greatest feasible segregation of duties is desirable. With that in mind, the really important requirements of the internal control by the accounting department over accounts payable should recognize which basic principles?

Source: W. A. Walker, "Internal Audit Procedures for Controlling Costs," *Journal of Accountancy,* May 1950, p. 383.

E-5

A manufacturing plant location was undergoing extensive construction. An internal auditor was requested to review the plant's security. The security supervisor explained that the area under construction was enclosed with a fence and that a special gate was installed for all of the contractors' employees' use. This gate was posted with a company guard. The guard was responsible for checking the badges of all of the people entering and leaving the area and for checking tool boxes, lunch boxes, and similar items that were being carried to and from the plant.

Upon observing the construction site, the auditor noticed that there were more contractors' employees in the plant than company employees. A staff of guards was assigned to the area in which company employees worked, but only one guard was assigned to the area under construction.

Required:

What control problems are likely to arise in this setting? How could the auditee effectively respond to such problems?

Adapted from The Round Table, Philadelphia Chapter, "Auditing on Your Feet," *The Internal Auditor,* Winter 1961, pp. 73–74.

E-6

The following is a list of internal controls:

1. Videotaped camera surveillance of the store's premises.
2. The clerk examines a check for completeness.
3. The clerk's supervisor approves checks for more than $50 after examining all of the checks and a list of people known to pass bad checks.
4. Telephone credit-card number for approval of charges exceeding $50.
5. The end-of-day total of sales compared with the totals of cash from the register, checks, and credit-card sales slips.

Required:

a. Examine the flowchart on the following page and place numbered symbols for the above controls at appropriate control points on the flowchart.
b. Determine whether each of the controls above might best be described as preventive, detective, corrective, directive, or compensative.
c. Name at least three additional controls that might be employed in the above process — one preventive, one detective, and one corrective.

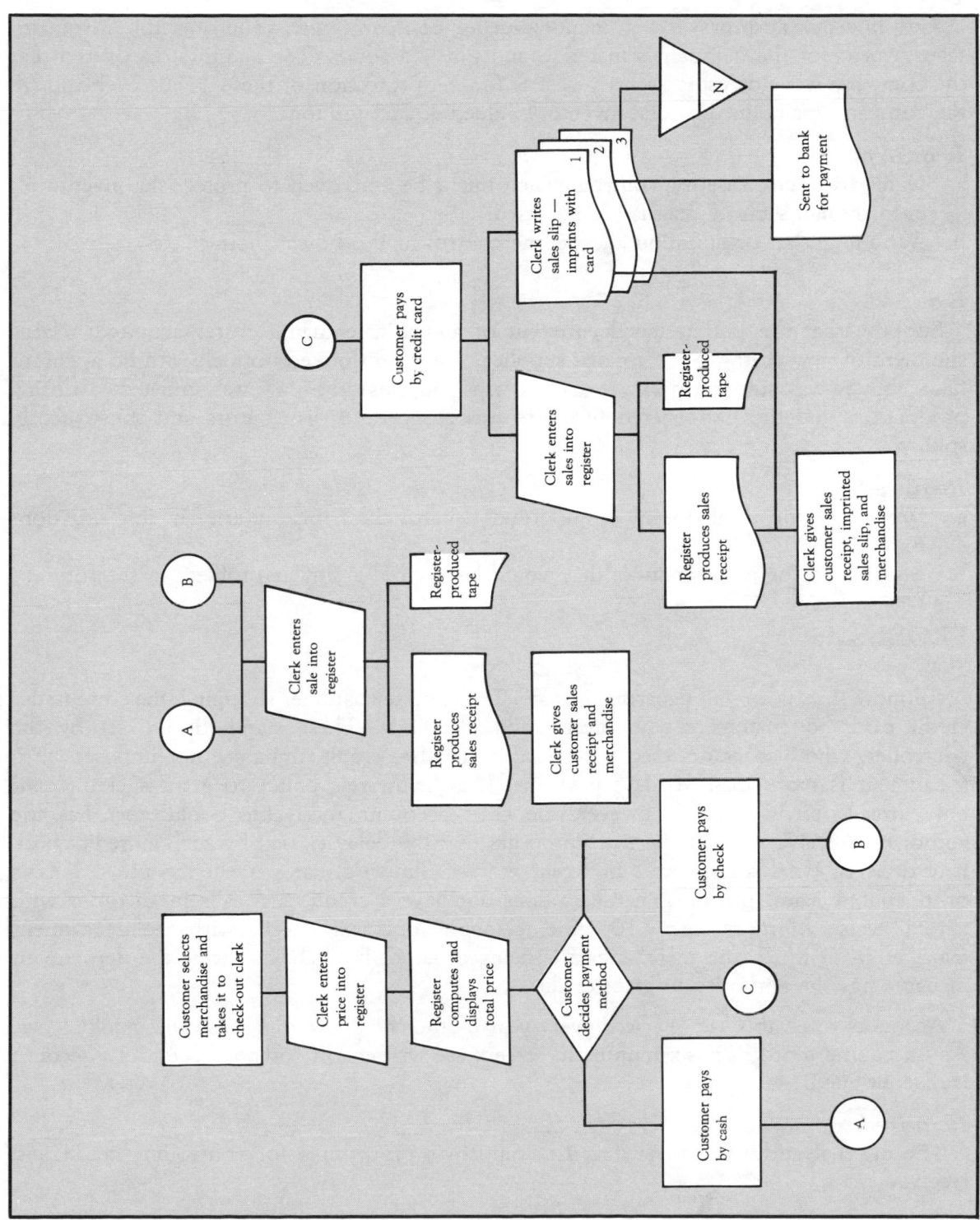

E-7

The internal auditors for a manufacturing company were auditing the inventory management for the company's materials and finished goods. The auditors discovered that the company was not using security guards for the protection of these assets, even though the company maintained a total inventory valued at $25 million.

Required:

a. Name five compensating controls which might be employed to protect the inventories even though security guards are not used.

b. Why might an organization choose one control method over another?

E-8

Suppose that the purchasing department of a furniture manufacturer acquired a large shipment of new cloth from a foreign supplier. The cloth looked normal, with no apparent flaws, but it was subject to easy tears and rips. Suppose the flaw was undetected during production, and the upholstered furniture was shipped to distributors and subsequently sold.

Required:

a. Where do you think the most important risks to the company arise in this situation? Explain.

b. Suggest one or more controls that would help avoid a similar problem in the future.

PROBLEMS

P-1

Sellmore, Inc. is a retail department store. To facilitate customer shopping, the store issues credit cards to customers who meet credit standards. These standards are set by the controller, who also grants credit. To encourage sales, credit limits are not imposed until a payment is more than 90 days past due. It is Sellmore's policy to grant a credit card only after a credit check. However, the chief accounts receivable bookkeeper has the authority to waive a credit check if it appears that the delay caused by such a credit check may deter or defer a large sale. In recent years, Sellmore's management has put emphasis on telephone sales. If a customer who does not have a credit card calls in an order with a retail value of more than $100, the telephone operator checks with the department manager from which the merchandise is being ordered. In such instances, the department manager has the authority to grant credit.

Accounts receivable are reviewed every year by the chief accounts receivable bookkeeper. Any accounts more than six months in arrears are written off and the customer's account is discontinued.

Required:

The internal auditor is reviewing the company's procedures for controlling credit and receivables.

a.   Identify five deficiencies that exist in Sellmore, Inc.'s credit-granting procedures.
b.   Recommend procedures that may be used to overcome the deficiencies mentioned in requirement (1) above.

(CIA Exam Adapted)

P-2

Following are two lists. The first is a list of control procedures; the second is a list of related control objectives for the lending function in a commercial bank.

Required:

On your answer sheet, write down numbers 1 through 10. Next to each number, write the letter of the Control Objective that most closely relates to each of the Control Procedures. Some letters may be used more than once, but each number should have only one letter.

Control Procedures

1.   Establishing a monitoring of lending limits for all loan officers.
2.   Assigning responsibilities for receiving and investigating all customers' inquiries about loan balances to individuals having no control over cash receipts and collection procedures.
3.   Sending periodic statements of loan activity to all credit customers.
4.   Monitoring geographic concentrations in the loan portfolio.
5.   Periodically reviewing and pricing the value of loan collateral to determine its adequacy in protecting the bank's investment.
6.   Requiring the approval by an independent officer of all waivers of loan fees.
7.   Reconciling the totals of the loan interest receivable ledgers to the corresponding control balance at least quarterly.
8.   Assigning responsibilities for maintaining and safekeeping actual loan instruments (notes, collateral receipts, etc.) to individuals who do not receive loan payments.
9.   Requiring that written appraisals be performed by competent, independent individuals to determine the value of real property that will be used to secure a loan.
10. Routing a copy of a computer-generated report of all changes made to loan payment due dates to a high-level, independent official for careful review on a daily basis.

Control Objectives

a.   To ensure that potentially uncollectible amounts are promptly identified, evaluated, and accounted for.
b.   To ensure that loan interest, fees, and other charges are recorded correctly as to account, amount, and period.
c.   To ensure that each loan and its terms are reviewed and properly authorized before the transaction is consummated.
d.   To ensure that physical loss or misuse of loan documents, collateral, and repossessed property is prevented or promptly detected.

e. To ensure that all completed lending transactions are recorded correctly as to account, amount, and period.

f. To ensure that loan interest, fees, and other charges are billed to customers in the correct amounts.

(CIA Exam Adapted)

P-3

An accountant in the treasury department of Health Plans, Inc. was disturbed by the changes made by management that affected work in the department. The changes were the result of recommendations made during a recent internal audit but were never explained to the accountant. The changes were as follows:

1. New responsibilities were assigned to the accountant for performing proofs of quarterly accruals of investment interest on securities.
2. The accountant must now prepare weekly proofs of cash receipts and disbursements.
3. The accountant will no longer have access to the security vault, the imprest cash fund, and the incoming mail.
4. Periodic review will be made of the accountant's work by the supervisor.

The accountant has expressed dissatisfaction with the above changes because of the constraints and dilution of job responsibilities and an indication of a lack of trust. You have been asked to discuss the rationale for the changes with the accountant.

Required:

Give a reasonable explanation for each of the changes listed above based on internal control considerations. Do not use the same reason for more than one change.

(CIA Exam Adapted)

P-4

The internal auditors for a large corporation interviewed the assistant manager of purchasing to find out how special orders are processed by the purchasing department. The auditors transcribed the assistant manager's statement as follows:

We get special orders every once in a while from different departments. Usually it's either production or the main office people who put in the special orders. But every once in a while we get special orders from other departments, too. Anybody putting in a special order usually calls us, and we tell them to come down and pick up a special-order form that they have to fill out. Because the main office has all the big shots, we just take them a handful of blank special-order forms every once in a while, because they don't want to come down and pick them up. The production department makes special orders often enough that we take them a stack of blank forms, too. The production secretary just calls when they get low and I send someone up with some more.

Well, anyway, after they fill it out, they give the form to one of our purchasing agents who checks and makes sure that all the right information is there. He checks stuff like what item is being ordered, who's authorizing the order, when it's needed, and the right code number. Stuff like that.

After the purchasing agent is satisfied that the form is okay, he'll call one of our suppliers, you know, the one that's most likely to have it, to see if they can get us the item when it's needed and to find out how much it costs.

Our policy states that we have to get at least two bids on all orders that are more than $1,000. The purchasing agent takes care of that. Our purchasing agents have gotten to know company suppliers pretty well and usually can pick the best one right off. The only reason they call some of the others is because of the policy. There have been a couple of times, though, when some of our agents were fooled and they did get better prices from their second or third call.

Well, anyway, after the purchasing agent gets the special-order form and calls the suppliers, he chooses the best one and makes out a purchase order. I sign it, or Mr. Tatum, the purchasing director, does. We keep a copy of the purchase order here. We send the supplier a copy. And we send the accounting department a copy. That's right, there are three copies: one for us, one for the supplier, and one for accounting. Then everybody just waits till the goods get here.

The shipping and receiving department gets the order, makes out a receiving report, and sends a copy to the accounting department. They send a copy to us, and I think they keep a copy, but I'm not sure. I think they ought to if they don't. But I'm pretty sure they do.

We call the department that put in the order and tell them that their stuff has arrived, and they go pick it up. Or somebody delivers it to them. Whichever way, they make the arrangements to get it from shipping and receiving. We check and make sure that the receiving report matches up with our purchase order and that what we ordered is what arrived. I understand that shipping and receiving takes out a packing slip from the items sent from the supplier and sends the packing slip with a copy of the receiving report to the accounting department. Accounting matches up the copy of the purchase order, the packing slip, and the receiving report, staples 'em together and waits for the invoice from the supplier. If the invoice checks out with everything else, then someone in the accounting department sends a check to pay for the special order. As far as I know, that's about it.

Required:

a. Write a well-organized narrative outlining the special-order process for the above company.
b. Prepare a horizontal flowchart with the following column headings: Ordering Department; Purchasing Department; Supplier; Shipping and Receiving; Accounting Department. Label key control points as given by the assistant purchasing manager.
c. Prepare a vertical flowchart of the special-order process. Label key control points as given by the assistant purchasing manager.

P-5

Three brothers worked for a very large manufacturing company. One of the brothers worked as a warehouse foreman, another as a bookkeeper, and another as a customer service representative. The warehouse foreman would leave work every day pushing a wheelbarrow full of old rags, with his lunch box balanced on top. The company guards became suspicious of this unusual behavior and began checking through the rags and the lunch box every day as the man left work. They never found anything hidden in the rags or in the lunch box. Every day, the man would take the wheelbarrow and sell it in a neighboring city to one of three different hardware stores. The brother in bookkeeping would write up a sales ticket for the sale of one wheelbarrow to a fictitious construction company. The paperwork would be completed as if every sale were made on credit. As payments were received from a real company that had done business with the company for many years, he would record part of each payment on the fictitious company's account and adjust all of the accounting records to cover the irregularities. The brother working in customer service would write up a complaint report each month explaining how the wheelbarrows sold to the fictitious company were falling apart on the construction sites. The report said the company demanded a refund for each of the faulty products. The brother in customer service would send the report to the brother in bookkeeping, who then would send a "refund" check to the brother in the warehouse for the total cost of the wheelbarrows. The three brothers split all of the proceeds — until they went to jail.

Required:
Explain how an audit might lead to the discovery and solution of this scheme.

P-6

Arrow Company makes almost 98 percent of its sales on credit, with an average purchase by its customers of $500. The sales-collection cycle may be summarized as follows:

1. Sale of goods.
2. Recording of the sale in the company's books.
3. Billing of the customer.
4. Receipt of payments.
5. Deposit of payments in the bank.

Required:
a. Identify at least one key control objective at each of the five steps in the sales-collection cycle.
b. Pick three of the steps and describe how your control objectives might be achieved.

4 Audit Evidence

The collection of evidence to support audit judgments constitutes a major part of the internal auditing process. Some auditors consider evidence to be the central focus of internal auditing. While the audit report is the product, evidence is what gives internal auditing its substance.

This chapter discusses the following:

- A general definition of evidence.
- Standards of audit evidence.
- Types of audit evidence.
- Considerations affecting the selection of audit evidence.
- Evaluating the adequacy of audit evidence.
- Documenting evidence in working papers.
- Evidence as a determinant of professionalism.

General Definition

The dictionary defines evidence as something that is intended to prove or to provide support for some belief. Everything collected by an internal auditor is a piece of evidence which by itself may have flaws in the form of personal bias, potential error of measurement, or less competency in its substance than is generally desired. However, by combining each piece of evidence into an information pool, the internal auditor can build a foundation — a "body of evidence" — from which audit inferences can be drawn.

Standards of Audit Evidence

The *Standards for the Professional Practice of Internal Auditing* stresses the importance of audit evidence. Standard 420 states that auditors "should collect, analyze, interpret, and document information [i.e., evidence] to support audit results." It goes on to state that:

- Auditors should collect information related to the audit objectives and scope of work.
- Audit evidence should be sufficient, competent, relevant, and useful to provide a sound basis for audit findings and recommendations.

- Procedures to collect and analyze audit evidence should be selected in advance, where practicable, and expanded or altered if circumstances warrant.
- In order to maintain objectivity and to meet the objectives of the audit, the collection, analysis, interpretation, and documentation of audit evidence should be supervised.
- Working papers documenting audit evidence should be prepared and reviewed.

Sufficient evidence is defined as "factual, adequate, and convincing so that a prudent, informed person would reach the same conclusions as the auditor."

Competent evidence "is reliable and the best attainable through the use of appropriate audit techniques."

Relevant evidence "supports audit findings and recommendations and is consistent with the objectives for the audit."

Useful evidence "helps the organization meet its goals."

The IIA's *Code of Ethics* also specifies that when expressing audit opinions, auditors "shall use all reasonable care to obtain factual evidence to warrant such expression . . . ."

In the following sections of this chapter, we discuss audit evidence in more detail and show how these standards of performance can be achieved.

Types of Audit Evidence

To assist internal auditors in evaluating the contribution of each piece of evidence in the information pool, various classification schemes for evidence have been developed. Four classifications are discussed:

- Source of evidence.
- Audit procedure.
- Persuasiveness.
- Legal rules.

Audit Evidence Classified by Source

One consideration used when classifying evidence is source. Who created the evidence, who processed the evidence once it was created, and who had access to the evidence?

Internal. Internal evidence refers to information that is created and processed by the auditee. For example, time cards for employees usually are classified as internal evidence because they typically are created, processed, and maintained within the entity being audited. Generally, internal evidence is considered less persuasive than evidence that has some external party involved in either the creating or the processing of information. At issue is: how objective is the audit evidence? Evidence from parties independent of the audit is viewed as more objective and less subject to distortion by the auditee.

Internal-External. Some information is created by the auditee and then processed through some external party's operations. Checks written by an entity will be processed by banks. The reasonableness of the check amount (in the sense that the entity is capable of covering the expenditure) will be evidenced by the bank's cashing the check. Auditors frequently examine cancelled checks when testing cash disbursements. While internal-external information is considered to be stronger than purely internal information, both are initiated by the auditee and are therefore subject to auditee bias.

External-Internal. Many types of information are initiated by third parties and then either processed or maintained by the auditee. The initial involvement of the third party contributes additional strength to the evidence. Invoices for purchased materials and services are representative of external-internal documents commonly examined by internal auditors. However, the fact that such documents pass through the auditee's system makes it possible for them to be altered or misplaced, creating the potential for flaws in their evidential value.

External. Information that is generated by third parties does not pass through an auditee's operations, but is received directly by the internal auditor. It is referred to as external evidence and has the greatest evidentiary weight. Deeds of trust filed at the county courthouse and examined by the internal auditor are one example of external information.

Audit Evidence Classified by Audit Procedure

An alternative classification scheme emphasizes the means by which the evidence is gathered. Later chapters discuss a more comprehensive list of audit procedures than is included here. The specific ones discussed here, however, illustrate the diversity of audit procedures that may be employed, depending upon the circumstances. The effectiveness of various audit procedures is considered when evaluating the strength of the evidence collected.

Interviews. Interview procedures involve discussions with the auditee, other employees who interact with the auditee in varied capacities, and independent parties. Testimonial evidence is particularly important to internal auditors in gaining an understanding of operations and in providing insight as to the possible reasons for exceptions and unusual fluctuations occurring in auditees' operations.

Successful audit interviews depend upon several factors. Interviewers must take care not to bias respondents' replies. The testimonies must be accurately recorded and, if possible, should be verified with corroborative evidence. Third-party testimonies may sometimes be sufficient.

Recomputation. Whenever an internal auditor recomputes figures in order to verify their accuracy, the evidence is considered to be factual, objective, and competent. However, the scope of information is rather narrow. The output of a recomputation procedure relies on the accuracy of the input. The output must be evaluated on its reasonableness relative to what is being measured. For example, the auditor may recompute interest income. If one-third of recorded loans receivable are unlikely to be collected, or if rates charged exceed usury ceilings for the state and are subject to appeal, the mathematical accuracy of interest income is of limited value.

Detailed Testing. To perform detailed testing means to examine documents that have been prepared to support activities and transactions. Such documents constitute direct evidence, in contrast to indirect evidence such as personal recollections of documented evidence. Also, the auditor may draw key distinctions between documents prepared by the client and those prepared by independent parties. As explained above, the latter would usually be considered stronger evidence.

In detailed testing, the evidence collected is determined by the audit objective; it is the basis for choosing the specific detailed test procedure to be performed. Two common audit procedures are referred to as *vouching* and *tracing*. Vouching means that recorded balances are tested by examining supporting documents. The audit objective is to determine whether all recorded transactions represent actual exchanges. In contrast, tracing procedures begin with original documents and follow them through the processing cycles into summary accounting records. The audit objective is to determine whether all actual transactions have been recorded.

The reason for emphasizing the differences between vouching and tracing procedures is to clarify the considerations that influence the auditor's evaluation of how relevant the pieces of evidence are to the audit questions being addressed. For example, an internal audit report on the completeness of accounting records would find vouching procedures to be of little relevance, because verifying that documentation exists for recorded transactions does not necessarily mean that all transactions are recorded. On the other hand, evidence acquired via tracing procedures could provide a strong basis for such conclusions.

Observation/Inspection. The idea that "seeing is believing" underlies the persuasiveness attributed to observation procedures. Any physical evidence that is examined, ranging from legal documents to physical assets on hand, constitutes evidence collected via observation or inspection.

A distinction is commonly made between observation and inspection procedures. An auditor *observes* activities such as system procedures. An auditor *inspects* physical assets.

The quality of observation or inspection evidence largely depends on the nature of what is being observed and the qualifications of the person doing the observing. For example, tires could be counted in a reasonably competent manner by most individuals, yet an inventory purported to be diamonds could really be glass and remain undetected by anyone other than a trained appraiser.

The internal auditor must appreciate the limited scope of information provided by observation and inspection procedures, just as he or she recognizes the narrow scope of information obtained from recomputation procedures. In particular, possession of assets does not constitute ownership, and the apparent condition of an asset may differ from the actual operating capacity of that asset.

The risk always exists that the documents being examined by an auditor may be fraudulently prepared forgeries. In such cases, direct observation or inspection can corroborate the documented evidence.

Scanning. Scanning is a less detailed observation procedure which is intended to detect the unusual. Its efficiency comes at the cost of a wide range of "acceptable" values in the audit conclusions that may be drawn. The effectiveness of scanning procedures depends on the auditor's ability to identify what is "unusual" and to sift through large quantities of data, flagging such unusual items. Obviously, the more abundant the data, the greater the likelihood of error when applying scanning procedures.

The ease with which unusual items can be detected will help the internal auditor evaluate the competence of evidence gathered through scanning procedures. For example, debit balances among accounts payable, outstanding receivables that are tenfold the norm reported on a computer-generated listing that lines up digits, or credit balances reported for bank accounts would all be easily detectable. In contrast, the identification of production amounts exceeding 70,000 units when averages range from 50,000 to 68,000 could be a time-consuming and error-prone process.

Statistical Sampling. Many audit inferences are based on sampling evidence. Although a separate chapter focuses on statistical sampling, it is nevertheless relevant to preview the advantages of a statistical sampling approach. If samples are drawn according to statistical sampling plans and are appropriately analyzed, then sampling risk can be controlled and quantified in accordance with widely accepted statistical theory. Sampling risk is the likelihood that the sampled items may not reflect the population sampled. Nonsampling risk exposure exists whether or not statistical sampling is applied. It refers to errors in performing an audit, including selecting an improper audit procedure, executing a procedure incorrectly, and drawing erroneous conclusions. To control such risk when performing statistical sampling, care must be used in planning, supervising, and executing statistical procedures. In most cases the ability to objectively determine risk levels enhances the value of statistical sampling relative to any nonstatistical sampling application.

Confirmation. A confirmation is a written representation, frequently prepared by the auditor, completed by some third party, and then delivered directly back to the auditor. Confirmation procedures are commonly applied to accounts receivable as a means of obtaining customers' confirmation that they owe the reported balances. Similarly, confirmations from banks are requested as to account balances, credit lines, collateral arrangements, and similar matters. Lawyers are frequently requested to confirm the reasonableness of contingency estimates. Such written representations, because of their external nature and the competence of the individuals completing the representations, are considered to be strong forms of audit evidence.

Analytical Review. Whenever the auditor compares interrelationships among data sets, he or she is said to be applying analytical review procedures. In effect, the auditor formulates expectations as to how data ought to be interrelated and then compares actual relationships to those expectations in order to isolate unusual or unexplained fluctuations.

Period-to-Period Comparisons. The most common analytical review procedure is often referred to as "flux analysis" (short for fluctuation analysis). Comparisons of this year to last year, this quarter to last quarter, or this quarter to the corresponding quarter of last year are all examples of period-to-period comparisons. The presumption is that these periods ought to be similar, which means that large swings across time warrant further investigation. The obvious limitations of period-to-period comparisons are that only two points in time are typically compared, and no explicit recognition is given to the effects of known changes in operations or in the entity's environment over time. These changes could easily account for observed fluctuations in productivity costs, growth, or whatever quantities are being analyzed. An example of a period-to-period comparison would be a five-year trend analysis of departmental travel expenses.

Budget-to-Actual Comparisons. Budgets often provide a convenient benchmark by which to measure and evaluate risks associated with many activities. Of course, such comparisons assume that the budget is prepared in a competent manner and represents a reasonable goal. If the budget is formulated in a haphazard manner, is consistently padded, or is otherwise unreasonable, its usefulness as a benchmark is highly questionable.

However, if budgets are stated fairly, comparisons of budgets-to-actual can highlight unexpected changes. Often auditees will have prepared variance analyses and will have followed up on exceptions relative to budgeted or standard benchmarks. These analyses can be the initial point of inquiry for internal auditors who can extend the investigation on an "as needed" basis. Cost-accounting variance analysis is an example of a budget-to-actual comparison.

Interrelationships Among Accounts. The double-entry accounting system results in numerous accounts with automatic interrelationships. For example, insurance expense should be reconcilable to prepaid insurance, just as interest expense should be traceable to various notes payable on the books. In addition, several accounts are expected to have a certain range of interrelationship. Suppose that advertising is expected to be a certain percentage of sales, and bad-debts expense is not expected to exceed a certain percentage of credit sales. By examining interrelationships across accounts, any misclassification of transactions or erroneous accounting treatments may be highlighted.

Comparisons to Industry Data. Industry data can provide useful external benchmarks as to how reasonable particular ratios and trends may be. For example, one manufacturer's yield of financial product per ton of raw material was well below the industry average, indicating severe inefficiencies in the production process.

The external nature of industry data often results in a more reliable benchmark than mere comparison to budgets or other standards prepared by the auditee. However, industry data usually are in the form of averages, and a wide range of actual performance may exist, even among successful organizations. Consequently, comparisons to industry data are not conclusive and require careful analysis and interpretation.

Comparisons to Operating Data. Data generated within operating departments provide valuable information for comparisons with data contained in accounting reports. For example, operating data as to the number of employees, the number of units produced, or the number of shipments made can be compared to recorded payroll, cost of sales, and inventory balances. Blatant frauds that result in recorded inventory in excess of productive capacity or payroll expenditures that are excessive for the level of output are likely to be uncovered through these types of comparisons. Even when no intentional wrongdoing is present, such comparisons help determine the quality of an organization's documentation and accounting system.

Comparisons to Economic Data. By comparing summary performance figures to economic data, auditors can assess overall trends and relationships, often uncovering possible risks to the organization that might otherwise go undetected. If, for example, an economic downturn has been experienced in a region in which the auditee operates, budgets may have been overly optimistic and sales may have fallen short of production schedules. The comparison of economic and operating data allows the auditor to evaluate the overall reasonableness of reported performance.

Comparisons to Nonfinancial Data. A variety of nonfinancial comparisons and trends may be valuable to the auditor. For example, employee turnover, production statistics, and population trends offer a perspective on organizational operations. Often such information enhances the relevance of financial information.

Externally generated data, beyond industry or economic data, can be usefully integrated into analytical review procedures. For example, if an auditee is involved in the utility industry in the northern regions of the United States, weather statistics could be valuable in assessing the reasonableness of fluctuations in recorded revenue. Again, the external generation of such nonfinancial data enhances its value to the auditor.

Exhibit 4-1 presents two examples of how audit procedures and the corresponding evidence are related to management assertions.

Exhibit 4-1

Examples of How Audit Procedures
and the Corresponding Evidence Are Related to
Reported Activities and Performance

ACTIVITIES AND PERFOR-
MANCE ITEMS

EXAMPLES OF AUDIT
PROCEDURES

The accounting system correctly
compiles all products, materials,
and supplies in appropriate inventory accounts.

Observe physical inventory
counts.

Analytically review the relationship of inventory balances to recent purchasing, production, and
sales activities.

Select a statistical sample of shipping and receiving documents and
test cutoff procedures.

Granting credit to customers follows prescribed standard
procedures.

Inquire from management of the
credit department if specific policies and procedures are incorporated into operations of the
credit department.

Analytically review trends in
credit sales, bad debts, and the relationships of these accounts to
the total revenue.

Select a statistical sample of customers' credit applications and
test them for conformance with
prescribed procedures.

Audit Evidence
Classified by
Persuasiveness

A third classification scheme for audit evidence focuses on the persuasiveness of the evidential matter. As noted earlier, individual pieces of evidence may have shortcomings. The key question is, how can the various pieces be combined to support an audit report? In choosing how to combine evidence or how to complement existing evidence, auditors consider three primary levels of reliance.

Full Reliance. Full reliance implies that no further corroborating evidence is required. The evidence supports an audit conclusion as is. Physical counts or personal observations by the auditors often are given full reliance. Such procedures typically may be judged as objective, competent, and sufficient.

Partial Reliance. Most evidential matter justifies only partial reliance, meaning that some corroboration is necessary. For example, inquiry procedures may require follow-up analytical review or detailed tests to verify the reasonableness of the explanations provided. In many instances of internal, internal-external, or external-internal evidence, it is likely that the auditor will be required to gain assurance that controls exist over the generation, processing, and maintenance of such evidence.

Some determinants of how persuasive certain kinds of evidence are likely to be are summarized in Exhibit 4-2.

No Reliance. Some evidence in and of itself warrants no reliance, although it may be useful in directing an auditor toward more reliable information. For example, inquiry procedures of auditee management may warrant little or no reliance in the absence of verification, since some bias is known to exist; the charge of the internal auditor is to test the auditee's operations, not merely to communicate the auditee's explanations as to what has happened. Of course, sometimes auditee management is quite knowledgeable about the issue or the practices under review. Even though it is often biased and not conclusive in itself, such management-supplied information is sometimes good supplemental evidence.

Audit Evidence
Classified by Legal
Rules of Evidence

The internal auditor may at times be asked to assist in a fraud investigation, litigation-support activities, or similar management service activities for which consideration will need to be given to legal rules of evidence. For that reason, distinctions across types of evidence common in a legal setting are described briefly.

Direct. Direct evidence means that the party offering the evidence acquired it directly. For example, that person either inspected the documents, witnessed the transaction, or testified as to what actions

Exhibit 4-2
Relative Persuasiveness of Different Kinds of Evidence

STRONG	WEAK
Objective	Subjective
Documents	Opinions
Knowledgeable or expert opinions	Poorly informed opinions
Direct	Indirect
From systems with good internal control	From systems with poor internal control
Independent of auditee's operations	Prepared by auditee
Statistical samples (usually)	Nonstatistical samples (usually)
Corroborated	Uncorroborated
From records prepared on a timely basis	From records prepared after a lapse of time

he or she took. Direct evidence is the strongest evidence and commonly entails original documents and eyewitness testimony.

Hearsay. In contrast to direct evidence, hearsay evidence is a secondhand account of what transpired; for example, "Joe said that he saw her do that." Such evidence tends to be shunned by the courtroom, because it is important that Joe is cross-examined as to exactly what he saw, how well he saw it, and under what circumstances.

Documentary. Any original record, deed, contract, or similar written instrument is documentary evidence. Originals are imperative unless peculiar circumstances (such as a fire) have made the originals unobtainable. In such cases, copies may be the only existing documentary evidence.

Opinion. Generally, opinions are not deemed to be useful evidentiary matter. The exception to this generalization is that experts' opinions are frequently solicited in areas that are beyond the layman's typical expertise. Of course, the credentials and the objectivity of such experts must be clearly demonstrated.

Circumstantial. When direct evidence is unavailable, circumstantial evidence is often cited as being consistent with a particular set of inferences. Although such evidence may be recognized as supportive, it is by no means persuasive in demonstrating fact. Corroboration is essential in narrowing the competing explanations that might similarly be consistent with circumstantial evidence.

Best Evidence/Secondary Evidence Considerations. As has already been suggested, courts prefer direct evidence and original documents. However, the courts acknowledge the need to focus on the best available evidence, which sometimes forces attention on secondary evidence for practical reasons. As an example, if a court's possession of books of original entry of a business over a long time period would bring undue hardship to the business, it is likely that permission will be granted to obtain copies of such records for the court's use.

Corroborative Evidence. Any evidence that supports other evidence is said to be corroborating in nature. Obviously, the greater the amount of corroborating evidence, the more persuasive it is. For example, five eyewitness testimonies are stronger than a single testimony, since each witness can corroborate the others' direct evidence.

Conclusive Evidence. Whenever evidence is deemed to be undisputable in arriving at a conclusion, it is said to be conclusive evidence. Obviously, by definition, circumstantial evidence is incapable of being conclusive, whereas direct evidence, well corroborated, may be conclusive.

Implications from the Courtroom

Although the auditor is by no means bound by legal rules of evidence when conducting the typical audit assignment, courtroom guidelines do have implications for the internal auditor's interpretation of evidentiary weight. For example, when provided with hearsay evidence, the auditor should try to obtain direct evidence from the individuals who are actually involved. Generally, when copies of documents or photographs of occurrences are provided, the auditor should ask about the whereabouts of the original documents and the circumstances under which the photographs were obtained. What is the likelihood that the evidence has been tampered with?

If presented with circumstantial evidence, the internal auditor should make every attempt to corroborate the facts and provide a basis for eliminating alternative explanations of how such circumstances might exist in the absence of any error or intentional wrongdoing.

As an example, suppose the auditor checks the numerical sequence of used and blank checks and finds a series of 100 checks missing. A logical explanation of how this could occur, in the absence of auditee error or misappropriation, would be the possibility that the printer inadvertently left out that 100-series when preprinting the numbers.

Legal rules of evidence do have implications for the auditor. The key message is to recognize potential shortcomings in the evidence acquired and try to maximize the objectivity and competence of any opinion evidence obtained. On the other hand, the legal burden is stronger than the audit opinion. Auditors must consider the cost/benefit aspects of gathering the evidence. Also, although audit evidence may be persuasive, it may not necessarily be conclusive.

Considerations Affecting the Selection of Audit Evidence

The auditor should explicitly plan the type of evidence to be accumulated. The diverse classification schemes for evidence which have been discussed to this point suggest the broad choices of evidential matter that are available.

The Desirability of a Mix of Various Types of Evidence

Generally, evidence should be composed of various types. In other words, all inquiry evidence or only detailed test evidence is unlikely to be optimal, both from the perspective of completeness as well as economy. Corroborative evidence — critical in reaching audit conclusions — will often come in a variety of forms and can be most effectively combined when generated from different sources through the application of varied audit procedures.

The Importance of Audit Objectives in Directing the Type of Evidence to Be Gathered

In large part, the type of evidence that is gathered will depend on the audit objective. For example, to determine the existence of assets, direct observation is effective; to evaluate documentation, detailed tests are effective; to evaluate the reasonableness of recorded values, analytical review procedures and experts' testimony are helpful; and to assess the accuracy of figures, recomputation is likely to be the most direct audit test.

Often, audit objectives are rather global in nature, such as *assessing* the effectiveness of controls over the entry of data into a computerized information system. Such general objectives may be subdivided into more detailed objectives, such as (in this case) examining and evaluating the accuracy of input, the reasonableness of quality control standards, the use of adequate manuals and training materials, and compliance tests with set policies and procedures. Each of these detailed procedures suggests different audit approaches that produce diverse types of evidential matter to fulfill the audit objective.

Risk Factors

A critical decision that auditors must reach is when the evidence is sufficient as a basis upon which to rest an audit conclusion. Sufficiency is assessed relative to risk. In other words, what is the risk of drawing an erroneous conclusion? Risk arises from sampling and nonsampling error. Specifically, the samples that are tested could be unrepresentative, the procedures that are performed could be ineffective or mismatched with the audit objectives of interest, or the competence of the evidence that is gathered could be lacking due to the presence of fraud or to an overall poor control environment.

The Cost/Benefit Considerations Implicit in Selecting Audit Evidence

The topics of risk assessment and audit planning cannot be discussed without considering the cost/benefit trade-offs affecting such decisions. Presumably, if cost were of no relevance, risk could almost be eliminated. However, no entity is likely to be able to afford a control system or an internal auditing function that totally eliminates risk. Instead, the entity balances the costs of controls and the internal audit staff against their benefits to the organization. Some tolerable risk level is defined in light of this balancing. In other words, reasonable assurance is sought, not assurance beyond any doubt. "Reasonable" connotes that cost/benefit evaluations or risk exposure are intended to be a facet of audit planning. Risk and cost/benefit evaluations typically require materiality considerations.

Materiality

The concept of materiality focuses on whether a piece of information is likely to change the opinion or the action of an individual. If information influences a decision-maker's actions, it is said to be material. *Statement on Internal Auditing Standards No. 1* explains that material errors should be prevented, or detected and corrected. *Professional Standards Bulletin 85-4* states that "all errors should be corrected where it is economically feasible to do so." Economic feasibility implies materiality considerations.

Auditors frequently confront decisions as to what is material and what is not. To make these decisions rationally and systematically, auditors often define materiality in quantitative terms using several different approaches.

Magnitude in Absolute Terms. Certain dollar amounts are commonly perceived as material, no matter how large an entity's operations are. For example, most people would consider a million-dollar error to be material, even for a billion-dollar operation.

Percentage Relationship to an Account of Interest. Once absolute dollar terms are evaluated, the next benchmark for evaluating materiality is to compare the amount of potential effect to the total amount in the account to which it relates. In other words, an error of $10,000 can be substantial relative to a $20,000 account balance, whereas it might lack significance within a $2,000,000 account balance. The first would represent an error of 50 percent; the second, an error of half a percent.

Percentage Relationship to Profit. Many people contend that an effect on the bottom line ought to be the primary basis for assessing materiality. In fact, the Securities and Exchange Commission has suggested that a 3 percent change in earnings per share is a material change. The effect of potential misstatements on reported profit merits special consideration when assessing materiality.

Percentage Relationship to Asset Base. The size of an entity often serves as a benchmark by which to assess materiality. Therefore, auditors look at total assets employed in an operation when planning what dollar amount of risk exposure is deemed to be material.

Qualitative Attributes. Aside from amounts, qualitative attributes of errors or misstatements make certain activities material. For example, any errors in employees' pension funds or in key executives' salaries and perquisite payments often are considered to be material because of their emotional effect on members of the organization and others. Likewise, legal violations, even small ones, generally are considered material.

Fraud tends, by its nature, to be material. The point is that no matter what the past or current losses are, the presence of fraud can grow into an enormous risk exposure unless preventive, if not punitive, actions are taken.

Other qualitative attributes that can influence the materiality of certain types of activities, regardless of their associated dollar amounts, include:

- Transactions involving related parties.
- Sensitive payments (e.g., "grease" payments facilitating foreign operations).
- Regulatory issues.
- Politically sensitive operations.

Cumulative Effect of Otherwise Immaterial Items. When numerous individually immaterial items are identified, the auditor should consider their cumulative effect. It is possible that when considered together, their combined effect could indicate serious internal control weaknesses.

Materiality of risk exposure and related cost/benefit trade-offs help auditors determine how much evidence they will collect. The more material an item is, the greater the possible risk, and the more likely the auditor is to collect additional evidence.

Evaluating the Adequacy of Audit Evidence

Evidence provides the support for audit reports. Standard 420 states that such evidence should possess four specific attributes — sufficiency, competence, relevance to audit objectives, and usefulness to the organization. This standard also states that audit evidence should be gathered on all matters related to audit objectives and scope of work. Before issuing a report and concluding an audit, the auditor must decide when these standards have been met. This decision is a judgment call, since the measures are not quantifiably defined. Consequently, different auditors accept different types and levels of evidence to support their conclusions and recommendations. Some guidelines are available to help make these judgments.

Sufficient Evidence

According to Standard 420, the criteria for sufficient evidence lead to the concept that "a prudent person would reach the same conclusion as the auditor." The point here is that evidence should be persuasive (discussed earlier in this chapter).

Basically, the auditor must answer the question of whether a normally intelligent, well-informed, and prudent person would be satisfied that a body of evidence related to a question is persuasive enough to support the auditor's conclusions and recommendations. As noted earlier, retracing procedures alone may be sufficient to demonstrate the completeness of records, but the objective of evaluating those records' reliability would require a greater evidential base prior to reaching a conclusion.

Competent Evidence

The tests for competent evidence are (1) reliability and (2) that it is the "best attainable" from "appropriate audit techniques." Evidence is reliable when, if different auditors were to gather evidence from the same places in the same ways, their results very likely would be consistent with one another and would reflect the true situation being examined. One of the major arguments for the use of quantitative methods in auditing is their inherent reliability.

The test of "best attainable" evidence imposes constraints upon internal auditors which emerge from severe practical limitations. While it may be possible to collect all available evidence, it is seldom cost-efficient to do so. The time and money required would be prohibitive, and the marginal value of each new piece of evidence decreases significantly in most cases as more evidence is gathered.

Consequently, internal auditing procedures have been developed to maximize the cost-efficiency of gathering evidence. Some of these procedures are interviewing, recomputation, detailed testing, observation, scanning, statistical sampling, confirmation, and analytical review.

When applying these various auditing techniques, however, auditors must be skilled in knowing which procedures are likely to yield the "best attainable" results. For example, one team of internal auditors examined the internal controls of a multibillion-dollar project and concluded that controls were in order. A year later, after several costly problems had occurred involving millions of dollars, a second team of internal auditors examined the same operation. Numerous internal control weaknesses that had existed for several years were discovered. When the director of internal auditing investigated why they had not discovered the control weaknesses, he found that the first team had not performed adequate detailed testing. The team had depended primarily upon inquiry and observation techniques and had not followed up on questionable results from these initial procedures. As a result, the evidence was neither competent nor the best attainable.

Relevant Evidence   Standard 420 states that auditors should collect relevant evidence which "supports audit findings and recommendations and is consistent with the objectives of the audit."

Auditee operations are almost invariably interesting; so interesting that auditors usually can find far more things to examine than the audit plan requires. The tendency for many auditors, especially inexperienced ones, is to pursue answers to these additional questions, sometimes at the expense of planned audit work. Internal auditors should plan what evidence is required to meet the audit objectives without spending undue effort collecting unnecessary and extraneous information.

While wisdom may suggest that auditors share their informal observations regarding activities outside the audit objectives and scope, the *Standards* indicates that no undue formal effort or audit time should be devoted to gathering such information. Even when such information is shared with the auditee and management, auditors must acknowledge its tentative nature and lack of substantiation.

On the other hand, internal auditors should, as stated in Standard 420, collect evidence in "all matters" related to the audit objectives and scope. In so doing, the internal auditors can avoid the embarrassment of not collecting adequate relevant information.

The decision regarding how much evidence is enough, without gathering too much, takes practice and study. The following chapters suggest a variety of techniques to help the auditor strike an appropriate balance.

Each piece of evidence that is considered to contribute to the overall audit report must be relevant. This means, as we demonstrated, that vouching evidence (i.e., checking documentation on reported activities and transactions) should not be looked to as support for the conclusion regarding the completeness of accounting records.

Useful Evidence

Useful evidence is defined as that which "helps the organization meet its goals." These goals can be defined as the five objectives of internal control:

- Reliability and integrity of information.
- Compliance with policies, plans, procedures, laws, and regulations.
- Safeguarding of assets.
- Economy and efficiency in the use of resources.
- Accomplishment of organizational objectives and goals.

All audit evidence not only should relate to one or more of these objectives, it should also pass the "so what?" test; i.e., it should enable management and the board to perform their duties better. The "so what?" test is perhaps the most important criterion for success in internal auditing. It is by passing this test that management and the board generally believe that internal auditors earn their pay.

Substantiating One's Assessment Through Feedback From Auditees

While far from unbiased, the auditee can be depended upon to challenge erroneous conclusions, to raise competing explanations for the evidence collected, and to question weak inferences. Such feedback can assist the auditor in shoring up the evidential base through additional work, if necessary. In contrast, positive feedback from the auditee that adverse findings were as expected, or at least appear to be reasonably supported, is a tough test to pass and can provide considerable assurance to the auditor that conclusions are warranted.

However, the auditee can only be relied upon to provide useful feedback when adverse findings are reported. The fact that an auditee agrees with positive findings should not be treated as a strong indicator that the evidence collected is sufficient — unless, of course, the auditee requested the audit due to suspected problems. The point is that auditors must be cognizant of auditees' incentives to challenge, versus approve, the audit conclusions that are to be reported.

Documenting Evidence in Working Papers

Auditors document the planning, gathering, analysis, interpretation, and summarization of audit evidence in "working papers" that support the information contained in audit reports. Working papers often contain *rationale memos* that explicitly describe how the risks were evaluated, the role of cost/benefit considerations, and the tie-in of objectives to particular pools of evidence in formulating overall conclusions that address the purpose of the audit.

Working papers should be able to stand alone without further explanation by the internal auditor. Once prepared, the rationale memos should be critically reviewed for completeness and coherency in order to be assured that the audit report is sufficiently supported by working paper documentation, including the linkage between specific audit tests and summary audit findings.

Although a separate chapter in this text covers working paper preparation, the topic is so closely linked to the evaluation of evidential matter that some basic concepts merit emphasis here. Working papers should be clearly labelled and should relate only to directives and procedures that are relevant to the audit project. In addition to having a descriptive heading, the auditor's initials, the date of preparation, and a reference number to facilitate the organization of files should be noted. All columnar schedules should be fully explained, with the purpose and scope of the audit tests described and the methods of sample selection specified. "Tick marks" are commonly used to document what audit procedures were performed on which amounts, and a clear legend of tick marks and symbols should be prepared. For example, an auditor was assigned to test a monthly production report showing daily production totals by department. She indicated with a check mark beside each department's daily total that she had vouched each day's production totals to daily production records. At the bottom of her working papers she explained the meaning of the check mark.

The audit program can be used to summarize audit work merely by adding cross-references to various working papers. All deficiency findings should be summarized in a manner that clearly communicates their nature and materiality. Documentation should be complete and should answer the obvious questions. Clear conclusions on audit findings should be provided in the working papers, with erroneous items traced from summary to detail. In this manner the working papers can stand alone as support for the audit report.

When preparing working papers, efficiency and clarity should be stressed. When possible, copies of procedures and instructions should be photocopied to save on manual documentation. Working papers should be uniform in size and appearance. Only one side of the paper should be used because the back of a page could be overlooked by a reviewer or by someone copying the working papers for reference by others.

In this day of microcomputers, numerous word processing and spreadsheet programs are available for generating working paper documentation. Such applications can substantially increase both the efficiency with which documentation can be prepared and its clarity.

Evidence as a Determinant of Professionalism

A number of factors related to the quality of audit evidence affect the professionalism of internal auditors.

Due Professional Care

Standard 280 states that "internal auditors should exercise due professional care in performing internal audits." A large portion of the section is devoted to the collection of audit evidence.

This standard specifies that due care "implies reasonable care and competence, not infallibility or extraordinary performance." While auditors should conduct reasonable examinations, they need not perform detailed tests of all transactions or all activities. Also, absolute assurance need not, and cannot, be given with regard to audited activities.

Standard 280 goes on to explain that when performing audits, internal auditors should consider the following factors which affect the nature and the amount of evidence needed for a prudent and competent audit:

- The extent of audit work needed to achieve audit objectives.
- The relative materiality or significance of matters to which audit procedures are applied.
- The adequacy and effectiveness of internal controls.
- The cost of auditing in relation to potential benefits.

The Consequence of Unsubstantiated Claims

If internal auditors were to prepare reports with unsubstantiated claims, the credibility of their work, future communications, and their professional stature would suffer. For that reason, due professional care must be exercised in collecting sufficient evidence to support reported findings. Speculation is unacceptable. If cost/benefit constraints or time pressures force an end to an audit project, only those findings that are supportable should be included in the report.

If additional evidence is required to substantiate other "apparent findings," it must be collected prior to communicating anything about the auditors' interim expectations. The profession's standard of due audit care implies that reported findings should be substantiated by available evidence.

Occasionally, internal auditors encounter information which cannot be substantiated, but which is critical enough to warrant management's attention. In such cases, the information is reported, sometimes informally. Auditors, however, must clearly communicate the unsubstantiated nature of such information.

The Scope of Services

While the necessity of sufficient evidence to support audit findings should be obvious, it becomes an important question as the scope of auditors' services expands. For example, if auditors are asked to check the reasonableness of reported oil reserves, which can be ascertained by petroleum engineers within only a 25 percent range, will third parties consider claims on existing reserves to be sufficiently substantiated?

Common Concepts of "Hard Data." The sufficiency of evidence is easier to determine when an auditor works with "hard data." For example, a physical inventory of raw materials that can be counted or weighed with precision represents "hard data" about which definitive conclusions can be drawn. Most dollar transactions between independent parties are similarly easy to audit.

Common Concepts of "Soft Data." In contrast, "soft" judgment areas, such as the appropriate level of insurance coverage, are more difficult to audit and frequently require reliance on experts such as actuaries. The reason is the uncertainty of future events requiring insurance claims. Many other examples could be offered. For example, "rapport with customers" may be an operational objective which is expected to be considered by the auditor in expressing an opinion on the effectiveness of performance. To avoid the adverse consequences of unsubstantiated claims, the internal auditor should obtain the consensus of the auditee and top management as to how "soft data" are to be evaluated.

"Planned" Obsolescence. One key consideration by the internal auditor must be management's intent. There may be problems that have in some sense been "planned" by top management and accepted as cost/benefit-justified. For example, higher-quality machinery could be acquired for production or administrative purposes. Yet if technological advancement is expected, planning earlier obsolescence through the purchase of lower-quality assets may be an intelligent approach to ensuring state-of-the-art facilities at minimal cost. Allowance for such plans should be explicitly recognized in the gathering of evidence and in the reporting of audit findings.

Different Levels of Assurance. One approach in adapting the auditor's scope of services to management's needs is to offer different levels of assurance to management. For example, the internal auditor may agree to provide assurance that no more than 5 percent of purchase orders are unapproved, at a 95 percent level of confidence, rather than expressing an opinion on the overall compliance level of the purchasing department with respect to prescribed policies. Obviously, the assurance that is provided is restricted in scope and relates to a very narrow objective, but it has the benefit of providing the desired service to management, with a clear definition of the extent of evidence collection required to substantiate the specific conclusion. Statistical sampling can be applied to arrive at an objectively verifiable conclusion as to compliance with approval requirements.

Often, no overall opinions are requested, but rather a summary report on the facts obtained. As an example, many internal audit departments are requested to review potential merger candidates' operations or joint venture participants, which involves only a small part of additional operations. These special engagements contribute to the effectiveness with which management can evaluate merger candidates and joint venture operations.

The internal auditor should exercise due care in making the scope of services explicit, the criteria for evaluating "soft data" evident, and the level of assurance to be provided obvious, *before* performing the audit work. Exercising such care helps to ensure that the professionalism of the internal auditor's product is maintained.

Supervision of Audit Work

Appropriate supervision also enhances the professionalism with which audit evidence is planned, collected, analyzed, interpreted, documented, and reported. According to Standard 230 on professional proficiency, supervision should begin with the planning of the audit and end at the conclusion of the audit assignment.

Audit supervision includes a variety of activities such as:

- Instructing the audit staff with respect to audit techniques.
- Reviewing individual work to ensure that planned audit work is performed.

- Reviewing working papers.
- Reviewing the audit report to ensure accuracy, objectivity, clarity, concise structure, constructive tone, and timely preparation.
- Determining that audit objectives are met.

Supervision should be documented, usually in the form of checklists, approval forms for planned audit work, and supervisors' approval signatures on completed audit work. Of course, the amount of supervision that is necessary varies depending upon the abilities of the auditors performing the work and the complexity of the work.

Such supervision helps develop the professionalism of individual auditors and provides a quality control over audit work, thereby enhancing the overall professionalism of the internal auditing department.

QUESTIONS

1. What is "evidence"?
2. What attributes characterize quality audit evidence, according to the *Standards?*
3. Rank the following types of evidence from most valued to least valued (generally speaking) and explain why this ranking tends to prevail.
   a. Internal-external evidence.
   b. Internal evidence.
   c. External evidence.
   d. External-internal evidence.
4. Compare and contrast the effect on the quality of evidence when applying the following audit procedures to collect that evidence:
   a. Inquiry procedures.
   b. Recomputation.
   c. Detailed testing.
   d. Observation.
   e. Scanning.
   f. Statistical sampling.
   g. Confirmation.
   h. Analytical review.
5. Which types of analytical review procedures produce more objective evidence? Explain your response.
6. How does the evidential standard "beyond a shadow of a doubt" relate to the internal audit process, and why?
7. Is evidence that warrants "no reliance" of any use? Explain your response.
8. How does direct evidence differ from hearsay evidence in a courtroom?
9. Define "corroborative" evidence.
10. In planning an evidentiary base, what type(s) of audit evidence is desirable? Why?
11. Provide three examples of audit objectives that clearly guide the manner in which evidence is to be collected, as well as the type of evidence required to substantiate an audit finding.
12. What is the role of risk and cost/benefit analysis in the evidence collection process?
13. Provide a thorough description of materiality. How does this concept relate to the internal auditor's plans to collect audit evidence?
14. What considerations warrant attention when evaluating the adequacy of evidence collected? What is meant by persuasive evidence? How can auditees aid the auditor in evaluating the sufficiency of audit evidence collected?
15. What are rationale memos? Why are they important?
16. What special problems are posed in terms of how to collect sufficient evidence in an internal audit setting?
17. Explain the concept of "due professional care" with respect to audit evidence.
18. What would be the consequences of issuing internal audit reports containing unsubstantiated claims?
19. Distinguish between "hard data" and "soft data."

20. How can the scope of services be adjusted to best meet management's needs and still preserve the professionalism of internal auditing?

21. How does supervision enhance the professionalism of internal auditing?

EXERCISES

E-1

Peggy Carlisle recently graduated from Goodwin University, where she majored in engineering with a minor in business administration. She was hired by Boardman Manufacturing Corporation as a junior staff internal auditor, and she reported to work this week for the first time. She was assigned to work with Robert Pointer, a newly promoted senior auditor, on an audit of the company's quality control program for production at one plant.

Robert is a little uneasy about this, his first assignment as a senior auditor. To make things even more challenging, he has been assigned to supervise Peggy's work.

Required:

Review Standard 420 and indicate which provisions Robert and Peggy may have the most trouble meeting. Explain your selection(s).

E-2

An internal auditor has been asked to investigate inventory control because of recent reports indicating that inventory turnover figures have fluctuated substantially and differ greatly from competitors' experiences. Inquiry procedures as to what has changed with respect to sales, shipping, or inventory management policies have uncovered only one significant change. Two new, major customers have requested drop shipments (i.e., direct shipments via our suppliers — since our enterprise is a wholesale operation).

Required:

a. How could this relate to the inventory turnover statistics that were recently reported?

b. What type of evidence needs to be collected to verify such a relationship? Be specific.

E-3

A team of municipal auditors is examining street-construction contracts. The team leader is especially concerned that (1) contracts are executed for all construction contracts, (2) contracts are awarded only after receiving at least three bids for each project, (3) the work meets specifications represented in the contracts, and (4) payments are made to the construction firms according to contracted provisions. Following are five pieces of evidence gathered on this audit:

● Copies of a sample of construction contracts that were prepared by the city's legal department and signed by the municipal director of transportation and representatives of the construction companies. The original contracts are kept by the legal department, one copy of each is filed in the Municipal Transportation Office, and another copy is delivered to the construction companies.

- A sample of invoices sent by the contracted firms for payment.
- A sample of cancelled checks made in payment of contracted work.
- A sample of inspection forms prepared by municipal inspectors for particular street projects.
- A sample of bids collected for a number of projects.

Required:

a. Classify the above pieces of evidence according to internal, internal-external, external-internal, and external evidence.
b. Rank the five according to evidentiary weight.
c. Identify which piece of evidence matches each of the four audit objectives.

E-4

As internal auditor, you have been asked to review an entity's control over cost. You determine that this means you must review the adequacy of cost accounting. You proceed to outline what you believe are the most important purposes of cost accounting:

- To enable all levels of management to localize and measure inefficiencies so that cost-reduction efforts can be applied intelligently.
- To produce accurate product costs so that management can set sales prices and policies and plan efficient production schedules.

Required:

What should you do to assess the adequacy of the cost accounting function? Be specific as to the audit procedures that you would perform to gather the evidence required to support conclusions in an audit report.

Adapted from W. A. Walker, "Internal Audit Procedures for Controlling Costs," *Journal of Accountancy*, May 1950, p. 386.

E-5

Peter Drucker, the author of *Management — Tasks, Responsibilities, and Practices,* has stated, "Efficiency is concerned with doing things right, whereas effectiveness is doing the right things."

Required:

Comment on the adequacy of this distinction in explaining the manner in which internal auditors collect evidence.

E-6

Required:

For the audit described in E-3, identify one possible analytical review comparison of each of the following types:

1. Period-to-period.
2. Budget-to-actual.

3. Interrelationships among accounts.
4. City-to-industry.
5. Operating data-to-account balances.
6. Operating data-to-economic data.
7. Operating data-to-nonfinancial data.

E-7

Internal auditors frequently use the audit technique of observation. Which of the following statements best reflects the auditor's view of observation?

a. It should be performed separately from any other audit fieldwork function.
b. It is essentially related to the review of work flow and plant layout.
c. It is generally considered to be less authentic evidence than copies of basic documents describing the control process.
d. It can be supported by photography, flowcharts, drawings, and narrative.
e. All of the above.

(CIA Exam Adapted)

E-8

Which of the following excerpts from working papers would adequately support a conclusion in an audit report?

a. "We are of the opinion that control over stores is adequate."
b. "A physical inventory disclosed a 9 percent shortage."
c. "The storekeeper appears to be doing a commendable job."
d. "We are of the opinion that requisitioning procedures are inadequate."
e. All of the above.

(CIA Exam Adapted)

E-9

Suppose that Boardman Manufacturing Corporation (mentioned in E-1) was being sued in a class action because of injuries to persons using products produced at the plant. The action alleges that poor product quality caused the injuries.

Required:
a. How would this circumstance affect the types of evidence Robert Pointer and Peggy Carlisle would seek in the audit?
b. Identify an example of at least one piece of evidence that could be collected in each of the classifications for legal rules of evidence relevant to this problem.

E-10

The internal auditors for a utility company discovered information from a file of customer complaints that suggests an unusually large number of overcharges on monthly bills.

Required:
Identify two additional pieces of evidence the auditors might seek to verify the problem.

E-11

The internal auditors for Atlantic Enterprises, Inc. are auditing the purchasing function for the company's Northeastern region. One audit objective is to examine and evaluate the regional purchasing office's compliance with prescribed procedures for purchase authorizations. The audit team leader is considering the choice of audit techniques. The following are four possible alternative procedures:

1. Flowchart the prescribed authorization procedures from a policies and procedures manual.
2. Interview the regional purchasing manager.
3. Examine a sample of purchasing documents for prescribed authorization signatures.
4. Test all available documents for prescribed authorization signatures.

Required:

a. Identify key risks associated with evidence collected by each one of the above procedures.
b. How would using two or more different audit procedures decrease the risk resulting from only one audit procedure?

E-12

An auditor who reviewed the efficiency of a small drug-manufacturing division of a multibillion-dollar conglomerate gathered the following pieces of evidence:

1. The total budget for the drug division employed approximately 1 percent of the company's total assets.
2. Three months before the audit, the Federal Drug Administration (FDA) approved the sale of a new drug produced by the division for treatment of arthritis. Although the company's researchers and the FDA had performed extensive tests, the auditor discovered a note in one company scientist's research papers indicating that a significant risk of hair loss was present for a particular group of patients who might use the drug. The FDA, however, had placed no restrictions on the sale of the drug, and the auditor discovered that although the scientist had voiced his concerns, management had decided to market the product without any warnings to patients or doctors. Management had decided on this strategy after two other researchers on the project said they believed the risk of serious side effects, including hair loss, was remote. Total expected sales of the drug were estimated by the marketing department to be $500,000 per year. The auditor, in consultation with the legal department, concluded that one class-action suit could cost the company at least 10 times that amount.
3. The drug division expensed two trucks, costing $25,000 each, that should have been capitalized.
4. Payments to suppliers often were delayed, causing $25,000 in lost discounts. That was 0.25 percent of net profits from the division's previous year's operations.

Required:

Assess the materiality of each of the above items.

E-13

An auditor notes a case of decreased production output. Based on discussions with and observation of employees, she attributes the decreases to low employee morale caused by low pay rates and poor working conditions.

Required:

Describe what should be demonstrable by competent and sufficient evidence in support of such a finding.

Adapted from Edward P. Chait, "Sufficiency of Audit Evidence in Differing Audit Environments," *The Internal Auditor,* August 1976, pp. 77-79.

E-14

As audit supervisor, you are reviewing a set of working papers covering a completed audit assignment. The working papers consist solely of columnar schedules without narrative comments. All the tests set forth in the audit program were carefully carried out.

All test items are listed and identified, and the tests that were performed are clearly indicated by appropriate tick marks that are properly identified in a legend on the worksheets. Items listed in the schedules to which the auditor took exception are underlined in red. The schedules contained proper headings, cross-references, dates, and initials.

Required:

Give three suggestions you would make to improve these working papers.

(CIA Exam Adapted)

E-15

As audit supervisor, you are reviewing the report draft of an auditor who has completed an audit of a research and development department. In the report draft, the auditor made the following statements:

> With the approval of top management, we obtained the services of a scientist who is an acknowledged expert in the field to help us in our evaluation of the research and development activities. The scientist's appraisal disclosed the following: (1) The new filtering process developed by the research and development department meets the technical requirements of the project authorization. (2) The costs of the project as detailed in the project-cost report included an appropriate proportion of R&D overhead.
>
> Based on the expert's appraisal, we concluded that the technical requirements have been met and that the costs may be considered acceptable.

Required:

a. State whether you will accept or reject statements (1) and (2) above for the final report.
b. Identify the applicable rules of evidence.
c. Explain the application of those rules to both statements in the report draft.

(CIA Exam Adapted)

E-16

In an effort to become more familiar with the internal auditing function, a newly hired high-level executive in a large, diversified company asked the company's director of internal auditing to have lunch. The new executive had been president of a smaller neighboring company before moving to his current position, but the former company, where he had spent his entire career up to that point, had not employed internal auditors. At lunch he made the following comments:

> Gerald, I just read two of your auditors' reports on a couple of my areas of responsibility, and there is something I don't understand. Neither report told me anything for sure. One said that if we revise our policies and procedures manual and train our people better we probably could improve our efficiency. The auditor said some other divisions had experienced some success that way and suggested that we might consider it.

> First, I don't understand what an auditor is doing making recommendations about operations anyway. Aren't you auditors supposed to make sure that no one is stealing our money?

> Second, I don't understand why the auditor couldn't tell us right out whether our operations are efficient or not, and if not, how to fix them. I am not used to people beating around the bush. I realize I am new here, and I was hoping you could help me understand what it is you guys do.

Required:

a. How would you answer the executive's first question?

b. How would you answer the second concern, using the concept of due professional care?

PROBLEMS

P-1

An audit report included the following section:

> Finding: Local newspaper and television advertising expenditures for 1986 exceeded those for 1985 by 20 percent, while sales increased only 12 percent in those markets. Company guidelines have suggested that all costs should be closely scrutinized and that managers should try to hold increases below 10 percent. Marketing management attributes the 20 percent cost increase to a strategy to reach a broader audience than did the previous strategy of limiting advertising to point-of-sale displays.

> We conclude that the increased cost has not been effective and is not cost-justified. We therefore recommend that the advertising expenditure be reduced for newspaper and television to no more than 12 percent above the 1985 amount.

Required:

a. Evaluate the evidence used to support the audit conclusion and recommendation above.

b. What additional evidence would you suggest in this case?

P-2

The auditors of an energy company with headquarters in Oklahoma City and divisional administrative and sales offices in Chicago, New York City, and San Francisco were assigned to audit the company's training program. Of particular interest was the orientation and training of new college graduates in management track and engineering positions. The audit team leader was considering what analytical review measures would be appropriate with respect to the following types of internal controls:

1. Organizational structure.
2. Lines of decision authority.
3. Objectives, goals, and standards.
4. Training procedures.
5. Training staff.
6. Facilities.

Required:

a. Identify some appropriate analytical review measures for the items above.
b. Specify what type of analytical review measure you are suggesting from the categories outlined in the chapter.
c. Identify the source from which you think the required information likely could be obtained.

P-3

An audit director reviewed the performance of his staff and determined that audits were taking too much time. Audit jobs consistently had been going well over the time allocated. He called a meeting of the audit managers to discuss the problem. This meeting resulted in a number of observations and suggestions, including the following:

- Managers of auditee operations have begun accepting the auditors as a valuable source of information and now often request additional information from the auditors that is outside the scope of planned audit work.
- Top management, under heavy pressure from the board of directors for improved performance, has cracked down on internal control. Top management also is stressing to the audit director that audits need to be thorough and should determine all sources of any insufficiencies or ineffectiveness that may be present in activities being audited.
- One manager suggested that perhaps less detailed testing could be performed and that the auditors could specify a lower level of assurance on audit results.
- Another manager mentioned that supervision and review procedures were taking an inordinate amount of time and suggested cutting back on these activities.

Required:

Comment on each of the four observations and suggestions with respect to professionalism and due professional care.

SECTION II
THE AUDIT PROCESS

5 Overview of the Internal Audit Process

Some auditors can best be described as "auditing mechanics." They can apply the various tools required to conduct an audit, but the process for them typically becomes one of mere rote. In this chapter we consider the audit as a process of critical thinking, analysis, and careful evaluation. The mechanical procedures must be integrated into a larger context of thoughtful inquiry.

The main body of the chapter is divided into nine sections corresponding to nine steps in the audit process. An appendix on audit working papers is included at the end of the chapter.

Overview of Audit Activities

Exhibit 5-1 illustrates a flowchart outlining nine steps in the internal audit process. The remainder of the chapter briefly covers each of these nine steps as a preview to more detailed discussions in later chapters.

Step 1 — Selection of the Auditee

"Auditee" can mean an organizational entity, subsidiary, operation, or program. The term may also refer to an isolated process, activity, or condition. An auditee is that part of the organization being audited.

An audit begins with the selection of the auditee. Auditors may select auditees in different ways and for different reasons. The selection of a particular auditee may not even be initiated by the auditors, but by someone else in the organization. Consequently, the selection of a particular auditee may not be as routine a matter as it might first appear.

We have suggested that risk should be the primary consideration when selecting an auditee. In Chapter 1, risk was defined as the product of the amount of exposure to possible losses (expressed in monetary units) and the probability of loss — i.e., R equals pr(E). Although this particular mathematical formulation for risk is not universally applied in auditing departments, the concept of risk usually does determine the selection process. As we mentioned before, it often is extremely difficult, sometimes even impossible, to

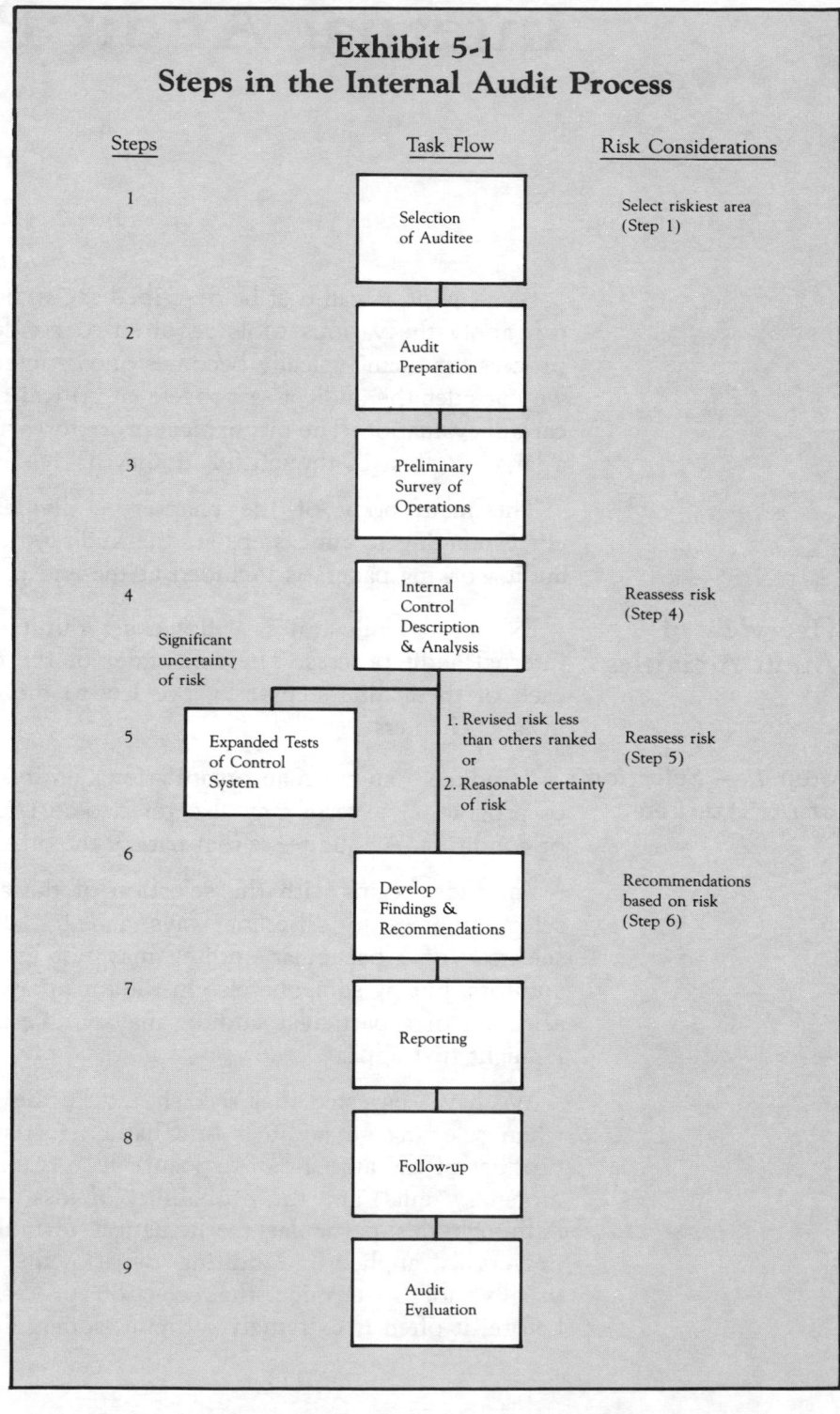

Exhibit 5-1
Steps in the Internal Audit Process

Steps	Task Flow	Risk Considerations
1	Selection of Auditee	Select riskiest area (Step 1)
2	Audit Preparation	
3	Preliminary Survey of Operations	
4	Internal Control Description & Analysis	Reassess risk (Step 4)
5	Expanded Tests of Control System	Reassess risk (Step 5)
6	Develop Findings & Recommendations	Recommendations based on risk (Step 6)
7	Reporting	
8	Follow-up	
9	Audit Evaluation	

Significant uncertainty of risk

1. Revised risk less than others ranked or
2. Reasonable certainty of risk

determine precisely how much exposure really exists. A precise probability of loss also may be difficult to compute. On the other hand, auditors and managers consider these two variables even when making a subjective assessment of risk; and the riskier the situation, the greater the need for management's attention.

Developing Audit Plans

Basically, there are three methods by which an auditee may be selected:

Systematic Selection. In the first method, auditing departments generally compile an annual schedule of audits in the sequence in which those audits are expected to be conducted. Typically, this schedule is developed with risk as the primary consideration. Potential auditees exhibiting higher levels of risk generally are the ones selected first. Those potential auditees exhibiting lower risks are selected later, after audit management is satisfied that the greater risks have been adequately addressed.

Ad Hoc Audits. Why does the selection of an auditee take other paths? If all operations were to go as planned, the systematic selection process would be the only one needed. However, operations do not always go exactly as planned, which leads to a second method of selecting an auditee. This method corresponds somewhat to the "squeaky wheel" method of management. The "squeaky wheel" is the one to get the grease. In other words, management and the board sometimes identify problem areas that, in their judgment, need immediate attention from the auditors. They, in effect, choose auditees for the auditors.

For example, one company unexpectedly received a large bill for immediate payment on a loan. Although the money had been received and used in production, for some reason there was no record of it in the company's accounting system. The required payment was so large that two managers were taken from their regular duties for almost a week to resolve the crisis created in the company's cash management system. At the next meeting of the board of directors, a report of this situation prompted the call for an immediate inquiry into internal controls in order to determine how such a gross mistake could have occurred.

In other situations, the auditors may identify areas in need of special audits that were not previously included in the auditing budget. For example, an EDP audit manager for a large international corporation recently returned from a computer security conference. Based on what he had learned at the conference, he suspected that the controls over the company's data files were dangerously weak.

Consequently, he interrupted existing audit plans and assigned a small team of auditors to investigate the controls over EDP data files. Their preliminary findings resulted in a much more in-depth investigation into what turned out to be a serious problem. Other examples might include discussions of previously unanticipated failure by a department to comply with corporate policies or government regulations, suspicious behavior by some personnel, or the acquisition of a new operation for which management needs information on internal controls.

Auditee Requests. A third way auditees may be selected is by a request from the auditee. Some managers feel that they need the input of auditors to evaluate the adequacy and effectiveness of internal controls affecting the operations under their supervision.

Regardless of whether an audit is proposed by management, the board, internal auditors, or auditees themselves, before interrupting the previously determined auditing plans, auditors usually evaluate whether the proposed audit is more important than the audits already scheduled. Theoretically, this importance may be evaluated by the same yardstick as the others in the plan — relative risk. If the risk appears great enough, an immediate audit is warranted. If not, the audit probably would be set in a queue with others according to its perceived risk.

Realistically, other considerations occasionally bear heavily upon auditee selection. One such consideration is internal politics. Occasions sometimes arise when relationships with management, the board, or the auditee may prompt internal auditors to select particular auditees over others. Independence of the internal auditing department, however, can help avoid undue political pressure on auditee selection.

In summary, auditees may be selected by three general methods: (1) a systematic risk analysis may be conducted in order to establish an auditing plan for the year, (2) unanticipated ad hoc audits may be scheduled, which sometimes arise as emergency audits, or (3) auditees themselves may request audits.

Step 2 — Audit Preparation

Preparation for the audit includes seven phases: (1) a tentative determination of the objectives and scope of the audit, (2) a review of audit files, (3) selection of the audit team, (4) preliminary communication with the auditee and others, (5) preparation of the preliminary audit program, (6) planning the audit report, and (7) obtaining approval of the audit approach.

Audit Objectives and Scope. Preparation requires the auditors to tentatively determine (1) what the objectives of the audit are to be and (2) the scope of the audit.

Determining Objectives. While the *Statement of Responsibilities of Internal Auditing* states that the objective of the internal auditing function is "to assist members of the organization in the effective discharge of their responsibilities," the objectives of an individual audit are more specific.

The objectives of individual audits may be classified into three general categories: (1) *review* of operations and the design of the internal control system, (2) tests of operational *compliance* with the designed control system, and (3) *evaluation* of the adequacy of the control system.

The review of operations and the internal control system generally includes a description of the two and usually a brief evaluation of how well the designed controls are coordinated with operations. The purpose of this review is to provide a basic understanding of the auditee and of the relevant operating controls.

Tests of compliance are designed to examine the auditee's operations to determine whether they conform to the prescribed control system. This examination compares the actual operations with the policies, standards, and established procedures of the organization.

Evaluation objectives for an audit require a substantive analysis and appraisal of the auditee in terms of (1) the adequacy and effectiveness of the control systems and (2) the organizational risks that are an inherent part of the auditee's operations.

The specific objectives for a single audit may include any or all three of these categories. Of course, a full audit would require objectives in all three classifications, while more limited audits may be more narrowly focused.

Notice that the objectives follow a logical sequence so that each subsequent category follows a previous category containing information requisite to the next level of objectives. Consequently, a review of operations and of the design of internal controls provides a logical step toward determining whether the operations are in accordance with established controls. Likewise, as auditors determine whether operations are in compliance with the designed controls, they can evaluate the design and the effectiveness of the controls more effectively. Usually, when an in-depth evaluation is required, the first two categories of objectives (review and compliance) are also included in the audit; and when a test of compliance is required, a review generally is required as a prerequisite.

Determining Scope. Scope relates to the specific parts of operations to be examined and to the extent of the examination. Some audits focus upon a very narrow aspect of operations. Other audits are quite broad. Some go into great depth, while others are more superficial. The scope of the auditing function is also outlined in the *Statement of Responsibilities.*

After selecting an auditee, it is important that the auditors have at least a tentative idea of the nature of the subsequent audit in order to plan effectively. By specifying both the objectives and the scope of the audit, the auditors are able to estimate the necessary resources (in terms of manpower, time, and travel) to conduct the examination. While later changes may be made in both the objectives and scope of the audit, this initial determination provides the basis for moving forward with assigning the audit team and then into the first steps of the preliminary survey work.

Review of Audit Files. Most audits are not first-time audits for particular auditees. Usually one or more audits have been conducted before, although the previous ones may not have examined the same aspects of operations. Before beginning a new examination, most audit team leaders prefer to review reports and other information from previous audit files for different types of information. The auditors try to acquaint themselves with the nature of the operations as a preview to the preliminary survey.

Such a preview allows them to anticipate special or unusual aspects of the operations that may need attention. It also permits them to acquaint themselves with operating policies and control procedures so that they will make a positive impression in the preliminary survey as being knowledgeable and prepared. The auditors look for previous concerns that may carry over to the present audit, especially where follow-up procedures may be deemed to have been inadequate. Finally, the auditors look for indications of the collective personality of the auditee and of the attitudes of the auditee toward previous audits. Such information is valuable in planning how to approach the current audit.

Some auditing theorists have argued that the review of files from previous audits should not be done until after completion of the preliminary survey and review of internal controls. This argument is based upon the auditor's need for an objective attitude during the preliminary survey. If the review of the previous files occurs before any examination is done, then the auditors may be unduly influenced by what the previous auditors did and thought. By completing the preliminary survey first, the auditors will stress their own observations, adding the insights of the previous auditors as the audit program is written.

Many auditors, on the other hand, believe in their own ability to maintain an objective attitude toward an audit even though they have studied previous audit files. They often point to the advantages of an early look at the previous files as outweighing any possible disadvantages. As long as the auditor is cognizant that the current operations and findings could be totally different from prior years' experiences, and strives to maintain an objective attitude toward evaluating current conditions, he or she is likely to benefit from being familiar with past audit work involving the auditee.

One auditor, for example, in a review of previous audits of a remote office of an energy company, discovered that the office manager resented having auditors in his office. The previous auditors had noted in a memo to the files that the manager believed that the auditors did not know enough about his operations to be able to effectively evaluate the office. This auditor was able to plan her audit in such a manner that she convinced the manager to teach her a great deal about the operations before her audit actually began.

While he was teaching her about operations, she was able to ask appropriate questions and to identify the documents that would be necessary for the later audit work. As they went through the various aspects of the operations, her insightful questions actually prompted the manager to notice weaknesses in control and to propose effective measures to correct the weaknesses. As a result, her audit was very brief, and in the final report she was able to state that the problems discovered during the audit were being corrected by the manager.

The audit was a success, and her strategy probably made future audits easier to conduct. Another advantage to her approach was that she really did learn more about the auditee's operations than did the previous auditors, thereby allowing her to conduct a better-informed audit.

Selection of the Audit Team. The vast majority of audits are performed by teams that include between one and eight auditors. A team of more than eight auditors constitutes a very large audit team. In fact, most audits are conducted by two or three auditors working at the audit site and one or two that oversee the work from the internal auditing department offices.

Each team has several functions to perform, usually by different members of the team. First, there is an audit executive who generally is responsible for selecting the auditee and for determining the objectives and scope of the audit. This audit executive is almost always an audit *director,* and even though the director may not actually do any of the on-site work for the audit, he or she is responsible for the outcome.

Second, the team includes a person responsible for the overall coordination of the work, including assigning team members, coordinating the audit projects with other work going on in the auditing department at the same time, serving as a troubleshooter when problems arise on the audits, and reviewing all of the documentation for the audit process. This person usually is a *manager* within the department, and may or may not travel to the audit site, depending on the size and routine nature of the audits.

Third, the on-site leader is called the *auditor-in-charge, lead auditor,* or *team leader,* and usually is a senior staff auditor. The lead auditor's responsibility is to conduct the audit and coordinate the day-to-day activities of the audit team.

Finally, the *audit staff* usually consists of junior staff auditors and senior staff auditors who are responsible for doing most of the routine audit work.

Naturally, on very small audits, or in departments where relatively few auditors are available for any single audit, these functions are combined so that a single auditor may be responsible for more than one of the functions. There are, in fact, some auditing departments that employ only one auditor who is responsible for all of the functions.

Different audit teams may be assigned, depending upon the nature and size of an audit. An operational audit of an engineering office requires different expertise than a financial audit of accounts receivable, for example. A computerized environment may require an EDP specialist, or a complex sampling approach may require the involvement of a statistical sampling expert. Obviously, larger audits take either more auditors or more time, both of which have ramifications for the scheduling of the audit tests.

Preliminary Communication. Courtesy as well as good business practice suggest that the auditors notify the auditee and selected others that an audit is about to begin. Such communication allows the auditee to make necessary preparations to accommodate the auditors' requirements for access to records, facilities, selected employees, materials, and so forth. The auditee also may be asked to prepare and supply certain schedules and other information for the auditors when they arrive. Usually, management to whom the auditee reports and the audit committee are notified of the upcoming audit.

The audit team leader usually makes a personal contact, often by telephone, with the auditee's management, and discusses briefly the purpose of the audit, the auditors who have been assigned to do the work, the timing of the audit, and the expected preparations. Adjustments to the timing, the scope of work, and the preparations may be negotiated at this time.

After the personal contact, the team leader will draft a memorandum or letter outlining the preliminary information pertaining to the upcoming audit. This letter confirms the agreements reached in the earlier discussion between the team leader and auditee management. Management above the auditee also is notified in writing, and sometimes the audit committee is notified. In some instances the notification is a copy of the memo or letter sent to the auditee. Other times the team leader will draft separate memos or letters for management and the audit committee.

Preparing a Preliminary Audit Program. The audit plan and schedule of activities required to complete the audit is called the "audit program." Although many auditors wait until after their review of internal control (Step 4) to prepare their formal audit program, we recommend preparing a preliminary audit program during the initial audit preparation phase.

An audit takes careful planning and coordination. The audit program outlines those plans. It contains such information as the objectives and scope of the audit, specific questions to be answered during the audit, procedures to be employed, and evidence to be examined. It may identify the auditors to be assigned to each of the audit tasks and specify when those tasks should be accomplished.

The preliminary audit program may be considered the first of two phases of program preparation. This first phase includes the work to be done in the preliminary survey and the review of internal controls (Steps 3 and 4). After these steps are completed, the program may be modified according to the information acquired during those steps. The value of the preliminary program is that it offers a systematic guide to performing the early stages of an audit.

Keep in mind that each step of the audit should be well integrated with all other steps. What is done in any one phase is dependent either upon what has happened in previous steps or upon what may be expected from subsequent steps.

Consequently, the preliminary audit program should be compiled and structured to include expectations of the rest of the audit work to be done. For example, suppose auditors know that their examination of one operation will also necessarily include how that operation interacts with another related function in the organization. The preliminary program very likely would include not only a review of the control system for the one operation primarily under examination, but also selected parts of the related function's control system.

Planning the Audit Report. The audit report communicates the results of the audit to the auditee and to others in the organization. Planning for the report begins at the preparation stage of the audit process. All audit work is done in anticipation of the audit report. Consequently, internal auditors begin thinking at the start of the audit assignment about how the report will be prepared, when it should be delivered, and who should receive it.

The objective is not to anticipate all of the details that will be presented in the report, but rather to develop some basic parameters. For example, the auditors know at the beginning of the assignment that they will be presenting their findings to the auditee at a closing conference. The auditors can begin considering the best place to conduct this meeting. They can determine who are the people most likely to be invited and tentatively set some alternative closing conference dates, as well as some limits on the length of the meeting. The auditors also can tentatively plan what visual aids would be appropriate for the presentation.

Similarly, for the written report, the internal auditors can plan who will bear the primary responsibility for writing the report. They can plan how the report will be reviewed, edited, and corrected before issuance. They also can tentatively decide to whom the report should be addressed and who should receive copies. Auditors can anticipate the relative format of their reports, the need for graphics, the approximate expected length, and the approximate delivery date.

Approval of the Audit Program. The director of internal auditing is responsible for the review and approval of the audit program before the audit team begins work.

Program review includes the audit objectives and scope as well as specific audit procedures. Such a comprehensive review helps ensure that the work procedures support the audit objectives and the proposed scope of work.

Once the auditee is selected, the tentative audit objectives and scope have been determined, the previous audit files have been reviewed, the audit team has been selected, the auditee and others have been notified, and a preliminary program has been prepared and approved, the auditors are ready to proceed with the next step in the audit process — the preliminary survey.

Step 3 —
Preliminary
Survey

The objectives of the preliminary survey are to gain some initial impressions of the auditee, to gather preliminary evidence for further audit planning, and to gain the cooperation of the auditee.

Opening Conference. During the preliminary survey, an opening conference will be conducted between the members of the audit team and auditee management. This meeting normally is held at the auditee's place of operation. It outlines the audit assignment with management and coordinates the audit activities with auditee operations.

On-Site Tour. A tour of the premises is customary and provides the auditors with an idea of such things as the nature of operations, the work climate, physical facilities, interrelationships with other departments, and work flow. The auditors also often have an opportunity to meet many of the personnel during this tour.

Document Study. The opening conference, tour of facilities, and further study of selected documents provide a basis for a written description of the auditee's operations, which will be included in the audit files. Auditors study such documents as organization charts, government regulations, statements of organizational objectives, job descriptions, policy manuals, summary reports, and even relevant periodicals. Key concerns at this stage of the audit are whether certain documents exist, how they are organized, how orderly they are kept, and whether they are adequately secured.

Written Description. Auditors must understand the auditee's operations in order to evaluate the adequacy of the internal control system. A written description of the auditee kept in the permanent files demonstrates such an understanding and provides a reference from which to evaluate the internal control system and the audit procedures. Descriptions of operations include narratives, flowcharts, floor plans, references to operational policies, and information about competitors and other elements of the auditee's environment.

Analytical Reviews. An integral part of the preliminary survey on audits of financial statements, and on a growing number of operational and other internal audits as well, is the analytical review. These reviews, which are discussed in Chapter 4, provide a brief analysis of summary numerical data contained in various financial and operating reports. When performing analytical review procedures, auditors compare actual results to budgeted activity; examine trends from year to year and over several years; scan records for unusual details; calculate approximate totals in account balances or volume of activity using various other correlated figures; and also compute financial, production, and operating ratios for comparison to those of previous years, other departments, or industry averages.

The analytical review not only helps the auditors to understand more about the auditee's operations, but it also helps them plan audit procedures. Unusual or unexpected results from these calculations and comparisons create questions which should be addressed specifically in later, more detailed audit procedures. Note that these procedures can be more than attention-directors. They can also provide positive evidence that certain operations and financial numbers are reasonable, permitting audit time to be allocated to other areas at risk.

Step 4 — Internal Control Description, Analysis, and Evaluation

Step 4 constitutes the following activities: preparing a reasonably detailed description of the auditee's internal controls related to the area under study; conducting a "walk-through" of selected transactions and operations at key control points; performing limited testing of controls; evaluating internal controls; and reassessing risks associated with the controls.

Description of Controls. The auditors describe the control system with flowcharts, answers to standardized questionnaires, and narrative outlines. Often the flowcharts of controls are integrated with the flowcharts describing operations, so that the auditors can more easily study the effects of controls on operations and evaluate the need for additional or modified controls. The control questionnaires and narrative outlines provide further analysis of controls so that the auditors can acquire a complete understanding of the control system before attempting to test and evaluate it. These descriptions often are prepared by updating documents already on file.

"Walk-Through." The first level of testing the controls is a "walk-through" of selected transactions and operations through key control points. The system of internal controls includes certain key or critical points where potential risks appear to be particularly high. The auditors make a step-by-step examination of auditee operations at these critical control points in one of two ways — either by tracing each step of a transaction through organizational records or by actually performing the procedures themselves. The first may be called a "documentation walk-through;" the second a "procedural walk-through." "Walk-throughs" usually include only one or two tests for any single procedure. For example, the auditors may "walk through" a quality control inspection of an item of finished goods coming off an assembly line.

Limited Testing. Auditors select a small number of transactions and examine how they actually were conducted. Such an examination provides the auditors with an understanding of how the controls are supposed to work as opposed to how they actually work in operation. The testing of actual transactions or operations indicates to auditors whether or not the controls seem to be effectively implemented. A limited amount of testing may be done during Step 4, and substantially more testing may be done in Step 5, as the need arises. In our quality control example, the auditors may perform limited tests by selecting a few completed items that have been approved and a few that have been rejected to see if quality control inspectors classified them properly. Although a limited test sample may include as many as 25 or 30 items, there are times when as few as two or three items may be selected, depending upon the circumstances.

Evaluation of Internal Controls. After describing the system of internal controls and doing some preliminary analysis, the internal auditors are in a position to make a preliminary evaluation of the control systems under review. One way of making such an evaluation is to prepare an internal control matrix and to outline important observations, risks, and standards of control that pertain to specific observations and risks. By studying these results, prepared from audit work performed so far, auditors can evaluate the quality of the internal control system with respect to control objectives and risks.

A variety of formats are used to prepare internal control matrices. One is to list four columns: (1) results of preliminary survey and internal control review; (2) key risks associated with specific results; (3) appropriate control methods and standards; and (4) the internal auditors' evaluation. Rows in this matrix comprise individual entries related to specific observations made up to this point in the audit. Exhibit 5-2 illustrates one such set of entries.

Risk Reassessment. At the conclusion of the description, analysis, and evaluation of internal controls, the auditors determine any needed changes in the objectives or scope of the audit. They also decide how much, if any, expanded audit work is required before drawing their conclusions, making recommendations, and writing the audit report. All of these considerations are based upon the auditors' assessment of risks associated with the auditee's operations.

Exhibit 5-2
Internal Control Matrix

IMPORTANT RESULTS	KEY RISKS	PROPER CONTROL METHODS/ STANDARDS	EVALUATION
An individual collects cash receipts, prepares and delivers bank deposits, and makes accounting journal entries for Skyview's branch office. These deposits average $15,000 per week. No improprieties or exceptions were discovered in our review.	(a) Significant risk exists of skimming by the employee and for this practice to go undetected. (b) The employee is also at risk because of temptation, physical danger if others discover his sole responsibility for branch funds, and blame if funds are lost or unaccounted for.	Appropriate controls in this case, which are specified in the company's policies, include (a) segregation of cash collections, preparation of deposits, and accounting; (b) dual responsibility for preparing and delivering deposits; and (c) supervision and review of each set of tasks.	(a) Adequacy of design: Cash controls are inadequate at Skyview's branch office. (b) Effectiveness of controls: No audit evidence indicated losses, although detailed testing was limited.

The first risk assessment was made for the purpose of selecting the auditee. This second risk assessment uses the additional information gathered from Steps 2, 3, and 4. The reassessment of risk leads to one of two possible paths for the audit. Sometimes additional work is considered to be unnecessary, either because the auditors feel they will learn very little additional information, or because even though they may learn more from further examination, other audits appear more pressing in comparison to their respective estimated risks.

Auditors usually decide to do some expanded testing, primarily because of uncertainties that remain after the preliminary survey and the description and analysis of internal controls. In fact, Steps 3 and 4 provide a foundation from which to plan the remaining majority of the audit work. Whatever the decision, it is based upon the results of the preliminary survey and the auditor's description and analysis of internal controls.

Step 5 — Expanded Testing

If the auditors decide to do expanded audit work, it is outlined in the audit program as an addition to the preliminary audit program. Any changes in the objectives and scope of the audit will be noted on the program, and additional procedures will be outlined. New auditor assignments and time schedules also may need to be entered.

Once complete, the audit program provides an outline of all of the activities to be performed during the audit. As each activity is completed, its completion date may be written directly on the program, with the initials of the auditors performing the work. This helps to document who is responsible for which audit procedures. When the audit is completed, the program provides a convenient reference. It is filed with other documents from the audit — the audit report and working papers — providing a comprehensive history of the work performed and the results.

In contrast to the preliminary survey and analysis of internal controls, the expanded tests represent an in-depth examination of the auditee. While the analysis of internal controls and the preliminary survey are designed to detect possible control strengths and weaknesses, expanded testing techniques are designed to confirm that information and to quantify the related risk exposure. While the analysis of controls often indicates the extent of possible control strengths and weaknesses, the expanded tests determine the extent and the effects of those strengths and weaknesses. These tests also provide a study of how the auditee interacts with other parts of the organization and with elements of the organization's environment. Auditors then are prepared to make a final evaluation of the control system and to formulate any necessary recommendations.

The testing in Step 5 represents the heart of most audits. It includes the examination of records and documents, interviews with auditee management and other personnel, observation and documentation of operations, examination of assets and review of the accounting for those assets, and other procedures aimed at providing the auditor with a detailed understanding of how well the organizational controls function.

There are essentially three dimensions to the nature of these activities that correspond to the objectives of the audit: (1) reviewing the operations and the various controls designed to make the operations both effective and efficient; (2) testing the operations to determine if they are in compliance with the designed control system; (3) evaluating the design of the control system and the effect of either compliance or noncompliance with the controls.

Depending upon the scope of the audit and the results of the various tests, the expanded testing phase of audits may take from a few hours to several months to complete.

This work provides the basis for any conclusions the auditors draw and for their recommendations. After acquiring a thorough understanding of the auditee's objectives, goals, and standards, and after gaining a familiarization with the auditee's operations, including internal controls and how well they are functioning, the auditors should be in a position to make some valuable observations about the system of controls. The auditors also should be able to reassess organizational risks and to make any necessary recommendations as to how the control system might be improved.

During this phase of the audit, the auditor has the opportunity to use his or her entire "tool kit" (if not on any one single audit, then certainly over the course of several audits). Auditors must have good interviewing and other human relations skills; they must understand how to organize and to use audit working papers that document the progress of the audit; they need a good understanding of statistical sampling and other quantitative methods; they must have an acute sense of logic and order; and a rapidly growing number of auditors are required to know how to use the computer as an auditing tool and how to evaluate controls in an EDP environment.

You will encounter the term "fieldwork" in internal auditing. This term is not precisely defined among most auditors. Some auditors use the term to mean the expanded testing phase of the audit. Others use the term more generally to mean any work that is done in the "field," i.e., any work performed outside the departmental offices during an audit. Because of the lack of uniform use of this term, we have substituted other terminology that we believe captures the nature of the actual work being performed in the various audit steps.

Step 6 —
Findings and
Recommendations

Once the study and evaluation of the auditee is complete, the auditors are ready to develop their findings and determine what changes are necessary to improve internal controls. From the various alternatives, the auditors can select and recommend the ones they believe to be most appropriate. The auditors' findings include *conditions* as actually observed, *criteria* by which to evaluate the condition, the *effect* (or risk) associated with any observed problems, and the *causes* of the problems.

Recommendations may take four forms: (1) Make no changes in the control system. Such a recommendation results when the current control system is adequate for the needs of the organization, and is cost effective. (2) Increase control, i.e., improve the cost effectiveness of control either by modifying current controls or by adding new ones. (3) The auditors may recommend adding insurance to cover certain risks for which it may be either impossible or infeasible to augment the operational control system. (4) Finally, the auditors may recommend changes in the required rates of return for certain investments in order to reflect differences in risks associated with those investments.

The selection of which recommendation to make sometimes is difficult. Auditors often are faced with alternatives or combinations of alternatives which appear to be similar in terms of their ultimate effect on the overall risk comparisons. When alternatives appear equivalent, it is important to consider those individuals for whom the recommendations are formulated. They may prefer one alternative to another. In fact, they may want to make the selections themselves.

In such cases, the auditors point out the different possible alternatives with their comparative risks. Some auditors prefer this practice even when their recommended alternatives are clearly preferable in terms of risk. The comparison of alternatives for the auditees allows those people who are studying the recommendations to follow the auditors' reasoning.

Step 7 —
Reporting

The reporting phase of the audit includes documenting and communicating the results of the audit. One director of a large internal auditing department contends that the audit report is the audit "product." When new recruits ask him what internal auditing is all about, he hands them a copy of an audit report and says that it is internal auditing's job to produce that product. His point is that the internal auditor's reputation largely is based upon the audit report because it represents the only formal presentation of his or her professional expertise and performance. Everything performed on an audit either leads to or results from the audit report.

The report contains an explanation of the *audit objectives, scope, questions, general procedures, findings,* and *recommendations.* The written report is signed by the auditors and usually is delivered to executive management, to the auditee's management, and to the audit committee. The auditors also file at least one copy of the audit report in the internal auditing department, and the external auditors often receive copies of internal auditing reports.

Different internal auditing departments use different strategies in assigning responsibility for the writing of audit reports. In some departments one person is assigned the responsibility to write the entire report for an audit. That person usually is the auditor-in-charge or team leader. He or she may be a senior staff auditor, a supervisor, a manager (if it is a large audit), or sometimes even a junior staff auditor assigned to a small one-man audit.

In other departments, writing the audit report is a team effort. The person or persons responsible for particular parts of the audit work are also responsible for writing the related sections of the report. In these departments, the auditor-in-charge is responsible for organizing and editing the various parts of the report so that it forms a unified and integrated composition — a single, whole piece, rather than merely a stack of shorter, separate reports.

The audit report also takes another form — the personal presentation. Usually this presentation is given at a "closing conference" with the auditee. Internal auditors generally discuss their major findings with the auditee's management at the closing conference. A member of the audit team, usually the lead auditor, makes a summary presentation of the audit results. Although these presentations are made orally, they can have a greater and more lasting effect if the oral presentation is supplemented with visual aids of some sort. Also, quantifying the results in terms that are understandable to the auditee can be effective in demonstrating the severity of problems and the importance of prompt action.

The auditee often has an opportunity to respond to the findings and recommendations contained in the audit report. Interaction takes place between the auditors and the auditee during the audit, and often includes the presentation of preliminary findings and recommendations before the final audit report is issued so that the auditee can have an opportunity to respond prior to the formal communication of the audit results. This interaction allows possible misunderstandings to be addressed and resolved before the final audit report is presented to other members of management.

Sometimes, however, misunderstandings and conflicts are not resolved. In many of these cases, the auditee will issue a formal statement responding to the audit report so that the response, as well as the report, can be registered with management. Many auditors, in fact, make it a general practice to include the auditee's responses — both positive and negative — in the audit report itself.

Auditors also may issue what are called "interim reports." These reports are issued during the audit and concern any issues that need immediate attention before all of the audit work is finished and the final report is issued. Such reports usually are relatively brief and are presented in a meeting with management, followed by a brief memorandum outlining the auditor's major concerns. The contents typically include the observed condition, criteria, effect, and cause of the problem, and often include suggestions for correcting it. Such interim reports are especially valuable on extended audits for which final reports may be issued several weeks after particular findings are developed.

Step 8 —
Follow-Up

After the audit report is delivered and presented to the auditee, and the auditee has had an opportunity to make an appropriate response to the report, the auditing process may appear to be complete. However, all of the activities related to an individual audit are not completed at that time. First, there is the follow-up to the audit.

This phase of the work can take three general forms: (1) Top management may consult with the auditee to decide if, when, and how any auditor recommendations will be acted upon. (2) The auditee may act on those decisions. (3) The auditors, after waiting an appropriate amount of time after the completion of the audit, may check back with the auditee to see if corrective actions have been taken and desired results are being achieved, or that management and the board have accepted the responsibility of not taking corrective action.

Notice that the auditors are not really involved in the first two forms of follow-up. After the audit report is written and delivered, the auditee and its management determine what effect, if any, the report will have. The last form of follow-up, however, places the auditor in the position of investigating, evaluating, and reporting the effect of the audit upon operations.

Some auditors contend that all follow-up work should be performed by executive management in conjunction with the auditee. These auditors insist that direct follow-up by auditors places them too close to the decision-making process and places undue pressure upon the auditee to implement recommendations. Some people insist that auditors should not make recommendations at all, but rather should present possible alternative actions that might be taken in response to a perceived problem in the control system. Management, then, would have the sole responsibility for choosing which action is most appropriate. They argue that such a position would preserve an even greater degree of auditor independence from operations than is normally achieved when auditors make such recommendations. However, even if auditors were not to formulate recommendations, they would assume a follow-up role to confirm that management's directives have been implemented.

In most cases, there is a combination of follow-up procedures. Auditees usually make a written response to auditor recommendations, especially when the auditee disagrees with audit findings. Some entities require a formal reply by all auditees. Managers above the level of the auditee's management will work out an approach with the auditee to solve the perceived problem, and the auditors may be called back to review the solution. Such a procedure helps to preserve the integrity of the decision-making process and, at the same time, takes advantage of the expertise of the organization's auditors.

Whichever follow-up procedures an organization decides are best, some kind of follow-up is necessary. Unfortunately, some organizations do not provide for adequate follow-up to audits. In these cases, audit reports tend to be stored away to gather dust, perhaps unread and unheeded. Without adequate follow-up, an organization's auditors lose their credibility and stature, and ultimately, their value to the organization.

Step 9 —
Evaluation of the
Audit

The final activity related to an audit is the evaluation made by the auditors of themselves. The team leader, the assigned manager, and often the director of auditing determine any ongoing concerns, including how effective the audit was, how it might have been performed better, and how future audits might benefit from the one just completed. The evaluation is documented and filed. When subsequent audits are conducted on the same auditee, the evaluation will be reviewed with the rest of the files.

Also, performance reports are completed on each staff auditor and on the team leader. These reports usually are completed after each audit and are used as a basis for future assignments, promotions, professional development, and pay decisions.

No audit is complete until the total process is complete. Auditors should not feel pressured into moving ahead too fast after the completion of an audit report. Follow-up and evaluation are imperative to maintaining an effective and efficient audit function.

Exhibit 5-3 outlines the general nine-step audit process.

Exhibit 5-3
The Audit Process

Step 1   <u>Selection of the Auditee</u>

Audit plan based on risk assessment (systematic selection)
"Squeaky wheel" (ad hoc) audits
Auditee requests

Step 2   <u>Audit Preparation</u>

Tentative overall purpose and scope of audit
Review of previous audit files*
Selection of audit team
Preliminary communication with auditee
Preparation of preliminary audit program
Planning the audit report
Obtaining approval of the audit approach

Step 3   <u>Preliminary Survey</u>

Opening conference
Tour
Document study
Written description
Analytical review (when appropriate)

Step 4   <u>Internal Control Description, Analysis, and Evaluation</u>

Controls description
Walk-through of transactions or decision process
Limited testing
Evaluation of internal controls
Risk reassessment

Step 5   <u>Expanded Testing</u>

Detailed review of operations and controls
Tests of auditee's compliance with control system
Evaluate design of control system
Evaluate the effectiveness of control system

Step 6   Findings and Recommendations

Findings:
    Conditions
    Criteria
    Effects (Risk)
    Cause

Recommendations:
    No changes
    Modify current controls
    Ensure against risks
    Rates of return to reflect risks

Step 7   Reporting

Written:
    Audit objectives
    Audit scope
    General procedures
    "Findings"
    Recommendations (alternatives and possible remedies)
Personal presentation

Step 8   Follow-up

Audit response
Management's follow-up
Auditor's review

Step 9   Evaluation

Evaluation of audit approach, techniques, etc.
Auditor performance reviews

---

*Some audit theorists have placed the review of previous audit files at the end of the preliminary survey procedures, just before preparing the audit program. However, practicing auditors usually review these files before the preliminary survey begins.

Appendix

DOCUMENTING AUDIT EVIDENCE: WORKING PAPERS

It is important that audit evidence is documented appropriately in the audit working papers. Audit working papers perform several functions that are important to a successful audit:

1. They document and organize the accumulated evidence used to develop the audit report.
2. They provide a central, ongoing reference during the audit, including planning information and a growing body of evidence, so that the audit can proceed effectively and efficiently.
3. They provide a convenient reference for audit follow-up. Follow-up work largely depends upon previous audit work, findings, and recommendations.
4. They facilitate a convenient, well-documented review of both the overall performance of the audit team and the individual auditors.

In short, a good set of working papers encourages an organized, disciplined audit.

This appendix discusses five aspects of audit working papers: (1) content and organization, (2) management, (3) preparation of individual working papers, (4) tick marks, and (5) computerization. It also includes *Statement on Internal Auditing Standards No. 6,* "Audit Working Papers."

Content and Organization

The specific content of a set of working papers will depend upon the operation or activity under examination, the objectives and scope of the audit, the nature of specific audit tests, and even the personal preferences of the auditors performing the work. Also, different auditors and auditing departments organize working papers in different ways. Our discussion presents one approach that describes the general content of audit working papers, their organization, and system of numbering. Exhibit 5-A outlines a set of working papers organized similarly to an approach used by one large international corporation.

Exhibit 5-A
An Outline of Audit Working Papers

WORKING PAPERS	EXPLANATION
I. Table of contents	
II. Planning checklist	An itemized checklist of the steps necessary to complete the audit such as audit preparation, initial survey, review of internal controls, etc.
III. Authorization form	A form designating the auditee, the objectives and scope of the audit, the assigned auditors, the estimated number of hours required to complete the audit, and the kick-off date. This form is signed by the director of auditing authorizing the work.
IV. Preliminary memo to the auditee	An interoffice memorandum to the auditee confirming the audit arrangements as discussed in the previous chapter.
V. A cross-referenced audit report, interim memoranda, and follow-up	Individual items contained in these reports are cross-referenced to specific working papers prepared during the audit and included in this file.
VI. Auditee's written response to audit findings and recommendations	Copies of the auditee's responses to the audit report and interim memoranda. Sometimes cross-referenced to the report and memoranda.
VII. Review notes on the working papers	The audit supervisor's and audit management's notes on the working papers indicating additional work, changes in the working papers, and other comments.
VIII. Audit program	The step-by-step procedures performed on the audit.
IX. Summary findings sheets	Brief summaries of significant auditing evidence, conclusions, evaluations, and alternative recommendations. These will be discussed in Chapter 9.
X. Preliminary survey	
A. Minutes of opening conference	
B. Summary of observations made during the on-site tour	

C. Notes from the study of background materials and copies of relevant documents

D. Written description of the auditee's operations

A copy of the description of the auditee's operations as described in this chapter. Another copy will be placed in the auditee's permanent file.

E. Analytical review worksheet

Copies may also be included in the auditee's permanent file.

XI. Review of internal control

A. Completed internal control questionnaires

B. Flowcharts and descriptions of internal controls

C. Worksheets and notes on walk-through tests

D. Worksheets on limited tests

Includes detailed lists of the items selected, the nature of the tests, results, conclusions, and the effects on further audit planning.

E. Internal control matrix

Working papers prepared to evaluate the auditee's internal control system.

XII. Worksheets from expanded testing

Various schedules, worksheets, reconciliations, copies of documentation, confirmation letters, interview schedules and notes, etc., organized according to the sequence of steps outlined in the audit program for specific areas being examined.

XIII. Miscellaneous papers

Papers not conveniently classified in the areas under study in the audit program. These include such items as notes or observations while performing the audit, notes on relevant telephone conversations and informal encounters with auditee's personnel and others, and other documentation of evidence acquired during the audit in addition to that outlined in the audit program.

XIV. Follow-up working papers

Various schedules, worksheets, changes in policy statements and procedures, etc., resulting from audit follow-up. This material will be discussed in Chapter 11.

As with the content and organization of the working papers, page numbering systems for working paper files also vary from company to company. Page-numbering systems range from the very simple — the numbering of pages sequentially from beginning to end — to a more elaborate system that differentiates working papers through combinations of letters and numbers in accordance with whether they relate to income statement accounts, balance sheet accounts, particular control systems, or specific aspects of the audit process. The following example illustrates a relatively elaborate page-numbering system designed for the set of working papers described in Exhibit 5-A.

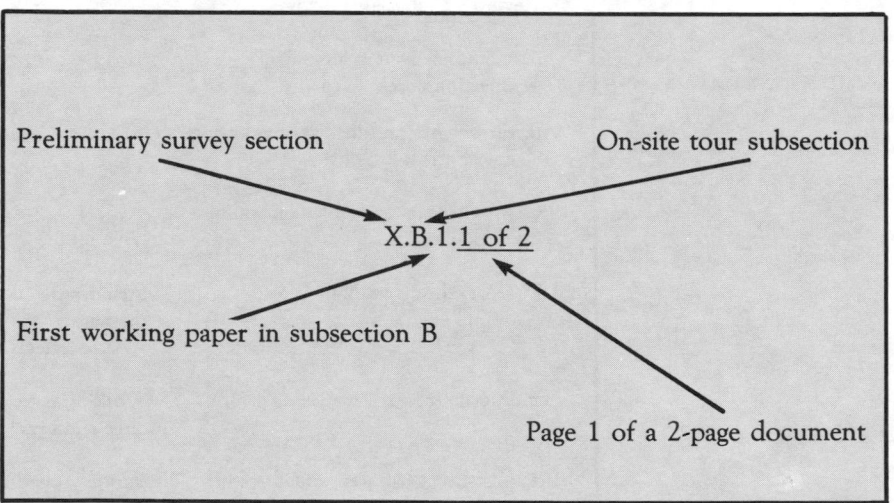

As the diagram indicates, the Roman numeral identifies the major section of a working paper; the capital letter identifies the subsection, where appropriate; the number immediately following the capital letter designates the specific working paper within the subsection; the first number in the "x of y" sequence indicates the specific page number within the document; the last number in the "x of y" sequence states how many pages are in the document. Where there is no subsection, the number might appear as follows:

IX. 3.2 of 2

This number indicates that this is the second of a two-page document which is a description of the third finding included in the summary findings section.

Management of Working Papers

Two important considerations in the management of working papers include (1) review and (2) ownership and security.

Review. As an audit progresses from step to step, the working papers are reviewed by the level immediately above the auditor who prepared them. For example, the authorization form is usually prepared by the audit manager assigned to the audit. This authorization form is reviewed and approved by the audit director. The audit program usually is prepared by the lead auditor. The program is reviewed and approved by the lead auditor's immediate supervisor. On new audits, or when unique or unusual audit programs are developed, an audit manager or the audit director may review the audit program. The reviewer should initial and date the working paper at the time of the review.

Ownership and Security. The audit working papers belong to the organization and are not the property of the individual auditor. If a person terminates employment in the internal auditing department of an organization, the working papers prepared by that individual remain filed in the department.

Auditors maintain controlled access to their working papers. *Professional Standards Bulletin 82-9* states that auditors may show auditees certain working papers to "substantiate or explain a finding or recommendation." Also, management may use systems documentation prepared by their internal auditors to avoid reconstructing such documentation. The *Standards* does not discourage making working papers available to auditees. However, as the bulletin points out, the auditors should assess the reasons why the auditee may or may not need them, and make them available on a selective basis. Certainly no one outside the organization has a right to examine the auditor's working papers except when subpoenaed by the court systems. There may even be a question as to whether the courts should have access to an auditor's working papers in some cases.

Because of the importance of the working papers to the audit and to the support of audit findings, and because of the highly confidential nature of the working papers, auditors are careful to protect their working papers from loss, destruction, and unauthorized use. Working papers are stored in locked file cabinets. When the auditors are on-site, they keep their working papers in locked briefcases when not in use. If they must leave their working papers overnight, they keep them secure from unauthorized access in locked briefcases, behind locked doors. Auditors do not leave their working papers out so that members of the auditee staff or others might view them in the auditor's absence. If auditors must leave their work stations during the day, they should either take their working papers with them or secure them.

Preparation of Individual Working Papers

As you have studied the importance of the auditors' working papers in general, you probably have surmised the care with which individual working papers are prepared. James W. Patillo in *Handbook for Auditors* (edited by James A. Cashin and published by McGraw Hill, 1982) outlined several guidelines for working paper preparation. These guidelines include the following:

1. Completeness and accuracy.
2. Clarity and understandability.
3. Legibility and neatness.
4. Relevance and an appropriate level of detail.
5. Attention to design and layout.

While these standards are quite general, they outline the various dimensions required for the preparation of quality working papers.

With the above standards in mind, consider the general format of individual working papers. Each working paper should have an appropriate heading, including the name of the auditee, the audit objectives and the item being examined (such as a review of supplier contracts, an examination of production controls, or an evaluation of inventory mangement), and the specific audit work being done (such as documentation of controls, physical counts, or collection and analysis of statistical samples). Individual working papers also include preparation and review information. The name or initials of the person preparing the working papers and the date of preparation are written in designated spaces. An additional space is provided for the reviewer's initials and the date of the review. Following is an illustration of an example heading:

Printing Services		Page Number:
Examination of Work Orders	Preparer:	Date:
Test for Production Quotas	Reviewer:	Date:

Notice the same general format used in all of the sample working papers shown in Exhibits 5-B through 5-G. These exhibits illustrate the following general types of working papers:

1. Lists (Exhibit 5-B).
2. Analytical working papers (Exhibit 5-C).
3. Reconciliations (Exhibit 5-D).
4. Computations (Exhibit 5-E).
5. Narratives (Exhibit 5-F).
6. Photographs (Exhibit 5-G).

While these types of working papers do not exhaust all of the possibilities, they are illustrative of general types that are frequently used. The working papers illustrated here represent those prepared by the internal auditors. Of course, there are other documents filed in the working papers, such as letters, copies of original documentation, copies of memoranda sent to or received from the auditee or others, and so forth. These documents would not have the same headings and spaces for the preparer and reviewer to place their initials. They would, however, receive assigned page numbers placed in the same general location as the other working papers, i.e., an upper or lower corner of the page.

Tick Marks

In these illustrative working papers, you see an assortment of check marks, tiny handwritten letters, and geometric figures written next to items related to specific information in the audit tests. These figures are called "tick marks." The tick marks represent specific audit tests performed on the items listed.

Because there are no standard or generally accepted tick marks, different auditors and audit departments tend to develop and use their own systems. Since there are many different systems in use, the auditor preparing working papers where tick marks appear should include a legend either at the bottom of the working paper or on a separate sheet attached to the working paper indicating the specific procedures associated with each tick mark used. You will notice that there are different tick marks on the working papers shown in the exhibits, with legends at the bottom of each.

Computerization of Working Papers

A separate appendix at the end of Chapter 17 discusses microcomputer-assisted auditing. There we illustrate how modern microcomputing techniques can be used to facilitate the audit process. In that section, we discuss how typical word processing, spreadsheet, data management, flowcharting, and statistical software can be used. One of the primary uses of portable microcomputers in auditing is in the generation of working papers. The advantages of using these machines to produce working papers are that they are fast, neat, and can communicate directly from remote sites with other machines in the department so that an entire audit can be reviewed while the auditors are still in the field. Interestingly, the nature of the working papers and their formats do not change substantially from those illustrated here.

Exhibit 5-B
Example Working Paper: Lists

Physical Plant Audit   Page: 8.3.1/1

Evaluate Annual Construction and Major Repair Costs   Preparer: KRS   Date: 12/8/86

List of Unfinished Projects   Reviewer: BMT   Date: 12/9/86

		Beginning	Projected Ending	Estimated Total	
Project	Type	Date (Mo/Yr)	Date (Mo/Yr)	Cost	
Wagner Greenhouse	C	11/86	3/87	$ 75,620	V E
Wagner Pump Station	C	9/86	2/87	250,182	V E
Wagner Office Wing	C	9/86	3/87	318,418	V E
Wagner Parking Lot	R	11/86	2/87	15,000	V E
Wagner Office – Roof	R	11/86	1/87	36,175	V E
Mount Entrance Rdwy.	C	10/86	5/87	2,967,856	V E
Mount Landscaping	C	8/86	6/87	52,000	V E
Mount Fencing	R	12/86	1/87	7,793	V E
TOTAL PROJECTS UNDERWAY				$3,723,044	
Authorized Projects Not Yet Started:					
Wagner Service Ctr.	C	3/87	8/87	$1,225,892	V E
Wagner S.C. Parking	C	3/87	6/87	68,743	V E
Mount Office Renovation	R	1/87	4/87	163,052	V E
TOTAL AUTHORIZED PROJECTS TO START				$1,457,687	

C = Construction projects   R = Major repair projects

Sources of Information – Project Log Book, minutes of Board
                                 of Directors' meetings

V = Authorizations verified in Board minutes

E = Estimated costs confirmed on Cost Projection Sheets

Conclusion: Project Log Book is current on all unfinished
                  construction and major repair projects.

Exhibit 5-C
Example Analytical Working Paper

New England Marketing Division   Page: VI. c. 4. 1/1

Evaluate Comparative Regional Sales Performance   Auditor: GG   Date: 1/15/87

Analyze Sales by Region   Reviewer: DK   Date: 1/17/87

Region	Total 1986 Sales	Total 1985 Sales	% Inc.(Dec.)
Maine	$6,845,215	$6,732,248	2%
Ver.-N.H.	3,263,070	3,998,729	(18.5)%
Mass.	7,496,134	6,820,050	10%
R.I.-Conn.	5,037,886	5,142,695	(2)%

Region	1986 Unit Sales	1985 Unit Sales	% Inc. (Dec.)	% Repeat 1986 Sales (A)
Maine	2,415	2,362	2%	66%
Ver.-N.H.	1,250	1,321	(5)%	35%
Mass.	3,126	2,989	4.6%	57%
R.I.-Conn.	2,242	3,130	5%	59%

Region	Average 1986 Sale (B)	Average 1985 Sale (C)	% Inc. (Dec.)
Maine	$2,834	$2,893	(2)%
Ver.-N.H.	3,610	3,027	(14)%
Mass.	2,398	2,282	5%
R.I.-Conn	2,247	2,414	(7)%

Sources of Information: 1985 and 1986 Annual Regional Sales Reports

1985 and 1986 Sales Receipts

(A) = Computed from a sample of 350 sales receipts in each region for 1986.

(B) = "   "   "   "   "   "   "   "   "   "   "   "   "

(C) = "   "   "   "   "   "   "   "   "   "   "   " 1985.

Conclusion: The Vermont - New Hampshire region appears to be

deteriorating compared to the other sales regions.

Exhibit 5-D
Example Reconciliation

Lakeworks Division   Page: D. 1/1

Accounts Payable Review   Auditor: QR   Date: 1/21/86

Reconciliation of Payables   Reviewer: SGO Date: 1/23/86

Beginning Balance at 1/15/85   #3,464,873.19 l

Add:

    Supplier Invoices   #1,965,437.73 √c

    Services   10,267.80 √c

    Payroll   3,614,000.40 √

    Miscellaneous   3,217.82 √

                   #5,592,923.75   5,592,923.75

Subtract Payments   (6,246,813.57) du

Ending Balance at 12/31/85   2,810,983.37 l

l = agrees with general ledger control amount balance

√ = calculated from original documentation (vendor invoices,
    service billings and contracts, payroll timecards and
    personnel contracts, and miscellaneous invoice file)

c = positive confirmations sent on all supplier balances,
    90% return with no material differences

d = calculated from cash disbursements journal

u = tested selected cash disbursements — tracing to check
    register and cancelled checks.

Conclusion: no exceptions.

Exhibit 5-E
Example Working Paper: Computations

Payroll

Page: VII. D. 1. 1/1

Review Executive Bonuses

Preparer: DMY   Date: 2/10/86

Verify Computations

Reviewer: jp   Date: 2/20/86

Policy:

Corporate policy specifies, as do contracts with executive-level personnel, that annual bonuses be paid according to the following formula 10 the company president and vice-presidents:

$$B = f (I - B)$$

B = Amount of bonus

f = percentage bonus (1% for 1986)

I = Income before deducting bonuses and income taxes
($3,671,400 for 1986)

Calculation of <u>total</u> bonuses paid for 1986:

Per person — $B = .01 (3,671,400 - B)$

$B = .01 (3,671,400) - .01B$

$1.01 B = .01 (3,671,400)$

$B = 36,350.50$

For 12 eligible executive personnel (President and 11 vice-presidents):

$36,350.50 \times 12 = \$436,206.00$ TOTAL BONUSES 1986

⊙ = verified provision in each of 12 contracts

✓ = checked journal voucher, posting, and cancelled checks — all agree with calculated bonuses

Exhibit 5-F
Working Paper Narrative

Office Administration	Page: 6.1.1/1
Meeting with Office Manager	Auditor: SM Date: 1/19/87
Memo to W.P. File	Reviewer: jp Date: 1/31/87

Date of Meeting : 1/19/87

Those Present : Clay Brown — Office Manager

Manuel Sanchez — Personnel Supervisor

Cary Thorn — Auditor

Purpose : To determine the standards used for merit pay increases and promotions of clerical office staff.

Mr. Brown stated that no formal criteria were being used to determine merit pay increases or promotions. He insisted that he and the office supervisors under his area of responsibility can assess the performance of clerical staff without guidelines from the Personnel Department. Mr. Sanchez informed Mr. Brown of a suit being filed against the company by a former file clerk with the headquarters staff. The basis of the suit, Mr. Sanchez said, was age discrimination. He asked Mr. Brown for some more formal criteria that could be applied objectively in the case of the former employee now filing suit. Mr. Brown said he could not supply such criteria — he just follows his "best judgment" at the time.

Conclusions: (1) If the suit is ultimately filed, Mr. Brown needs to consult with company lawyers as soon as possible. There is significant risk to the company in this area. (2) Establishing formal criteria for promotions and merit pay raises can help prevent future problems.

Exhibit 5-G
Photographs in Working Papers

Property Management	Page: VIII.A.4.3 of 7
Examine Titles and Ownership	Auditor: JBB Date: 8/5/86
Photograph of Illegal Fence Placement	Reviewer: jp Date: 8/12/86

Photograph of company-owned fence along approximately 1000' of SE boundary of property. Surveys show fence 3' beyond boundary, on Williams land adjacent. Survey stake in picture indicates true property line. Photograph was taken on 8/5/86 by JBB.

Conclusion: After consulting with our legal staff (See VIII.A.5), the company may be subject to legal action by Williams.

Recommendation: Alternatives would include (a) notifying Williams of the error and offering either to buy the enclosed land at a fair price or to move the fence; (b) moving the fence and then notifying Williams; or (c) notify Williams, ask if the error poses a problem, and if not, leave the fence as it is and ask Williams to accept a nominal rent. I prefer (a). It is cleaner.

STATEMENT ON INTERNAL AUDITING
STANDARDS NO. 6
Audit Working Papers

Foreword

The Institute of Internal Auditors issued the *Standards for the Professional Practice of Internal Auditing* in 1978 "to serve the entire profession in all types of business, in various levels of government, and in all other organizations where internal auditors are found . . . to represent the practice of internal auditing as it should be . . . ." The *Standards* have been widely accepted and remain current despite continuing changes in business, society, and the profession of internal auditing.

This statement interprets guideline 420.01.5 which addresses the subject of audit working papers.

Summary

This statement provides guidance to internal auditors in the preparation and use of audit working papers. It includes interpretations of existing guideline 420.01.5 related to the functions and contents of audit working papers; audit working-paper preparation techniques; the working-paper review process; and guidelines for the ownership, custody, and retention of audit working papers.

Major conclusions of this statement are:

- Audit working papers provide the principal evidential support for the audit report and demonstrate the internal auditing department's compliance with the *Standards for the Professional Practice of Internal Auditing.*
- Support for audit conclusions should be included in the audit working papers.
- The director of internal auditing should establish policies on working-paper preparation techniques.
- Evidence of supervisory review should be documented in the audit working papers.
- Audit working papers are the property of the organization.
- Requests by parties outside the organization other than the independent outside auditor for access to audit working papers and reports should be approved by senior management and/or legal counsel, as appropriate.

Interpretations

Guideline 420.01.5 states: Working papers that document the audit should be prepared by the auditor and reviewed by management of the internal auditing department. These papers should record the information obtained and the analyses made and should support the bases for the findings and recommendations to be reported.

FUNCTIONS

.5.1   Audit working papers generally serve to:

a.   Provide the principal evidential support for the internal auditor's report.

b.   Aid in the planning, performance, and review of audits.

c.   Document whether the audit objectives were achieved.

d.   Facilitate third-party reviews.

e.   Provide a basis for evaluating the internal auditing department's quality assurance program.

f.   Provide support in circumstances such as insurance claims, fraud cases, and lawsuits.

g.   Aid in the professional development of the internal audit staff.

h.   Demonstrate the internal auditing department's compliance with the *Standards for the Professional Practice of Internal Auditing.*

CONTENTS

.5.2   The organization, design, and content of audit working papers will depend on the nature of the audit. Audit working papers should, however, document the following aspects of the audit process:

a.   Planning.

b.   The examination and evaluation of the adequacy and effectiveness of the system of internal control.

c.   The auditing procedures performed, the information obtained, and the conclusions reached.

d.   Review.

e.   Reporting.

f.   Follow-up.

.5.3   Audit working papers should be complete and include support for audit conclusions reached.

.5.4   Among other things, audit working papers may include:

a.   Planning documents and audit programs.

b.   Control questionnaires, flowcharts, checklists, and narratives.

c.   Notes and memoranda resulting from interviews.

d.   Organizational data such as organization charts and job descriptions.

e.   Copies of important contracts and agreements.

f.   Information about operating and financial policies.

g.   Results of control evaluations.

h.   Letters of confirmation and representation.

i.   Analyses and tests of transactions, processes, and account balances.

j.   Results of analytical review procedures.

k.   The audit report and management's responses.

l.   Audit correspondence if it documents audit conclusions reached.

.5.5   Audit working papers may be in the form of paper, tapes, disks, diskettes, films, or other media. If audit working papers are in the form of media other than paper, consideration should be given to generating backup copies.

.5.6   If the internal auditor is reporting on financial information, the audit working papers should document whether the accounting records agree or reconcile with such financial information.

.5.7   Some audit working papers may be categorized as permanent or carry-forward audit files. These files generally contain information of continuing importance.

PREPARATION TECHNIQUES

.5.8   The director of internal auditing should establish policies for the types of audit working-paper files maintained, stationery used, indexing, and other related matters. Standardized audit working papers such as questionnaires and audit programs may improve the efficiency of an audit and facilitate the delegation of audit work.

.5.9   The following are typical audit working-paper preparation techniques:

    a.   Each audit working paper should contain a heading. The heading usually consists of the name of the organization or function being examined, a title or description of the contents or purpose of the working paper, and the date or period covered by the audit.

    b.   Each audit working paper should be signed (or initialed) and dated by the internal auditor.

    c.   Each audit working paper should contain an index or reference number.

    d.   Audit verification symbols (tick marks) should be explained.

    e.   Sources of data should be clearly identified.

REVIEW PROCESS

.5.10   All audit working papers should be reviewed to ensure that they properly support the audit report and that all necessary auditing procedures have been performed. Evidence of supervisory review should be documented in the audit working papers. The director of internal auditing has overall responsibility for review but may designate members of the internal auditing department to perform the review. Review should be conducted at a level of responsibility higher than that of the preparer of the audit working papers.

.5.11   Evidence of supervisory review should consist of the reviewer initialing and dating each working paper after it is reviewed.

.5.12   Other review techniques that provide evidence of supervisory review include completing an audit working-paper review checklist and/or preparing a memorandum specifying the nature, extent, and results of the review.

.5.13   Reviewers may make a written record (review notes) of questions arising from the review process. When clearing review notes, care should be taken to ensure that the working papers provide adequate evidence that questions raised during the review have been resolved.

OWNERSHIP, CUSTODY, AND RETENTION

.5.14 Audit working papers are the property of the organization.

.5.15 Audit working-paper files should generally remain under the control of the internal auditing department and should be accessible only to authorized personnel.

.5.16 Management and other members of the organization may request access to audit working papers. Such access may be necessary to substantiate or explain audit findings or to utilize audit documentation for other business purposes. The director of internal auditing should approve these requests.

.5.17 It is common practice for internal and independent outside auditors to grant access to each other's audit working papers. The practice of granting the independent outside auditor access to audit working papers should be approved by the director of internal auditing.

.5.18 There are circumstances when requests for access to audit working papers and reports are made by parties outside the organization other than the independent outside auditor. Prior to releasing such documentation, the director of internal auditing should obtain the approval of senior management and/or legal counsel, as appropriate.

.5.19 The director of internal auditing should develop retention requirements for audit working papers. These retention requirements should be consistent with the organization's guidelines and any pertinent legal or other requirements.

QUESTIONS

1. What is the primary factor that distinguishes what may be described as an auditing "mechanic" from the true auditor?
2. Outline the general steps of an audit.
3. How is an auditee selected for a specified audit? Why might the selection be made in different ways?
4. Why might there be multiple objectives for a single audit? Explain the logic of the sequence of the objectives outlined in the text.
5. Describe the different functions that must be fulfilled on an audit team.
6. Why conduct a preliminary survey for an audit?
7. What is a "walk-through"?
8. What is the "audit program"? How is it prepared?
9. What is an "analytical review"? What type of implications can be drawn from analytical review procedures?
10. What is the purpose of an internal control matrix?
11. What are the three dimensions of expanded audit work?
12. What kinds of recommendations do auditors make regarding the control system?
13. Why is the audit report so critical to the auditor's performance and reputation? When do auditors begin planning the audit report? Why?
14. What information does the audit report contain?
15. What are the different forms of follow-up to an audit? Explain why an organization might prefer each one of these forms to the others.
16. What are the advantages of combining the different forms of follow-up?
17. Explain the different types of evaluation that must be done at the completion of an audit.
18. What are the functions of audit working papers?
19. Outline the contents of audit working papers.
20. Illustrate one type of numbering system for audit working papers.
21. Discuss two important aspects of working paper management.
22. Outline a set of five guidelines for the preparation of working papers.
23. What are "tick marks"? Show three examples.
24. What information is typically included at the top of working papers prepared by auditors?

EXERCISES

E-1

The director of internal auditing for a state government drove into his parking spot in the basement of the capitol building. As he opened his door to get out, he heard one of his auditors yell from across the parking lot that the director of public safety had been trying to contact him for the last half-hour, and it was an emergency. When he arrived at his office a few minutes later, the director of auditing called to find out what the emergency was. It seems that the payroll checks for the department had been issued during the past two months with gross errors in them, often amounting to several thousands of dollars. The director of public safety had called the State Accounting Office to inquire why the errors had occurred and when the checks could be corrected. Personnel at the State Accounting Office said that a new computerized payroll system had been installed, and they were still working out the bugs, but they would correct any checks made out for the wrong amounts within a week. This promise had been made each of the last two months, and still the checks that were in error had not been corrected. The employees in public safety were complaining loudly. After calling the State Accounting Office and several other state offices to check for similar mistakes, the director of auditing decided an immediate audit was necessary, but all of his auditors were already on assignment, except for one three-man team which had been assigned to begin an audit of the State Tax Commission the following day.

Required:

a. Suppose the director of auditing decides to audit the State Accounting Office. What other steps would be necessary to prepare for this audit?
b. How do you suppose the director of auditing might decide whether or not to audit the State Accounting Office?
c. What kinds of skills would be most important for the audit team he assigns?
d. What kinds of problems may arise from postponing the audit of the State Tax Commission? (Integrate the ideas presented in Chapter 4.)

E-2

Gene Roberts, audit manager for Commercial Enterprises, Inc., is selecting a three-man team to audit the Region II headquarters office of the firm. The office is responsible for marketing the company's full line of products, including electrical appliances, powered lawn care products, snowblowers, and ski accessories. The Region II headquarters conducts market tests of new products as they are introduced to its clients. The office sells its products wholesale to retail outlets and takes orders from three months to a year in advance of delivery. The Region II office also assists its clients in cooperative advertising promotions, and sends a corps of 50 salespeople throughout the region to call upon clients and to stage special demonstrations at fairs and other special public occasions. An assistant controller works in the office to keep all of the accounting records and sends them via computer to the company's headquarters. The office is responsible only for sales and is managed as a revenue center. The regional offices of the company do not maintain inventories; the products are shipped to the clients from a main warehouse in Chicago. The audit will examine the full scope of activities that are conducted through the regional office. Roberts is selecting a supervisor, a senior staff auditor, and a junior staff auditor. The following auditors are available to go on the audit:

Supervisors:

Kenn Griffith has been with Commercial Enterprises for seven years. He is 36 years old and has a bachelor of science degree in industrial engineering. He spent four years in the Navy immediately after completing his degree and is a specialist in computer auditing.

Mark Church is a 28-year-old MBA who has worked with the company for four years. His undergraduate degree was in accounting, and he pursued general business studies in his MBA work. He is highly regarded for his understanding of the interrelationships among the company's different elements.

Senior Staff Auditors:

Deborah Vandenbergh is a CPA who worked in auditing for two years with a public accounting firm before joining Commercial. She has been with the firm less than a year and is still learning how the different operations are organized, although she has developed a good reputation for her knowledge of financial internal control.

Billy Coe is a management trainee who has worked in the auditing department for a year. He previously spent six months in sales and another 18 months in financial management. He is scheduled to transfer out of the auditing department in another three months to assume a position as an assistant sales manager of Commercial's Eastern Regional office.

Junior Staff Auditors:

Claude Mann and Judy Torres are both recent graduates of State University. Judy was an accounting major who concentrated her elective courses in human resource management. Claude majored in communications and is now studying for the Graduate Management Aptitude Test. He plans to begin an evening MBA program in the spring.

Required:
If you were Gene Roberts, which of the available auditors would you choose for the three-man team? Explain your answer.

E-3
Required:
For Exercise E-2, outline the three types of objectives required for the audit of the Region II office. Discuss.

E-4
Required:
Compare and contrast the scopes of the audits of the State Accounting Office in Exercise E-1 and the Region II office of Commercial Enterprises, Inc. in Exercise E-2.

E-5
The director of auditing for a large utility company just assigned his last available auditors to examine the company's coal-mining operations in a neighboring state. They were scheduled to leave on a flight the following morning. At three o'clock in the afternoon the operations vice president called expressing his suspicion that a fraud was being committed in one of the company's supply warehouses. He demanded an immediate audit.

Required:

a. Assuming the only possible auditors that might be assigned were those scheduled to leave the following morning, what major considerations would determine whether they should be rescheduled immediately for an audit of the warehouse?

b. How would your response be influenced by the presence of a security department within the entity?

E-6

A Western nutrition company owns three large Florida citrus-fruit farms. Each farm produces oranges and grapefruit that are graded (1) to be sold to grocery store chains, (2) to be sold for fruit juice to food processing companies, and (3) to be used in the production of natural vitamins by the parent company in its Western facilities. The three farms are managed under a central management team that includes a "farm manager," an accountant who is an assistant controller to the company controller, and a marketing and transportation specialist in charge of selling and shipping the fruit. These three members of the management team live in Florida and have offices in Orlando. In addition, each farm has an overseer who is directly responsible for the operation of his farm. All of the three overseers have homes on the farm properties where they live with their families. While some of each year's crop is harvested by machine, each farm continues to employ migrant workers during the harvest season. The overseers also have sizable truck farms where they harvest fruits and vegetables for their own families and for the families of the management team. Excess produce from these truck farms is sold to local grocery stores in Orlando. Each farm overseer is allowed to keep any proceeds from these sales to augment income from the company fruit farms.

A team of auditors has been assigned to audit the farm operations and the record-keeping system.

Required:

a. Plan a preliminary survey for this audit, outlining in general what could be expected from each step in the preliminary survey.

b. Similarly, prepare a general outline of the auditors' plan to describe and analyze internal controls for the farm operations, and specify what the auditors should learn from each step.

E-7

Two internal auditors met at a national conference and were discussing their respective departments and some of their personal ideas about auditing. One of the auditors made the following statement:

> I don't understand why any auditor would ever do a preliminary survey or a description and analysis of controls. We just take our audit programs either from previous audits that we've done, or from a set of books of audit programs published for the utilities industry. All that preliminary work to the real audit work is just a waste of time and the company's good money.

Required:

How would you answer this auditor in terms of (a) the specific contents of an audit program and (b) the possible advantages and disadvantages of referring to old audit programs or standardized ones from books?

E-8

Suppose the following three audits are to be performed:

1. An audit of the notes collection department of a bank.
2. An audit of checkout counters for a grocery store chain.
3. An audit of security operations for a large warehousing operation.

The following is a brief explanation of each type of department:

The notes department of a bank is responsible for collecting all of the payments made by persons or businesses who owe monies on loans extended by the bank. This department has a record of all of the loans, the payment schedules, and the payment records for each one. The personnel in this department enter all customer transactions into the bank's computerized accounting system. Weekly, monthly, and quarterly reports are made to management outlining the status of various accounts, highlighting past-due accounts with the associated amounts, reporting the number of new loans and their amounts, and summarizing the loans that have been retired.

Grocery store checkout counters total all of the individual purchases from the stores. A record of the purchase is kept inside the adding machine or the computerized checking system, and a receipt is given to each customer. The cash at the end of each shift and at the end of the day is compared to the respective sales totals.

The security department for a warehouse is responsible for protecting the warehouse property and its contents. An alarm system links the warehouse with both the police department and the fire department. Also, hired guards tour the warehouse area and punch clocks located at various places throughout the property according to a predetermined schedule. If a guard fails to punch a clock within a certain time, an alarm automatically goes off. Some warehouses also have guard dogs for enclosed areas.

Required:

a. Would analytical review procedures be appropriate for each of the above audits? Explain.
b. Explain how an analytical review might be used in an audit of the checkout counters.

E-9

Following are three auditing procedures:

1. Determining if emissions at a production plant meet Environmental Protection Agency (EPA) standards.
2. Flowcharting plant production operations and identifying key control points.
3. Assessing the propriety of certain controls in the firm's hiring practices.

Required:

a. Identify each of the three procedures above as (a) a review procedure, (b) a test of compliance, or (c) an evaluation.
b. How might each of the three examinations (1, 2, and 3) be converted to either of the other two types of examinations? Suppose, for example, you stated that comparing plant emissions to EPA standards is an evaluative procedure. How could this examination be converted either (a) to a review procedure or (b) to a test of compliance?

E-10

The following report was issued to management at the conclusion of a recent audit of a petty cash fund:

AUDIT OF PETTY CASH
Completed 5/30/87

Recommendations:

After having examined the petty cash fund at the three different locations within the headquarters building, we recommend that all of the managers receive in-depth training in the management of petty cash. We further recommend that strict controls be established to ensure that each request for replenishment to the fund be signed by a departmental manager, because the petty cash custodians demonstrate a severe lack of judgment in their expenditures and requests for funds. A third recommendation is to institute a voucher system so that each expenditure is approved by the immediate supervisor of the custodians.

Findings:

Control over petty cash is dangerously inadequate, due primarily to the incompetence of the custodians over those funds. Funds often were expended for trivial items or for items that should have been purchased from other funds in other departments. Because a voucher system has not been established, approval is seldom obtained for any expenditure, and replenishments are made solely upon the authority of the custodians.

Required:

a. What topics were covered in the report?
b. What additional topics might have been addressed?
c. What is the tone (or climate) of the report?
d. How would you respond if you were one of the petty cash custodians?
e. Based upon your knowledge of petty cash (imprest) funds, evaluate the findings and recommendations. (A review of these funds in an introductory financial accounting textbook may be helpful.)

E-11

It had been two years since the last audit of the Hanning branch of Wendell Furniture Company, Inc. Wendell manufactures a budget-priced line of household furnishings and retails its line through a regional chain of furniture stores. The stores also sell Jeremy G. Manchester furniture as its better line. During the last audit, the Hanning branch had come under severe criticism for its inventory management. Inventory records were incomplete, and an inordinate amount of damage occurred to furniture in the branch's storage warehouse. When the auditors recently began a new audit of the branch, they were surprised to discover evidence indicating that nothing had been done to correct the previous problems. Inadequate inventory accounting and careless handling of goods apparently had continued since the last audit. The lead auditor became disturbed by what he and the junior staff auditor had found. The lead auditor asked his audit manager, "Why perform an audit at all if nothing is going to be done to correct the problems we find?"

Required:

What aspect(s) of the previous year's audit process seems to have been neglected in the above example? Explain.

E-12

A member of the audit committee questioned the director of internal auditing about how the company's internal auditing function is being developed. The director of internal auditing answered that the primary factor in the development of the function is risk to the organization. The audit committee member appeared a little confused by this answer and asked, "How can you develop the entire function based solely upon the principle of risk?"

Required:

Flowchart the steps included in directing the audit function. Identify those steps that help auditors to (a) locate the areas of greatest risk, (b) determine the order of audit areas, (c) examine and evaluate the risks, and (d) decide and report on how to manage the risks.

E-13

Suppose that you are the director of internal auditing for a large utility company and you recently assigned one of your younger auditing staff members to lead a new audit. This was his first opportunity to plan and lead an audit from the beginning. About 10 days after the audit began, he called you and explained that he had finished the initial survey, but he doesn't remember what comes next.

Required:

a.   What are the possible next steps?
b.   How does he know which of those steps to take? Explain.

E-14

The following is a working paper prepared by an auditor assigned to examine the branch operations of a large bank:

Bookerville Branch   Page Ref. 22.1

I have examined all loan agreements and noted the following exceptions:

LOAN CONTRACT	EXCEPTION
Love, W. M.	No signature
Kyle, A. J.	Calculation error in interest payments
Cummingham, D. Q.	Delinquent
Kimball, C. R.	Address missing

Conclusion: Controls on loan agreements need improvement.

Auditor: Date:

Reviewer: Date:

Required:

Evaluate this working paper according to the five standard guidelines outlined in the appendix to the chapter.

E-15

The auditor in E-14 (above) examined 15 loan contracts for the Bookerville branch of the bank. The auditor performed five tests on each loan contract, checking for: (1) complete identification for each customer; (2) appropriate loan approval by a bank officer; (3) calculations of interest and payment schedules; (4) appropriate collateral; and (5) comparisons of actual payments (as shown in the branch's subsidiary accounts receivable ledger) to the contracted payment schedule shown on the loan contract.

Required:

a.   Create tick marks that the auditor might use for each of the five tests.

b.   Suppose the auditor found that one of the loans was not properly approved by a bank officer. How might this exception be shown in the working papers? What information would be required in the working papers with regard to the exception?

PROBLEMS

P-1

The flowchart on the following page depicts the audit process as presented by R. I. Anderson in "Analytical Auditing: Does it Work," published in *The Internal Auditor*, July/August 1972. We have added the numbers in the bottom right-hand corners of the boxes to allow you to complete this exercise more easily.

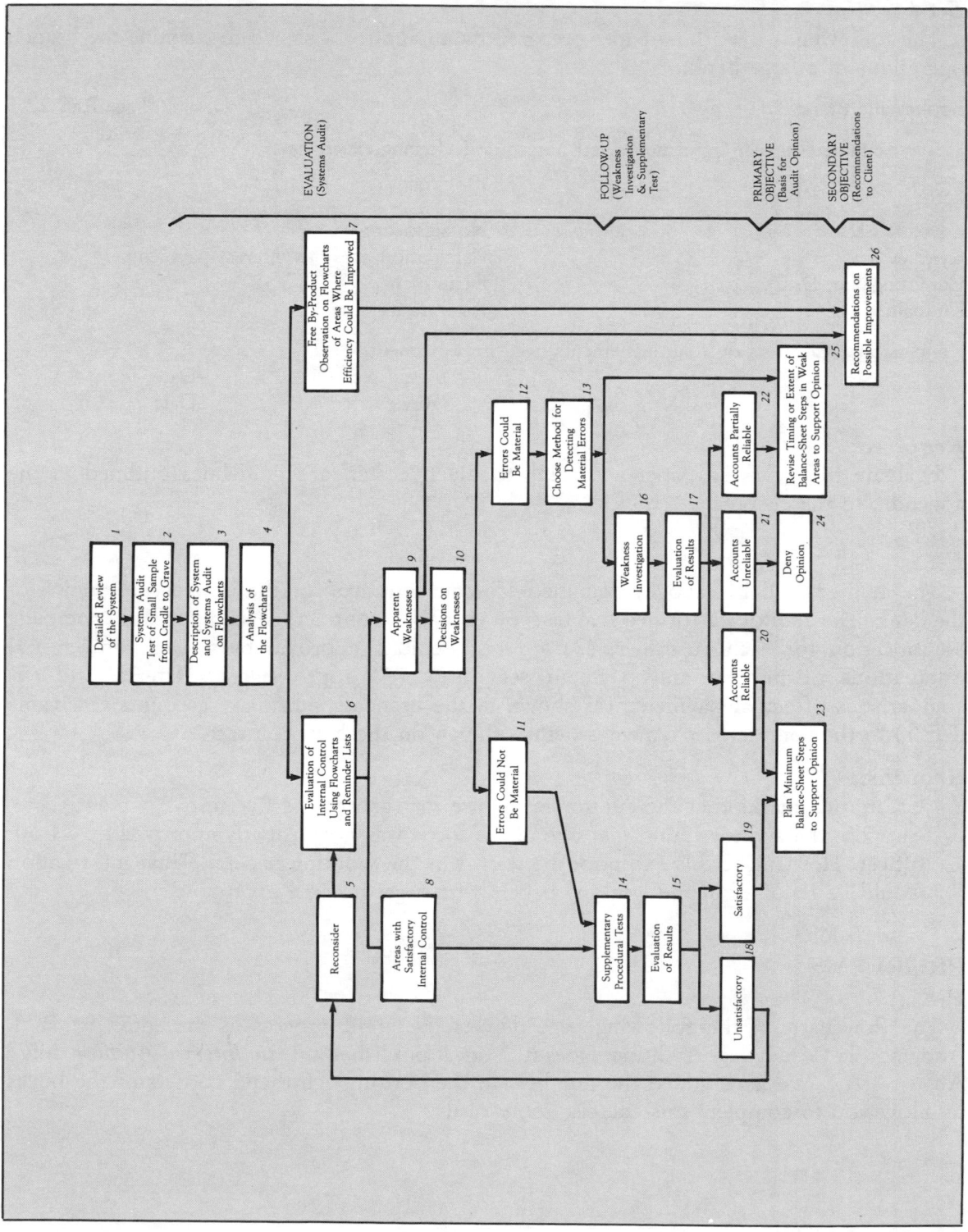

Required:

a. Identify which of the boxes are associated with each of the nine steps of the audit, as discussed in this chapter.

b. Do you see any boxes that you cannot associate with any of the nine phases of the audit?

c. Are all of the nine phases of the audit covered by this flowchart? If not, which ones are missing in the diagram? Why do you think these phases of the audit would be left out of such a flowchart?

P-2

A commercial airline company's new jumbo jets have had a series of mechanical problems with the engines. Although the problems so far have been minor, the company's management was concerned that there was the potential for dangerous problems to occur. An argument had been growing between the company's top management and the manufacturer's management about the source of the problems. The commercial airline company argued that the planes were deficient due to poor quality control during production. The manufacturer argued that the airline company was doing an inadequate job of servicing the aircraft when preparing for flight. The airline's management had counterargued that its crews had been following the exact procedures recommended by the manufacturer, and that if those procedures were deficient, the manufacturer was still to blame.

The board of directors of the airline company decided to have an audit conducted on the service procedures to determine (1) whether or not appropriate controls were designed into the service procedures to ensure that they were being done correctly, and (2) whether the procedures were complete.

In reference to the second question, the board wanted to know if perhaps the problems on the planes were occurring in areas of the engine for which service procedures were either incomplete or totally omitted. Also, the board members wondered what future problems might occur if the procedures were incomplete.

Required:

a. Define what you think are the appropriate review, compliance, and evaluation objectives for the above audit, as dictated by the board of directors.

b. Evaluate the scope of the audit as given by the board. Would you increase the scope of the audit? Why or why not?

c. Would you trust auditors to conduct this study? What skills will be needed by the audit team? If the auditors do not possess those skills, how might they increase their knowledge in order to complete the work satisfactorily?

d. How important are the results of this audit? Explain.

P-3

The following scenario describes the various phases of a fictional audit for a utility company:

I. Selection of the Auditee

The vice president of operations for a large utility company demanded an immediate audit of water usage for the company's lawn sprinkler system. The sprinklers at the headquarters building had been running when he arrived at work the day before, when he left for lunch, when he returned from lunch, and when he left to go home from work. The director of auditing agreed to begin an examination of the sprinkler system immediately.

II. Audit Preparation

A. Tentative audit objectives.

Determine whether more water is being used this year, on the average, per day, than last year when the company won a citation from the city for its beautiful grounds.

B. Tentative scope of the audit.

1. Sprinklers at all offices and branches throughout the city.
2. Time cards for the lawn maintenance crew.
3. Monthly water bills from November of last year through August of this year.

C. Audit team.

The director of auditing assigned one of his two audit managers as a one-man team for the audit. The audit manager's expertise lay in computerized accounting systems. The director's reasoning was that the sprinkler system is computerized.

III. Preliminary Survey and Analysis of Internal Controls

The audit manager went out on the grounds and spoke with one of the groundskeepers, who said the way the sprinkling was scheduled was crazy. He said he couldn't possibly get all the mowing done because the sprinklers were started and stopped at odd hours throughout the day and night. The audit manager examined the time cards and found that the groundskeeper was a part-time employee who worked four days per week from 7 a.m. to noon. The audit manager also discovered that the water bills for four of the months this year were approximately 5 percent greater, on the average, than for last year. He determined from this preliminary information that the controls over the sprinkler system were inadequate.

IV. Expanded Tests

The audit manager concluded that he had enough information from the preliminary survey and the analysis of controls to make the necessary recommendations. He did not perform any additional work.

V. Reporting

The audit manager issued the following report and sent it to the vice president and to the chief groundskeeper for the company:

After a thorough investigation of the company's sprinkler system, the internal auditing department recommends that all company lawn sprinklers be regulated to run during the summer months from 4:30 a.m. to 6:30 a.m. daily and from 7:30 p.m. to 8:30 p.m. every other day.

This plan will reduce the number of hours of sprinkler service by 10 percent, still provide daily watering, and allow proper lawn care and maintenance by grounds crews.

We recommend that these changes be documented in writing and posted on the maintenance shop doors immediately.

The report was signed by the audit manager.

VI.   Follow-up
The following week the audit manager sent a new junior staff auditor to the maintenance shop to check to see that the new policies had been posted on the door. They had been posted, and the audit manager sent a memo to the vice president saying that the lawn sprinkler problem had been resolved.

V.   Evaluation
There was none.

Required:
Evaluate each phase of the above audit.

P-4
Raymond Grisson, an internal auditor for Chickadee Industries, Inc., was investigating the efficiency at the company's Columbus plant. One of the audit questions was how effectively overtime hours were being managed at the plant. The audit procedures chosen to answer this question were as follows:

1.   To calculate the percentage of overtime hours used over and above the total vacation and sick leave hours.
2.   To compare the cost of the excess overtime hours to what costs would have been at regular rates.
3.   To compare total hours for each of the last three periods to production levels in those periods.
4.   To calculate how many full-time employee equivalents (FTEs) were used in overtime hours during each of the last three periods. One FTE is 2,080 hours per period, computed at 40 hours per week for 52 weeks.

Mr. Grisson took the following information from payroll records for the plant:

	1983	1984	1985
Number of plant workers	21	21	23
Vacation days carned	294	294	345
Vacation days taken	294	275	320
Average hourly wage	$8	$9	$10
Total vacation pay	$18,816	$19,800	$25,600
Days of sick leave	75	90	92
Total sick pay	$4,800	$6,480	$7,360

Overtime hours	4,250	4,040	5,105
Overtime pay rate (average)	$12	$13.50	$15
Total overtime pay	$51,000	$54,540	$76,575
Total units produced	50,600	51,000	52,000

Required:

a. Prepare one or more working papers for the required audit procedures.
b. Show how your working papers meet the criteria outlined in the guidelines presented in the text.

6 Selection of Auditees

This chapter, the first of six to cover the audit process in detail, discusses Step 1 in the audit process — the selection of activities to be audited. As you studied in Chapter 5, there are three primary ways that auditees are selected:

1. By systematically setting up a schedule of audits for the planning period.
2. By requests from executive management or the board.
3. By requests from auditees.

The main consideration when selecting auditees is risk. This chapter considers the various aspects of auditee selection, including the effect of risk on auditee selection by all three methods. Major chapter headings include:

- Standards related to auditee selection.
- Developing audit schedules.
- Audits requested by management or the board.
- Audits requested by auditees.

Standards Related to Auditee Selection
Standard 520 in the *Standards for the Professional Practice of Internal Auditing* states that the director of the internal auditing department should establish audit plans "consistent with the internal auditing department's charter and with the goals of the organization."

This standard goes on to include audit work schedules as an important part of the audit planning process. Guideline 110.5 states that these work schedules and any significant changes in the work plans should be approved by management and submitted to the board of directors for its information. Guideline 520.04 says that the "audit work schedules should include (a) what activities are to be audited; (b) when they will be audited; and (c) the estimated time required." This guideline states that these schedules should be flexible enough to allow for unanticipated demands on the internal auditing department.

Guideline 520.04 adds that auditors should consider seven factors when considering audit priorities:

1. *The Date and Results of the Last Audit*
   Basically, auditors can presume that the longer the time since an audit was performed on an activity, the greater the risk and, therefore, the higher the priority. Likewise, the more weaknesses found on a previous audit, the greater the presumed likelihood of continued control weaknesses.

2. *Financial Exposure*
   Funds tend to attract attention and indicate risk. When comparing different activities to determine how best to allocate audit resources, auditors usually favor those involving more dollars because of the higher levels of potential risk.

3. *Potential Loss and Risk*
   This consideration focuses on the internal control system. Weaker controls indicate greater potential losses and higher risk, whereas stronger controls indicate less potential loss and, therefore, lower risk for comparable levels of exposure. Some seemingly nonfinancial risk may also be considered, such as legal exposure, loss of public image, or public embarrassment. Although the initial effect may appear nonfinancial, these risks may ultimately bear financial consequences.

4. *Requests by Management*
   Auditors take management requests seriously. When management requests particular audit work, auditors usually can assume some perceived risk by management. Usually, management is closer to operations than anyone else and is in a good position to know where risks exist.

5. *Major Changes in Operations, Programs, Systems, and Controls*
   Major changes increase the priority of an audit of the underlying operations for several reasons. The process of change tends to cause complexities and risks that do not necessarily exist in a steady state. After changes have been made, many adjustments are likely to be required before the new operations are well integrated into the organization, which causes increased risk during the early implementation period. Also, the new activities would not have been audited before, causing significant uncertainty regarding the adequacy of related control systems.

6. *Opportunities to Achieve Operating Benefits*
   Failure to take advantage of potential benefits causes as real a loss to the organization as an actual loss of assets or some other damage. Consequently, internal auditors and management are

interested in continuing improvements, even where controls or performance have been adequate. Another consideration with respect to this provision is how receptive management is to the audit results. Given equally risky circumstances, the auditors give a higher priority to situations where audit results are more likely to have a positive effect.

7. *Changes to and Capabilities of the Auditing Staff*

    The mix of skills on an audit staff affects the concentration of audit work. Auditing departments generally are better equipped to audit certain operations than others. Auditing departments that comprise only CPAs probably would be better able to examine financial and accounting systems than engineering systems, for example. As a result, departments strive for an appropriate balance of experience, training, and ability in order to audit a range of activities within their respective organizations.

Naturally, internal auditors must consider all of these factors simultaneously as they set audit priorities. One or two of these seven factors may be more significant than the others in a given case, but as auditors compare a number of possible auditees, considerations for each one probably will be different.

Given the number of considerations possible for each potential auditee, as well as the large number of possible auditees, how can auditors make rational comparisons for an appropriate selection of auditees and audit priorities?

Unfortunately, internal auditors can busily go about their work while timely and serious problems may go undetected, and consequently uncorrected, because the auditors have not gotten around to those operations or processes yet. In many ways, the selection of auditees remains something of an art form (more subjective intuition than science), although in recent years some progress has been made toward more systematic selection procedures.

Developing Audit Schedules

The process for scheduling audits for a planning period may be analyzed in four general steps, as shown in Exhibit 6-1. Let's examine each of these four steps in turn.

Step 1: Set Strategy to Identify Potential Audits

A myriad of audits are possible within almost any organization large enough to employ an internal auditing staff. Auditors determine how they will divide the organization into its natural operations, activities, or processes before the selection process begins. One way of gaining insight into activities that may be audited is to look at the organization relative to:

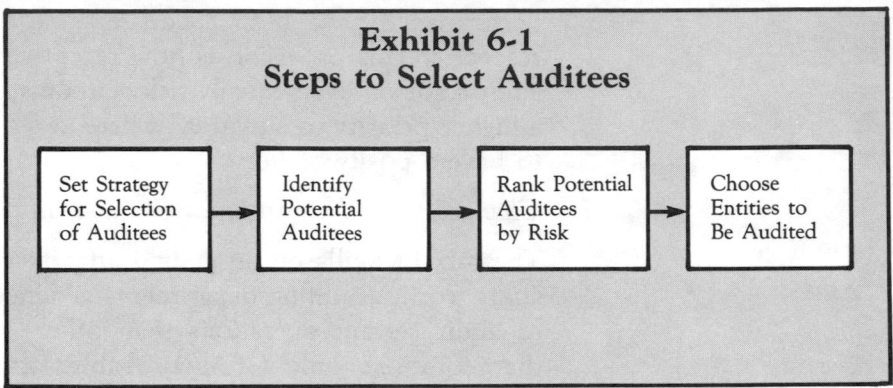

Exhibit 6-1
Steps to Select Auditees

Set Strategy for Selection of Auditees → Identify Potential Auditees → Rank Potential Auditees by Risk → Choose Entities to Be Audited

1. The location of plants, stores, assets, etc.
2. The total dollar amounts associated with each location or with types of operations.
3. The level of detail or complexity of the various activities, operations, or processes.
4. Available manpower in the audit department.
5. The degree of management concern regarding the various activities, operations, or processes.
6. Functional organizational units.
7. Transaction cycles.
8. Decision centers.

Location. Often, location readily defines potential audits because of natural separations. Production plants, regional operations, branch offices, sales operations, consignments, warehouses, and many other examples may illustrate the clear distinctions among potential auditees simply by locating them on a map. Similarly, the layout of many office buildings defines potential auditees by respective locations of different divisions and departments within the building complex. Such a strategy is simplistic and usually is inadequate without additional considerations.

Total Dollar Amounts. Consideration of total dollar amounts provides a kind of materiality measure by which to evaluate and compare potential auditees. Suppose, for example, a company's internal auditors and management decide that it isn't worth the auditors' time to audit any function with less than $1 million either in total assets or total cash flow during any one accounting period.

Suppose, however, that a small service department was responsible for servicing a large number of electrical appliances that are sold to several companies located in a nearby industrial park. The total assets for the service department may be only $250,000 and the payroll may total no more than $300,000 annually. However, service may have been the key factor in more than $15 million in sales to companies in the industrial park during the previous year, and thus it plays a key role in the success of the organization.

Consequently, the auditors are likely to combine the service department with some other potential auditee entity, such as marketing, in order to meet the total dollar requirement. A problem with this strategy is that it often results in illogical combinations of functions that are subject to the same audit assignment.

A singular focus on dollar amounts tends to lead auditors away from activities with an indirect yet substantial effect on revenues and profits. This could result in audits that are narrowly focused on a relatively small set of organizational activity, and lead to serious risks in some unexamined areas.

Required Detail and Time Constraints. The amount of detail required to audit an entity and the number of available auditor man-hours impose constraints on the auditing function, limiting the total amount of work that can be performed in any given period. Of course, the same level of detail is not required on every audit. An audit of a company's credit management, for example, would require considerably more detailed work than an audit of stock transactions for a closely held company.

As a result of the limitations caused by this combination of demand for detail and limited auditing staff resources, auditors often define the auditees so that an audit can be completed within a specified time. Typically, these audits are estimated in terms of total man-hours needed for the audit.

For example, an audit might require 400 man-hours to complete. This measurement means that a total of 400 hours of work performed by the auditors is expected to be required to complete the audit, from the initial preparation to the final report. Audits may range from 40 or 50 hours to several thousand hours.

By defining auditees so that the audit work can be done within certain time parameters, auditors are able to complete a variety of audits in different parts of the organization during the budget period. Seldom can auditors justify spending an entire budget period on one audit. The decision of how many man-hours to budget for an audit depends upon expected benefits to the organization in different amounts of assigned hours. The decision is made based upon the best trade-off of audit costs (including opportunity costs) to expected benefits.

Management Concern. There are occasions when the primary factor that determines what is to be audited is management concern. The internal auditors, management, or the board may consider a question to be sufficiently important that the question itself defines the auditee. Such concern may focus upon a readily identifiable function within the organization, which may occupy a specified space in the building and fit neatly into the organizational chart. Examples include product marketing, various accounting functions, the personnel department, and purchasing.

In other cases, however, management's concern may focus on aspects of the organization that are less well-defined. Examples include information management, labor relations, and customer service. Information now is considered an organizational resource to be managed like other resources, such as labor, materials, facilities, and money. Information permeates the entire organization and is influenced by many individuals using various media. Labor relations involve far more than labor-contract negotiating teams. And customer service in many organizations involves every person in the organization, not just the sales and product service departments.

Functional Organizational Units. Functional organizational units relate to specific types of activities of the organization. Typical functions for service organizations include marketing, financial management, accounting, personnel, facilities management, and the particular service being performed. Retailing organizations may add purchasing and inventory management. Manufacturers may add the manufacturing function (raw materials, work-in-process, and finished goods inventories), and often large transportation functions.

These functions are further subdivided into subfunctions. For example, the accounting function for a manufacturing firm may comprise general ledger accounting, accounts receivable, accounts payable, payroll, and cost accounting for a number of products.

Because of the integrated nature of functional activities, they often form convenient auditees, especially when they have separate locations. Some organizations are subdivided into divisions, each of which may administer its own functional areas. In such cases, the auditee likely would be the divisional areas of marketing, accounting, financial management, and so forth.

A similar application of the functional operating unit method of defining potential auditees is project management. Numerous projects arise in most organizations, such as building projects, research projects, product development, etc. They generally are organized temporarily for the completion of a particular task, after which the projects are disbanded.

Systems of internal controls are of particular importance and can be conveniently developed and integrated into these organizational units. This important link between internal controls and the functional areas provides another reason for selecting potential auditees along functional lines.

Transaction Cycles. Many activities of organizations, however, cross functional boundaries, so that the cycles involve more than a single function. In fact, external auditors often view an organization as a highly integrated set of five overall cycles known as transaction cycles. Auditing textbooks provide a number of examples of how such cycles might be illustrated. One example is provided by Alvin A. Arens and James K. Loebbecke in their auditing textbook, *Auditing: An Integrated Approach,* Third Edition (Prentice-Hall, Inc., 1984), and is illustrated in Exhibit 6-2, which also includes the general cash function.

The firm acquires capital, usually in the form of cash, and allocates it to various acquisitions and payments (e.g., raw materials, equipment, legal services, etc.) and to the company's labor needs. The combined activities of acquisition (and payments) with labor generate inventories, which then are sold. The money from these sales is used to pay dividends and the other costs of capital acquisition. Then the cycles begin again.

While this diagram represents the activity cycles for a profit-oriented firm, the principles of transaction cycles also apply to governmental and other not-for-profit organizations. The point is that many transactions cross organizational boundaries. It often is more convenient and meaningful to consider these larger cycles of activity than to stick strictly to an organization's functional boundaries. For example, general cash management usually crosses the boundaries of all of the organization's functional activities. The inventory and warehousing cycle crosses production, warehousing, accounting, and electronic data processing for a manufacturing entity. Exhibit 6-3 outlines typical steps in the five transaction cycles.

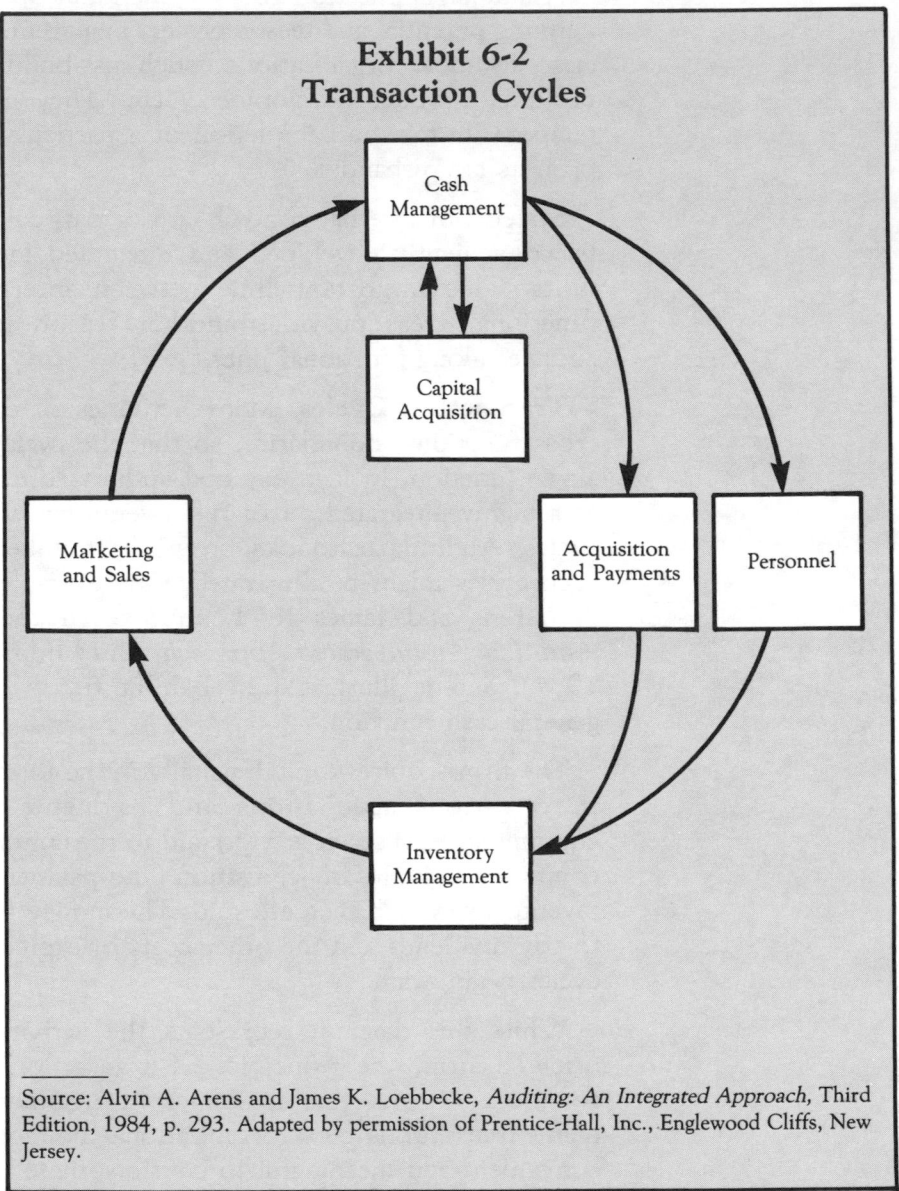

Exhibit 6-2
Transaction Cycles

Source: Alvin A. Arens and James K. Loebbecke, *Auditing: An Integrated Approach,* Third Edition, 1984, p. 293. Adapted by permission of Prentice-Hall, Inc., Englewood Cliffs, New Jersey.

Also, internal control systems, especially financial internal control systems, often follow these transaction cycles more closely than they do functional operations. By reducing the organization to these five cycles and to cash management, auditors can test rather large segments of related activities. Although the five cycles are clearly linked in the overall cycle of activities, each of the five cycles and general cash management are treated independently.

Exhibit 6-3
Steps in the Transaction Cycles

MARKETING AND SALES	INVENTORY MANAGEMENT	CAPITAL ACQUISITION	PERSONNEL AND PAYROLL	ACQUISITION AND PAYMENTS
Processing customers' orders	Receipt of goods	Issuing long-term debt and stock	Hiring employees	Processing purchase requests
Credit granting	Storage of goods	Paying interest and dividends	Authorizing payroll rates, deductions, etc.	Issuing purchase orders
Shipping goods	Accounting for receipt and storage	Repurchasing securities and paying at maturity	Timekeeping	Receiving goods and services
Recording sales	Processing goods (manufacturing)	Accounting for financing transactions	Payroll preparation	Processing vendors' invoices, receiving reports, and purchase orders
Billing customers	Accounting for costs of production processing	Maintaining detailed records for payment of interest and dividends and filing proper tax forms	Payroll payment	Disbursing cash
Receiving, processing, and recording cash receipts	Storage of processed or manufactured goods		Paying payroll taxes	Recording goods receipts, liabilities, and cash disbursements
Providing for bad debts	Shipment		Filing payroll-tax returns	
Writing off bad debts				
Receiving, processing, and recording sales returns				
Providing other credits, adjustments, and allowances				

Extracted from Irvin N. Gleim, *CIA Examination Review*, Volume 1, Second Edition (Gainesville, Florida: Accounting Publications, Inc.), 1984, pp. 248-49.

Decision Centers. Decision centers provide a final variable in possible strategies to identify potential auditees. While the trend has been toward large segments of an organization as possible auditees, decision centers may represent more narrowly defined parts of the organization. A divisional vice president's office, including the vice president and his or her support staff, composes an administrative decision center. The foreman in charge of the production of a key part used in a rocket engine also may be considered a decision center.

The primary factor in this approach to defining possible auditees is *decision authority* — not necessarily operating or transaction cycles or any other method of aggregating pieces of the organization. The focus is on key decisions that have significant effects upon the organization. Auditors may, for example, be interested in the recruiting practices for design engineers who will be privy to extremely sensitive information. In such a case, the auditors likely would focus their attention on the decision process to recruit and hire these key personnel.

As you review the eight factors used in defining potential auditees, it should be apparent that no one factor is likely to provide the ideal single strategy in auditee selection. Rather, most internal auditing departments consider all of these factors before selecting a particular strategy.

Contrast, for example, the approaches taken by two large international corporations. The audit director for one typically uses a dual strategy of identifying auditees. For audits that examine financial controls, auditees are identified according to transaction cycles for particular corporate divisions. For audits of operations, auditees typically are identified according to their geographic locations. The company's auditing executives state that different regional and international offices operate somewhat independently of one another. Assigning audit teams to do extensive examinations within these geographic units provides well-coordinated audit information. It relates various operations at each location without having to send, at different times, several different audit teams who would have a problem trying to integrate their various findings.

Auditors for the second corporation go through an annual process of dividing the company in three different ways:

1. By functional organizational units.
2. By transaction cycles.
3. By decision centers.

The audit executives then consider the other five factors on an informal basis, evaluating subjectively the most beneficial strategy for examining each part of the organization. The result often is a separate strategy for each part of the organization rather than a single strategy applied to all segments. Recently the auditors have started to examine large divisional segments of the company using all three strategies in order to perform a more comprehensive examination. These large audits can take more than 3,000 hours to complete.

Step 2:
Identification of
Possible Auditees

Once an organization's internal auditors have developed a strategy (or in some cases, as we have shown, strategies) for identifying potential auditees, the next step is to divide the organization into auditable units. This process usually results in a list — often a long one — of potential auditees.

An Example

An example will help illustrate these first two steps in establishing an audit schedule. Suppose that the corporate auditors for Timberland Industries, Inc. are scheduling audits for the coming year. Timberland has two primary divisions — lumber and paper manufacturing. The company also has a large plywood plant administered within the lumber division. Company headquarters are located in east Texas, the company's paper mill is located nearby, and two lumber mills and the plywood plant are located in Arkansas. Exhibit 6-4 shows Timberland's organization chart through five layers of management. The respective management levels are shown in the lower right-hand corners of the rectangular boxes indicating the various positions.

Timberland management treats the two divisions almost as independent enterprises. Each one is organized with its own accounting, operations management, and personnel functions. The headquarters group includes legal, corporate auditing, corporate accounting, and financial management functions.

The auditors decided to use functional organizational units as the primary factor in defining potential auditees. The functional organizational units follow Timberland's organization chart. A secondary factor is determined to be the level of detail required to complete an audit, and is measured in terms of expected audit man-hours. The level of detail required for each audit could be controlled by selecting operating units of predetermined sizes from among the five administrative levels of management.

Interestingly, although Timberland's auditors did not consciously choose other potential strategies for selecting auditees, the particular

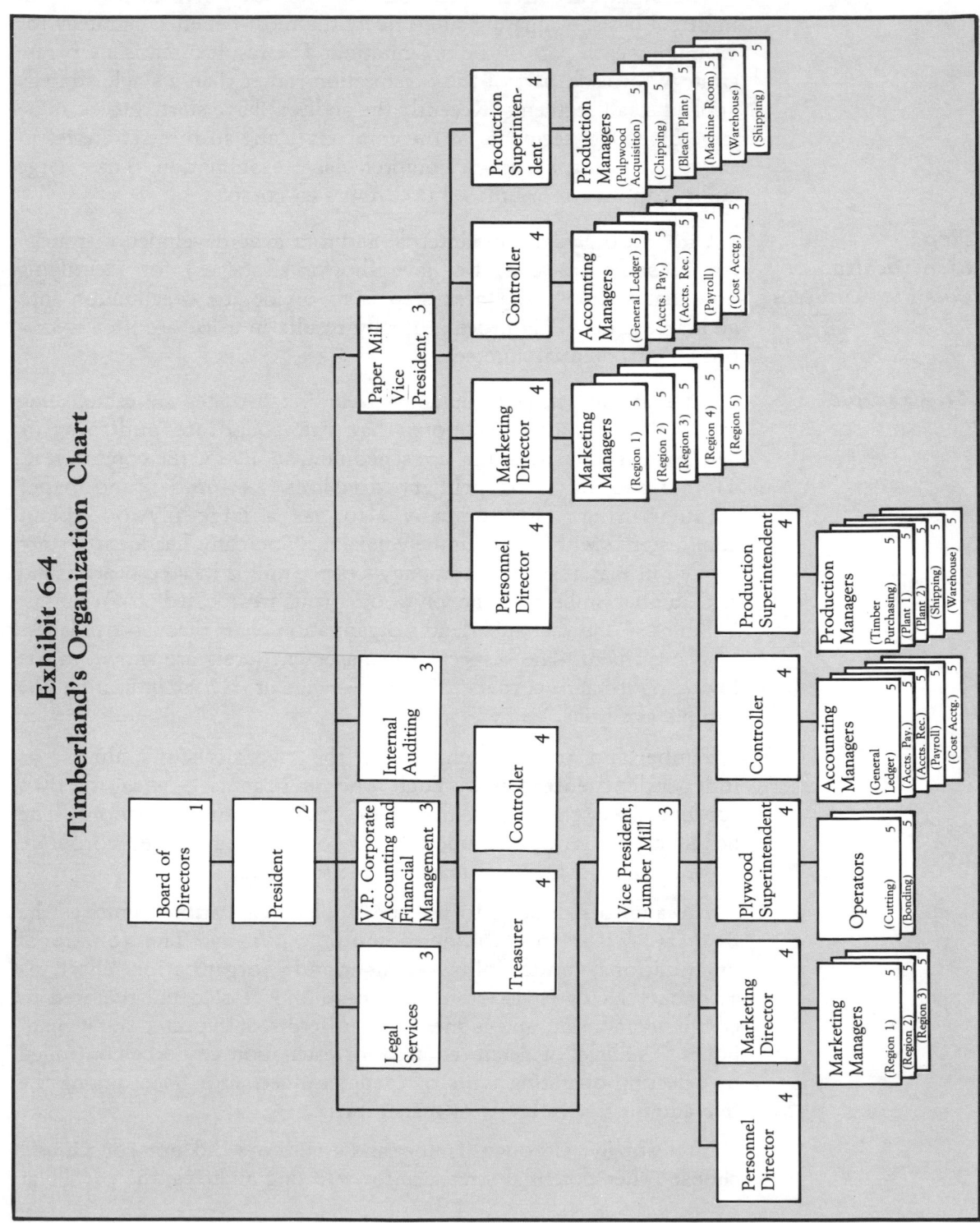

Exhibit 6-4
Timberland's Organization Chart

strategy they did choose results in a division of the organization that conforms to at least three other strategies. Because of their relative independence, the different operating units of the company follow fairly rigid geographic divisions as well as administrative decision centers. Also, significant dollar amounts flow through each of the functional organizational units.

Exhibit 6-5 shows units that are classified by organizational segment, management level, and estimated audit man-hours. Timberland's auditors have chosen to restrict the sizes of their audits to a maximum of 500 hours. They argue that larger audits are difficult to manage effectively, and their managers prefer shorter, more frequent audit reports to longer, more infrequent ones. The fourth column of the exhibit ("Estimated Audit Hours") shows several of the functions that require considerably more than 500 hours — corporate accounting and financial management, corporate controllership, lumber controllership, lumber production, paper marketing, and paper accounting. These functions, however, come under either the third or fourth management level. By dividing audits of these functions into several audits of their respective subfunctions (at management level 5), auditors can maintain the desired audit size and still ensure coverage of the larger functions.

For example, the controllership function of the lumber division is estimated to require 560 hours, which is beyond the 500-hour limit. Separate audits of the general ledger (160 hours), accounts payable (160 hours), accounts receivable (160 hours), payroll (80 hours), and cost accounting (140 hours) cover the various subfunctions of the controllership function in more manageable pieces. Although the total of these audits is 700 hours when doing them separately, each individual audit remains below the 500-hour ceiling.

Not all organizations use the same guidelines to govern the sizes of their audits. As mentioned before, there are some audits requiring several thousand hours. These audits may require more than a dozen auditors. As you can see from the example, some organizations keep audits much smaller. Each organization establishes its own guidelines in keeping with its management style and auditor preferences.

Another observation about Exhibit 6-5 is important. Some functions are estimated to require less than 500 hours. How do auditors decide whether to audit the overall function or to divide the audits into separate audits of subfunctions? For example, the auditors would decide whether to conduct one audit of the lumber marketing department (360 hours), or three separate audits for the three sales

Exhibit 6-5
Classification of Potential Auditees

Segment	Function	ML[1]	EAH[2]	EHE[3]
Headquarters	Legal Services	3	180	
	Auditing	3	230	
	Corp. Acctg. & F.M.	3	740	X
	Corp. Controller	4	560	X
	EDP Manager	5	200	
	General Ledger	5	160	
	Receivables	5	160	
	Payables	5	160	
	Financial Management	4	220	
Lumber	Personnel	4	140	
	Marketing	4	360	
	Region 1 Sales	5	140	
	Region 2 Sales	5	120	
	Region 3 Sales	5	120	
	Plywood Plant	4	110	
	Plywood Cutting	5	60	
	Plywood Bonding	5	60	
	Controller	4	560	X
	General Ledger	5	160	
	Accounts Payable	5	160	
	Accounts Receivable	5	160	
	Payroll	5	80	
	Cost Accounting	5	140	
	Production	4	510	X
	Timber Purchasing	5	120	
	Plant 1	5	160	
	Plant 2	5	160	
	Shipping	5	140	
	Warehouse	5	80	
Paper	Personnel	4	140	
	Marketing	4	420	
	Region 1 Sales	5	100	
	Region 2 Sales	5	120	
	Region 3 Sales	5	100	
	Region 4 Sales	5	100	
	Region 5 Sales	5	120	
	Accounting	4	620	X
	General Ledger	5	160	
	Accounts Payable	5	140	
	Accounts Receivable	5	160	
	Payroll	5	80	
	Cost Accounting	5	200	
	Production	4	390	
	Pulpwood Acquisition	5	120	
	Chipping Plant	5	60	
	Bleach Plant	5	80	
	Machine Room	5	80	
	Warehouse	5	72	
	Shipping	5	120	

[1]ML means "management level."
[2]EAH means "estimated audit hours."
[3]EHE means "estimated hours exceed 500."

regions (region 1 — 140 hours, region 2 — 120 hours, and region 3 — 120 hours). While this choice is a judgment call and differs from case to case, there is a key factor that usually helps the auditor decide: the degree of integration among the subfunctions, and consequently, the amount of joint risk existing among the subfunctions.

Highly integrated subfunctions share similar levels of risk because risk for one affects risk for the others. On the other hand, highly differentiated, independent subfunctions share little risk. For example, Timberland's cutting and bonding processes for the plywood plant are highly integrated. Consequently, the auditors are likely to audit the plywood plant as a single auditee. Timberland's different sales regions, however, operate somewhat independently of one another. As a result, rather than auditing marketing as a single auditee, the three sales regions probably would be considered as three separate auditees.

Timberland's auditors then set their strategy for identifying potential auditees as follows:

1. Select functional operating units.
2. Define potential auditees so that no more than 500 hours are required for any one audit.
3. Where a choice exists of whether to select a larger function or its several subfunctions separately, define the auditee according to the relative independence (or integration) of the subfunctions.

This strategy sets the parameters that define the potential auditees for the budget period.

Step 3: Ranking Potential Auditees According to Audit Priority

The most important determinant in ranking the potential auditees is their relative risk. Standard 520 outlines seven factors, reiterated here, that auditors consider when assessing the comparative risk associated with different potential auditees:

1. Time and results of the previous audit.
2. Financial exposure.
3. Potential loss and risk.
4. Requests by management.
5. Major changes in operations, programs, systems, and controls.
6. Opportunities to achieve operating benefits.
7. Changes to and capabilities of the auditing staff.

A study performed by James M. Patton, John H. Evans, and Barry L. Lewis (*A Framework for Evaluating Internal Audit Risk,* Research Report Number 25, The Institute of Internal Auditors, 1982) concluded that there are more than these seven factors that auditors use to compare the relative risks associated with various activities. The study outlined 18 risk factors considered to be important by professional internal auditors. This list is reproduced below, with the various risk factors listed in their overall rank order as reported in the study.

Risk Factors

1. *Quality of the auditee unit's internal control system.* The overall effectiveness of the internal control system that results from both the design and implementation of the system. The lower the effectiveness, the greater the risk.

2. *Competence of management.* The overall, combined effect of management's training, experience, commitment, and judgment. Increased competence decreases risk.

3. *Integrity of management.* Management's willingness to compromise a high ethical code of behavior in order to protect itself and/or its area of responsibility. Management's willingness to compromise these standards of ethics increases risk to the organization.

4. *Size of unit (revenues, assets).* The combined total of the assets invested in an area and the total of financial resources flowing through the area in the form of expenditures and revenues. The greater the assets, the greater the risk.

5. *Recent change in accounting system.* Changes in accounting policies, EDP systems, or management. Recent changes in the accounting system usually increase risk due to errors.

6. *Complexity of operations.* Either the technical sophistication of operations or the degree of detail required to manage the operation effectively. Greater complexity increases the risk for errors.

7. *Recent changes in key personnel.* Changes in decision makers within the organization who are responsible for critical factors relating to the success of operations. Often such changes increase risk or, at the least, cause uncertainty about the level of risk.

8. *Liquidity of assets.* Susceptibility to being taken from the organization and easily converted to cash. The greater the liquidity, the greater the chance for loss.

9. *Deteriorating economic condition of a unit.* Increasingly worse performance. As performance deteriorates, management may tend to become more reckless and to distort performance information.

10. *Rapid growth.* Growth in workload. As the workload becomes larger, the risk of emphasizing productivity at the expense of controls increases.

11. *Extent of computerization of a unit.* The degree of control over significant aspects of operations by computer systems. EDP expertise normally rests within the hands of relatively few people, and as computerization spreads, the risk of losing control over assets and information to this relatively small group increases.

12. *Amount of time since the last audit.* Frequent audits usually decrease risk.

13. *Pressure on management to meet objectives.* Expectations to meet higher levels of performance, as perceived by management of the area under review. As management feels increased pressure to meet overly ambitious objectives, the risk of emphasizing productivity at the expense of controls increases.

14. *Extent of government regulation.* The degree of federal and state government laws and regulations directly affecting operations and performance of the organization. These forces are often somewhat unpredictable. Therefore, the greater the level of regulation, the greater the potential risk.

15. *Level of employee morale.* Low morale increases risks to the organization.

16. *Audit plans of independent (i.e., outside) auditors.* Anticipated audits by government auditors/examiners or CPA firms — including the timing, frequency, and coverage of the audit work. Usually, more frequent audits with greater coverage reduce risk.

17. *Political exposure/adverse publicity.* The amount of exposure an area gets through the various media. Increased exposure/ publicity might lower the risk. Less exposure may increase the likelihood of improprieties or ineffectiveness.

18. *Distance from the main office.* The greater the distance from general management's direct observation, the greater the tendency for local management to fail to coordinate its efforts with the overall organization and to neglect controls.

While these 18 risk factors have been listed in their overall ranks, the research team was careful to point out that different organizations rank them somewhat differently. Exhibit 6-6 shows the top 10 risk factors selected by auditors in the banking and insurance industry, manufacturing firms, and other organizations.

Exhibit 6-6
Top 10 Risk Factors by Industry

Ranking	Banking and Insurance	Manufacturing	Other
1	Quality of internal control	Quality of internal control	Quality of internal control
2	Competence of management	Competence of management	Competence of management
3	Integrity of management	Integrity of management	Integrity of management
4	Recent change in accounting system	Size of unit	Recent change in accounting system
5	Size of unit	Deteriorating economic position	Complexity of operations
6	Liquidity of assets	Complexity of operations	Liquidity of assets
7	Change in key personnel	Change in key personnel	Size of unit
8	Complexity of operations	Recent change in accounting system	Deteriorating economic position
9	Rapid growth	Rapid growth	Change in key personnel
10	Government regulation	Pressure on management to meet objectives	Rapid growth

While the researchers suggest a mathematically sophisticated method of ranking potential auditable units using the above risk factors, the following simpler process can provide similar results:

1. Select the five most important risk factors for units in the organization.
2. Score each auditable unit on each of the five selected risk factors, using a scale from 1 to 5 points for each factor, with 5 points indicating maximum risk and 1 point indicating minimum risk (3 points would indicate either medium risk or unknown risk).
3. Total the points for each auditable unit to compute a "risk score." (A maximum risk score of 25 points — i.e., 5 points for all five risk factors — would indicate maximum risk for the auditing units).
4. Rank the units according to their risk scores.

When ties occur among risk scores, the auditors consider other factors in determining ranks. For example, one such factor would be the number of hours required to conduct an audit. All other things being equal, the cost/benefit trade-off would improve with fewer required hours. Another factor might be the organizational levels of the different entities. An audit usually can have a greater effect at higher levels than at lower levels because changes at higher levels tend to trickle down through the organization. Other factors from the list of 18 might also break some of the ties.

The risk evaluations are made from the auditors' experience with specific auditable entities and, when necessary, from additional information gathered from management and other sources.

Upon completion of the ranking exercise, it is wise to review the comparative rankings to be sure that they seem reasonable. Individual rankings may seem different when considered in the larger context of the rankings of other auditable units. This overall review of the rankings allows the auditors to check for any inconsistencies that might have occurred in the process.

Less systematic methods of ranking auditable units are employed in most organizations. Typically, auditors (and sometimes management) meet to consider the auditable entities and the comparative risks on an informal basis. Internal political considerations often may strongly influence how auditees are selected.

Analytical methods similar to the one suggested, however, have been successfully employed in some internal auditing departments. The advantage of such an approach is the systematic consideration of several key factors affecting organizational risks. Such consideration helps increase auditors' confidence in selecting auditees for the budgeting period, and reduces the temptation to let political or otherwise distorting forces gain too much influence in the selection process.

An Example

Exhibit 6-7 lists the potential auditees for Timberland Industries in the left column. The five most important risk factors for manufacturing firms are listed across the top of the table. Points are assigned to the five risk factors for each entity. The two right-hand columns total the points to provide a risk score for each entity and then rank each potential auditee according to the total risk scores. Of course, the points assigned to each risk factor vary for each potential auditee.

The auditors review the comparative rankings and conclude that they are reasonable. The auditors now are prepared to conclude the auditee selection process for the budget period.

Of course, the auditors may choose whichever risk factors seem most appropriate to the situation, including those specified in the *Standards.* Another refinement in the process that often proves helpful is to prepare a short narrative justification for each ranking. This reference can be valuable when questions arise regarding why certain judgments were made. The disadvantage of keeping these notes, however, is that they can become somewhat voluminous for large organizations.

Step 4: Selection of Auditees for a Budget Period

The final step in the auditee selection process is to determine how many of the audits can be completed during the budget period. It is impossible for auditors to audit everything in an organization in one budget period. Auditors operate with scarce resources like other parts of an organization. The scarce resource for auditors is audit hours. There simply are never enough audit hours available to do everything auditors would like to do. That, of course, is the point of ranking the different potential audit entities. By prioritizing audits, the auditors can be reasonably confident that they are conducting the most important audits.

An Example

Continuing with the Timberland Industries example, examine Exhibit 6-8. The entities are reorganized according to their ranked risk scores in decreasing order. The two columns to the right of the listed entities show:

1. The estimated number of audit hours required to audit the entity.
2. The cumulative hours required to conduct the audits in the order given.

Exhibit 6-7
Ranking Potential Auditees

ENTITIES	IC[1]	MC[2]	MI[3]	SIZE	EP[4]	RST[5]	RANK*
Corporate:							
Legal Services	3	1	2	5	1	12	14T
Auditing	1	1	1	2	1	6	28
Financial							
Mgt.	4	5	4	5	4	22	3T
EDP	5	2	2	5	2	16	10
General							
Ledger	2	3	1	5	2	13	13
Receivables	2	2	1	2	3	10	18
Payables	2	2	1	3	1	9	19T
Lumber:							
Personnel	3	3	3	2	1	12	14T
Marketing	5	3	4	5	4	21	5T
Plywood							
Plant	1	1	1	3	1	7	24T
General							
Ledger	2	4	2	5	1	14	12
Payables	2	2	1	2	4	11	16T
Receivables	3	1	2	5	4	15	11
Payroll	3	3	2	2	1	11	16T
Cost							
Accounting	1	1	2	3	1	8	22T
Timber							
Purchasing	5	1	4	5	4	19	7
Plant 1	5	3	1	4	4	17	8T
Plant 2	5	4	4	4	5	22	3T
Shipping	5	5	4	5	5	24	1T
Warehouse	5	5	4	5	5	24	1T
Paper:							
Personnel	2	1	2	1	1	7	24T
Marketing	5	1	2	5	4	17	8T
Production	4	5	3	5	4	21	5T
General							
Ledger	2	1	1	4	1	9	19T
Payables	2	1	1	2	1	7	26T
Receivables	2	1	1	3	1	8	22
Payroll	1	1	1	3	1	7	26T
Cost							
Accounting	1	1	1	3	3	9	19T

---

[1]IC means "internal control."
[2]MC means "management competence."
[3]MI means "management integrity."
[4]EP means "economic position."
[5]RST means "risk score total."
*T means "tie."

Exhibit 6-8
Selecting Auditees

RANK*	AUDIT ENTITY	EAH[1]	CAH[2]
1T	Lumber: Shipping	140	140
1T	Lumber: Warehouse	80	220
3T	Corporate: Financial Mgt.	220	440
3T	Lumber: Plant 2	160	600
5T	Lumber: Marketing	360	960
5T	Paper: Production	390	1,350
7	Lumber: Timber Purchase	120	1,470
8T	Lumber: Plant 1	160	1,630
8T	Paper: Marketing	420	2,050
10	Corporate: EDP	200	2,250
11	Lumber: Receivables	160	2,410
12	Lumber: General Ledger	160	2,570
13	Corporate: General Ledger	160	2,730
14T	Corporate: Legal Department	180	2,910
14T	Lumber: Personnel	140	3,050
16T	Lumber: Accounts Payable	160	3,210
16T	Lumber: Payroll	80	3,290
18	Corporate: Receivables	160	3,450
19T	Corporate: Payables	160	3,610
19T	Paper: General Ledger	160	3,770
19T	Paper: Cost Accounting	200	3,970
22T	Paper: Receivables	160	4,110
22T	Lumber: Cost Accounting	140	4,390
24T	Paper: Personnel	140	4,250
24T	Lumber: Plywood Plant	110	4370
26T	Paper: Payables	140	4,530
26T	Paper: Payroll	80	4,610
28	Corporate: Auditing	120	4,730

*T means "tie."
[1]EAH means "estimated audit hours."
[2]CAH means "cumulative audit hours."

Suppose Timberland Industries' internal auditing department employed two auditors. Each auditor may be scheduled for 40 hours per week, 45 weeks per year (each auditor takes two weeks vacation each year and perhaps another five weeks for holidays, sick leave, and professional development), for a total of 1,800 hours of direct audit effort per year, per auditor. The total available hours for the two auditors is 3,600. Assuming 10 overtime hours, the last audit the auditors would have time to perform would be the payables function at the corporate level. The line at that point in the table indicates the cutoff for one year's audit plan. It would not be possible to audit the final eight potential audit entities in this planning cycle of one year.

In the next period, all of the entities would be reevaluated according to the risk factors. The rankings probably would change, the order of audits would be different, and some of the entities not included in the last period's schedule likely would be included in this one. Also, the strategy to divide the organization may change from period to period in order for the auditors to view operations from different perspectives.

Should a particular entity consistently be placed at the bottom of the list, the auditors would probably desire some coverage of its operations within a five- or 10-year cycle. Consequently, these entities probably would be included in audit schedules on a periodic, although infrequent, basis, even though their risk scores may not place them in a higher priority.

One other item for scheduling involves examination of the auditing department itself. This often is either a self-evaluation performed by the auditors or a peer evaluation performed by an outside review team hired by the company. In either case, some time will have to be allocated to this quality control dimension of operations.

The auditee selection process is complete at this point. The auditors for Timberland Industries, Inc. have developed a strategy for identifying potential auditee entities; they have identified those entities; they have performed a risk analysis and ranked the entities; and finally, they have allocated the available audit hours to those entities possessing the highest levels of risk.

Audits Requested by Management or the Board

There are many occasions when top management will request specific audits to be performed. Such requests arise from management's concern over particular aspects of the organization's performance and operations. Such concern might arise unexpectedly when some aspects of operations seem out of control. In such cases, the preliminary risk analysis may need reevaluation. The problem that has gained management's attention may, in fact, pose a higher risk to the organization than other audits already scheduled. If so, then the auditors likely will interrupt their scheduled audits and honor management's request.

If it is unclear whether or not the area for which management has requested an audit poses greater risk to the organization than other scheduled audits, then the decision to interrupt the audit schedule becomes one of negotiation between management and the auditors. In some organizations, management has the authority to require the auditors to perform the requested audit. In other organizations, where the auditors fall more under the authority of the board of directors, the auditors have greater influence over the decision.

Usually, however, unless crucial problems are apparent in other areas scheduled for audits, the internal auditors, as a matter of professional courtesy, will honor management's requests. Similarly, the board of directors may request specific audits. The internal auditors almost always are obliged to honor these requests from the board.

Management and board requests may not follow the same organizational boundaries used by the auditors in the budget scheduling process. Management's concern does not always follow convenient dividing lines, as we discussed in the section on auditee selection strategy.

An Example

Timberland Industries provides an example of a somewhat unusual and unexpected management request of the company's auditors. Management suddenly became aware of new computerized technology that vendors claimed could increase the plywood mill's productivity by 25 percent and profits from plywood sales by as much as 10 percent, as a result of decreased costs.

Although the lumber mill's management was intrigued by the new technology, there were serious concerns about how production controls would be affected if a change were made. The auditors were asked to perform a specific evaluation (with the company's engineers) of the production controls presently in place for equipment being used in the plant, and further, to examine the control system proposed by the vendor for the new technology. The requested study was for a particular subsection of the plywood plant, with respect to a specific machine and its operation.

When they earlier had considered the plywood plant for possible inclusion in the audit schedule for the budget period, the auditors evaluated the plywood plant as a whole. They also considered the cutting plant and the bonding plant as potential auditees. The auditors did not, however, break the plywood plant down into units small enough to consider the operation of a specific machine, and certainly not in the context of possibly replacing the machine. Consequently, the auditors did not consider this particular audit earlier when preparing the audit plan. They performed this work as a courtesy to management.

Notice the unique nature of this management request. While the requested work is not an audit in the traditional sense, the work involves an evaluation and comparison of controls. The auditors were called to work with the engineers in this case because of the unique perspective auditors have on controls.

Audits Requested by Auditees

Many times auditees may have specific concerns regarding their own operations. When auditees have developed a good working relationship with internal auditors, and when the auditors have the necessary skills to assist, the internal auditors may decide to conduct the specially requested audits. The auditors must be careful to maintain their independence in these cases, however, and not participate in the decision-making process.

The decision whether to interrupt the audit schedule again depends upon the perceived risk. The auditors can conduct a risk analysis on the requested audit similar to what was done when they set up the budgeted audit schedule. The requested audit is then prioritized along with the other auditees. Higher risk scores usually lead to earlier audits. Lower risk scores tend to lead to later audits, or in some cases, a tactful refusal by the auditor to do the requested work.

QUESTIONS

1. What are the three primary ways that auditees are selected for audits?
2. What primary factor determines the selection of particular auditees for audits?
3. Explain how the *Standards for the Professional Practice of Internal Auditing* addresses the selection of auditors.
4. Why is the selection of auditees critical to the successful performance of the audit function?
5. Identify the four steps in selecting auditees for a budget period.
6. Outline and discuss briefly eight factors that help to define an organization's strategy for selecting auditees to be included in the budget period.
7. Why do you think that a single "best strategy" for selecting auditees has not been agreed upon?
8. How does the identification of possible audits follow directly from the particular strategy selected by the auditors? Give an example.
9. How is risk used to rank potential auditees according to audit priority?
10. A study by Patton, Evans, and Lewis, published by The IIA, identified 18 factors used to rank potential auditees according to risk. Identify these 18 risk factors. How does this list compare to a similar list in the *Standards?*
11. Many organizations use relatively informal methods of ranking potential auditees. Describe their usual method.
12. How are auditees selected for a budget period once potential audits have been ranked?
13. How is it possible to use risk as the predominant consideration when deciding upon an audit that has been requested by management? What other factors may play a role?
14. How is risk used to decide upon an audit requested by an auditee? What potential benefits do you think might accrue by conducting such audits?

EXERCISES

E-1

The organization chart on the following page depicts the decentralized structure of Baxter's, Inc., a medium-sized chain of large department stores located in six cities in the western part of the United States. The director of internal auditing has decided upon the following key factors to guide the selection of auditees for the 1985–86 budget year: location and transaction cycles.

Required:

a. Study the organization chart and state why you think the audit director would choose location and transaction cycles as selection factors.
b. Name at least one other strategy that you think might be appropriate in this case for identifying potential auditees. Defend your strategy(ies).

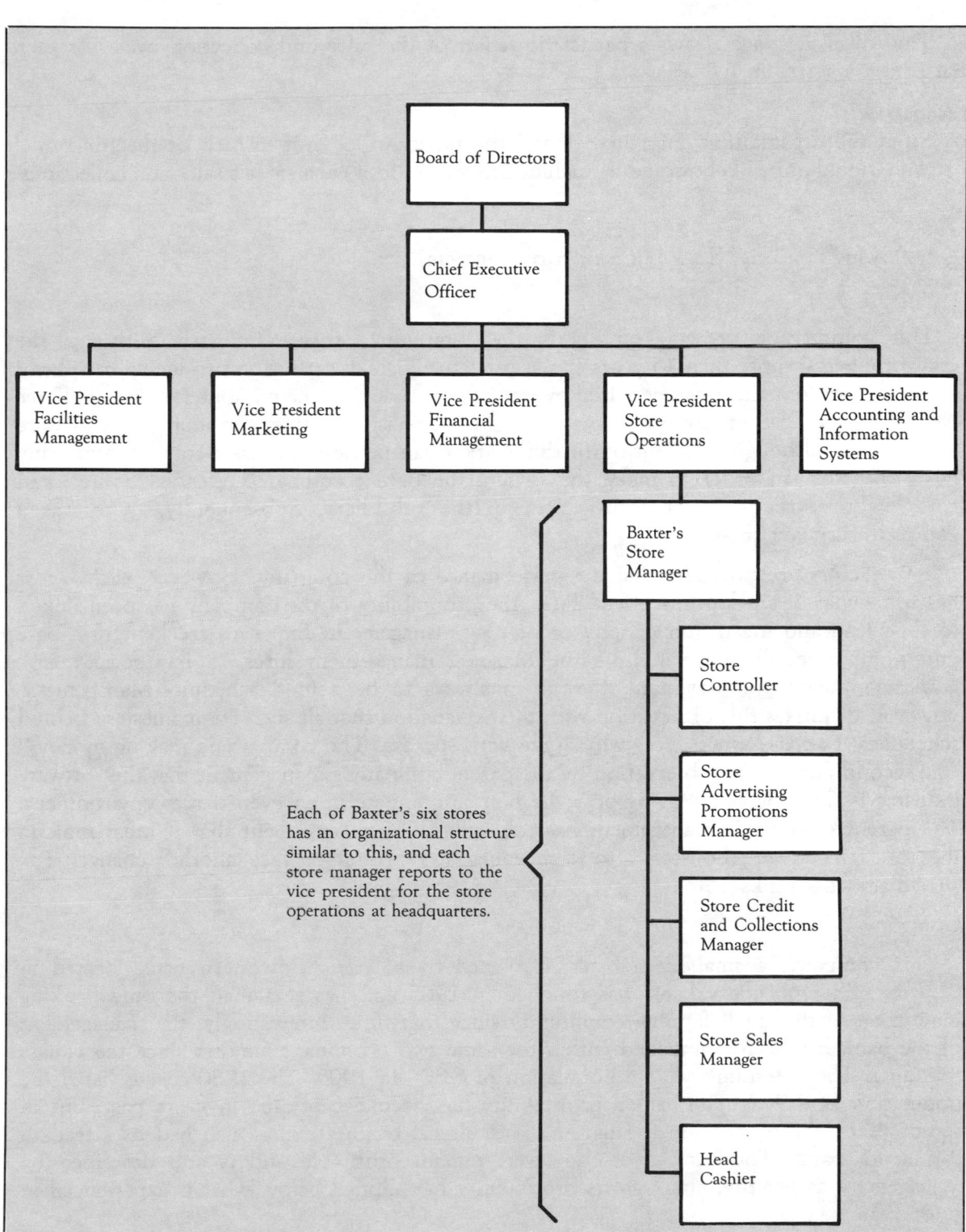

Each of Baxter's six stores has an organizational structure similar to this, and each store manager reports to the vice president for the store operations at headquarters.

E-2

The following page shows a partial flowchart of the sales and collection cycle for each of Baxter's stores in E-1 above.

Required:

From the organization chart in E-1 and the flowchart, identify which of the functional organizational units likely would be included in the audit of each store's sales and collections.

E-3

Following is a brief description of two companies:

Company A

This company is growing rapidly in the computer software industry. Although the company began more than 15 years ago as a relatively small operation producing peripheral computer equipment, it was acquired by one of the leaders in the computer industry. Three years ago the parent company switched the emphasis in this subsidiary to software production. Although competition in this market can be described as fierce, the company has done well. In order to make the switch, the parent company "cleaned house" and completely restructured the management of the subsidiary. Subsequently, there was a complete turnover in staff.

Two factors are now affecting the performance of the company. However, each factor has somewhat of an opposite effect. First, the profitability of the company has been linked to the "lean and mean" philosophy of its new management. Expenses are kept to a bare minimum, especially payroll. Like the Marines, management hires "a few good men." Although they work very hard, they seem always to be behind schedule. Management, however, dismisses this observation with the explanation that all such companies are behind schedule. "Besides," they say, "why argue with success? The company is making money." The second factor is an observation by the parent company's management that the software industry is thinning out, leaving only the best to compete in an even fiercer environment. The parent company's management has told subsidiary management that it must rank in the top 10 software houses in total revenues and profits or face another change. The subsidiary now ranks 15th.

Company B

This company, a small-town bank, is owned by a large Midwestern bank located in Chicago. The subsidiary bank was founded in 1905 and has remained the only banking institution in the small farming community since that time. Interestingly, the management of the bank has been maintained within the same two prominant families since the bank's founding. The community had a population of 6,804 in 1905. The 1980 census listed the population as 7,967. The bank's profitability has been exceptional in years past, but in recent years, the squeeze on the nation's agricultural businesses has also had its effect on this small bank. The bank does, however, remain profitable and is still described by management as healthy, although its profitability has slipped below what it experienced in prior years.

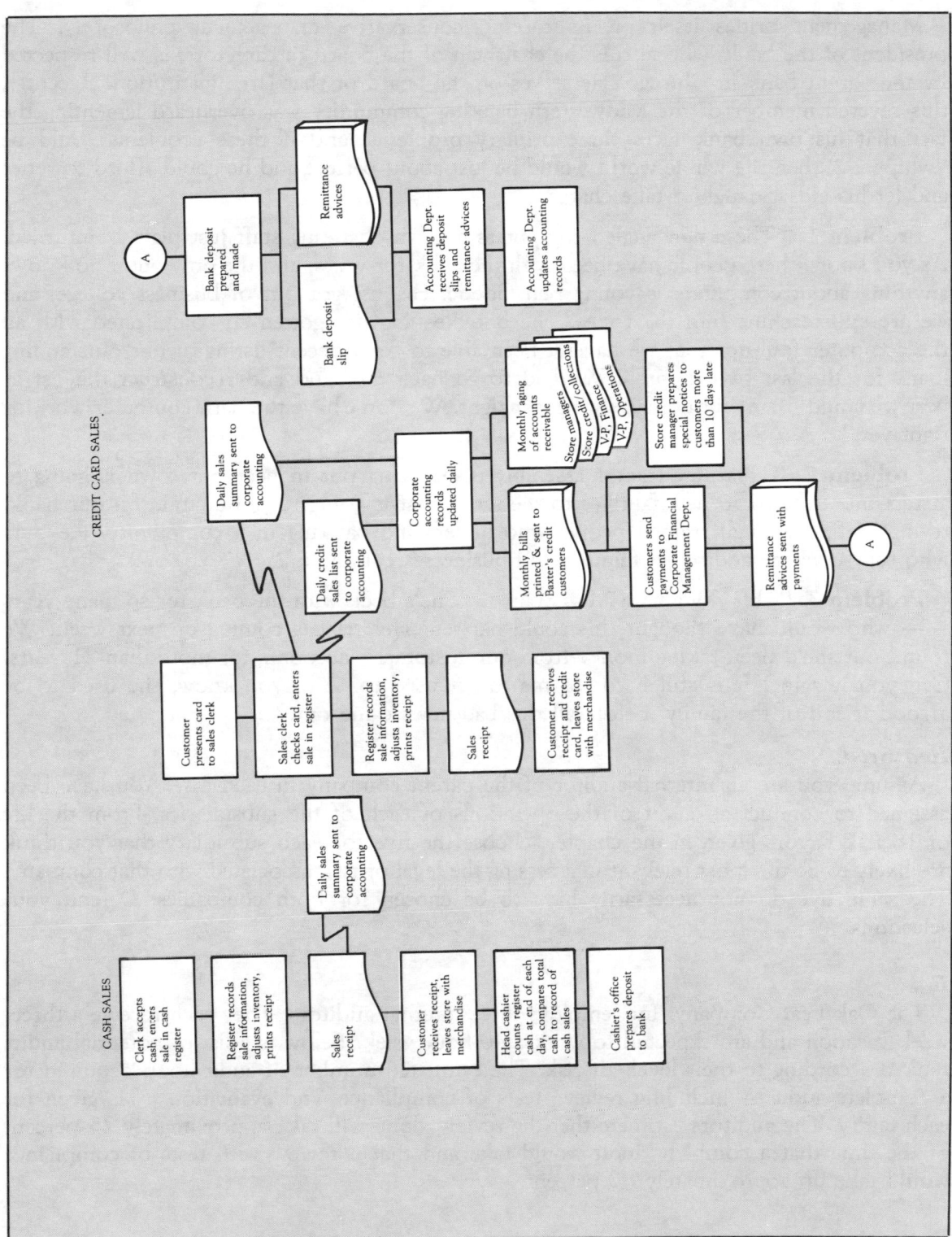

Management prides itself on its careful, conservative management philosophy. The president of the bank, who also is the chairman of the board of directors, is well respected by the parent bank in Chicago. He serves on the board of that large institution. Recently, this revered member of the Midwestern banking community was overheard lamenting the fact that his own bank faces three primary problems, and if these problems could be "whipped," then the whole world would be just about perfect and he could afford to retire and let his eldest daughter take charge.

Problem 1. "These newfangled computers have my banking staff just plain bumfuzzled. As you know, these people have been with the bank for years, and the only one who knows anything about computers is young Ben Goode. He just got out of business college, and we are still teaching him the ropes. The bookkeeping has gotten so complicated with all the computer foul-ups that we haven't been able to get a decent listing of our outstanding loans for the last two months. We had to go back by hand and reconstruct the list as best we could. I am still not sure we got it right. We don't have the darn computer working right yet."

Problem 2. "This new tractor assembly plant being put in near our town is going to attract more than 150 new families to the area. That is going to put a strain on our bank, trying to find enough trained people who understand banking in a community like ours who can serve the additional families and businesses coming in."

Problem 3. "This thing with Miss Sparrow. She's been with the bank for so many years —— who would have thought this could happen? Her trial is coming up next week. We found out she'd been taking money from our customers' accounts for more than 21 years. Can you imagine? It is still hard for me to get used to. And you know, she used to be a good friend of the family, before all this bad news came out."

Required:

Assume you are an internal auditor of the parent company in each case. You have been assigned to conduct an audit of the operations of each of the subsidiaries. From the list of 18 risk factors given in the chapter, choose the five for each subsidiary that you think are likely to be the most relevant in assessing the level of risk associated with that company. The same five do not necessarily have to be chosen for both companies. Defend your selections.

E-4

The Oak Leaf Company, Inc. employs three internal auditors. They each receive a three-week vacation and are expected to work a 40-hour week. Below is a list of potential audits ranked according to their levels of risk. The estimated number of audit hours required for a complete audit — including review, tests of compliance, and evaluation — is given for each entity. The auditors estimate that the review alone will take approximately 25 percent of the time that a complete audit would take and that a review with tests of compliance would take up approximately 80 percent.

AUDITING ENTITY	RANK	ESTIMATED AUDIT HOURS
Accounting	5	1,500
Data Processing	2	1,500
Mechanical Engineering	14	250
Commercial Research	7	550
Plant Engineering	8	500
Purchasing	4	1,500
Industrial Engineering	13	350
Assembly Plant	15	250
Processing Plant	6	500
Facilities	9	1,000
Customer Service	12	800
Eastern Region Sales	1	1,750
Western Region Sales	3	1,250
Transportation	10	1,600
Personnel	11	500
Training and Services	16	250

Required:

a. Create a worksheet listing the potential audits in their ranked order with four additional columns, as shown below:

Potential Auditee	Rank	Review Hours	Compliance Test Hours	Evaluation Hours

Using this worksheet, determine at least two strategies the auditors might use to allocate their total available audit-hours among the seven riskiest auditing entities.

b. Suppose the auditors were asked to evaluate and show the effect that bypassing evaluations of systems would have on total audit coverage in the budget period. Do you see any dangers in such a policy if the auditors decide not to perform the evaluation portion of an audit?

PROBLEMS

P-1

Listed below are two auditing entities within Hollyfield, Inc., with the risk scores on each of three factors:

Auditing Entity	Quality of Internal Control	Competence of Management	Computerization of Unit
Residential Sales	1	2	5
Purchasing	4	5	2

The range of possible scores on each of the risk factors is 1 to 5 — 5 indicates the maximum possible risk associated with a factor, and 1 indicates the least possible risk. Numbers up and down this scale indicate either less risk or more risk, according to the direction.

The scores for residential sales and purchasing were given by the company's auditors at the beginning of the last auditing period (June 1, 1985–June 1, 1986). Recently the auditors developed some new information related to three of the risk factors and have decided to reevaluate the risks associated with these two entities resulting from the three areas of potential risk. This information includes flowcharts, job descriptions for the managers of each function shown in the flowcharts, information on the managers themselves, and minutes of a board of directors' meeting.

Management Job Descriptions (Partial)

Residential Sales Manager — Responsible for the following:

1. Recruiting, training, compensation, supervision, performance, and general management of the company's sales force, including zone sales managers and the sales staff.
2. Sales forecasting.
3. Sales promotions and residential advertising.
4. Development of the general sales plan for the department.
5. Budgeting and financial management of the sales department.

Purchasing Manager — Responsible for the following:

1. Purchasing all company materials, supplies, out-of-plant services, merchandise inventory, and furnishings.
2. Recruiting, training, compensation, supervision, performance, and general management of purchasing department personnel.
3. Optimizing cost and quality of all purchases.
4. Budgeting and financial management of the purchasing department.

Manager of Inventories and Delivery — Responsible for the following:

1. Managing the warehousing and delivery function of the company.
2. Recruiting, training, compensation, performance, and general management of warehouse and delivery personnel.
3. Maintenance and repair of delivery vehicles.
4. Maintenance of adequate levels of inventory, monitoring inventory levels, and requisitioning additional inventory as needed.
5. Budgeting and financial management of the inventories and delivery department.

Controller — Responsible for the following:

1. General administration and control over the corporate accounting and financial management functions.
2. Maintaining accurate, up-to-date accounting records.
3. Overseeing the preparation and compilation of corporate budgets.
4. Administration of corporate collections, cash receipts, and disbursements functions.
5. Providing quarterly and annual financial statements to management and the board of directors.

6. Recruiting, training, compensation, performance, and general management of accounting and treasury department personnel.
7. Budgeting and financial management of accounting and treasury department.

Managers:

Residential Sales Manager — William (Willy) Gardner recently was hired as residential sales manager. He graduated from a well-known Midwestern university in 1965 with a degree in history. Since graduation, he has worked in door-to-door residential sales for various appliance companies. Prior to joining Hollyfield, he held a similar position at the regional level for a major vacuum cleaner company for five years. Everyone agrees that Willy's two main strengths are (1) an ability to get along well with people and (2) great attention to details.

Purchasing Manager — Claude (Skipper) Yardley is the great-great-grandson of a now infamous U.S. senator who amassed a fortune in questionable business dealings with the government of a Caribbean country. Skipper is heir to the fortune, but in the meantime has decided to work, applying his Ivy League business education down at the grass roots. Skipper is active in local and state politics and thinks that his business experience will be helpful to his own political career someday. His general intelligence, integrity, and willingness to work hard have enabled him to move quickly within the ranks of Hollyfield. At 27, he is the youngest manager in the company. He has been with the company for only five years and was promoted to the position of purchasing manager about a year and a half ago.

Manager of Inventories and Delivery — Wayne (Kip) Newell has worked for Hollyfield for more than 30 years. He began as a night janitor when he was in high school and worked his way up through the ranks in the early years, when promotions were based primarily upon seniority. He did not attend college and resents the influx of all the "college kids who," he says, "don't know nothing but what they read in them college books." Kip tries not to let this attitude affect his work, however. For the last 10 years Kip has been manager of inventories. Just last year Kip was given the responsibility for delivery, which was combined at that time with the inventory management. Under Kip's management, delivery costs have more than doubled, and complaints are up 25 percent over the average for the three years before the change in organizational administration. Kip insists he can bring the costs and the complaints down, given enough time.

Controller — Nancy Wallace is a 1955 graduate of a local college, with a double major in marketing and finance. Nancy was married to Gregory Wallace, the former vice president of marketing for Holleyfield, when she joined the company's accounting staff in 1960. Gregory died in 1970. Nancy stayed on with the company and was promoted to controller in 1979. She insisted at that time that it would be much more efficient to combine the accounting and treasury function into one department. It was combined last year.

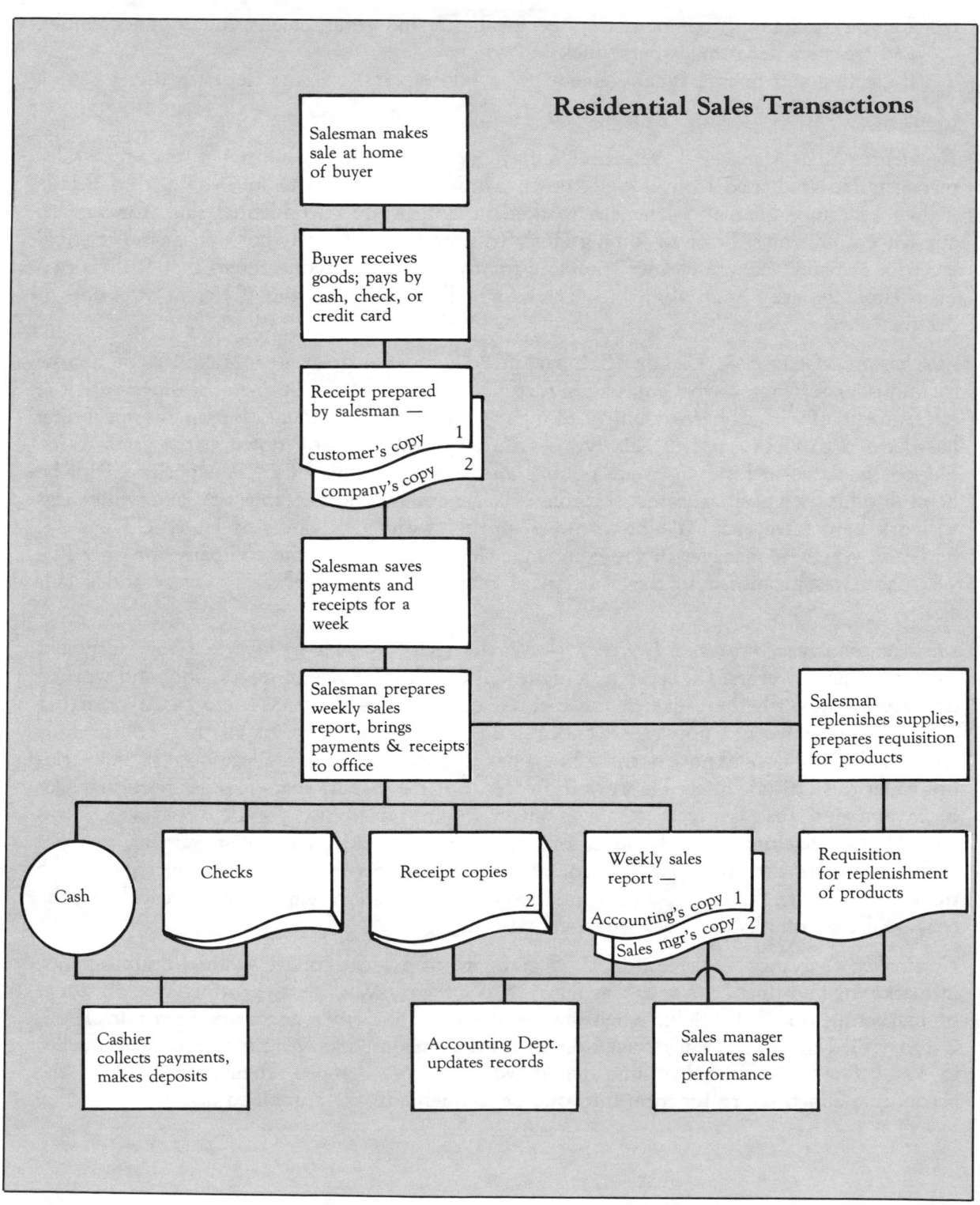

Residential Sales Transactions

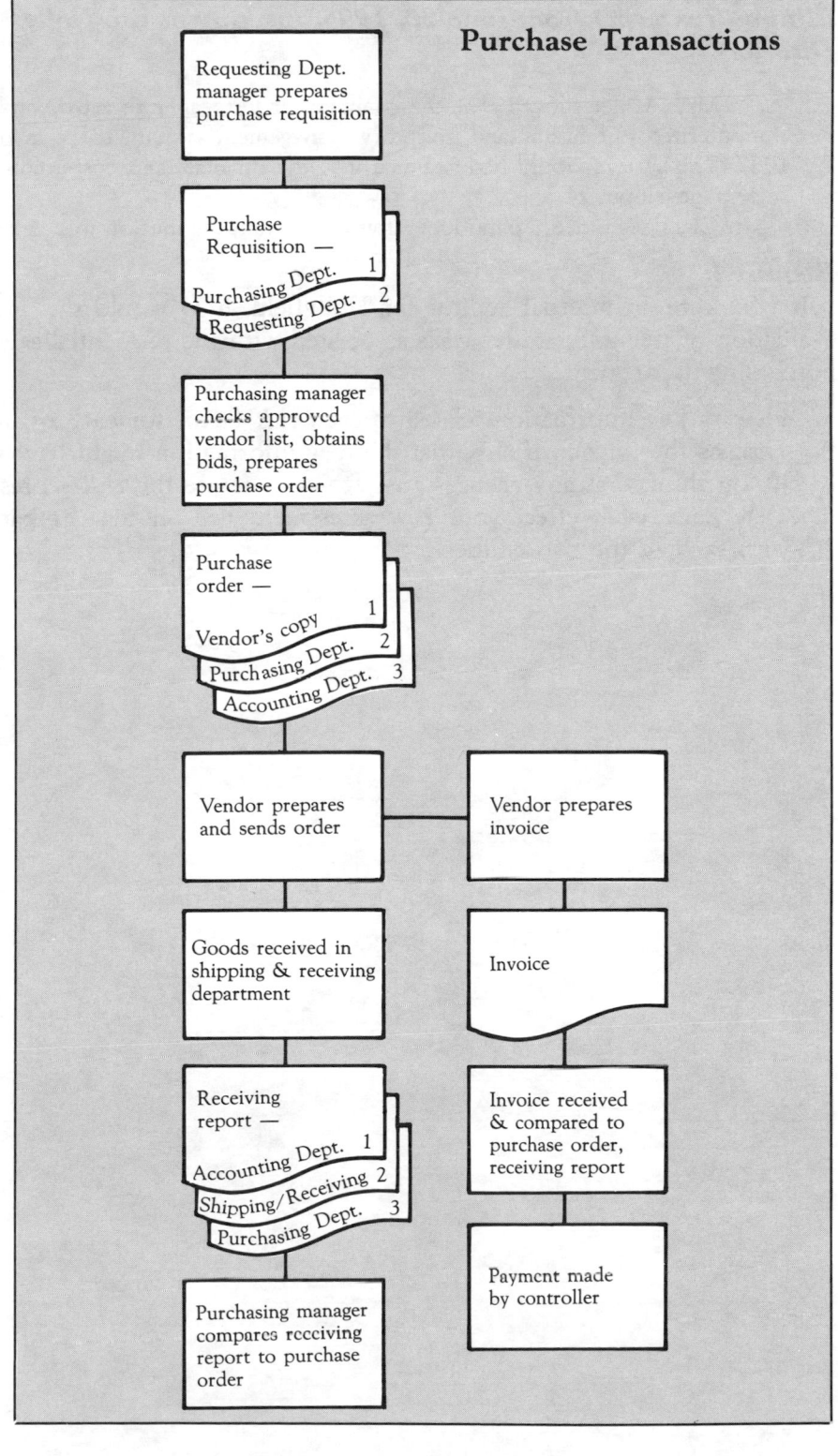

Minutes (excerpt) from June 20, 1985, meeting of the Hollyfield, Inc. Board of Directors

... Mrs. Miller moved that the company acquire an integrated, on-line, state-of-the-art computerized purchasing and inventory management system, to be in operation by July 1, 1987. The system would be integrated into the financial and cost-accounting systems under current development.

Mr. Clark seconded the motion. After discussion, the motion was carried unanimously. ..

Required:

If you were an internal auditor for Hollyfield, how would this information affect your evaluation of the comparative risks associated with the residential sales department and the purchasing department?

a. Identify key information related to each risk factor for each of the two entities.
b. Discuss the impact, if any, that the new information might have on your assessment.
c. If you think that any changes are necessary, revise the risk scores appropriately.
d. Determine what effect your new assessment has on the comparative risks associated with each of the two entities.

7 Preparation for the Audit

After determining what to audit, the auditors begin preparation for the audit. According to Standard 410, "Planning the Audit," preparation comprises the following parts:

- Establishing audit objectives and scope of work.
- Reviewing audit files and other materials.
- Selecting the audit team and other audit resources.
- Preparing a preliminary audit program.
- Informing the auditee that an audit is to be performed.
- Determining how, when, and to whom the audit results will be communicated.
- Obtaining approval to do the audit.

This standard also lists on-site surveys (what we have referred to as "preliminary" or "initial" surveys) as part of the planning or preparatory phase of audits. Because these surveys contribute valuable information regarding the current operations of auditees, we consider them separately as more of a beginning step in the audit work than as a preparatory step to that work. The initial survey is covered in more detail in Chapter 8.

Establishing Audit Objectives and Scope

Audit preparation begins with determining what the auditors intend to accomplish and what aspects of the organization's operations are to be examined. Remember that Standard 300, "Scope of Work," reads as follows:

> The scope of the internal audit should encompass the *examination* and *evaluation* of the *adequacy* and *effectiveness* of the organization's *system of internal control* and the *quality of performance* in carrying out assigned responsibilities.

We have italicized six key words and phrases that provide guidance in establishing the objectives and scope of work to be performed in the audit of the selected auditee.

Establishing Audit Objectives

The key terms identifying audit objectives are *examination* and *evaluation*.

Basically, there are two primary types of audit examination. The first can be described as a "review" and comprises a variety of work performed by the auditors to describe and to help understand the auditee. Sample review objectives might be:

- Review the Eastern Regional Sales Office's procedures for customer service after closing sales.
- Analyze the composition of the company's investment portfolios.
- Locate all of the microcomputers being used at headquarters' offices and describe how they are being used.

A second type of examination is for the auditors to determine the auditee's level of "compliance" with established policies, plans, procedures, laws, and regulations. A few examples of compliance objectives include:

- Determine whether the company's London office is complying with British labor laws.
- Investigate whether finished-goods inventory meets company quality-control standards.
- Examine whether the purchasing department is complying with policies relating to receiving bids from approved vendors prior to purchase.

Auditors also are called upon to evaluate auditees' operations. While every audit may not require an evaluation, most do call for some type of auditor judgment relating to quality. Even when a stated audit objective does not specifically call for an evaluation, there is usually an implied evaluation objective.

As an extension of one of the examples, after the auditors identify all of the microcomputers at headquarters and learn how they are being used, they probably will evaluate several aspects of their findings — perhaps the method of purchase, the efficiency and effectiveness of microcomputer use, and the preparation of employees in the use of these small computers.

As another example, once the auditors determine the purchasing department's level of compliance regarding policies on receiving bids from approved vendors, the auditors will evaluate the quality of performance. The auditors also may evaluate the appropriateness of the policies governing those procedures.

Objectives may be stated broadly or narrowly, depending upon the scope of audit work. Regardless of how broad or narrow an audit objective is, it should relate directly to organizational risk. For example, the audit objective to determine whether finished-goods inventory meets company quality-control standards relates directly to the company's ability to accomplish established sales and revenue goals.

Further, a combination of review, compliance, and evaluation objectives may be established for any one audit.

The decision to limit the objectives of an audit affects the number of audit hours that are to be allocated to the audit work. A review, for example, takes fewer audit hours than performing both a review and tests of compliance. When auditors decide to limit their audit work, they also need to reassess which additional activities may be included in the audit plan. Narrower audits free up additional audit hours that may be applied to other activities.

It is important that audit objectives are committed in writing. The discipline of writing down audit objectives helps formulate a clearer understanding of what needs to be done; it facilitates executive review and satisfies documentation requirements for the audit.

Scope

Audit scope identifies what the auditors are examining and evaluating. Notice in the examples shown for audit objectives that each objective was to examine or evaluate something. The "something" implies the scope of the audit work to be performed.

The key words in Standard 300 pertaining to scope are *adequacy, effectiveness, system of internal control,* and *quality of performance.* Stating these a little differently, the scope of examination might include the following:

- The adequacy of the organization's system of internal control.
- The effectiveness of the organization's system of internal control.
- The quality of performance in carrying out assigned responsibilities.

According to *Professional Standards Bulletin 82-2,* "adequacy" refers to the design of the internal control system. Auditors are called upon to examine and evaluate the design of systems which have been established by management. The design refers to how the internal control system is supposed to operate. The auditor's primary concern is whether the design includes adequate controls for the prevention, detection, and correction of "material errors and irregularities and to assure that the organization's objectives and goals will be met."

Professional Standards Bulletin 82-3 indicates that the "effectiveness" of the internal control system refers to the "degree of compliance with key control procedures . . . . An effective system is one which, in the auditor's opinion, is functioning in accordance with management's intentions."

Obviously, some systems may be designed well, but the organization may not be following the designed system. On the other hand, some systems may not be designed very well, but employees compensate for the inadequate design to bring about an adequate control environment.

Professional Standards Bulletin 81-2 says that not only should internal auditors evaluate whether the organization's system of internal controls is functioning as intended, but also, to evaluate effectiveness, internal auditors should "determine whether individual controls taken together provide the necessary level of control." This determination is as much a design question as it is one of effective performance. The close association between design and performance of the internal control system is apparent in this bulletin.

The "quality of performance," according to *Professional Standards Bulletin 81-5,* refers to how well management is accomplishing established objectives and goals. Auditors frequently assist management by providing information relating to the accomplishment of goals and objectives by individual entities within an organization. Of particular interest in many cases is whether the various subunits of an organization are working together to accomplish the overall objectives and goals of the organization.

In determining the scope of an audit, auditors refer to the primary objectives of internal control systems, as stated in Guideline 300.05:

1. Ensure the reliability and integrity of information.
2. Promote compliance with policies, plans, procedures, laws, and regulations.
3. Ensure the safeguarding of assets.
4. Promote the economical and efficient use of resources.
5. Ensure the accomplishment of established objectives and goals for operations or programs.

Study the following table that outlines the scope of audits examining each of the five control objectives:

CONTROL OBJECTIVE	NATURE OF EXAMINATION
Reliability and Integrity of Information	*To Be Examined:* financial and operating records and reports and controls over recordkeeping and reporting. *Nature of Examination:* reviews, compliance tests, and evaluation of the organization's system of internal control over recordkeeping and reporting.
Compliance with Policies, Plans, Procedures, Laws, and Regulations	*To Be Examined:* control systems established to ensure compliance; the policies, etc., themselves. *Nature of Examination:* review of control system; tests of compliance with policies, plans, procedures, laws, and regulations; evaluation of controls.[1]
Safeguarding Assets	*To Be Examined:* control systems over assets; assets themselves. *Nature of Examination:* review the control and security systems and the existence of assets; compliance tests on controls; evaluation of controls.
Economical and Efficient Use of Resources	*To Be Examined:* operating and performance standards; auditee's understanding of operating and performance standards; operating results; and control measures for detecting, correcting, and communicating deviations from standards. *Nature of Examination:* review of operating standards and corrective measures; compliance tests on how well auditee meets standards and how well corrective measures are followed; and evaluation of auditee's operations with special attention to underutilized facilities, nonproductive work, procedures that are not cost justified, and either over- or understaffing.
Accomplishment of Established Objectives and Goals	*To Be Examined:* auditee's objectives and goals; auditee's operating results. *Nature of Examination:* review of objectives, goals, and operating results, including (1) that objectives and goals have been established and (2) that they conform to organizational objectives and goals; determination of whether the auditee is achieving the established objectives and goals; evaluation of the performance review system, including evaluation of the objectives and the goals as effective control and performance measures.

[1]*Professional Standards Bulletin 81-4* qualifies the nature of the internal auditor's examination of compliance with laws and regulations. According to this bulletin, "Internal auditors are not responsible for ensuring compliance with . . . laws and regulations. Management is responsible for designing and establishing systems for this purpose." Internal auditors determine whether such systems have been established. Inquiries of the organization's legal counsel may be necessary to determine whether all applicable laws and regulations have been considered by management in establishing the necessary systems.

Most auditors attempt to examine all five control objectives, at least to some degree. There are occasions, however, when auditors narrow their scope for particular audits. *Professional Standards Bulletin 82-16* states that "the director of internal auditing should select the internal control objectives which are most suitable for the purpose and scope of the audit activity and the area under review." The director has two choices. First, he or she can limit the scope of an audit to fewer than the five control objectives. Second, he or she can choose to do a less comprehensive examination of the objectives. These more limited examinations usually occur for special audits, where particular questions have come to the auditors' attention, or when the auditors' time is limited. Otherwise, for regularly scheduled audits of a more general nature, all five control objectives are included in the audit scope.

An Example   Suppose auditors for Timberland Industries, Inc. (introduced in Chapter 6) were planning audits of the lumber shipping department, lumber accounts receivable, and the lumber cost accounting function. After some consideration, the auditors decide upon the following objectives and scope for each of the three audits.

Lumber Shipping Department. Because the lumber shipping department currently represents one of the two riskiest activities in Timberland Industries, the auditors will review operations and internal control, test compliance with established controls, and evaluate the control system.

An objectives and scope statement for this audit might be formulated as follows:

> Review shipping department operations and internal controls, test compliance with established controls, and evaluate the internal control system.

Lumber Accounts Receivable. Basic internal controls for accounts receivable are generally well understood and accepted in the business world. Consequently, internal auditors will review operations and ascertain whether controls have been adopted. Further, the auditors will test the department's compliance with established controls. If standard controls have been adopted, there probably will be little need for an evaluation of the controls themselves.

An objectives and scope statement for lumber accounts receivable might be as follows:

1. Review the lumber division's policies and procedures for managing and accounting for accounts receivable.
2. Test compliance with generally accepted controls as well as established policies and procedures over receivables.
3. Evaluate the effectiveness of the internal control system over accounts receivable and the quality of performance in the management of accounts receivable.

Lumber Cost Accounting. The relatively low risk associated with the cost accounting function likely would lead to an audit that is limited to review procedures only, unless the auditors discovered evidence suggesting higher levels of risk that would justify further testing.

An objectives and scope statement for this audit might be written as follows:

> Review the policies, procedures, accounting system, and reporting for cost accounting information at the lumber division. Evaluate the reliability and the integrity of cost accounting information provided to management.

Reviewing Audit Files and Other Materials

Before specific work on any audit is either planned or conducted, auditors should gather the appropriate background materials. Part of this work is accomplished by selecting auditees, but more in-depth review almost always is required. Many times, the review of background material is performed even before establishing the objectives and scope of the audit.

By reviewing the audit files that relate to an auditee, the auditors can acquaint themselves with the nature of operations and any special concerns that may arise from previous audits. There are two types of files which auditors may review — (1) permanent files and (2) files from previous audits.

Permanent files provide basic information about auditees, including organization charts, descriptions of operations, information on management personnel, articles published about the auditee or its employees in company publications or the news media, periodic financial reports, and budgets. These files are updated as necessary to remain current. This information provides valuable background material for auditors before they begin an audit. Of course, auditors who have not participated in previous audits of a particular auditee will rely more upon these materials than auditors who have participated.

Files from previous audits include descriptions of previous audit work. This information includes auditor working papers, previous audit reports, and the auditee's response to audit findings and recommendations. This information from previous audits helps the auditors stay alert to any continuing problems or concerns related to previous findings and recommendations, and to understand the nature of previous audit work. It also prepares the auditors for unusual problems they may encounter on an audit, such as unusual personality characteristics of auditee management or peculiar record-keeping procedures.

Selecting the Audit Team and Other Audit Resources

In Chapter 5 we discussed the make-up of audit teams. Such teams include the team leader, lead auditor or auditor-in-charge (who is responsible for managing the on-site work and for preparing the audit report), and the audit staff, which usually includes one or more additional auditors to help conduct the audit and prepare the report. The team leader usually is an audit manager, supervisor, or senior, depending upon the size and complexity of the audit. The audit staff usually comprises junior and senior staff members. On larger, more complex audits, supervisors also may serve as staff. An audit director bears the overall responsibility for the audit, but he or she usually remains at the auditors' offices. Exceptions might be special conferences with auditee management and perhaps an occasional visit to the audit site, unless the audit is unusually complex or highly sensitive, in which case the director may be more involved.

More important than the particular ranks of the auditors assigned to conduct an audit are the requisite skills necessary to complete the work satisfactorily. Guideline 220.02 states that auditors should possess the necessary knowledge and skills to meet audit responsibilities. Such knowledge and skills include auditing, accounting, economics, finance, statistics, electronic data processing, engineering, taxation, management, and law.

When the auditors themselves do not possess the adequate knowledge and skills in the required areas, this guideline says consultants should be used. Often, the "consultants" may come from within the organization, but from another department or division. The advantage of using internal consultants is that they already are familiar with the organization. Also, there is less risk of sensitive information being communicated outside.

Different audits require different kinds of knowledge and skills, and audit teams reflect these differing needs. For example, an audit of accounts receivable typically requires auditing, accounting, EDP, and sometimes legal expertise. An audit of corporate investments would require knowledge of finance, investment portfolio management, economics, and taxation in addition to basic auditing and accounting skills. When selecting audit teams, the internal auditing department's management must be alert to these differing needs.

Another important consideration when selecting an audit team is the required *audit hours.* The auditee selection process specified an estimated number of audit man-hours required to complete the audit. These hours must be allocated so that the proper coverage is given to each area of audit interest. More audits today require *computer support,* and *travel funds* also may be required for auditors. Planning for the necessary resources to conduct an audit, then, typically includes the team of auditors (including the necessary consultants), the allocation of audit hours, computer support, and travel funds.

Preparing a Preliminary Audit Program

The audit program is the written plan for conducting an audit. The program usually is prepared by the audit team leader and often is approved by the audit executive assigned to the job — typically the audit director. In general, it identifies the objectives and scope of the audit and the procedures to be employed. When the audit has been completed, the program also serves as a record of what was done.

Three approaches traditionally have been taken in the development of audit programs:

1. Writing the program during the preparation stage of the audit.
2. Writing the program as the audit progresses.
3. Using standard audit programs for specific operations.

Even when standard programs are used, auditors generally modify them to suit a specific application. While standard programs offer valuable guidance in considering generalized situations, such programs usually only provide auditors with general guidance for a specific application. Consequently, we will elaborate only upon the first two approaches to program preparation.

Auditors generally write their audit programs after a preliminary survey reveals the activities that are to receive attention. Programs written at this time typically contain all of the audit procedures that are to be employed from the beginning of the audit work to the end. As the audit progresses, the lead auditor may determine that some procedures are not necessary or should be modified. At such times, notes are written on the program to indicate any change in the audit plans.

When experienced auditors are directly involved and circumstances preclude the performance of an adequate initial survey or some similar preparation, the development and writing of the audit program can be done as the audit takes place. This might be done when an audit is expected to be relatively simple or routine and, again, when experienced auditors are involved. It might also be done in a situation where advance notice and preparation is not desirable or possible, and the guiding objectives are "surprise" or investigatory in nature.

For example, management might ask the auditors to look into certain operations en route to or from another location *if* they have time or if certain circumstances exist. In instances such as these, an experienced auditor can assess the operational environment relatively quickly upon arrival, and "audit sense" acts as the directive influence. The audit program, then, is written as the audit approach unfolds.

A combination of these two approaches for developing audit programs is common in practice. A preliminary audit program is developed during the audit preparation; an initial survey is conducted and the control objectives are outlined; detailed tests are developed to evaluate the effectiveness of existing controls.

A preliminary audit program usually includes the following sections:

1. Audit preparation.
2. The initial survey.
3. A description and analysis of the auditee's internal controls.
4. Expanded audit tests. Audit tests can be developed only after the auditors have outlined the control objectives and determined what processes and actions have been designed into operating activities to achieve the control objectives. Consequently, a convenient time to determine detailed audit tests is upon completion of the review of internal controls.
5. Instructions concerning the audit report.
6. Wrap-up procedures.

Program Preparation Process

The audit team leader generally is responsible for preparing the audit program. Others may assist, and even prepare some subsections, but the team leader usually bears the responsibility for the overall compilation even in these cases.

Actual preparation requires a determination of what audit evidence is required, what the most appropriate sources of the evidence are, and what procedures are best to collect and analyze the evidence. The team leader also determines at what step in the audit process each procedure should be performed.

The program then is written down in a single document and kept by the team leader with the audit working papers. Individual auditors usually are given copies of the sections of the audit program for which they are to do the audit work.

Sources of Audit Information

Although there are many possible sources of information, they fall into a relatively few general categories, as discussed in Chapter 4 on evidence. Exhibit 7-1 outlines some general sources of audit evidence and some specific examples of each type. The exhibit offers insight into the variety and number of possible sources of information. It also provides some general categories by which to classify the various sources.

Audit Procedures

Audit procedures are what auditors *do* to gather audit evidence. Exhibit 7-2 provides a list of various procedures included in audit programs. The terms themselves may be familiar, but because many of them have specific meanings within the auditing context, we have included brief descriptions of typical procedures and an example of an audit program statement using each term. The list is not exhaustive. It is, however, representative of typical terminology used in audit programs.

The previous discussion outlines the general nature of audit programs. Subsequent chapters outline and illustrate specific program applications.

Program Format

Audit programs may be prepared in many different formats. Exhibit 7-3 illustrates a format that is consistent with the audit process we have described. The program identifies the auditee and the date of the audit. It identifies the document as an audit program and shows the approval by audit management, with the associated date of approval.

Columns are provided for the audit procedures to be performed during the steps of the audit, for space to designate the auditor assigned to the different procedures, for dates when each procedure is completed, and for cross-references to working papers that are associated with the different audit procedures. The final column provides space for comments related to different audit steps and procedures. For example, suppose the lead auditor decided to skip a procedure for some reason or to switch assignments among staff members. Notes of such changes would be entered in this "comments" column.

Exhibit 7-1
Sources of Audit Evidence

GENERAL SOURCE	EXAMPLES OF SPECIFIC SOURCES
Auditee's managerial personnel	Division Manager Production Supervisor Financial Vice President
Auditee's nonmanagement personnel	Shipping Clerk Sales personnel Design Engineer
Personnel outside the auditee's organization	Supervisor of the manager responsible for the operations being audited Clerk receiving documents prepared by personnel in the unit being audited Warehouse clerk sending materials to the auditee
Outside parties	Customers Suppliers or vendors Government regulators Bankers or creditors
Operating documents:	
Prepared by the auditee	Production schedules Performance reports Vouchers, sales slips, etc.
Prepared within the organization but not by the auditee	Budgets, transfer documents, and performance reports
Prepared outside the organization	Invoices Bills of lading Shipping schedules Letters of inquiry
Documented policies, standards, and procedures	Policy manuals and production flowcharts Generally accepted accounting procedures Internal accounting guidelines
Auditee's activities and transactions	Machine maintenance operations Production operations Preparation of reports Background checks on new applicants Processing of accounts receivable
Legal documents	Contracts Corporate charter Notarized documents Bylaws

Exhibit 7-2
Audit Procedures

PROCEDURE	DESCRIPTION OF ACTIVITIES	EXAMPLE OF AUDIT PROGRAM STATEMENT
Describe	Flowcharts, graphs, tables, and narrative outlines of particular operations, procedures, resources, etc.	Describe the internal controls for project approval.
Compare	Identify similar and dissimilar characteristics of two or more information sources relating to a particular audit objective.	Compare documented procedures with observed procedures.
Calculate, compute, and recompute	Mathematical computations; recomputations involve checking figures already derived by others to verify their accuracy.	Calculate direct and overhead costs of monthly production.
Examine	Inspect, investigate, or scrutinize the physical audit evidence such as materials, facilities, and documents.	Examine suppliers' contracts.
Observe	Watch auditee's activities and procedures in operation.	Observe customer checkouts at stores.
Walk-through	Perform certain procedures in a prescribed, step-by-step manner.	Walk through data-input procedures.
	Trace specific operations or transactions step by step through documentation, determining if effective control measures are built into the system and if the controls are being documented.	Walk through two credit reports.
Tour	Personally survey the auditee's facilities and operations on site.	Tour warehouse facilities.
Count	Enumerate.	Count the raw materials, work-in-process, and finished-goods inventories.
Foot	Add figures contained in documents in order to compare the document totals with those calculated by the auditor.	Foot monthly sales totals.
Confirm	Correspond with outside parties to verify information documented by the auditee.	Confirm investment-portfolio balances.

Reconcile	Show mathematically, with supporting documentation, the changes in beginning and ending totals.	Reconcile monthly bank balances.
	Identify and explain the reasons for differences between related amounts.	Reconcile differences in departmental and central office totals.
Scan	Quickly observe, being alert for any unusual or suspicious evidence.	Scan minutes of executive committee's meetings for possible improprieties in project selection.
Trace	Proceed through accounting records and track the documentation of specific transactions.	Trace daily inventory issuances to account balances in the general ledger.
Vouch	Examine the underlying written evidence to support final reported amounts.	Vouch payments to the company's independent contractors.
Read	Make a detailed examination of documents.	Read annual employee performance reviews done by divisional management.
Analyze	Show how a single, aggregated figure may be broken down into several components.	Analyze inventory totals and identify subtotals by product line and location.
	Make calculations to show trends and interrelationships among figures.	Analyze performance efficiency in terms of units completed per hour in each of the last 12 months.
Inquire, ask, and request	Question.	Inquire of management concerning the existence of stock option or management-bonus plans.
Verify and determine	Make sure that particular activities, amounts, procedures, etc., are as they are represented to be.	Verify that maintenance procedures are being performed.
Test and sample	Examine a sample in order to draw conclusions about a larger population.	Test vouchers for authorized signatures.
Evaluate	Judge the quality.	Evaluate internal control procedures for nightly deposits.
Prepare	Put into writing.	Prepare a schedule of weekly production costs for March.

Exhibit 7-3
Modern Industries, Inc. Audit Program

MODERN INDUSTRIES, INC.
AUDIT OF CASH DISBURSEMENTS — 1986
AUDIT PROGRAM

Approval_____ Date _____

Audit Steps and Procedures	Assigned Auditor	Date Completed	Working Paper Ref.	Comments
AUDIT PREPARATION				
Objective: become generally familiar with auditee's operations, background, and possible concerns.				
Procedures:				
(1) Review permanent file materials and previous audit reports.				
(2) Interview vice president of finance at headquarters to identify possible concerns and audit emphasis.				
INITIAL SURVEY				
Objective: identify areas of current, critical risk.				
Procedures:				
(1) Conduct opening conference.				
(2) Administer and analyze internal control questionnaire.				
(3) Examine disbursement files for location, organization, and order.				
(4) Perform analytical review.				
Objective: update permanent file materials.				
Procedures:				
(1) Review and compare current information with permanent file material.				
(2) Update permanent file.				

Informing the Auditee That an Audit Is to Be Performed

Before an audit begins, auditors should inform the auditee that an audit is to take place, when it will begin, and what its purposes are. The auditors should provide a list of schedules and documents and other information that the auditee should have available for the audit. The list may identify employees that the auditors expect to interview. The auditors also will inform the auditee's executive management and the audit committee about the timing and purposes of the audit.

This communication is both a matter of courtesy and good audit practice. Auditors should not interfere with the organization's operations. They should plan and conduct their audits around the organization's operations so that routines can proceed as normally as possible. This awareness permits the auditee to plan for the audit, gather the required documents, prepare necessary schedules, and notify those employees who will be most affected by the audit.

For example, the auditee, given the choice, might postpone a special project that requires management's total concentration and the employees' effort until after the audit is finished. There are occasions when the auditee might even request that an audit be postponed until after some planned operation has been completed because of the interruption an audit would have on that operation. In these cases, the auditors might either postpone the audit or concentrate their efforts on the parts of the audit that are the least likely to interfere with operations while the special work is being performed.

If the auditors sense that the auditee is merely trying to avoid being audited, however, the auditors may decide to conduct the audit anyway. In these cases, the auditors would inform the auditee that the audit will take place. As a matter of courtesy, they probably would get the approval of the auditee's managers, although it may not be necessary to have that approval. These cases are unusual, however, and auditors typically are able to coordinate their activities with the auditee so that both the audit and the auditee's operations can proceed smoothly.

At times, auditors conclude that a surprise audit is necessary for some reason. In these cases, they would not give the auditee prior notification, although top management and the audit committee would probably be informed.

In summary, the key aspects of preliminary communication are:

1. The auditors inform the auditee.
2. The auditors inform the auditee's superiors and the audit committee.

3. The auditee assembles any required information and plans operations so that the audit can proceed as scheduled.

Auditors typically use either letters or interoffice memoranda for this preliminary communication. In most cases the auditors also will either telephone or personally visit with the auditee's management to coordinate these preliminary activities. Exhibit 7-4 illustrates a typical interoffice memorandum informing an auditee of an upcoming audit.

When auditees actively resist audits, auditors sometimes either state a company's policy requiring auditees to cooperate, or receive a written statement directly from top management giving authorization for an audit. Fortunately, auditors seldom need to resort to this strategy, although it usually is available when needed.

Determining How, When, and to Whom Audit Results Will Be Communicated

Because all audit work proceeds toward the preparation of a report, internal auditors begin planning for the report from the beginning of the assignment. Obviously, it is impossible to know the detailed information that will be included in the final report. The auditors know enough, however, from the general nature of the risks involved, the audit objectives and scope, the hierarchy of management interested in the audit, and relevant previous audit results to establish some parameters for the report.

Almost all audits require both a presentation of audit results and a written report. As the auditors plan the audit, several considerations bear upon how to plan this communication. Where should the presentation be made? Who should be there? Should audiovisual devices be used? If so, how? How long should the presentation last? Will interim presentations be necessary to report significant findings before the final report?

Similar questions are relevant to the written report. How should the report be delivered? Some highly sensitive reports require special handling. To whom should the report be addressed, and who should receive copies? How long is the report likely to be? Will graphic illustrations be helpful? Will interim reports be helpful? What is the target date for issuing the audit report?

Obtaining Approval to Do the Audit

Approval for audit work can be given in essentially three ways. First, after the auditors complete the audit schedule for a particular budget period, the audit committee generally reviews the schedule and approves the audits for the period all at once. In those organizations where the internal auditors report to executive management, the approval of the audit schedule would be given by that level of management and then reported to the audit committee or the board of directors.

Exhibit 7-4
Audit Notification

DATE: October 3, 1986

TO: Allen Montgomery, Superintendent, Timber Purchasing, Lumber
                 Division

FROM: J. Mayer Cornett, Director, Corporate Auditing

SUBJECT: Scheduled Audit to Begin First Week of November

Michael Anderson, my assistant, and I are planning an audit of the Timber Purchasing Section. An opening conference will be conducted on November 7 at 9:00 a.m. in your offices, as per our telephone conversation yesterday afternoon. The purposes of our audit are to review the section's operations and system of internal controls; test compliance with established policies, procedures, standards, and State land-management regulations; and evaluate the adequacy and effectiveness of controls. In performing the audit, we expect to test the following aspects of timber-purchasing operations:

1. The reliability and integrity of accounting and timber management information.
2. Compliance with established policies, plans, procedures, etc.
3. Safeguarding the company's timber and monetary assets.
4. The economical and efficient use of the company's resources.
5. The accomplishment of established objectives and goals.

We would appreciate your willingness to help facilitate this audit by having available the following schedules, documents, and records upon our arrival:

1. All of Timberland's leases, deeds, and harvesting contracts.
2. A list of all timber harvested during the last 12 months that is itemized by the number of board-feet from each land sector, the distribution of harvests between lumber and paper operations, and sectors under restricted harvesting programs.
3. A schedule of reforestation efforts by land sector indicating the number of acres affected, the number of trees planted, other land-management programs, and estimated number of board-feet to be produced from reforestation efforts. Also, a breakdown of the estimated future board-feet into expected growth and harvesting periods.
4. A schedule of all harvesting costs, including any unexpected costs, incurred during the last two years.
5. A schedule of planned harvesting activities over the next five years indicating the sectors, expected board-feet, and expected distribution of the timber.
6. A schedule of activities, including expected costs, to support the harvesting efforts (such as clearing, road building, investment in equipment, etc.).
7. Original documents supporting information regarding section activities: cutting orders, transportation routing slips, sector photographs and inventory documentation, seedling purchase orders and receiving slips, labor time cards and assignment schedules, road-building permits, and monthly performance and cost reports.
8. Cutting selection guidelines and procedures.
9. Policies and procedures outlining security of timber properties.

In addition to preparing these materials prior to our arrival, we hope that other documents, reports, and schedules kept in your section will be open to our examination.

We would like to schedule interviews with you; your assistant, Wally Johnston; each of the sector managers; your security chief, Clancy Reynolds; and your secretary, Jewel Masters. Please notify these individuals that we will be scheduling one-hour interviews with each of them. We also will be touring each of the land sectors by car. We hope to schedule these visits at convenient times when a member of your staff can escort us to the different sectors. If necessary, you can provide us some alternative times when we meet on November 7. The final request we have is for either you or Mr. Johnston to come with us in the company's plane to fly over and examine the timber properties.

We look forward to doing this work with the members of your section. We expect to complete our work by November 21 and to have a finished audit report for your review by December 1. A final report will be completed by December 15. This final report will be distributed to you, Harold Williams (Production Manager), and Claude Smythe (Vice President, Lumber Operations). We shall keep a copy of the report, and an executive summary will be sent to Timberland's Corporate Audit Committee. If you have any questions about the upcoming audit work, please call.

J. Mayer Cornett, Director
Corporate Auditing

cc: Harold Williams, Production Manager
     Claude Smythe, Vice President, Lumber Operations
     Gerald Oakley, Chairman, Corporate Audit Committee

The second type of approval for audit work may be given for individual audits by either management or the board, depending on to whom the auditors report. This approval for individual audits usually is required when the auditors interrupt the previously-approved schedule to conduct a special audit or where general approval for an entire schedule is not given at one time. Such approval for individual audits is especially important where wrongdoing is suspected and outside law enforcement officers may be involved, when highly sensitive company operations or documents will be reviewed, or when operations will be significantly interrupted by the audit.

The third type of approval for audit work is given within the internal auditing department itself. The director of auditing usually approves each audit before it begins. He or she reviews the preparatory work for the audit and pays particular attention to the objectives and scope of the audit, the selection of the audit team, the allocation of estimated audit hours, and the preliminary audit program.

Recall that one of the biggest dangers for the internal auditing function is the loss of its independence. Should the board or executive management unduly interfere with the auditor's decisions regarding what audits to conduct, there is the danger that the auditors will lose the necessary independence to perform their duties effectively. In the best auditing organizations the approval given by management and/or the board is more in the form of a review for information purposes rather than giving permission.

Where management or the board disagrees with the selection of auditees, it may try to persuade the auditors to change the schedule somewhat. But when either management or the board attempts to keep auditors from conducting particular audits, the auditors then should interpret these attempts as danger signals and press forward in conducting those specific audits. The distinction should be whether management or the board might have different priorities than the auditors, or when management or the board is attempting to hide something. Different priorities may cause the auditors to make changes in the schedule. Attempts to hide information or operations lead to attempts to block the auditor's efforts. Auditors must resist such attempts.

Conclusion

Like most other activities, good preparation makes the rest of the work easier. Most internal auditors can testify to difficulties that arise on those audits when, for some reason, adequate preparation was not made. Such audits generally take longer than expected, they are more difficult to coordinate with the auditee, there usually is unnecessary slack time among the audit staff, and there is a higher likelihood of conflict with the auditee. On the other hand, good preparation can help avoid such problems and actually promote higher quality work in fewer total hours.

QUESTIONS

1. The chapter identifies six preparatory activities to an audit. This list is somewhat different than that given in the *Standards for the Professional Practice of Internal Auditing.* Compare and contrast these two lists.
2. Identify and discuss briefly three objectives for an audit.
3. How are these three objectives related?
4. How does the *Standards* describe the scope (in general terms) of an internal audit?
5. What are the five objectives of internal control systems?
6. What are the two types of files that auditors review in preparation for an audit? What are the contents of each file?
7. What types of audit resources are assigned to different audits? Discuss each type briefly.
8. The chapter identifies two general approaches to writing audit programs. It also advocates a combination of the two approaches. Identify and discuss each of the two approaches and the recommended combination.
9. What are the general categories of sources for audit information? Give an example of each category.
10. List the types of audit procedures used in audit programs. Give an example of each type.
11. Outline the key aspects of the preliminary communication for an audit.
12. How do internal auditors begin planning for the final report at the preparatory stage of an audit? Why?
13. What three types of audit approval are given for audits? Discuss each briefly.

EXERCISES

E-1

The internal auditors for Pinewood National Bank were planning an audit of the bank's lending policies and procedures. The auditors were especially interested in the quality of the bank's loan portfolio and the effect that controls over the lending process had on the quality of the portfolio.

Required:

a. Identify at least three *review* audit procedures for this audit.
b. Identify at least two *tests of compliance* that probably would be required for this audit.
c. Identify at least two *evaluation* procedures that you think would be required for this audit.

E-2

Required:

a. What performance audit objective might be included in the audit of the Pinewood National Bank's loan portfolio described in E-1 above?
b. Identify at least one procedure that you think would help determine the level of performance of the bank's loan portfolio. What audit evidence would be required to perform that procedure?

E-3

For the Pinewood National Bank audit (described in E-1 and E-2), explain how you think the scope of the audit might include (1) each of the five internal control objectives and (2) the nature of the examination, as specifically as you can, so that the auditors are *examining* and *evaluating* the *adequacy* and *effectiveness* of the bank's internal control over its loan portfolio.

E-4

Binky Collins is the lead auditor on an assignment to examine the internal controls over a large agricultural firm's grain inventories being transported to, held by, and distributed from cooperative facilities in the Panhandle of Texas and in Nebraska. Mr. Collins called the firm's home offices in Columbus for some additional information needed in preparing part of the audit program. Mr. Collins wanted to know the following:

1. Specific services to be provided by the co-op in the handling and marketing of the grain. Mr. Collins says that the co-op's management has a copy of a 1976 contract between the firm and the co-op, but he understands some amendments were made to the contract in 1981.
2. A schedule prepared for the previous year's audit that shows the distribution of grain to various buyers. Mr. Collins' figures and those of the co-op conflict, and he feels that last year's audit papers may help resolve the issue.
3. Was the firm's management aware of a change in the management structure of the co-op? He especially wanted some information about the co-op's new vice president in charge of marketing and distribution.

Required:

For each of the three items requested by Mr. Collins, determine whether it might be found in the permanent files, the audit files, or neither. If neither, where would you suspect the information might be found?

E-5

A real estate development company was building an industrial park near Oklahoma City. An audit team was assigned to examine and evaluate the internal controls for the construction and development of that complex. The internal auditors assigned to the audit were:

Candy Wharton — BBA in accounting, MBA with six years of internal auditing experience, Certified Internal Auditor.

Alan Clarkson — BS in civil engineering, LLB, retired from a law firm that specializes in real estate, auditing part-time to get out of the house once in a while, he says.

Diane Lamar — BS in computer science, new graduate, preparing for CIA exam.

The following is a list of procedures to be performed on the audit:

1. Describe the internal controls for the development company's MIS and accounting system, which will be computerized and is being designed specifically for the development and operation of the industrial park.
2. Examine the builder's documentation for construction specifications and test compliance with these specifications.
3. Prepare a schedule of the cost variances in construction so far and evaluate the materiality of these variances individually and in the aggregate.
4. Examine and test the materials inventories at the site and compare your estimated totals, for reasonableness, with totals in the accounting records.
5. Calculate the estimated percentage of completion on the various sectors of the building project. Compare your estimates with the builder's master building schedule.
6. Vouch a sample of materials purchases and subcontracted costs-to-date on the project.
7. Verify the builder's payroll expenditures to date and test, with observation, at least one distribution of payroll checks.
8. Examine the county records specifying the property boundaries and the builder's survey record. Scan the county records for restrictions and covenants affecting the property.

Required:
a. How would you allocate the above procedures among the three auditors?
b. What sources of information would help the auditors perform each of the eight audit procedures? Include both the general classification of evidence and the specific source. Define your selections based on the quality of your sources and the persuasiveness of the evidence.

E-6
Following are 10 audit procedures taken from several audit programs:

1. Observe customers purchasing merchandise at counters throughout the store, being alert for indications of impoliteness on the part of store employees and for details related to courtesy in the treatment of customers.
2. Examine last year's audit findings and list items needing follow-up in this year's audit.
3. Count the vehicles in the motor pool, being sure to account for all of those in the lot, the maintenance shop, and those checked out to company employees. Compare this inventory count to accounting records.
4. Foot the monthly production records and check their accuracy.
5. Tour plant facilities, observing operations and scanning for unusual or unproductive activities.
6. Prepare flowcharts that describe operations and identify key control points.
7. Vouch a statistical sample of divisional disbursements.
8. Evaluate the adequacy of the internal control system.
9. Evaluate the effectiveness of the internal control system.
10. Request the original production documents to support the department's monthly report totals.

Required:

Identify the audit procedures that are most likely to be included in the review phase of an audit, the compliance testing phase, and the evaluation phase. You may find that some of the procedures could be included in more than one of the phases. If so, state which phases and explain why.

E-7

Phil Larsen, the director of auditing for Graham Manufacturing Enterprises, sent the following letter to Kevin MacGregor, manager of the hydraulics division:

October 16, 1986

Mr. Kevin MacGregor, Manager
Hydraulics Division
Graham Manufacturing Enterprises
5678 Park Boulevard
Ogden, Utah 45678

Dear Mr. MacGregor:

The corporate audit department is scheduling an audit of the hydraulics design department. The audit team is scheduled to arrive in Ogden on October 25, at which time they have been instructed to contact you to coordinate their work. The auditors are scheduled to begin another engagement on November 8 in Calgary, so your assistance and cooperation would be greatly appreciated.

I am sorry for the delay in getting this letter to you, but our work here has stacked up so much that we are almost a month behind. Earlier this year we discussed beginning the audit in July. I am sorry I was not able to get back to you before now.

As the audit team leader, I am sending Goober Watkins, whom you met in Los Angeles last year at our annual company party. As you know, he has a great sense of humor and will be great to work with on the audit. If I can be of any further help, please let me know. My greetings to your family.

Sincerely,

Phil

Phil Larsen
Director of Auditing

Required:

a. Critique the letter to Mr. MacGregor in terms of its content and style. Evaluate the letter in terms of its effectiveness as a communication device for audit preparation.
b. What suggestions would you make to improve the letter?

PROBLEMS

P-1

The internal auditors for Longhorn Foods Corporation had scheduled an audit of one of the company farms in Southern California and also an audit of a livestock feedlot that was recently purchased by the company and is located near the farm. The purpose of these audits was to review the operating controls in effect at each location.

Required:

a. List the steps in preparation for this audit that you think would be necessary.

b. Discuss how each of the steps might be performed in this case. For example, what kind of preliminary communication would be necessary, who would receive it, and what messages should be contained in the communication?

P-2

The internal auditors for a large electronics manufacturing corporation were planning an audit of the central purchasing department. More specifically, the auditors intended to study the department's approved vendor listings to: (1) determine whether the approved vendors were being used; (2) evaluate the individual vendors approved for the listings in terms of availability of desired products, quality of products, prices, and timeliness of delivery; (3) examine any potential conflicts of interest among corporate employees and approved vendors; and (4) evaluate how vendors are selected from the listings for individual orders when more than one approved vendor is listed.

The auditors have decided to interview the purchasing director, his assistant, and two purchasing clerks. The auditors also will examine a statistical sample of purchase orders from the past three years and the first six months of this year. They plan to examine the approved listings and catalogues from the last four years for each of the approved vendors. Questionnaires also will be distributed among other departments that receive goods through the purchasing department. The auditor plans to begin the audit on January 8, 1986. Two auditors — Mary Lou Cantwell and Lewis Cary — have been assigned to do the work, which is estimated to take seven days on-site. The audit report will be distributed to Bill McFinney, vice president of operations; Carl Gordon, director of central purchasing; and the corporate audit committee.

Required:

Assuming the audit already has been prearranged by telephone with Mr. Gordon, draft an engagement letter or interoffice memorandum explaining the upcoming audit. Address your letter or memo to him with copies going to all others who will receive the audit report.

8   Preliminary Survey and Internal Control Review

After selecting the auditee and preparing for the audit in steps 1 and 2, the next steps are to perform a preliminary survey and a review of internal controls.

This chapter covers the following aspects of the preliminary survey:

- The opening conference.
- On-site tour.
- Study of documents.
- Written description of the auditee.
- Analytical reviews.

These procedures make up the preliminary survey and provide the auditors and the auditees with an introduction to the more detailed examination that will follow. The auditors must be careful, however, not to rely on the preliminary survey to compensate for inadequate prior preparation. Step 2 of the audit process (preparation for the audit) should, in fact, facilitate the preliminary survey and minimize the time required before actual audit work begins. In many respects, the preliminary survey is an extension of audit preparation. What distinguishes it from earlier preparation is that it is performed on site. These on-site procedures are important enough to the overall performance of the audit that we will consider them separately.

The second major section of the chapter is devoted to a review of the auditee's internal control system. The topics include:

- Description and analysis of internal controls.
- Preliminary evaluation of internal controls.
- Reassessment of auditee risk.

This initial review of internal controls is the first of what might be considered "the real audit work." It is the *review phase* described in the previous chapter.

Preliminary Survey

Preliminary surveys give auditors the opportunity to get some initial on-site information which can be extremely valuable in becoming familiar with current operations of the auditee and the controls to be audited. The auditors can review how best to approach the audit, consider possible new information that was not available during the audit preparation, and evaluate comments and suggestions by the auditee. Failure to perform an effective survey can cause inefficiencies when conducting audit work, and may cause the auditors to overlook important audit work that should be done.

In this section, we discuss each of the five types of survey activities.

The Opening Conference

The auditors should contact the auditee and schedule an opening conference as a kind of "kick-off" meeting prior to beginning the audit. The meeting usually includes the audit team and members of the auditee's management. The audit team leader usually conducts this meeting. When additional senior executives of the auditee are likely to attend, an audit manager or the audit director may be present as a matter of protocol, but even in these cases the audit team leader usually conducts the meeting.

The objectives of the opening conference are to:

1. Elicit a spirit of cooperation.
2. Convey information that will help the audit go well.
3. Obtain information needed for the audit.
4. Promote a feeling of credibility.

We will now examine the opening conference in terms of how these objectives can be realized.

Planning the Opening Conference — Preparing a Written Agenda. The agenda outlines the information that will be covered in the meeting. The information includes an explanation of the audit; i.e., the audit scope and the general purposes and nature of the audit, who will be conducting it, and approximately how long the work will last. It is important to allay any of the auditee's concerns regarding the coordination of the audit work with operations so the audit will interfere as little as possible with the auditee's work activities.

Internal auditors usually do not discuss specific audit procedures with the auditee. They may discuss what types of documents are to be reviewed, which employees will be interviewed, which operations will be observed, and perhaps some audit techniques. But if the auditors tell the auditee what specific audit procedures are to be employed, the auditee has an opportunity to manipulate the audit results.

Although the sequence of opening conferences may vary, a typical agenda might be outlined as follows:

1. Introduction of those present at the conference.
2. An outline of the audit assignment (scope, objectives, etc.).
3. Addressing any auditee concerns.
4. Coordination of the audit with auditee operations.
5. Discussion of the kinds of information needed during the audit and the extent of auditee assistance.
6. Timing and form of the audit report.

Regardless of which particular aspects of the engagement and the auditor's concerns are discussed during the conference, both the audit team and the auditee must understand what is required of them by the end of the meeting.

Establishing an Appropriate Conference Climate. The climate for an opening conference must foster a spirit of *professional courtesy*. It should be neither too informal nor too formal and stiff. If it is too informal and overly relaxed, the auditors may jeopardize their authority. If the meeting is too stiff and formal, there is a chance of alienation and the loss of auditee cooperation. By showing a spirit of professional courtesy, the auditors can establish their authority in a reasonably relaxed atmosphere of respect and cooperation. To achieve the desired atmosphere, the following things need to be considered:

1. Setting a specific time and place for the meeting.
2. Conducting it in a relatively quiet setting where interruptions can be avoided.
3. Distributing a written agenda at the start of the meeting.
4. Leading the conference in a confident but respectful and courteous manner.
5. Maintaining a relaxed tone of conversation.
6. Projecting an open and cooperative attitude.
7. Keeping the meeting within reasonable time limits to allow the business to be conducted efficiently, yet not allowing conversation to wander from the subject.

Of course, the auditors' dress and appearance must be professional and appropriate to the situation.

Building a Feeling of Credibility. Auditors gain credibility from being associated with the internal auditing profession, from their reporting line within the organization, and from their own demonstration of professionalism. There is little auditors can do in the opening conference itself to acquire additional credibility from the profession or the organization. But there is a great deal the auditors can do through their actions to either enhance or diminish their own credibility. Personal sources of credibility include appropriate dress and grooming, manners, composure, preparation, respect for the auditee and his or her ideas, and demonstrating competence without being overly technical.

In cases where auditees actively resist audits, it may be important for audit notification to come from a line officer who oversees the operation that is to be audited. In other cases the auditors might bring copies of organizational policies or letters from top management that set forth the auditors' responsibility and authority. But such documents do not eliminate the need for the auditors to generate their own credibility. The auditees still are likely to be only minimally cooperative if the auditors do not establish credibility. The efficiency and effectiveness of the audit is then jeopardized.

Documenting the Opening Conference. The importance of the opening conference justifies having adequate documentation. The agenda, notes taken during the meeting, any handouts given to the auditee, and similar supporting data should be retained in the working papers. The agenda copy to be filed in the working papers might show the time, place, and persons present.

On-site Tour

On-site tours provide firsthand observation of the auditee's facilities, equipment, personnel, and operations.

Auditee management usually escorts the audit team and provides brief explanations of the operations. Tours are usually relatively brief, lasting between a few minutes for small operations to several hours for large companies. The objective of the tour is to obtain an overview of operations.

Although the auditors may be introduced to some personnel during the tour, this is not the time to pursue questions in depth. The auditors should, however, "scan" the operations for unusual activities, indications of inefficiency, unused facilities, idle workers, poor maintenance of machinery and facilities, and so forth. The auditors also should observe the employees' attitudes toward their jobs and how they relate to each other and to management. Such observations often affect the development and preparation of the audit program.

Study of Documents

Although the auditors may already have examined documents from their own permanent file, they will study additional documents on site. The on-site perusal provides updated information that indicates changes in the organizational structure, responsibilities, and operations. The documents that are of most interest to the auditors include descriptions of current policies and procedures, organizational charts, operational flowcharts, job descriptions and specifications, performance reports, and government regulations.

This study of documents will not be performed in detail. The primary goals of this study are to locate documents on site to determine how they are organized, and to scan them for indications of how well they are maintained. In some audit organizations, permanent files are kept up to date and actually provide more and better information than the auditors are likely to find on site. Of course, in those cases, the on-site document study may be either abbreviated or eliminated altogether.

Written Description of the Auditee

With the information that was acquired from the opening conference, the on-site tour, and the document study, the auditors are prepared to write a description of the auditee or to update a description that is already in the permanent file. Such descriptions include narrative explanations, flowcharts, and organization charts, as well as financial and operating performance information. A convenient outline that may be used for these descriptions includes:

1. Objectives of auditee operations.
2. Environmental restrictions.
3. Functional components comprising the organization.
4. Resources (number and classifications of employees, cash flows, land, buildings and equipment, information systems, etc.).
5. Management.

Exhibit 8-1 illustrates a brief written description of the investments department for a relatively large corporation. Descriptions often may be much larger than the one illustrated here. Some auditing departments do not prepare written descriptions, but depend upon other documents to provide this information. The advantages of having these descriptions include:

1. The auditors have a convenient source of this introductory information.
2. They can make sure they acquire and organize the information in a manner that is the most suitable to their needs.

Analytical Reviews (Comparisons, Ratios, and Trend Analysis)

As described in Chapter 4, analytical reviews are performed by calculating a number of ratios and trends from financial and production data. These ratios and trends provide comparisons of auditee operations with past performances, industry averages, performance of other companies, and similar auditing entities within the organization. Here you will study a more detailed application of that material.

Exhibit 8-1
Written Description of an Auditee

INVESTMENTS DEPARTMENT   Prepared by: Rydalch
General Description — November 3, 1987   White
Audit Department   Oeknick
Permanent File

1. OBJECTIVES OF OPERATIONS

    The Investments Department has the responsibility to:

    a. Maintain investment portfolios containing approximately 80 percent of the company's liquid assets: 30 percent in current marketable securities and 50 percent in long-term investments.

    b. Earn approximately 2 percent above the average annual prime rate on current marketable securities and 3 percent above the average annual prime rate on long-term investments.

2. ENVIRONMENTAL CONSTRAINTS

    Corporate policy constraints imposed by top management:

    a. Investments in current marketable securities must be limited to over-the-counter stocks, bonds, and commodities.

    b. Long-term investments may include over-the-counter stocks, bonds, commodities, commercial real estate, and merged subsidiary operations with corporate ownership equal to or greater than 20 percent of the common stock.

    c. A maximum of 85 percent investment of the company's nonfixed assets in portfolios managed by the investments department.

    No unusual constraints apparent from outside the company excepting the usual market constraints.

3. RESOURCES

    In addition to the personnel shown in the above organization chart, the Investments Department has the following resources to perform its assigned responsibilities:

a.   Budget for 1987:

Departmental Operations
 Salaries $600,000
 Travel $100,000
 Other $200,000

 TOTAL $900,000

Investment Funds
 Current portfolio $120,000,000
 Long-term portfolio $280,000,000
 New funds $ 10,000,000

 TOTAL INVESTMENTS $410,000,000

b.   Computer Facilities

 (1)   GREAT computerized investments accounting and control software package.

 (2)   MANO computer system.

4.   FUNCTIONAL COMPONENTS

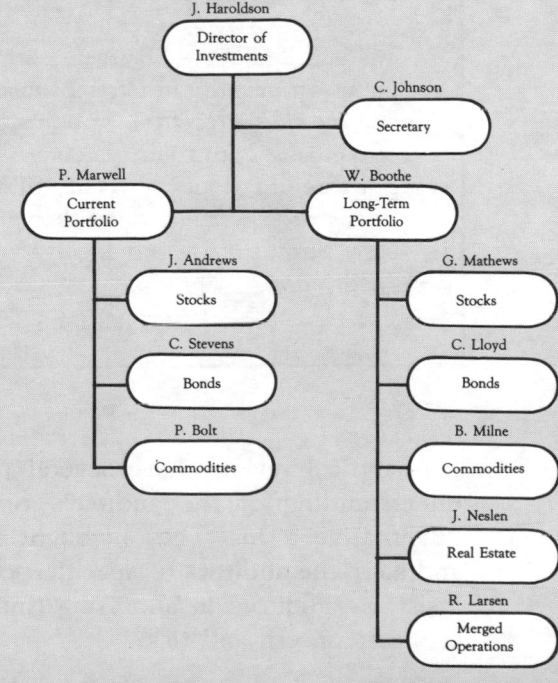

5. MANAGEMENT

The management of the investments department has complete authority to manage the company's portfolios under the few constraints outlined above. A brief description of each manager is given below:

Judy Haroldson — Director, Corporate Investments. Ms. Haroldson is a 1970 MBA graduate of the University of North Carolina. She has spent her entire professional career in the Investments Department. She has been director for the last three years, during which the portfolios have exceeded the target return rates. Ms. Haroldson manages with a firm hand and is very strict with subordinates — perhaps one reason for an increased turnover in personnel during her time as director.

Paul Marwell — Manager, Current Portfolio. Mr. Marwell transferred from the Accounting Department two years ago and was promoted to portfolio manager last year. He first worked as assistant manager over current stock investments. He is a 1975 graduate of Pepperdine University with majors in accounting and finance. Mr. Marwell is generally easygoing; but upon being moved to portfolio manager under Ms. Haroldson, he has exacted tighter control over the assistant portfolio managers.

William Boothe — Manager, Long-Term Portfolio. Mr. Boothe is an unknown quantity in terms of management style and personality. He was recently hired from Coopers Bank, where he managed a portion of the bank's portfolio. He comes highly recommended. He is a 1959 graduate of Purdue University with a major in chemistry and has had extensive experience since then in investments management. He is past president of the local chapter of the Portfolio Managers Association.

Analytical reviews have several purposes. They provide a better understanding of the auditee's operations that are expressed in quantitative terms. They highlight significant variations and trends and alert the auditors to specific potential problem areas. They also assist the auditors in allocating time to those areas that are of the greatest concern and risk.

These reviews are performed by a number of methods. The following is one example:

1. Compare current period totals with totals from preceding periods.
2. Analyze the totals of the current period, break them down into their various subparts, and compare these subtotals with those of previous periods.
3. Compare operating results with budgeted amounts.
4. Examine interrelationships among related accounts.
5. Compare financial and production ratios, percentages, and trends with industry averages.
6. Relate financial information to operating data.
7. Compare ratios, percentages, and trends to other similar organizational divisions or departments.
8. Compare organizational performance to economic data.
9. Scan financial and production information for unusual items.

A distinct difference between an analytical review by internal auditors and one that is performed for review services by external CPAs is the level of standardization. CPAs perform a relatively standardized set of financial ratio, trend, and comparative analyses when performing an analytical review. Internal auditors, on the other hand, must relate such review measures to many different kinds of audits. Because of the varied nature of internal audit problems, internal auditors must tailor analytical measures to each audit. The analysis is just as valuable for internal auditors; however, the specific measures are less predictable than for a CPA's review engagement.

Exhibit 8-2 lists several areas of interest for which analytical review procedures might be performed. The exhibit also includes example analyses and possible sources of information for each area.

An Example   Suppose the internal auditors for a large school and office supply company are conducting an examination of the company's advertising department. Exhibit 8-3 provides an illustrative analytical review for this audit. It includes valuable insights into the nature and results of the department's operations and an analysis of various performance and operational trends over the five-year period from 1982 through 1986.

Observations that are likely to be of interest to the auditors in this case include the following:

1. Increasing advertising expenditures, including increasing percentages of the company's total expenses.
2. Steadily increasing or declining revenues over the period.
3. A dramatic rise and fall of revenues per dollar of advertising cost.
4. Variations in the mix of advertising expenditures.

Exhibit 8-2
Examples of Analytical Review Procedures

AREA OF INTEREST	ANALYSIS	POSSIBLE SOURCES OF INFORMATION
Profits	Compare profits for several periods for trends.	Financial performance reports
	Compare gross profit margins for several accounting periods.	
	Compare monthly profits for seasonal trends.	
	Compare profits to industry averages, to other companies, and to other similar divisions or departments within the company.	
Costs	Compare total costs of several accounting periods.	Monthly and summary financial performance reports
	Analyze and compare components of costs, breaking down as to labor, materials, machine, and overhead for several accounting periods.	
	Compare costs per unit and percentages of cost components to totals over time.	
	Compare direct costs and allocated overhead costs of several accounting periods.	
	Analyze and compare cost variances to those of several budget periods.	
	Analyze monthly costs for observed trends.	
	Compare cost figures to industry averages, to figures for other companies, and to those for other similar divisions or departments within the organization.	Trade and professional societies, either in special reports or in trade journals

Return on Investment	Compare ratio of profits/total investment in auditee's operations for several accounting periods.	Monthly and periodic summary financial reports
	Compare ROI for auditee to industry averages, to other companies, and to other units within the company.	
Productivity	Analyze total units of production for several budget periods.	Monthly and periodic summary performance reports
	Analyze average cost per unit of production for several budget periods.	
	Analyze the average number of units produced per labor- and machine-hour for several budget periods.	
	Analyze monthly productivity figures during budget period.	
	Analyze revenue generated per labor-hour for several budget periods.	
Resource Management	Calculate and compare the number and percentage of employee turnover for the period with several other periods.	Personnel records
	Analyze and compare the ratio of inventory purchases to usage for several budget periods.	Summarize financial and production reports
	Compare total downtime for labor and machines for several budget periods.	Production reports and records

Exhibit 8-3
Five-Year Chart

AREAS	1982	1983	1984	1985	1986
Trends					
Total expenses	$ 2M*	$ 2M	$1.5M	$2.5M	$3.5M
Percentage of total company expenses	2%	2.5%	2.0%	2.6%	3%
Total revenues	$100M	$150M	$150M	$160M	$200M

Information Source: financial statements

Productivity					
Revenue/dollar advertising cost	$50	$75	$100	$64	$67

Information Source: financial statements

Media Expenditures					
Trade journals	$ .5 M	$ .2M	$ .1M	$ .5M	$ .5M
Newspapers	$ .25M	$ .3M	$ .1M	$ .3M	$ .2M
Direct mail:					
institutional	$1 M	$1 M	$ .75M	$1.5M	$2.05M
residential	$ .25M	$ .5M	$ .55M	$ .2M	$ .25M

Information Source: summary financial reports for advertising
department

Customer Analysis					
Institutional: all revenue	$ 75M	$100M	$ 90M	$100M	$125M
Revenue/dollar advertising: institutional	$ 50	$ 83	$106	$ 50	$ 49
Individual: all revenue	$ 25M	$ 50M	$ 60M	$ 60M	$ 75M
Revenue/dollar advertising: individual	$ 50	$ 63	$ 92	$120	$167

Information Source: financial statements and summary financial reports
for advertising department

Number of Responses to Direct Mail Promotions					
Total:					
Institutional	37,000	40,000	25,000	30,000	35,000
Individual	100,000	166,667	200,000	250,000	300,000

Percentage of responses to direct mailings:

Institutional	.12	.14	.09	.10	.10
Individual	.02	.02	.03	.03	.03

Information Source: summary end-of-period performance reports

---

*M means "million."

5. Significant differences in the patterns of revenue from institutional and individual sources.
6. The remarkable increase in responses from individuals to direct mail promotions, while the number of institutional responses remains stable.

These observations may cause the auditors to examine the reasons for increased advertising spending, the dramatic drop in productivity during 1985–1986 per advertising dollar, and the differences between advertising programs aimed at individuals and those aimed at institutional sales. The auditors may find that some of these differences are due to changes or errors in the accounting and information system. Differences may represent actual differences in operating results and management strategy. The auditors will need to investigate and analyze possible explanations, with implications for the design and effectiveness for the internal control system, before they can reach any audit conclusions.

Summary

The preliminary survey typically comprises an opening conference, an on-site tour, an on-site study of relevant documents, and a written description of operations that often includes an analytical review. This survey provides the auditors with a good understanding from which to begin the actual audit work in the review of internal controls.

Review of Internal Controls

The review of internal controls includes a description and analysis, an evaluation, and a risk reassessment. The results of the risk assessment determine whether the auditors will extend their testing or go directly to Step 6, where they will develop findings, conclusions, and recommendations for the auditee. As we discussed previously, the description and analysis of internal controls may comprise the completion of an internal control questionnaire, preparation of flowcharts, narrative descriptions, walk-throughs, and limited testing of the system. Many auditors also include the evaluation of policy and procedure manuals and other documents that outline internal controls.

Internal Control Questionnaire (ICQ)

Usually the first step auditors take in describing and analyzing the internal control system is to interview selected employees within the auditee's operations. One good way to conduct these interviews is to prepare an "internal control questionnaire" (ICQ) before the interview and use it to guide the interview process.

ICQs contain questions pertaining to the internal control system. They may be designed to investigate organizational, operational, personnel, review, and facilities and equipment controls. They also may be set up to differentiate among preventive, detective, corrective, directive, and compensating controls. Further, they may encompass a very narrow to a very broad scope to include the reliability and integrity of information; compliance with policies, plans, procedures, laws, and regulations; the safeguarding of assets; the economical and efficient use of resources; and the accomplishment of established objectives and goals for operations and programs.

Often, ICQs can be quite long and may require one or two hours, or even more, of interview time to complete. They generally are designed to elicit simple "yes/no" answers. The questions are usually written so that a "yes" answer indicates appropriate control and a "no" indicates a potential weakness. After each question there is a space for a brief comment or explanation as the auditor deems necessary.

ICQs may be prepared for various aspects of the control system. For example, one ICQ may cover the auditee's financial control system. Another ICQ may apply to the EDP system. Still another may cover the auditee's system of management controls. Auditors usually do not administer all of these ICQs on a single audit, but rather, use one or more particular ones most suited to that audit.

Because of the general nature of controls, however, auditors frequently use generalized ICQs from various published sources or those that have been prepared by members of their own staff, and then adapt these generalized questionnaires to specific audits.

The advantage of ICQs is that, because of their extensive nature and formal structure, auditors are less likely to omit important questions than if they obtained their information without them. Also, the "no" responses provide an easy guide in directing the audit team to potential control problems within the auditee's operations.

Exhibit 8-4 illustrates an example of an internal control questionnaire. This particular questionnaire is designed to study the auditee's management control system. Notice the level of detail in the questions.

Exhibit 8-4
Questionnaire Concerning Management Control
(General)

AREAS	YES, NO, N/A	COMMENTS OR W/P REFERENCES

A. Role of the Department or Function

1. Has the role of the department been defined in writing?

2. Is the role related to:
   Statutory authority?
   Legislative intent?
   Federal intent?
   Federal regulation?

3. Are you satisfied with the department's overall performance?

4. Are there particular areas or problems in the department that you would like us to review?

B. Objectives of the Department

1. Have departmental objectives been established?

2. Are they in writing?

3. Are they prioritized according to importance?

4. Is accomplishment reported regularly?

5. Is nonaccomplishment reviewed with management:
   Verbally?
   In writing?

Adapted from Questionnaire for Review of Managerial Control developed by Honeywell, Inc. Used with permission of Honeywell, Inc.

AREAS	YES, NO, N/A	COMMENTS OR W/P REFERENCES

C. Planning

1. Does the department have:
   An annual operating plan?   _____   _____
   A long-range operating plan?   _____   _____
2. Have responsibilities been as-
   signed to carry out the plan?   _____   _____
3. Is performance against the plan
   measured?   _____   _____
4. Does the plan have units of
   measure such as costs, number
   of employees, dates, etc.?   _____   _____
5. Are reports of progress against
   the plan issued?   _____   _____

D. Organizing

1. Do you have any staff
   problems?   _____   _____
2. Are you satisfied with the
   quality of personnel in the
   department?   _____   _____
3. Does the department have a
   formal on-the-job training
   program?   _____   _____
4. How is a person's performance measured:
      Objectives?   _____   _____
      Work measurement?   _____   _____
      Other standards?   _____   _____
5. Do employees know how they
   are measured?   _____   _____
6. Is performance measured
   regularly?   _____   _____
7. Is it reviewed with the
   employee?   _____   _____
8. Are job descriptions written
   for each position?   _____   _____
9. Has employee turnover been a
   problem? (Determine the turnover rate.)   _____   _____

AREAS	YES, NO, N/A	COMMENTS OR W/P REFERENCES

10. Does the department have formal organization charts?

11. Do you have an excessive number of people and/or functions reporting to you? (Determine the number.)

12. Have you changed your organization in the last:
  Year?
  Two years?
  Three years?

E. Controlling

1. Policies

A policy is a guide for carrying out action in order to achieve objectives. It is effective today and thereafter, until it is replaced or declared invalid.

  a. Does the department have written policies?
  b. Are they organized in a manual?
  c. Are they up to date?
  d. Are they enforced?
  e. Are they distributed to personnel in the department?
  f. Is the format standardized?

2. Procedures

A procedure is a document that explains how the work will be done to carry out policies. Procedures minimize the chance for irregularities or improper practices and act as a reference

AREAS	YES, NO, N/A	COMMENTS OR W/P REFERENCES

in determining that policies are carried out.

a. Does the department have written procedures?
b. Are they organized in a manual?
c. Are they up to date?
d. Are they monitored for compliance?
e. Is a procedure written for all policy statements?
f. Are procedures distributed to department personnel?
g. Is the format standardized?

3. Forms and Files

"Forms" is a general term and refers to the information and the media used in the formal communication system of the department, with the exception of the reporting structure. It includes such items as time records, personnel files, case files, applications, complaints, etc. "Files" constitute the formal storage of information in a department. It includes filing cabinets, tub files, notebooks, etc., for the purpose of reference.

Forms:
a. Does the department have a forms-control program?
b. Is form design handled within the department?
c. Do all forms require management's approval?

AREAS	YES, NO, N/A	COMMENTS OR W/P REFERENCES

Files:

a. Is access to departmental files restricted?

b. Do files document accurately entire transactions in one place?

c. Are files purged according to a planned record-retention program?

d. Is there a procedure covering record retention?

e. Does it comply with the stated policy?

4. Standards of Performance

Control is impaired unless steps are taken to measure results against anticipated standards of performance. These indicators point out situations requiring management's attention. They include forecasts, budgets, standard costs, cases processed, clients served, transactions handled, inventory levels, etc.

a. Has management specified how the department's performance is to be measured?

b. Has the information (operating data and statistics) been defined that must be accumulated to measure performance?

c. Has provision been made to accumulate the data required to evaluate the performance of:

    Individuals?

    Organizational units?

AREAS	YES, NO, N/A	COMMENTS OR W/P REFERENCES

d. Has a reporting structure been established that identifies program effectiveness?

e. When was the last audit made of your department (or portions of your activity) by:
    Federal auditors?
    State auditors?
    Survey team?
    Management?
    Other? (Specify.)

5. Budgets

a. Does the department prepare a detailed annual budget based on the appropriation?

b. Are regular reports showing revenues, expenditures, and variances received in the department?

c. Are large variances explained?

6. Reporting

a. Does the department prepare and issue written reports to management for its use in review and control?

b. Are these reports issued regularly?

c. On statistical reports, do the dollar figures "tie in" to the books?

d. Are reports issued on unusual items such as overtime, overload help, long-distance phone use, travel, etc.?

AREAS	YES, NO, N/A	COMMENTS OR W/P REFERENCES
e. Are any of the department's reports directed specifically to:		
Dept. management?	_____	
Division management?	_____	
Federal agencies?	_____	
f. Are these reports issued for information only?	_____	
g. Is any action taken as a result of these reports?	_____	
h. Does the department prepare most of its report material by hand, or is it obtained as a by-product of accounting or by an automated process?	_____	

7. Facilities, Equipment, Layout, and Location

AREAS	YES, NO, N/A	COMMENTS OR W/P REFERENCES
a. Are quarters adequate in terms of:		
Space?	_____	
Noise level?	_____	
Lighting?	_____	
Other? (Specify.)	_____	
b. Does the layout of the department seem logical?	_____	
c. Is equipment up-to-date and adequate to do the work efficiently and accurately?	_____	
d. Are appropriate records kept of fixed assets?	_____	
e. How often are fixed assets inventoried?	_____	
f. Is departmental management apprised of fixed assets that cannot be accounted for?	_____	
g. Does departmental management approve all fixed-asset acquisitions and dispositions?	_____	

The disadvantages of ICQs are:

1. They are tiring because of their length. As a result, auditees sometimes give superficial consideration to their answers simply to complete the interview. This can lead to errors or faulty assumptions.
2. Because it is usually clear that the desirable answers are all "yes," the people being interviewed may hesitate to give a negative response.
3. By interviewing auditee personnel, the auditors are acquiring indirect audit evidence which usually must be corroborated in some way.

Despite these weaknesses, auditors usually consider ICQs to be a valuable tool in the description and analysis of the auditee's internal control system. The other three procedures (flowcharts, walk-throughs, and limited testing) used in the review of internal controls help to counter the weaknesses of the ICQ.

An Example

Suppose the internal auditors for a state government were to use an internal control questionnaire in an audit of the State Highway Maintenance Department. Suppose further that the auditors adapted the generalized management control questionnaire shown in Exhibit 8-4 to this particular audit. Exhibit 8-5 shows how one page of the generalized questionnaire may be adapted in this case. Notice that most of the questions are identical to those in the generalized ICQ; the biggest difference is simply the identification of specific organizational positions and program elements within the generalized questions. You will also notice, however, that there are a few questions added to the questionnaire. These additional questions are identified by an arrow to the left of each number.

When adapting a generalized questionnaire for specific use, the auditors may make specific reference to organizational units, personnel, and functional elements. The auditors also may ask questions regarding concerns that are unique to the auditee's operations. Fortunately, in many cases, the generalized nature of internal controls is such that few specific and unique questions are required.

Flowcharts and Narrative Descriptions

As you will recall from Chapter 3, flowcharts provide a graphic representation of systems operations and internal controls. As was discussed and illustrated in that chapter, two basic types are horizontal and vertical flowcharting. This chapter describes how flowcharting is used for the specific purposes of describing auditees' operations and internal control systems.

Exhibit 8-5
Questionnaire Concerning Management Control
(Specific)

AREA	YES, NO, N/A	COMMENTS OR W/P REFERENCES

A. Role of Department

1. Has the role outlining the general areas of responsibilities for the State Highway Department been defined in writing?

2. Is the department's role related to:
  Statutory authority?
  Legislative intent?
  Federal authority?
  Federal regulations?

➤ 3. Are there apparent conflicts among the State Highway Department's role and areas of responsibility as defined in the four groups outlined in 2?

4. Are you satisfied with the department's overall performance?

5. Are there particular areas or problems in the department that you would like us to review?

B. Objectives of the Department

1. Does the State Highway Department have a written set of general objectives?
  Short run?
  Long run?

2. Is accomplishment reported regularly?
  Short run?
  Long run?

AREAS	YES, NO, N/A	COMMENTS OR W/P REFERENCES
→3. Are objectives evaluated periodically to review their continued need?	_____	
→4. Does the State Highway Department's management participate in setting objectives?	_____	
C. Planning		
1. Does the State Highway Department have a written annual operating plan?		
For specific construction projects?	_____	
A financial budget?	_____	

As an example, suppose the auditors of a large clothing manufacturer and distribution company were reviewing the inventory management function of one of the company's regional distribution and warehousing centers. Exhibit 8-6 shows the auditors' flowchart for the distribution of the company's products from this warehouse. Notice the legend for abbreviations and the brief description of specific key control points within the flowchart.

The flowchart is followed by the narrative description of additional controls that are related to this distribution function. While the controls discussed in the narrative description are important to the distribution function, they are not considered to be a part of the routine distribution cycle, and thus are difficult to include in the flowchart itself. However, since the review of internal controls should include all of the relevant controls related to an auditee, it usually is necessary to flowchart the routine cycle of operations and to describe the other related controls in narrative form.

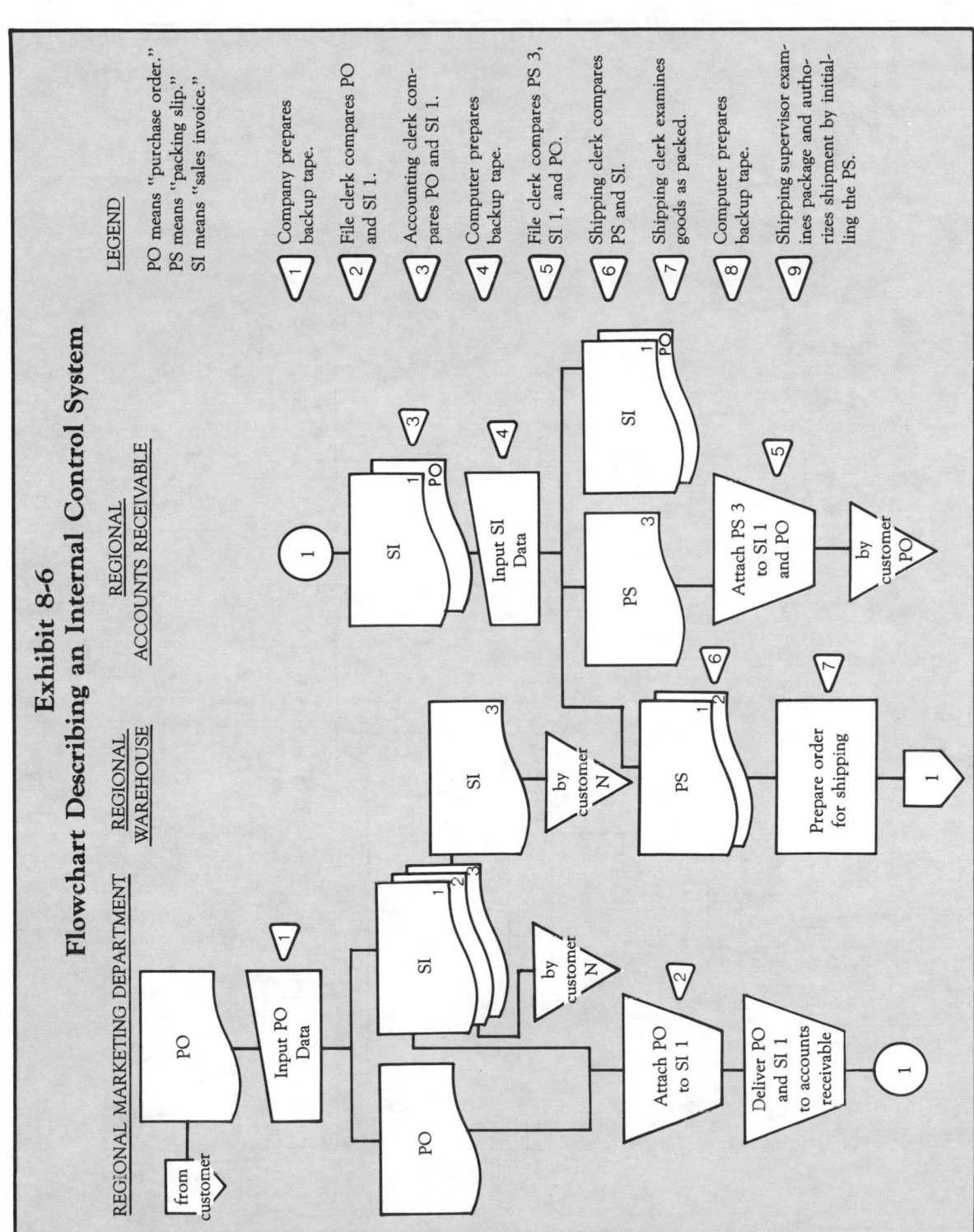

Exhibit 8-6
Flowchart Describing an Internal Control System

LEGEND

PO means "purchase order."
PS means "packing slip."
SI means "sales invoice."

1. Company prepares backup tape.
2. File clerk compares PO and SI 1.
3. Accounting clerk compares PO and SI 1.
4. Computer prepares backup tape.
5. File clerk compares PS 3, SI 1, and PO.
6. Shipping clerk compares PS and SI.
7. Shipping clerk examines goods as packed.
8. Computer prepares backup tape.
9. Shipping supervisor examines package and authorizes shipment by initialling the PS.

ADDITIONAL CONTROLS

Because of the highly competitive environment of the company, management is very concerned that customers are satisfied with the quality of service, including whether they received what they ordered in good condition and promptly. A marketing clerk conducts monthly surveys of a rotating sample of 25 customers, inquiring about the company's shipping services. Regular internal audits examine the warehousing operations, and annual audits by the company's CPA firm also test the accounting controls.

REGIONAL WAREHOUSE

1

Enter shipping data into shipping log

2   8

Attach SI to PS, copy 1, and place in order box

9

Load order on trucks

to customer

PS

by customer N

2

Daily shipping log — for review by management

by date

Some auditors combine more extensive narrative descriptions with flowcharts so that a running narrative is presented parallel to the flowchart itself. Such a practice provides the auditor with two perspectives of the operations and control system. This combination of a running narrative with a flowchart is usually done only with vertical flowcharts. An example of this practice is shown in Exhibit 8-7 for the shipping function of the clothing company mentioned above.

Usually the auditors choose either one form or the other for the description of a particular system — the horizontal approach or the vertical approach.

Walk-Throughs

Procedural. As we have discussed, procedural walk-throughs take the auditors step by step through particular processes. For example, the auditors of a large bank were examining the management of the bank's securities portfolios. They discussed with the portfolio managers how individual purchases were documented and entered into the accounting system. They decided to walk through the process from the point at which a decision was made to make a purchase to the point when the portfolio managers were to sign a journal voucher authorizing the transaction to be entered into the accounting records.

The auditors walked through the process as it was described in the investment department's procedures manual. They discovered that none of the forms indicated for which of the bank's five portfolios the purchase was being made. The auditors were unable to enter the purchase in a particular portfolio, as the manual prescribed, from any of the documentation.

The auditors discovered that the keypunchers had created a "suspense" account where all of the new purchases were entered until individual managers sent memos stating which securities were to be moved to specific portfolios. These memos might be several days in arriving. In the meantime, particular securities might begin to perform badly, and none of the managers had listed those securities in the portfolios. Consequently, the securities that were performing poorly remained in the suspense account and no one was assigned to trade or sell them. As a result, while individual portfolios were performing satisfactorily, the bank's overall securities package was performing poorly, solely because a large number of these securities had accumulated in the suspense account.

Previous auditors had questioned the need for a suspense account, but it was only when the auditors walked through the process that they discovered the central role of the account. Further examination

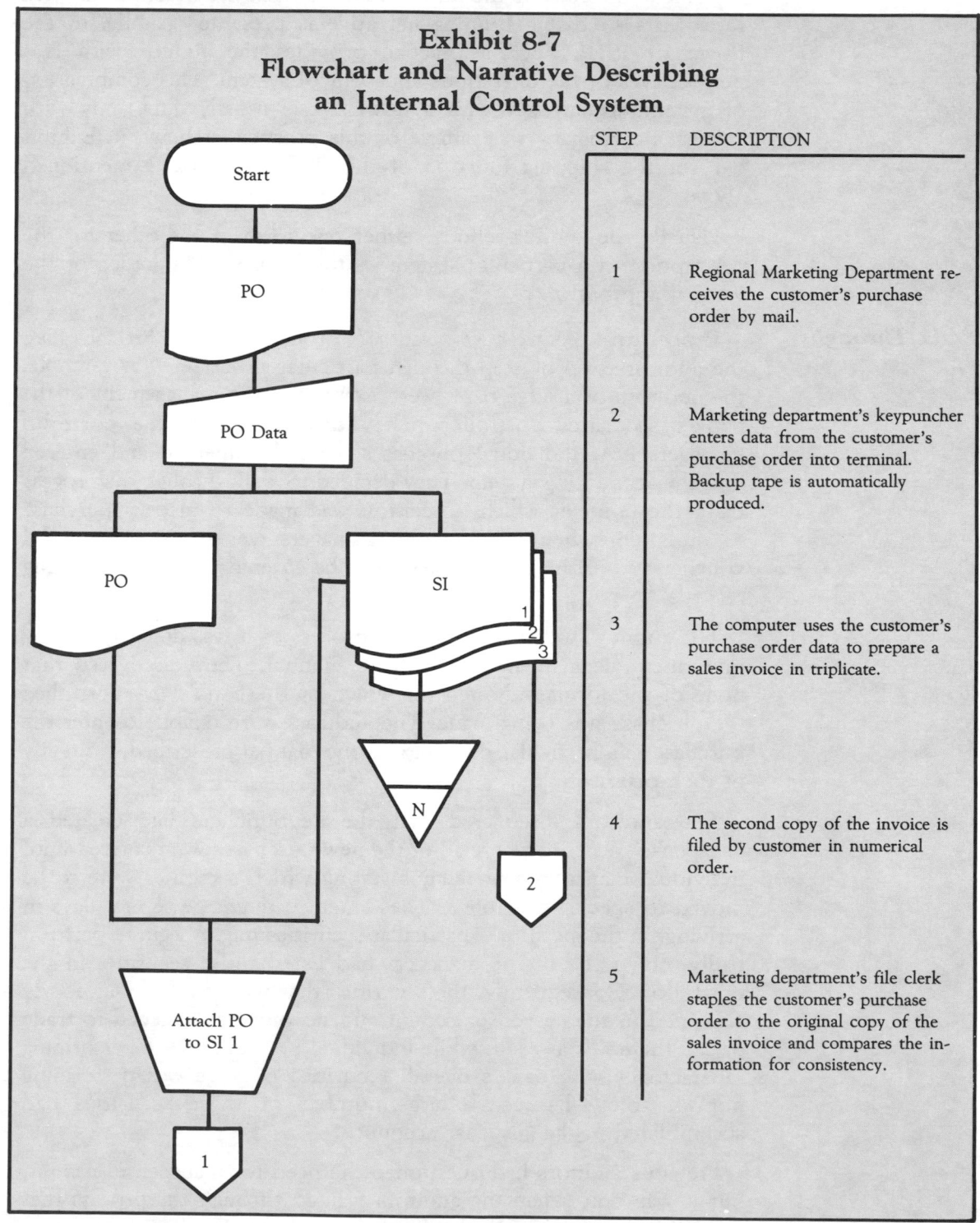

Exhibit 8-7
Flowchart and Narrative Describing
an Internal Control System

STEP	DESCRIPTION
1	Regional Marketing Department receives the customer's purchase order by mail.
2	Marketing department's keypuncher enters data from the customer's purchase order into terminal. Backup tape is automatically produced.
3	The computer uses the customer's purchase order data to prepare a sales invoice in triplicate.
4	The second copy of the invoice is filed by customer in numerical order.
5	Marketing department's file clerk staples the customer's purchase order to the original copy of the sales invoice and compares the information for consistency.

uncovered the devastating effect the recording procedures were having upon the performance of the bank's securities investments.

In order to perform a walk-through, the auditor needs to know what steps to perform. This information may come from policy and procedure manuals (as in the example discussed above), from flowcharts prepared by the auditee or by the auditors themselves, or from personal observation. Auditors document a walk-through by listing the steps to be performed, as illustrated in Exhibit 8-8, and by providing a check-off column that indicates whether each step has been performed. A section for comments and observations may also be included.

The primary advantage of procedural walk-throughs is the firsthand, comprehensive knowledge of how a particular procedure is performed. There are many occasions when no amount of documentation, study, or discussion with members of the auditee's staff can offer the same level of experience and knowledge as simple walk-throughs.

Documentation Walk-Throughs. This second kind of walk-through allows internal auditors to follow particular operations or transactions from beginning to end through documentation. This documentation walk-through is one form of vouching transactions to check whether specific controls are present in a system, although it usually is limited to only one or two transactions.

For example, an internal auditor may walk through the authorization of a pay raise for an employee. The auditor would examine the original request prepared by the employee's supervisor to verify the details of the pay raise, the approval of the supervisor, and the review by executive management. The auditor would then determine whether the original request was sent to the personnel department for review and a copy was kept in the employee's file in the department where he or she works. The next step would be to check the documentation sent from the personnel department to payroll accounting authorizing the changes in the employee's payroll record. A final step would be to examine a check stub subsequent to the change to verify that it did take place as authorized.

Limited Testing of the System

Testing the system means to sample and examine various elements of the system: documents, materials, outputs, etc. The auditor tests those parts of the system that are the most critical in answering the audit questions. Limited testing means that only a few items will be sampled. The purpose of limited testing is to acquire a general initial

Exhibit 8-8
Walk-Through Sample Document

Walk-through of pressure and viscosity tests for
liquid stock entering production process

Steps	(i*)	Comments
1. Take wrench from wall hook and open valve A. (Procedure to be performed hourly.)	1 ✓	Wrench found on operator's observation table, not on wall hook.
2. Read pressure gauge and record in log book the peak pressure registered on gauge during a 10-second interval.	3 ✓	Gauge very dirty and hard to read — chance for significant error. Log book dirty and messy, missing many entries.
3. Open valve B with wrench.	3 ✓	
4. Read pressure gauge and record in log book the peak pressure from combined effects of opening valves A and B during a 10-second interval.	4 ✓	
5. Turn off both valves and return wrench to wall hook.	5 ✓	
6. Read viscosity of mixture from test gauge.	6 ✓	Gauge dirty and hard to read.
7. Record viscosity in log book.	7 ✓	

*(i) means the order in which steps were performed.
The checkmark indicates that the step was performed by the auditor.

understanding of how well the systems are operating and how well controls appear to be functioning. The auditor may or may not choose to use statistical sampling techniques for this procedure. Usually the auditor subjectively selects a few items for examination without taking a formal sample. The auditor may examine as many as 25 or 30 items or as few as three or four, depending upon the circumstances.

For example, suppose the auditors were reviewing the internal controls for warehousing operations in the flowchart illustrated in Exhibit 8-6. One of the critical controls is the set of checks to determine whether information on customer's purchase orders (P.O.), sales invoices (S.I.), and packing slips (P.S.) is consistent. The auditors can perform a limited test of the effectiveness of these checks by quickly thumbing through the files of the attached documents in the accounts receivable area. First the auditors would observe whether the files were in order and whether documents were filed under the customer's name in the numerical sequence of purchase orders. Then the auditors would pick a few of the P.O./S.I./P.S. sets — perhaps a dozen or so — to compare for the consistency and completeness of information.

Another limited test that might be performed would be the observation of three or four boxes of goods being prepared for shipment. The auditors might examine the packing slip and observe that all of the goods listed are indeed put into the box for shipment. At the same time, the auditors are observing the efficiency with which the order is prepared, the neatness of the packaging, the general orderliness of the warehouse operations, and the manner in which the supervisor examines the package before mailing. These observations also may be combined with a walk-through.

A summary of the results of this limited testing is written up as a file memo and included in the audit working papers.

Preliminary Evaluation of the Internal Control System

Upon completion of the preliminary survey, the ICQs, flowcharts, narrative descriptions of controls, walk-throughs, and limited testing, the internal auditors have enough information to make a preliminary evaluation of the internal control system. Internal control matrices often are used in making these evaluations.

Internal Control Matrices. Internal auditors use a variety of formats in preparing internal control matrices, but their basic purposes are generally quite similar. Such matrices systematically organize important results of the audit work up to that point and record the auditors' evaluations of those results with respect to specific internal control objectives. Exhibit 8-9 illustrates an example of an internal control matrix. Its columns reflect the following information:

- Specific audit objectives.
- Important results itemized by audit objectives from the preliminary survey, description, and preliminary testing of internal controls.
- The nature and seriousness of risks associated with each result.
- Appropriate control methods and types of control relevant to each result.
- The internal auditor's evaluation of each result.

Notice that both positive and negative results may be recorded in the matrix. Item 1 for objective 1 in this exhibit indicates a management policy problem with respect to the approval and installation of microcomputer systems in local offices. Item 1 for objective 2 indicates good design and performance of reconciliations. Although item 1 for objective 3 appears problematical with respect to cutting travel expenditures, it is more questionable.

An audit team is likely to prepare only one matrix as the final step in the review of internal controls. In the case of a large audit, perhaps one matrix may be prepared for each major portion of the audit. For example, suppose a team of internal auditors was examining a major warehouse operation. The auditors may divide the audit into several segments, such as shipping and receiving, inventory storage and handling, accounting, facilities and equipment management, and personnel. A separate internal control matrix may be prepared for each segment of this audit.

Control matrices require preparation procedures similar to the following:

1. The auditors review all of the materials prepared so far on the audit and determine key results that are likely to be reported or that are likely to need additional testing.
2. The auditors determine the criteria by which to evaluate the results, including specifying the risks associated with each result and the specific controls that should be at work in the situation. This information probably will be included in the working papers prepared for each previous step in the audit. In this case, entering it onto the internal control matrix may simply be a matter of reorganization.
3. The auditors evaluate the results with respect to the risks and good internal control standards.

Exhibit 8-9
Internal Control Review Matrix

AUDIT OBJECTIVES	RESULTS OF PRELIMINARY SURVEY AND INTERNAL CONTROL REVIEW	RISKS (NATURE AND SERIOUSNESS)	APPROPRIATE CONTROL METHODS AND TYPES	AUDITOR'S EVALUATION
(1) Examine and evaluate the performance of local office accounting systems.	(1) By policy, the purchase of all computer equipment, including microcomputers, must be separately authorized by a senior vice president. This is a carryover policy from the 1970s, when computer equipment costs were higher. The policy has not been changed, resulting in a serious bottleneck in processing small computer purchases.	(1) These current practices create several problems whose combined effects could be serious: (a) an extraordinary effect on the senior vice president's time and diminished ability to perform other administrative tasks; (b) a slowdown in implementing the recently approved interoffice data-management and reporting systems; and (c) without microcomputers, local offices are unable to implement the new local inventory control and cash-management programs. Current programs bear unnecessarily high risks of loss in both areas.	(1) Budgetary controls upon local division managers, including: (a) annual budget review and approval with detailed allocations for equipment and specific classifications of expenditures, (b) local decision authority for items under a specific amount, and (c) review by the budget exception review board for items exceeding a specific amount.	(1) The current policy appears inadequate, although with only the survey and the review information it is difficult to determine the extent of the effects of the current policy.
(2) Review internal accounting controls at headquarters.	(1) Reconciliation of all bank accounts and of general ledger control accounts is current as of the examination date. Reconciliations are performed monthly by persons without access to cash or the ability to manipulate accounting records. Reviews and approvals were in order.	(1) Failure to reconcile bank accounts and general ledger control accounts exposes the company to increased risks, such as accounting errors, undetected bank errors, and undetected misuse of funds.	(1) Reconciliations should be (a) performed by accounting personnel without access to cash or the ability to manipulate accounting records, (b) timely and performed at specific times, and (c) reviewed and approved.	(1) Reconciliation controls appear excellent.

AUDIT OBJECTIVES	RESULTS OF PRELIMINARY SURVEY AND INTERNAL CONTROL REVIEW	RISKS (NATURE AND SERIOUSNESS)	APPROPRIATE CONTROL METHODS AND TYPES	AUDITOR'S EVALUATION
(3) Examine and evaluate travel by headquarters personnel.	(1) Budget variances appeared satisfactory, except for travel expenditures, which are less than half those budgeted for the year. This cut in travel expenditures is a result of top management's new emphasis on cutting travel by headquarters personnel to local offices.	(1) While cutting travel budgets has reduced these related expenditures by more than $300,000, other risks may increase, such as (a) inadequate training of local office personnel, restricted feedback from local offices, and restricted ability to monitor adherence to the company's policies and procedures and (b) too much dependence on indirect information from summary field reports for headquarters decision-making.	(1) Planning for the level of travel needed to optimize the trade-off between travel costs and improvements in internal control is essential. Because of frequent conflicting points of view with respect to how much travel is needed, executive management should set guidelines and review travel budgets, including amendments to budgets. Other means of contact with local offices may be used to good advantage — telephone, memos, and letters — and should be considered in planning.	(1) Executive management's instruction to cut travel costs is a weak control and could cause other more severe problems. We must remember, however, the advantages of decentralized and local decision authority. Too much headquarters "interference" is equally unattractive. The objective should be an appropriate, well-defined balance of local authority with headquarters' assistance and monitoring of activities.

Preparation of an internal control matrix aids in the transition to the next step in the audit process, which begins with determining what expanded testing may be necessary. The control matrix provides an excellent reference for determining where additional information may be needed for the auditors to be more confident in their judgments, conclusions, and recommendations.

Summary of Review of Internal Controls

The review of internal controls, then, is likely to include several documents prepared by the internal auditors:

1. A completed set of internal control questionnaires.
2. Flowcharts and narratives illustrating the nature of operations and key controls.
3. Descriptions of walk-throughs performed by the auditors.
4. A file memo summarizing the results of the auditor's limited testing of the system.
5. One or more internal control matrices that show the auditors' evaluations of specific aspects of the internal control system.

This set of materials offers a quick exploration of the auditee's internal control system. An evaluation of the results of this review determines whether testing needs to be expanded in order to perform more comprehensive compliance tests and evaluations.

Risk Reassessment

In Chapter 5 we noted that after the internal control description and analysis, auditors should reassess the level of risk associated with the auditee's operations. One of three things is likely to happen during this reassessment:

1. The revised risk may be less than that for other potential audit entities. If so, it is prudent for the auditors to go on to higher-risk areas. They would, however, write up any findings and recommendations and discuss them with the people in charge of that operation.
2. The auditors may determine that there is very little additional information that they could learn from further audit tests. In this case, the auditors again would note their findings and recommendations, discuss with the auditee, and move on to the next audit project.
3. The final possibility is that the auditors will continue to have significant unanswered questions that arise, perhaps from the preliminary examination of internal controls. Consequently, the risks will appear to remain high and the auditors will not have made any final determinations regarding their findings or recommendations simply because they need more information.

This situation leads to Step 5 in the audit — expanded tests of the control system.

This reassessment is likely to be informal and involve non-numerical comparisons with the previously ranked auditees. Some auditors use numerical comparisons of risks associated with potential auditees. They reevaluate each of the risk factors and compute a new risk score. This score is compared and ranked with the previously assigned scores to determine whether or not the auditors should move on. In either case, the preliminary survey and the internal control review prepare the auditor to reassess risk in more specific terms. The decision on whether to continue the audit with expanded testing or to go directly to the development of findings, recommendations, and the reporting process will depend upon this risk reassessment.

Interestingly, the risks may conveniently be categorized according to the five basic objectives of internal control, or some combination thereof:

1. The reliability and integrity of information.
2. Compliance with policies, plans, procedures, laws, and regulations.
3. The safeguarding of assets.
4. The economical and efficient use of resources.
5. The accomplishment of established objectives and goals for the operations or programs.

QUESTIONS

1. What procedures typically are included in preliminary surveys?
2. What distinguishes preliminary surveys from other audit preparation?
3. Describe the opening conference.
4. What is an on-site tour? What is its purpose?
5. Why do internal auditors study additional documents on site at the auditee's place of operations?
6. What is the value of a written description of the auditee as a part of the preliminary survey? What information is included?
7. What is an analytical review? How are such reviews performed? Why are they performed?
8. What audit procedures are performed on a typical review of internal controls?
9. Name several advantages and disadvantages of internal control questionnaires.
10. Why is it usually necessary to combine flowcharts with narrative descriptions of internal controls?
11. Why is it often helpful to walk through some operations in addition to flowcharting and narration?
12. What does it mean for auditors to do "limited testing" of internal controls?
13. What are internal control matrices, and how do internal auditors use them to evaluate internal control systems?
14. Why is risk reassessment such a critical part of the review of internal controls?
15. Identify five types of risk with which auditors are particularly concerned.

EXERCISES

E-1

The West Agribusiness Company recently purchased three large fruit farms and a dairy operating under the name of Newberry Farms. All of the company's products had been marketed through the previous owner, Coe County Farm Cooperative. The farms were managed by local personnel, none of whom had any formal training in either agriculture or agribusiness. They had been more like caretakers than managers, and had let the co-op run the business. The co-op provided marketing and accounting services to the co-op members. West had not decided how it wanted to manage the Newberry Farm properties. West's management decided to wait for the results of an internal audit of operations before deciding whether to replace Newberry's management, provide training, or simply let them proceed.

Required:

Prepare a set of audit program steps for the preliminary survey portion of this audit. Discuss the purpose of each step and what information about the auditee each step would provide.

E-2

The secretary knocked sharply on Clark Dailey's office door. Clark was the audit manager in charge of an upcoming audit of corporate investments. He was reviewing a report prepared for an audit that had just been completed. When the secretary entered, she seemed a little confused and said that several financial executives were waiting in a conference room on the 14th floor for the auditors who had scheduled an opening conference that morning. The executives had been waiting for more than 15 minutes. The secretary asked what she should tell Bill Merkley, the vice president of finance, who was on the phone asking where the auditors were.

Clark knew that this audit of investments was important and that his director, William J. DeVries, was especially interested in attending the opening conference. The normal practice had been for auditees to respond in writing to the final audit report. Mr. DeVries wanted to be sure to discuss a new policy with the financial executives. The auditors would be issuing a follow-up evaluation of the auditees' written responses. He knew this would be a sensitive issue and planned to discuss the need for appropriate responses to audit findings in order to avoid unfavorable follow-up evaluations. Mr. DeVries, however, was on vacation, because Clark had told him that the opening conference was scheduled for the following week. Clark's calendar also showed the opening conference scheduled for the next week.

Clark hurriedly pulled together some preliminary notes and audit programs to take to the opening conference. He and Janet Knox, the audit supervisor who was assigned to the audit, went to the conference room. Needless to say, he was unprepared, appeared more than a little confused, and was somewhat disheveled. Janet also was unprepared. Consequently, the opening conference served little purpose but to make the financial executives irritated. They insisted that Clark had called one of their departmental secretaries to set up the appointment. She had informed each of them the day of his call, and they all had the same day and time on their calendars. More than 15 minutes of the half-hour meeting was spent discussing the mix-up in scheduling. They never discussed the new follow-up procedures.

Required:
a.   Discuss what went wrong with this opening conference.
b.   How might the difficulties of this opening conference have been avoided?

E-3

The auditors for Middlebrook Company toured the production site of one of the company's regional divisions. Several things came to the auditors' attention as they toured the facility:

1.   A "graveyard" for old machinery was spotted behind the plant. Heavy weeds were growing around the machinery, much of which was rusty and stacked in a heap. The auditors knew that a healthy market existed for used machinery of this type.

2. A separate warehouse was used to store the inventory of raw materials used in production. A six-month supply of materials was often on hand. The warehouse was located almost 100 yards from the main plant, and a separate road went to the warehouse through a gate in the chain-link fence around the plant site. The road to the main plant had security guards placed at the entrance 24 hours a day. A padlock was used to secure the warehouse gate at night after production shut down.

3. One of the auditors slipped in a puddle of water on the tile floor at the foot of a staircase in the plant. The auditor had not noticed the water and suggested that it be cleaned up before someone fell and was injured. The manager conducting the auditors' tour said it would be difficult to clean up because of a small fracture in a pipe near the staircase. He said it wasn't serious and everyone knew about the water and just went around it or over it.

Required:
a. Suggest some of the questions raised by these observations.
b. What effect would these observations have upon the audit program?

E-4

The following is a list of documents the auditors examined on a recent audit of the purchasing function of a large drug retailer:

- Supplier contracts.
- A sample of customer receipts.
- A sample of purchase orders.
- Resumes of inventory clerks.
- Flowcharts of purchasing transactions, including internal controls.
- A written description of purchasing operations for the company.

Required:
Identify which of the documents are most likely to have been examined as part of (a) the on-site tour, (b) the preliminary survey, (c) neither of the two, or (d) both the on-site tour and the preliminary survey.

E-5

Following is a description of the research and development department for the chemical fertilizer division of a large agribusiness company. The description was found in the division's permanent file.

Chemical Fertilizer Division
Research and Development

The research and development department is responsible for the development and improvement of fertilizer compounds to be used on various commercial farm crops. The department is to be funded from division revenues. The departmental organization should include a manager of research and development and a staff of scientists, with a chief of research and a chief of product development to lead the two arms of the department's responsibilities. The department, organized five years ago, successfully introduced two new fertilizer compounds and made improvements in three of the company's other products already on the market. The department's operations are located on the second floor of the old Charity complex. Last year's budget was $2.5 million for operations, excluding salaries and administrative expenses.

Required:

Critique the description in terms of its value to the auditors who are planning an examination of the research and development department's operations.

E-6

The internal auditors of a large university were assigned to audit the student aid office. Three audit questions were:

1. What are the comparative proportions of funds processed for (a) student loans and (b) student scholarships for the federal government, the state government, and private sources?
2. Are student loans and student scholarships growing adequately to meet student demands and to attract top scholars?
3. How efficiently are student loans and scholarships being administered in terms of cost to the university?

Required:

Prescribe analytical review tests to answer each of the three questions. You may have more than one test for each question, since each question contains more than one subquestion.

E-7

The preliminary survey for an audit of the psychiatric unit of a hospital produced the following information:

> The hospital administrator had mentioned at the opening conference that she was especially concerned that some critically ill psychiatric patients had been able to leave the unit unattended, without permission. On more than one occasion, these unattended patients had caused problems in other areas of the hospital. She said the problem seemed to be with the security measures for the entrance door to the unit, but so far the problem was something of a mystery, and nobody knew exactly what was causing the breakdown in controls. Another problem mentioned at the opening conference was the use of an excessive number of overtime hours in the unit. With less than two-thirds of the year over, the unit already exceeded the annual budgeted overtime pay. On the on-site tour of the unit, the auditors observed two doors to the unit — one outer door separating the psychiatric unit from the rest of the floor, and an inner door to a high-security section of the unit.

The auditors asked if any of the patients who had left the unit without authorization were from the high-security area. They were told that all of those who had left were from the high-security area. The auditors were informed that all of the patients had gotten out during meal time, either just prior to the time or just after the food carts came into the area. The nurses felt that the problem lay with the food distribution procedures.

PSYCHIATRIC UNIT

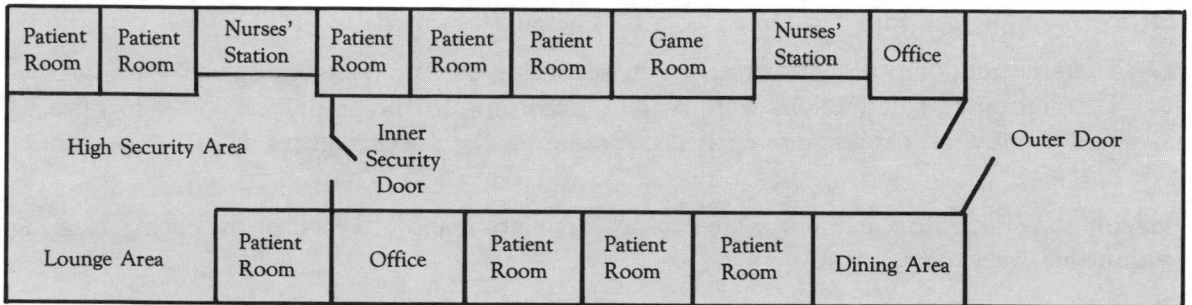

Required:

a. What problems do you see from the administrator's comments that need investigation on the audit?

b. Write three specific audit steps that you would include in the review of internal controls. These steps need not necessarily relate directly to the problems mentioned in your response to (a) above.

E-8

State auditors were examining a project where Nealson Company had subcontracted with the State Highway Department to landscape the entrance to a state park. The auditors prepared the following narrative description of Nealson's payroll system:

> Project time-tickets are prepared weekly by the project supervisor for each hourly employee who checks and initials his or her time-ticket before the batch of tickets is delivered to the main office. Information for the tickets is keypunched onto a magnetic tape, which then is used to process the weekly payroll from the payroll master file. An earnings statement and a paycheck is printed for each employee, and a payroll register is printed as a part of each weekly run. Management scans the register for potential problems and errors. Afterwards, problems are followed up and the register is filed. An error report is prepared manually for follow-up items. These error reports are attached to and filed with the payroll register. Project supervisors pick up the paychecks weekly and distribute them to the employees at their respective project sites.

Required:

a. Prepare a flowchart, with a parallel narrative, for Nealson's payroll system.

b. Identify preventive, detective, and corrective controls in this system.

E-9
Required:

a. Prepare a walk-through worksheet for E-8, where the auditors walk through the documentation only.

b. Prepare a walk-through worksheet for E-8, where the auditors actually perform the outlined procedures.

E-10

As part of the auditors' limited testing for the audit described in E-8, they examined one of the weekly payroll registers. They compared payment information from the register for three employees with personnel records. The auditors made the following observations:

1. The amounts of payment were correct, according to employee contracts.
2. The amounts of deductions were correct, according to the employees' W-4 forms.
3. The employees' names were spelled the same on the check register as in the personnel files.

Tracing the checks to the appropriate bank reconciliation showed each of the checks clearing within one week of payment.

Required:
a. How much confidence would you place in the above payroll system as a result of this limited test?
b. What effect would these results have on further testing of the system?

E-11

An internal auditing team for a chain of supermarkets was assigned to examine the sales performance at one store location. One audit objective was to determine whether sales performance met company standards. Preliminary analytical tests showed the store sales per square foot at about 75 percent of the company standard of $130 per year. A study of the store's layout and customer traffic patterns along display aisles and checkout counters revealed exceptionally wide aisles measuring about 10 feet.

Standards prescribe a maximum of eight feet. The average inventory for a store of that size was $1 million; the store being audited had an average inventory of about $800,000 for the period under audit. The wide aisles left less space for shelves, and the store tended to have less inventory on hand. Management concentrated mostly on basic staples. There also were frequent stockouts of goods.

The average sale per customer was about $20. Other stores in the chain averaged more than $25 per customer. An analysis of sales led the auditors to conclude that too many customers were using the supermarket primarily as a quick-stop convenience store rather than as a supermarket, resulting in poor profitability. The store was barely breaking even. The auditors attributed this trend to the concentration on basic staple goods and failure to provide the variety of products customers typically expect from supermarkets. The wide aisles and smaller purchases did, however, allow customers to move about easily in the store and to check out more quickly, on the average, than at any other store location.

Required:
Prepare an internal control matrix for the items, showing five columns — audit objectives, preliminary results, risks, appropriate controls, and auditor evaluation. You will need to determine your own evaluations for the last column.

PROBLEMS

P-1

Cornwallis Research Labs were established at State University in 1967 to study the ecological effect of man's intrusion into primitive areas, especially desert regions. In addition to administrative offices and three large laboratories, the facilities include a five-acre controlled environment built and developed by the labs to simulate desertland. The following is an organization chart for the Cornwallis labs. Notice the link between the director and the university's vice president in charge of research.

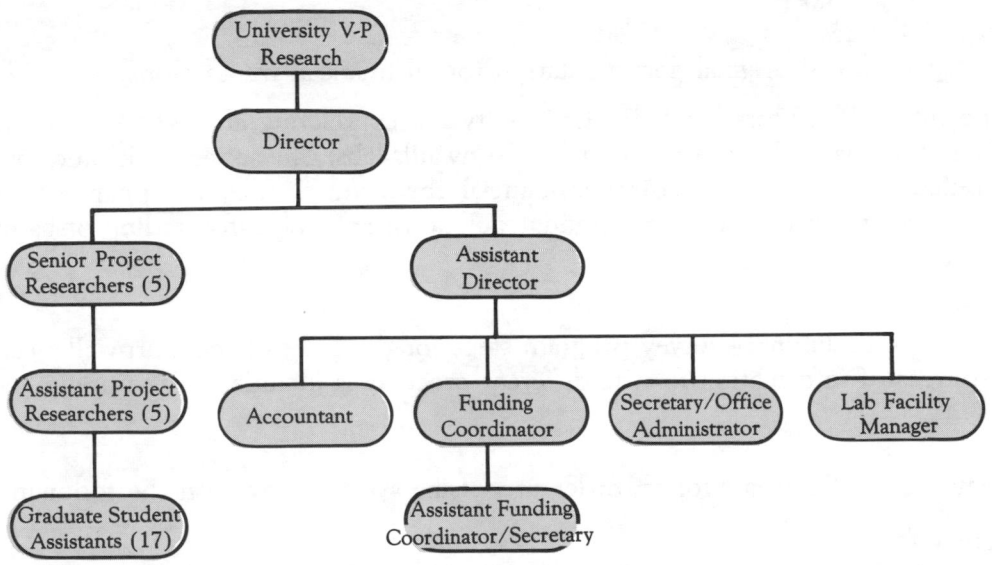

There are four sources for funds used by the research facility:

10%	Endowed gift to the university for ecological research.
15%	Funding from state government.
65%	Funding from federal government.
10%	Private industry.
100%	

Financial management and accounting policies and procedures are dictated by the State University Controller's Office, and also to some extent by state and federal funding agencies. Notice the separation of the financial management function and the accounting function under the assistant director position shown in the organization chart. The accounting function includes:

1. Recording all financial transactions.
2. Preparation of monthly project cost reports.
3. Preparation of quarterly and annual statements of receipts and disbursements.
4. Preparation and mailing of financial reports required by the various funding sources.

The financial management function includes:

1. Coordination of funding.
    a. Budget preparation.
    b. Solicitation of private funds from individuals and industry.
    c. Preparation of project fund proposals for state and federal funding agencies.
    d. Collection and receipt of all funds.
2. Disbursement of funds.
    a. Payroll.
    b. General and administrative costs.
    c. Project costs.
    d. Facilities.
3. Preparation of original documentation for all financial transactions.

The internal auditors for State University are conducting an audit to review, test, and evaluate the financial control system for Cornwallis labs. The scope of the audit is to include the reliability and integrity of the financial reporting system; compliance with policies, approved plans, procedures, laws, and regulations; and the safeguarding of assets used by the labs.

Required:
Write the preliminary survey program steps for the audit of the Cornwallis labs. Indicate the sources of information for the different procedures included in the preliminary survey.

P-2
Examine the flowchart for an order processing system shown on the following page.

Required:
a. In a review of internal controls, which of the *procedures* could you walk through to test for control weaknesses?
b. What *documents* would you walk through in the examination of a single transaction in the order processing cycle shown in the flowchart?
c. The flowchart reveals at least one control weakness that increases the possibility of a defalcation. Explain the nature of the control weaknesses that you find.
d. Correct the weaknesses and reconstruct the flowchart showing your corrections.

(CIA Exam Adapted)

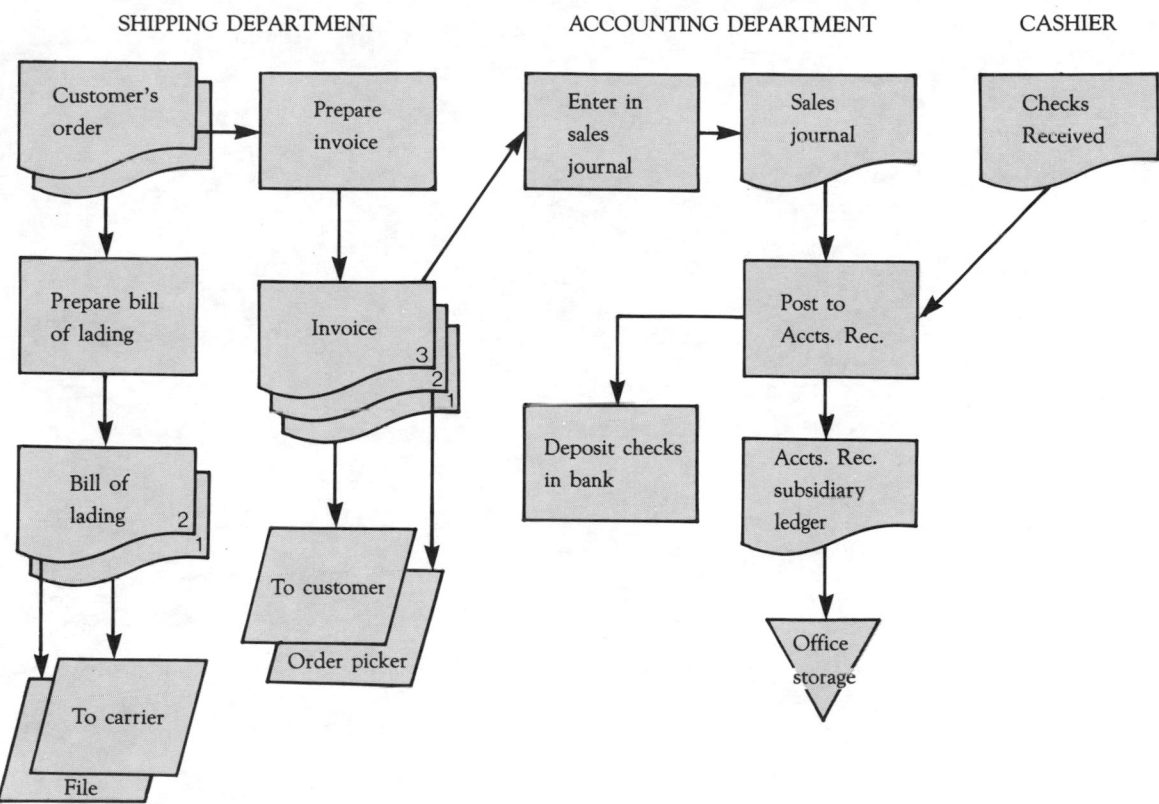

SHIPPING DEPARTMENT   ACCOUNTING DEPARTMENT   CASHIER

9   Expanded Testing and Audit Findings

Step 5 in the audit process expands the audit tests beyond the preliminary survey and the review of internal controls. As we already have discussed, not all audits include these expanded tests. Guideline 420.3, on examining and evaluating information, states that "Audit procedures . . . should be selected in advance, where practicable, and expanded or altered if circumstances warrant."

The decision of whether to expand the audit tests depends upon evidence acquired from the previous audit steps and the auditors' reassessment of risk. When the decision is made to expand audit tests, the auditors must modify the audit program. The first part of this chapter discusses how the audit program is likely to be extended to perform the required tests, and includes the following topics:

- The meaning of expanded testing.
- Risks.
- An example.
- Developing audit programs for expanded testing.
- Criteria for expanded tests.
- Quantitative approaches to expanded testing.

The second part of the chapter addresses Step 6 — the development of audit findings and recommendations which result from the performance of the various audit tests. In discussing audit findings, the chapter addresses the following topics:

- The components of audit findings — condition, criteria, effect, cause, and recommendation.
- Considerations for auditor recommendations.
- Types of audit recommendations.
- Development of audit findings.

Expanded Testing

This section covers the meaning of expanded testing, discusses related risks, and provides an extensive, detailed example.

The Meaning of Expanded Testing

What expanded testing amounts to is gaining additional information so that the auditors can have more confidence in their conclusions. The preliminary survey and review of in.ernal controls provide important information for the auditors, but in most cases the information is inadequate for final conclusions or the development of findings and recommendations. In many cases the evidence represents auditee opinion. In the case of analytical review, it is a set of summary indicators of risk. The evidence may include established policies and procedures, but there is usually limited evidence pertaining to how the auditee actually operates and what specific performance has been attained.

There are three ways that auditors can expand audit tests. They can (1) make a more detailed examination of evidence studied in the preliminary survey and review phase of the audit; (2) increase the number of items previously examined; or (3) broaden the scope of their examination beyond the specific types of evidence examined in steps 3 and 4 of the audit process. Or, the expanded tests may comprise some combination of all three methods. The specific nature of the expansion of audit tests depends, of course, upon the results of the reassessment of risks following the review of internal controls.

The expanded audit tests have three primary purposes. They (1) perform a more *detailed review,* (2) *test compliance* with established controls or performance objectives, and (3) help *evaluate* the control system or the quality of auditee performance.

Of all the topics discussed in this textbook, this particular section may be the most difficult to explain, because everything in the process of expanding audit tests depends upon the results of previous audit work in steps 3 and 4. Knowing how and whether to expand the audit tests requires training, experience, insight, and mature judgment. It is impractical to provide step-by-step guidelines and there are no simple formulas. We can offer, however, some guidance in the form of a logical approach to determining what kinds of tests are most likely to be required in following up certain results in the preliminary survey and the review of internal controls.

Standard 420 states that "internal auditors should collect, analyze, interpret, and document information to support audit results." This standard goes on to state that audit information "should be sufficient, competent, relevant, and useful to provide a sound basis for audit findings and recommendations." Even though the four criteria for audit information, that is, the terms "sufficient," "competent," "relevant," and "useful" are defined, the standard is general and does not provide specific guidelines or rules indicating precisely how much of what kinds of audit information are required. It is mostly a matter of judgment.

Later in this chapter we emphasize how the preliminary results from Steps 3 and 4 might logically be expanded and what evidence will be most beneficial.

Risks

The auditors relate their findings to specific risks, as we have stated. There are five general kinds of risks with which the auditors are concerned, and they relate directly to the objectives of internal control. Internal control is designed to manage these risks. Remember the types of internal controls — preventive, detective, corrective, directive, and compensating — and the 17 methods of internal control (see Chapter 3).

Expanded testing examines the various types and methods of internal control as they relate to the five kinds of risks:

1. The reliability and integrity of information is low.
2. There is inadequate compliance with policies, plans, procedures, laws, and regulations.
3. Operations are uneconomical and inefficient.
4. Assets are inadequately safeguarded.
5. The auditee jeopardizes the achievement of the organization's objectives and goals.

An Example

Perhaps the best method of illustrating the expanded testing step in the audit process is with the analysis of a specific case. Suppose Candlestick Land Enterprises purchases Crabapple Farms, a small corporation with four farming and ranching units. One of the units produces primarily fruits and vegetables; another raises cattle; and two raise sheep. These farms are spread throughout a western state. Candlestick's management asks its internal auditors to examine the internal controls of Crabapple Farms in an effort to help assess the management needs of the newly acquired company. The auditors perform a preliminary survey and a review of internal controls. Exhibit 9-1 outlines some of the results of these audit steps.

After studying the results from the preliminary survey and review of internal controls, the auditors determine whether to expand their audit procedures. Some of the results will lead to expanded testing and some will not, depending upon the level of risk and the quality of evidence obtained. After each preliminary survey and internal control review procedure (outlined in the exhibit with its results) is a brief discussion of considerations related to *expanded test procedures.* Notice the direct relationship between preliminary results and any expanded testing. The next section in this chapter discusses a method to develop expanded testing procedures from preliminary results.

Developing Audit Programs for Expanded Testing

The information on the Crabapple Farms audit helps illustrate a method for developing audit programs for expanded testing. The method essentially schedules, in outline form, the logical steps from the preliminary results to the selection of particular expanded audit tests. The schedule format is similar to that of the internal control matrix, and includes the following five steps. Notice the logical progression from the first to the last of these steps. The auditors:

1. Determine the results from the preliminary survey and the review of internal controls.
2. Determine what, if any, risk is indicated by the result.
3. Determine what types of controls best manage the risks.
4. Determine what, if any, additional evidence they would like to have in order to assess the effectiveness and efficiency of the controls.
5. Select their tests to acquire the additional evidence.

The columns of the schedule in Exhibit 9-2 correspond to these five steps in developing the expanded testing procedures. The first three columns correspond to information prepared for the internal control matrix. The last two columns are specifically prepared to develop the necessary expanded audit procedures. In fact, these last two columns may simply be added to the control matrix. The three sample entries in the exhibit are taken from the narrative description of the audit of Crabapple Farms.

Schedules such as this one offer a systematic approach to developing the expanded program procedures. By developing the procedures using this method, the auditor is forced to consider each preliminary result and what specific audit test would provide the best information related to the risk and the central factors associated with the result. The method does not replace the need for training and good judgment. Rather, it enhances the auditor's ability to exercise his or her judgment.

Criteria for Expanded Tests

While these expanded testing procedures are not exhaustive of everything the auditors might do during the audit, they do offer several examples of how expanded testing might be performed on various items. It should be apparent that there is no set formula for precisely what to do and when.

Exhibit 9-1
Partial Results of Preliminary Survey and Review of Internal Controls With Expanded Test Procedures

AUDIT PROCEDURES

PARTIAL RESULTS

Opening conference with Crabapple management.

Extreme reluctance of the controller for the auditors to closely examine financial controls.

Expanded Test Procedures. Because of the controller's hesitancy for the auditors to examine the financial controls, the auditors suspect that either appropriate financial controls are not in place or that Crabapple's financial management and accounting are not in compliance with policies. Therefore, after the auditors document the financial and accounting controls in the review procedures, they expand their tests to include procedures to test compliance. For example, they may test a random sample of 25 expenditures examining the authorization, supporting documentation, payees shown on the checks, and check signatures.

AUDIT PROCEDURES

PARTIAL RESULTS

On-site tours of Crabapple headquarters and each of the farms.

The general condition of the farms is good with the exception of the sheep farms. The animal shelters appeared to be badly deteriorated and fencing around much of the property is in need of repair. Also, the farm equipment on the sheep farms appeared to have been badly maintained.

Expanded Test Procedures. No additional testing is needed on the fruit and vegetable farm and the cattle ranch. Although problems are apparent from preliminary audit work at the sheep ranch, no new testing is likely to be needed. The auditors should already have documented conditions.

AUDIT PROCEDURES

PARTIAL RESULTS

Study of documents including corporate charter, bylaws, minutes of board of directors' meetings, previous financial statements, and des-

Since incorporation, the financial statements show nine years of generally increasing revenue and income until the purchase of the

AUDIT PROCEDURES	PARTIAL RESULTS
criptions of properties and their operations, and accounting policies and procedures.	sheep ranches three years ago, which greatly increased the company's expenses and failed to provide expected revenues. The board minutes reveal serious questions related to the competence of the manager responsible for the sheep ranches. While the accounting policies and procedures seemed relatively comprehensive, they were badly outdated; in fact, the controller had difficulty finding the policies and procedures manual.

Expanded Test Procedures. The auditors will expand their procedures to analyze the expenses related to the sheep ranch operations, paying particular attention to unusually large expenses and the degree to which various expenses are controllable. They also might compare the expense items to industry averages for similar operations.

While no specific tests are included to examine the competence of the manager of the sheep ranches, the combination of all the audit procedures related to these operations provides substantial evidence related to the quality of sheep ranch management.

Expanded audit tests are needed to determine what accounting procedures are being used, since it is obvious that little attention is paid to the documented accounting policies and procedures. The auditors would test various transactions in order to determine how these transactions are being recorded in the company's records and whether the entries conform to current generally accepted accounting principles.

AUDIT PROCEDURES	PARTIAL RESULTS
Written description.	The only change in corporate management since the founding of the company 12 years ago is the change of the executive secretary at headquarters four years ago. All Crabapple management had extensive agricultural experience and education. Although they desired to continue ownership of the enterprises, Candlestick's offer to pur-

AUDIT PROCEDURES	PARTIAL RESULTS
	chase was very attractive; so they decided to sell their ownership with the contractual understanding that there would be no change in corporate management personnel for at least two years.

Expanded Test Procedures. The auditors probably already will have examined the contract outlining the conditions of sale, so no further testing is needed to confirm these arrangements. No detailed tests appear to be indicated for management's tenure, training, or experience.

AUDIT PROCEDURES	PARTIAL RESULTS
Analytical reviews of Crabapple's financial statements.	A trend analysis of income showed rapid increase in income over the first nine years of operation with the exception of the fifth year, when income was about equal to that of the preceding year. Although income decreased three years ago at the time of the purchase of the sheep ranches, return on equity in all 12 years ranged between 5 and 15 percent. Inventories on the sheep ranch seemed suspiciously high with an unusually low level of sales. Five years ago, mutton and wool markets were exceptionally good, and inventories were increased markedly. Prices were relatively high; however, when the market prices fell four years ago, the sheep ranch was left with over-valued inventory and the prospect of substantial losses. The market continues to be poor. Also, a relatively high turnover of farm employees below the manager level was evident.

Expanded Test Procedures. The auditors already know from previous audit procedures that the sheep ranch operations have decreased the overall corporate income. This information alone does not, however, lead to further testing of the internal control systems. The information informs them of the relative success of the operations and was prepared by the auditors because the figures had not been provided in the financial statements.

The information regarding the sheep inventories and the low level of sales would lead the auditors to test the inventory and sales management policies for the sheep ranches. The expanded tests might include a determination of what performance standards are for inventory management and sales management and whether the high level of inventories and low level of sales are intentional. If so, why?

In addition, the auditors might determine what training and supervision the sheep ranch manager had received. These tests are likely to be in the form of interviews with Crabapple's headquarters management and with the sheep ranch manager. Perhaps the auditors also would acquire documentation provided by the industry, related to sheep farm management practices.

No additional audit procedures would be scheduled for high employee turnover, since this is common among farm workers.

AUDIT PROCEDURES

Internal Control Questionnaire related to Crabapple's financial controls administered to the corporate controller.

PARTIAL RESULTS

Bank reconciliations are supposed to be performed monthly, immediately upon receipt of the company's bank statement. Reconciliations, however, usually are performed and caught up only quarterly, prior to the filing of tax forms with the IRS.

Expanded Test Procedures. The auditors will expand their tests to examine the bank reconciliations. They probably will reconstruct at least one of the reconciliations to test its accuracy and completeness. Another typical test in the area of reconciliation of bank accounts is the examination of segregation of duties, especially on farms when managers assume responsibility for most operational and accounting activities.

AUDIT PROCEDURES

Flowcharts and narrative descriptions.

PARTIAL RESULTS

Journal entries are made by the company's bookkeeper without

AUDIT PROCEDURES	PARTIAL RESULTS
	the review and the approval of the controller.

Expanded Test Procedures. No additional testing is needed to document this control weakness. On the other hand, the auditors are likely to expand their tests to determine the effect of this control weakness. A large sample of journal entries might be selected to examine their documentation to support the entry and the accuracy of the entry. Further, because there is no review or approval of journal entries beyond the bookkeeper, the auditors will likely search for unrecorded transactions such as unrecorded liabilities or purchases.

Unrecorded liabilities may be tested by several procedures:

- Vouch balances in liabilities accounts to supporting documents from creditors.
- Reconcile liabilities with monthly statements from creditors.
- Confirm selected balances with creditors where monthly statements or invoices are not available.
- Compare cash disbursements after the accounting period with a listing of accounts payable as of the end of the period.

AUDIT PROCEDURES	PARTIAL RESULTS
Walk-throughs.	A walk-through of documentation for sales at the fruit farm revealed that sales receipts were not being used.

Expanded Test Procedures. The auditors would likely expand their testing in this case to estimate the total market price of the harvest and the actual sales revenue from the harvest. A comparison of these two figures provides them with a measure of whether all the revenues have been properly accounted for. The auditors also might confirm the amount recorded for sales with the buyers of large quantities from the farm.

AUDIT PROCEDURES	PARTIAL RESULTS
Limited testing of invoice files for the cattle ranch.	Files appeared complete. The five invoices examined were marked "paid" and showed the date of payment and the check number.

Expanded Test Procedures. The five invoices examined do not provide enough evidence for the auditors to make a firm conclusion. Even though invoices appeared in order, they might expand their tests to take a larger sample in order to have more confidence in their conclusion regarding the processing of suppliers' invoices. Other weaknesses in the system would cause them to have less confidence here without further testing.

AUDIT PROCEDURES

Reassessment of risks.

PARTIAL RESULTS

Reliability and integrity of financial statements. Uncertain.

Compliance with policies, plans, etc. Low risk except for accounting, which is uncertain.

Economy and efficiency of operations. Low risk for fruit and vegetable farms and cattle ranch. High risk for sheep ranches.

Safeguarding assets. Medium risk for financial assets. Low to medium risk for produce. Low risk for fixed assets. High risk for the sheep.

Achievement of objectives and goals. Medium risk for sales and collection of revenues. Medium risk for management of expenses except for sheep ranches, which have high risks.

Expanded Test Procedures. The high-risk items include the economy and efficiency of sheep ranch operations and the safeguarding of the sheep themselves. These high-risk matters would likely lead to expanded testing. The auditors might test the accuracy and efficiency of operations by comparing operational expenses to industry averages or other sheep farms known to be well managed and financially successful. To test the safeguarding of the sheep, they might arrange for a count at a time reasonably convenient for them to be present to observe and test its accuracy. The inventory would then be compared to company records. The auditors would evaluate the consistency and fairness of valuation methods and compare that number to the total balance of the sheep inventory accounts.

The auditors might also examine the identification marks on a sample of the sheep to determine if they had been marked appropriately. They would examine records to determine the number of new lambs; the purchase of new sheep; the sale of sheep; the personal use and consumption of others; or losses due to theft, weather, disease, and predators. They might examine the facilities used to house, dip for parasites, corral, and pasture the sheep. The auditors might also confirm the sales figures and purchase of sheep to other farms, the farmer's co-op, and others with whom the farm has done business.

Note: This type of audit is frequently described as an "acquisition" audit, which focuses on three primary factors:

1. Are existing assets as represented in the sale?
2. What accounting practices are used, and is valuation of the assets appropriate in the financial records?
3. What control weaknesses exist in the system?

Management uses the information from these audits to decide what management strategy is most appropriate for the newly acquired assets. Acquisition audits also may be performed *prior* to purchases. Although the audit objectives likely will be similar, management would use the information to decide whether to proceed with the purchase, and if so, what management strategies to implement.

There are, however, logical and reasonable links between the preliminary evidence (with its associated risks) and the selected expanded tests. The selection criteria for these tests may be summarized as follows. Expanded tests should be:

1. *Direct,* relating directly to the risk being examined; i.e., reliable, relevant, and useful.
2. *Efficient,* requiring no more time and expense than is necessary.
3. *Feasible,* within the auditors' abilities (or the abilities of consultants retained by the auditors); i.e., attainable through the use of appropriate audit techniques.

For example, the auditors for Candlestick desired to test the condition of the facilities of the sheep ranches. The auditors could have chosen to find out when all of the various buildings, fences, and so forth, were erected; determine how old each one was; compare that age to the normal expected life of each asset; calculate the total maintenance and repair costs on each; and evaluate the adequacy of these expenditures. But why not simply go look at them?

Exhibit 9-2
Development of Expanded Audit Test Procedures

RESULTS OF PRELIMINARY SURVEY AND INTERNAL CONTROL REVIEW	NATURE OF RISKS APPARENT FROM RESULTS	CONTROL METHODS APPROPRIATE TO MANAGE THE APPARENT RISKS	DESIRED EVIDENCE TO TEST CONTROLS	EXPANDED AUDIT TEST PROCEDURES
Extreme reluctance of controller for auditors to closely examine financial controls.	(a) Compliance with accounting policy and good procedures and (b) quality of accounting information.	(a) Documentation of compliance, (b) effective supervision, and (c) maintenance of accounting records.	(a) Evidence of documentation showing compliance, (b) evidence of effective supervision, and (c) accounting records.	(a) Testing for documentation of employment of good control procedures and (b) testing of accounting entries and balances for accuracy and appropriateness.
Infrequent bank reconciliations.	(a) Possible loss of assets (cash).	(a) Segregation of duties related to handling and accounting for cash and (b) prompt, monthly reconciliation of bank accounts.	(a) Description of duties related to handling and accounting for cash; (b) evidence of timely, complete, and accurate reconciliations; and (c) up-to-date assurance of proper cash stewardship.	(a) No new evidence required related to duties (ICQ information should be enough) and (b) verify two latest bank reconciliations.
Sheep inventories high.	(a) Overstatement of inventories and profits; (b) unsound inventory valuation methods; and (c) losses due to overinvestment in inventories.	(a) Performance standards and (b) supervision and review.	(a) Evidence of existing performance standards, (b) evidence that Crabapple management supervised and reviewed the management of sheep ranch operations, and (c) industry averages and recommended inventory levels.	(a) Compare industry averages, recommended inventory levels, performance standard, and inventory levels and (b) examine documentation of supervision and review or otherwise verify such supervision and review.

*Quantitative
Approaches to
Expanded Testing*

A great deal of research has been performed determining quantitatively how much audit evidence is required to gain certain levels of confidence. We include an introduction to the subject in Chapter 15. A complete treatment of the subject is beyond the scope of this textbook, however.

Audit Findings

As the audit work is performed for the review of internal controls and the expanded testing, the auditors develop their "findings," sometimes also called "points." The findings usually are documented on "Summary Findings Sheets." A single audit may have many findings, and for every finding a separate summary sheet is desirable. These summary sheets provide a convenient, concise, and well-organized source of information for the audit report. They are included in the auditors' working papers.

Guideline 430.04.5 states that "Reports may include findings . . . " which may be both positive and negative. Negative findings are called "exceptions," and admittedly tend to attract more of the auditors' attention than does satisfactory performance or previous corrective action. Exceptions represent areas of current risk. Auditors usually prefer, however, to present a balanced perspective of the auditee's operation, showing good work as well as exceptions. Auditees nearly always prefer a balanced reporting of positive as well as negative audit findings.

Listed below are the five components of an audit finding. (See Exhibit 9-6 for an illustration of a Summary Findings Sheet for the Crabapple Farms audit.)

1. Condition.
2. Criteria or expected practices.
3. Effect.
4. Cause.
5. Recommendation.

Technically, only the first four components are a part of the finding; recommendations are developed from the findings. Auditors, however, often discuss their recommendations as a part of audit findings, and Summary Findings Sheets usually include auditor recommendations. We discuss audit recommendations in some depth later in the chapter. Let's first examine briefly the form of other attributes of audit findings.

Condition

The condition is what the auditors found to be the actual circumstance. This circumstance could be the actual procedure being performed (or not being performed) in an operation, the actual condition of an asset, or the actual amount recorded.

For example, the Candlestick auditors discovered that sales receipts were not being used by the fruit and vegetable farm manager. The farm's customers included a local farm cooperative, several local grocers, and individual customers at a larger farmer's market in a nearby city. There was no documentation of how much merchandise the farm's customers actually received, or the amount and manner of payment. The only documentation of payment was the remittance advices attached to the checks that were received from the co-op after delivery and sale of the commodities.

Notice that even though the condition is presented in summary form, it is still specific. The more specific the description, the more informative it will be. Compare, for example:

1. "Payroll records were disorganized."
2. "Payroll registers were out of sequential order, and two (January and March 1986) were misfiled with employee contracts."

The second statement, although concise, is more informative and helpful than the first.

Criteria or Expectation

The criteria represent the prescribed policies, procedures, standards, laws, and/or regulations to which the auditee should be adhering. It is the performance, behavior, or standard against which the actual practices are being measured by the auditor. This information is almost always needed to avoid communication foul-ups. The auditor should not assume that everyone knows what is expected. In one example, all sales should be documented with a receipt prepared by the person selling the products. The receipt should document the type and amount of goods sold, the amount and method of payment, any applicable tax, the person making the sale, the buyer, and the date of the transaction. These are the practices (criteria) that are expected to exist.

Effect

The effect is the actual or potential impact associated with the condition. How serious is the condition? Is it serious in and of itself, or does the condition make the organization vulnerable to loss? Information that is responsive to questions such as these helps in judging the relative importance of the matter as a finding.

Risks are of five types and correspond to the objectives of internal controls. In our example, the primary risk of not preparing sales receipts is that some sales may go unrecorded and the money collected from these unrecorded sales may not be deposited to farm accounts. Even portions of the collections from recorded sales may be taken and a lesser amount remitted to the company.

Notice that the primary risks in this example are of two types:

1. Inadequate safeguarding of the company's assets (in this case, cash).
2. Unreliability of the financial statements in reporting actual sales from the property.

After identifying the type of risk associated with a condition, the auditor then assesses the severity of the risk. Is it relatively minor? Is it serious? Is it of critical importance? In the example, the failure to issue sales receipts is relatively serious. The auditors can make a somewhat indirect test of sales by confirming sales with each of the customers purchasing large quantities of the farm's produce. The auditors also could estimate sales by estimating the amount of crops harvested, perhaps from harvest records. These procedures provide only an estimate, however, and also are more time consuming than a direct examination of sales receipts.

Cause

The cause of the existing condition indicates why the problem has occurred. There are occasions when the auditee has deliberately chosen to assume the risks that are associated with particular conditions, because alternative decisions may have increased the overall risk to the organization, or because the risk seemed small compared to the cost of correcting the problem. Also, the cause of one problem may be the result of a seemingly unrelated decision. There may be many possible causes of a problem. Although the auditee is responsible for determining the most direct cause(s) in order to know where to focus any remedial action, the auditor is keenly interested and usually assists in pinpointing the cause.

Following the above example, the failure to issue sales receipts at the fruit and vegetable farm is the result of the accounting system used at the farm before it was incorporated by Crabapple Farms. The Crabapple controller had not redesigned the system after the farm's purchase, and there was no review of accounting procedures used for the farm.

Recommendations

The next attribute of audit findings is recommendations. Let's first understand what an audit recommendation is *not*. An audit recommendation *is not* an admonition "to consider the problem for possible action." Such a "recommendation" is really no recommendation at all, because the auditee is no closer to a possible solution after considering the statement than before. An audit recommendation *is* specific to the problem and, ideally, should offer some alternatives or other advice for solving the problem.

When making recommendations, auditors are wise to avoid dictatorial connotations through use of words such as should, ought, or must. Rather, they are generally better received by emphasizing needs and alternatives relative to specific control objectives.

Exhibit 9-3 lists two example conditions and illustrates a possible audit recommendation for each one.

While most internal auditing departments make recommendations in their reports, some auditors and theorists argue that making recommendations can pose a problem because of the potential loss of objectivity. Suppose that internal auditors for a company make recommendations for a control system, and the recommendations are accepted and implemented. Although the auditors do not actually make the decision to take the specific action recommended, some auditing authorities contend that the auditors could become so involved in the decision that their independence would be jeopardized. Consequently, some auditors avoid making recommendations on audit findings.

Guideline 430.5, on communicating audit results, implicitly recognizes the propriety of making recommendations by stating that "reports *may* include recommendations for potential improvements . . . ." (Italics ours.)

Management and auditees are obligated to take audit findings seriously. On the other hand, they are not always obligated to accept audit recommendations. This fact has influenced auditors to recognize that their recommendations sometimes may be more like "suggestions of possible action" that are designed to help the auditee solve problems.

Caution is needed in presenting remedies. The auditors may appropriately suggest reasoned or obvious remedies, but there is risk in offering anything other than well-thought-out alternatives. It is wise for auditors to avoid "off-the-cuff" recommendations just because they might be expected. Further study may be required. Sometimes it is better to suggest ways to approach finding an answer than to recommend a specific solution. This circumspect attitude regarding recommendations is especially important at the report-writing step of the audit process, which is discussed in depth in the next chapter.

Considerations for Auditor Recommendations

When making recommendations, auditors must consider several factors. For example:

1. Does the recommendation solve the problem; i.e., resolve the risk?

Exhibit 9-3
Example of Recommendations

CONDITION

(1) Company vehicles are often taken from the motor pool and used for personal errands of employees. This practice is against company policy and causes unnecessary expenditures.

(2) Many clerical errors are occurring in completing forms and filing office papers. Office work appears to be delayed because of these errors. This condition seems to be the result of a lack of adequate training and/or supervision of office personnel, who appear to be diligent employees.

RECOMMENDATIONS

A possible remedy for this problem would be for departmental supervisors to approve specific use of company vehicles taken from the motor pool and to sign an authorization form to be presented to an appropriate motor-pool person at the time of receiving a vehicle.

Alternative actions to remedy this condition might include the following:

Training. (1) Development of a more thorough job orientation and training program for clerical employees upon their employment but before their assuming job responsibilities. (2) More careful on-the-job training, especially during the early period of employment.

Supervision. (1) More careful assistance and supervision of clerical employees during the workday as specific tasks are being performed. (2) Establishment of a more rigorous review of work performed by clerical employees.

2. Is the auditee capable of implementing the recommendation? Does the auditee have the necessary expertise? Is the necessary technology available?
3. Is the recommendation compatible with the rest of the auditee's operations?
4. Is the recommendation cost effective; i.e., will the benefits exceed the costs of implementation?
5. Does the recommendation represent a long-term, short-term, or merely a stop-gap solution to the problem?

The ultimate consideration is that, if accepted, the auditee is the one expected to live with the decision. The auditors soon will leave, only to return periodically to reexamine the results of the decision. Whatever recommendations are made should be suited to the auditee's needs and operations.

For example, suppose the real estate division of a large investments company was being audited. The auditors were unhappy with the informal methods currently being used to establish the values of potential purchases. The auditors determined that formal appraisals would be more appropriate. Two types of appraisals were considered:

1. External appraisals could be contracted with certified independent appraisers.
2. Internal appraisals could be performed and documented by company experts.

Further, if internal appraisals are performed, either real estate division appraisers may be employed or appraisers may be used from other divisions of the company in order to maintain the desired objectivity.

After studying the problem carefully and conferring with the auditee, the auditors determine that the quality of external appraisals varies significantly. Also, because properties are being purchased throughout the United States and Canada, a number of different appraisal firms would be required. Auditee management argued that the division's own procedures provided more consistent and dependable results than would the practice of requiring external appraisals.

The auditee's management included one of the nation's foremost experts in land appraisal. Auditee management asked if this individual's expertise could not be utilized to help solve the problem. The auditors concluded that, in light of the auditee's recognized expertise and the variable quality of external appraisals, internal appraisals would be appropriate in three conditions:

1. A standard documentation package would be compiled for each appraisal.
2. Each appraisal would be reviewed by the auditee's appraisal expert and by the company's legal staff.
3. An in-house program would be developed to train those doing the appraisals. These individuals also would be required to complete a professional certification program.

The auditors' recommendations were presented in the form of two alternative solutions. External, certified, independent appraisals would be appropriate, or internal appraisals could be performed, given adequate controls.

Auditee management determined that the second alternative would solve the problem less expensively than the other alternative, and was well suited to the auditee's unique situation. The second alternative also represented a relatively long-term solution, assuming that the resident expert remained healthy and on the job. As other company appraisers began to acquire similar expertise, the program would be less dependent upon the one person.

Types of Audit Recommendations
Depending upon the results of the audit tests and procedures, the attitude of management, the nature of the findings, and the resources available, the auditors can make four kinds of recommendations:

1. No changes in the current system.
2. Modification of the current internal control system.
3. Purchase insurance, or self-insure, against the risks discovered during the audit.
4. Adjust the required rate of return on certain activities to reflect the associated risks.

Sometimes the decision as to which type of recommendation to make is relatively straightforward, given the circumstances. Exhibit 9-4 illustrates four problems, with associated audit recommendations, to illustrate different kinds of recommendations.

Some problems require a combination of recommended actions. For example, suppose that because of problems with the transportation and storage of a toxic chemical, one company's internal auditors recommended that:

1. The company should purchase additional liability insurance to cover the risks of spillage during transportation from the supplier to the company's storage facility.
2. The chemical reserve inventory should be moved inland from a riverfront facility to one that is more remote.

Exhibit 9-4
Audit Results with Recommendations

AUDIT RESULTS	RECOMMENDATIONS
No significant exceptions; control system is well designed.	No recommendation for changes.
Cash is collected, deposited, and booked by the same person.	Segregation of collecting, depositing, and accounting responsibilities.
Despite adequately designed control procedures, significant risks remain of defalcations by employees handling large amounts of cash.	Purchase bond insurance on each employee handling large amounts of cash.
Despite adequately designed control systems, business risks remain high for international sales of electronic equipment. More losses have occurred than were expected, and too many offices are only marginally successful.	Increase the required expected rate of return on investment to open or maintain an international sales office.

Other problems may not yield such immediate, clear-cut solutions. When one of these problems arises, the auditors may discover that several alternative recommendations appear equally applicable. In such cases, the internal auditors usually present each alternative recommendation and outline its advantages and disadvantages.

Remember, too, that the auditee may offer the best solution to a problem, in which case the auditors should acknowledge the solution and its origin.

Development of Audit Findings

You may have observed that the Summary Findings Sheets contain no new information that is not already in the audit working papers. Then why prepare summary sheets? The summary sheets briefly outline information that may be scattered in several places in the working papers. The sheets are organized so that all of the findings elements are organized logically. An audit executive, for example, can review the results of an audit quickly and not have to study the detailed working papers, which not only contain information found in the audit findings, but also the detailed support. Of course, the executive must be satisfied that the detailed support is there. But usually, with the review of the individual's working papers by the lead auditor and supervisory auditors, the executive would need to review the detailed working papers only when questions arise as to the quality of the supporting evidence or the appropriateness of particular audit procedures.

Summary Findings Sheets also provide well-organized notes from which to write the audit report.

Examine how an auditor might prepare a Summary Findings Sheet from audit working papers. Exhibit 9-5 shows working papers from the Crabapple Farms audit. From these working papers the auditor prepares a Summary Findings Sheet like the one shown in Exhibit 9-6.

Exhibit 9-6 illustrates how the findings sheet concisely summarizes the detail contained in the working papers. Notice the cross-reference on the write-up sheet to the two working papers. It can be quickly reviewed and evaluated in terms of how the finding should be presented in the final report.

Unfortunately, some auditors prepare only partial findings and do not include all five elements. We have explained why some auditors may not write up their recommendations, but the other four elements usually would be required for a complete finding.

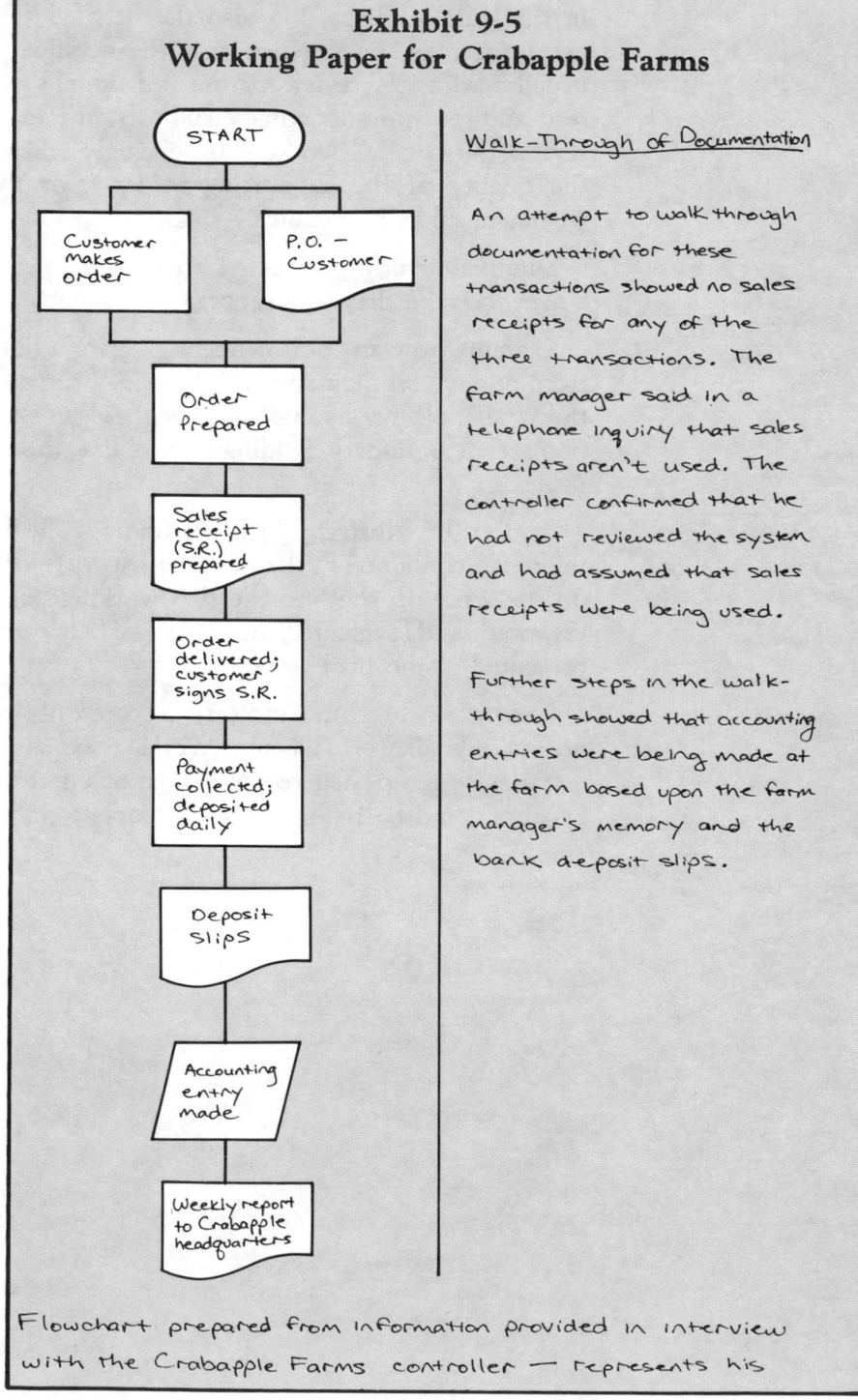

Exhibit 9-5
Working Paper for Crabapple Farms

START

Customer makes order

P.O. — Customer

Order Prepared

Sales receipt (S.R.) prepared

Order delivered; customer signs S.R.

Payment collected; deposited daily

Deposit Slips

Accounting entry made

Weekly report to Crabapple headquarters

Walk-Through of Documentation

An attempt to walk through documentation for these transactions showed no sales receipts for any of the three transactions. The farm manager said in a telephone inquiry that sales receipts aren't used. The controller confirmed that he had not reviewed the system and had assumed that sales receipts were being used.

Further steps in the walk-through showed that accounting entries were being made at the farm based upon the farm manager's memory and the bank deposit slips.

Flowchart prepared from information provided in interview with the Crabapple Farms controller — represents his understanding of sales transactions on fruit and vegetable farms.

The farm manager reconstructed each of the day's transactions from bits and pieces of paper collected during the day and from the bank deposit slip, which is broken down into cash and individually listed checks. The farm manager says that entries are usually constructed from memory. He says he makes sure the total sales are correct and that cash and checks deposited are entered correctly in the "cash receipts" portion of the weekly transaction report. He has worked at the farm since he was 12 years old and says that these transactions have been handled the same way since then.

<u>Risk</u> — High risk of errors in the sales entries. High risk of skimming cash off the deposit and using it for the manager's own purposes.

<u>Recommendation for further audit work</u> — ① Confirm sales figures with large customers. ② Compare total sales to the total of confirmed sales.

<u>Audit recommendation</u> — ① Prepare sales receipt for each sales transaction. ② Periodic review by controller of documentation for sales transactions, to ensure that controls are in place.

Exhibit 9-6
Findings Write-Up Sheet for Crabapple Farms

Prepared by _____   Date _____
Reviewed by _____   Date _____
Working Paper Reference _____

Condition	Sales receipts are not being prepared for sales from Crabapple's fruit and vegetable farm (for 12 years).
Criteria	Standard control procedures for sales, including Crabapple's controller's control policy, require sales receipts of some kind to document the sales transaction.
Effect	(1) Serious risk of skimming and defalcation, (2) serious risk of misstatements on the income statement, and (3) condition existing for 12 years — a 12-year effect.
Cause	Failure of controller to review and enforce accounting control procedures.
Recommendations	(1) Each sale from Crabapple's fruit and vegetable farm should be documented with sales receipt indicating buyer, person making sale, type and amount of products being sold, price for each separate type of item, total price, applicable tax, date of transaction, type of payment, and signature of buyer indicating receipt of goods. (2) Periodic review by controller of sales documentation to ensure that controls are in place.

QUESTIONS

1. What are the three ways that audit tests may be expanded?
2. Why do internal auditors perform expanded testing?
3. What is the chief factor determining if and how audit tests should be expanded? Explain.
4. List the types of controls that expanded audit tests might address.
5. Describe the method discussed in the chapter that is used to develop an audit program for expanded testing procedures.
6. Identify three criteria for expanded audit procedures.
7. Which of the three general audit objectives do expanded tests primarily address?
8. What is an audit finding? How is an audit finding typically documented in the working papers?
9. What are the five components of an audit finding?
10. What problem is associated with including recommendations in audit findings? How does the *Standards for the Professional Practice of Internal Auditing* address the question of making audit recommendations?
11. What alternatives does an auditor have to making audit recommendations?
12. Given the controversy, why do auditors make recommendations?
13. Outline some key factors to consider when making specific audit recommendations.
14. Give an example of a properly stated audit recommendation. What distinguishes a properly stated audit recommendation from the following "recommendation"? — "The auditee should address the control weakness as soon as possible."

EXERCISES

E-1

The internal auditors for Royal Travel Tours included the following three procedures in their audit program for expanded testing to be done on an audit of one of the company's offices:

1. Confirm the balances of a sample of accounts receivable.
2. Test an additional 50 payroll checks for authorized deductions.
3. Expand the testing on previously examined customer-service forms to include documentation of clients' airline and lodging preferences.

Required:

Match the three audit procedures with the following three types of expanded testing:

a. A more detailed examination of evidence studied in the preliminary survey and the review of internal controls.
b. An increase in the number of items previously examined.
c. An examination of entirely new evidence not included in the preliminary survey or in the review of internal controls.

E-2

Suppose a team of internal auditors for a large construction company completed their review of internal controls on an audit of one project's construction costs. The preliminary survey and review of internal controls revealed that the project manager was not taking bids from potential suppliers before purchasing materials. In order to determine the effect of this practice on construction costs, the auditors were considering two procedures:

1. Interview the project manager and ask if, by his not receiving bids on materials, he was able to speed up completion of the project. If so, by how much?
2. Compare the prices paid for materials on this project to prices for similar materials on other similar projects where the project managers took bids.

Required:

a. How might each of the procedures help the auditors determine if construction costs are affected?
b. Which procedure likely would be better, if given a choice of only one? Why?
c. Given the choice, would you perform only the one procedure, or would you perform both? Why?

E-3

Consider the following results from preliminary surveys and reviews of internal controls:

1. Office records are in disorder and some important documents appear to be missing.
2. There recently has been an unusually high turnover of key technical personnel.
3. Appropriate approval signatures are missing on a large number of work orders.

Required:

To what extent does each of the results above expose the organization to the five types of risk? Discuss each of the three results above in terms of all five types of risk.

E-4

Following are two lists: (1) sample audit procedures and (2) several methods of internal controls.

Audit Procedures

1. Test the documentation for a sample of 25 expenditures and verify the recorded amounts.
2. Examine the divisional organization charts for improper lines of authority.
3. Examine personnel background forms on key personnel, match their backgrounds with their respective job descriptions, and evaluate the suitability of these key employees to their positions.
4. Test the budgeting director's compliance with budget review procedures.
5. Test a sample of new sets coming off the production line for quality control.
6. Foot and crossfoot the division's payroll register.
7. Flowchart the purchasing, receiving, and payment functions for regional operations.

Methods of Internal Control
1. Organizational structure and responsibilities.
2. Segregation of related duties.
3. Proper authorization.
4. Budgeting and accounting.
5. Standards of performance.
6. Policies and procedures.
7. Selection, training, and supervision of personnel.
8. Review.

Required:
Identify which type of control is being tested by each of the audit procedures.

E-5
The internal auditors for a city government were preparing a schedule to develop the expanded testing procedures for an audit of the city's fire department. One part of the schedule is shown below:

Result	Risk	Controls
Response time on last five fires from one station averaged three minutes longer than standard.	Significant property losses to fires.	(a) Truck preparation (b) Ability of men (c) Preparation of men (d) Communication lines (e) Traffic and street access

Required:
a. If you were an internal auditor assigned to this case, what additional evidence would you want?
b. What audit procedure would you use to gather the evidence?

E-6
A team of internal auditors developed the following finding, except for their recommendation:

Condition	Current production rate per machine is 120 units per day, leading to more than two-week delays in job deliveries.
Criteria	The standard production rate is an average of 150 units per day per machine.
Cause	The variable quality of the current supply of raw materials results in inconsistent product quality, numerous rejects, and machine breakdowns.
Effect	In addition to production delays, 10 percent of all orders have been cancelled over the last three months. New orders have decreased from an average of 100 per week to 90. The combined effect of cancelled orders and the loss of new sales decreases revenues by approximately $200,000 monthly. Production costs also have increased by $15,000 per month in materials wastage and $5,000 average monthly repair cost on machinery.

Required:

a. Evaluate the following alternative recommendations for this case. Justify your answers in terms of the criteria outlined in the chapter.

   1. Production's management should consider the problem and possible solutions.
   2. Production's management should increase the overtime that is necessary to meet production standards.
   3. Purchasing should change suppliers of new materials.
   4. Production should test materials from several suppliers in the quantities needed to determine which supplier can best meet the required materials standards of quality and consistency.

b. What recommendation would you make in this case?

E-7

Study the following audit finding:

Condition	An analysis of inventories revealed a frequent periodic shortage of a dye that is important in the preparation of a particular cloth that is popular for draperies.
Criteria	Inventories should be examined and reordered monthly to replenish supplies.
Effect	Frequent periodic shortages in the dye occur, causing a stoppage in production of the particular clothing that requires the dye.
Cause	Reordering is too infrequent to maintain the necessary supplies.
Recommendation	Purchasing should set up a special reordering schedule to replenish the dye weekly.

Required:

Critique the finding, paying particular attention to its logical development.

PROBLEMS

P-1

The claims department of National Insurance Company has instituted some new claims procedures for local offices. The new procedures have been designed to improve the review of claims and to prevent both overpayment and payment of false claims. Management mentioned concern about the new procedures at the opening conference of an audit. Management told the auditors that three complaints had been received recently about the excessive time it took to receive the insurance proceeds for their claims. The company advertises 48-hour claims service. Each of the three claims that generated complaints took seven days. Management said these were the first complaints of this type and were received only after the new procedures were implemented. Management feared that if claims took too long to process, many clients would switch to another company. The auditors decided to find out if processing time really had increased, and if so, whether it was because of the new procedures. The auditors decided to test 25 randomly selected claims made since the change in procedures and 25 claims from before the changes and compare them statistically. If the claims since the change were taking significantly longer, the auditors decided to walk through both processes — before the change and after the change — and stay alert for differences in time requirements. If there were no significant differences in the two samples, the auditors decided to find out why the particular claims responsible for the complaints had been delayed.

Required:

Prepare a schedule showing the development of the expanded audit procedures from the result of the opening conference.

P-2

The audit tests in P-1 revealed that the new procedures had indeed caused an increase in claims processing time for two reasons. First, there was a learning effect with the new forms required. The headquarters' claims department often had to correct the forms and request additional information before a claim could be processed. Also, the new procedures require a more extensive review than before, sometimes even including a field visit by one of the claims staff in addition to the regular inquiry by one of the company's claims adjusters. The auditors estimated that the delayed disposition of claims seriously eroded the marketability of the company's policies, perhaps decreasing sales by as much as 10 percent the first year and up to 25 percent in subsequent years. The new procedures also would increase the cost of servicing claims by 5 percent to 10 percent, depending upon whether an additional inquiry is conducted by one of the claims department staff members. The estimated savings on payment of improper claims was equivalent to a maximum of 10 percent of total expenditures in any one year. The company's internal auditors determined that returning to the previous claims service procedures, with minor review modifications, would serve the intended purpose and avoid the problems associated with the revised procedures. The additional review procedure recommended by the auditors was a computer scan of company records to ascertain any previous claims by the claimant and the nature as well as the amount of the prior claims.

Required:

Prepare a Summary Findings Sheet from the information given in P-1 and P-2.

P-3

Required:

a. For the previous problem, identify at least three possible alternative recommendations, including the one chosen, that the auditors might have given. Evaluate and rank each of your alternatives in terms of the criteria outlined in the chapter.

b. Identify at least one alternative audit procedure the auditors might have chosen for their expanded testing other than the ones selected. Compare your procedure(s) with the ones in the problem in terms of the criteria listed in the chapter.

10 Reporting the Internal Audit

Everything related to an audit either is directed toward the preparation and delivery of the audit report or occurs as a result of the audit report. While a great deal of attention is given to the various other steps, the focus of the total auditing process is on Step 7 — the preparation and delivery of the internal audit report.

Usually, results of the internal audit are reported in two ways:

1. At meetings where findings are discussed orally.
2. In a formal, written document.

The oral presentation is made at what is called a *closing conference,* which takes place soon after the audit team completes the audit work. The written report follows later. Some findings that are developed during the audit work require communication before the end of the audit. In these cases, auditors often make *interim reports.*

This chapter outlines reporting standards and discusses closing conferences, interim reporting, and various aspects of the process of creating written reports.

A word of caution is appropriate here. The principles discussed in this chapter apply generally to almost all internal audit reports. Specific applications of these principles, however, vary among different internal auditing departments. The applications discussed in this chapter are designed to illustrate the principles. Students should realize that there are other approaches and that all reports do not conform precisely to these illustrations.

Reporting Standards

The importance of the audit report is manifest in the *Standards for the Professional Practice of Internal Auditing* as follows:

430 Communicating Results
Internal auditors should report the results of their audit work.

.01 A signed, written report should be issued after the audit examination is completed. Interim reports may be written or oral and may be transmitted formally or informally.

.02 The internal auditor should discuss conclusions and recommendations at appropriate levels of management before issuing final written reports.

.03   Reports should be objective, clear, concise, constructive, and timely.

.04   Reports should present the purpose, scope, and results of the audit; and, where appropriate, reports should contain an expression of the auditor's opinion.

.05   Reports may include recommendations for potential improvements and acknowledge satisfactory performance and corrective action.

.06   The auditee's views about audit conclusions or recommendations may be included in the audit report.

.07   The director of internal auditing or designee should review and approve the final audit report before issuance and should decide to whom the report will be distributed.

Statement on Internal Auditing Standards No. 2 (SIAS 2) on "Communicating Results" is reprinted in an appendix to this chapter.

In the following pages we discuss how these various standards may be met so that the internal audit report effectively communicates the results of the audit.

Audit Closing Conferences

Guideline 430.02 states, "The internal auditor should discuss conclusions and recommendations at appropriate levels of management before issuing final written reports." These discussions are an important part of the reporting process and generally take place at *closing conferences.*

As the audit work draws to a finish, the audit team leader schedules a closing conference with auditee management to discuss the results of the audit. It is best to schedule the closing conference as near to the completion of the audit work as possible. Otherwise, the auditee will have pursued normal operations after the audit work, and the closing conference may have less of an effect. The meeting is usually held at the offices of the auditee. The audit team leader, other members of the audit team, and sometimes (especially on controversial audits) an audit executive will attend.

At the closing conference, the team leader typically reviews audit objectives and then the findings. Major findings — those that involve more risk — are reviewed first. The ensuing discussions help the auditors determine if their information is complete and accurate. Discussions frequently touch on possible implications and risks to the organization, and on alternative actions that might be taken to rectify any observed problems. The auditors should take care to make a balanced and fair presentation, and make comments about good control as well as any observed weaknesses. It is at this meeting that the more controversial issues tend to surface, and the auditee is more likely to indicate what responses might be forthcoming to the audit findings.

Key Factors to Successful Closing Conferences

As discussed in earlier chapters, the primary factor in successful communication is adequate preparation.

Exhibit 10-1 illustrates one internal audit organization's suggested agenda for closing conferences. The list of reminders and the agenda incorporate principles of effective communication.

The agenda shown in Exhibit 10-1 is for the exclusive guidance of the auditor. If it seems desirable to give the auditee an agenda at the start of the meeting, one such as the following would generally cover matters to be discussed:

1. Objectives and scope of the audit.
2. Basic audit approach.
3. Observation regarding operations, systems, and procedures.
4. Audit findings.
5. Response to findings.
6. Written report:
    a. Expected completion date.
    b. Distribution list.
    c. Review process.
7. Written response for auditee.
8. Follow-up to audit findings.
9. Questions, observations, suggestions for auditors.

Written Audit Reports

Aside from the technical task of clearly communicating audit results, there is an ever-present reality: *the audit report is a reflection of the competence and professional image of the auditor.*

The power of the report is influenced not only by the technical soundness of the findings and recommendations, but by its communicative qualities as well — things such as clarity, tone, and style.

The writer of any document is responsible for communicating the message, and must be clear. Questions must be anticipated and addressed in the document. In personal presentations there is a flexibility that is not available in written reports. In face-to-face encounters, auditors can use their power of personality. There is the captivating power of voice and manner — body language, gestures, voice modulation, etc. Questions can be asked and responses can be offered. Reactions and moods can be observed and responses can be given. But in written reports there are only words, numbers, and graphic illustrations. Therefore, the written report must be clear, and the desired mood must be created by words and other skills that are covered in later sections.

Exhibit 10-1
Agenda for Closing Conference and
Reviews of Report Drafts

A Reminder: Display Professionalism

1. Be courteous and polite always:
   a. Refuse to engage in bickering or name-calling.
   b. Avoid impolite comments such as "you are wrong," "I don't buy that," "I disagree." It is unthinkable to use words such as "dumb," "crazy," "stupid," "ridiculous," or "asinine."
2. Be neutral and objective, fair, and balanced in tone and profile.
3. Be prepared and anticipate objections. Have adequate evidence ready: notes, references, etc.
4. Be positive in attitude:
   a. Build up, improve, encourage; don't tear down, defeat, or destroy.
   b. Leave room for auditee to save face.
   c. Don't treat airing of views as being disagreement.
5. Show restrained confidence and speak audibly with eye contact and calm authority.
6. Listen carefully for feedback.

Suggested Agenda

1. Explain audit scope and objectives. _____
2. Briefly explain the audit approach. _____
3. Make appropriate, positive comments about cooperation and assistance. _____
4. Make appropriate, positive comments concerning operations, systems, and procedures. _____
5. Discuss findings and recommendations and receive needed feedback. Be willing to modify wording if appropriate. _____
6. Point out to whom the report is or will be addressed and who is to receive copies or portions of it. Obtain auditee's view as to the propriety of this. Stress confidentiality measures. _____
7. Tell the auditee when report will be ready to review or when it will be released. _____
8. Inform the auditee of expectation of response. _____
9. For report draft reviews, ask auditee if there is a need to hold on to the discussion draft. Take back or politely ask the auditee to be cautious about its use and eventual destruction. _____
10. Consider asking if they have any suggestions regarding the conduct of the audit. _____
11. Extend thanks for feedback. _____

Uses and Importance of Audit Reports

Audit reports may serve several parties, including the auditors, operating management, executive management, the organization's outside auditors, and often government regulators or courts. Internal auditors should keep the various needs of these groups in mind when preparing audit reports.

How the Report Serves the Auditor

1. *The audit report communicates the purpose, scope, and results of the audit work.* It is a powerful communicating device that draws, if not commands, the attention of management.

2. *It demonstrates that the auditors have discharged their responsibilities.* The report informs management of audit activities and is written evidence of audit performance. It is the primary evidence to which a prudent person would refer in assessing what an auditor had done.

3. *It stimulates action to bring about needed improvements.* When matters are reported formally, auditors can communicate a level of commitment, seriousness, and resolve which commands respect and attention. As a result, there is a greater likelihood of action.

4. *It governs and controls the end product of the audit.* The end product is the report, and it is subject to review and approval. This review process allows the auditors to control the content, organization, and style of the audit report.

5. *It is a means of teaching and training audit staff members.* The disciplines of organizing and presenting ideas can be developed as the report evolves. The writing, editing, review, rewriting, and presentation of the internal audit report help refine the auditor's technical auditing as well as general communication skills.

6. *It is a means of selling oneself.* Communication and technical skills are generally exposed in the report; indeed, they cannot be hidden. To the audit executive it is an opportunity to evaluate individual skills and the performance progress of audit staff members.

7. *It helps in audit follow-up.* What has been reported? What is to be done? When? The written report serves as a readily available reference.

How the Report Serves Operating Management

1. *The audit report amounts to an independent and objective review of operations* by people who have been trained to focus on important control activities, processes, and procedures.

2. *It can stimulate action toward necessary improvements.* The audit function is a type of self-corrective device within the organization that prompts action on matters that need attention. Specific findings and recommendations can serve as a plan of action.

3. *It can be a means of gaining support for issues that require the attention of upper management.* There are times when operating managers would like to bring certain issues to the attention of upper management, but hesitate because of internal politics, fear of reprisals, etc. Auditors can do so without such fear and hesitancy.

4. *It can serve as a window into operations* for busy operating managers. Because time is scarce, they tend to focus more on the daily processing of work than upon specific controls. The audit report helps management to monitor the controls over operations and risks.

5. *It can assist in evaluating operating performance.* The audit report usually is not intended as a performance report card, but it can be a resource for such a purpose. For management to assess performance adequately, it must understand the factors contributing to the operating results. One key factor is the internal control system. Performance audits focus primarily on evaluating auditee performance when management, for some reason, needs this independent evaluator.

How the Report Serves Top Management

1. *The audit report provides details about operations and controls that are not contained in other reports.*

2. *It provides independent, often unfavorable, information that otherwise may not reach top management.*

3. *It provides top management with information on audit activities.* In addition to informing management about auditees, the report tells top management what the auditors did to reach their conclusions.

4. *It helps promote appropriately disciplined and ordered operations.* The knowledge that audit reports go to top management encourages auditees to maintain good control over other activities.

5. *It results in improved control.* The audit, as part of the internal control system, provides a detective control and alerts management to risks and weaknesses. Corrective action can then be taken.

6. *It provides evidence about prudence and compliance with the law.* Executive management is especially sensitive to legal provisions such as those contained in the Foreign Corrupt Practices Act. The audit report alerts management to violations of such laws that may have been found during the audit.

Use of Audit Reports by Others

The internal audit report can be an important source of information for external auditors. In addition to providing insight into specific operations, it can help them evaluate the extent to which the internal auditors' work can be relied on for segments of their examination. The report can also alert them to special problems and help them avoid duplication of work.

Internal audit reports can sometimes provide reassurance to regulatory agencies regarding practices that are of interest to them.

When internal audit reports address especially sensitive affairs of the organization, both management and the auditor need to be aware that the report is "discoverable" by outsiders. That is, where there are disputes with governmental regulatory and taxing agencies or other parties, information in an audit report could be detrimental in some way to the organization or to individuals. Awareness of a report's discoverability is needed to avoid potential conflicts. Although the internal auditors should inform management of such problems, in some cases these matters need not be documented in the audit report. Some auditors feel, however, that where management may otherwise ignore a potentially serious problem, documenting it in the report is more likely to prompt corrective action, which may help avoid even more serious consequences.

Clear Writing Techniques

The objectives of writing are to inform and to influence. Whether these objectives are met depends on the quality of the writing, often described in terms of its clarity.

There are many materials published on the subject of clear writing. Most writing experts agree on the following principles:

1.   Gather the necessary information before starting.
2.   Use a conversational style.
3.   Keep most sentences short and simple.
4.   Use active voice verbs.
5.   Use clear, familiar words.
6.   Use appropriate captions.
7.   Use emphasis — underlining or italics.
8.   Use white space for a more attractive appearance.
9.   Use short paragraphs.
10. Use graphics.

Gather the Necessary Information Before Starting

Trying to perform any task without the necessary tools or supplies is frustrating and inefficient. Trying to write without having an ample array of facts and figures is also wasteful. Information fuels ideas and speeds word flow. Also, by gathering information before writing, the auditor can avoid time-consuming reorganization and rewriting that otherwise might occur.

*Use a
Conversational
Style*

There is a misconception that writing must be scholarly, technical, and formal to be authoritative. However, research has shown that writing tends to be more precise and more retainable when it is conversational in style.

An auditor in a relaxed mood at the water fountain, face-to-face with his team leader, is likely to explain a situation in a clear and interesting manner. Then he picks up a pencil and suddenly becomes stiff, formal, and dull. One reason is because there is spontaneous feedback in conversation. "What do you mean?" "Why didn't it jam up?" "Anyone see it?" "Who said that?" "I understand." "Wow, how could that happen?"

When you're writing, however, feedback isn't immediately available, so it is essential to *anticipate where misunderstandings might occur.* Ask yourself, "How would I say this if I were trying to explain it face-to-face?" Keep asking yourself what, when, why, where, who, and how?

As you write, try to anticipate the reaction of the reader. Remember, the reader wasn't there and does not have the mental images that you have.

With a conversational style, the names of people often are included. Don't go out of the way to keep them out. After naming people, use "he," "she," or "they." But don't keep repeating "he" over and over again — go back to the proper name as a natural break. Also, avoid names and personal references when deficiencies are the subject and the tone begins to suggest personal inadequacies. Criticize practices, not people.

*Keep Most
Sentences Short
and Simple*

Much of the information included in audit reports is of a technical nature. The jargon used to explain how systems work and how employees do what they do tends to include many polysyllabic words. Technicians and workers in one function or agency frequently have a "work language" that differs from others in some ways. Managers and administrators also have their special business and operating language. Auditors tend to use the technical business and systems' terms. The writing, therefore, tends to be relatively complex.

Under these circumstances, it is important to keep most sentences short and simple. A rule of thumb is to use an average of 15 to 20 words and one main idea per sentence. Long sentences are often foggy, awkward, and tend to be dull. Observe what can happen when this simple principle is ignored: "Assuming the material to be converted in the Apex Company 100-gallon mixer in their plant and in its present operating condition (three batches per hour, stopping the machine five minutes to empty and refill) and with the condition of shipping the material from Apex to Acme packing in one-quart containers, reshipping to Apex labeling and hand-packing 12 cans per carton, including adequate amounts for waste, delays, trucking, etc., the cost amounts to $0.432 per carton of 12 one-quart cans." Although other writing principles are violated in this example, the placement of two or three periods would have made the information clearer.

Use Active Voice Verbs

Use the passive voice sparingly. The active voice is usually shorter, more lively, and more conversational. It is also more natural.

Active: The subject of the sentence performs the action specified by the verb. Example: "The operations manager asked for several special assignments."

Passive: The subject undergoes the action of the verb. Example: "Several special assignments were asked for by the operations manager."

The passive voice tends to be dull and synthetically formal. It is also less emphatic and frequently is not as clear as the active voice.

Passive: "It was recommended by general counsel that the wording changes be made."

Active: "General counsel advised us to make the wording changes."

Passive: "It was found that money was being lost through the ownership of agency offices and that leasing them would be preferable."

Active: "Figures showed that the agency could save money by leasing its offices instead of owning them."

The passive voice is not wrong, but it frequently is vague. When vagueness is desired, passive voice is the answer. For example: "It was recommended that the wording changes be made," or "Wording changes were recommended." Who recommended the changes? The passive voice permits this vagueness, whereas the active voice usually forces disclosure. The active voice would be, "General counsel recommended wording changes."

When used sparingly, the passive voice can add variety. A natural way to use the passive voice is to place the object first in a sentence. For example: "Purchase requisitions are submitted by agency directors; the purchase orders are prepared by the purchasing department."

**Use Clear,
Familiar Words**

Precision and ease of understanding are the dual objectives in selecting words. For example, the word "indicated" may be perceived by some as "proved," when you really intended it to mean "suggested." "Indicated" is familiar but not *precise.*

The word "noted" is short and familiar but frequently imprecise. Does it mean you personally observed something, or that you heard about it from others? The word "consonance" may be precise enough, but "harmony" is more familiar to most people and more easily understood (e.g., "in harmony with division policy . . .").

The auditor must constantly challenge the selection of words. Be specific and precise. If an entire sentence is needed because you can't find a precise, familiar word, sacrifice brevity for clarity by using a sentence.

The auditor must not let anyone influence him or her into thinking that the reader is responsible for understanding. *The burden is on the writer.* Sophisticated ideas and complex procedures and conditions should be expressed clearly and simply without sacrificing accuracy.

**Use Appropriate
Captions**

Captions, also called "headings" or "subtitles," help the reader locate specific information in the report. They help to speed the review, facilitate scanning, and help the writer control what the reader gets out of the written material. Captions also speed up the reading process by providing transition from subject to subject.

While there are a variety of styles for captions, three guidelines may be helpful in determining how best to use them:

1. When a section of a report is relatively short and contains an expansion of a basic idea or theme, a *descriptive caption* that states the idea or theme with the utmost brevity is appropriate. For example, a descriptive caption might read something like this: "Inaccuracies in Cost Control Records." On the other hand, when sections are relatively long and contain a variety of information on a particular subject, a *topical caption* is appropriate. An example of a topical caption would be "Computer Security." Sometimes a large section of a report will have a topical caption followed by several descriptive captions for the various subsections. For example:

   Travel Advances
   (topical caption for overall section)

   Travel Advances Not Settled on a Timely Basis
   (descriptive caption for subsection)

Unnecessarily Large Travel Advances
(descriptive caption for subsection)

2. Captions tend to make reading easier. Pages with no captions tend to be forbidding, even tiring, for many readers. Too many captions, however, will make the page look cluttered and disorganized. As a general guideline, every page of the report should have one or two captions but no more than four, although circumstances may cause some variation in these limits. The point is to make reading easier by using captions to break up the mass of text in the report, and to manage what the reader should receive from the material.

3. Where the sequence of captions follows logically from one to the next, a numbering system will help the reader link the ideas together. Compare, for example, the two lists of captions below:

Control Procedure Steps	Control Procedure Steps
Open document	(1) Open document
Verify signature	(2) Verify signature
Calculate results	(3) Calculate results
Record results	(4) Record results

The list of captions on the left itemizes a set of control procedure steps. The list on the right, however, implies a sequence to the procedures. If the sequence is important, numbered captions help make that point clear.

Use Emphasis

The auditor may want to emphasize certain points or ideas which may not be set apart through captions or graphic illustrations. The use of underlining or italics directs the reader's attention to specific wording and adds emphasis. Too much underlining, however, becomes confusing. Auditors who use underlining for emphasis must be careful to sprinkle enough in their reports to emphasize key points, without using so much that the reader is unsure of what the key points really are.

Use White Space

Effective use of white space makes a page appear inviting. Adequate white space makes captions and illustrations stand out. Ample margins — usually one to two inches wide - are also important. Surrounding a single statement with extra white space adds emphasis to the statement. Remember that adding some white space to pages in a report can also enhance the reader's understanding, and paper is cheap compared to the alternative of not being understood.

**Use Short
Paragraphs**

Readers tend to prefer short paragraphs rather than long ones. Shorter paragraphs tend to add white space and serve as resting or stopping places for the reader. Six to twelve lines are common for paragraphs, although a paragraph may sometimes constitute a single sentence of one or two lines. Occasionally a long paragraph may be appropriate when discussing a single idea or concept in detail, but a good general guideline is to use short paragraphs.

Use Graphics

The use of charts, graphs, drawings, diagrams, and even photographs in internal audit reports helps the auditor to communicate more effectively and efficiently. Auditors frequently include graphics to add variety, interest, and additional information to their reports.

Preparing to
Write the Report

Preparation for writing the report starts at the beginning of the audit — not at the end. Like every worthwhile creation, the report should be conceived and pictured in the mind before it is structured tangibly. This sets the creative thought processes in motion. If the auditor thinks about the report while planning and preparing for the audit and while performing the initial work, a mental image of the report will begin to form.

In keeping with Standard 410 on planning the audit, some internal auditing departments require that an audit executive and the team leader get together at the start of an audit to discuss the following report characteristics:

a. General or specific format of report.
b. Likely addressee.
c. Possible wording of audit objectives, scope of the audit work, and similar formalities.
d. Likely or tentative distribution.
e. Approximate or desirable length in number of pages.
f. How findings may be presented.
g. Possible types of information that can be used to supplement findings, and the use of appendices, exhibits, and graphics.

When the team leader has a relatively clear picture of what the report format is likely to be, the report can be partially formed as the audit progresses. Also, the team leader will have a high level of confidence that at least these aspects of the report will be acceptable to the audit executives who must approve the report.

From the mental process, the auditor might picture the finished product. For example, the writing style will be relaxed and inviting. Topics will be descriptively worded. Facts and circumstances will clearly set forth just the right amount of detail for the reader. The report format will permit the reader to quickly scan and gain key information. The more important matters will be covered up front. An executive summary will outline key points. The wording will be simple yet powerful. The tone will be objective, fair, natural, and balanced. Salient facts will be presented in just the right sequence. Illustrations and analyses will complement the wording and add to clarity and interest. Questions that would naturally occur to the reader will be answered at just the right time.

Coordinating the Efforts of Other Writers

Frequently, two or more auditors participate in writing the report. One person should take the lead to ensure that format and style are consistent. The use of Summary Findings Sheets is an effective tool for this purpose, since the findings constitute the bulk of the report. The team leader should get together with contributing writers early in the audit to decide on the format of the findings write-ups. The team leader normally adds the finishing touches, refines and polishes the report, and prepares the formalities (or introductory) section.

Later, each contributing writer should read the entire report, or at least the part he or she wrote, to ensure that editing and refining changes did not adversely affect accuracy.

Basic Audit Report Model

Internal audit reports from different organizations take many different forms. The following basic model illustrates one acceptable format that is highly flexible and has proven successful in a variety of settings. This model contains the following components:

1. Cover.
2. Formalities section.
3. Executive summary or highlights section.
4. Detailed findings.
5. Exhibits and attachments (if any).

Cover

A cover is almost always desirable. Covers range from simple file folders to fancy binders. If the information to report is very short, a letter may be more appropriate. For the more typical audit report, however, the cover should include the following:

1. Report title.
2. Name and location of auditee.
3. Date of audit.

Title. The title identifies the subject of the audit, the name of the auditee, or both. It should provide the reader with an immediate image of the nature or character of the audit. The number of words should be limited to those that are essential to get the meaning across. The wording of the title deserves careful thought because it will probably be referenced as such for filing and indexing purposes. See examples in Exhibit 10-2.

```
┌─────────────────────────────────────────────────────────┐
│                                                         │
│                    Exhibit 10-2                         │
│        Examples of Cover Information for Audit Report    │
│                                                         │
│                                                         │
│                    (Example A)                          │
│                                                         │
│                   Special Audit                         │
│                Accounts Receivable                      │
│                  State University                       │
│                September 30, 19XX                       │
│                                                         │
│                    (Example B)                          │
│                                                         │
│                   Report of Audit                       │
│        Red Butte Division Purchasing Function           │
│                  Atlanta, Georgia                       │
│                   August 19XX                           │
│                                                         │
│                    (Example C)                          │
│                                                         │
│               Report of Internal Audit                  │
│      Medical Claims Paid by Metro Health Maintenance Plan │
│                  Oakland, California                    │
│          From May 20, 19XX, to December 31, 19XX        │
│                                                         │
│                    (Example D)                          │
│                                                         │
│                   Report of Audit                       │
│         Acquisition, Use, and Control of Microcomputers │
│            in the Information Systems Department         │
│                  February 19XX                          │
│                                                         │
└─────────────────────────────────────────────────────────┘
```

Name and Location of Auditee. Specific identification of the auditee may be included in the title or it may be separate.

The corporation, division, department, section, or other name of the entity should be shown as it officially exists. For example, distinguish between "Incorporated" and "Inc.;" "and" and "&;" "Company Inc." and "Company, Inc." If "The" is not part of the legal name, it should not be used when referring to the organization by name. When the full official name is not being used in the body of the report, the auditee may be referred to as Company, Division,

Section, School, City, Plant, Project, or other similar designation (capitalizing the initial letter).

The name of the city where the auditee is located should not be abbreviated on the cover, and the preference is not to abbreviate the name of the state or country. See examples in Exhibit 10-2.

Date of Audit Coverage. The nature of the report will dictate how to disclose the date on the cover. The following guidelines should be helpful for most situations:

1. Use the month and year of the activities being audited, unless financial reports are the subject.
2. Use only the *balance sheet date* in cases where the balance sheet alone or balance sheet schedules and analyses are the subject of the audit.
3. Use the *balance sheet date* where balance sheet *and* operating statements for the fiscal year ended at the balance sheet date are included.
4. Use the *period dates* in cases where statements of operations or similar financial data are for periods that are longer or shorter than a fiscal year.

Examples of period dates:

Year ended December 31, 1987.
Period of six months ended June 30, 1987.
Period of one year and four months ended April 30, 1987.
From March 1, 1987, to September 24, 1987.

5. Use *"ended"* when the period has passed. Use *"ending"* when the date is in the future (such as for projections and forecasts).

Formalities Section   There are certain formalities that must be covered, usually at the beginning of the report. The formalities constitute an introduction, often in the form of a "transmittal letter." For a large audit the introduction may require several pages. In most reports the formalities can be covered in one to three pages.

These formalities normally include the following:

1. Date of report or date transmitted.
2. Addressee (name, title, address, etc.).
3. Preface, foreword, or background.
4. Audit scope or objectives.
5. Brief opinion and nature of findings.
6. Reply (or other action) expectations.
7. Signature.

8. Names of participating auditors.
9. Distribution disclosure.
10. Contents reference or index.

Exhibit 10-3 illustrates such a transmittal letter. The case on which this example was patterned provided a separate table of contents for the report.

Date of Report or Date Transmitted. When the introduction or formalities are presented in a transmittal letter, the date of the letter will usually serve as the report date. This date usually is included at or near the top of the first page. A transmittal date will not necessarily correspond to the date on the cover. The cover date represents the time of the audit or the time being audited. The report date is the date on which the report is released for distribution, which sometimes may be more than a month after completion of the audit.

Addressee. The addressee may be an entity or an executive group, such as the board of directors or executive committee. The addressee may also be a single executive, such as administrator, executive director, manager of operations, etc.

Usually, during the planning phase of the audit, it is determined to whom the report will be addressed. A guideline that is frequently followed in the absence of other prevailing influences is to address the report to the executive person or body to whom the audited function reports.

Auditors avoid addressing the report to anyone who is powerless to influence the necessary changes.

Preface, Foreword, or Background. This section provides just enough information to identify the organization or function that will be reviewed and explain its objectives and significance. This information also can help establish the tone and setting. It is sometimes appropriate to explain why the audit took place — e.g., transition of new management, special request or requirements, part of an ongoing program, high risk, etc. In this section, auditors avoid inferences of inadequate management, distrust, or anything that could offend the auditee.

Audit Scope or Objectives. The facts of the operation that have been reviewed, audited, or studied are explained here, along with a brief disclosure of the depth or breadth of the review. If the audit approach is unique, it may be desirable to briefly explain that approach. Special care must be taken to avoid language that is overly technical or too detailed. Any limitations should be explained so that no one can assume that more audit work was done than actually was.

Exhibit 10-3
Transmittal Letter

[date] February 17, 19XX

Morton L. Fepplemeyer, Vice President *[addressee]*
West Coast Operations
Oakland, California

We recently completed an audit of medical claims processed and paid by Metro Health Maintenance Plan (Metro Plan) from May 20, 19XX (date of inception of the plan) to December 31, 19XX. *[preface]*

Metro Plan was recently organized as a wholly owned subsidiary to administer all health plans for Hawker Industries' employees living in the Bay Area. Prior to May 20, 19XX, health services to employees living in the Bay Area were provided by outside companies. *[preface]*

The audit was made for the initial period of operation to provide a basis for comparing claim costs with past and future periods. It was also made to assess the effectiveness of internal controls pertaining to the processing of medical claims. Our work was limited to analyses of systems, processes, and procedures and audit tests that we considered appropriate under these circumstances. *[audit scope or objective]*

In general we found that claim processing and payment procedures are well designed and implemented. Claims are generally paid in conformity with the "new plan," but claim-processing time is excessive. Completed claim files are well designed and generally orderly, but a problem exists in the manner of filing and locating claims in process. Also, the extended absence of a key data-processing employee, as a result of an automobile accident, has strained the system and has resulted in delays in obtaining key reports. *[brief conclusions and nature of findings]*

The accompanying report is provided for your information. A copy is also provided to the controller of Metro Plan, who is required by corporate policy to respond to the audit report within 60 days of its receipt. *[reply expectations]*

We acknowledge the full cooperation and helpful assistance given by executives and staff of Metro Plan.

_____
[signature]
Audit Team Leader
(or audit executive)

Participating Auditors:
D. K. Michels
L. M. Hill
M. Summerhays
[names of auditors]

Distribution:
W. G. Edling, Chairman, Corporate Audit Committee
D. Andersen, Corporate Personnel Director
R. C. Edglee, Corporate Controller
M. U. Stewart, President, Metro Health Maintenance Plan
D. Karenski, Controller, Metro Health Maintenance Plan
[distribution disclosure]

Brief Opinion and Nature of Findings. A paragraph or two stressing the *nature* of the findings, as contrasted with the *specifics,* should be included. In a short report this explanation may serve as the audit highlights or executive summary. In a longer report an executive summary might also be included, usually as the first page or few pages after the introduction section.

The following is a brief statement of opinion with regard to certain activities. The paragraph illustrates how one internal auditing report presented the nature of the audit findings:

> Production processes are operating smoothly and quotas are being met without overtime. However, we found a need for clarification of policies in sales and marketing and in executive compensation practices. We also found a need to formalize banking and investment strategies. The report presents these needs and the associated risks in fairly comprehensive detail.

Reply (or Other Action) Expectations. It is appropriate to let the auditee know what is required with respect to a reply to the audit report. For example:

> Division policies require a written response to the audit report within 60 days after the report is received. Responses should be addressed to the division controller, and a copy should be sent to the division audit director.

Signature. The report usually is signed by the auditor-in-charge, supervisor, lead auditor, or by an audit executive. *Professional Standards Bulletin 82-1* notes that the *Standards* does not specify who should sign the audit report. While the director of internal auditing (or designee) should approve the report before it is issued, it may be signed by different persons within the auditing department.

In a very short report, the signature can be included at the end of the report. In a long report the signature is usually placed at the end of the formalities section. Some audit groups require the auditor or audit team leader *and* an audit executive to sign the report.

Names of Participating Auditors. While there is no professional obligation to disclose the names of all of the audit team members, some audit groups do. The disclosure is usually included at the end of the formalities section near the signatures.

There are three advantages to including auditors' names:

1. It is a matter of courtesy to let management know who has been working within the auditee's operations.
2. Such disclosure gives recognition to individual auditors, who will tend to associate themselves more closely with the final product of the audit. This recognition enhances quality control on the audit if individual auditors know their names are going to be included in the report.
3. Questions often arise regarding aspects of an audit after the report has been issued. The names provide a quick reference for information or insights not provided in the audit working papers.

Distribution Disclosure. Who receives copies of the report? Auditees usually have the right to know to whom their affairs are to be exposed. As a general rule, the report should not be sent to anyone who does not have a right to and a need for it. The disclosure is usually made at the end of the introductory (or formalities) section near the auditors' names.

Since the report is usually confidential, there can be "painful repercussions" if the report gets into the hands of people who have no right to or need for it. This is particularly true when auditees are touchy or unhappy about certain findings. Disclosure of report distribution helps the auditor stay sensitive to this matter.

Sometimes only sections of a report will be distributed to certain people. In these cases the selective distribution is disclosed.

For example, suppose a team of auditors conducted an audit of production costs for a manufacturing process comprising two plants.

The vice president of production certainly would have both a right and a need to know the combined audit results. Each plant manager, however, may require only that portion of the audit report pertaining to his or her separate operations. In such cases, the report is prepared so that the results may be conveniently divided and distributed. The distribution of the separate pieces would be shown in the formalities section.

Contents. A contents page is helpful for a long report. It is usually not needed for a report of less than about 20 pages, particularly if the findings are well captioned.

Executive Summary or Highlights Section

Some people receiving an internal audit report, especially those in upper management, have less interest in detailed audit findings than in issues and concerns of a more general nature. A brief executive summary is prepared for this purpose. Another advantage of a summary is that readers can acquire a good grasp of the key issues addressed in the report before sifting through the various details. The summary provides a preliminary perspective from which to understand the details. The focus is upon risks to the organization and how specific control weaknesses increase those risks.

Executive summaries usually are only one or two pages long and almost never more than 5 percent of the total length of the report. Often executive summaries are not prepared for reports of less than 10 to 12 pages.

There are two general approaches to writing these summaries:

1. *The "condense-and-eliminate" approach.* Summaries prepared by this approach are abbreviated explanations of the major audit findings. This process involves assessing which of the findings are the most important. These findings and any recommendations are then highlighted in summary terms in order of their importance, following the auditors' overall opinions or conclusions. It is helpful to include page references within the report where the reader can find additional information.
2. *The "briefings" approach.* An auditor who uses this approach to writing summaries assumes the position of advisor, consultant, and confidant. The auditor is not just listing findings; he or she is informing, advising, and interpreting.

Compare Exhibits 10-4 and 10-5. These exhibits illustrate the two different approaches, both of which might have been prepared for the same audit report.

Exhibit 10-4
Condense-and-Eliminate Approach

EXECUTIVE SUMMARY

Our audit of Jacob Company's financial management and investments portfolio has resulted in the following findings:

1. Bank reconciliations have not been performed regularly; at the time of the audit work, they were three months behind. Failure to promptly perform bank reconciliations seriously weakens control over the company's funds (pp. 3-5).

2. More than $60,000 in dividends and interest income have not been collected because of a failure to follow up on delinquent investment income accounts (pp. 9-12).

3. Our auditors discovered 1,560 shares of Bohreman, Inc. stock, purchased on April 16, 1986, for $70,200, which have never been entered into the accounting records. This error occurred because documentation apparently has been lost and because security counts have failed to disclose the error (pp. 6-8).

Detailed Findings   The detailed findings that usually compose the body of the internal audit report are typically taken from the Summary Findings Sheets, which were discussed in the previous chapter. These Summary Findings Sheets state the condition, criteria, effect, cause, and auditor recommendation pertaining to a particular audit finding. The audit report discusses each major finding. Exhibit 10-6 illustrates how a section of the report may be taken from a findings sheet.

Each detailed finding may be summarized, presented, and arranged in order of its relative importance.

Introductory and summary comments, as well as commentary on various findings, may also be included in the report. These comments provide a perspective on the detailed findings and allow the auditors to address global issues related to the findings.

In the illustration where the auditors discovered that bank reconciliations had not been performed, dividend and interest income was not being collected, and transactions were going unrecorded, the

---

**Exhibit 10-5
Briefings Approach**

EXECUTIVE SUMMARY

The detailed findings of our audit of financial management and the investment portfolio appear symptomatic of what we consider to be a more general problem. Unprepared bank reconciliations (see pp. 3-5), the failure to follow up on delinquent dividends and interest income (see pp. 9-12), the loss of documentation of a major securities purchase, and the resultant failure to record that purchase (see pp. 6-8) suggest a general breakdown in internal controls. We do not believe this breakdown is a result of purposeful wrongdoing or irresponsibility. The results of our audit indicate that both financial management and the investment portfolio seriously need additional qualified and experienced personnel (see pp. 1–2).

---

auditors concluded that the primary cause of these problems was a lack of manpower. In addition to an individual section on each of the separate findings, the report would include a discussion of this more general finding. In fact, the more general finding probably would be presented first, followed by the separate findings.

The length of a report is determined in large part by the amount of detail included. Some internal auditing departments require that reports be no longer than a set number of pages — perhaps 20 pages or so. Other auditing departments place no specific limits on audit reports, and some reports may total more than 100 pages. Regardless of the specific length of an audit report, the presentation of the detailed findings should include enough information for the readers to understand the findings, as well as what the auditors say might be done to correct any problems. Even for the most abbreviated reports, the detailed information should include the condition, the effect (or risk) of the condition upon operations, and appropriate alternative recommendations.

Exhibits and Attachments

Graphs, tables, charts, financial tabulations, etc., (if any) should be placed on the page where the discussion is covered. This information should be placed in an appendix only if it is so numerous or extensive in length that it would interfere with readability if interspersed throughout the report.

Exhibit 10-6
Detailed Reporting from Findings Write-Up Sheet

FINDINGS WRITE-UP SHEET

Audit: Finance Department

Working Paper Page No. _____
Prepared by _____ Date _____
Reviewed by _____ Date _____
Working Paper Reference _____

Condition	An examination of reconciliations of the company's five major bank accounts for May 1986 to September 1986 revealed that reconciliations for all five accounts were current only up through June 1986.
Criteria	Monthly bank reconciliations, by policy, should be performed within 30 days of the receipt of the bank statement.
Effect	Failure to maintain current bank reconciliations increases the risk of financial loss, due both to unintentional errors and irregularities.
Cause	The finance staff has an extremely heavy workload. The number of financial transactions has tripled in the last three years, whereas the number of staff members has remained constant.
Recommendation	Expand staff of qualified, experienced professionals.

(Excerpt from Detailed Report of Findings)

Bank Reconciliations Three Months Behind Schedule

Examination of the bank reconciliations for May through September 1986 revealed that reconciliations had been completed for all five of the company's major bank accounts only through June. The company's policy states that reconciliations are to be completed within 30 days of the end of the previous month. Failure to perform reconciliations promptly exposes the company to serious financial losses.

The failure of the finance department to maintain current bank reconciliations appears to be caused by a shortage of well-trained, experienced personnel. While the number of transactions has tripled in the last three years and the number of management reports has almost doubled, the number of professional staff members in the department has remained unchanged.

Recommendation: We recommend the addition of qualified professional staff members in the finance department to adequately perform the responsibilities of the increased workload.

All exhibits and attachments should be clearly labeled or introduced. If the information is not easily understandable with only cursory study, an explanation or interpretation should be provided to the reader.

Internal Audit Opinions

Many internal auditors advocate writing internal audit opinions that provide management with an overall summary evaluation of the activities being audited. Management often asks the question, "What do you [the auditors] think about the activities you have audited?" In these cases, management is seeking an overall opinion from the auditors. Are things okay, or not? The purpose of such an opinion is to offer management some assurance that operations are in order, or to alert management to potential or existing problems.

Guideline 430.04 states that " . . . where appropriate, reports should contain an expression of the auditor's opinion." *Professional Standards Bulletin 82-13* recommends using standard wording for internal audit opinions, although no suggested wording is given. Each internal auditing department can determine (a) whether it wishes to make a practice of providing opinions on a routine basis, (b) whether the opinion statements should be standardized, and (c) what standard wording should be used if such opinions are given.

This bulletin recommends using a two-paragraph statement when the auditors want to issue a favorable opinion, with no qualifications or exceptions. The first paragraph would describe the scope of the internal audit project, and the second paragraph would present the opinion. An opinion that contains qualifications or exceptions would expand these basic paragraphs. The following examples illustrate how such opinions may be presented.

**Example 1
(Favorable)**

"We have examined and evaluated the adequacy and effectiveness of shipping controls in the Holladay warehouse. We used audit methods and procedures appropriate to the circumstances. Our examination included the warehouse shipping operations and the accounting for shipping transactions.

"Based on our examination, we believe that adequate internal controls are in place and operating satisfactorily; the correct goods are sent promptly in the correct amounts and to the correct places. We also believe that shipping transactions are properly recorded in the company's accounting system."

**Example 2
(Unfavorable)**

"We have examined and evaluated the adequacy and effectiveness of the internal controls for marketing and production that may have affected the company's loss of market share from June 1986 through March 1987. We used audit methods and procedures appropriate to the circumstances. Our examination included buyer perceptions of products, production controls, product distribution, and coordination between marketing and production.

"In our opinion, the company's loss of market share is due primarily to inconsistent product quality resulting from inadequate production control. Based on the results of our examination, we believe that the formal system of controls is poorly designed; in an effort to meet the marketing department's increased sales projections, production management has been unable to exercise the informal control it once did for consistent product quality."

Presentation

These opinions, especially where standard wording is used, may be set apart in a separate section of the audit report labeled "Internal Audit Opinion." Otherwise, the statement may be made in the introductory section of the audit report before the presentation of detailed findings, or it may be integrated into summary sections, such as in the formalities section and the executive summary.

**Advantages and
Disadvantages of
Internal Audit
Opinions**

The primary advantage of including an internal audit opinion in the audit report is that it provides management with an overall perspective from which to view the rest of the report. The opinion tells management the auditors' general conclusions after carefully studying and evaluating the auditee's activities. Management can interpret any further commentary from this basic perspective. The overall opinion provides busy managers with a quick reference to relative risks to the organization.

The disadvantages of including internal audit opinions in reports arise from the advantages themselves. There often is the tendency among executive management and auditees to overreact to audit opinions and to ignore other important information in the report. Since audit results are almost always mixed, it may be difficult to issue an overall opinion without balancing positive and negative conclusions.

For example, auditors may conclude that internal controls for a system are generally good, but that certain improvements still are necessary. A favorable audit opinion in this case may lead the auditee to conclude that since the opinion is favorable, it is not necessary to act on the problems or recommendations identified in the report. On the other hand, the internal auditors may issue an unfavorable overall opinion, which would overwhelm the effect any positive comments might otherwise have on the auditee.

Conclusions

When making opinion statements, internal auditors should remember the purpose of the audit — to assist management and the board in the performance of their respective responsibilities. The objective is to assist, not just to make a statement. Consequently, an opinion statement will sell the internal audit report to management and the board only if it is fair, informative, and constructive. The following example illustrates a more balanced second paragraph of an internal audit opinion.

Example 3 (Balanced)

"Based on the results of our audit, we believe that, overall, the inventories are managed well and there is adequate internal control. Inventory management and staff seem to be well qualified and conscientious, and inventory control systems appear to be well designed and executed. Our findings suggest, however, a few concerns that we believe deserve the prompt attention of management. These concerns, outlined in our report, relate primarily to periodic stockouts and possible theft."

Auditee Responses in Audit Reports

To make a balanced and complete presentation of audit results, many internal auditing departments include in their reports the auditee's responses to audit findings. Guideline 430.06 states, "The auditee's views about audit conclusions or recommendations may be included in the audit report."

Notice the phrase ". . . *may* be included . . . ." The term "may" implies some discretion on the part of the internal auditor with regard to including the responses of auditees. Some internal auditing organizations do, some do not. Some include auditees' views on some audits, but not on others, depending on their own preference and often on other means by which auditee views may be communicated to management.

Auditors usually learn the auditee's views on findings at the closing conference. When such responses are included in the audit report, auditors have a choice of methods by which to make the inclusions. The auditors can include a brief, general summary statement, such as the following:

> Auditee management expressed general agreement with the audit findings and recommendations, with the exception of the finding that inventory reorder points are so high that most items are overstocked. The auditee states that the inventory reorder points are in accordance with the company's conservative policy to protect itself against stockouts. A more detailed response to this point will be drafted and issued by the auditee within 30 days of the issuance of the audit report.

A natural place for this statement would be at the end of the introductory section of the report. Notice that this summary statement of the auditee's response is drafted by the auditors. Such a statement would need to be reviewed by auditee management to ensure that it includes an accurate portrayal of the auditee's views.

Another method of including the auditee's response in the report is for the auditors to state an individual response to every audit finding. Again, the auditee would review these statements.

Still another method is for the auditee to draft a response to the findings and for the auditors to attach the response to the report itself upon issuance. However, since auditees usually wait until the final draft of the audit report to prepare their formal, written responses to audit findings, this method is used less frequently than the others.

Reviewing and Editing — Polishing the Report

The *Standards* suggests the importance of appropriate review and editing of the internal audit report. Pertinent standards include the following:

230.02.4	The director of internal auditing is responsible for . . . making sure that audit reports are accurate, objective, clear, concise, constructive, and timely.
430.07	The director of internal auditing or designee should review and approve the final audit report before issuance . . . .

Review and Edit Process

Before internal audit reports are issued, they generally go through a rigorous review process. Although the process may differ from organization to organization, the flowchart in Exhibit 10-7 illustrates the preparation and review process for one large internal auditing department.

Exhibit 10-7
Preparation and Review Process
for Internal Audit Report

Preparation of the initial draft of the report.

Review and edit by members of the audit team.

Preparation of the revised audit report.

Review and edit by the manager of the audit assignment.

Preparation of the second revision of the report.

Review and edit by the director of the auditing department.

Preparation of the third revision of the report.

Combined review and edit by the audit team leader, manager, and director.

Preparation of the "discussion draft" of the report for review by auditee management.

Review by auditee management for accuracy. NOTE: The auditee does not have authority to edit or change the report. This review is a matter of courtesy and provides a final check for possible inaccuracies in factual data.

Preparation of the final draft of the audit report for distribution.

The old adage that "writing is rewriting" certainly holds true in most internal auditing organizations, as illustrated in Exhibit 10-7. As one can readily see, in such an environment there is little room for personal pride of authorship. The preparation of an internal audit report usually is a combined effort of several people, although as the *Standards for the Professional Practice of Internal Auditing* indicates, the director of internal auditing bears the final responsibility.

A Review and Edit Checklist

A checklist may be used for reviewing and editing reports. An example of such a checklist is illustrated in Exhibit 10-8. By following a checklist, reviewers are less likely to overlook important considerations for effective communication in the internal audit report. These checklists are used for reviews within the internal auditing department, not for reviews by auditees. Notice that the exhibit includes consideration not only of basic content and language, but also appearance and organization to help make the report easier and more appealing to read.

Distribution and Retention of the Report

Distributing Copies of the Report

The final steps in the reporting process are: (1) distributing the report and (2) filing the report in the internal auditing department.

The distribution of the report is tentatively determined early in the audit and finally decided when the report is reviewed and approved. The names of the recipients are shown, often on the last page of the introduction section of the report. This disclosure contributes to control and security over the report and satisfies professional courtesy considerations.

Being aware of the auditee's chain of command helps the auditor to ensure that appropriate executives, as well as the audit committee, get a copy of the report. As a general rule, those persons whom the auditor must contact before the audit begins will be those with a right to and need for a report copy when the audit is completed.

In deciding how to transmit reports, the auditor can be guided by two simple questions:

1. For each alternative conveyance method, what is the relative risk of the report being delayed, lost, or falling into the wrong hands?
2. What are the likely repercussions of delay, loss, or possession by others?

After assessing the risks, the delivery method can be chosen. It is a good idea to hand-carry any reports that contain highly sensitive information. Other methods include mail, special courier services, fee delivery within an office complex, and interoffice delivery. Once the report leaves the custody of the auditor, control over it quickly fades.

Exhibit 10-8
Review and Edit Checklist

Cover

1. Title of audit — accurate and descriptive?
2. Auditee's name and address — accurate?
3. Date — correct form and accurate?

Introduction Section

1. Addressee — appropriate person, correct title, spelling, address?
2. Preface — appropriate content, length, and tone?
3. Audit scope or objectives — clear and includes limitations of scope?
4. Nature of findings — covered at all, too detailed, tone?
5. Expectation for reply by auditee to report — present?
6. Signature — who will sign? Is the level of the signer consistent with the level of the addressee?
7. Name of participating auditors — are they shown, and is the order correct?
8. Distribution disclosure — any inappropriate recipients, anyone overlooked?
9. Contents page — needed? Placement location appropriate?

Executive Summary or Highlights Section

1. Have the weightiest matters been addressed first?
2. Is the relative length about right for each subject?
3. Is the overall tone constructive and fair?
4. Are references made to page numbers where detail write-ups are located in report?

Detailed Findings

1. Are appropriate captions used?
2. Are explanations clear; are facts and circumstances concise?
3. Are there imprecise words or vague phrases?
4. Is the matter important enough to include in the report?
5. Is wording fair and polite in tone?
6. Is too much or too little space allocated relative to the matter's significance?
7. Are there unnecessary words or trite expressions?
8. Are there appropriate recommendations or alternative solutions?
9. Do the pages look inviting? Can the reader effectively browse?
10. Has someone checked all computations and crosschecked amounts, etc., to working papers?

Writing and Composition

1. Is there at least one caption or heading per page (preferably two to four)?
2. Does the paragraph length and mixture look about right (no long paragraphs)?
3. Do sentences average about 15 words with appropriate variety in sentence length?
4. Is there effective use of emphasis such as underlining or italics?
5. Is active voice and conversational tone used? Or is the report stuffy and boring?
6. Is there effective use of white space?

Documenting Transmittal of the Report

The transmittal letter, dated as of the issuance date, accompanies the internal audit report. When the transmittal is separate from the formalities section (discussed earlier in the chapter), the transmittal letter typically is quite brief, as shown in Exhibit 10-9. Each person receiving a copy of the report usually receives a personally addressed transmittal letter.

Retention of the Internal Audit Report

The internal auditing department keeps at least one copy of each internal audit report issued. These copies are filed differently in different organizations. Sometimes they are filed separately from the audit working papers, sometimes *with* the working papers, sometimes both.

A typical method is to keep a clean, unmarked copy in one file and place another copy in the working paper file. This second copy may be marked so that each finding in the report is cross-referenced to the relevant Summary Findings Sheet in the working papers, and perhaps directly to the individual working papers themselves.

Interim Reporting

Circumstances associated with some audits give rise to the need for "interim reports," i.e., reports that are prepared and issued while audit work is still being performed, prior to issuance of the final report. These reports usually occur when (1) an audit continues over an extended time period, or (2) a finding during the audit is significant enough to warrant immediate attention rather than waiting to include the point in the closing conference and final report.

Exhibit 10-9
Brief Transmittal Letter

September 5, 1986

Willard C. Benson, Agency Director
Area Social Services Agency
Atlanta, Georgia

Dear Mr. Benson:

Here is a copy of the June 30, 1986 report for our audit of the Atlanta
Agency. If you have any questions about the report, please call me.

Sincerely,

R. S. Turk

R. S. Turk
Director of Auditing

RST: sm

Interim reports offer at least four advantages:

1. Timely feedback to the auditee.
2. A high probability of more immediate action than would be
    possible by waiting for the final report.
3. With prompt action by the auditee, a more favorable final report.
4. An opportunity for the auditors to follow up on the report
    during the audit itself.

Because of these advantages, many internal auditing departments
make extensive use of interim reports.

As stated in Guideline 430.01, "Interim reports may be written
or oral and may be transmitted formally or informally." An informal,
oral interim report usually constitutes little more than a meeting
between an auditor and someone among the auditee's management
or staff who is in a position to act on the information. The only
documentation of the meeting would be a file memo indicating who

met, when, where, what information was communicated to the auditee, and what the response was. A more formal oral report usually is documented by a written agenda as well as the file memo. Also, the more formal oral report usually is accompanied by a written report as well. Seldom is a written interim report prepared and delivered without some form of oral presentation, even if it is by telephone.

A written interim report may take at least two forms — letter or memorandum. Exhibit 10-10 illustrates the memorandum format. Notice that this memo is relatively short and does not include all of the various sections discussed for the final report. Also, it is typical for the review and editing process to be somewhat abbreviated for interim reports. While the report may indeed be reviewed by the team leader, manager, and director, the emphasis is on speed or timeliness.

Distribution of the interim report will vary from organization to organization and from situation to situation. Some organizations prefer that interim reports be distributed to the same people who receive the final report. Other organizations prefer that interim reports be delivered only to auditee management, giving them the opportunity to take some positive actions prior to the issuance of the final report. Obviously, when a situation poses a serious, immediate risk to the overall organization, executive management has a right and a need to know as soon as possible.

A single audit may yield several interim reports, all of which would be included in the audit working papers. The final report typically will make reference to the particular findings that are addressed in the interim reports, and state the issuance of the reports and the auditee's responses.

Exhibit 10-10
Example of Internal Audit Report

DATE: July 14, 1986
TO: Vernon Callender, Director of Purchasing
FROM: Kenneth Poe, Manager of Internal Audits
SUBJECT: Interim Audit Report Regarding Vendor Selection
               Procedures

Our audit, currently underway, has disclosed that the vendor selection process for heavy machinery has resulted in the purchase of more than $2,400,000 of obsolete equipment from an obscure manufacturer that is not able to maintain the equipment. At present, the equipment is sitting unused in a warehouse at our Bluffs plant.

Company policy states that all relevant criteria are to be considered in the purchase of assets, implying that the low bid should not be the sole criterion for selection. Our evidence suggests, however, that price alone has dictated the purchase of heavy equipment.

The results of following a price-only decision have been a significant waste of company funds and general inefficiency when inappropriate purchases have been made. Our calculations estimate more than $4,000,000 in excessive costs required to correct prior purchase decisions and more than $15,000,000 in lost sales.

Recommendation: We suggest that the Purchasing Department formulate guidelines for the purchase of equipment that include other factors in addition to price. Such factors might include date of availability, support and maintenance, serviceability, reliability of the technology, service life, and so forth. Because negotiations are currently underway for the installation and replacement of heavy machinery in three of our plants, the resolution of this problem seems critical.

Appendix

STATEMENT ON INTERNAL AUDITING
STANDARDS NO. 2
Communicating Results

Foreword

The Institute of Internal Auditors issued its *Standards for the Professional Practice of Internal Auditing* in 1978 "to serve the entire profession in all types of businesses, in various levels of government, and in all other organizations where internal auditors are found . . . to represent the practice of internal auditing as it should be . . . ." Experience and success have demonstrated the credibility of the basic principles promoted in the *Standards*.

The *Standards* establishes a basis for the guidance and measurement of internal auditing performance. For Communicating Results, this basis is delineated in the *Standards* by seven guidelines related to the types, contents, and attributes of audit reports. This statement interprets guidelines 430.01 through 430.07.

Summary

This statement provides guidance to internal auditors in communicating audit results in the form of oral and written reports.

It includes interpretations of Standard 430 (Communicating Results) related to types, contents, and attributes of audit reports; discussion of findings, conclusions, and recommendations with management; and audit report approval and distribution.

Interpretations
Guideline 430.01

Guideline 430.01 states: A signed, written report should be issued after the audit examination is completed. Interim reports may be written or oral and may be transmitted formally or informally.

.1 Interim reports may be used to communicate information which requires immediate attention, to communicate a change in audit scope for the activity under review, or to keep management informed of audit progress when audits extend over a long period. The use of interim reports does not diminish or eliminate the need for a final report.

.2 Summary reports highlighting audit results may be appropriate for levels of management above the head of the audited unit. They may be issued separately from or in conjunction with the final report.

Guideline 430.02

Guideline 430.02 states: The internal auditor should discuss conclusions and recommendations at appropriate levels of management before issuing final written reports.

.1 Discussion of conclusions and recommendations is usually accomplished during the course of the audit and/or at postaudit meetings (exit interviews). Another technique is the review of draft audit reports by the head of each audited unit. These discussions and reviews help ensure that there have been no misunderstandings or misinterpretations of fact by providing the opportunity for the auditee to clarify specific items and to express views of the findings, conclusions, and recommendations.

.2 Although the level of participants in the discussions and reviews may vary by organizations and by the nature of the report, they will generally include those individuals who are knowledgeable of detailed operations and those who can authorize the implementation of corrective action.

Guideline 430.03

Guideline 430.03 states: Reports should be objective, clear, concise, constructive, and timely.

.1 Objective reports are factual, unbiased, and free from distortion. Findings, conclusions, and recommendations should be included without prejudice.

.2 Clear reports are easily understood and logical. Clarity can be improved by avoiding unnecessary technical language and providing sufficient supportive information.

.3 Concise reports are to the point and avoid unnecessary detail. They express thoughts completely in the fewest possible words.

.4 Constructive reports are those which, as a result of their content and tone, help the auditee and the organization and lead to improvements where needed.

.5 Timely reports are those which are issued without undue delay and enable prompt effective action.

Guideline 430.04

Guideline 430.04 states: Reports should present the purpose, scope, and results of the audit; and, where appropriate, reports should contain an expression of the auditor's opinion.

.1 Although audit report format and content may vary by organization or type of audit, they should contain, at a minimum, the purpose, scope, and results of the audit.

.2 Audit reports may include background information and summaries. Background information may identify the organizational units and functions reviewed and provide relevant explanatory information. They may also include the status of findings, conclusions, and recommendations from prior reports. There may also be an indication of whether the report covers a scheduled audit or the response to a request. Summaries, if included, should be balanced representations of the audit report content.

.3 Purpose statements should describe the audit objectives and may, where necessary, inform the reader why the audit was conducted and what it was expected to achieve.

.4 Scope statements should identify the audited activities and include, where appropriate, supportive information such as time period audited. Related activities not audited should be identified if necessary to delineate the boundaries of the audit. The nature and extent of auditing performed also should be described.

.5   Results may include findings, conclusions (opinions), and recommendations.

.6   Findings are pertinent statements of fact. Those findings which are necessary to support or prevent misunderstanding of the internal auditor's conclusions and recommendations should be included in the final audit report. Less significant information or findings may be communicated orally or through informal correspondence.

Audit findings emerge by a process of comparing "what should be" with "what is." Whether or not there is a difference, the internal auditor has a foundation on which to build the report. When conditions meet the criteria, acknowledgment in the audit report of satisfactory performance may be appropriate. Findings should be based on the following attributes:

Criteria: The standards, measures, or expectations used in making an evaluation and/or verification (what *should* exist).

Condition: The factual evidence which the internal auditor found in the course of the examination (what *does* exist).

If there is a difference between the expected and actual conditions, then:

Cause: The reason for the difference between the expected and actual conditions (*why* the difference exists).

Effect: The risk or exposure the auditee organization and/or others encounter because the condition is not the same as the criteria (the *impact* of the difference).

The reported finding may also include recommendations, auditee accomplishments, and supportive information if not included elsewhere.

.7   Conclusions (opinions) are the internal auditor's evaluations of the effects of the findings on the activities reviewed. They usually put the findings in perspective based upon their overall implications. Audit conclusions, if included in the audit report, should be clearly identified as such. Conclusions may encompasss the entire scope of an audit or specific aspects. They may cover but are not limited to whether operating or program objectives and goals conform with those of the organization, whether the organization's objectives and goals are being met, and whether the activity under review is functioning as intended.

Guideline 430.05

Guideline 430.05 states: Reports may include recommendations for potential improvements and acknowledge satisfactory performance and corrective action.

.1   Recommendations are based on the internal auditor's findings and conclusions. They call for action to correct existing conditions or improve operations. Recommendations may suggest approaches to correcting or enhancing · performance as a guide for management in achieving desired results. Recommendations may be general or specific. For example, under some circumstances, it may be desirable to recommend a general course of action and specific suggestions for implementation. In other circumstances, it may be appropriate only to suggest further investigation or study.

.2   Auditee accomplishments, in terms of improvemewnts since the last audit or the establishment of a well-controlled operation, may be included in the audit report. This information may be necessary to fairly represent the existing conditions and to provide a proper perspective and appropriate balance to the audit report.

Guideline 430.6

Guideline 430.6 states: The auditee's views about audit conclusions or recommendations may be included in the audit report.

.1 As part of the internal auditor's discussions with the auditee, the internal auditor should try to obtain agreement on the results of the audit and on a plan of action to improve operations, as needed. If the internal auditor and auditee disagree about the audit results, the audit report may state both positions and the reasons for the disagreement. The auditee's written comments may be included as an appendix to the audit report. Alternatively, the auditee's views may be presented in the body of the report or in a cover letter.

Guideline 430.07

Guideline 430.07 states: The director of internal auditing or designee should review and approve the final audit report before issuance and should decide to whom the report will be distributed.

.1 The director of internal auditing or a designee should approve and may sign all final reports. If specific circumstances warrant, consideration should be given to having the auditor-in-charge, supervisor, or lead auditor sign the report as a representative of the director of internal auditing.

.2 Audit reports should be distributed to those members of the organization who are able to ensure that audit results are given due consideration. This means that the report should go to those who are in a position to take corrective action or ensure that corrective action is taken. The final audit report should be distributed to the head of each audited unit. Higher-level members in the organization may recieve only a summary report. Reports may also be distributed to other interested or affected parties such as external auditors and audit committees.

.3 Certain information may not be appropriate for disclosure to all report recipients because it is privileged, proprietary, or related to improper or illegal acts. Such information, however, may be disclosed in a separate report. If the conditions being reported involve senior management, report distribution should be to the audit committee of the board of directors or a similar high-level entity within the organization.

QUESTIONS

1. What are the two primary modes of reporting audit results?
2. Which of The IIA's standards address personal presentations of audit results, written reports, and both personal presentations and written reports?
3. What is an audit closing conference?
4. What are the key factors to conducting a successful closing conference? What is a *successful* closing conference?
5. Describe how the audit report reflects the competence and professional image of the internal auditor.
6. How is the internal audit report important to the following groups: The auditors? Operating management? Top management? External auditors? Government regulators?
7. List at least 10 guidelines for achieving effective, crisp, clear writing.
8. How does the internal auditor prepare to write the audit report?
9. Outline and briefly describe the elements of the basic model of internal audit reports.
10. What is the difference between the "condense-and-eliminate" approach and the "briefings" approach to writing an executive summary for an internal audit report?
11. What options does the internal auditor have in including the auditee's views regarding audit findings?
12. Describe the reviewing and editing process for the audit report.
13. To whom is the internal audit report distributed? How should it be distributed?
14. What is a transmittal letter?
15. How does marking a copy of the audit report with cross-references to working papers help to preserve the integrity of the auditing process?
16. What is an interim audit report? Why issue an interim audit report?

EXERCISES

E-1

Scenario 1. The manager of public relations for Eason Company sent a memo to the director of internal auditing complaining bitterly that a recent audit report was unfair. The major complaint was that the report was one-sided and presented only the auditors' views.

Scenario 2. The auditors sent a letter to the chief of batching operations for Lichter Ice Cream Company's Monroe plant stating that a written audit report would not be prepared. The letter further stated that the chief of batching operations had enough information from the closing conference to correct the observed weaknesses in internal controls.

Scenario 3. The director of internal auditing for Big Foot Courier Services left the following note for one of the department's managers:

Bill:

I have had to leave unexpectedly this afternoon due to an illness in my family. I will be out of town for approximately a week. We promised Carl that we would get the marketing audit report out by Friday. I have not been able to get to it, so I have left it with your secretary. Please review it, make any necessary changes, and distribute it. Thanks for your help.

Doug

Required:

Identify The IIA's reporting standards that are applicable in each of the three scenarios and note any violations of these standards.

E-2

At the closing conference of a recent audit, the audit team leader became confused as the auditee continued to interrupt the presentation of audit findings. The team leader had trouble maintaining the continuity of the meeting and several times looked puzzled, nervously rubbing his forehead with his fingertips. He muttered something like, "Now, what do we do?"

Required:

List at least three things the team leader could have done to avoid this problem.

E-3

The internal auditors for Pepper International, Inc. recently completed an audit of the shipping and receiving department in the industrial products division. The report outlined a major control weakness that was discovered when taking an inventory count of materials received by the division. The director of internal auditing sent copies of the report to the following individuals:

Craig Wallace, Manager, Shipping and Receiving Department
Gill Hart, Manager, Industrial Products Division
Stewart Gibbons, Vice President in charge of Operations,
  Pepper International, Inc.
Clark, Bailey, and Roberts (the company's CPAs)
Audit Committee, Pepper International, Inc.

Required:

Explain how each of these recipients is likely to use the audit report outlining the control weakness.

E-4

The following is an excerpt from an audit report:

> The audit tests were performed by the auditors in order to accomplish several important objectives — verify the existence of the engines contained in the inventories kept at the warehouse, determine whether any of the engines had been damaged during storage at the warehouse, review the handling procedures being performed by personnel at the warehouse, determine whether proper accounting procedures are being followed for engines kept in inventories at the warehouse, calculate the current fair market value of warehouse inventories, and compare the total value of the inventories to company accounting records. It was confirmed by the assigned auditors that of the 37 engines selected from purchasing records for their sample, eight were present on the warehouse floor. Another five were on the loading dock ready for conveyance to the assembly plant. Still another 22 already had been conveyed to the manufacturing plant at prior times, and two were unaccounted for in the warehouse

records. A sample of 25 engines were examined for possible damage, and all but two were in good condition. The handling procedures outlined in the warehouse policy manual appeared to be adequate, and warehouse personnel apparently were following those procedures, except for the examination of items being received for inventory. Warehouse workers usually unload crates from the rail cars, unpack the crates, and stack inventory items without a systematic examination of the items. An examination by the auditors of the accounting procedures being used at the warehouse revealed the failure by the warehouse accounting clerk to reconcile inventory records monthly, as required by policy. Instead, the clerk reconciled quarterly, required excessive overtime, and failed to find errors in the records promptly. The auditors calculated the current market value of the warehouse inventories to be $3,845,640.

Required:

a. For the previous excerpt, identify any violations of the 10 principles for clear writing given in this chapter.
b. Explain the effects of each of the violations.
c. Show or explain how you would improve the passage.

E-5

The audit report for a major state university contained the following sections:

Purchase of Landscaping Services for New Buildings

The university purchasing department requests bids from five local landscaping companies prior to constructing any major landscaping work for new buildings or renovations. According to policy, the specifications for each job are contained with each request for a bid in order to maintain comparability among bids. The purchasing department then contracts the work to the lowest bidder.

Strong competition exists among the landscaping companies. Consequently, a significant amount of work has been performed by each of the companies during the past three years. Expenditures for landscaping services totaled more than $2 million during the three-year period.

Once a bid is offered and accepted, the bid price becomes the contract price. Additional costs for this work can occur in two ways:

1. The landscaping company can request and receive special approval for changes in specifications once a job begins.
2. Once jobs are complete, university grounds crews may be assigned to perform minor modifications and clean-up work.

The following table outlines the differences in the amount of additional costs that are associated with the work performed by each of the five landscaping companies:

| | Additional Costs | | | | |
Company	All Accepted Bids	Contracted Changes	University Crew Repair Work	All Other Costs	Total Added
The Garden House	$ 345,000	$ 41,400	$ 6,900	$ 48,300	14%
Landscaping, Inc.	130,000	3,090	13,000	16,090	12%
East's Nurseries	402,000	8,040	4,020	12,060	3%
Trees & Things	820,000	49,200	32,800	82,000	1%
Bud's Landscaping	301,000	60,200	39,130	99,330	33%
TOTALS	$1,998,000	$161,930	$95,850	$257,780	12%

The figures indicate the large amount of additional costs incurred by the university associated with work performed by Bud's Landscaping Services — 33 percent of the total contracted work. Not quite as high, but still excessive, are the 14 percent and 12 percent associated with work performed by Garden House and Landscaping, Inc., respectively.

Inquiries to the four other major universities in the state who have a similar procedure for landscaping services indicated that the maximum that might normally be expected would be additional costs of 5 percent. Assuming there are additional costs of 5 percent for the Garden House, Landscaping, Inc., and Bud's Landscaping, and assuming the 3 percent for East's Nurseries and 1 percent for Trees and Things, the total savings would have amounted to $124,920 ($257,780 — $132,860).

University grounds officials also state that most of the additional costs for work performed by the Garden House, Landscaping, Inc., and Bud's Landscaping resulted from poor quality work, not because of major design changes. Each of the three companies has been allowed to use the provisions for design changes to pay for rework when the companies failed to meet the predetermined specifications.

Recommendations

Based on the information, we believe that two approaches would save considerable funds for contracted landscaping services:

1. Eliminate any company from requested bids whose work consistently results in more than 5 percent in additional costs.
2. Hold the companies to the contracted price for contracted work, and do not approve payment for rework required to meet specifications.

Required:
Prepare a Summary Findings Sheet for the above section of the audit report.

E-6

The internal auditors for Executive Hotels, Inc. just completed an audit of the company's billing system. All bills are sent from company headquarters in New Belle City, Iowa. The auditors began their work on May 6 and held a closing conference with the company controller and assistant controller in charge of billings on June 26.

Required:
Prepare, in good form, the information to be shown on the report cover.

E-7

Of the three items shown below, which one(s) would be found in the formalities section of the report? The executive summary? Neither?

1. "A copy of this report is being provided to the manager of customer relations who is expected to make a written reply within 30 days of receiving the report."
2. A photograph of a warehouse that was damaged by a hurricane three years ago and left unrepaired.
3. "Several findings with regard to management of the company's effluent indicate a potential threat to City Creek and, consequently, to Meyer's Fish Hatchery."

E-8

Prepare an appropriate section of an audit report for the following Summary Findings Sheet, written for an audit of the Post Oak Road Store of Big G Supermarkets, Inc.

Findings Write-Up Sheet

Audit: _____

Working Paper Page No.: _____

Prepared by: _____   Date: _____

Reviewed by: _____   Date: _____

Working Paper Reference: _____

Condition	Cashiers at the Post Oak Road Store continue to use manual cash registers, and our study revealed an average error rate of 8 percent.
Criteria	The average error rate at all 12 of our other stores using computerized point-of-sale entry is 3 percent.
Effect	While errors may occur in either direction, few customers call attention to errors in their own favor. Our calculations, based upon industry data, indicate losses from an 8 percent error rate in comparable stores can total $70,000 per annum.
Cause	While a number of factors contribute to the high error rate, the underlying cause appears to be use of manual cash registers. The store manager has strongly resisted computerized registers for several years.
Recommendation	Persuade store manager to install cash registers with computerized point-of-sale entry.

NOTE: Remember that the store manager likely will receive a copy of the report. The objective should be to persuade, not abuse.

E-9

The internal auditors for a large corporation have issued a discussion draft of their report which states that nepotism is seriously jeopardizing the efficiency of operations in the company's Pacific office. The manager of Pacific operations disagrees with the audit finding.

Required:

Identify at least two ways that the auditee's views may be fairly represented in the final draft of the audit report.

E-10

The director of internal auditing for a commodities company was concerned that too much time was being required to prepare and issue audit reports. He was reviewing a chart similar to Exhibit 10-7 to identify some possible ways to shorten the process. He concluded that by eliminating one of the reviews, the process could go faster.

Required:

1. Identify potential problems that are associated with eliminating any one of the reviews.
2. How might the preparation of Summary Findings Sheets help speed up the report-writing process?
3. How does the auditee receive information on audit results before issuance of the final report?

E-11

Internal auditors for a mining company recently completed an audit of the company's safety standards for three of its mines. The audit report outlines key safety policies imposed by specific company policies and procedures. The report also outlines a few of the violations of those policies and procedures. The primary reason noted for the violations was management override in the interest of operational efficiency.

A partial company organization chart follows:

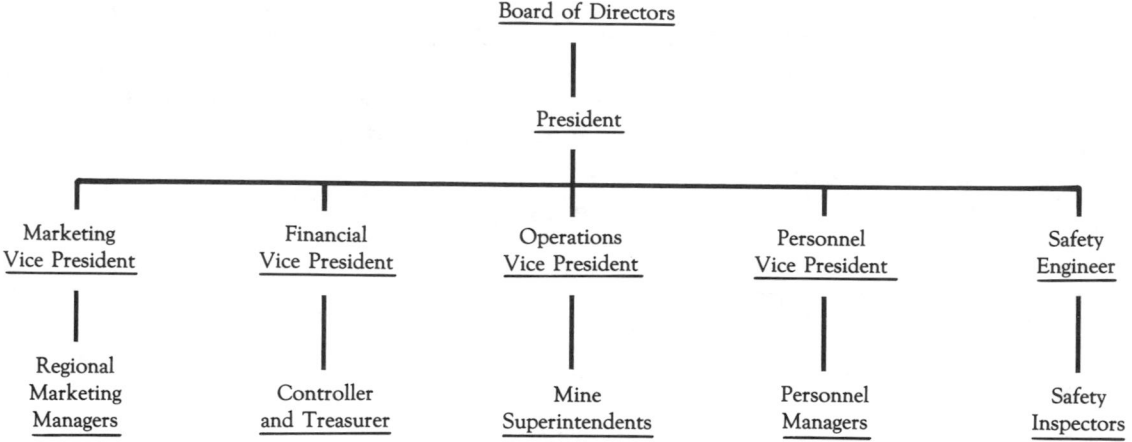

Required:

1. Identify to whom you think the auditors' report should be distributed.
2. If the auditors were to discover what they consider to be violations of federal safety regulations, to whom should they report these apparent violations? Should a copy of the report be sent to a regulatory agency of the federal government? Explain.

E-12

The internal auditors developed the following two findings during an audit of a company's investments:

1. The company has a policy to retain the securities (stocks and bonds) contained in its investment portfolio in a large safe housed in a nearby bank. A count of the securities

in the safe showed a shortage of $2.8 million of a particular stock compared to company accounting records. The auditors determined that a major weakness was present in the control system which allowed several company personnel and bank employees to have individual access to the safe without anyone else present. Due to the disorder, the auditors suspected the securities might have been misplaced.

2. The auditors also discovered that the securities housed in the safe were not well organized and catalogued. Securities could easily be misplaced, making transactions in a particular security difficult. The personnel who are responsible for the investments portfolio attribute the disorder to an extremely heavy workload.

Required:

Should either one (or both) of the above findings be reported on an interim basis prior to the final audit report? Why?

PROBLEMS

P-1

You are conducting the first audit of the marketing activities of your organization. Your preliminary survey has disclosed indications of deficient conditions of a serious nature. You expect your audit work to document the need for substantial corrective action. You feel certain that your audit report will contain descriptions of a number of serious defects.

Your preliminary meeting with the director of the marketing division and the principal subordinates gave you reason to believe that they will be defensive, that the draft of the audit report will receive a chilly reception, that your stated facts are likely to be challenged, and that any deficient conditions reported will be denied or minimized.

Required:

Identify and explain five techniques you might use to improve the chances that your draft report will be well received and that appropriate corrective action will be taken.

(CIA Exam Adapted)

P-2

The following is part of an interim audit report:

Subject: Controls over the billing of charges for parts/repair work.

Current procedures provide for the use of prenumbered sales order forms and recording sales orders for repairs in logs that are manually maintained. These procedures also provide for creating manually-serialized shipping documents and for the recording of such shipping documents in the sales order log. The recording of the shipping document numbers in the sales order log serves to close the sales order. This may give rise to a billing for the repair work. (Some work is done on a "no-charge" basis.)

Our examination of the sales order log disclosed a significant number of sales order numbers that were not matched up with shipping document numbers for the past two years. As a result, it is uncertain whether the repair work performed had been authorized for those orders. Specifically, we found that the sales order logs showed "no entry" for 71 (about 18 percent) sales order serial numbers spread randomly over a range of about 400 serial numbers covering a recent twelve-month period. This indicated that billing personnel had not received sales orders for, or information about, the disposition of those serial numbers. Further investigation disclosed that 50 of the serial numbers showing "no entry" related to sales orders which had been voided or to billings which had been closed at no charge. In addition, 16 other serial numbers related to sales orders which, in fact, were issued and were still open. However, we were unable to account for the remaining 15 serial numbers.

Required:

The interim audit report contains errors made by the internal auditor. The errors involve numbers, computations, and logic. Identify three errors made by the internal auditor and state how you would correct each one.

(CIA Exam Adapted)

P-3

The chief executive officer of your company is about to retire. He has always required that the audit reporting function be limited to final, formally written reports not to exceed two pages in length. The executive who has been designated to succeed the present CEO has asked department heads to submit comments and suggestions concerning this policy.

Required:

Prepare a memo that explains the limitations inherent in using only final, formally written, short audit reports to communicate with executive management. Discuss alternative report formats that can be used to supplement a formal reporting system.

(CIA Exam Adapted)

P-4

You have just received the draft audit report shown below. It was prepared by one of your staff auditors.

AUDIT OF THE PURCHASING DEPARTMENT

Introduction

The purchasing department is responsible for all procurements except those involving executive approval. During the past months, purchasing issued 19,736 purchase orders for a variety of products. Our audit covered only four of the 12 separate product classifications for which purchasing is done.

Purpose and Scope

We made our audit to determine whether:

1. Competitive bidding was employed.
2. Purchase orders were being approved at an appropriate level.
3. Buyers were following up appropriately.

Findings and Opinion

1. New procurement procedures prescribe an adequate control system which is designed to require supervisory review of all bidders' lists to see that all qualified suppliers are permitted to bid.
2. We found that 43 purchase orders for more than $25,000 had been approved only by the buyer. We reported this to the purchasing agent.
3. Follow-up action on late shipments has been ineffective because shipments continue to be received late.
4. Based on a random sample of 200 items, there should not be more than a 2 percent error rate in the purchase orders issued.

_____

(Signed) Auditor

Required:

Evaluate the quality of the report and recommend improvements. Please use the format below:

Line Number	Weaknesses in Report	Improvement Suggested

(CIA Exam Adapted)

11 Follow-Up Reviews and Audit Evaluation

After the audit results have been communicated (as discussed in Chapter 10), there are still two remaining steps in the audit process: follow-up reviews (Step 8) and evaluation of the audit process and results (Step 9).

The first major section of this chapter covers the following topics pertaining to follow-up reviews:

- Standards for follow-up.
- Follow-up roles of the auditor, the auditee, and executive management.
- Types of follow-up actions.
- Some practical considerations and helpful hints.
- Audit follow-up policies.
- Additional keys to follow-up success.

The second major section of the chapter addresses audit evaluation. The overall audit is evaluated in terms of its effectiveness and efficiency, as well as possible implications for future audits.

Follow-Up Reviews

There is an old adage that says "the road to despair is paved with good intentions." Success in any endeavor requires follow-through, or in the case of internal auditing, follow-up. The audit is considered to be successful when action is taken on the auditors' findings. While some action may be taken to correct central weaknesses, an alternative action may be a determination by management or the board that they will assume the risk of not correcting deficiencies that are reported in the findings. This latter action represents a conscious, knowledgeable choice.

Standards for Follow-Up

Exhibit 11-1 reproduces internal auditing Standard 440 on following up. Notice the two phases of the follow-up process. First, management and/or the board of directors either takes action on the auditors' findings, or they assume the risk of not taking action. The second phase of this process is for the auditors to find out what

---

Exhibit 11-1
IIA's Standard for Follow-Up Reviews

440   Following Up

Internal auditors should follow up to ascertain that appropriate
action is taken on reported audit findings.

.01   Internal auditing should determine that corrective action was
taken and is achieving the desired results, or that management
or the board has assumed the risk of not taking corrective
action on reported findings.

---

action, if any, was taken and assess its appropriateness. The auditors
usually are expected to report their findings from the follow-up
review. This follow-up report usually is delivered to the same people
in the organization who receive the original audit report.

Standard 440 specifies that auditors should follow up on audit
findings. As was discussed in a previous chapter, audit findings and
recommendations are directly linked. Findings identify the problem;
recommendations suggest possible solutions to the problems.

In practice, auditors usually think of follow-up in terms of findings
and recommendations. They often incorporate follow-up tests for
their recommendations as a stage in assessing the auditee's corrective
actions. Recommendations result from extensive study and usually are
discussed at length during the closing conference. Often there are
good reasons for follow-up on these recommendations; however, it
should be remembered that the recommendations evolve from audit
findings. The key focus should be on the findings and the resolution
of problems, not necessarily on specific audit recommendations.

Follow-Up Roles
of Auditors, the
Auditee, and
Executive
Management

The following case illustrates the differences in the follow-up roles
of auditors, the auditee, and executive management.

Suppose that internal auditors for a publishing company discovered
that one of the company's printing plants had a high percentage of
projects that were severely past the deadlines for various job orders.

They also found that overtime labor hours were unusually high. Suppose further that the auditors recommended that the plant install a new computerized job and labor scheduling system similar to one being used satisfactorily at another plant. The auditors delivered their report to the plant manager, the company's production vice president, and the audit committee. The audit committee, in turn, reported the findings and recommendation to the rest of the board of directors.

The plant manager opposed the installation of a computerized scheduling system for the present. He already was trying to implement new computer applications for the plant's printing processes and cost accounting system. He argued that adding another new system, especially one that would have to be integrated with the other two systems, would further hinder their completion. He argued that development of the third new system would only prolong current adverse effects on productivity. The plant manager presented his opposition in a report that was sent to the same group receiving the audit report.

After meeting with the plant manager, however, the vice president of production concluded that the new system would indeed help eliminate much of the inefficiency in scheduling printing jobs and labor assignments. He emphasized that since the scheduling system already had been written and implemented at another plant, it would be an easy matter to adapt the system to this plant. To minimize interference with the development of the other two systems, he suggested that the scheduling system be set up independently at first. Once the major bugs were worked out of all three systems, they could decide whether or not to integrate them into a single system.

The plant manager and the production vice president agreed on a plan to install the new scheduling system within three months, with another two months allotted for debugging the program. The plant manager sent a memorandum to the board, the production vice president, and the internal auditors outlining the decision to use the system. The memorandum also presented a timetable for its implementation.

The internal auditors performed a follow-up examination of the new system six months later. They found significant improvement in meeting production deadlines and in decreasing the amount of overtime hours. The auditors did not follow up with a full-scale audit, but focused their examination on the scheduling system. Their follow-up report was distributed to the plant manager, the production vice president, and to the audit committee as before. The auditors noted that even though there had been problems since the audit with the other two computerized systems, the scheduling system had worked successfully and had been implemented in an even shorter time than anticipated.

In this case all three parties — the auditee, executive management, and the auditors — were involved in the follow-up. The plant manager and vice president laid plans for implementation, the internal auditors did a post-facto check, and the audit committee exercised general oversight. All actions were documented and communicated so that each of the responsible parties was kept informed.

Exhibit 11-2 summarizes and outlines the different roles for the auditors, auditees, and executive management as they would be performed in an ideal situation.

There are four key ideas relating to these roles:

1. Follow-Up Assurance. When each of these three groups fulfills its role, follow-up is assured. Auditee management is responsible for doing something about deficiencies that are discovered by the auditor. Executive management oversees the process and sometimes directs and helps the auditee to respond. The auditors perform an independent review to assure that appropriate action has been taken. The auditors then report the results of the review to the auditee, executive management, and the board.

2. Communication and Cooperation. As all three roles are performed, effective communication and cooperation take place among the auditor, the auditee, and executive management. Imagine the potential for difficulties if auditees simply did what they felt was needed, executive management later observed that the action was incongruent with corporate objectives, and the auditee ended up doing something different. The auditors returned only to fault the second response, which precipitated animosity, confusion, more delay, and another start. Unfortunately, such things happen.

3. Timing. Timing and coordination of the three roles are important to the success of audit follow-up. The ideal role functions outlined in Exhibit 11-2 also suggest an efficient and effective sequence for follow-up activities. The auditee formulates a plan and works with executive management as necessary to implement the plan. The auditors then can decide when to conduct their review. Sometimes this follow-up review may be conducted relatively soon after the audit report is released. Other times, especially on less critical items, follow-up reviews may be performed much later as a part of a subsequent audit.

Exhibit 11-2
Follow-Up Roles:
Auditor, Auditee, and Executive Management

Ideal Auditor Role

1. Auditors perform follow-up review to assure that appropriate action is taken in response to audit findings.
2. Auditors inform the auditee, executive management, and the board in writing of judgments and evaluations made during follow-up reviews. They also may answer queries from auditees who are contemplating certain actions in response to an audit.
3. Auditors respect the auditee's responsibility and stewardship. They do not force specific corrective measures upon the auditee. *Professional Standards Bulletin 83-17* states that internal auditors should make management aware of actual and potential risks but that they have no further responsibility when management or the board elects to accept the risk and not take corrective action. The same principle applies if management chooses an alternative corrective measure to one recommended by an internal auditor.
4. Auditors respect the auditee's operations and time demands while conducting any on-site follow-up review in order not to interfere unnecessarily with the auditee's operations and employees.

Ideal Auditee Role

1. Auditees provide timely, complete responses to the audit report.
2. Auditees cooperate with and assist auditors making follow-up reviews.
3. Auditees keep auditors and executive management informed of corrective actions, both contemplated and actually made.
4. Auditees inform executive management and auditors of major disagreements with auditors about the adequacy of corrective measures. They acknowledge responsibility for the resultant risks of remedial measures believed by the auditors to be inadequate.
5. Auditees assess the cost effectiveness of alternative corrective measures and choose an appropriate alternative.

Ideal Executive Management Role

1. Executive management monitors the follow-up process, checking with

and encouraging the auditee to assure an appropriate response to the audit report.
2. Executive management assesses the adequacy and cost effectiveness of auditees' corrective actions and takes needed steps to rectify observed inadequacies.
3. Executive management avoids interference with auditors' follow-up reviews, thereby encouraging their objectivity and independence.

4. Integrity of the Organizational Functions. Each of the three groups — auditor, auditee, and executive management — preserves the integrity of the decision process without compromising the performance of any of the groups' responsibilities. The auditors respect the auditee's responsibility and stewardship and avoid unduly interfering with operations during the follow-up review. Likewise, the auditee respects the auditor's right to make an independent follow-up review, and cooperates and assists as needed. Executive management's role is that of an overseer.

Types of Follow-Up Actions

There are three general types of actions taken by auditors in the follow-up reviews: (1) they review auditees' responses and corrective actions on audit findings; (2) they evaluate the adequacy of those responses and corrective actions; and (3) they report their follow-up findings.

These three actions appear to be straightforward. They may, however, be applied quite differently under different circumstances. On one audit, the follow-up review may be short, almost perfunctory. On another audit, the follow-up may seem more like another audit, involving a wide range of audit procedures. The breadth and depth of the follow-up depend on the importance of the findings and the scope of the audit itself.

Breadth. Some follow-up reviews focus narrowly on specific points of concern. For example, a recent audit of one company's accounts receivable ledger resulted in a recommendation that an aging of accounts be performed monthly. The auditors' follow-up review focused only upon whether the recommended aging of accounts was being performed and communicated to management.

Conversely, the interaction of some operations is so great that follow-up leads the auditors into parts of the organization other than the original auditee's department. Such an occasion occurred when a team of auditors recommended a renegotiation of payment schedules, interest rates, and delivery schedules from the company's suppliers. The auditors' follow-up examination took them into the company's legal department, accounts payable, the warehouse, and the marketing department.

Depth. The extent of follow-up examinations also varies with respect to the kind and the amount of study undertaken on a single point of concern. The review may examine (1) the documentation of corrective actions and (2) the performance of those actions. By examining both the documentation and the performance, the auditors conduct a more in-depth review than by reviewing either one alone.

For example, suppose two audits for a large utility company were completed at about the same time. The results of one audit led to a recommendation that service districts be classified on management reports according to their respective sizes. The second audit resulted in a recommendation that certain maintenance work on company vehicles be done more frequently.

Both audit teams followed up on their audits approximately six weeks after the release of their reports. The first team merely requested a sample document and an explanation of the new format used in the management reports. The second team discussed the auditee's response by telephone and then visited the motor pool to observe the work being performed. They also reviewed the documentation of the motor pool's new policies, standards, and procedures. Their follow-up was more in-depth than that of the first audit team. The auditors in the first case examined only the documentation of the change. The auditors in the second case examined both the documentation and the performance. We cannot necessarily say, however, that one follow-up was more effective than the other, since both audit teams verified that corrective action had taken place.

What determines the breadth and depth of audit follow-up procedures? As with other audit decisions covered throughout this book, risk is the primary factor governing the nature and extent of follow-up. The greater the risk, the more extensive the follow-up procedures are likely to be.

The table shown below illustrates the effect of risk on the follow-up performed on the four audits discussed previously. Without discussing how the risks in the table were determined, consider the effect of the risk upon the follow-up procedures. In both cases where the risk was high, the follow-up work was more extensive — in the first case broader, and in the second case more in-depth. In the two cases where risk was relatively low, follow-up was less extensive — in the first case narrower, and in the second case less in-depth. Both the breadth and depth must be considered for every follow-up review.

	Auditor's Recommendation	Exposure	Probability of Loss	Risk	Follow-up
1	Classify service districts by size in reports	Low	Low	Low	Limited
2	Expand vehicle-maintenance procedures	Medium	High	Med/Hi	Extended
3	Monthly aging of accounts receivable	Medium	Low	Med/Low	Limited
4	Renegotiation of payment schedules	Medium	High	Med/Hi	Extended

Follow-Up Plans. The above considerations — i.e., risk and the resultant considerations of breadth and depth — lead to specific decisions about how the three follow-up actions will be performed. These decisions are then reflected in the specific follow-up plans.

The easiest, quickest, and least expensive follow-up plan is simply to ask the auditee what corrective action has been taken. This inquiry may be made by telephone or in person. In such cases the auditors should prepare a written summary of the auditee's answer. Although this is the easiest form of follow-up, it might not be acceptable by itself for high-risk situations. Auditees tend to take corrective action more seriously when a written response is required. Exhibit 11-3 illustrates how an auditor might document a follow-up inquiry.

Another simple follow-up approach is to request and review a written response by the auditee. Such responses should explain what, if any, corrective action has been taken. These written responses vary in formality, but frequently are in the form of an interoffice memorandum addressed to the director of internal auditing and to the auditee's supervisor. Exhibit 11-4 illustrates a short memorandum from the director of office administration for an insurance company. This memorandum recounts an audit team's finding and recommendation and explains the director's response.

Notice the date of receipt handwritten on the memorandum with "JM," the initials of the auditor who reviewed the memo.

A third type of follow-up plan includes on-site review. Methods of on-site review include interviews, direct observation, and examining the documentation of corrective actions. The auditors document these reviews in the working papers in support of the follow-up report.

Exhibit 11-5 illustrates a sample of a brief follow-up report for an audit of the employee training program of an electronics manufacturer. This report states its purpose and reiterates the previous audit findings and recommendations. It also outlines the actions taken, the follow-up findings, and finally, the auditor's evaluation of the corrective measures. Even though this sample of a follow-up report is brief, it may not always be short and may even approach the length of the original report, especially when the original findings are serious.

Practical Considerations Dealing with Follow-Up

The above discussion focused on general principles governing follow-up procedures. Two important practical considerations affect how those principles are applied. These considerations include (1) time and (2) the roles actually assumed by auditees, executive management, and auditors. Let's examine each in turn.

Time. Internal auditing departments almost always are pressed for time. Audit plans and budgets often assume there are ideal audit working conditions. Sometimes audit plans simply are too optimistic. Consequently, auditors seek ways of squeezing the most work out of the available time, and follow-up procedures often are a convenient place to take shortcuts. Although this attitude can adversely affect the audit function, it is possible to plan these procedures so that they may be performed efficiently.

The worst possible case occurs when occasionally internal auditors neglect to follow up an audit, sometimes in the name of more pressing work elsewhere. An audit for which follow-up work has not been performed is unfinished. So important is this work that most auditing departments include follow-up as a required step for almost every audit with significant findings, often as a part of subsequent audits.

Since follow-up procedures sometimes may be considered a bit of a nuisance, you can understand auditors' preoccupation with more efficient methods. The following guidelines can help reduce the time necessary for follow-up reviews:

Exhibit 11-3
Written Summary of a Follow-Up Inquiry

MEMORANDUM

Date: November 16, 1986

To: File
               Ronald Baker, Vice President of Operations
               Herman Adamson, Assistant Manager, Lincoln
               Warehouse
               Ann Isuko, Audit Committee, Board of Directors

From: Linda Jeffries, Senior Auditor

Subject: Follow-up interview with Herman Adamson, Assistant
               Manager, Lincoln Warehouse, in reference to the
               recommendation in the audit report dated August 12,
               1986.

Audit Report Recommendation. A significant number of inventory tags in the warehouse were not properly dated or numbered. The team recommended that the warehouse obtain a special stamping device to number each item with a code, including the date, inventory classification, supplier, and shelf life.

Follow-up Action and Auditee's Response. I spoke with Mr. Adamson this morning on the telephone. He said that the warehouse acquired four of the new stamps in October and that, beginning November 1, a new policy had been implemented requiring all inventory items to be stamped before stacking. He said he personally checks once each week on a random basis to confirm that the stamps are being used. He further confirmed that the new stamps help the warehouse workers rotate the inventory stock more systematically with less effort.

Exhibit 11-4
An Auditee's Written Response

MEMORANDUM

Date: July 1, 1986

To: Clyde Stringer, Director of Internal Auditing
                 Gale McGregor, Executive Vice President
                 Delbert Adamson, Controller

From: Jim Madsen, Director of Office Administration

Subject: Change in payroll distribution policy in response to
                 audit report of June 15, 1986

The audit report recommended that departmental secretaries return undistributed payroll checks to the personnel department for distribution. Departmental secretaries currently distribute payroll checks to employees between 9 a.m. and 10 a.m. on the first workday of each month; but when employees are out of the office (sick, vacation, business, etc.) on payday, our secretaries have been returning the undistributed checks to the payroll department, where employees later pick them up.

The change has been made to conform with the audit recommendation and will go into effect on August 1, when all undistributed checks will be delivered to the personnel department at 4:30 p.m.

An office memorandum explaining the change has been sent to each employee, and a notice has been placed on office bulletin boards.

Because of the recent significant losses discovered by the auditors (a payroll clerk had subverted the system and cashed several returned checks for fictitious employees), our office staff understands the need for the change.

I also understand that several additional controls have been implemented in payroll accounting to help avoid similar losses in the future.

Exhibit 11-5
Follow-Up Report

AUDIT FOLLOW-UP REPORT

Date: December 8, 1986

Auditee: Employee Training Center

Date of Report: July 19, 1986

Auditor in   Nancy Logan, Senior Staff Auditor
Charge:

Follow-up Audit   Brandon Gray, Internal Audit Manager
Leader:

Distribution: Carl Davis, Director, Employee Training Center
                         Gilbert Tobias, Vice President, Human Resources
                         Susan Patten, Manager, Employee Training Center
                         Mandy Kantor, Director, Internal Audit
                         Joseph McConkie, Chairman, Audit Committee

A team of internal auditors made an on-site review of the administration policies governing the Employee Training Center. This review was conducted as a follow-up measure to evaluate the center's response to a previous audit report recommending changes in sizes, instruction, and examination of certain classes.

Audit Findings and Recommendations. The audit found that a significant number of assembly employees, especially those for whom English is not their native language, were being sent back to the training center for retraining after they already had completed the company's prescribed course. Calculations of the previous cost of retraining the employees, including the rework and waste in the assembly plant, totaled almost $60,000 annually. The auditors recommended smaller classes with more intensive personal supervision in the practice segments of the course and a more stringent evaluation process upon course completion.

Response of Employee Training Center. The center has since added an instructor's aide to assist in these classes, although class sizes have not been reduced. The center says that the aide provides more personal supervision, especially since he speaks the native language of the trainees as well as English. The center also has rewritten its examination procedures so that a more careful screening of the trainees is possible upon completion of the course.

Follow-Up Findings. The auditors reviewed and verified the changes made in the Employee Training Center. The manager of the assembly plant confirms that trainees entering plant service since the training changes were made have performed significantly better, and none has required retraining. The cost of the changes is estimated as follows:

Instructor's Aide salary (annually)	$14,500
Employee benefits, etc. (annually)	$ 2,000
New examination (consultant's fee)	$ 2,500

Follow-Up Evaluation. Our conclusion is that the corrective measures are satisfactory and rectify the observed problem.

1. Follow up as many items as feasible during the audit.
2. Review written responses to every major audit finding prior to a follow-up review. This feedback allows the auditors to preview auditee responses and to focus follow-up procedures on the most critical problems or potential problems.
3. Review only the documentation of corrective action for less critical findings.
4. Do not perform follow-up work at all on very minor items (other than reading auditee responses).
5. Limit follow-up tests to the specific problems noted. For example, a random sample of 500 sales transactions in the regular audit work showed that a high percentage of a certain type of customer required an inordinately high number of service calls. These customers all had the same brand and type of machine for which the product was being purchased. A relatively minor adjustment prior to delivery would eliminate most of the service calls. As a result, the auditors recommended, and the auditee agreed, that a procedure be established to identify these customers at the time of sale and make the adjustment prior to delivery.

Audit follow-up procedures would not require examination of another 500 randomly selected sales transactions. After the new procedure was implemented, the auditors would limit their tests to transactions involving only the one type of customer. The tests would involve a much smaller sample of transactions to investigate than before. Of course, before taking the follow-up sample, the auditors would determine if a procedure had been established to correct the problem. Also, any follow-up inquiries of customers likely would focus only upon the particular problem rather than upon the much broader array of concerns present in initial tests.

Assumed Roles. In an earlier part of this chapter, we outlined "ideal" roles for the internal auditor, the auditee, and executive management with respect to follow-up procedures for a given audit. As you might suspect, many situations are not ideal. The role distinctions and requirements often become blurred or confused. Executive management, for example, may not monitor the follow-up process, but instead may expect the auditors to assume total responsibility for follow-up. Such an expectation would place an improper burden upon the auditors, who could become involved in the decision-making process. If executive management does not get involved, the auditee may not feel compelled to do anything at all in response to the audit, in which case the effectiveness of the audit may be critically weakened.

Similarly, should the auditee fail to keep the auditors well informed and to cooperate with the follow-up procedures, the auditors may have difficulty in planning and executing effective, efficient follow-up reviews. Should executive management neglect its responsibility, and should the auditee refuse to cooperate with the follow-up review, the auditors could find adequate review impossible. Should the auditors neglect their proper role in the follow-up review, the overall effectiveness of the audit function could be jeopardized.

The most effective method of dealing with these problems is to establish written policies governing the internal auditing function within the organization. Policies should outline the roles of auditees and executive management as well as that of the auditors in follow-up reviews. While most audit policies regarding follow-up do not include all of these prescribed roles, the inclusion of such policies can facilitate this important aspect of the audit process. Often, when the specific roles relating to the follow-up procedures are not included in the follow-up section, a general description of the respective roles is included elsewhere in the policies. This general description may be adequate to infer the more specific roles in the follow-up review process.

Audit Follow-Up Policies

Although they may differ somewhat, follow-up policy provisions might possess characteristics that are similar to the following:

1. Audit follow-up is required for all audits for which exceptions are reported.
2. Internal auditors are given the authority and the responsibility to evaluate the effectiveness of corrective actions.
3. Follow-up reviews should be adequately documented and include (1) a written response by the auditee and (2) a follow-up report by the internal auditing department on major issues.
4. The roles and responsibilities for follow-up reviews are outlined for the auditors, the auditee, and executive management. These roles and responsibilities should be outlined specifically for follow-up reviews, or they at least should be obvious from more general role and responsibility descriptions in other parts of the internal auditing policies.
5. The policies are in writing.
6. The follow-up policy states executive management's commitment to the principle of follow-up reviews.
7. The policy specifies to whom auditee responses and follow-up reports are to be addressed and distributed.
8. The policy statement is addressed to all management-level executives, both operating and staff.
9. The statement is clearly identified as coming from the highest level of authority within the organization.
10. The statement specifies that the auditee respond in writing to audit findings and recommendations within a specified period of time.
11. The policy suggests the format of the response to be made.

An audit response policy such as that described above can help maximize the effectiveness of the internal auditing function. Exhibit 11-6 illustrates a follow-up policy statement incorporating the above characteristics.

Additional Keys to Follow-Up Success

Three additional sets of guidelines can help strengthen the effectiveness of follow-up reviews. They are:

1. Discriminating between auditee responses to symptoms and responses to causes.
2. Guidelines for documenting follow-up reviews.
3. Guidelines for rejecting an auditee's corrective measures.

Exhibit 11-6
Illustration of an Audit Follow-Up Policy

TO: All Division and Department Heads

The Board of Directors has approved the following policy regarding audits by the Internal Auditing Department and the responsibilities for related audit follow-up. We urge your full support.

Responsibility for follow-up. It is the responsibility of the manager of the operation audited to write a response to the report and to implement appropriate corrective action when needed. Responses should be prepared and distributed within 60 days of the receipt of the report. The response, developed by the manager with the help of his or her staff, should include:

a.   Synopsis of audit point.
b.   Comment on audit points (agreement or disagreement).
c.   Action to be taken. If no action, why not.
d.   Timing as to when action will be taken, if applicable.
e.   Person responsible for implementation, if applicable.

Distribution of a formal response. Responses are to be addressed to the executive officer to whom the auditee operation reports. Distribution is to be the same as that of the audit report with a copy provided to the Internal Auditing Department.

Evaluation of corrective action. The Internal Auditing Department is responsible for evaluating the corrective action to determine its effectiveness. It is also responsible for reporting in writing the results of the follow-up review to the management of the operation audited, executive management to whom the management of the audited operation reports, and the audit committee of the board of directors.

Facilitation of audit follow-up. Management of the operation audited must facilitate the follow-up review by cooperating with the internal auditors in providing them access to documents, facilities, personnel, and operations necessary to conduct the review. Executive officers are responsible for providing them with the necessary resources to conduct appropriate follow-up review of audits and to encourage adequate administrative independence for them to preserve their objectivity during audit follow-up. The Internal Auditing Department is responsible for providing the auditee operation with appropriate notification of follow-up so as not to unduly disrupt company operations.

Decision making. As in the primary audit, all decision-making responsibility relating to follow-up audit findings rests exclusively with operational and executive management.

Symptoms vis-à-vis Causes. Consider the following paragraphs from an audit report:

> There has been a continuous lag of three to four months in the reconciliation of division bank accounts. The Security Commercial Bank account had not been reconciled since it was opened 10 months ago. Also, reconciliations contain numerous outdated reconciling items and outstanding checks — some a year old or older. Internal control is seriously weakened when bank accounts are not reconciled promptly and errors are not corrected immediately.
>
> We recommend that all bank statements be reconciled within 10 working days after receipt. We further recommend that all errors be corrected immediately upon discovery and that all outdated items be researched and cleared.

The auditee's response arrived the month following the exit conference. The part of the response pertaining to the above situation reads as follows:

> We are aware of this situation. Our accounting clerk is working on the reconciliations to correct the problem.

Unfortunately in this case, the auditors accepted the response without further follow-up. Another audit of the division 15 months later found essentially the same conditions.

Among several deficiencies in the auditee's response in this case is that it does not address the cause of the problem. A more appropriate reply would have been:

> Divisional management has established a policy whereby all bank statements must be reconciled within 10 working days from the date of receipt. Accounting procedures also have been implemented so that the accounting clerk receives each statement directly from the mail clerk. The accounting clerk then is responsible for all reconciliations. Upon completion, they are to be approved by the division's assistant controller, who will review calculations and check the date of the statement to assure prompt reconciliation. Any errors are to be corrected immediately. The accounting clerk is responsible for follow-up of any unusually outdated items to determine the cause of their being late. All reconciliations are to be filed with copies of the bank statements in chronological order.
>
> This new policy, along with the associated accounting procedures, is scheduled to go into effect October 1.

Notice that the alternative reply not only states that corrective measures have been taken, but also specifies what actions have been taken to correct the cause of the problem and when the measures will go into effect.

Auditors should be alert to this distinction between symptoms and causes and to how the auditee plans to address the causes rather than just the symptoms. Exhibit 11-7 lists a few symptoms with possible causes to illustrate the differentiation.

Exhibit 11-7
Comparison of Symptoms and Causes

SYMPTOMS	POSSIBLE CAUSES
Loss of purchase discounts	Slow review and processing of invoices
Poor product quality	Inadequate inspection procedures
Discrepancies between shipment quantities and quantities recorded on customers' invoices	Poor coordination between accounting and shipping
Unusually high downtime for machinery	Inadequate maintenance
Employee discontent and high turnover with associated high recruiting and training costs	Comparatively low wages

Follow-Up Documentation Guidelines. Two sources generally provide the documentation of the follow-up review. Auditors generate their own documentation, including correspondence and other memoranda, that outlines the nature of the review and its results. Auditees also generate documentation in the form of written responses to the audit, including descriptions of proposed actions and corrective actions actually taken to address the problems identified in the audit report. Generally, documentation of the follow-up is attached to the audit working papers, and the follow-up report is attached to the original audit report.

Documents contained in the working papers may include the following:

1. Copies of transmittal letters on the audit report.
2. Correspondence regarding matters in the audit report.
3. Memoranda summarizing follow-up conferences and meetings, telephone conversations, document reviews, calculations, etc.
4. Letters and memoranda from the auditee responding to the audit report.
5. Correspondence to the auditee expressing the auditors' opinion regarding anticipated corrective actions.
6. A copy of auditee plans on corrective actions.
7. Letters and memoranda sent to the auditee that contain the follow-up report and express approval or disapproval of the measures being taken.

Of course, all of the above documentation may not be generated for every follow-up review. Various reviews will require varying amounts and kinds of documentation. Keep in mind, however, that good documentation is essential to effective follow-up.

How the documentation generated during follow-up reviews is distributed also affects the success of these reviews. It is essential that auditee responses outlining final decisions and corrective actions are distributed both to the auditors and to executive management, especially on controversial findings. It is important for the follow-up report to be distributed to the recipients of the original audit report. Such communication ensures that a complete history of the audit is made available to the various interested parties.

It is not so important, however, that all of those people in the original distribution of the audit report receive each piece of documentation in the follow-up file. Much of this information is tentative and represents something of a negotiation process before final actions are taken. The executive immediately above the auditee in the organization often receives the correspondence generated between the auditor and auditee in order to remain well informed about the review process. Other people in the original distribution of the audit report usually do not need to maintain such close observation, but should receive final responses by auditee management and the final report from the auditors.

Rejections of Auditee Responses. The auditors and the auditee, even with executive management's assistance, do not always reach an agreement on corrective measures. The auditors' objective in these situations is to recognize the differences of opinion while still maintaining a workable relationship with the auditee and with executive management. A few guidelines can help accomplish this dual objective:

1. Auditors must not force their preferences upon management.
2. Auditors must focus their attention upon control objectives and control principles and allow management to choose from acceptable alternatives.
3. Auditors must avoid assuming the responsibility for corrective action.
4. Auditors should avoid assuming the role of inspector, regulator, policeman, or approver whose blessing must be obtained before any action is taken. Management has the authority to make decisions. The auditors should review, evaluate, advise, and report.
5. Auditors should decide in advance which deficiencies are most critical and attempt to resolve plans of action with the auditee before the audit report is released.
6. Auditors should never attack individuals in their reports. They should evaluate decisions and actions.
7. Auditors should not become emotionally entangled in disagreements with the auditee.
8. Auditors should state specifically in their written rejections why they believe the auditee's response is deficient and which specific control objectives are in danger. This information should be written as matter-of-factly as possible. Emotional language should be avoided.

By keeping the above guidelines in mind, particularly in controversial situations, auditors can better maintain their professional posture and maximize their overall benefit to the organization. It is important that the auditor and the auditee be able to recognize differences of professional judgment without jeopardizing their working relationship.

The auditors are in a position of independent and objective review and appraisal. The audit and the follow-up reporting function should present (1) the results of the reviews (with the auditors' conclusions and recommendations) and (2) the auditee management responses (including any apparent differences). Resolution of conflicts in judgment between the auditee and the auditors almost always is the responsibility of executive-level decision-makers and the auditee management.

This section of the chapter has covered audit follow-up in some detail, with an emphasis on the importance of effective follow-up in order to follow through on the audit process. While the audit process may appear to be complete at this point, one more step is necessary.

Audit Evaluation

The final step in the audit process is evaluation — a critique of the overall audit.

Not all auditing departments evaluate their work, but increasing numbers of auditors are discovering the value of doing so. These evaluations help maintain effective quality control. Although we have referred to evaluation as the final step, it usually is completed before the follow-up. It is important for evaluation to be done while the audit is fresh on the minds of the audit team. When done immediately after the audit, evaluation tends to be more specific and insightful than if it were performed later. Also, the lessons learned as a result of the evaluation can be applied on a more timely basis.

Audit Critiques

A critique of an audit usually is performed during a meeting between the lead auditor, the audit manager or supervisor assigned to the audit, and the audit director. Some critiques also include staff auditors.

One approach to critiquing an audit is to provide each assigned auditor with a simple "critique sheet" at the beginning of the audit. The auditors use the sheets to write down things they believe would be valuable to know for future audits, such as particularly effective or ineffective audit procedures. The sheets are kept for the duration of the audit and are turned in at a meeting held when the audit is completed. The various concerns noted on individual sheets may be discussed at this meeting and a summary critique can be prepared. This summary sheet then may be filed with the audit report and/ or working papers.

The summary critique sheet would include such information as:

- The date of critique.
- Who attended the meeting.
- The identification of the auditee.
- The date of the audit report or period covered.
- The purpose of the audit.
- The nature of the findings and recommendations (with risk considerations and cost/benefit expectations).
- The nature of the auditee's response.
- The name of the lead auditor.
- Whether the audit was completed on schedule.
- Notes regarding the overall performance of the audit, with special attention to items that are important to future audits.

Another approach to audit critiques begins with a meeting of the same group after an audit is completed. The group discusses the audit in its entirety, including such issues as the audit plan, objectives, overall team performance, individual performances, communication with the auditee, quality of the audit evidence, expected effects of recommendations, and lessons for future audits. Obviously, these meetings may be more abbreviated for routine audits than for more critical and unusual ones. A written summary of conclusions resulting from this meeting is prepared and filed. Although many auditing departments use only an informal critiquing process with no summary documentation, we believe that a written summary of the auditors' impressions is too valuable to ignore.

Suppose, for example, that a team of auditors discovered that the plant manager whose operations were being audited was cooperative and helpful toward experienced auditors, but often hostile to younger staff auditors. Only after the lead auditor met with the plant manager to discuss the problem were the team's two junior staff members able to complete their assignments. The lead auditor discussed this problem with his supervisor at the post-audit meeting. They decided to include a statement in the audit critique that explained the manager's apparent bias in dealing with the auditors. Exhibit 11-8 illustrates the critique summary that resulted from this meeting. This critique sheet was filed with the auditors' working papers for future reference. The information contained in this summary helped the next lead auditor to avoid similar friction between his team and the manager.

Exhibit 11-8
Audit Critique Sheet

Audit: Chemical Prep Plant

Date of Report: October 24, 1986

Lead Auditor: Willie Patten

Supervising Auditor: Kirk Gallion

The audit of the Chemical Prep Plant was a routine audit of plant operations, resulting in relatively minor findings and recommendations. It began and ended on schedule. The auditee accepted the auditors' recommendations, which were implemented prior to the closing conference.

Although the audit did not uncover major deficiencies in the operations of Chemical Prep Plant, its manager's response to the junior staff assigned to the audit was troublesome. The manager displayed great impatience with these less experienced members of the audit team. At one point, he tried to prevent them from reviewing some of the plant's papers, insisting that the auditors weren't competent to interpret them. Only after a lengthy meeting with the lead auditor was the manager persuaded to cooperate with the junior staff.

We recommend that future lead auditors thoroughly brief any assigned junior staff on the audit procedures to be used in order to avoid the appearance of incompetence. We also recommend that future lead auditors assigned to this audit explain at the opening conference with the plant manager the qualifications of each of the assigned auditors. Should a particularly inexperienced auditor be assigned, the manager will likely need to be assured that the new auditor will be adequately supervised.

QUESTIONS

1. Name the two phases of the audit follow-up process and explain each one.
2. What are the four aspects of the ideal auditor role in the follow-up process?
3. What are the three aspects of the ideal auditee role in the follow-up process?
4. What are the four aspects of the ideal executive management role in the follow-up process?
5. How do the three ideal roles help to assure that the follow-up process is carried out?
6. How do the three roles help communication and cooperation among the auditor, the auditee, and executive management during the follow-up process?
7. What effect do the ideal roles have upon the timing of the various responsibilities for the two phases of follow-up? Explain.
8. Explain how the three ideal roles help to preserve the integrity of the auditing, operational, and management functions of the organization.
9. What does it mean that one follow-up review has more breadth than another? More depth?
10. Why are auditors concerned about the documentation of corrective actions as well as the performance of those actions? Explain the effect upon follow-up procedures.
11. What is the primary factor governing the nature and extent of audit follow-up? Explain.
12. List the three primary types of follow-up plans. Explain each one and discuss the advantages and disadvantages of each.
13. List and discuss two important practical considerations affecting how follow-up reviews are conducted.
14. What are some of the important characteristics of an internal auditing policy for follow-up reviews? Discuss briefly why each of your listed characteristics is important to the policy.
15. What difference does it make to the auditor if the auditee addresses symptoms rather than causes in response to audit findings and recommendations?
16. What are the two primary sources of follow-up documentation? Give some examples of documents from each source.
17. Name one guideline for each of the following aspects of rejecting an auditee's follow-up response — (a) auditor role, (b) potential emotional disagreements with the auditee, and (c) language used in the written rejection.
18. Name two major benefits of evaluating an audit upon its completion.
19. What are post-audit critiques? What do they contain? How are they prepared?

EXERCISES

E-1

The auditors for a chain of wholesale food distribution outlets conducted an audit of the company's produce management. They discovered what appeared to be high levels of spoilage in the three oldest storage facilities. Although all three of these facilities experienced almost identical levels of spoilage, which were only slightly greater than the estimated industry standard, these levels were significantly greater than the five newer storage facilities owned by the company. The obvious difference was the refrigeration equipment and the handling procedures of the older facilities compared to the state-of-the art operations in the newer facilities. Executive management recently had adopted plans to renovate the older plants in order to reduce spoilage and improve handling and shipping procedures. The auditors, however, computed some cost comparisons of maintaining the old system as opposed to making the proposed changes. They concluded that the new system would cost far more than the possible benefits the company might receive in cost reductions. The auditors recommended that the company keep and maintain the old system, at least until new technology made such a change more cost-effective. The produce department managers of the eight storage warehouses favored the change and already had begun their own plans for the changeover.

Required:

a. Describe and compare the roles of the auditors, the auditee (i.e., the produce department managers of the eight distribution outlets), and executive management in any future follow-up to the audit.
b. What problems might you anticipate that could interfere with the successful fulfillment of these three different roles?
c. How might you avoid such problems as an auditor?

E-2

Phil Scranton is the auditor-in-charge of an audit of corporate research and development of Faecit Metals Company. Phil and his team of two staff auditors have just completed their exit conference with Henry Wilson, director of research and development, and his assistant, Antonio Calontino. The auditors felt that the documentation of the various research projects was inadequate in terms of allocating their costs and identifying future potential benefits. Several specific audit recommendations were given at the exit conference through the presentation of the audit report. Both Wilson and Calontino argued vigorously with Scranton and vowed to ignore the recommendations. They failed to make any response to the audit and continued to conduct the affairs of the research and development center as before. The auditors tried to set up meetings for a follow-up review and to persuade Wilson to respond to the audit in writing. These efforts were ignored. Finally, Wilson told his secretary not to accept any calls from the auditing department and to return any interoffice memoranda or other written communication from the auditing department.

When top management requested information about the conclusion of the audit, the auditors explained that they were meeting stiff opposition from the auditee, who refused to participate in any follow-up procedures. Kell McDugan, vice president of operations, sent word to the director of the internal auditing department that a team of auditors absolutely must visit the R&D center to see what, if anything, was being done to correct the problems found during the audit. Further, McDugan said, if Wilson and Calontino were unwilling to fix the problems, the auditors should undertake their own corrective measures and inform the R&D managers that "McDugan sent word that you can either do what the auditors say or take a permanent walk."

Required:

Identify which of the four benefits of proper role fulfillment in follow-up reviews are in jeopardy in this case. Explain your answer for each one.

E-3

It is the policy of your company that the internal auditing department follow up its audit reports to ensure that appropriate action has been taken on findings of deficiencies. You are on an audit team that recently completed an audit of the marketing division of a large book-publishing company. One of your team's findings was that promotion costs for trade books consistently ran at least 20 percent over budget, and often by as much as 40 percent. The causes of these overruns were determined to be (1) an unsystematic method of determining the budgeted costs and (2) the failure of marketing personnel to use the budgeted amounts as realistic guidelines for spending. These personnel argued that the budget was always ridiculously low and totally unrealistic. And besides, they said, the budget was being prepared by an individual who had spent the past 10 years in the same job in the same office doing the same thing, and had never participated in any actual promotion work.

The audit report made two recommendations for correcting this situation. First, the report recommended that the employees planning the promotion of the trade books meet with the budget planner, who also worked as an accounting clerk, to prepare more realistic budgets. Second, it was recommended that a cost variance report be prepared for each book by the marketing department employee responsible for managing the promotional effort. Not only would more realistic financial planning be possible, but stewardship comparisons would be easier with respect to the performance of different promotional personnel.

Required:

List and explain the steps you think would be necessary to satisfy the company policy for follow-up.

E-4

Suppose that in an audit of accounts receivable the auditors find an unusually high number of accounts being written off as uncollectible. They determine that the cause is management's lack of awareness of the aging patterns of various accounts. Because of this lack of information, management has not taken steps to collect older accounts. Consequently, the accounts are written off after a certain period of time. The auditors recommend a monthly aging of accounts for management's study. They further recommend a policy specifying steps to be taken for the collection of accounts that become delinquent. The auditors perform a follow-up review six months after the close of the audit.

Required:

a. Develop very narrow review procedures for the aging of the accounts.
b. Develop broader follow-up review procedures to include both the aging of the accounts and the effect of the aging procedure upon credit collections.

c. Develop a set of less in-depth follow-up procedures so that the auditors may determine whether an effective collection policy has been established. Focus the review upon the policy statement itself.

d. Develop a set of more in-depth follow-up review procedures to verify the establishment of the new collection policies and to determine the effect of those policies.

E-5

The Eagle's Nest Resort Communities, Inc. is a diversified company with three luxury resort communities (one each in Hawaii, Texas, and Maine); a ski apparel production division located in Denver, Colorado; a travel business specializing in high adventure, hunting, and fishing expeditions in Alaska, Canada, and Mexico; and a luxury cruise ship operating in the Carribean. Headquarters are located in Denver. Last year's gross revenue from each division of the business may be summarized in round figures as follows:

Division	Gross Revenue
Resort Communities	$25,000,000
Ski Apparel	3,000,000
Travel Business	12,000,000
Cruise Ship	20,000,000
TOTAL GROSS REVENUES	$60,000,000

The company's internal auditors recently completed an audit of the Mexico High Adventure operations. It seems that a number of complaints had been received from clients who said their accommodations were not comparable with those advertised in the company's literature. Clients also complained about bad food, and one group actually got lost for a week in the southern jungles of Mexico because of a reportedly ill-prepared expedition leader. The group was rescued by another of the company's expedition leaders who led the search after the group was two days late returning.

The auditors found that revenues from the Mexico operations had declined over the past three years and that the operations manager had been trying to improve profits by minimizing costs. As a result, he had hired inexperienced expedition leaders who would work for less money, and he had changed the hotel chain where expedition members gathered before and after their adventures. The new hotel chain was advertised as a luxury chain, but was willing to sign a less expensive contract with the company than the previous chain. Although the new chain was not quite of the ultra-luxurious quality that the original chain was, the operations manager felt that the clients would not object. He also felt that they might even prefer the new one, since the decor was a bit more rustic and would suit the atmosphere of an outdoor adventure.

The auditors recommended an immediate change in policies so that more highly qualified expedition leaders would be recruited and hired and the previous hotel chain would be retained. The auditors also recommended that a new advertising and promotional campaign be designed to counter the diminished reputation of the company's operations in Mexico.

Required:

a. If the auditors decide to review only the documentation of the auditee's corrective actions for the follow-up procedures, what documents would be the most appropriate to examine in order to evaluate (1) the actions regarding the qualifications of expedition leaders, (2) the change in hotel accommodations, and (3) the advertising and promotional campaign?

b. What would be the determining factors in your decision as an auditor to review documents only or to conduct an on-site review of performance in this case?

c. Would you perform an on-site performance review, review documents at your Denver offices, or combine your review of both documentation and on-site performance? Why?

E-6

a. For the previous exercise (E-5), which of the two types of follow-up review would represent the greater risk to the company — the document review at headquarters or the on-site review?

b. Suppose the auditors decided that three procedures should be used to follow up the recommendation that more highly qualified expedition leaders be hired. The first procedure is to determine which of the expedition leaders employed at the time of the audit had unacceptable levels of experience. The second procedure is to verify that those leaders with unacceptable levels of experience had been replaced by leaders who were better qualified. Suppose further that the auditors perform both of these steps by reviewing resumes and employment records. What additional step or steps might the auditors perform in order to decrease the risk that (1) the new leaders do not possess the level of expertise that their resumes purport and (2) that they may not be qualified to lead the company's expeditions in Mexico?

E-7

SOUTHOCO is a major energy company that operates worldwide, primarily in fossil-fuel exploration, production, and distribution. One of the company's distribution methods is through consignees, who contract as independent agents to operate as wholesale distributors of SOUTHOCO's products. The company's auditors in the southeastern region recently completed an audit of consignee operations in the northern sales district of one state in the three-state region. The auditors focused their examination on gasoline, diesel fuel, and oil. Price differentiations have been established during the past year for different types of customers — private contractors, service stations, and local and state governments. The consignees were supposed to have received notification of the changes in pricing policies nine months prior to the beginning of the audit. New bookkeeping procedures for the changes required the use of new forms with additional space for the classification of the customers. These forms would allow the company to keep track of both the actual charges and the amount that should have been charged on each sale.

The auditors found that approximately one-half of the consignees were still using the old forms. Further investigation showed that erroneous pricing by many of the consignees had cost the company more than $200,000 in lost revenues since the new pricing policies went into effect. The consignees said the reason they were using the old forms was that the new forms were slow in arriving and because they wanted to use up the old forms first. Further, they claimed that they had not received adequate communication about how to apply the new pricing policies. Consequently, they did not feel they had much choice but to use the old forms and prices, and since no one had complained, they thought it was okay.

The auditors made the following recommendations:

1. The company should make a concerted effort to see that all of the consignees receive and learn how to use the new sales forms.
2. The company should send representatives to each consignee office to inform and train the managers about the new pricing policies and how to use them.
3. Headquarters accounting personnel should check the consignee sales documents to see that the new procedures are being used properly.

Required:
a. Plan a simple inquiry follow-up review. What key questions need to be answered?
b. Plan a follow-up review at the auditees' headquarters to verify that the corrective measures have been taken. What key questions need to be answered? What documents do you think should be reviewed?
c. Plan an on-site follow-up review to examine both the documents and the performance of corrected procedures. What key questions need to be answered? What methods would you use?

E-8

Refer to the previous exercise and complete the following:

Required:

a. Identify at least one specific time-reducing method for this case that corresponds to each of the six follow-up time reduction principles.
b. For at least three of the six principles, explain the trade-off between time and risk in their application.
c. Which of the six principles seem to have the greatest time-reduction effect and yet provide the least risk to the company in this case? Explain your answer.

E-9

Corporate auditors for a large hotel chain completed the audit of one of its hotels located in Stamford, Connecticut. The auditors reported that local hotel management relations with the housekeeping personnel had deteriorated badly since the previous audit four years before. The auditors determined that the cause of the problem was the contract negotiated between the hotel management and a local housekeeping and janitorial service.

Originally, the hotel hired and managed its own housekeeping staff. Three years ago the hotel manager decided that it would be simpler and less expensive to contract with Jiffy Maids, Inc. for all of the housekeeping service for the hotel. At the time the contract was signed, Jiffy Maids did not have enough personnel to meet the hotel's contract. They decided to hire the existing workers who were already familiar with the jobs. Both the hotel and Jiffy Maids' management felt that it would be a good arrangement for the workers, who otherwise would be out of work. The logic was that Jiffy Maids would increase revenue, the workers would keep their jobs, and the hotel could simplify its management responsibilities at less cost.

The transition, however, left the housekeeping staff with less income, since the hourly wage paid by Jiffy Maids was less than the hotel was paying. Although most of the workers had decided to go to work for Jiffy Maids at the hotel, they were unhappy. The high turnover and poor morale among the workers resulted in poor housekeeping service at the hotel.

In their report, the auditors agreed that hiring Jiffy Maids had caused a decrease in housekeeping costs, but that hotel revenues could suffer, and much of management's time still was being spent trying to resolve the housekeeping problems. The auditors recommended that the local hotel managers renegotiate the contract with Jiffy Maids and stipulate that the workers be paid on a scale at least equal to the wages they were previously making. The auditors also recommended that Jiffy Maids should improve the employee benefits.

The auditee argued that these recommendations infringed upon Jiffy Maids' own labor-relations policies and that the hotel had no right to tell Jiffy Maids how to manage its own employees.

The auditors said that if such a contract were not negotiated with Jiffy Maids, company management would be notified that the auditee was being uncooperative.

The local manager became annoyed with the auditors' attitude and decided to ignore their recommendations. Instead, the manager decided to meet with Jiffy Maids' management to discuss the problem, explain the hotel standards in detail, and outline what would be required from the housekeepers in order for the hotel to continue using the service. The manager did not think it would be wise to inform the auditors of such action, since they already had taken such a strong position. Besides, he did not want to be reported to executive management as being uncooperative. He reasoned that if the problem was solved before the auditors returned, that should be good enough.

Company management had a policy that all problems should be resolved between the auditors and the auditees, and only in extreme circumstances should executive management be involved in the correction of difficulties arising from any internal audit. It was also their policy to receive final reports and to review those reports with the audit committee in semi-annual meetings.

Required:
a. Evaluate the roles assumed by the auditors, the auditee, and management in this case.
b. What problems do you foresee arising from the assumed roles in this case in terms of follow-up assurance, communication and cooperation, timing, and the integrity of organizational functions?
c. How might the roles be improved to correct the problems?

E-10

Read the following company policy regarding audit follow-up reviews:

REVIEW POLICY

The internal auditing department has adopted the following policy regarding follow-up on corporate audits. All division and department heads are urged to support this policy to ensure adequate performance of the department.

The internal auditing department is responsible for conducting a follow-up investigation for each audit in which deficiency findings are reported. The purpose of such follow-up investigations is to determine whether corrective actions have been taken, to report such actions, and to evaluate their effect on the deficiencies found during the audit. The auditors are also responsible for distributing the follow-up report to the same recipients who receive the audit report. The follow-up report should be completed and distributed within 30 working days from the completion of the follow-up reviews.

Required:
List which of the 11 policy characteristics outlined in the chapter are contained in the previous policy statement and which of the 11 characteristics are not included.

E-11

The auditors for a greeting-card company became concerned when, during their audit of production operations, they discovered 10 percent more waste and 5 percent more rework on jobs than for the same period two years before. Further examination revealed that these excessive costs were being caused by relaxed standards and two faulty machines that needed either major repair or replacement. The auditors requested a follow-up statement from the production manager within 30 days explaining the corrective measures that had been taken. The production manager's reply follows:

> We have corrected the waste and rework problem. Our calculations show that these two costs are now in line with our best performance periods in the past.

Required:
a. Evaluate the production manager's follow-up response. Explain your evaluation.
b. What questions do you think should be addressed in this auditee's response?

E-12

Malcolm Stewart, chairman of Kelly Company's audit committee, received the following communication from Norman Hall, Kelly's director of internal auditing:

MEMORANDUM

Date:	January 16, 1986
To:	Malcolm Stewart, Chairman of the Audit Committee
	Ken Kelly, Vice President of Operations
	Jan Dexter, Controller
	Curtis Kelly, President and Chairman of the Board
From:	Norman Hall, Director of Internal Auditing
Subject:	Rejection of Ms. Fess's proposed action to correct weaknesses in production control reports.

It is becoming increasingly difficult to work with Ms. Fess since she assumed responsibility for the company's control reporting procedures. A team of auditors led by Vicky Checker, one of our best senior auditors, recently conducted an audit of production control reports. This audit was specifically requested by Ken Kelly, because he claimed that he and his managers were having difficulty understanding some critical information contained in the reports. He has tried to meet with Ms. Fess on several occasions to discuss the reports, but she has been most unapproachable in the matter. She claims that the reports are identical to those of Masters Corporation, where she used to work. Since the auditors have the authority to impose an audit on any office or department, Ken suggested that we investigate these reports for him. He is right. Ms. Fess's reports are totally inadequate. We recommend that they be changed, but she has been uncooperative from the beginning. She says she is willing only to make a token change in her reports.

I have written this memorandum in the hopes that something could be done to correct the problem with her reports, and we could move on to other assignments.

Required:

Critique the above memorandum as a rejection of the auditee's response. Which of the guidelines outlined in the chapter for rejections of auditee's responses seem to be violated?

E-13

Paul Adamson, audit director of North American Airlines, assigned Maxwell Cannes and Leanne Shoemaker to audit the company's Salt Lake City terminal operations. Maxwell was designated the lead auditor. The audit included ticket sales, freight, passenger boarding, baggage handling, customer relations, and the terminal's accounting system. The audit began July 16, 1986, with an opening conference on that date. The closing conference was conducted on July 31, 1986.

The objectives of the audit were (1) to test compliance of the terminal operations with company policy, (2) to evaluate the effectiveness and the efficiency of the terminal operations, and (3) to evaluate the integrity (accuracy and completeness) of the terminal accounting records.

The audit team had several significant findings. In general, company policies were being followed in each of the six areas reviewed, although there were a few exceptions. First, air freight items were being collected in the same work and storage area as passenger luggage, and although freight items were clearly tagged and marked, there were problems with some shipments. Second, rather than training someone or hiring a specialist, the terminal manager for the airline was handling customer relations. The result was that many complaints were either not attended to or were resolved unsatisfactorily.

The auditors concluded that the effectiveness and efficiency of the Salt Lake City operations appeared to be satisfactory with the exception of freight handling and customer relations. These areas had suffered badly. In fact, ticket sales had decreased 4 percent over the last year's sales, while overall ticket sales for the company had increased 8 percent over the same period.

They also found that the integrity of the accounting system appeared to be satisfactory. The few errors and inaccuracies that did occur in the system were minor and were corrected by routine internal review procedures. The auditors found no discrepancies in the accounting records.

As a result of their review, the auditors made three recommendations: (1) the deposit and collection areas for freight and passenger baggage should be separated; (2) the terminal manager should train or hire a customer-relations specialist to handle special problems and complaints; and (3) due to the time demands of his other responsibilities, the terminal manager should become involved with customer problems and complaints only in the most extreme cases.

The terminal manager was cooperative with the auditors during the audit and agreed to all recommendations, which were implemented within 30 days after the closing conference.

The auditors believe that if the customer-relations problem is solved, this terminal operation could become a sales leader in the company because of rapidly increasing air traffic through Salt Lake City. Further, the auditors think that future audits should correlate overall passenger growth for the Salt Lake City Airport to North American's passenger growth at the terminal, in an effort to monitor a turnaround in the sales downturn.

Required:
Write a critique for this audit, using the following outline as a format:

Auditee:
Date of Audit Report:
Lead Auditor:
Audit Objectives:
Nature of Findings and Recommendations:
Auditee Response:
Comments:

PROBLEMS

P-1

The auditors for Drawing Heavy Industries, Inc. recently completed an audit of the company-owned store used by its employees and their families. Following are the findings and recommendations reported by the auditors:

Findings

The overall evaluation of the company store was favorable. The auditors concluded that the store was providing a valuable service to the company and its employees and that store operations generally were being conducted in a professional and businesslike manner. However, there were three critical exceptions:

1. Cash receipts were not being reconciled with cash register totals on a daily basis. Rather, a courier from the company's accounting office went to the store at 5:00 p.m. every day to pick up the day's cash receipts. Since the store closed at 6:30 p.m. every day, some cash from the day's sales remained in the store overnight and was counted as part of the following day's cash totals picked up by the courier. Consequently, cash register totals did not correspond to any single day's count. Rather than make the necessary calculations for adjusting the totals so that they might be easily reconciled, both the cash register totals and the daily pickup totals were tallied by store management for a full month. The store manager then would send all of the cash register totals with the record of daily pickups by the courier to the accounting department to reconcile for management's monthly reports. Often the totals did not correspond, and in three of the past 12 months examined the totals differed by more than $2,500.

2. The company store's accounting system did not have an accounts receivable subsidiary ledger. The store maintained only a handwritten log of the names of employees who bought on credit and the amounts of their credit purchases. When these employees paid their store bills, the amounts were recorded in the log. When the full payment was received, the employees were crossed off the list by a single line drawn through their names. Each credit transaction and payment was simply added in the next available line on the log sheets. No dates were recorded for any of the transactions. Store management said the dates were recorded on the receipts and were not necessary on the log, since it was only an informal record.

3. The company store had no credit collections system. There was no aging of accounts, and a few employees had outstanding bills with purchases made as many as five years prior to the beginning of the audit. One of these employees no longer worked for the company, and had left owing the store more than $1,500. Employees never received any bills, and payment arrangements were made on an informal basis with no interest charges. It was apparent that some employees had received hundreds of dollars of merchandise without making arrangements for payment within a reasonable time period.

Recommendations

The auditors made the following recommendations as a result of these findings:

1. A daily reconciliation of cash and credit sales with cash register totals is needed. If it is impossible for the courier to pick up the daily cash receipts at the end of the store hours, then the receipts between the time of pickup and the store's closing time could be kept separate from the following day's cash receipts. They could be counted separately, and the amount could be added appropriately so that each day's receipts could be accounted for and checked against cash register totals. It is appropriate for such reconciliation to be performed both at the store and in the accounting department, and the two results should be compared to ensure that they agree.

2. The store needs an accounts receivable subsidiary ledger. Entries into the subsidiary ledger can be made on a daily basis, using copies of customer's receipts as documentation.

3. A formal collections system is needed for the store's charge accounts. A monthly aging of accounts and customer billing is needed to improve the collections of these accounts. Specific follow-up by company and store management would enhance the collection of excessively old accounts. In the case of the former employee who left owing the store more than $1,500, a special effort is needed to find him and collect the money he owes.

4. It was recommended that management consider making payments on store accounts a part of the company's payroll deduction program, especially for excessively old accounts.

Required:

Outline a plan for follow-up procedures to review each of the findings and recommendations. You will need to determine three things in your analysis:

a. What information is needed for the review?
b. What type of review is most appropriate — simple inquiry, written auditee response, and/or an on-site review?
c. What specific procedures are required?

P-2

Auditors for Mainland Dairy Products, Inc. completed an audit of the company's computer operations and issued a report on January 27 of this year. That report was distributed to the manager of the EDP department, the vice president of operations, the internal auditing department, and the board of directors. The auditors reported the following problems in these operations:

Forms that were used by various departments for their computerized information systems frequently were not completed correctly, leading to inaccurate reports and, consequently, complaints from numerous managers about the company's EDP department. An analysis of the forms led the auditors to the conclusion that the forms themselves were defective. The forms were formatted poorly, they contained numerous items that were never used by any managers, and directions were either ambiguous or completely left off the forms.

These problems were not unique to any one group or type of form; the problems seemed to be almost universal to all forms used by the company in its EDP operations. In fact, the auditors came to the conclusion that what previously had been observed as a general suspicion and dislike of the EDP department and its personnel had been caused primarily by a general dislike of the forms, which in turn led to the unsatisfactory reports. They also discovered that all of the objectionable forms had been designed by a former systems analyst who had been employed when the EDP department was first formed. This employee recently had left the company.

The auditors recommended that a complete study of the company's EDP system forms used by various managers be undertaken by an analyst experienced in forms design. The auditors recommended that, upon completion of this study, the systems analyst propose the necessary changes in the forms and test new designs with the company managers to provide more suitable forms for the EDP department to use in providing improved reports to the managers. It was further recommended that the analyst also meet with company managers to determine whether the new reports were better than the ones produced from the previous forms. Once an agreement is reached between the managers and EDP personnel regarding the forms and reports, the auditors recommended that those employees who are affected by the changes be trained appropriately.

The auditors conducted an on-site follow-up review on July 17, six months after the close of the audit. They found (1) all of the company's EDP forms used by management personnel had been redesigned, and (2) management reports had been reformatted as a result of the study and the information contained in the reports. The auditors interviewed EDP management, the managers of the departments who were using the forms and reports, and the systems analyst who had done most of the work. Shortly after the conclusion of the audit, the analyst had been recruited from a nearby university where he had specialized in management information systems. The auditors also discovered a more positive attitude among company managers toward the EDP department and a much more cooperative relationship between EDP personnel and the other company managers.

Required:

a. Write a one-page follow-up report for this review, and date it July 20 of the current year. In your report you should include the auditee, previous audit findings, auditor recommendations, the nature of the follow-up review, and the follow-up findings. Be sure to include a distribution list (you can make up the names and titles, but be sure to include the important functions that you think should receive this report), the date of the original audit report, the date of the follow-up report, and the auditor who will sign the follow-up report (that would be you).

b. Do you see any aspects of the follow-up review that appear to be inadequate? Discuss them.

12 Internal Auditing Management

Like other activities in organizations, the success of the internal auditing function depends upon good management. Whereas other chapters have discussed a variety of management issues within the context of the overall audit function and audit process, this chapter focuses exclusively upon internal auditing management. The first part of the chapter is devoted to the management of an audit. Topics include:

- IIA standards pertaining to audit management.
- Roles of the audit director, team leader, and audit staff.
- Audit management aids.

The second part of the chapter is devoted to management of the internal auditing department. Discussion parallels the *Standards* and addresses the following topics:

- Responsibility of the director of internal auditing.
- Purpose, authority, and responsibility of the internal auditing department.
- Planning.
- Departmental policies and procedures.
- Personnel management and development.
- Coordination with outside auditors.
- Quality assurance.

Management of the Internal Audit

Good audits are the result of well-coordinated activities that have been well planned and executed. This requires good management, which begins before the audit work starts and extends beyond delivery of the audit report, or even the follow-up report. Management in this sense means those decisions and activities related directly to running an audit project, including auditor assignments, supervision, review, and evaluation. While management, broadly defined, encompasses all of the information in this text, the focus here is upon a narrow subset regarding how to run an audit.

Standards Related to Audit Management

The *Standards for the Professional Practice of Internal Auditing* recognizes the need for effective management. Several provisions in the *Standards* apply specifically to managing an audit project.

Standard 120. This standard states that in order to achieve auditor objectivity, assignments should avoid placing auditors in situations where they might have conflicts of interest or bias. This standard goes on to state that "internal auditors should report to the director any situations in which a conflict of interest or bias is present or may reasonably be inferred." Appropriate reassignments may then be made.

As discussed in Chapter 2, conflicts of interest may occur in any situation in which a person is likely to sacrifice the interests of the organization in favor of personal aggrandizement or welfare, friendship, or some other loyalty. Almost everyone has multiple loyalties, giving rise to potential conflicts of interest in audit assignments. Potential conflicts become a factor in making auditor assignments when the organization's interests might be jeopardized. Likewise, everyone has biases. The ones of concern are those that are likely to cloud the auditor's professional judgment regarding the auditee.

Professional Standards Bulletin 84-7 suggests that one way to obtain conflict of interest information would be to request that each auditor complete and sign a statement each year regarding personal activities, conditions, interests, and relationships with potential auditees that might constitute a potential or actual conflict of interest.

Standard 120 goes on to state that auditors should be periodically rotated from assignment to assignment. These rotations may be made as often as deemed appropriate by the audit director. Rotations may be made every time a particular auditee is audited, or (especially on audits requiring special training or a particular expertise) auditors may continue for several iterations before rotations are made.

The objective of these rotations is to avoid the development of a bias toward a given auditee. *Professional Standards Bulletin 82-5* states that "internal auditors may not continue to use professional skepticism in reviewing areas with which they are familiar." After rotation, new auditors usually bring a fresh perspective to the auditee's operations. Moreover, *Professional Standards Bulletin 82-5* suggests that rotation is valuable for an auditor's professional development because of the resultant well-rounded audit experiences.

Standard 120 qualifies this provision on rotation, however, by stating that rotation be done "whenever it is practicable to do so." It may be impossible to practice auditor rotation in very small internal auditing departments, or among a small group of audit specialists such as EDP auditors. In such cases, internal auditors must take extra care to exercise objectivity.

In some circumstances it may be impossible to avoid assigning internal auditors whose personal objectivity may be questionable with respect to an auditee. When the audit must be done regardless, the easiest way to maintain auditor objectivity is to use objective audit techniques. Such techniques include:

- Use of documented organizational objectives, standards, activities, and performance to determine the relevant facts pertaining to the situation.
- Use of quantitative rather than qualitative measures.
- Use of statistical rather than judgmental sampling.
- Reporting facts rather than opinions so that management can form its own opinions and recommendations.

Additional guidance on the relative quality of different kinds of evidence is provided in Chapter 4.

Standard 120 also states that auditors "should not be assigned to audit those activities they previously performed until a reasonable period of time has elapsed. Such assignments are presumed to impair objectivity and should be considered when supervising the audit work and reporting audit results."

Professional Standards Bulletin 81-3 provides a guideline regarding what is a reasonable time to wait before assigning an auditor to examine activities for which he or she previously had major responsibility. Such assignments "should be delayed until their successors have had the time and the opportunity to influence the system of control for the activity. Such work should never involve making audit judgments about the accuracy or integrity of data which the internal auditor generated while employed in the audit area."

Finally, Standard 120 states that "internal auditing work should be reviewed before the related audit report is released to provide reasonable assurance that the work was performed objectively." Even in cases where auditor bias or a lack of objectivity may be present, proper supervision by an objective supervisor who works with the assigned auditors to establish audit objectives and procedures, and carefully reviews the resultant audit work, helps prevent individual auditor biases from overcoming good judgment. Audits also typically employ extensive reviews of working papers and reports to further ensure quality control.

Standard 230. This standard, on audit supervision, addresses the following five issues:

1. *The role of the audit director with respect to audit supervision.* All internal auditing assignments and related supervision are the responsibility of the director. Of course, the director may not be on site supervising all audit activities, but the director does assign team leaders who directly supervise the audit work. The director monitors the work through meetings with and reports from the team leader. On critical and sensitive audits, the audit director may become more closely involved with direct supervision of the work.

2. *The expected duration of supervisory activity.* Standard 230 states that "supervision is a continuing process, beginning with planning and ending with the conclusion of the audit assignment."

3. *Supervising activities.* According to this standard, five kinds of activities constitute audit supervision: (a) providing appropriate instructions to the auditors; (b) seeing that the approved audit program is performed, including any authorized changes to the program; (c) reviewing audit working papers to ensure that they adequately support audit findings; (d) reviewing the report; and (e) seeing that audit objectives are achieved.

4. *Documentation of supervisory activities.* In order to ensure quality control, internal auditing departments should document the supervision performed on audits. For example, the team leader may prepare a checklist of administrative tasks to be done during an audit, including supervisory tasks. As each one is completed, it is initialled and dated. Also, as working papers and audit reports are reviewed, the reviewer generally initials and dates his or her approval. The section in this chapter on audit management aids discusses several additional documented supervisory activities.

5. *The amount of supervision required.* Standard 230 explains that "the extent of supervision required will depend on the proficiency of the internal auditors and the difficulty of the audit assignment." Clearly, some auditors require more supervision than others, because of differences in training, experience, objectivity, and perhaps commitment. Likewise, some audits are

more technical, politically sensitive, or complex than others, and thus require more supervision to ensure quality control and to demonstrate due professional care.

Guidelines 420.01.4 and 560.02. These two guidelines also address audit supervision. The first reiterates the requirement that audit work be supervised to ensure objectivity and the achievement of audit objectives. The second reiterates the point that audit supervision is a continual process of ensuring "conformance with internal auditing standards, departmental policies, and audit programs."

Guideline 430.7. According to this guideline, "the director of internal auditing or designee should review and approve the final audit report before issuance and should decide to whom the report will be distributed." This provision goes a step beyond Guideline 230.02.4, which requires the review of the audit report. Guideline 430.7 specifies that the director is responsible for the approval and distribution of the report. Although the director may delegate the task, this standard indicates that the report is so important that it deserves the highest level of attention.

Professional Standards Bulletin 82-14. A concern sometimes is expressed that management and the board decide what is to be audited and "the director of internal auditing influences only the scope (of work)." This bulletin stresses that the director should establish sufficient authority in the internal auditing department charter for him or her to be responsible for the selection of auditees, as well as the scope of audit work. Although the director should be open to suggestions and should consult with management and the board in these decisions, he or she should bear the responsibility.

The extensive nature of these various provisions reflects the importance of good audit management. They span auditor assignments, supervision and review of audit work, supervision and review of preparation of the audit report, selection of auditees, and determination of the scope of the audit. The following section outlines the typical division of responsibilities among team members in the performance and management of an audit project.

Roles of the Audit Director, Team Leader, and Audit Staff

Exhibit 12-1 provides an extensive outline showing the audit tasks performed by the audit director, team leader, and audit staff. The respective tasks outlined define the three different roles performed in a typical audit. The outline corresponds to the audit process described in previous chapters.

Exhibit 12-1
Comparative Roles of Audit Positions

AUDIT STEP	AUDIT DIRECTOR	TEAM LEADER	AUDIT STAFF
Selection of Auditee	Selects the auditee, assigns audit team leader, and briefs team leader on audit.	Consults with the audit director on audit emphasis and preliminary details.	
	Signs form for job authorization.	Prepares form for job authorization with the audit director.	
Audit Preparation	Advises the team leader on possible background materials to examine and meets with him/her to review this material.	Gathers and reviews available background materials and meets with audit executive to review this material.	
	Discusses audit objectives and scope with the team leader.	Prepares objectives and scope of the audit with the audit director.	
	Selects or approves team members with the team leader.	Consults with the audit director about the selection of the audit team.	
	Notifies team members of their assignments.	Allocates audit hours among assigned staff.	
	Attends the preliminary team meeting and prepares for the team meeting in consultation with the team leader.	Conducts a preaudit team meeting and consults with audit executive on preparation.	Attend the preaudit team meeting.
	Consults with the team leader and decides who will be notified of the audit and how they will be notified.	Notifies the auditee and others about the audit as assigned.	

AUDIT STEP	AUDIT DIRECTOR	TEAM LEADER	AUDIT STAFF
	Reviews and approves the preliminary audit program.	Prepares the preliminary audit program with the audit director and team members as appropriate. Also prepares a working paper index.	Review background materials and help prepare audit program as assigned.
	Discusses with the team leader the audit approach and likely format, nature, and distribution of the audit report.	Develops the audit approach and outlines the report expectations with the audit director.	Assist in developing the audit approach and report expectations as assigned.
Initial Survey	Directs arrangements of the opening conference.	Arranges the opening conference as assigned.	Attend and participate in the opening conference as requested.
	Conducts or presides at the opening conference with the auditee if appropriate.	Conducts or participates in the opening conference as assigned.	
	Participates in on-site tour as desired.	Participates in on-site tour and ensures that appropriate notes are taken.	Participate in the on-site tour as appropriate.
	Reviews the update of permanent files.	Supervises the update of permanent files.	Update the permanent files as assigned.
	Reviews the analytical review.	Performs and/or supervises the analytical review.	Assist in the analytical review.
Review of Internal Controls	Informed by the team leader of progress and results of the review of internal controls.	Supervises the performance of the review of internal controls, reviews working papers, and assists as needed.	Perform the review of internal controls as assigned.
	Evaluates the results of the review of internal controls with the team leader.	Informs the audit director of progress and results of the review of internal controls.	
Expanded Tests if Needed	In consultation with the team leader, determines the need for expanded testing.	Consults with the audit director about the need for expanded testing.	Consult with the team leader on the need for expanded testing.

AUDIT STEP	AUDIT DIRECTOR	TEAM LEADER	AUDIT STAFF
	Reviews and approves the expanded audit program and amendment to job authorization form.	Amends the job authorization form if needed.	Perform audit procedures as assigned.
		Prepares audit program changes for expanded testing.	
		Supervises expanded testing, reviews working papers, and assists as needed.	
Review of Audit Findings and Recommendation	Reviews summary findings sheets.	Reviews and comments on summary findings sheets during the audit.	Prepare summary findings sheets as audit work is performed.
		Organizes summary findings sheets and reviews them with the audit director.	Submit summary findings sheets for review by the team leader.
		Ensures orderly compilation of working papers.	
Reporting the Audit	With the team leader, discusses planning, organizing, and setting the agenda for the closing conference.	Plans and organizes the closing conference with the audit director; prepares the agenda.	Attend the closing conference as requested.
	Conducts or attends the closing conference as desired.	Participates in and usually conducts the closing conference.	
		Ensures adequate documentation of the conference and that the auditee's views are properly noted.	
	Consults with the team leader on the initial draft of the report.	Organizes and drafts the audit report from the summary findings sheets, consults with the audit director, and clears wording of findings with applicable auditors.	Assist in drafting the relevant sections of the audit report.

AUDIT STEP	AUDIT DIRECTOR	TEAM LEADER	AUDIT STAFF
	Reviews the "discussion draft" of the report.	Submits the draft for review by the audit director and makes needed changes.	Review the relevant sections of the audit report for accuracy and presentation.
	Communicates suggestions for report revisions with the auditee as needed.	Sends the "discussion draft" for review by the auditee; prompts auditee for feedback as needed.	Assist in evaluating the auditee's responses and comments and help determine the needed modifications in the final report.
	Reviews and approves the final draft of the audit report.	Incorporates the auditee's input as needed while consulting with the audit director and the audit staff.	
		Clears wording changes with the auditee as needed.	
		Ensures the distribution of the final report according to policy.	
		Cross-references the final copy of the report to summary findings sheets and files the final copy of the report.	
Audit Follow-Up	Monitors the auditee's reply status.	Enters "tickler" into a personal calendar to check the status of the auditee's written reply after an appropriate period after issuing the report; monitors the status of response thereafter as needed.	
	Reviews the auditee's reply with the team leader.	Reviews the auditee's written reply with the audit director.	Review the relevant sections of the auditee's response to the audit report.
	Discusses and approves follow-up procedures with the team leader.	Determines the need for audit follow-up in consultation with the audit director.	

AUDIT STEP	AUDIT DIRECTOR	TEAM LEADER	AUDIT STAFF
	Reviews and approves the follow-up report if prepared.	Prepares the program for any immediately needed follow-up and supervises audit follow-up procedures.	Perform audit follow-up procedures as assigned.
	Attends follow-up meetings with the auditee as needed.	Plans and conducts follow-up meetings with the auditee as needed.	Review the follow-up report for accuracy and presentation.
		Compiles any needed follow-up memos and obtains the approval of the audit director.	
Evaluation	Meets with the team leader to critique audit performance.	Meets with the audit director to critique the audit.	Review the relevant sections of the audit critique sheet prepared by the team leader.
	Reviews the critique sheet prepared by the team leader.	Prepares the critique sheet for the audit and files it with the working papers.	Each individual reviews his/her performance evaluation form.
	Reviews the individual performance evaluation forms and files them in the personnel files.	Completes the performance evaluation form for each auditor supervised.	

Different internal auditing departments may define these roles and tasks somewhat differently than shown in Exhibit 12-1, and there is some variation even from job to job within a single department. The exhibit illustrates, however, typical relationships among the three levels of responsibility.

Even more important than the specific tasks is the nature of the different responsibilities. For example, the role of the audit director is that of an overseer. The audit director usually is responsible for several audit projects at the same time, as well as for a variety of departmental administrative functions.

Due to time constraints, the audit director simply is unable to provide the direct day-to-day leadership required to manage all audits and also perform his or her other executive responsibilities. Of course, there may be an exception to this when a particular audit is highly sensitive. For example, the internal auditors of a large utility company were assigned to audit the company's billing system after government regulators threatened legal action for unlawful billing practices. The results of the audit were to be used by a variety of parties involved in the case, including a state regulatory agency, company executives, the board of directors, the company's legal counsel, and its external auditors. The case involved several millions of dollars in billings and additional millions in potential losses from lawsuits and fines. The director of internal auditing assumed personal responsibility for day-to-day management of this audit.

More typically, however, the director assigns a team leader from the department's professional staff. Depending upon the complexity of the audit and the abilities of the assigned auditors, the team leader may be an audit manager or a senior staff auditor.

Exhibit 12-1 outlines the detailed management tasks required of the team leader during each step of the audit process. For example, when selecting the auditee, the team leader consults with the audit director on the final selection and the allocation of audit hours. The team leader also typically prepares the job authorization form, which is approved and signed by the audit director. Notice that the team leader has more tasks in the performance of the audit than either the audit director or the audit staff. Consequently, the team leader spends more time on the audit.

The audit staff becomes partially involved in the audit preparation work and then becomes fully involved in the audit during the audit survey, review of internal controls, expanded testing, and reporting of the audit. The staff then plays a relatively small role during the evaluation and close-out of the audit project. Where follow-up audit work is required, staff auditors are likely to be assigned to perform this work, again under supervision of the team leader.

Audit Management Aids

Audit team leaders utilize several devices to help manage the audit. The following paragraphs describe a variety of these devices and how they may be used to expedite quality audit work. Although not all internal auditing departments use all of these devices, and although some internal auditing departments use audit management devices not included in these descriptions, the management tools detailed herein are common.

Job Authorization Form. These forms, similar to the one shown in Exhibit 12-2, set some basic parameters for an audit, and also document the formal approval of each audit project. Job authorization forms identify the auditee or project name, such as "Hills Road Plant Review" or "Cash Transfer System Audit." Often a project number is assigned, and the number of allocated hours, start date, expected end date, and team leader are specified. The audit team also may be listed, as well as a few preliminary determinations, such as the purpose of the audit, persons needing to be contacted before audit work begins, and to whom the final report will be addressed. Space for an approval signature and date also is provided.

Audit Checklists. Team leaders often use checklists to keep track of the numerous administrative details required to perform the audit. Exhibit 12-3 illustrates such a checklist. Other checklists, such as opening and closing conference checklists and agendas, were illustrated in previous chapters.

Auditor Assignment Forms and Assignment Boards. In small internal auditing departments, auditor team assignments usually are made informally by the director. In larger departments a director is likely to prepare written or printed forms to be distributed to audit team members, showing their work assignments. Many departments also post assignments on a centrally located wallboard, usually near the departmental bulletin board.

Job Time Control Sheets. Exhibit 12-4 illustrates a job time control sheet, which accumulates all of the audit hours performed on a specific audit project. The hours are itemized by auditor for each day of the audit. The time control sheet allows the team leader to monitor the progress of the audit and keep the time within the authorized budget hours. Budget hours may be established for the initial steps of the audit and then expanded as necessary. Even where expanded testing is unnecessary, budgeted hours may be adjusted as the audit progresses. Consequently, the time control sheet becomes a dynamic planning device as well as a record of hours worked.

Exhibit 12-2
Job Authorization Form

1. Job Name _____ Project No. _____
2. Preliminary authorized hours _____
3. Start date _____ End date _____
4. Expanded hours authorized _____
   Approval/Date _____
5. Lead auditor _____
   Probable assigned auditors _____
   _____
   _____

6. Why are we doing this work? _____
   _____

7. Who should be contacted before job begins?
   Name   Position   Who will make contact?
   _____
   _____
   _____

8. To whom will the report likely be addressed? _____
   _____

9. Other (comment as appropriate) _____
   _____
   _____

Submitted by _____
Date _____
Authorization and approval _____
Date _____

Working Paper Index. The working paper index is prepared before audit work begins, and typically is presented at the team meeting. This information helps the auditors organize and number their working papers as they are prepared. Both the organization and numbering of working papers are discussed more fully in the appendix to Chapter 5.

Audit Program. The audit program, discussed at length in previous chapters, is the chief management device of the audit. It helps the team leader and the audit director organize and distribute the audit work among the audit team, and it charts the progress through the detailed procedures required for each step in the audit process.

Exhibit 12-3
Audit Checklist

DAILY
1. Review audit checklist.
2. Monitor performance of relevant sections of the audit program.
3. Check which auditors report for work and which are out because of illness, etc. Notify the departmental secretary of any absences.
4. Update the job time control sheet.

WEEKLY
1. Conduct a team meeting to monitor and coordinate the status of audit work.
2. Brief the audit executive as to the status of the audit work.
3. Brief the auditee management as to the status of the audit work and monitor the auditee's attitude toward the audit.

BY AUDIT STEP

INITIALS/DATE OF
COMPLETION

AUDIT PREPARATION

_____ 1. Determine the preliminary objectives and the scope of the audit.

_____ 2. Submit the job authorization, obtain approval and get a job charge number.

_____ 3. Assign the audit team members.

_____ 4. Notify the auditee and others.

_____ 5. Prepare and send the preaudit package.

_____ 6. Arrange the necessary travel and accommodations.

_____ 7. Prepare and obtain approval of the preliminary audit program.

_____ 8. Prepare the job time control sheets.

_____ 9. Determine the likely addressee and distributees of the report.

_____ 10. Obtain approval for the preliminary report specifications (what kind of information is desirable to include in the report and what its format is likely to be).

_____ 11. Set up a report preparation folder.

_____ 12. Prepare a working paper index.

_____ 13. Hold an audit strategy meeting with the audit team.

INITIAL SURVEY

_____ 14. Prepare the opening conference agenda and checklist.

_____ 15. Notify the people who should attend the opening conference.

_____ 16. Review and approve the working papers prepared to date.

_____ 17. Ensure that the time control sheet is up to date.

TECHNICAL REVIEW OF INTERNAL CONTROLS

_____ 18. Review and approve any additional working papers.

_____ 19. Ensure that the time control sheet is up to date.

EXPANDED AUDIT TESTING

_____ 20. Amend the audit program as needed.

_____ 21. Ensure that findings write-up sheets are being prepared and reviewed currently and that appropriate information for the report is being accumulated.

_____ 22. Amend job authorization form and get approval if needed.

_____ 23. Arrange additional travel and accommodations if needed.

_____ 24. Meet with the auditee's management to discuss the expanded audit testing.

_____ 25. Review and approve the working papers to date.

DEVELOPMENT OF FINDINGS AND POTENTIAL REMEDIES

_____ 26. Collect and organize the findings write-up sheets.

_____ 27. Meet with the audit executive to finalize the rankings and the order of audit findings.

_____ 28. Refine and adapt the wording of the findings write-up sheets to permit evolution into the first draft of the report.

_____ 29. Compile and index the working papers.

REPORTING THE AUDIT

_____ 30. Prepare agendas for the closing conference.

_____ 31. Notify all who should attend the closing conference.

_____ 32. Complete the report discussion draft.

_____ 33. Distribute the report discussion draft for feedback.

_____ 34. Check the status of the auditee's review of the discussion draft.

_____ 35. Revise the report draft as appropriate.

_____ 36. Submit the final draft of the report to the audit department.

_____ 37. Distribute the report upon the approval of the audit executive.

_____ 38. Cross-reference a copy of the audit report to the findings write-up sheets and/or working papers. File this cross-referenced report with the working papers.

_____ 39. Enter "tickler" in calendar to check the status of the auditee's written response about a month after distribution of the report.

FOLLOW-UP

_____ 40. Check the status of the auditee's written response at the tickler date.

_____ 41. Ensure that the auditee's written response is date-stamped and logged into the report filing system.

_____ 42. Acknowledge the receipt of the response from the auditee.

_____ 43. Review the auditee's written response.

_____ 44. Consult with the audit executive as to the adequacy of the response and decide what, if any, follow-up action is needed.

EVALUATION

_____ 45. Meet with the audit executive to critique the audit strategy and performance. Document the critique.

_____ 46. Complete the auditor performance evaluation forms.

_____ 47. Prepare and submit the job completion transmittal form.

Exhibit 12-4
Job Time Control Sheet

Job Name and Number _____

Team Leader _____

AUDIT STEP	AUD*	7/1	7/2	7/3	7/4	7/5	7/8	7/9	7/10	7/11	7/12	7/15	7/16	7/17	7/18	7/19	7/20	7/23	7/24	7/25	Budgeted Hours
Job Preparation 30	TJD																				20
	OPR																				5
	APW																				5
Initial Survey 35	TJD																				15
	OPR																				15
	APW																				5
Internal Control Review 60	TJD																				20
	OPR																				20
	APW																				20
Expanded Testing 100	TJD																				30
	OPR																				40
	APW																				30
Finding and Recommendations Development 10	TJD																				5
	OPR																				3
	APW																				2
Reporting 130	TJD																				80
	OPR																				30
	APW																				20
Follow-up 5	TJD																				5
	OPR																				
	APW																				
Evaluation 5	TJD																				3
	OPR																				1
	APW																				1
Total Budgeted Hours 375																					375
Daily Totals																					
Cumulative Totals																					

*AUD means "auditors."

Meeting Agendas. A variety of meetings are conducted during an audit, including at least one team meeting, an opening conference, interim meetings with the auditee, and a closing conference. Planned agendas, preferably written down, help keep these meetings on the subject and help ensure that all of the items of business are addressed during the meeting. Without agendas, meetings often take too long, and important items may be forgotten. Generally it is wise to alert meeting participants to a planned agenda long enough before the meeting to give them a chance to suggest changes and additions to agenda items.

Even if time runs short and it is not possible to cover all of the planned agenda items, subsequent meetings can be scheduled, using the agenda as a guideline with respect to the urgency of the matters needing attention and the time required. Planned agendas for opening and closing conferences have been illustrated in previous chapters.

Working Papers. Previous chapters have discussed working papers in some detail. Most relevant to this chapter is the role that working papers play in managing the audit. They provide a convenient way to monitor the progress and the quality of the audit. Working papers are reviewed regularly throughout an audit to ensure that adequate audit work is being done and that the work is progressing in accordance with the audit program. If questions arise after the audit, working papers also provide an easy reference to the evidence gathered to support audit findings and recommendations.

Working Paper Review Sheets. Exhibit 12-5 illustrates a working paper review sheet, used by the team leader to inform the audit staff of necessary changes in the working papers and of additional audit procedures required. These sheets often are called review "point sheets." A "point" is a suggestion noted on the sheet by the team leader. Working paper review sheets typically are written up informally and may even be discarded after all of the review points have been cleared by the auditor.

Summary Finding Sheets. Previous chapters discussed and illustrated Summary Finding Sheets and their role in the audit process. These sheets help improve management of the audit by facilitating the report-writing process, as discussed in Chapters 9 and 10. These sheets also can improve the quality of an audit. By forcing the auditor to address the various facets of a finding — i.e., observed condition, criteria, effect, and cause of any observed problems — these sheets encourage the auditor to be thorough.

Exhibit 12-5
Working Paper Review Sheet

INTERNAL AUDITING DEPARTMENT
WORKING PAPER REVIEW FORM

Auditee _____

Section Being Reviewed _____

Audit Date _____

Reviewer and Date _____

Supervisor's Review Notes	Working Paper Ref.	Auditor Response

Report Review Sign-Off Sheets. Chapter 10 illustrated the extensive review procedures often imposed upon the written internal audit report. One method to monitor and facilitate this process is to have each reviewer sign and date the completion of his or her review.

A simple format works well. The sign-off sheet should identify the audit name and the report date and should provide space for each reviewer's signature and the date of review. If desired, the names of the audit team leader and the typist may also be included. This sign-off sheet may be attached and filed with the audit report. Separate sheets may be used for the "discussion draft" and the final report, but often only the review sheet for the final report is kept.

Report Release Control Sheet. The report release control sheet identifies each person receiving a copy of the internal audit report, the authorization for release, the date delivered, mode of delivery, and the person receiving the report. This control sheet helps ensure that (1) the report goes only to those people who have a right to recieve it and (2) it is distributed in a timely manner.

Exhibit 12-6 illustrates a report release control sheet. Not all internal auditing departments use a formal report release control sheet. These sheets are especially valuable in large departments issuing many reports to a large number of individuals in the organization. Without control sheets, some of the details of this important step in the audit — i.e., delivery of the audit report — can be overlooked and mismanaged.

For example, an auditee in one organization became critical of the company's internal auditing department, complaining to executive management that the auditor's report was never delivered. Several months had elapsed since the audit, and executive management was inquiring whether measures had been taken in response to the auditors' findings. The audit team leader insisted that a copy of the report had been delivered to the auditee. The auditors made another copy and had the team leader hand-deliver it to the auditee management, who blamed the auditors for their own embarrassment before top management.

Cool, strained relations continued between auditee management and the internal auditing department for several months, until a new secretary for the auditee called the auditing department wondering to whom she was supposed to give an old audit report she had found in a stack of papers stored in her desk drawer. The report was the one delivered earlier, which the previous secretary had carelessly

Exhibit 12-6
Report Release Control Sheet

Report Name _____
Report Number _____
Project Number _____

RECIPIENT	RELEASE AUTHORITY	DATE CONVEYED	HOW AND BY WHOM CONVEYED	RECEIVED BY

misplaced. Although the auditors felt redeemed, and perhaps a little satisfied at the auditee's embarrassment, the director of internal auditing began using report release control sheets after each report to avoid future embarrassment by either the auditors or auditees. An even more embarrassing situation can occur if a report gets into the hands of people who are not entitled to it. Control sheets help prevent, for example, a clerk or secretary from giving a copy of a report to anyone who simply requests it.

Summary Documents. Finally, audit directors often utilize several summary documents for planning and monitoring departmental performance. A few of these include:

- The master schedule of all audits planned for a budget period.
- An audit project log showing the status of each project underway.
- A time report summary itemizing each auditor's hours and each audit project's hours.
- A master file of audit reports listing sequentially all internal audit reports issued.
- An annual activity report for the audit committee and executive management.

Management of the Internal Auditing Department

Extensive treatment of departmental management is beyond the intended scope of this introductory textbook. However, a general overview of the topic is appropriate, and so this part of the chapter briefly addresses management of the internal auditing department. The material in this section is intended to outline the dimensions of the management function by offering perspective on section 500 of the *Standards for the Professional Practice of Internal Auditing.* Each subsection of section 500 is addressed in turn.

Responsibility of the Director of Internal Auditing

Standard 500 states that "the director of internal auditing should properly manage the internal auditing department." In order to fulfill this charge, the standard specifies three overall responsibilities:

1. The director should ensure that "audit work fulfills the general purposes and responsibilities approved by management and accepted by the board."
2. The director should effectively and efficiently employ departmental resources, including funds, manpower, equipment, and supplies.
3. The director should ensure that "audit work conforms to the *Standards for the Professional Practice of Internal Auditing.*"

This standard designates the internal auditing director as the executive bearing the overall administrative responsibility for the department. It implies a dual standard of performance. First, the director is responsible for seeing that the department meets organizational purposes and responsibilities. Second, the director is supposed to hold to a professional standard of performance as well: that outlined in the *Standards for the Professional Practice of Internal Auditing*. When these two responsibilities are consistent, the director encounters little conflict. On the other hand, if inconsistencies arise, the director may experience some role conflict which must be resolved with management and the board.

Purpose, Authority, and Responsibility of the Internal Auditing Department

Standard 510 states that "the director of internal auditing should have a statement of purpose, authority, and responsibility for the internal auditing department." It goes on to specify that this statement should be in the form of a charter, which should be approved by management and accepted by the board of directors. *Professional Standards Bulletins 82-15* and *83-19* state that the charter should be in writing. Internal auditing department charters generally are prepared within the departments and subsequently reviewed and approved by management and the board.

Exhibit 12-7 illustrates an example of such a charter. This charter comprises a "Statement of Internal Auditing Purpose, Authority, and Responsibility" and a "Message from the Board of Directors" communicating the board's endorsement of the statement. The board calls on management to cooperate with the internal auditing department and "related parties," including corporate legal counsel, the company's CPA firm, managers of subsidiary businesses, and perhaps others. The chief executive officer for Bountiful National Corporation, Maurine W. Winston, also serves on the board of directors, so endorsement by the board also includes top management's approval.

Many similar documents are titled "Charter." The specific word is not necessarily required, however, to establish the internal auditing department's official purpose, authority, and responsibility.

Charters also frequently establish the internal auditing department's position in the organization's hierarchy. In the illustration, the director has a direct reporting line to the company's chief executive officer and an indirect line to the board, as outlined in the statement's introduction.

Exhibit 12-7
Internal Auditing Charter

BOUNTIFUL NATIONAL CORPORATION
MESSAGE FROM THE BOARD OF DIRECTORS

To the Internal Auditing Department:

We endorse the Statement of Internal Auditing Purpose, Authority, and Responsibility as presented in the attached document. We are confident that the various corporate divisions and departments will increasingly seek help that can be furnished through effective internal auditing, and we call upon all corporate managers and related parties to cooperate in the internal auditing effort.

Sincerely,

Board of Directors

_____

Claude P. Walker
Chairman

_____

Maurine W. Winston
Chief Executive Officer

_____

E. Robert Nielsen

_____

Glenda W. Marsh

_____

Wayne Neyland Bancroft III

_____

Ernest J. Draper Jr.

BOUNTIFUL NATIONAL CORPORATION
STATEMENT OF INTERNAL AUDITING
PURPOSE, AUTHORITY, AND RESPONSIBILITY

Introduction

Internal auditing is an important tool of management and is one of the ways by which Bountiful National Corporation maintains the integrity, efficiency, and effectiveness of financial and other management control systems. The internal auditing department carries out its activities within the organizations of the company consistently with the missions of the company.

A director of internal auditing is hired by the company's chief executive officer, with concurrence by the board of directors' audit committee, to administer the internal auditing department. Although the internal auditing department is an integral part of the organization, it functions independently of all other divisions and departments. Independence and accessibility to information sources are essential elements which permit audit work to be performed freely and objectively. The director of internal auditing is to submit an annual budget and a schedule of planned activities to the chief executive officer and the audit committee for approval. Substantial changes from the budget and the schedule are to be approved. The director of internal auditing is also to submit periodic activity reports to the chief executive officer and the board of directors.

Purpose

The mission or purpose of the internal auditing department is to provide objective audit and review services within the company for management and the board of directors. The objective is to assist various levels of management in the effective discharge of their responsibilities.

Authority

In harmony with the policies of the board of directors and executive management, the internal auditing department has authority to audit all functions, and has accessibility to all records, personnel, and physical properties relevant to the performance of audits. However, internal auditors have no authority over, nor responsibility for, the activities they audit.

As a tool of management, internal auditing may be concerned with any activity. Hence, it goes beyond examining accounting controls and records. It involves the comprehensive review and appraisal of financial, operational, and data-processing systems.

Responsibility

The internal auditing department accomplishes its purpose of assisting management by examining and evaluating activities and furnishing analyses, appraisals, recommendations, counsel, and similar information in a manner consistent with the *Standards for the Professional Practice of Internal Auditing.* Information is furnished to appropriate stewardship levels as established by executive management and the board of directors.

Management of an activity is apprised of the nature of information prior to its release so that an opportunity exists for inclusion of alternative data or differing points of view.

The information provided to management primarily concerns the adequacy and effectiveness of financial and operational internal control systems. The internal auditing department also may be called upon to assist the company's independent auditors, and it should coordinate its activities appropriately with the independent auditors to maximize their joint effectiveness and efficiency. The need for internal auditing in the Bountiful National Corporation's environment is not primarily a matter of distrust but, rather, of developing and maintaining systems of order.

There is a practical limitation to auditing all functions on a routine, periodic basis. Consequently, internal audit priorities and scheduling are established by the internal auditing department in consultation with the company's chief executive officer, the audit committee, and other management as appropriate.

The primary factor governing the scheduling, performance, and reporting of internal audits is *risk.* Risk may be said to "drive" the audit function and takes a variety of forms:

- Poor financial or operating information.
- Failure to comply with company policy, plans, procedures, or legal requirements.
- Loss of or damage to assets.
- Diseconomies or inefficiencies.
- Failure to accomplish established objectives and goals.

The internal auditing department also has the responsibility to perform audit work with due professional care. The following departmental requirements are indicative of the level of professionalism expected of its members:

- Appropriate education, certification, and experience.
- Professional image and neat work habits.

- Personal integrity.
- An attitude of service, professional courtesy, and consideration of the feelings and needs of other people.
- Relevant, timely, and quality work.

Bountiful National Corporation
BNC document file A-032, May 16, 1987

Planning

Planning for the internal auditing department is the responsibility of the director. Guideline 520.01 states that "these plans should be consistent with the internal auditing department's charter and with the goals of the organization." Guideline 520.02 goes on to identify four aspects of this planning:

1. Establishment of departmental goals.
2. Preparation of audit work schedules.
3. Preparation of staffing plans and financial budgets.
4. Preparation of activity reports.

Guideline 110.01.5 states that a summary of the department's work schedule, staffing plan, and budget should be submitted to management annually for approval and to the board for its information. Guideline 110.01.6 says that activity reports should be submitted to management and to the board "annually or more frequently as necessary." These activity reports should highlight significant findings and recommendations and inform management and the board of any significant deviations from approved audit work schedules, staffing plans, and financial budgets.

Professional Standards Bulletin 83-10 specifies that a formal, written audit plan should be in effect, identifying overall objectives and the functions and activities to be audited. This bulletin outlines three steps in developing the audit plan:

1. "Development of a comprehensive, long-range, strategic plan which outlines the overall objectives to be achieved by the auditing department."
2. "Identification of all functions and activities which the auditing department is responsible for auditing."
3. "Determination of which of those functions and activities should be audited and why, through evaluation of the risk associated with each function and activity."

Chapter 6, on selecting the auditee and audit preparation, discusses much of this material at some length. *Professional Standards Bulletin 83-10* provides additional insight, however, on establishing audit goals, work schedules, staffing plans, financial budgets, and activity reports:

> Goals and objectives should be long- and short-term. The long-term objectives should generally include those authorized within the internal auditing department's charter. In addition, they should include organizational development objectives such as to make the auditing organization a leader in the profession, to expand the service to management, to help the individual auditor to achieve greater dimension and stature, to increase the level of professional competency, and to improve the audit approach.

> The short-term goals should include emphasis on specific objectives such as increasing the staff's computer and quantitative skills via both in-house and external training programs and to expand the coverage of operational audits.

> The audit work schedules should include those audits that are to be done and the scope and purpose of those audits. This schedule should generally include such information as project number and report date, the last time the particular audit was performed, identification number of applicable permanent or master program files, area of coverage, evaluation of audit priority and risk, frequency with which the audit should be made, years in which the audit should be made, and number of audit days allotted to each project. This schedule is then used in developing staffing plans and financial budgets.

> After individual audit arrangements are established, an overall plan should be discussed with the board or audit committee. A monitoring mechanism should be put in place to assure actual activity is progressing in accordance with the plan.

Professional Standards Bulletin 84-8 suggests that major changes in the audit plan should be reviewed and approved by the same level of management reviewing and approving the original plan.

Guideline 520.05 states that staffing plans and financial budgets should include the number of auditors and the knowledge, skills, and disciplines required for the work. This guideline states that staffing plans and financial budgets should be determined from a variety of considerations: audit work schedules, administrative activities, education and training requirements, and audit research and development efforts.

With respect to activity reports, Guideline 520.06 specifies that these reports should be submitted to management and the board periodically and should "compare (a) performance with the department's goals and audit work schedules and (b) expenditures with financial budgets. They should explain the reasons for major variances and indicate any action taken or needed."

Departmental Policies and Procedures

Standard 530 states that "the director of internal auditing should provide written policies and procedures to guide the audit staff." This section qualifies this basic provision by stating that the form and content of the written policies and procedures should be tailored to the needs of the department in terms of formality, complexity, size, and content. In fact, small departments may need only "close supervision and memoranda" rather than extensive policy and procedure manuals.

Exhibit 12-8 lists the contents of one such policy and procedure manual used by a large internal. auditing department.

Personnel Management and Development

Personnel management and development is an important part of the management responsibility in any organization, as indicated by the emphasis given this area in the methods of internal control. The principle is as true for internal auditing as for other organizational areas. Standard 540 states that the director of internal auditing is responsible for the effective management of internal auditing personnel, and includes the following activities in this responsibility:

1. Preparation of written job descriptions for the different internal auditing positions.
2. Recruiting and selecting qualified and competent auditors.
3. Providing training and appropriate educational opportunities for the staff.
4. Evaluating the auditors' performance at least on an annual basis.
5. Counseling each member of the staff with respect to his or her performance and professional development.

All of these activities are important to effective recruitment and development of the audit staff. Job descriptions not only assist the auditors in understanding their responsibilities, but also provide support to company personnel review boards for establishing suitable salary levels to attract quality candidates for internal audit staff positions. Job descriptions include such information as job titles, reporting relationships, qualifications, and responsibilities.

Exhibit 12-8
Policy and Procedure Manual Contents

1. Statement of purpose, authority, and responsibility.
2. Departmental organization, administration, and job descriptions.
3. *Standards for the Professional Practice of Internal Auditing.*
4. *Code of Ethics.*
5. The general audit process.
6. Management of the audit:
    a. Director, team leader, and staff responsibilities.
    b. Audit management aids.
7. Concepts and tools:
    a. Internal controls.
    b. Planning and scheduling.
    c. Auditee relations.
    d. Communication guidelines.
    e. Interview techniques.
    f. Auditee's preparation.
    g. Computer-assisted audit tools.
    h. Principles of audit evidence.
    i. Analytical review.
    j. Flowcharting guidelines.
    k. Working paper guidelines.
    l. Findings and recommendations.
    m. Development of audit programs.
    n. Report-writing guidelines.
8. Investigative and fraud auditing responsibilities.
9. Departmental quality control:
    a. Self-analysis.
    b. Supervision.
    c. Quality control officer.
10. Personnel matters:
    a. List of employee names and addresses.
    b. Conflict of interest.
    c. Performance appraisal.
    d. Career development.
    e. Salary and benefits.
    f. Employees' association.
    g. Personal standards.
    h. Time reporting.
    i. Office administration.
    j. Security and confidentiality.

k. Travel.
l. Expense reimbursement.
m. Parking.
11. Forms.
12. Index.

Recruiting is done on university campuses, within the organization, from CPA firms, from professional recruiting organizations, and from other organizations. The point of recruiting is to seek out well-qualified, competent staff. The integrity of the entire internal auditing function is jeopardized when a poorly qualified staff gives auditees and executive management reason to question the auditing function.

The dynamic nature of internal auditing technology, related disciplines, and the business environment make it imperative that internal auditors continue their professional development through training and education. The director of internal auditing is responsible for providing such opportunities for all of the department's staff. Such training can be in the form of self-study courses, professional journals, in-house instructional programs, attendance at conferences and seminars, university classes, or other appropriate classes provided outside the organization. Ideally, auditors participate in a variety of these activities for well-rounded development.

Performance evaluation and counseling help identify the strengths of staff members as well as areas where development would be appropriate. These sessions also provide the auditor with an opportunity to plan his or her career path with a supervisor who is in a position to help. This information also is important to the director, who will use it in evaluating and planning manpower needs for the department.

While management-level auditors (i.e., directors and managers) usually receive annual performance reviews, staff auditors (i.e., junior and senior staff) usually are reviewed after each audit. At this time, supervising auditors generally complete a performance appraisal for each staff auditor on the audit team. These appraisals may cover a variety of performance issues, such as:

- The auditor's ability to think systematically, logically, and creatively.
- How well the auditor develops and documents audit findings.
- Writing ability.
- Communication with other members of the audit team and with auditee personnel.
- Effective use of time.

Sometimes the supervising auditors also meet with individual team members to discuss important aspects of their performance. These performance appraisals are important to the internal auditor's training, retention, and promotion. They also are helpful to audit management in making assignments.

Perhaps the most important use of these appraisals is to provide feedback on an auditor's professional development. Internal auditors should view this feedback as an opportunity to determine how best to develop themselves professionally — to build upon strengths and to minimize weaknesses. Many directors consider this written evaluation so important that they require auditors to read and sign the appraisal form before it is filed. More important than merely providing a basis for assignments and promotions, evaluations offer guidance for training and development.

Coordination with External Auditors

Standard 550 states that "the director of internal auditing should coordinate internal and external audit efforts . . . to ensure adequate audit coverage and to minimize duplicate efforts." This standard lists the following four ways in which this coordination may be accomplished:

1. The internal auditors should hold periodic meetings with external auditors "to discuss matters of mutual interest," such as scope of audit coverage, results of recent audit work, and planning and coordination of upcoming audit work.
2. Internal and external auditors should have access to each other's audit programs and working papers. Although internal and external auditors often may exchange these materials, especially audit programs, this provision does not necessarily mean that each must routinely provide the other with copies of audit programs and working papers, but rather, in order to coordinate their work most effectively, it may be necessary to refer to the other's work from time to time. Sometimes copies may be provided back and forth, but this normally should be done only upon the formal approval of the director of internal auditing or an authorized partner from the external auditor's office, respectively.

3. The internal auditing department and the external auditing firm should exchange audit reports, in the case of the internal auditors, and management letters, in the case of the external auditors. External auditors' management letters usually are provided to the audited organization along with a formal audit opinion in order to communicate observations and evaluations of internal accounting controls, with recommendations for improvements. Clearly, the exchange of these reports and management letters allows both internal and external auditors to plan their work more effectively and efficiently, to evaluate audit results more effectively, and to communicate with management and the board more knowledgeably.

4. Internal and external auditors should have a "common understanding of audit techniques, methods, and terminology" in order to communicate effectively.

Quality Assurance   Again, management and the audit committee may ultimately be held responsible for the quality of the internal audit function, although Standard 560 states that "the director of internal auditing should establish and maintain a quality assurance program to evaluate the operations of the internal auditing department."

This standard states that the purpose of this program is "to provide reasonable assurance that audit work conforms with [the] *Standards,* the internal auditing department's charter, and other applicable standards." Such a program should include adequate supervision, internal reviews, and external reviews.

> *Supervision* of [internal audit] work . . . should be carried out continually to assure conformance with internal auditing standards, departmental policies, and audit programs.

> *Internal reviews* should be performed periodically by members of the internal auditing staff to appraise the quality of the audit work performed. These reviews should be performed in the same manner as other internal audits.

> *External reviews* of the internal auditing department should be performed to appraise the quality of the department's operations. These reviews should be performed by qualified persons who are independent of the organization and who do not have either a real or an apparent conflict of interest. Such reviews should be conducted at least once every three years. On completion of the review, a formal, written report should be issued. The report should express an opinion as to the department's compliance with the *Standards for the Professional Practice of Internal Auditing* and, as appropriate, should include recommendations for improvement.

Audit supervision has been discussed at some length in other sections. Explanations throughout the text provide guidance in performing an internal review "in the same manner as any other internal audit."

In 1984 The IIA published the *Quality Assurance Review Manual for Internal Auditing* as a "self-assessment workbook." This manual provides step-by-step procedures for conducting an internal review of the internal auditing department. The manual also contains sections on external reviews. External reviews, sometimes called "peer reviews," are controversial in internal auditing. While their value in acquiring an outside, objective opinion with respect to the quality of the internal auditing function is well recognized, organizational managements generally are reluctant to open internal auditing department records to persons outside the organization unless it is absolutely necessary. Lawyers may require internal auditing documents, as may the organization's external CPAs. But lawyers can claim client confidentiality, and CPA firms generally exercise similar privilege. Also, both lawyers and CPAs perform legally required functions, and many managements would hesitate to provide even these two groups access to documented "secrets" of the organizations' inner workings if such access were not required for them to satisfactorily fulfill their legal responsibilities. Peer reviews of internal auditing departments are not legally required.

Also, management and boards frequently contend that they are in the best position to evaluate the performance of the internal auditing department. Since the department is charged with serving their management needs, they often feel that they can best assess whether those needs are being met adequately. As a result, internal auditing departments often do not undergo external reviews by outside review teams.

Where such reviews are performed, teams may consist of external auditors, members of internal auditing departments from other organizations, or qualified consultants. *Professional Standards Bulletin 82-8* specifies that a review by a team of individuals who are part of the organization, but who are independent of the internal auditing department, is not considered independent for the purposes of an external review.

A. S. Glazer and H. R. Jaenicke, in *A Framework for Evaluating an Internal Audit Function,* published by the Foundation for Auditability, Research, and Education, Inc. established by The IIA, suggest how peer reviews may be conducted. They suggest a rigorous two-step evaluation approach divided into four sections: (1) developing a profile of the internal auditing organizational environment; (2) examining and evaluating policies and procedures of the department; (3) conducting interviews with a variety of people in the organization, both inside and outside the internal auditing department; and (4) reviewing individual audits.

Statement on Internal Auditing Standards No. 4, "Quality Assurance," is included as appendix to this chapter.

Conclusion

Obviously, the successful manager of an internal auditing department must be more than the office's "super auditor." In fact, some of the more successful directors of internal auditing may not be the absolute best auditors in their respective departments. Certainly they must be competent auditors, but they must also be able to oversee and manage the various administrative aspects of the internal auditing department's activities. Therefore, those who desire to become managers and directors of internal auditing departments should plan on developing general management skills in addition to their auditing skills.

Appendix

STATEMENT ON INTERNAL AUDITING
STANDARDS NO. 4
Quality Assurance

Foreword

The Institute of Internal Auditors issued the *Standards for the Professional Practice of Internal Auditing* in 1978 "to serve the entire profession in all types of business, in various levels of government, and in all other organizations where internal auditors are found . . . to represent the practice of internal auditing as it should be . . . ." The *Standards* have been widely accepted and remain current despite continuing changes in business, society, and the profession of internal auditing.

As a general term, "quality assurance" is usually understood to mean the process of objective reviews of overall effectiveness and compliance with relevant policies and standards. The concept of quality assurance encompasses a broad range of objective reviews, from routine supervisory functions to independent appraisals. Such reviews may therefore encompass various levels of responsibility and detail.

This statement provides guidance on these issues by focusing on guidelines 560.01, 560.02, 560.03, and 560.04.

Summary

This statement provides additional guidance for implementing a quality assurance program in an internal auditing department. These guidelines define a program which includes adequate supervision, internal review under the control of the director of internal auditing, and external review by qualified persons who are independent of the organization. This *SIAS* gives more detailed interpretation and guidance in separate sections on each of these elements of quality assurance.

Quality assurance is essential to maintaining an internal auditing department's capability to perform its functions in an efficient, effective manner. Quality assurance is also important in achieving and maintaining a high level of credibility with management, the audit committee, and others who rely on the work of the internal auditing department.

Guideline 560.04 states that external reviews should be conducted at least once every three years. However, there may be circumstances which could justify a different interval or which currently preclude the director of internal auditing from obtaining an external review. In circumstances where the external review is delayed, the director has the responsibility to ensure that an adequate level of quality assurance is achieved through alternative means.

The Institute has supplemented the applicable standard and guidelines with both objective criteria and examples of the tools, such as questionnaires, interview guides, and audit procedures, needed for full implementation of a quality assurance program. These materials are intended to be advisory and should be tailored to the particular internal or external review.

Interpretations
Guideline 560.01

Guideline 560.01 states that the purpose of a quality assurance program is to provide reasonable assurance that audit work conforms with these *Standards,* the internal auditing department's charter, and other applicable standards. A quality assurance program should include the following elements:

Supervision

Internal reviews

External reviews

.1   The "reasonable assurance" mentioned in this guideline serves the needs of several constituencies in addition to that of the director of internal auditing. These may include senior management, the independent outside auditors, the audit committee, and regulatory agencies, each of whom may have reasons to rely upon the performance of the internal auditing function.

.2   Conformity with applicable standards is more than simply complying with established policies and procedures. It includes performance of the audit function at a high level of efficiency and effectiveness. Quality assurance is essential to achieving such performance, as well as to maintaining the internal auditing department's credibility with those it serves.

.3   As cited in Guideline 560.01, a key criterion against which an internal auditing department should be measured is its charter. Consideration of the department's charter should also include an assessment of the charter in terms of the elements specified in Standard 110, Organizational Status (110.01.4).

.4   The following are examples of "other applicable standards" and potential measurement criteria that should be considered in evaluating the performance of the internal auditing department:

- The Institute's *Code of Ethics.*
- The internal auditing department's objectives, policies, and procedures.
- The organization's policies and procedures that apply to the internal auditing function.
- Laws, regulations, and government or industry standards which specify auditing and reporting requirements.
- Systems for establishing the audit universe, assessing risk, and determining frequency and scope of audits.
- Audit planning documents, particularly those submitted to senior management and the audit committee.
- The plan of organization, statements of job requirements, position descriptions, and professional development plans of the internal auditing department.

Guideline 560.02

Guideline 560.02 states that supervision of work of the internal auditors should be carried out continually to assure conformance with internal auditing standards, departmental policies, and audit programs.

.1 Adequate supervision is the most fundamental element of a quality assurance program. As such, it provides a foundation upon which internal and external reviews can subsequently be built.

.2 The nature of and responsibility for supervision are set forth in the *Standards,* particularly 230, and related guidelines. As indicated in the guidelines under Standard 230, supervision includes among other things:

- Adequate planning and providing suitable instructions to subordinates.

- Determination that the approved audit program has been carried out and documented in the working papers and that the resulting report comments are appropriate.

- Adequate and properly documented supervision of all internal auditing activities, which is ultimately the responsibility of the director of internal auditing.

.3 In Guideline 560.02, the word "continually" indicates that supervision should be performed throughout the planning, examination, evaluation, report, and follow-up process for all assignments. Supervision should also extend to training, employee performance evaluation, time and expense control, and similar administrative areas.

Guideline 560.03

Guideline 560.03 states that internal reviews should be performed periodically by members of the internal auditing staff to appraise the quality of the audit work performed. These reviews should be performed in the same manner as any other internal audit.

.1 Formal internal reviews are periodic self-assessments of the internal auditing department. These reviews generally are performed by a team or an individual selected by the director of internal auditing. Larger departments may have a person designated as "manager of quality assurance" or with a similar title and responsibilities.

.2 Internal quality assurance reviews primarily serve the needs of the director of internal auditing, but can also provide senior management and the audit committee with an assessment of the internal auditing function. These reviews should be structured so as to indicate the degree of compliance with the *Standards,* level of audit effectiveness, and extent of compliance with the organization and departmental policies and standards. The review should also provide recommendations for improvement.

.3 An internal review program, particularly in smaller internal auditing departments, will require adaptations that take into consideration the structure of the department and degree of involvement of the director in individual audits.

.4 When the foregoing formal internal reviews are not appropriate to the internal auditing department's needs, or to supplement such reviews, the following methods can provide elements of internal review coverage:

a. Reviews by the director of internal auditing, audit managers, or supervisors, of a sample of audits (and areas of audit administration) where the work was performed under the direction of other managers or supervisors. As an ongoing process this can provide training, exchange of ideas, and greater uniformity, as well as provide assurance to the director of internal auditing.

b. Feedback from auditees (in addition to that from personal contact) through the use of questionnaires or surveys, either routinely after each audit or periodically for selected audits. This process will elicit operating management's perception of the audit function and may also result in suggestions to make it more effective and responsive to management's needs.

.5 The director of internal auditing should initiate and monitor the internal review process. In selecting and instructing the team for an internal review, the director of internal auditing should ensure that the team is qualified and as independent as practicable.

.6 The director should receive a written report of the results of each internal review and ensure that appropriate action is taken. Although the purpose of internal reviews is to assess the effectiveness of the audit function for internal purposes, it may be appropriate for the director to share ther results with persons outside the department, such as senior management, the audit committee, and the independent outside auditors. Internal reviews can also be useful as part of the self-assessment process in preparation for an external review.

.7 More detailed information about internal reviews is contained in other IIA pronouncements and publications, including the *Quality Assurance Review Manual for Internal Auditing* which was published by The Institute of Internal Auditors in 1984.

Guideline 560.04

Guideline 560.04 states that external reviews of the internal auditing department should be performed to appraise the quality of the department's operations. These reviews should be performed by qualified persons who are independent of the organization and who do not have either a real or an apparent conflict of interest. Such reviews should be conducted at least once every three years. On completion of the review, a formal, written report should be issued. The report should express an opinion as to the department's compliance with the *Standards for the Professional Practice of Internal Auditing* and, as appropriate, should include recommendations for improvement.

.1 External reviews can have considerable value to the director and other members of the internal auditing department. Another important purpose of external reviews is to provide independent assurance of quality to senior management, the audit committee, and others such as the independent outside auditors who rely on the work of the internal auditing department.

.2 The director of internal auditing should discuss with senior management and the audit committee the nature of an external review in the context of the overall quality assurance program and should involve them in the selection of an external reviewer.

.3 This guideline (560.04) states that external reviews should be performed by qualified individuals who are independent of the organization and who do not have either a real or an apparent conflict of interest. "Qualified individuals" are persons with the technical proficiency and educational background appropriate for the audit activities to be reviewed and could include internal auditors from outside the organization, outside consultants, or independent outside auditors. "Independent of the organization" means not a part of, or under the control of, the corporate entity or other organizations to which the internal auditing department belongs. In the selection of an external reviewer, consideration should be given to a possible real or apparent conflict of interest which the reviewer might have due to present or past relationships with the entity or its internal auditing department.

.4 Organizations of independent outside auditors in various countries have specified certain limited review procedures that they should consider in evaluating and using the work of the internal auditing function. These relate primarily to quality of work and degree of independence from auditees. These limited review procedures by independent outside auditors usually relate only to their audit of an organization's financial statements and generally would not constitute an "external review" for the purposes of Guideline 560.04.

.5 Upon completion of an external review, the review team should issue a formal report containing an opinion as to the department's compliance with the *Standards.* The report should also address compliance with the department's charter and other applicable standards and include appropriate recommendations for improvement. The report should be addressed to the person or entity who requested the review. The director of internal auditing should prepare a written action plan in response to the significant comments and recommendations contained in the report of external review. Appropriate follow-up is also the director's responsibility.

.6 Guideline 560.04 states that external reviews should be conducted at least once every three years. However, there may be circumstances that justify a different interval. These circumstances include: (a) significant review and monitoring by the audit committee, (b) in-depth reviews by the independent outside auditors or others, and (c) the relative stability of the audit department's charter, organization, staff, and audit universe. The nature, scope, degree of independence, and overall results of the internal review program should also be considered in determining the external review interval.

.7 External review is an important element of the program for achieving quality assurance. However, if resources are limited, or for other reasons discussed above, the internal auditing department may be currently unable to obtain an external review. In these circumstances, more emphasis should be placed on supervision, periodic internal reviews, and other quality assurance methods that are available to the department. It is the responsibility of the director of internal auditing to annually assess the conditions which restrict an external review. Another interim method is the use of qualified internal groups to conduct a review (e.g., former audit manager in the employ of the organization, other audit directors in a decentralized audit organization, or internal management advisory personnel). However, such a review should not be expected to achieve all of the objectives of an external review.

.8 More detailed information about external reviews is contained in other pronouncements and publications including the *Quality Assurance Review Manual for Internal Auditing* which was published by The Institute of Internal Auditors in 1984.

QUESTIONS

1. Discuss how each of the following official pronouncements relates to internal auditing management:
   a. Standard 120.
   b. Standard 230.
   c. Standard 420.
   d. Standard 430.
   e. Standard 560.
   f. *Professional Standards Bulletin 82-14.*
2. In general, how would you compare the relative responsibilities of the audit director, the audit team leader, and the audit staff assigned to an internal audit?
3. Why do you think the audit team leader is likely to spend more time on a given audit than others who may be assigned?
4. Compare the respective responsibilities of the audit director, team leader, and audit staff for each of the nine steps in the audit process.
5. What information is likely to be included on a job authorization form? Why prepare such a form?
6. How does an audit checklist differ from the audit program?
7. How is an auditor likely to find out to which audit projects he or she is to be assigned?
8. What is a job time control sheet? What information is contained on this sheet?
9. Why prepare a working paper index before an audit begins?
10. How does the audit program help manage an internal audit?
11. What advantages are there to preparing meeting agendas for an internal audit?
12. How do working papers improve audit management?
13. What are working paper review sheets? What information is likely to be included on a working paper review sheet?
14. How does a summary finding sheet help facilitate report writing?
15. Why prepare a report review sign-off sheet and a report release control sheet?
16. Prepare a table identifying on which steps of the audit process the various management aids are likely to be used. (Some may be used on more than one audit step.)
17. What is a statement of purpose, authority, and responsibility, and how does it improve management of the internal auditing department?
18. What activities are included in departmental planning? What are the three types of planning, as discussed in *Professional Standards Bulletin 83-10?* Briefly discuss each of the three.
19. How are policy and procedures manuals likely to differ for large and small internal auditing departments? What kinds of information are likely to be included in such manuals?
20. Discuss how each of the five kinds of personnel management and development activities, as prescribed by Standard 540, contributes to effective management of the internal auditing department.
21. Who is responsible for coordinating internal and external auditing activities? Who bears the ultimate responsibility of all auditing activities? How does the director coordinate internal and external auditing efforts?

22. List the three methods outlined in Standard 560 that should be utilized in a quality assurance program for the internal auditing department. What is the controversy involving external reviews?

EXERCISES

E-1

A medium-sized Southwestern community started a new internal auditing department. After screening several candidates, the city council hired the city's assistant city manager as director of the department. The council decided not to provide any additional professional staff at that time, but did provide for a secretary.

As assistant city manager, the new director of internal auditing had been closely involved with the development of several important computerized systems and the installation of a new water treatment plant.

Required:

a. What potential conflicts of interest do you see in this scenario?
b. Which of The IIA's standards apply in this case?
c. What steps can the new director of internal auditing take to maintain objectivity when auditing those functions for which he previously had some responsibility?

E-2

The director of internal auditing is out of the country on a critical audit assignment in Brazil. Another team leader is finishing an audit report which is scheduled for distribution in two weeks. The director is scheduled to return in three weeks and will be unable to review the report before its scheduled release.

Required:

a. According to the *Standards,* what is the director's responsibility for the review of audit reports? (You may need to refer to the *Standards* reprinted in Chapter 2.)
b. How can the director fulfill his or her responsibility, complete the assignment in Brazil, and still see that the report is issued on time?
c. What risks do you see if the director does not review the report?

E-3

The director of internal auditing for a large Eastern banking corporation was preparing the annual schedule of audits, which would be presented to the audit committee and to executive management the following month. The company's chief executive officer called and asked for a meeting with the director the following day.

At that meeting, the CEO told the director that he (i.e., the CEO), in consultation with the company's senior vice presidents, would prepare the audit schedule instead of delegating that responsibility to the director.

It seems that two senior vice presidents had complained that the internal auditors scheduled some audits during the previous year at inconvenient times for auditee operations.

The CEO also said that it would be more appropriate for him to determine the scopes of audits on the schedule, since he needed this information to determine how long each audit should take. He argued that since the audits were primarily for management's benefit, it would be more appropriate for management to schedule the audits and determine what should be audited.

Required:
a. Which of The IIA's standards apply in this case? Explain.
b. What dangers do you see in the CEO's decision?
c. How do you think the director should handle this situation?

E-4
Paul Adams is a new senior auditor for Brown Enterprises, Inc., a large Northeastern heavy-equipment manufacturer. Paul is an industrial engineering graduate who had two years of industrial engineering experience prior to being transferred to the company's internal auditing department 18 months ago. He is about to lead his first audit project and is wondering how he is supposed to exercise his leadership role in the audit.

Required:
a. Study Exhibit 12-1 in the chapter and outline the specific team leader tasks that require the team leader to directly supervise the staff auditors in some way.
b. Outline the tasks in which the team leader is being directly supervised by or reporting directly to the audit director.
c. Outline the tasks in which the team leader is essentially acting alone, neither directly supervising the audit staff nor being directly supervised.
d. What measures are taken in these various role relationships to assist Paul in doing a good supervisory job, to assure a quality audit, and to give Paul confidence as a team leader?

E-5
On his first team leader assignment, Paul Adams of Brown Enterprises (introduced in E-4) is to head an audit of the production employee time-card system. Bob Schwabb, a new junior staff auditor, has been assigned to work with Paul on this project. The director responsible for the project is Frances T. Burger.

Required:
a. Prepare a standardized preliminary audit program for this audit, as Paul might be expected to do, through the preliminary survey.
b. Prepare an audit checklist appropriate for Paul through the preliminary survey.
c. How does the audit program differ from the checklist?

E-6
Required:
The following page shows a job time control sheet for an audit project by a team of three municipal auditors. How would you evaluate the progress of the audit project as of 7/16? Explain.

Job Time Control Sheet

Job Name and Number _Library Purchasing Controls #86-032_ Team Leader _Jerry J. Donaldson_

AUDIT STEP	AUD*	7/1	7/2	7/3	7/4	7/5	7/8	7/9	7/10	7/11	7/12	7/15	7/16	7/18	7/19	7/20	7/23	7/24	7/25	Budgeted Hours
Job Preparation	TJD	3	8																	20
30	OPR			2	2															5
	APW			2	1															5
Initial Survey	TJD					4	2	1												15
35	OPR					2	6	1												15
	APW					1														5
Internal Control Review	TJD						3	3	8	10	10	4	2							20
60	OPR						2		8	8	8	6	8							20
	APW								10	8	8	2	4							20
Expanded Testing	TJD																			30
100	OPR																			40
	APW																			30
Finding and Recommendations Development	TJD																			5
10	OPR																			3
	APW																			2
Reporting	TJD																			80
130	OPR																			30
	APW																			20
Follow-up	TJD																			5
5	OPR																			
	APW																			
Evaluation	TJD																			3
5	OPR																			1
	APW																			1
Total Budgeted Hours 375																				375
Daily Totals		3	8	4	3	7	13	5	26	26	26	12	14							
Cumulative Totals		3	11	15	18	25	38	43	69	95	121	133	147							

*AUD means "auditors."

E-7

An internal auditing supervisor for a chain of drugstores assigns a senior auditor to audit a very large drugstore that the company recently purchased. The supervisor gives a time budget to the senior auditor and suggests that the senior refer to permanent files for other store audits for guidance.

During the next several weeks, the supervisor telephones the senior to ask if there will be any problem in meeting the time budget. On each occasion, the senior replies that there should be no problem in meeting it. Subsequently, the senior submits the working papers and the final audit report to the supervisor. The supervisor gives the working papers back to the senior and explains that they will not be needed for the review. No other planning, directing, or supervising was performed by the supervisor.

The *Standards for the Professional Practice of Internal Auditing* includes a number of references dealing with supervision. One of these states: "The internal audit department should provide assurance that internal audits are properly supervised."

Required:

Describe three elements of good internal audit supervision set forth in the *Standards for the Professional Practice of Internal Auditing* that were not complied with during this audit.

(CIA Exam Adapted)

E-8

An internal audit manager is preparing to send an audit team to perform an initial audit of a technical operation in a newly created government agency.

Required:

List six important subjects that the manager should discuss with members of the audit team before they start the audit.

(CIA Exam Adapted)

E-9

Rhoda Phillips was assigned as team leader of an audit to examine and evaluate the internal controls over cash disbursements. The audit program called for preparation of a flowchart for cash disbursements and limited testing of five disbursements.

The flowchart prepared by a staff auditor revealed that all invoices are approved by an assistant controller prior to check preparation. All disbursements of more than $100 are reviewed by a controller for appropriate invoice processing and check preparation. Checks of less than $100 for approved invoices need not be reviewed prior to actual disbursement.

Four of the five disbursements selected for testing were processed according to the prescribed procedures. The fifth invoice, for $80, showed no approval signature prior to payment. The check was made out in the correct amount to the company shown on the invoice and appeared properly signed and recorded.

As the team leader, Rhoda is evaluating the results of these preliminary audit procedures.

Required:
a. How would you evaluate these results?
b. Is additional testing appropriate in this case? Why or why not?
c. Based upon this information, what instructions should Rhoda give the staff auditor?

E-10

Teddie Wayne prepared the working paper shown on the following page for an audit of the 1st Street store of Ogalvie's Stores, Inc. The specific audit objective Teddie is working on is to evaluate the sales performance of the household appliances department. The audit program called for a comparison, by major product category, of budgeted sales to actual sales for at least one randomly selected month of the previous year.

Required:
Review this working paper, making your review notes in a format similar to the one shown in Exhibit 12-5.

E-11

A Midwestern corporation hired a new director of internal auditing. The director began his duties by interviewing all of the professional staff and departmental secretaries, one at a time. He discovered that his staff included the following backgrounds:

6 CPAs	All are from different public accounting firms, and two were hired within the last six months. Two are CIAs.
1 attorney	Employed in the department for seven years. CIA.
1 MBA	A former high school English teacher; hired one year ago. Recently passed the CIA exam.
2 EDP auditors	One is a computer science graduate who had seven years of EDP experience before joining the department three years ago. The other is a new business administration graduate, recently hired, who learned about computers as a hobby and has no audit experience yet.

These personnel expressed some frustration over the lack of departmental policies and procedures. No formally adopted policies and procedures existed, and each team leader established his or her own. The former director had intended to prepare a departmental manual of guidelines and standards, but because of what he considered more pressing needs, he never did.

Later interviews with company management and former auditees revealed similar frustrations with respect to the internal auditing department. They all said they got the feeling that they could not establish a consistent relationship with, and expectations of, the department.

Required:
What do you think are going to be the major effects, beyond the frustrations expressed, of not having established departmental policies and procedures? Explain.

Auditee: 1st Street Store   Auditor: MW Date: 2/21

Objective: Evaluate Sales Performance – Household Appliances   Reviewer: Date:

Procedure: Comparison of Budgeted Sales to Actual Sales   WP Index: D-4-1

Interview Notes

Date: 2/21/87

Interviewee: Marianne Johnson, Household Appliances Sales Manager

Place: Ms. Johnson's office

Ms. Johnson made the following comparison of actual sales to budgeted sales for November of last year:

Week	Explanation
1	Achieved budgeted sales.
2	Did not meet budgeted sales because advertising department failed to place a scheduled ad in the newspaper.
3	Did not meet budgeted sales because sales clerk was terminated by personnel department — had to work short-handed.
4	Did not meet budgeted sales because (a) extra time was required to train new sales clerk and (b) poor position of appliance information in newspaper ad.

Conclusion and Recommendation: Budgeted sales are set too high for household appliances under normal working conditions. These budgeted figures should be decreased by approximately 10 percent.

PROBLEMS

P-1

John Fuentes is the director of internal auditing for a large regional sales distributor of auto parts and accessories. The company purchases directly from manufacturers and markets the products through a chain of stores throughout the multi-state region. The company has its own line of products, which are made by manufacturers to its specifications. Other brands also are marketed through the company stores. In some towns and small cities where the company does not operate stores, consignment sales are contracted with locally owned auto parts dealerships.

Mr. Fuentes has a staff of seven auditors who have been assigned to a variety of jobs during the first quarter of the year.

Illustrated on the following page are portions of the internal auditing department's annual Master Budget and Job Status Log. The Master Budget shows the job number assigned to each audit project, the job name (or auditee), the initials of the assigned auditors, the budgeted hours for each project, and the calendar time scheduled for each project, from the beginning of preparation to the target date for release of the audit report. The Job Status Log is updated and reviewed weekly by Mr. Fuentes. It contains job numbers, job names, assigned auditors, budget hours, actual hours to the date of log preparation, the target report date, and the current job status as of the log date. Job status classifications include the following:

- *Pending* — scheduled, but not yet started.
- *Preparation* — audit preparation has begun, but no audit work has been performed.
- *In progress* — audit work is being performed.
- *Writing/review* — audit work is concluded, and the written report is being prepared.
- *Wrap-up* — filing of working papers, audit evaluation, and follow-up.
- *Closed* — audit project is finished.

Mr. Fuentes is studying these reports as of February 14.

Required:

a. How would you evaluate the progress of audit work so far in 1987? Explain.
b. How would any problems you identified in part (a) affect other operations in the department during the year?

P-2

A rapidly growing manufacturing corporation is about to establish an internal auditing department at the suggestion of its external auditor. The corporate controller has proposed a charter for the internal auditing department that contains, among other things, the following provisions:

1. The internal auditing department is a staff function that is headed by a director who reports to the controller.
2. The internal auditing department has the primary responsibility for the adequacy of the internal accounting control system.
3. Internal auditing department personnel have full access only to accounting records.

MASTER BUDGET: 1987 (PARTIAL)

JOB NO.	JOB NAME	AUDITORS	BH	JAN	FEB	MAR	APR
87-1	Purchasing	TPJ*, JBO, ABQ	400	1/3	2/15		
87-2	Cash Management	RTL*, VJB	300	1/7	2/15		
87-3	Shipping/Receiving	JRS*, ABQ, HLC	450	1/3		3/5	
87-4	Delta Warehouse	TPJ*, JBO	200		2/10	3/12	
87-5	Consignment Contracts	RLR*	200		2/15		4/1
87-6	Sales Travel Expenses	JRS*, VJB, HLC	300		2/15	3/15	

JOB STATUS LOG (PARTIAL): FEBRUARY 14, 1987

JOB	JOB NAME	AUDITORS	BH	AHD	TRD	STATUS
87-1	Purchasing	TPJ*, JBO, ABQ	400	410	2/15/87	in progress
87-2	Cash Management	RTL*, VJB	300	300	2/15/87	wrap-up
87-3	Shipping/Receiving	JRS*, ABQ, HLC	450	410	3/05/87	in progress
87-4	Delta Warehouse	TPJ*, JBO	200		3/12/87	pending
87-5	Consignment Contracts	RLR*	200		4/01/87	pending
87-6	Sales Travel Expenses	JRS*, VJB, HLC	300		3/15/87	pending

---

The asterisk (*) means "team leader."
BH means "budgeted hours."
AHD means "actual hours to date."
TRD means "target report date."

4. The internal auditing department supports the work of the external auditor as directed by the controller.
5. Activities to be performed by the department include:
   a. Participating in the design and implementation of financial control systems.
   b. Ascertaining the extent to which company assets are accounted for and safeguarded from losses of all kinds.
   c. Ascertaining the extent of compliance with established accounting and financial policies.
   d. Reviewing and appraising the soundness, the adequacy, and the application of internal accounting controls.
   e. Ascertaining the reliability of accounting data developed within the organizations.
   f. Recommending improvements in the internal accounting control system.

A candidate being considered for the position of director of internal auditing has reviewed the proposed charter and has noted some problems with it. The candidate has pointed out that the proposed charter greatly restricts the scope of internal auditing and thus reduces its potential benefits. The candidate also noted that the proposed charter contains some provisions that are contrary to the *Statement of Responsibilities of Internal Auditing.*

Required:

For each of the provisions 1 through 5 above, discuss:

a. Any inhibiting restriction on the internal auditing department's scope of work.
b. Any aspect of a provision that is contrary to the *Statement of Responsibilities of Internal Auditing.*

(CIA Exam Adapted)

P-3

An insurance company expanded significantly by purchasing smaller companies. A new director of internal audit was hired and charged with providing extensive professional audit services. The new director prepared a charter which granted appropriate status, access, and support for internal auditing, and top management approved this charter. They also promised support for expanding and professionalizing the internal auditing staff.

The new director developed a long-range audit plan based upon a systematic risk analysis and ranking of each potential audit area. This plan was fairly specific as to subjects of audit coverage within the identified areas.

During the first annual revision of the audit plan, the director found it necessary to modify significantly the planned coverage scheduled for audit during the next year.

Required:

a. Describe briefly the three major types of planning and how they relate to internal auditing.
b. Explain the major purposes of long-range audit schedules.
c. Discuss three issues that the director of audit should consider when reviewing the long-range plan.
d. For each of the above issues, describe what (if any) effect it would have on the other two types of plans.

(CIA Exam Adapted)

SECTION III
TECHNICAL MATERIALS

13   Human Relations

It seems universally accepted among persons connected with auditing that good human relations skills are requisite to professional success. Recruiters on university campuses consistently insist that the two primary characteristics they are seeking in accounting students are (1) technical skills (business, accounting, and auditing) and (2) human relations skills. In fact, some business executives and auditors believe human relations skills may be the single most important factor that leads to success and advancement on the job. Certainly, without these skills, any chance of success as an auditor is little more than a glimmer of hope.

Internal auditors work throughout the organization, at all levels of administrative authority, examining and evaluating how people do their work. Auditors report their findings to auditees' superiors, often making recommendations on how the work can be improved. Because auditors are looking for things that are wrong, ineffective, and inefficient, it is not difficult to understand the potential for interpersonal conflict.

Some auditors seem continually involved in interpersonal strife with various people in their organizations, while other auditors develop relationships leading to requests for audits from the very people to be audited. This latter group values the auditors' insights and feedback, and yet does not necessarily feel threatened by the auditors' presence. The ability to cultivate such a positive attitude in auditees is a result of developing auditors' human relations skills.

Stephen R. Covey reported in *Spiritual Roots of Human Relations* (Deseret Books, Inc., 1976) that an extensive research study at a famous graduate school of business strongly suggested that successful business executives consistently possess two powerful personal characteristics. First, these executives are motivated by an intense desire and determination to excel. Second, and of greater interest here, these executives have exceptional people skills.

Like other successful business people, internal auditors need to develop the ability to relate well with others. Good human relations skills take studied effort to develop and practice.

On the other hand, there are as yet no final and definitive answers regarding effective human relations. Psychologists and other researchers currently spend much of their energy in this area. Many different theories abound regarding this important aspect of our lives, but despite the current confusion and uncertainty, two things are commonly accepted. One, good human relations are vital to effective social interaction. Two, depending upon which model one wishes to utilize, certain variables in human relations seem to compose a logical set by which to approach an understanding and development of good human relations skills. It does appear that most people who get along exceptionally well with others seem to share some common characteristics. Exhibit 13-1 represents a model of one perspective of those characteristics.

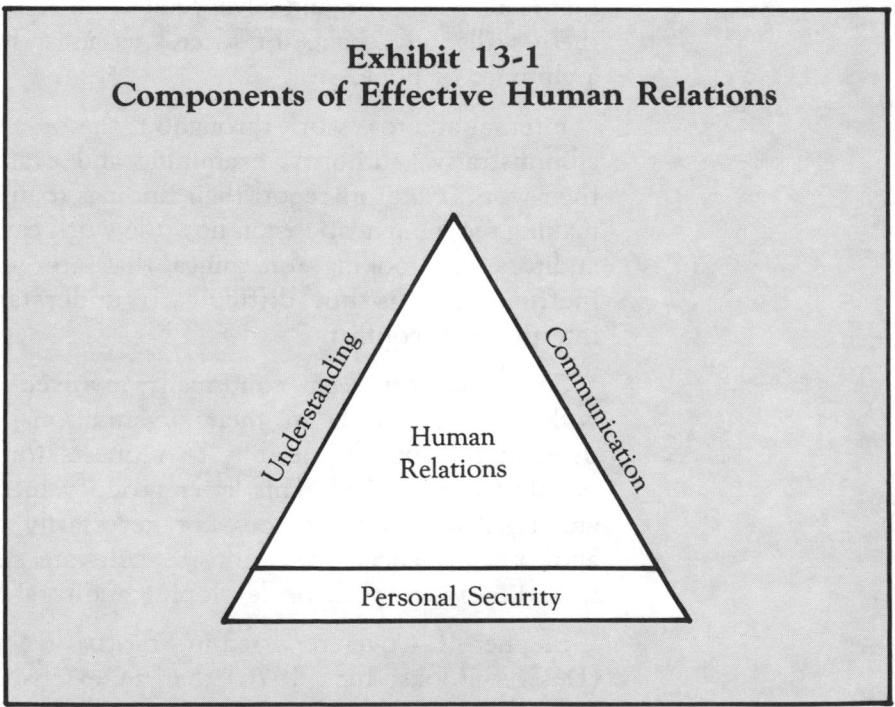

Exhibit 13-1
Components of Effective Human Relations

As this model illustrates, a primary foundation for good human relations is to have a strong self-image. It is much easier for a person to develop good relationships with others when he or she begins with a sense of personal worth, ability, and self-confidence. The give and take of relationships can be difficult for auditors, and without an adequate self-image, relationships can fail simply because the auditor may be too fragile and unprepared for the required commitment. As the auditor is able to achieve a strong self-image, he or she then is prepared to develop productive and mutually respectful relationships with auditees, management, and others.

Effective human relations depend upon two general capabilities — the ability to understand others and the ability to communicate. Communication is a human relations skill. Although some researchers and writers separate the two, communication is really a subset of the more general field of human relations. The remainder of this section discusses the nature of self-image, the importance of understanding other people, and the critical role of communication as tools to help internal auditors develop effective human relationships.

Understanding Self-Image

Because they work in an environment where there is a constant potential for interpersonal conflict, internal auditors must maintain a strong self-image. While they should not be overbearing or arrogant, they need the confidence of management, the auditee, and members of the audit committee in addition to a sense of their own character and integrity.

A strong self-image may be considered the product of six factors. These factors include the following list, which is adapted from Covey's:

1. Knowledge of one's own strengths and weaknesses.
2. A sense of belonging.
3. A sense of natural order in the world and one's environment.
4. A high priority on serving the needs of others.
5. A feeling of personal productivity.
6. A high degree of integrity.

These sources of a strong self-image represent a state of being; i.e., characteristics of a psychologically and emotionally secure individual. In a secure person these characteristics usually are balanced, with the individual possessing a reasonable degree of all six. An inadequate level of any one of the six jeopardizes a person's ability to achieve his or her potential in the other areas. Let's consider each of these aspects of personal security in a little more detail.

Self-Knowledge

The first element of a strong self-image can be described as "self-knowledge," i.e., a realistic understanding of one's own strengths and weaknesses. This knowledge includes mental, physical, emotional, and personality characteristics. Such knowledge enables one to accept responsibility wisely and to know when to seek help, when to yield, and when to assert authority. Of course, an individual's strengths and weaknesses are dynamic. This condition means that the secure person is aware not only of what his or her strengths and weaknesses are at any one time, but also how they may be changing. Thus, Covey suggests that the secure individual can feel able to deal with the present and to prepare for and meet the future.

Sense of Belonging

A second element contributing to one's self-image is a sense of belonging, which may be derived from groups. In most work-related situations, an internal auditor's self-concept is enhanced when he or she feels a sense of belonging to a unified, harmonious work group. An auditor's self-image may be threatened within the audit group context if the group lacks unity and harmony among its members. Harmony does not necessarily mean total agreement; in fact, the most effective groups are likely to be receptive to disagreements, new ideas, etc. The harmony is derived not from consensus, but rather from the group's common purpose and receptiveness toward improvements.

Sense of Natural Order

The third source of a strong self-image is a sense of natural order in one's environment. This concept can be considered both literally, in terms of nature, as well as figuratively. You do not necessarily have to be an outdoors enthusiast to have an appreciation of nature. The necessary sense of natural order would seem to come from an understanding and appreciation of some fundamental principles of nature, regardless of how they are learned.

For example, some apparent contradictions in nature may be quite in harmony with a fundamental natural order. Herds of deer help illustrate this point. In a herd of deer, there is a definite pecking order. The strongest animals, having proven their strength in individual combat, lead the rest. The herd, however, often is dependent upon the weaker animals for its survival. The weaker animals are forced to stay on the outer fringes of the herd, while the strongest ones tend to congregate in the center. The weaker animals suffer more stress, thereby secreting more adrenalin, and consequently they remain more alert to danger. These weaker deer keep watch for potential dangers to the herd and alert the others as danger approaches. This control system benefits the entire herd.

Likewise, in business organizations, control systems help management remain alert and avert dangerous risks.

This is only one example of many lessons to be learned about natural order. Such an understanding can give the internal auditor a more philosophical and wiser approach to his or her job, the result being a stronger self-image and better relationships with others.

A Feeling of Service

The fourth source of a strong self-image is to have an attitude of wanting to serve, placing a high priority on the needs of others. Internal auditing has a relatively low public profile, and its focus, according to the introduction to the *Standards for the Professional Practice of Internal Auditing,* is upon "assisting members of the organization." The internal auditing function is naturally service oriented.

Probably none of us has much trouble recalling an example of a self-centered person whose life focused on serving only his or her wants. Invariably, these people easily feel threatened, which indicates insecurity. In the worst cases, they can become paranoid and dangerous to other people and to themselves.

On the other hand, people who focus their greatest energies on serving others seem to be healthier psychologically and emotionally. Ironically, as these people help other people, the other people respond by trying to help them. Acceptance by others leads to a feeling of personal worth.

Of course, the person who smothers other people with attention and imposes his or her will upon them really isn't serving their needs at all, but rather is probably seeking self-gratification. For example, an internal auditor who becomes emotionally entangled in an audit situation and insists beyond professional reason on the implementation of a particular recommendation would seem to display such self-gratification at the expense of others. True service is not an imposition. True service requires an attitude of genuine interest in the welfare and the success of others.

Feeling of Productivity

A fifth source of a strong self-image is a feeling of personal productivity. A person who feels productive is more likely to feel in control of his or her future than is a person who feels unproductive. This feeling of control generally yields a willingness to accept and meet new challenges. Perhaps few things can drain a person's sense of self-worth more quickly and more completely than a feeling of powerlessness. While total control and independence is neither possible nor desirable, the secure individual needs to feel that he or she has earned a place in this life. This feeling, in large part, is one of productivity. It is as if "the organization (family, community, business, etc.) is better off for my being here."

Internal auditors often feel especially productive and gratified when their work results in significant improvements in operations. It is not uncommon to hear internal auditors telling success stories. On the other hand, auditors who tend to dwell on their failures often seem to lack confidence.

Sense of Integrity   A sixth source of a strong self-image is a high degree of personal integrity, i.e., living consistently with an ethical, upright value system. The *Code of Ethics,* discussed in Chapter 2, exhorts internal auditors to exercise integrity.

A person who lacks integrity not only risks embarrassment or discipline, but even ill-health. Persons who believe one thing, but do another, may suffer what is called "cognitive dissonance," an uncomfortable feeling of psychological and emotional disharmony. If unresolved, this internal conflict can cause personality problems, depression, and even physical illness, ranging from the relatively mild to the severe.

Researchers have discovered various methods of decreasing this cognitive dissonance, but in every case the resolution centers on reducing the distance between the person's beliefs and actions. A secure individual successfully maintains personal integrity, living consistently with his or her values.

Daniel Yankelovich, in his book *New Rules* (Random House, 1981), noted a rapidly growing trend among people in the U.S. work force to place more and more emphasis upon gaining strong self-concepts. The internal auditor who possesses a good balance of the six personal characteristics outlined above generally is well prepared to take the next step toward understanding and developing interpersonal skills.

Understanding Other People

Exhibit 13-1 illustrated the importance of understanding people to develop and maintain good human relations. For auditors to understand people, they should study not only individuals, but groups as well.

There are different kinds of understanding. First, and the easiest to learn, is an intellectual understanding of other people. A second kind of understanding is an emotional response to specific needs and situations involving other people. We have all heard the comment that a particular individual is "very understanding." Generally, what is meant by such a statement is that not only does the person have knowledge of others, but the person can also offer an appropriate emotional response to other people's needs.

Because internal auditors constantly interact with a variety of people and groups inside and outside the organization, they must understand other people and the dynamics of their respective groups. Usually, internal auditors are in a position to threaten the security of other people in the organization. Consequently, auditors must be sensitive to other people's needs and how to integrate the needs of the individuals and subgroups with the overall needs of the organization.

This section discusses the characteristics of individuals and groups and examines the role of the internal auditor's emotional responses in the exercise of effective human relations skills.

Characteristics of Individuals

As reflected by Robert M. Fulmer in *Practical Human Relations* (Irwin, 1983), a generally accepted notion about individuals is that their behavior is a result of (1) personal needs, (2) their abilities to meet those needs, and (3) personality types. The previous section outlined six needs that individuals seem to have to develop a strong self-image. Of the various other analyses proposed to explain personal needs, one that is widely recognized is that of Abraham Maslow, who outlined a five-step hierarchy of needs, as illustrated in the following diagram:

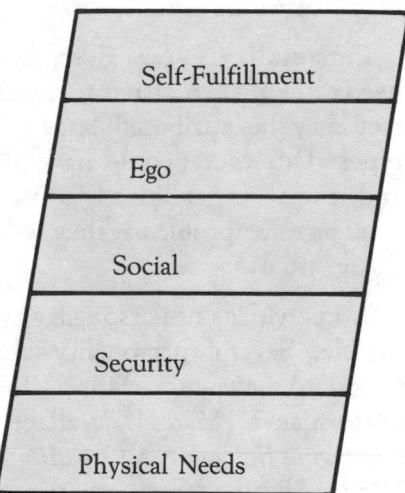

Maslow's Hierarchy of Personal Needs. Very briefly, Maslow argues that the first concern of the individual is meeting immediate physical needs such as hunger and thirst. As these needs are met, the individual then seeks future safety and security, after which the individual is likely to feel the need to associate with other people. The fourth level of need is the ego. The individual needs to have a sense of self-esteem, to like himself or herself and to be liked by others, and to feel important in a larger setting with other people. Finally, the individual feels the need for self-fulfillment or self-actualization. At this final step, the individual will turn inward for standards of fulfillment. Self-actualized people feel secure in their opinions and in what they are, and are able to work toward those things of importance to them personally.

While all of these needs exist simultaneously within the individual, one or another of the needs is likely to dominate the others at any one point in time. Of course, the movement may not always be upward through the hierarchy. Consider, for example, a successful business executive who appears to be well on the way toward self-actualization when he is suddenly struck with a heart attack. The executive is forced to revert immediately to the lowest level of physical concern — survival.

As individuals become aware of these various needs, they may strive to meet more than one simultaneously. A predominant need, however, likely will generate the primary motivation for their behavior at a particular time, while the other needs will generate secondary motivations.

Personality Types. Even though different people may have similar needs, they often strive to meet those needs in different ways. This fact may be attributed largely to different abilities and personality types. Different people have different physical, mental, emotional, and social capabilities. Consequently, when faced with identical challenges or problems, they will choose different methods of meeting those situations.

A knowledge of personality types also helps in understanding other people. Several personality characteristics have been studied and found to have important influences upon individual behavior and performance. Marc J. Wallace Jr. and Andrew D. Szilagyi Jr., in *Managing Behavior in Organizations* (Scott, Foresman, and Company, 1982), discuss three of the most prominent characteristics: (1) authoritarianism, (2) individual focus of control, and (3) risk aversion.

Different people are more or less authoritarian in their attitudes and behavior. People who are more authoritarian maintain status differences between themselves and others. They also tend to emerge as leaders in situations requiring autocratic, decisive, and structured performance. On the other hand, people who are less authoritarian are more apt to work well in participative efforts where joint responsibility is assumed by more than one individual.

Some people tend to believe that they have significant control over their lives. These people are termed "high internal control" types. Other people tend to believe that external forces control events in their lives. These people are described as "high external control" types. High internal control types generally prefer participative management styles, while high external control types generally work best under more directive management.

Risk aversion refers to a person's unwillingness to take chances. A highly "risk averse" person will avoid risky situations. This type of person tends to make decisions more slowly and to seek much more information before making decisions than a person who may be described as a "risk taker." Most people fall somewhere between the two extremes, with a tendency toward one direction or the other. Of course, different situations can elicit different risk responses from the same individual. In some cases the individual may appear more risk averse and in other cases appear more risk taking.

We must issue a word of caution here. Be very careful in basing judgments or decisions upon personality characteristics before you feel you really know the individual and how the characteristics are related to the work situation. Nevertheless, by being aware of different personal needs, abilities, and personality types, as well as the effects these factors can have upon risk, internal auditors can enhance their ability to assess the internal control environment.

For example, suppose the internal auditors were to audit two production plants whose operations were comparable, except for the two plant managers. One plant manager could be characterized as authoritative, a high external control type, and risk averse. The other was more participative, a high internal control type, and tended to be more of a risk taker than the first.

The auditors discovered an almost oppressive control environment in the first plant. Controls were so burdensome because of their excessive design that productivity and profits were substantially below those of the second plant. The auditors ended up making several strong recommendations for less stringent production controls in the first plant and a few minor recommendations for quality control and inventory management at the second plant. Control at each plant seemed to reflect the personality of its manager.

These areas of personal needs, abilities, and personality types are important to understanding the individual and should be carefully considered as you develop your interpersonal skills and relationships. This is not an exhaustive treatment, however, and you may want to study additional topics such as individual perception, learning theory, and motivation.

Characteristics of Groups

Although groups can be characterized as organizations of individuals, groups take on specific characteristics of their own, so much so that groups can have their own unique personalities and traits apart from the individuals involved. What are the general characteristics of a group? What makes one group more effective than another? Answers to these questions help improve internal auditors' understanding of how to relate to organizations as well as to people.

Fulmer identifies several general characteristics found in all groups:

1. There is interaction among group members. Perhaps all group members do not interact with every other group member, but they all do interact with at least some of the other group members.
2. The members of groups share common goals, at least as far as the group itself is concerned. Of course, members may have goals outside of the group context, but as part of the group, the various members will have at least some common goals.
3. Groups establish systems, norms, and rules of acceptable behavior. Some of these standards may be formally recognized and documented and others may be informally established; generally there are some of both.
4. Groups form stable role relationships among their members to fulfill the various functions necessary for group activity. Some of these functional roles include decision makers, gatherers of information, workers, "cheerleaders," and those responsible for maintaining group resources.
5. Finally, networks develop within groups among members who tend to interact among themselves more than with others in the group. These networks often are described as "networks of attraction" and may evolve informally. A change in these different networks can change the dynamics and operation of the entire group.

Internal auditors interact with individual people within the organization, yet these people represent and are parts of various groups. Thus, relating to the individual is in many ways interacting with the group.

As internal auditors interact with the various members of groups, they need to be conscious of the effectiveness of the groups' activities. After all, the primary responsibility of the internal auditor is to monitor the control system of the organization in terms of its effect upon the organization's (and its subunits') effectiveness and efficiency, not necessarily individual performance.

Not only is it valuable to understand that individuals are members of groups, it is also valuable to understand something about the particular group that an individual represents. Some groups simply perform better than others. These more effective groups tend to share some things in common. Generally, they make progress toward achieving their own goals, which are consistent with the larger organization's goals, and at the same time they tend to help the individual members of the group achieve their personal goals. Notice the goal congruence among individual members, the immediate group, and the larger group as an organization.

Fulmer lists seven essential functions in a successful group:

1. Some group members request information while other group members supply the necessary information.
2. Personal opinions from group members are requested and given regarding a wide range of topics, such as ideas, techniques, and procedures. Sometimes opinions are given without being requested, while at other times specific individuals are asked for their opinions on particular matters.
3. New ideas, plans, and suggestions come from members of the group, sometimes from a single individual or small subgroup and other times from the group as a whole.
4. Confusing or complicated issues are clarified and their implications extended into the future and into other aspects of the group activities. Sometimes this function is performed primarily by a single member, and other times by more than one member.
5. Group activities are organized and coordinated into a unified and cooperative effort.
6. As problems are addressed, their resolutions are briefly and clearly summarized so that group members may understand what has occurred.
7. Consensus is achieved among group members on matters of significant importance to group function and activity.

A breakdown in one or more of these group functions jeopardizes the success of the group, regardless of the personal strengths of individual members. Even when the objectives of an audit do not specifically include an examination of these group functions, it is wise to observe whether or not they are being fulfilled. If various subunits within the organization do not fulfill these group functions well, other areas within the organization may falter as a result.

Finally, effective groups interact well with other groups, especially with other groups within the organization. In fact, the better the interaction among the various groups within an organization, the more likely the whole organization is to succeed. Internal auditors examine this interface among related groups within the organization.

This brief discussion outlines some of the important aspects of individual and group behavior and their effect on developing effective human relations skills. But, as we mentioned at the beginning of the chapter, understanding people involves an emotional response in addition to an intellectual understanding.

Emotional
Understanding

Regardless of how well the internal auditor understands intellectually how and why other people behave the way they do, unless the auditor's emotional response is appropriate to the situation, he or she still can fail to develop effective human relations skills.

Psychological research into emotions has identified what are described as basic emotions, such as joy, fear, and anger. Generally, however, emotions arising from interpersonal relationships tend to be more complex, and there is yet much to be learned about emotional responses to different situations. The following diagram illustrates how such responses may take different directions (positive or negative), in different degrees of intensity, from absolute noninvolvement (or disinterest) to total emotional involvement.

TOTAL EMOTIONAL INVOLVEMENT

Love   Hate

Compassion   Hostility

Empathy   Distrust

Curiosity   Curiosity

DISINTEREST/NONINVOLVEMENT

In the positive direction of emotional responses, a person may begin a relationship with a mere intellectual *curiosity* and little emotional involvement or commitment. As the emotional response becomes greater, however, the two people involved in the relationship may experience similar feelings. This step is known as *empathy*. As a person begins to desire to act on the behalf of others, the person may be described as having *compassion,* which represents a still higher level of emotional involvement. Finally, as an individual becomes totally involved and absorbed in a relationship to the extent that the other person's welfare actually becomes the paramount concern, then the emotional response may be described as *love.*

Negative emotional responses also tend to range from noninvolvement to total involvement. Like the positive scale, the first step is *curiosity,* with little emotional involvement or commitment. As feelings become stronger, however, *distrust* may arise, or at a still higher level, *hostility,* where a feeling of antagonism may even prompt some kind of action against another person. Finally, the strongest negative emotion is described as *hate,* and it can be as all-absorbing in the negative direction as love is in the positive direction.

Of course, these descriptions are not exhaustive, but are illustrative of different levels of emotional responses to different situations. Notice that the greater the emotional involvement, the greater is the commitment of energy and effort by the person.

A person with good human relations skills reacts appropriately to the circumstances. A person with inadequate human relations skills generally reacts inappropriately. For example, a middle-level executive for a large corporation supervised a staff of professional-level employees. The supervisor reacted the same way to every situation — with compassion and intense efforts to work with people and to assist personally at the slightest indication of difficulty.

The staff of trained professionals, however, desired more independence, and the supervisor found that few employees would discuss any of their projects with him. His own supervisors eventually noticed that he emotionally isolated the staff from departmental activities. He was dismissed and replaced by one of his staff members. The replacement appeared little more than curious about what his employees were doing and let them work uninterrupted. Later, top management noticed that the professional staff had actually increased their interactions with the new supervisor and frequently sought his advice.

Another supervisor in a smaller organization frequently become hostile on those occasions when anyone opposed his views. Frictions mounted often, and the emotional climate of the organization was so negative that the supervisor could not keep employees for more than a few months before they quit and sought employment elsewhere.

Although all of the emotional responses illustrated above may be appropriate at various times, the trick to effective human relations is to match the appropriate emotional response to the situation.

Relevance to the Internal Auditor

The information in these sections on strong self-image and understanding others certainly is not designed to equip internal auditing students to become psychoanalysts. The issues of human relations are complex, and it is impossible to delve into a complete study of them here. What we have tried to present is a reasonably well-recognized set of information that may assist in developing good human relations skills. Good internal auditors possess these skills, and auditors without such skills limit their own progress.

Two important studies indicate that internal auditors face a challenge of improving their relationships with others in the organization where they work. In 1972, F. E. Mints published the results of a survey he conducted regarding how auditees feel about internal auditors. These results, published in The IIA Research Committee Report 17, *Behavioral Patterns in Internal Audit Relationships,* suggested that auditees at that time most often regarded internal auditors either neutrally or unfavorably.

In the June 1980 issue of *The Internal Auditor,* D. L. Clancy, Frank Collins, and Selimo C. Rael published an article titled "Some Behavioral Perceptions of Internal Auditing." They also suggested that internal auditors often are regarded questionably by auditees.

Given these indications, it is essential that internal auditors establish positive, constructive relationships with other people in the organization. The easiest way to accomplish this objective is to achieve common attitudes and goals in those relationships. For example, if an auditee remains intent on undermining the results of an audit, the internal auditor's relationship with that auditee is probably not going to be positive or constructive. The auditor's responsibility is to strive for and maintain a common understanding with the auditee about the objectives of the audit and how to achieve those objectives. When conflicts occur, the auditor should reestablish a spirit of understanding and cooperation with the auditee so that constructive progress is again possible.

How can this understanding and cooperation be accomplished? Primarily through resolve and effective communication.

Communication

The third primary factor of human relations is communication — the expression of a person's understanding of other people.

Since most students using this textbook will already have completed course work in communication theory, the emphasis here is upon methods of communicating more effectively. This section first reviews some relevant theory and then devotes the rest of the discussion to how to communicate.

Communication Model

A communication exchange, or encounter, can be diagrammed as follows:

ORGANIZATIONAL ENVIRONMENT

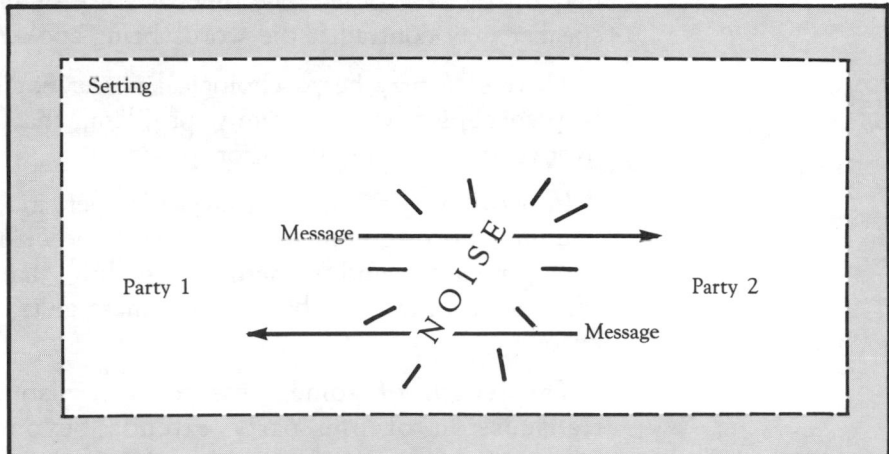

The exchange takes place in a particular setting within the larger overall environment. In business communication, the environment may be thought of as the *organizational environment,* which includes such things as a set of organizational objectives and goals, the organizational personality and style of operation, and the history of relationships among organizational units.

The *setting* is the more immediate environment in which the encounter takes place. In a face-to-face encounter, the setting would include the physical surroundings of each of the individuals. In a written encounter, the setting would include the surroundings of the writer and the reader. However, far more important than the physical surroundings are the immediate organizational climate, the organizational function out of which the communication originated, and the administrative relationship of the parties involved.

The focus of the model is upon the encounter itself. The encounter involves two parties in a two-way exchange of messages. The exchange may include some intended and some unintended messages, and the messages may be verbal, nonverbal, or both. These messages are sent through various media or channels, such as voice, actions, or written documents.

Noise in the encounter is anything that interferes with the sending or receiving of the intended messages. The noise may be physical — for example, loud machines operating in the area may make hearing difficult — but there are other sources of noise as well. A speaker's bad use of language can cause others to discount anything of substance that he or she may say. A nervous twitch by one party may distract the other. The tone of voice or facial expression of the speaker may contradict the words being spoken.

There also may be psychological noise. For example, if one party is preoccupied with a family problem, that preoccupation might overwhelm the communication process.

In written encounters, a messy paper may discredit the word content. Poor grammar may interfere with the thought being communicated, and sometimes spelling, language, and sentence construction can be so bad that the message is distorted or the reader becomes angered.

The length of some messages can also create noise. If the transmission of one party extends beyond the other party's expectations, then impatience may interfere and create enough noise to impede effective communication.

Obviously, communication can become quite noisy, even when efforts are made to avoid noise. The point is to be careful and to practice good communication habits.

Planning Communication

The best way to ensure effective communication is to plan encounters and to be aware of the communication process as these exchanges develop.

Situational Factors. Two types of factors affect the communication planning process: (1) situational factors over which the person may have only limited control and (2) characteristics of the message over which the person has substantial control. Although a person may have only limited control over situational factors, that does not mean there is no control. Consider the following situational factors and how they may be influenced:

- Audience.
- Obectives.
- Environmental setting.

- Noise.
- Timing.
- History.

Audience. Important considerations regarding the audience are the number of people, their personalities, their technical and job skills, their psychological and emotional maturity, and their expectations of the encounter. There may be little the internal auditor can do to change any of these things, but there may be a great deal he or she can do to allow for these considerations and thereby make communication more effective.

For example, one-to-one communication is generally more personal, with more personal references than typically are made in communication with larger groups. Even in more formal settings, one-to-one communication usually is more informal than communication in larger groups in similar settings. Sometimes the auditor may write a formal business letter to a single person, but it may be filed for reference by a much larger intended audience. For example, the internal audit report is usually addressed to one member of management, but is filed and read by several others.

When planning communication, the auditor needs to consider the total audience for which the communication may be intended. When meeting with small groups, the auditor needs to plan for participation by the other members of the group. Audit opening and closing conferences provide examples of these participative meetings. On the other hand, larger audiences generally require a presentation-style format. When writing to larger audiences, the auditor must have as broad an appeal as possible and not narrow the presentation to a select subgroup within the larger audience. An organization's published financial statement is one such example.

An audience's personality may be extroverted, introverted, open, cautious, or dominant. The problem with a more extroverted audience is maintaining control over the communication encounter so that the intended messages are sent and the communication objectives are achieved. On the other hand, the problem with more introverted audiences is that it can be difficult to elicit adequate response.

Communication from a more open audience requires the auditor to filter out the irrelevant messages, whereas cautious audiences generally require the auditor to probe more thoroughly for additional information. When communicating with a dominant audience, the internal auditor must take measures to ensure that his or her objectives are achieved and that he or she does not lose control of the encounter to the extent that the purposes are frustrated. This is true even when the encounter rightfully should be controlled by the other party. If the auditor's purposes are not achieved, then the encounter is a failure as far as he or she is concerned.

The technical and job skills possessed by the audience will affect the level of sophistication with which internal auditors communicate. For example, an auditor wouldn't explain the results of audit tests the same way to an employee with the equivalent of an eighth-grade education as he or she would to someone with an MBA.

The audience's psychological and emotional maturity will affect the attitude and the personal sensitivity the auditor assumes during an encounter. Here is where an internal auditor must be careful to exercise understanding of other people and offer an appropriate emotional response.

The expectations of the audience are critical to planning and conducting a communication exchange. If the audience's expectations contradict the auditor's, then the outcome of the encounter will be questionable before it even begins. Mutually compatible expectations must be set before any substantive issues are addressed.

Objectives. The objectives of a communication exchange in business usually are dictated, or at least highly influenced, by the particular operational setting in which the encounter occurs. Various steps of any audit are performed and the communication flow from each step is determined by the audit steps. The auditor does not have much control over the overall objectives of an exit conference, for example.

It is up to those parties involved in the communication to understand the objectives from the outset of the encounter, so that it can be conducted both effectively and efficiently. Meeting agendas are designed for this purpose.

While the overall objectives of the communication exchange may be determined by the function being performed, some specific objectives may be set by the individual people doing the communicating. However, the principle is the same. The objectives are more likely to be achieved if both parties understand the objectives from the beginning.

Environmental Setting. The environmental setting for the interpersonal encounter includes such things as the space, furnishings, and facilities available, as well as the functional use, physical arrangement, orderliness, and atmosphere of the setting. Whose "turf" the setting is in must also be considered.

The question of "turf" is especially important to internal auditors because audits almost always are conducted on the auditees' "turf." Auditees are generally possessive of their "ownership" and control of their area of responsibility and they tend to feel threatened by the auditors' presence. Realizing this tendency, internal auditors generally are careful not to intrude beyond the specific needs of the audit, and they generally express a cooperative attitude toward the auditee.

Although the question of "turf" may not be as critical in some interpersonal situations as in others, it is essential that the auditor command the environment in situations that require him or her to exercise authority. It is not necessary that the other party actually be on the auditor's turf, but the auditor's control of the setting is important. Internal auditors learn to be courteous and respectful at the same time they exercise the authority required to perform their job.

For written encounters in which the auditor is sending memos or reports, he or she may not be able to control the environmental setting of the person receiving the document. The auditor can, however, sometimes determine the document's time of arrival (morning or afternoon, before or after a vacation, etc.), and take into consideration how busy the recipient might be. Also, the auditor may have a choice of places to send the document — directly to an office, through a secretary, or sometimes even to one of several offices. To tailor a message to the circumstances of the reader, the auditor must think carefully about the environment in which the message will be read, and time its delivery appropriately.

Noise. As stated before, noise is anything that interferes with the effective communication of intended messages. The auditor should strive to eliminate as much noise as possible so that the intended messages have a greater chance of being communicated. This includes elimination of physical noises and distractions.

Timing. The flow of audits often determines the timing of communication, which then is not the prerogative of the internal auditor, except within relatively narrow limits. Good communicators learn to manage these narrow spans of time. When given a choice, a well-timed encounter will (1) provide adequate time for both parties to effectively complete the encounter, (2) allow adequate preparation by both parties, (3) be coordinated with the flow of other operations, and (4) be conducted when both parties can devote adequate attention to the matters at hand and not be distracted.

Auditors may not be able to anticipate all of the factors affecting these four requirements, but it is possible to take some important precautions:

1. The auditor can plan each encounter by rehearsing the objectives and how to achieve them before the encounter begins. This plan is easier to do when the auditor initiates the communication. It is more difficult when someone else initiates the communication. As an internal auditor becomes familiar with the operations of the organization, however, he or she will be able to anticipate communication exchanges, even when they are initiated by someone else. Successfully anticipating such exchanges allows the auditor to rehearse his or her participation in them. For example, if an audit report is particularly critical, the internal auditor generally can expect a reaction by the auditee. Realizing this, the auditor can plan how to handle the reaction.

2. In order to schedule enough time to allow adequate preparation for interpersonal encounters, the auditor can preview a proposed agenda with the other party. Specific time constraints for either party need to be communicated along with the agenda items.

3. The auditor needs to keep in mind the overall context of an exchange so that it will provide an integral link to the operations of the organization.

4. It is a good rule to try to avoid scheduling critical meetings or interviews to start immediately before or immediately after lunches, vacations, or just before the end of the work day. Also, if the auditor is aware of some other consideration that might interfere with the meeting or interview, perhaps a brief wait would be appropriate so that when the meeting does take place, it can be more productive.

History. History includes all prior events relating to the current encounter and the attitudes held by members of the organization about those events. Sometimes neither party may have taken part in any of the events. Other history more directly involves the participants in the communication exchange, who are likely to have predisposed attitudes toward the current encounter based upon their personal experiences.

Previous communication between the parties is especially important. If that communication was friendly and cooperative, they may begin where they left off. If the previous encounters were less friendly, and if suspicions on either side were aroused, they both should plan accordingly. Peace offerings may seem trite, but they often work. A display of genuine interest in and admiration for the other person's work (without being ingratiating) can sometimes help. The point is to join together in a common concern with mutual understanding.

This section has outlined six situational factors of communication over which the internal auditor generally has only limited control. They are (1) audience, (2) objective, (3) environmental setting, (4) noise, (5) timing, and (6) history. In every case, even though complete control is impossible, planning for each one can significantly increase the auditor's influence over what can be achieved in communication encounters.

Message Characteristics. Situational factors greatly influence the messages being sent. In fact, the messages may be considered direct results of the situational factors. This relationship is illustrated in the following diagram:

Situational factors are not always controllable by the auditor. These message characteristics may be divided into seven categories — method, trait, sequence, substance, emphasis, polish, and feedback.

Method. A basic question in any communication exchange is: which method is most appropriate? Choices include written, oral, pictorial or graphical, and nonverbal communication methods. Each has advantages and disadvantages.

Written communication offers the advantage that the reader can usually choose the time to read written messages. Also, if the material is complex, the reader can spend as much time as he or she chooses to study it. In addition, written communication may be filed for later reference.

There are also disadvantages to written communication. If the reader has questions about the information contained in the message, the paper cannot answer with more than it contained in the first place. Consequently, follow-up and clarifications are much slower, and sometimes misunderstandings occur that might have been avoided if the reader had been able to ask questions and the writer had been available to answer them.

Oral communication permits immediate feedback and allows the auditor to study the listeners and to adapt the message to them. The disadvantage of oral communication is that there tend to be more sources of noise, because the listener is receiving many messages from different sources in the environment. When reading, people tend to focus their attention more directly on the message itself. Another disadvantage of oral communication is that it may not be edited before its transmission. Once something is spoken, it cannot be retrieved, whereas a written message may be edited many times before it is delivered. Also, written messages provide documented evidence that spoken communication does not.

Pictorial or graphical communication, such as diagrams, pictures, drawings, graphs, and charts, can have a dramatic and immediate effect. On the other hand, it often is more difficult to communicate subtle complexities if only these means of communication are used.

Nonverbal communication is discussed in more detail later.

Generally, the choice is not necessarily which one communication method should be used, but rather which combination is most appropriate, since one method can reinforce another. Francis J. McHugh (in *Graphic Presentation,* published by Technifax Corp., Holyoke, Massachusetts, 1956) has shown, for example, that people remember an average of 72 percent of a visual message three hours after seeing it. Recall drops to 20 percent of the message after three days. Recall of vocal messages averages 70 percent after three hours and drops to 10 percent after three days. On the other hand, when messages are both seen and heard, three-hour recall averages 85 percent, with recall after three days averaging 65 percent. The two methods tend to reinforce a person's ability to recall messages.

Trait. The second message characteristic, message trait, has three dimensions — credibility, climate, and content. Credibility in communication refers to the believability of a message. The climate is the emotional attitude with which the encounter is conducted and the message sent and received. Climate comprises different degrees of such variables as formality, authoritativeness, participativeness, friendliness, and concern. The content trait previews the message; i.e., it briefly announces for the audience, at the beginning of the encounter, the information to be contained in the message. A letter, for example, may begin something like this:

Dear Mr. Williams:

I have been considering your proposal to provide our company with a new electronic climate-control system . . .

After this first sentence, Mr. Williams is prepared to read more about what the writer thinks about the proposal. Similarly, audit reports generally include an "executive summary" at the beginning, sometimes even when a report is not very long. Such a summary serves to preview the content of the report as a whole.

A number of factors govern the climate of a communication encounter. Such things as word selection, voice intonation (in interpersonal encounters), the environmental setting, and predisposed attitudes all have important effects upon communication climate. In fact, the climate may be the easiest of the various message characteristics to ascertain in communication.

Message credibility, however, may be more subtle. Two people can deliver the same message in exactly the same way and one will have credibility and the other will not. The primary source of credibility in most communication is the credibility of the person sending the message. People receive messages from other people and attribute credibility to those messages based upon their perceptions of the people who sent them. Even when messages are sent from unknown parties, readers generally try to determine who the senders are before making any final conclusions about the messages.

Auditors have essentially three sources of credibility — professional, organizational, and personal. The professional designations of Certified Internal Auditor and Certified Public Accountant were created to give the auditor credibility by satisfying commonly recognized standards, established in part to promote status for the auditing profession. Organizational credibility comes from the recognized authority and relationships enjoyed by the auditing department within the organization. This credibility may be documented in the form of a charter and written authorization from management to conduct particular audits.

These first two forms of credibility largely lie outside the individual auditor's control, except that he or she is able to pursue professional certification and thereby acquire any credibility attached to such certification. However, regardless of professional and organizational considerations, in the individual encounter the auditor's personal credibility is of paramount importance. Without personal credibility, neither of the other two sources of credibility is enough to successfully carry the message. Also, personal credibility can overcome deficiencies in other forms.

Personal credibility is based upon attitudes, behavior, physical appearance, and competence. The best communicators prepare themselves personally for each encounter and plan the use of their personal attributes in such a way as to maximize their effectiveness. "Winging it" almost invariably will show the lack of preparation and thereby discredit the auditor.

Sequence. To sequence the elements of a message is to order them. Complex messages are more understandable if they follow a logical sequence. This principle is just as true for spoken communication as it is for written communication. Standardized formats help the proper sequencing of business letters, memoranda, and reports. Likewise, planning both the form and the sequence of messages can increase the understandability of messages in interviews and meetings.

Logic follows a step-by-step process. The logical presentation of audit recommendations, for example, follows a general format:

- A brief identification of the problem area.
- Existing conditions found during the audit.
- Presentation of the principles, policies, or procedures governing the problem area.
- A comparison of the governing principles, policies, or procedures with the existing conditions.
- Conclusions.
- Recommendations.

Such a sequence leaves little doubt about how the recommendations came about. The main point is that every element of a message occurs in some larger context than the isolated element itself. The audience of the message needs to understand the larger context.

Proper sequencing of messages also can increase their acceptability to the audience. Simple courtesy would suggest that "good news messages" should begin with the good news, followed by the conditions or reasoning leading to the good news. The message should end with a final note of goodwill. A "bad news message," however, is generally easier to accept if good news and/or a buffer precedes it, and if the message is concluded with a final note of encouragement. Dishonesty of any sort can prove devastating, but an honest and positive statement can be valuable to the acceptance of bad news.

Substance. The substance is the main body of a message. Substance is the information to be communicated, and it is closely related to the content trait. If the content trait stated, for example, that the message would contain five steps leading to better internal control of accounts payable, then the substance of the statement would provide the five steps.

A second purpose of substance is to support individual message statements. Some messages have face validity and require no special treatment to justify the messages. Other messages require validating evidence. Audit findings are an example. A good strategy in planning a message is to communicate enough information to be convincing, but not so much as to be intimidating or boring.

Emphasis. Emphasis helps a reader focus on the substance of the message. In any communication, some messages get through more clearly and efficiently than others. The internal auditor should plan so that the messages that get through are in fact the ones intended. Proper organization can help, but several other methods are equally important.

If there are three key points, say so, and number them 1, 2, and 3. Graphic illustrations emphasize particular information. Underlining, italics, indention, and repetition all help give emphasis. In face-to-face encounters, pauses and gestures also emphasize key points, as does speaking more softly or more loudly than normal. The objective is to set the important parts of the message apart from the rest.

Polish. There is a familiar saying, "Details count." Polish is a matter of detail. Details such as good grammar, word selection, and appearance can be as important as other communication factors. Polish generally makes the difference between a successful encounter and an unsuccessful one. Two things can increase polish — (1) planning and (2) practice. It is not only a matter of what is done or said, but also how it is done or said.

Feedback. The ultimate test of any communication is whether its purposes are achieved. Feedback provides such a test. Feedback requires that each party in the encounter respond in some way so that the other party can assess the success of the communication process. The nature of the responses will differ, depending upon the nature of the encounter and the communication objectives of the parties.

Feedback may come in different stages. Initial feedback may come at the meeting where information was first delivered. Follow-up feedback may come later. During a meeting, for example, an auditee may make a commitment to study a proposed action before making a decision about whether to act on the proposal. Even in such cases (perhaps especially in such cases) it is important to seek feedback before ending the meeting, so that both parties understand what to expect later as a result of the meeting. The auditor may receive subsequent feedback about whether or not the auditee actually acted upon the proposal. Without adequate feedback, either party may leave the meeting with uncertainty and be confused about whether the meeting fulfilled its purpose.

Feedback in written communication may take different forms. A return letter, note, memorandum, telephone call, or even a personal meeting may be requested. If it is important that communication get through and be understood for future reference and/or action, some type of feedback will help to avoid possible misunderstandings.

This section has outlined seven characteristics of messages that should be planned for communication exchanges — (1) method, (2) trait, (3) sequence, (4) substance, (5) emphasis, (6) polish, and (7) feedback. These aspects of the message are more controllable than the situational factors.

Nonverbal Communication

A great deal has been written and said about nonverbal communication and how important it is to effective communication. Certainly, any discussion of communication would be incomplete without recognition of this principle. The nonverbal messages contained in encounters are at least as important as the verbal ones — regardless of whether the encounters are in writing or in person. Often what is not said bears a stronger message than what is said.

Exhibit 13-2 illustrates the differences between verbal and nonverbal aspects of an office memorandum. The verbal messages are contained in the words, sentences, telephone number, organization of the sentences into a logical flow, and in the friendly style of writing. The nonverbal messages are contained in the paper type, color, and size; the time the memorandum was received; the fact that the memorandum is typed rather than handwritten; that it is neat and clean; and that it is initialled by the sender.

Compare this memorandum with the note presented in Exhibit 13-3, which contains essentially the same verbal message. Believe it or not, some important business messages have been known to be as unintelligible as this one. The words are almost the same, but as you can see, the nonverbals are clearly different. The nonverbals in this case make the difference between being understood and not being understood.

Not only is the memorandum in Exhibit 13-2 more understandable than that shown in Exhibit 13-3, but it also possesses greater credibility, demonstrating more thoughtful consideration of others by the sender. Sometimes a personal note may be even better to communicate a friendlier tone.

**Exhibit 13-2
Memorandum**

Date: February 12, 1987
To: Wes Johnson
From: Carl Billings (CB)
Subject: Audit Supervisors' Seminar in Cleveland

   I checked with Buddy Andrews, Streeter Co.'s director of auditing, who says he is sending two of his supervisors to next week's seminar. They will be leaving Friday morning by car, and you are welcome to ride with them if you want. If you decide to ride with them, you are to contact Bill Smith on Mr. Andrews' staff. The number is 456-8946. Mr. Andrews said you should call by 10 a.m. on Wednesday. Bill is going out of town then and won't be back until Friday and probably will not be coming into the office before he leaves for the seminar.

   As I told you before, these programs have been a big help to me. I will be interested to know what you think. Call me on the 26th, and we'll plan lunch so that we can talk. Good luck and have a good time. I'll look forward to talking with you when you get back.

Nonverbal communication also is important in interpersonal encounters. Examine the pictures in Exhibit 13-4. How much do you know about the individuals in the two photographs, without having any information about them other than what you see in the pictures?

Business students at a large university were shown these photographs. One group saw the top picture, another group saw the bottom picture. No one saw both pictures. If you look carefully, you will see that the same person is pictured in the same office in both photographs. The differences are in personal appearance, the orderliness of the office, and in camera angle. Each student was told that the person in the picture was an internal auditor for a large local firm, and each was asked a series of questions about the individual pictured. Compared to the auditor in the bottom photograph, the results suggested that the internal auditor in the top picture has worked longer for his employer, has more education, and participates in higher-status sporting activities.

Exhibit 13-3
Nonverbal Attributes Affect Written Communication

Wes,

I have checked with Bradley Andrews Shecter Co.'s director of architecture, who says he is sending two of his supervisors to next week's seminar. They will be leaving Friday morning by car and you are welcome to ride with them if you want. If you decide to ride with them, you are to contact Bill Smith on Mr. Andrews' staff. The number is 452-8141. Mr. Andrews says you should call by 10 a.m. on Wednesday. Bill is gone for a tour, then and won't be back until Friday and probably will not be coming into the office before he leaves for the seminar.

As I told you before, these programs have been a big help to us. I will be interested to know what you think. Call me on the 25th and we'll plan things so we can talk. Good luck and have a good time. I'll look forward to talking with you when you get back.

Cris

Exhibit 13-4
Examples of Nonverbal Communication in Personal Appearance

In many cases it doesn't matter as much what the truth *is* as it does what others *perceive* it to be. For the audience, the perceived "truth" is critical. We are responsible for communicating the truth as accurately as possible. Our nonverbal communication sends many messages about us and about the message we may be trying to communicate verbally.

Verbal and nonverbal messages should complement, not contradict, each other. Different audiences require different nonverbal messages. John T. Molloy, author of *Dress for Success* (Warner Books, 1975) and *Live for Success* (Bantam Books, 1981), stresses that effective communication is so dependent upon nonverbal messages that he recommends many of his clients hire acting coaches for instruction. He recommends acting coaches because they are so well trained in nonverbal communication. Other people write the script. Actors interpret the script nonverbally. Their livelihood depends upon nonverbal communication, even moreso than others who may be better trained in communication as an academic discipline.

The objective is to communicate the intended message as effectively, accurately, and honestly as possible. The purpose is to coordinate all communication, verbal and nonverbal, in such a way as to be understood. Interestingly, one practical guide to effective nonverbal communication is a book on etiquette.

Auditor–Auditee Relationships

Although internal auditors must develop effective relationships with many individuals and groups within the organization, perhaps the most critical relationships are those with auditees. Cooperation between the auditor and auditee is essential for the development of a constructive auditing function within the organization. Unfortunately, there also is great potential for conflict between the two.

There are two primary sources of conflict: (1) the auditee's fear of audit consequences and (2) the auditor's own behavior.

Auditees often fear that audit findings will adversely affect future performance appraisals. Unfavorable findings generally lead to questions about who was responsible for any problems discovered during the audit. There then is the possibility of flawed performance records, reprimands, or even dismissals. Audit findings represent a threat and, therefore, a potential conflict.

Another factor sometimes compounds the emotional reaction to this threat. Many auditees believe that auditors are not qualified to review the auditee's activities. The assumption seems to be that the auditor's lack of expertise increases the chance that deficiencies will be reported even when they do not exist.

Auditees often express complaints such as: the auditors disrupt auditee operations; the audits are likely to result in unnecessary changes in familiar routines among auditee personnel; and auditors use such technical jargon that it is almost impossible to understand them. Generally, these complaints can be resolved to minimize serious conflict. Auditors usually can coordinate audit activities with the auditee so that minimum disruption results. A review of audit findings and recommendations with auditee management usually will uncover any unnecessary proposed changes. Also, auditors can learn to be careful not to use unnecessarily technical auditing language with auditees. When such language is unavoidable, auditors should carefully explain the unique terminology to the auditee in order to avoid misunderstandings.

The second major source of conflict between the auditor and the auditee is the auditor's behavior. Some auditors increase the chance of conflict simply by the way they do their jobs. These auditors tend to work in an atmosphere of secrecy. Their interviews with auditees often resemble an attorney's interrogation of a hostile witness in court. They emphasize deficiencies, errors, and mistakes, without giving a fair perspective of the overall effectiveness of the controls. They generally seek to attach blame to deficiencies, often naming individuals whom they believe to be at fault. They seem smug, aloof, and often assume an attitude of superiority. They seem insincere and lack a genuine interest in understanding the auditee's problems.

You can imagine the effect of mixing an auditee's fear with the above actions of an insensitive, ill-informed auditor.

Conflict Management

The behavioral science literature outlines three broad approaches to resolving conflict when it occurs within an organization: (1) avoidance, (2) defusion, and (3) confrontation.

Avoidance. Conflict generally may be avoided with three strategies. First, the persons involved simply can look the other way and ignore the conflict situation. Second, they can be physically separated. Finally, interactions between conflicting parties can be limited, restricted to only a relatively narrow range of subject matter and for limited periods of time. Often these avoidance techniques only put off the conflict, rather than offering a permanent resolution to the problem.

Defusion. By defusing a conflict situation, the parties may set aside the critical issues and concentrate on other, less controversial issues. This approach may be implemented either by downplaying differences and emphasizing similarities or by compromising so that the respective parties make concessions on some points in order to gain others.

An effective compromise is achieved when both parties agree to a "fair" exchange. Although such strategies allow the parties to work together, the ideal resolution may not be achieved if the real source of conflict remains. In addition to "give and take," the sharing of views and information can help achieve consensus.

Confrontation. This final approach often allows the conflict to be resolved at its core. The sources of conflict are identified and addressed by the conflicting parties with the aim of recognizing and establishing common interests. Rather than decreasing the communication exchanges between the conflicting parties, these exchanges are increased, and the people involved search out the overall goals of the organization which circumscribe individual goals.

Within the context of internal auditing, avoidance may be impossible, as may be defusion. If the auditors are to conduct an effective audit, they must work with the auditee. Because the audit is designed to discover the very issues of ineffectiveness and inefficiencies that are likely to cause the conflict, it is difficult to avoid or defuse them by concentrating on something else.

At times, the only approach left open to the auditor is confrontation, which points out another reason that human relations skills are so important to the auditor.

Participative Approach to Auditing

One method some auditing departments use to minimize conflict situations is to develop "the participative audit approach." This approach does not mean that members of the auditee staff conduct the audit jointly with the auditors, but it does mean that the auditor seeks to establish a more cooperative working relationship with the auditee. Here are some suggested methods that auditors can use to develop such a relationship:

1. The auditor can identify with the auditee the joint organizational goals they have in their work, and how one complements the other.

2. The auditees may be allowed to consult with the auditors on matters where the auditee's expertise and insight may be of help in carrying out the audit more effectively, as well as on matters that may be of special importance to the auditee.

3. The auditors may discuss the objectives of an audit with the auditee to minimize the aura of secrecy and mystery and to establish a better rapport.

4. Auditors may inform the auditee of all audit findings, favorable and unfavorable, and include in the audit report recognition of the auditee's participation and cooperation in the audit process and in resolving perceived deficiencies in the system.
5. Auditors may allow the auditee to review a preliminary draft of the audit report, providing an opportunity to respond to possible objectionable points. Also, the auditors may meet with the auditee to resolve perceived differences between them before the final report draft is written.

The participative approach to auditing helps resolve the two primary sources of conflict between the auditee and auditor — auditee fear and auditor behavior. The auditee has an opportunity to be an active part of the audit process rather than being merely the subject under review. Also, the auditor assumes a more cooperative posture with the auditee, thereby avoiding some of the objectionable behavior that we described earlier.

However, the auditors' independence may be jeopardized as the auditee becomes more involved in a cooperative effort involving operations, the review of operations, evaluations, and recommendations. Again, to successfully establish the participative audit approach while at the same time maintaining adequate independence, the auditor must possess excellent human relations skills.

Some auditors maintain their independence and objectivity while developing good rapport and cooperation with auditees, who seem to perceive the auditors as a resource rather than a threat. These auditors have the ability to find and report deficiencies in such a way that everyone involved benefits. Of course, it would be foolish to pretend that any internal auditor can successfully accomplish his or her duties to the organization without creating some uneasiness, and occasionally outright conflict. Good auditors, however, minimize these negative experiences, maximize the positive ones, and still fulfill their responsibilities. The key is effective people skills.

QUESTIONS

1. Personal security (i.e., a strong self-image) is described in the chapter as the foundation for effective human relations. Why?
2. What are the important sources of personal security? Explain each one briefly.
3. Why is it important to have an adequate balance of each of these factors (cited in your response to question 2) contributing to personal security?
4. What might be some consequences of an inadequate amount of each of these sources (cited in your response to question 2) of personal security?
5. What is the value of an intellectual understanding of other people? Why is it important to have more than just an intellectual understanding of other people?
6. What are the three factors that tend to motivate an individual's behavior? Explain each of the three briefly.
7. Why is it important for the internal auditor to understand groups as well as individuals?
8. Outline the general characteristics of a group.
9. What functions are performed in effective groups? Illustrate how a breakdown in one of these functions can jeopardize the success of the other functions. As your example for class discussion, use the coordination function outlined in the text.
10. What does it mean to have an emotional understanding of other people?
11. Explain the relationship of (1) emotional feelings and (2) commitment in a person's emotional response.
12. Diagram and explain the elements of the model of communication encounters illustrated in the chapter.
13. What situational factors affect communication encounters? Briefly explain each.
14. Outline and briefly discuss the seven message characteristics presented in the chapter.
15. Compare and contrast the situational factors and message characteristics in terms of control.
16. What is the relationship between situational factors and message characteristics in communication encounters?
17. Explain the importance of nonverbal communication in encounters. Give three examples of its importance.
18. What are the primary sources of conflict between auditees and auditors? Discuss each.
19. Outline three approaches to conflict management when it occurs within an organization.
20. What is participative auditing? How might it help improve auditor–auditee relationships? Do you see any dangers?

EXERCISES

E-1

Norman White has been a staff auditor for LIN, Incorporated for six months. Norman completed an MBA degree at the William B. Harding Graduate School of Business and has an excellent background in quantitative methods and financial analysis. He views his tenure in the internal auditing department as a brief step toward a management position in corporate planning. Despite his fine academic credentials and neat appearance, Norman is abrasive to his fellow auditors and to clerks and others whom he views as inferior. His work on audits is competent insofar as technical performance is concerned. On the other hand, several managers have requested that he not be allowed back in their departments, and fellow auditors have complained to the audit manager, Mel Hansen, who reported these complaints to the corporate audit director, Dick Michaels. Mr. Michaels has scheduled a meeting with Norman to discuss the situation. Mr. Michaels knows you are taking a course in internal auditing and invites you over to his house to discuss the upcoming conference with Norman. He doesn't reveal the individuals involved in the problem, but does explain the essence of the situation in general terms. He then asks your advice.

Required:
a. List a person's personal needs as outlined by Maslow's hierarchy. List the kinds of abilities that might be used to meet those needs. Also, list the personality variables outlined in the chapter that could be used to analyze and improve Norman's situation.
b. How would you describe Norman's personality type?
c. How would you handle the situation with Norman? Explain.

E-2
The audit director of Miles Corporation set an extremely tight schedule for a particular audit. During the course of the audit, he reassigned one of the staff auditors to another audit in a different city. The supervisor assigned to the first audit questioned how he could accomplish the audit on time without a full team, especially when the time constraints already were so severe. The audit director's reply was, "Get them to work harder."

Required:
a. What important factors, in terms of understanding individuals and groups, might the supervisor keep in mind to resolve this problem?
b. Identify which of the functions of an effective group seems to be most in danger in this situation.
c. How might the other functions of an effective group be utilized to strengthen the weakness created by the loss of the auditor from the team?

E-3
An audit of the personnel department of a large company is being conducted. A new staff auditor is assigned to review the departmental budgets and copies of employment contracts. The staff auditor has requested the documents from the personnel director on several occasions. The personnel director consistently promises to get the documents for the auditor, but never seems to get around to it. He is courteous, but he acts as if the audit is very low among his priorities.

Required:
If you were the staff auditor, how would you plan a meeting with the personnel director to resolve the problem? In your plan, be sure you consider both situational factors and message characteristics.

E-4

Three auditors just joined an audit team after having worked for several years under another supervisor who had grown lax before retiring a month before. Soon after they joined the new audit team, it became evident that these three auditors expected long breaks and extended lunch hours, and that they had poor work habits and low productivity. The other auditors in the group also observed that the three often returned after lunch appearing to have been drinking.

Required:

Analyze how you think the three auditors are likely to affect the effectiveness of the new audit group to which they have been assigned.

E-5

Auditors have discovered a budget overrun of $500,000 in a particular department. The overrun has been attributed to internal control weaknesses. The department manager, however, has been cooperative and helpful throughout the audit. He has taken steps to correct the control weaknesses, but it is apparent that he had not been careful to avoid the losses prior to the audit. The auditors have included all of this information in their report. The manager had worked for the company for 21 years, and he was well liked by his subordinates and managers from other departments. His performance in the past has been adequate, but he will find that his job may be in jeopardy when the losses are reported to his superiors in the audit report.

Required:

a. How might conflict be prevented in this situation, if at all?
b. If conflict does occur between the auditors and the manager, how might the auditors minimize it?

E-6

An auditee, a state government office, continually fails to provide information to the auditors. The auditors earlier discovered a significant unfavorable variance in the office, and the office management has displayed an uncooperative, even antagonistic attitude since then.

Required:

a. How might participative auditing have prevented such a conflict?
b. What precautions may be taken by the auditors to preserve their independence while still using the participative approach?

E-7

Mary Micheaux, an audit supervisor, is scheduled to present audit findings to senior management in less than a week. Skip Kelly, a senior staff auditor, is badly behind in compiling evidence regarding several key issues to be covered in the report, and Mary believes Skip may not have been as diligent in his work as he might have been. If the information is delayed one more day, Mary doubts that the report can be completed on time.

Required:

a. What do you think is the most appropriate emotional response for the audit supervisor in this scenario?

b. What would be the short-term and long-term objectives of her interaction with the senior auditor regarding the problem?

E-8

Community Federal Bank recently hired Alfred Day as one of its branch managers. Alfred had been an internal auditing manager with First Federal Bank before taking the new position. Last week, Community Federal Bank auditors began an audit of Alfred's branch, and within moments after the audit team arrived the first day, Alfred began criticizing everything the auditors did. At least once a day since then, Alfred has made the comment to the audit supervisor, "Boy, if I were still an auditor and you guys worked for me, I would fire you all. Why don't you go learn what you're doing before coming to audit my branch?" The audit supervisor knows that the team is well trained; in fact, the auditors are as well trained as Alfred. He knows because he has instructed auditing classes for the State Banking Association, where Alfred studied auditing. The supervisor knows some of the instructors Alfred studied under and actually reviewed some of Alfred's work with one of the other instructors three years before. The supervisor considers his present team members to be at least as knowledgeable and skilled in internal auditing as Alfred, whose attitude is proving a hindrance to the successful completion of the audit.

Required:

Suppose you are the audit supervisor. Plan a meeting with Alfred to discuss the problem. Remember both situational factors and message characteristics in your plan.

E-9

Leonard Bailey is director of internal auditing for a large retail chain with headquarters in Atlanta. Wilma Lawrence is vice president of operations for the firm. She has worked for the firm for 25 years and is extremely protective of what she considers her domain. The very first audit of her office has been scheduled to begin in two weeks. Leo has taken Claire Nunn, his new audit manager (whom he hired from a rival firm in San Francisco) with him for a preliminary meeting with Wilma. Wilma appeared courteous but somewhat uneasy during the meeting. After the meeting, Leo and Claire were leaving Wilma's office when Wilma called Leo back inside. Claire went into the outer office to wait for him. Wilma partially closed the door and said, quietly but firmly, "Leo, I have long respected your business sense. I know you've never audited my territory before, but I have watched from a distance, and you do good work. But where did you get that girl? She should be sent home to knit! And you intend to let her lead an audit?" Leo knows that Wilma has a history of conflict with other female employees in the firm, but he also knows Claire is a competent auditor and supervisor.

Required:

a. What should be Leo's emotional response to Wilma's reaction to Claire? Why?

b. Should he take Claire off the audit, especially since this is the first audit of the executive management of operations? Explain.

E-10

Robert Cutberth recently joined the internal auditing staff of a medium-sized manufacturing company in the West. He previously had worked for five years with a regional CPA firm. He had been successful with the CPA firm and was considered to be a fine auditor, extremely well-versed in financial accounting and auditing standards. He joined the manufacturing firm only because of what he felt was a very attractive offer in terms of pay and benefits, as well as future opportunities. Since Robert joined the company, however, he has restricted himself to the accounting aspects of audits. He seems unsure of himself when trying to review operational efficiency and effectiveness, and he often avoids those aspects of audit assignments. Last week he spoke with his audit manager and expressed some personal concerns about his ability to succeed as an internal auditor. He also had overheard two of the young staff auditors commenting on what they considered to be his inadequacies, and he mentioned this occurrence to the audit manager as well. The audit manager had noticed that Robert seemed to be becoming more and more withdrawn.

Required:
a.   What factor (or factors) of personal security seems to be inadequate in Robert's case?
b.   What do you think can be done to help?

E-11

The auditing department of Brown Enterprises, Inc. comprised 21 professional staff members, two secretaries, one file clerk, and two word processing/computer operators. Bob Nelson has worked for the department for three years. He had been hired after graduating from the University of Pinkham School of Accountancy.

Bob was adequate in terms of his technical skills, and he seemed to get along well with other people, but his verbal skills were terrible. He often said that he went into accounting because that field didn't require him to write so many term papers at school. He had his roommate edit and help him rewrite the required papers in other classes. In addition, Bob never looked quite right. He didn't like anything tight around his neck, so his shirts were always much too big, and for some reason he had never learned to tie a necktie properly. And on top of it all, he had terribly bad breath. Bob always was assigned work that could be done in a private room away from the rest of the team and members of the auditee's staff. He did a great deal of computations, recalculations of figures, reviewing documents, and the like. Bob was getting restless, however, and had been saying openly that he wants to have more responsibility.

Required:
a.   What effect do you think Bob has had on the group's effectiveness?
b.   With your understanding of groups, what effect do you think Bob's promotion to supervisor would have on his audit teams? (Analyze his effect upon those factors most contributing to a group's effectiveness.)

E-12

Marianne is the only woman auditor on Granville Company's internal auditing staff. She joined the staff approximately six months ago after having worked as an assistant controller for N.C. Hill Manufacturing, Inc. Ever since Marianne came to Granville, she has appeared very nervous on the job. When she makes a mistake, regardless of how small or large it may be, she apologizes to almost everyone in sight — the auditee, her supervisor, the other staff auditors — and when she leaves at the end of the day, she apologizes again for the various mistakes she has made, and she promises to do better the following day. Marianne recently started smoking, she says, to try to lose some of the extra weight she has picked up since taking the position with Granville. Her senior auditor overheard her telling a clerk on the auditee's staff that her father is very ill and isn't expected to live more than another month. Marianne is afraid that if she loses this job she may have to move away to find another job, leaving her mother by herself.

Required:
a. Review Maslow's needs hierarchy and evaluate Marianne's needs at this time.
b. Discuss Marianne's personality type in terms of the three personality variables presented in the chapter.
c. What might be done to help her situation?

E-13

Since Collin became separated from his wife, he has missed a lot of work because of his divorce proceedings. He appears tired when he does come in, and his audit work seems to have suffered considerably. He has told the audit manager that it is imperative to be at the meetings with his attorney and the courts in order to win custody of his children. He has even said that if custody is awarded to his wife, he is afraid for the welfare of his children.

Required:
What elements of Collin's personal security appear threatened by these circumstances? Discuss.

PROBLEMS

P-1

An internal auditor should be conscious of the obligation to be objective and of the need for constructive and practical audit opinions and recommendations. The auditor also should be conscious of the need for good auditor/auditee relationships.

Assume that an auditor is concluding an audit of the engineering division. The major audit findings indicate a tendency to bypass other departments that should be involved in decision making; some shortcomings in control practices; and a lack of liaison among the engineering, purchasing, and accounting departments.

Required:
Describe five actions the internal auditor should take to avoid unnecessary conflict and to preserve a workable relationship with the auditee.

(CIA Exam Adapted)

P-2

A large manufacturer of ladies' clothing recently acquired three manufacturing subsidiaries. As the director of internal auditing, you plan to have members of your staff review the internal controls over finished goods inventories and inventory costing practices in each of the newly acquired subsidiaries. You recognize that the initial contact with the auditees will be important to facilitate conduct of the proposed audits.

Required:

Discuss five steps that you, as the director of internal auditing, would take to develop a cooperative atmosphere (participative approach) between the auditees and the internal auditors.

(CIA Exam Adapted)

P-3

As Stephen delves into each of his auditors' work to determine the sources of some errors that have come to his attention, he discovers that Juanita, one of the brightest young staff auditors, has made some mistakes in her audit working papers. He calls her into his office to confront her, hoping not only to "take her down a peg or two," but to put her up as an object lesson for the other auditors, whom he thinks are getting too careless in their work.

As Stephen begins his talk with Juanita, he wastes no time in coming to the point. "I've been going over your work, and it looks like you've made some mistakes." Juanita is taken aback, embarrassed, and incredulous, since she considers herself one of the best auditors in the department. Stephen then accuses her of taking shortcuts in her work and being generally irresponsible and careless.

As she protests, he confronts her with the audit test results reported in the papers and tells her, "You ought to know better than this! I won't stand for work like this going out of here. You just see that it doesn't happen again, you hear?" After Juanita apologizes begrudgingly, still not understanding how the mistakes could have happened, Stephen simply says, "Okay. Now get back to work. Remember our audit goals and the deadline on Thursday."

Required:

Analyze this communication encounter in terms of the message characteristics outlined in the chapter. You should include an analysis of both Stephen's and Juanita's communication.

Adapted from Robert M. Fulmer, *Practical Human Relations,* Revised Edition (Irwin, 1983), p. 109.

14 Sampling

The necessity of using sampling procedures during the course of internal auditing should be obvious from merely considering the volume of transactions processed by the control system of a typical corporation. If it takes a full year for the accounting department to process such transactions, often with a 40-person staff, how can a team of three to five auditors possibly examine all of these transactions in the course of the typical audit project — a one- to two-month assignment? They cannot. However, it is possible to take a sample or subset of transactions processed and to draw accurate and useful inferences from that sample to the total set of transactions occurring during the time period under audit.

Professional Standards Bulletin 82-6 recognizes that "statistical sampling is *not* required when performing audit procedures . . . . Nevertheless . . . internal auditors are constantly faced with the assignment of drawing conclusions about entire populations based on . . . only a portion of the items in the population." Consequently, internal auditors must choose either judgmental or statistical sampling techniques. The auditor exercises his or her professional judgment in making the choice. This chapter helps clarify the choice, and it describes in some detail how statistical sampling may be used.

Historical Perspective

The idea of sampling has evolved due to necessity. Practically speaking, it is not possible for auditors to examine every transaction in a large entity. Whenever less than 100 percent of the items within an account balance or a class of transactions are examined, sampling is being performed. This notion of looking at a "few book items" was mentioned in a 1917 memorandum prepared by the American Institute of Accountants (the predecessor of today's American Institute of Certified Public Accountants). It was not until 1955 that the AICPA issued a professional publication on sampling, titled *A Case Study of the Extent of Audit Samples,* and not until 1962 that statistical sampling was the subject of an official pronouncement. Governmental auditors, however, began using statistical sampling several years before the 1955 AICPA publication.

The evolution of sampling in external and governmental auditing had a parallel development in internal auditing. Operational auditors observed the application of a variety of "acceptance sampling" procedures within engineering and production departments and gradually adopted such techniques into the audit process.

Sampling involves the examination of less than an entire set of data in order to express a conclusion about that entire set of data. Risks always exist that a sample drawn may not be representative of the entire data set and could lead to inappropriate conclusions. If these sample risks are not measured by using the laws of probability — due to the design of the sampling plan, execution of the sampling procedure, or evaluation of the sample — then a nonstatistical application has been performed.

There are many occasions when internal auditors may take a nonstatistical sample intentionally. This subject is discussed more extensively later.

Statistical Sampling

Any basic statistics book is likely to include an example of how a manufacturer of light bulbs or some other product might test the acceptability of a production lot. The approach is called "acceptance sampling" and is a familiar technique in quality-control testing.

An Example of Acceptance Sampling from Quality Control

Assume that a producer of machinery parts typically produces a certain part with an average diameter of 2.5 inches. When the manufacturing process becomes faulty in some manner, the average diameter will tend to vary either above or below the desired diameter. By periodically sampling from the manufactured parts, quality control can detect flaws in production on a timely basis. The sample size to be drawn depends upon how certain the quality control department wants to be that flaws will be identified if present. Assume that the department wants to be 90 percent certain that if the diameter is 2.49 inches or less, or 2.501 inches or more, such variations will be detected. At the same time, the department does not want to be under the misconception that flaws exist when none are present. Therefore, it wants to be 90 percent certain that when the sample indicates a flaw, such a flaw will actually be present.

Sample size is essentially computed by balancing two concerns — avoiding "false alarms," and at the same time detecting "real problems." Suppose the appropriate sample size based on statistical theory for the above acceptance decision is nine. Nine items would be selected at random, measured, and evaluated with the following decision rule:

If the average diameter of the sample is less than 2.4994555 inches or greater than 2.5005445 inches, do not accept the production process.

Therefore, in this example a 90 percent probability exists that a flaw is present in the production process if the acceptance criteria for the nine items are not met.

The Advantages of a Statistical Approach

A statistical sampling approach quantifies sampling risk. In the acceptance sampling example, both the risk of false alarms and the risk of nondetection were quantified. Moreover, a statistical sample provides assistance to an auditor in designing an efficient sample, measuring the sufficiency of evidence, evaluating sample size, directing sample selection, and evaluating findings, including the quantification of sampling risk. A statistical sample is an objective, verifiable technique for gathering audit evidence. Furthermore, due to the wide availability of software that calculates statistical sample sizes and aids in evaluating "acceptance regions," the formulas that underlie this type of problem rarely need to be calculated manually by auditors in the field.

The Influence of Audit Objectives upon Sampling Approaches

Numerous approaches may be taken to statistical sampling. The choice among alternative approaches should be directed by the audit objective.

Attributes Sampling. Attribute techniques focus on the existence of some attribute on a dichotomous (two-way) scale. Attributes sampling is particularly well suited to the audit objective of testing compliance with internal control. For example, if the attribute of interest is whether some item is properly authorized, the two-way scale would be *yes* or *no*.

This approach will result in a conclusion regarding the rate of error occurrence in the population. The error commonly involves a deviation from designed controls and exists whenever an occurrence of noncompliance is found, even if no dollar error or asset loss results. All deviations are given equal weight no matter what the size of the transaction containing the error or the size of an error resulting from a deviation.

Controls over purchasing, inventory pricing, and payroll are just a few of the areas in which attribute techniques are commonly applied.

Discovery Sampling. Discovery sampling is a subset of attribute techniques. If an auditor is concerned that a critical control is operating and expects very low noncompliance, a discovery sampling approach may be effective. This technique quantifies the sample size that, if it contained one error, would demonstrate that the noncompliance rate was too high.

To apply discovery sampling, the auditor should expect no noncompliance. Discovery sampling is frequently applied to compliance test work where a control system is expected to be very effective. This technique is also applied to fraud detection engagements. Obviously, fraud is an infrequent occurrence which constitutes a critical problem. The auditor would want assurance that if fraud occurred at a particular level, one incidence would be observed in the selected sample.

Sequential Sampling. One means of improving the efficiency of sampling is to apply sequential sampling, often referred to as "stop-or-go sampling." If a low population deviation rate (i.e., low noncompliance) is expected, sequential sampling will result in a minimum sample size.

A sample may be drawn with any number of stages, with each stage after the initial one being dependent on the outcome of the prior stage. For example, if the first group of sampling units resulted in no deviations, that group alone may be sufficient to support the strength of controls, whereas some deviations may require that a second group be examined before a sufficient basis is available to support the effectiveness of controls.

After each group, an assessment is made as to whether the internal auditor should "stop or go." If the population's compliance deviation rate is high, a sequential approach would result in a larger sample size than a typical fixed sampling plan. In contrast, the sequential approach will yield a smaller sample in the presence of a low deviation rate.

Variables Sampling. If, instead of simple occurrence, the auditor wants to assess a monetary amount or any measure of quantity, a variables sampling approach is required. The auditor may want to estimate the dollar amount of transactions that contain deviations from prescribed controls. To answer this audit objective, variables sampling techniques would be appropriate. Common applications of variables sampling include the testing of recorded receivables, inventory, and fixed assets.

Dollar Unit Sampling or Sampling with Probability Proportional to Size (PPS). If an auditor is only concerned about overstatements, dollar unit sampling or sampling with probability proportional to size can be more efficient in meeting the audit objective than a variables sampling plan. A probability-proportional-to-size (PPS) sample represents a hybrid method since it is based on attributes sampling theory, but expresses a conclusion as a dollar amount rather than an error rate.

Simplistically, each dollar is viewed as a sampling item and is either correct or incorrect (hence, a two-way scale). Then the dollar "attributes" of *correct* or *incorrect* are aggregated to draw a total dollar conclusion.

A smaller sample size is required for PPS than for a classical variables approach if no errors are expected. The PPS approach is simpler to apply, gives greater dollar coverage due to its emphasis on larger dollar amounts, and can be used at interim with more ease than a variables sampling approach. Areas in which PPS is commonly applied include receivables, loans, investments, and fixed asset additions.

Sampling Terminology and Concepts

As is the case with most technical auditing tools, sampling has its own jargon and set of fundamental concepts that must be mastered to understand how to apply sampling in an internal auditing context.

Population. The population is the account balance, class of transactions, or group of items of central interest about which an internal auditor wants to reach a conclusion. As an example, if an internal auditor wants to verify that competitive bids were obtained on all purchases exceeding $5,000, the population would be all such purchases. Obviously, identification of the population of interest will be directed by the auditor's objectives, and, in turn, will direct the auditor in identifying the appropriate sample.

Sample. In large entities, an examination of the entire population of purchases exceeding $5,000 is likely to be impractical. Therefore, the auditor will draw a portion of the population for examination, and this portion is referred to as a sample. In effect, any subset of a larger group of transactions, dollars, or other items of interest can be viewed as a sample of that population.

Representativeness. Since the intent is to examine the sample for the purpose of drawing inferences to the larger population, it is imperative that the internal auditor obtain a representative sample. This means that the sample has characteristics similar to those of the population and is therefore capable of representing that larger population's balance, error rate, or similar attribute of interest. Obviously, the representativeness of a sample is critical to drawing accurate conclusions about the larger population.

Assume that the auditor wanted to estimate the recorded inventory balance by taking the quantity of units observed and multiplying that quantity by the average inventory value per unit. To obtain an estimate of the latter, a sample of inventory units was drawn. If the sample drawn was from Warehouse A, and the entity had four warehouses, of which Warehouse A was known to store lower-valued units, the internal auditor would not have drawn a sample that was representative of all inventory stored in the four warehouses. In fact, if he or she made an estimate of the inventory value per unit, it would be expected to be an understatement of the actual average value of the population.

Sampling Unit. Just as the representativeness of a sample is important, the selection of the sampling unit is critical to the effective use of sampling. The term sampling unit refers to that item which is actually selected for examination. The selection of the sampling unit should be directed by (1) the objective of an audit test, (2) the correspondence of the sampling unit to the population units, and (3) the practicality of obtaining and evaluating the items sampled.

To demonstrate the importance of an audit test's objective, consider the appropriate sampling unit for determining whether all sales are recorded. One can assume that the population of interest is total sales. However, if a sampling unit of "recorded sales transactions" were used, it would not be capable of identifying unrecorded sales and would not address the audit objective. On the other hand, a sampling unit of "all shipping orders" could lead to the discovery of goods shipped but not recorded, indicating unrecorded revenue. Such a sampling unit could address the audit objective.

The question of the sampling unit's correspondence to the population units is a two-phased issue. First, will total shipping orders be likely to identify all unrecorded sales? In other words, do the sampling units relate to the population of interest (actual total sales in this example)? Assuming this correspondence of sampling units to the population of audit interest, the next question is whether the units from which the auditor intends to sample are complete.

For example, if an auditor samples from three filing cabinets which, according to the auditee, store all shipping orders for the relevant period, is there assurance that these orders in fact correspond to the population? Too often, employees have total access to filing cabinets, removing records for various purposes without keeping track of which documents are filed and which are pulled. The inevitable result is lost documents. Preferably, no original documents would be permitted to leave the files; instead, copies should be made. As a minimum, a log system should be established, whereby files checked out are logged and responsibility for their return is formally documented.

To provide assurance that the population from which the sample is to be drawn is the desired population, the auditor should test the files' completeness; this would be required as a prerequisite to determining the sampling unit's definition. Often, samples are drawn from lists such as journals or subsidiary ledgers; in such settings, completeness requires footing and reconciliation procedures.

The final concern is whether the shipping orders of interest are obtainable, at reasonable cost, to facilitate the sampling process. If an auditee had numerous geographically dispersed shipping points, each of which retained shipping documents, the cost to accumulate these documents for sampling could be prohibitive, suggesting the preferability of some other sampling unit. For example, as an alternative approach to identifying unrecorded sales, customers' orders might be compared to recorded sales, and discrepancies could be followed through to shipping documentation. If customers' orders were centrally maintained, this alternative could be preferable in cost/benefit terms.

Sampling Plan. The identification of a sampling unit is one component of developing a sampling plan. The plan should quantify the number of units to be drawn as a sample, specify the technique by which the sampling units will be drawn, and define the risk level provided for by the design of the sampling application. The audit objective of the sampling should be documented, as well as the intended type of evaluation to be performed on the sample. In other words, the following items should be documented:

- The population definition.
- Sampling unit specification.
- The nature of the errors to be identified.
- The method of selection.
- Sampling risk.
- The sample size.
- Both the evaluation and the interpretation of sample results that constitute the sample process.

Exhibit 14-1 summarizes these components and outlines the earlier acceptance sampling example involving the detection of flaws in a production process to depict the key components of that sampling plan. How the population is to be sampled is the focus of any sampling plan.

Exhibit 14-1
Components of a Sampling Plan

COMPONENTS	SAMPLING PLAN FOR QUALITY CONTROL EXAMPLE
Population definition	All machinery parts produced
Sampling unit specification	Each machinery part
Nature of the errors to be identified	Is diameter other than the desired 2.5 inches?
Method of selection	Random
Sampling risk	10 percent (90 percent confidence of detecting unacceptable variations)
Sample size	9
Evaluation phase	Compare to acceptable region from 2.4994555 to 2.5005445
Interpretation of sample results	Reject if outside acceptable region

Random Samples. Typically, the greatest assurance of a representative sample is gained by drawing what is known as a random sample. When every unit in a population has an equal chance of being sampled and every combination of sampling units has an equal probability of being chosen, the selection process is said to be random. Numerous approaches are commonly used in the selection of random samples.

Random Number Table. Numerous textbooks and reference manuals have tables of random numbers. An internal auditor can take such tables, arbitrarily select a starting point, and then establish a one-to-one correspondence of the random numbers to the sampling units. The internal auditors then draw the specified number of sampling units by moving down the columns of the random number table. An example of how documents can be tied to random numbers is to utilize the preprinted number of the shipping documents as the basis for choosing which documents are to be tested.

Assume that the shipping documents are numbered from one through 3,500. If the random numbers read from the random number table were 690021, 390861, and 253009, the auditor would note that only the last four digits of each number are relevant to this sampling plan. The valid sampling unit numbers are one through 3,500, meaning that the units selected, based on the three random numbers listed, would be #21, #861, and #3,009.

In lieu of a random number table, a computerized random number generator may be used. Such generators mechanize the process described for the use of tables.

Systematic Selection (Interval Sampling). Both a random number table and a random number generator require a one-to-one correspondence between sampling units and random numbers. However, when the documents of interest are not prenumbered, a systematic selection technique known as interval sampling can be used.

Interval sampling is systematic selection at certain intervals throughout the potential sampling units contained in the population.

If the shipping documents in this example were stored in filing cabinets, an interval sampling approach would be to draw a shipping order every 10 inches of the drawer's length.

Such an approach assumes (a) a random ordering of the shipping documents in the drawers, or an ordering that does not affect the attribute of the orders that is of interest to the auditor, (b) homogeneous width or storage space of each shipping order, and (c) the capability of translating the interval width to the desired sample size.

Such an interval sampling approach is frequently used due to its ease of application and is referred to as the taking of every "*i*th" sample. The "*i*th" in the example just described would be the "10th inch." Often the "*i*th interval" relates to the number of items, such as "every 100th" document. When applying interval sampling, the auditor takes a random start and then proceeds through the population systematically.

To enhance the likelihood that the sample drawn is effectively a random sample, multiple random starts can be used. For example, if an auditor initially planned a random start with an interval of every 100th unit, a shift to every 400th unit, with four random starts — passing through the population four different times — would decrease the risk that a nonrandom sample is selected.

As implied, the intent of an auditor who applies systematic selection is to obtain a sample that is likely to be representative of the population of interest. The intent is to draw a sample that will behave like a random sample. To assess whether this is the case, the auditor should gain assurance that the ordering of the items selected using interval sampling is independent of the attribute being tested.

For example, if the value of inventory were being estimated by sampling from suppliers' invoices that are filed alphabetically, the auditor would need to consider the possibility that the alphabetic order of suppliers was related to the value of inventory. Obviously, inquiry procedures and an understanding of the types of suppliers and inventories carried would be essential to such an evaluation. If inventory was fairly homogeneous in nature and value, and if prices were considered to be competitive across suppliers, an "ith" sample would most likely produce a sample that was essentially random.

Sometimes systematic sampling can be facilitated by randomizing the population. For example, if a population is contained on a computer tape, it might be randomized and then sampled through an interval sampling plan.

Stratified Sampling. A stratified sampling plan refers to a process whereby a population is broken into subpopulations called strata. The objective of defining strata is to minimize the variability of population units within a particular stratum, while maximizing the variability across strata. This approach permits the selection of a smaller sample as a basis for drawing the same type of inference to the population as would be possible from an unstratified sample. The strata may be defined by dollar size, control system attributes, or other aspects of the population that are expected to be relevant.

Often the auditor will want to sample items based on relative dollar value. Rather than designing a sample that gives each unit in a population an equal probability of selection, the auditor might specify that higher dollar values are to have a higher probability of selection than lower dollar values. The rationale for such an approach is to increase the audit coverage over recorded dollar balances. Stratified sampling is frequently utilized, with strata specified from which sampling units are drawn. For example, the strata could be units representing sales less than $5,000, units representing sales from $5,000 to $20,000, and units representing sales greater than $20,000. Frequently auditors will sample 100 percent of sales for high dollar amounts. Hence, 100 percent of sales greater than $50,000 might be audited, with sales from $20,000 to $50,000 forming the top stratum to be sampled.

Essentially, dollar unit sampling (i.e., sampling proportionate to size) serves a purpose similar to stratified sampling based on dollars. Both intend to get greater dollar coverage from the sample drawn.

Stratification does not have to be based upon dollar values. For example, a change in a control system could be the basis for stratifying the population for compliance testing: pre- and post-change in controls. Strata are frequently defined based on the likelihood of error, whereby an auditor is able to sample more units from those strata expected to contain a greater amount of error. Whenever a population is subcategorized for sampling, no matter what the basis is for such a division, stratified sampling is said to be in use.

Sample Size. This term is self-explanatory: how many sampling units are required to enable the auditor to draw meaningful inferences to the population? Certain attributes of a population influence the sample size requirements.

The sample size increases for larger population sizes. However, this increase is not proportional, and once the population reaches 5,000 units, little effect on sample size is observed. To demonstrate the sample size variation in relation to changes in population size: under certain conditions, if all other factors are held constant, a population of 50 would require a 33-unit sample, a population of 500 would require 78, a population of 1,000 would require 85, and a 55,000 to 100,000-unit population would require a 93-unit sample. Clearly, for large populations, the *size effect* of the population upon sample size is negligible.

In contrast, the *variability of the population* can have a substantial effect on required sample sizes. Variability is frequently defined as the standard deviation of a population. Recall from your basic statistics courses that standard deviation is computed by:

- Taking the difference of each item in the population from the average value of the population.
- Squaring that difference.
- Adding the squared values together.
- Taking their average.
- Then taking the square root of that amount.

To illustrate the calculation, assume the population contained only three values: 2, 6, and 13. The average value would be 2 plus 6 plus 13 or 21, divided by 3, yielding a mean estimate of 7. The difference from the mean would be -5(2-7), -1(6-7), and 6(13-7). The sum of squared differences would be 25 plus 1 plus 36 or 62; the average would be 20.7, yielding a square root of 4.5.

As the standard deviation increases, the required sample size increases. Consider variables sampling, in particular. Imagine the variability in inventory values which commonly exists across product lines and its effect on the accuracy in estimating average inventory value from a small sample. A range of $1 to $2,000 or even $20,000 may be common. Given such high variation, the sample size to produce reasonably accurate mean estimates would be very large; therefore, auditors typically use stratification as a means of reducing the effect of population variability on sample size.

As a general rule of thumb, *any change in a population's variability affects the sample size by the square of the relative change.* For example, if the above standard deviation of 4.5 were doubled to 9.0, the required sample size would be four times that required for the standard deviation of 4.5. It should be obvious that for unstratified samples, the implied sample size would frequently be cost prohibitive.

More generally, whether dealing with variables or attributes sampling, the auditor can expect that the more widespread the values in the population, the larger the sample needs to be to obtain a good representation of those values.

Required sample sizes increase as an auditor wants to make more *precise* estimates. Similarly, as an auditor wants to form more *reliable* estimates, the required sample sizes increase. The technical meanings of both precision and reliability are developed later in this chapter; however, the intuitive meanings of each are *accuracy* and *confidence,* respectively. The more accurate an estimate, the more precise. The more reliable an estimate, the greater confidence one can have in its accuracy.

Mean-per-Unit Estimation. The variability of the population is likely to be most troublesome in mean-per-unit estimation. This sampling approach merely estimates the mean value per audited unit of the sample and multiplies by the number of units in the population to estimate the total population value. The formula for estimating sample size follows:

$$n = \left(\frac{U_r \times \sigma_x \times N}{A} \right)^2$$

where   n   =   sample size

   U_r =   reliability factor

   σ_x =   estimated standard deviation of the population

   N   =   population size

   A   =   desired precision

These terms will be defined later in this chapter. However, the formula clearly depicts the idea that as standard deviation (σ_x) increases, sample size increases.

Difference Approach. To decrease the effects of variability, auditors have developed a difference approach. "Difference" refers to the result of comparing recorded book values to audited values; any time they are not identical, a nonzero difference has been observed. When they are identical, the difference has a value of zero. Generally, differences are expected to have less variability than the original set of population book values. For example, a population of inventory could easily contain values ranging from $1 to $20,000, whereas errors or "differences" in recorded balances may only range from $0 to $2,000, with many of them zero. The mean-per-unit technique is applied to the observed average difference to extrapolate the expected difference in the recorded value of inventory and the audited value.

This technique requires (1) that the book value per unit be known, (2) that total book value be known, (3) that the total number of items in the population be known, and (4) that a sufficient number of differences occurs to compute a reliable sample estimate. Although different auditors establish various floors, we recommend a minimum of 20 nonzero differences to apply the difference approach. This obviously has an effect on sample size. If an auditor expected that only 30 percent of the population would have differences between audited and book values, yet a total of 30 differences was needed for estimation, the auditor would have to draw a sample size of at least 100.

Ratio Approach. A similar approach to reducing the effect of population variability on sample size is referred to as the ratio approach. In this technique, the auditor calculates the ratio of the sum of all audited amounts over the sum of all recorded amounts and then multiplies this ratio times the total recorded amount for the population.

As with the difference approach, the variability of the ratio amounts is expected to be far less than the variability of items within the population. The same basic information is required to apply the ratio approach that is essential for applying the difference approach: book value per unit, book value in total, number of units in the population, and a sufficient number of ratios that vary from a 1-to-1 ratio. Note that these approaches do not change the sampling units of the population; they merely change the sampling distribution from which estimates of the population are to be made. Exhibit 14-2 provides examples of a mean-per-unit extension and an application of the ratio approach.

Exhibit 14-2
Examples of Mean-per-Unit Extension
and the Application of the Ratio Approach

Given:

Total book value of a population	$1,260,000
Average book value in the sample	$210
Average audited value in the sample	$224
Population size	6,000
Sample size	200

What is the mean estimate of the total population value:

- according to the simple extension method?

  $224 × 6,000 = $1,344,000

- according to the ratio statistical method?

  $\dfrac{\$448,000}{\$420,000} \times \$1,260,000 = \underline{\$1,344,004}$

Note: Since $224 is the average audited value and since averages are computed as the sum divided by the number of items added, the sum must have been $224 times 200 or $448,000. The same logic translates the $210 to $420,000. However, the use of $224/$210 as the ratio would produce identical results.

In choosing between the difference approach and the ratio approach, the auditor should consider whether he or she expects errors to vary by the size of the individual sampling unit. If the difference between the audited value and book value is expected to vary in proportion to size, the ratio approach is preferred. If homogeneous error amounts are expected, regardless of the magnitude of the value being estimated, the difference approach would be preferred.

The Pilot Sample. Drawing a pilot or preliminary sample is a popular means of anticipating the number of differences, the tendency of such differences to vary with the sampling unit, and the standard deviation or variability of the sample. Any initial sample of units from a population is termed a pilot sample. Generally, its size ranges from 30 to 50 sampling units. If properly planned, a pilot sample can be evaluated with the remaining sample in drawing inferences to a population.

In lieu of a pilot sample, it is often possible to rely on past years' audit work or experience with the auditee's operations as a basis for estimating standard deviation.

Error Rates. Rather than focusing on the standard deviation of a population, attributes sampling focuses on error rates. The auditor has to assess the error rate expected to be found in the population. This assessment is referred to as the expected population error rate, the expected deviation rate, or the expected rate of occurrence. Just as a higher standard deviation increases sample sizes in variables sampling, a higher expected population error rate increases the required sample size in compliance testing. To illustrate the effects on sample size: if all other factors are held constant, an expected population error rate of 1 percent would yield a sample size of 93, while an expected rate of 3 percent would require a sample of 361.

Precision. Precision refers to the accuracy with which one has generated sample estimates. Desired precision is often termed the desired allowance for sampling risk. For example, if the auditor were estimating recorded inventory with an expected balance of $1,000,000, he or she may desire a precision of $200,000 in the estimation process. This would imply that it was deemed likely that the true value of the inventory would not exceed or be less than the sample's estimate by $200,000. The tighter the desired precision, the higher the required sample size. Specifically, the sample size will increase by the square of the relative change in precision: the sample would increase by 16 times (or 4^2) if the desired precision were reduced to one-fourth of its original size.

When shifting from variables sampling to attributes sampling, precision is measured in percentage rather than dollar terms but is still referred to as "tolerable error."

In planning a sampling application, precision can be viewed as an uncertainty or risk assessment which should tie into the auditor's evaluation of materiality. In a compliance test mode, the auditor needs to consider the risk of incorrectly accepting a control system as effective when, in fact, it is ineffective.

Distinct from *desired precision* is the term *achieved precision.* The former connotes planning, while the latter refers to the evaluation stage of a sampling application. Precision is quantified in the evaluation phase — typically as an interval or acceptable range around the sample mean or as an upper error limit on the sample's error estimate. If the interval includes recorded book values or if the upper error limit is deemed to be tolerable, then the recorded values are accepted as reasonable or the control is deemed to be operating effectively.

Tolerable Error. The tolerable error rate is defined as the maximum rate of deviation that auditors would accept and still assess controls to be effective. Generally, a strong control system would be expected if the tolerable error rate were 2 percent to 5 percent. A reasonable control system would be expected if the tolerable error rate were 6 percent to 10 percent. At times, a control system may be deemed acceptable with a tolerable error rate of 11 percent to 20 percent, but it would be rare to deem a control system to be acceptable if the error rate exceeded 20 percent. Of course, different circumstances may call for tighter or looser tolerable error rates, depending upon the risks involved. When considering which rate is acceptable, auditors should keep in mind that a deviation from control does not constitute an error in recorded dollar amounts or any type of asset loss. For example, a supervisor may have failed to initial a purchase order which he reviewed and found to be correct. The noncompliance with the initialing procedure would not have resulted in any error or loss, though it would clearly be a deviation from prescribed controls.

Note that if you are willing to tolerate more error, the sample size required for drawing inferences diminishes. For example, under certain conditions, with all other factors held constant, a 2 percent tolerable error rate would require a sample size of 149, whereas a tolerable error rate of 10 percent would require a sample size of only 29.

Upper-limit Approach. In compliance testing, the auditor typically uses an upper-limit approach, meaning that the sole concern is whether the estimated compliance deviation rate is understated. In evaluating a sample, the number of observed deviations is divided by the sample size; this computes the deviation rate in the sample. This rate is an estimate of the population rate. If this actual error rate does not exceed the upper-limit rate, the sample is acceptable as support for the effectiveness of the control(s) being tested.

However, to draw conclusions regarding a compliance test, the qualitative nature of deviations also should be reviewed. Patterns, as well as clues of errors, irregularities, competency problems, or errors likely to result in further errors in related account areas, will all require follow-up to ensure that the population deviation rate implied from the sampling techniques is reasonably accurate.

Dollar Precision Measures. The dollar precision measures are likely to vary across account areas, as they are tied to the dollar amounts in particular account balances and/or the dollar transactions passing through the accounts.

As an example of an internal auditor's interest in determining dollar precision, assume that he or she first tested compliance with sales commissions and discovered a number of errors, to the point that the error rate was deemed to be unacceptable. Further assume that the internal auditor wants to estimate the audited value of commissions for comparison to the recorded book value, as a basis for reporting the effect of the discovered flaws in the control system.

In this setting, the internal auditor would consider what would constitute an acceptable precision level for the estimate of audited value. Perhaps 5 percent of recorded value is the desired precision, leading to a precision level of 5 percent times $3,000,000, or $150,000. Hence, the audit sample's mean estimate of $3,500,000 would have precision of $150,000. This would imply an interval of $3,350,000 to $3,650,000 for the sample estimate of sales commissions. Since the recorded value was $3,000,000, the audited value indicates that the book value was understated: sales commissions were likely to be higher than recorded, by at least $350,000 (that lower dollar limit on the range or interval formed around the sample's mean estimate) and by as much as $650,000 (based on the upper limit of the interval).

Confidence Levels and Reliability. A confidence level may be illustrated by an internal auditor drawing repeated samples from a particular population. Assume the auditor drew 800 different samples from the 100,000 sales commission transactions that are recorded within a year's time. If these 800 samples were plotted on a graph, 95 percent of the samples' interval estimates could be expected to contain the true commission value.

Reliability is the complement of risk. For example, if a 5 percent sampling risk is desired, reliability would be specified as one minus 5 percent, or 95 percent. Reliability is often referred to as the *confidence level.* With all other factors held equal, a higher level of confidence requires a larger sample size. The confidence level quantifies the likelihood that the sample interval estimated will contain the true population value of interest. For example, the interval estimate around sales commissions was $3,350,000 to $3,650,000; if that range were formed at a 95 percent level of confidence, it would mean that only a 5 percent risk existed that the actual sales commission amount would lie outside this interval. The auditor can rely, with 95 percent confidence, that the true population value lies between the upper and lower precision limits.

Confidence Interval. This interval or range is referred to as the confidence interval, since its width jointly reflects precision and confidence. For example, if the internal auditor wanted to have 99 percent confidence that the true population value would lie within the confidence interval, less precision would have to be accepted, and a wider confidence interval would result. On the other hand, if an 80 percent confidence level were deemed to be acceptable, precision could be improved, and a narrow confidence interval could be formulated.

A confidence interval is formed by multiplying a reliability factor, based on an underlying sampling distribution, by the standard deviation of the estimate adjusted for sample size, and then adding it to and subtracting it from the sample estimate. If a normal distribution is assumed, the internal auditor is stating that a plot of sample mean values would tend toward a symmetric curve, as follows:

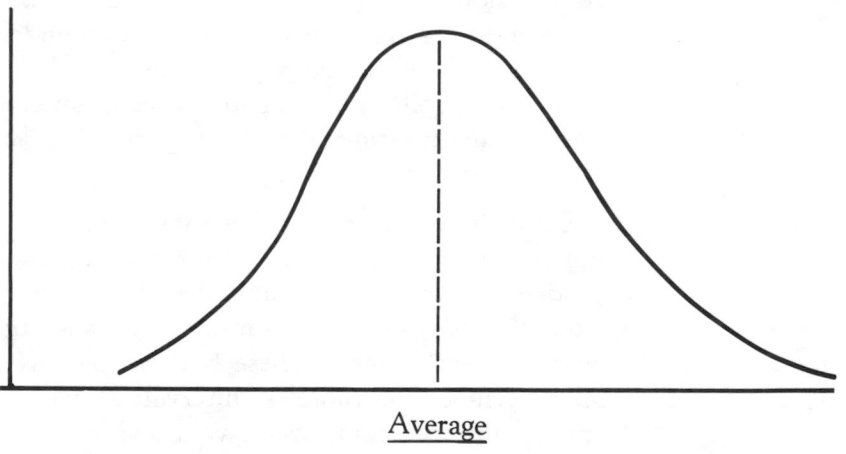

Average

A 95 percent confidence level results in a 1.96 reliability factor, based on the normal distribution. Hence, any sample estimate's standard deviation divided by the square root of the sample size would be multiplied by 1.96 to generate a confidence interval which would be interpreted as above. If the standard deviation for the sample estimate of sales commissions divided by the square root of the sample size were $765,306, the confidence interval described earlier would result: $3,500,000 ± (1.96 x $765,306). When rounded, this interval would range from $3,350,000 to $3,650,000.

The 1.96 reliability factor is commonly referred to as a t- or z-statistic, depending on how large the sample is. Smaller samples are said to have t-values which will assume values greater than 1.96 to reach 95 percent confidence. Larger samples are said to have z-values.

Consistent with the earlier discussion of the width of a confidence interval given varied levels of confidence, the t- or z-statistics drop as the confidence level is lowered. At a 90 percent level, the z-statistic is 1.645.

Bounds. For dollar unit (or PPS) sampling, bounds are formed which serve a purpose similar to that of confidence limits. Upper and lower bounds are derived by multiplying the upper precision limit (in percentage terms) and the total population value, weighted by the average percent of error for population items that contain an error.

For example, if the upper precision limit is set at 2 percent for a population valued at $3,500,000, and the maximum percentages of errors expected are 20 percent overstatement errors and 40 percent understatement errors, the following calculations would produce the applicable bounds:

Upper Error Bound = $3,500,000 × 2% × .20 = $14,000
Lower Error Bound = $3,500,000 × 2% × .40 = $28,000

Obviously, the auditor's assessment of percent of error (or tainting) is a critical determinant of the bounds. A conservative approach which is common in field use of dollar unit sampling is to assume 100 percent error for both overstatements and understatements, thereby permitting the results to be driven by the upper precision limit.

Once a sample is drawn, error bounds can be calculated based on actual errors found. Software is available for PPS evaluation.

Risk. Risk assumes meaning by tying uncertainty measures in dollars and error rate terms to plausible outcomes of testing. The possible outcomes of compliance and substantive testing can be described as depicted in Exhibit 14-3. The alpha risks (incorrect rejection) primarily relate to audit efficiency, while beta risks (incorrect acceptance) focus on audit effectiveness. It is generally accepted that beta risk is more critical to the auditor, and it tends to drive sample size.

Hypothesis Testing. Whenever sampling is directed at a question such as, "Is an account materially misstated?" the auditor is said to be hypothesis testing. This approach means that the auditor will accept an amount if it is reasonably correct. The risk of incorrect acceptance (beta) can be specified to arrive at a sample size. The greater the accepted risk, the smaller the required sample size. For example: under certain conditions, with all other factors remaining the same, a 5 percent risk would result in a sample size of 200, whereas a 10 percent risk would require 144 sampling units.

Exhibit 14-3
Possible Outcomes of Testing

VARIABLE	Test results indicate that population is reasonably stated	Test results indicate that population is not reasonably stated	CONSEQUENCE OF ERRORS
Population is reasonably stated	Accept population: correct decision	Type I error: incorrect rejection α risk (alpha)	Unnecessary testing
Population is not reasonably stated	Type II error: incorrect acceptance β risk (beta)	Reject population: correct decision	Misstated amounts

ATTRIBUTE	Test results indicate that control system is operating effectively	Test results indicate that control system is not operating effectively	
Control system is operating effectively	Deem controls to be effective: correct decision	Type I error: incorrect rejection α risk (alpha)	Overinvestment in controls or underreliance on controls
Control system is not operating effectively	Type II error: incorrect acceptance β risk (beta)	Deem controls not to be effective: correct decision	Insufficient control operations or inappropriate reliance on controls

The Interrelationships of Precision, Reliability, Risk, and Sample Size

A summary of how the various terms and concepts introduced in this chapter interrelate is provided in Exhibit 14-4. Generally, trade-offs will arise. If an auditor wants to be more precise, the cost is less confidence in estimation. On the other hand, a more reliable measure will result in less precision (all other factors remaining equal). Since risk is the complement of reliability, it moves inversely with confidence.

Exhibit 14-4
The Interrelationship of Statistical
Terms and Sample Size

As population size increases	Sample size increases
	But not proportionately as no ef-fect is discernible when popula-tion exceeds 5,000 units
As population variability increases	Sample size increases
	Increases by the square of the rel-ative change in variability
As expected error rate increases	Sample size increases
As desired precision (i.e., accu-racy) is tightened	Sample size increases
	Increases by the square of the rel-ative change in precision
As expected error gets closer to tolerable error	Sample size increases
As tolerable error increases	Sample size decreases
As reliability (i.e., confidence level) increases	Sample size increases

---

Examples of Sampling Applications

It is difficult to understand sampling applications without reviewing some examples, so we will now proceed with a demonstration of each of the major sampling alternatives described. These examples help clarify how to formalize, execute, and evaluate a sampling plan and its results.

Discovery Sampling

As stated earlier, the objective of discovery sampling is to select a sample which will have a specified probability of containing at least one occurrence of an attribute within the population, given that it is expected to occur at a certain rate. Most often, the attribute of interest in a discovery sampling application is compliance with internal controls, or the occurrence of an irregularity or fraud.

Assume that an evaluation of controls has revealed weaknesses that make it possible for a foreman to set up fictitious employees on the payroll. While fraud is not suspected, the auditor wants to gain statistical assurance that his or her assessment of risk is appropriate.

Audit Objective. The objective is to determine whether fictitious employees have been added to the payroll.

Sampling Plan. In accordance with the outline presented in Exhibit 14-1, the sampling plan can be summarized as follows:

- Population Definition: All employees on the payroll during the past year.
- Sampling Unit: Each employee on the payroll during the past year.
- Nature of Errors to Be Identified: Entering of fictitious employees.
- Method of Selection: Random.
- Sampling Risk: 5 percent, or 95 percent confidence level.
- Sample Size: 300 (see details that follow).
- Evaluation Phase: No fictitious employees were identified.
- Interpretation of Sample Results: Fraud is not present at the critical rate of occurrence, at a 95 percent level of confidence.

Sampling Unit. If fictitious employees are on the payroll, they could be identified by sampling from all employees on the payroll. Since foremen can be expected to vary fraudulent practices when existent, no reason is apparent for sampling in other than a random manner. Hence, each employee on the books at some time during the past year seems to be a reasonable sampling unit. Note that this sampling unit will result in no assurance that all employees are on the books (although this risk is likely to be controlled by employees' complaints if they did not receive appropriate compensation).

Sample Size Determination. The sample size is a function of population size, the rate of occurrence deemed to be critical, and the auditor's desired level of confidence that at least one occurrence of the possible fraud will be detected if fraud at the critical level is present. Tables are widely available for determining sample size; they typically appear in the following format:

9,500 Employees Sample Size	Probability for Rate of Occurrence		
	.5%	1%	2%
300	78	95	99+
400	87	98	99+

This table excerpt indicates that for the specified population size, if the auditor would consider a 1 percent occurrence rate (i.e., the presence of 95 fictitious employees) to be material, and wants to be 95 percent confident that if fraud were occurring with 1 percent of employees, it would be revealed through one occurrence in the sample, then the required sample size would be 300. As the table excerpt clearly shows, sample size increases with the desired level of confidence.

Sample Selection. Since each employee has an employee number, ranging from 1,000 to 15,500, the auditor decides to utilize a random number generator to draw the desired sample of 300. The range of numbers exceeds population size because of terminations of employees in prior periods. The auditor has a list of employee numbers not in use during the past period and draws a sample of 300 numbers currently in use.

Interpretation of Findings. No fictitious employees were identified, meaning that the auditor's expectations of no fraud were appropriate at a 95 percent level of confidence. Had only one fictitious employee been detected, the interpretation would have been that fraud was occurring at or above the critical rate of occurrence, i.e., 1 percent or more.

Appropriate Inferences. Note that the auditor cannot state that "no fraud is present." All statistical inferences tend to be ranges at specified levels of confidence. In this setting, fraud could exist at less than a 1 percent level, and a 5 percent risk still exists that fraud is present at a 1 percent or higher level.

Alternative Means of Responding to Findings. Assume that upon reviewing this sampling application, an audit supervisor questions the propriety of using employee numbers for selection. Since numbers are assigned as people are hired, risk is expected to vary across employee numbers. Little likelihood exists that fictitious employees have been on the books without detection for longer than a three-year period. This assessment is based in part on the fact that a discovery sampling application was performed three years ago, with clean results. Besides, greater opportunity for detecting such defalcations exists over longer time periods. After discussing this risk profile, the auditor decides that the relevant population is not 1,000 to 15,500 but instead ranges from 10,000 to 15,500. This range encompasses all new employees in the past three years, as well as all but 50 terminated employees during that same period. In other words, a feedback loop connects the reviewer's comments back to step one of the sampling plan: population definition.

The manager approved the redefined population, but also required the staff auditor to compare listings of terminated employees with employee numbers below 10,000 to those employee numbers receiving pay during the past period. The idea, of course, was to detect either reuse of such numbers to enter fictitious employees, or maintenance of terminated employees on the books beyond their proper final pay periods.

The redefinition of population size would have a relatively small effect on sample size. For example, even if the 10,000 to 15,500 range contained only 1,000 active employee numbers, the implied sample size would be 250. Given the probable higher frequency of employee numbers active in the past year, the sample size requirements are effectively the same. However, if the auditor's assessment that no risk is present in numbers below 10,000 — outside of the terminations which are being separately tested — is accurate, the new sampling plan is far more capable of detecting irregularities, should they exist.

Note that this revision reflects a reduction of nonsampling risk, rather than sampling risk. The former pertains to errors in auditing — expressing the audit objective, selecting the relevant population and sampling units, and appropriately recognizing deviations — while the latter relates to the sample's representativeness of the specified population.

Attributes Sampling

As described earlier, attributes sampling typically involves tests of the effectiveness of controls. For example, the internal auditor may want to assess whether the credit department is complying with required procedures. In particular, all customers requesting credit exceeding $1,000 are to be checked through a credit-rating agency before such sales are authorized.

Audit Objective. The objective is to determine whether the credit department is complying with the control procedure which requires a credit check for credit sales or receivable balances exceeding $1,000.

Sampling Plan. Again, using the outline from Exhibit 14-1:

- Population Definition: All credit sales or accounts receivable balances exceeding $1,000 over the past year. Note that the latter population encompasses the former.
- Sampling Unit Specification: All customers with balances exceeding $1,000 sometime during the year.
- Nature of Errors to Be Identified: All receivable balances exceeding $1,000 for which credit checks were not performed.

Note that this requires each sampling unit to be tied to formal documentation of credit-check results.

- Method of Selection: Random. Note that an if/then sort routine will be used on each computer tape that reports receivable balances over the past year in order to copy those accounts exceeding $1,000. From the auditor's computer tape thus generated, it will be a simple matter to select balances for testing.
- Sampling Risk: 5 percent, or 95 percent confidence level.
- Sample Size: 300 (see details that follow).
- Evaluation Phase: Prior to sample selection, the auditor designed rules as to what constituted a compliance deviation. By applying such rules, five deviations were identified.
- Interpretation of Sample Results: For all attribute tests, the auditor looked for patterns in errors or other information of a qualitative nature which might suggest a problem. Based on the observed deviations in this example, the auditor concluded that the credit department is complying with the prescribed procedure.

Sampling Unit. Sampling from receivables balances is sufficient since no credit extended would be omitted from all monthly statements mailed to a customer. While it would theoretically be possible for a customer to have a credit balance and purchase more than $1,000 worth of goods, resulting in a receivable balance of less than $1,000, this is unlikely; its omission from the population is not deemed to be problematic.

Cost/benefit considerations make the receivable balances a far more effective sampling unit than sales transactions. Innumerable low-dollar sales could easily aggregate to credit exceeding $1,000. Yet many customers never reach such a credit balance. The risk of concern is most related to "owed balances," as distinct from sales transactions.

Sample Size Determination. Tables based on a binomial distribution are widely available for determining sample sizes for compliance testing. These tables focus upon population size, desired confidence level, the desired upper precision limit, and the estimated error rate for the populations. Assume that 30,000 customer balances exceeded $1,000 over the past year. Also assume that the auditor wants to be 95 percent certain that the true population error rate is not more than 4 percent. Furthermore, based on past years' testing of the credit department, the sample error rate is expected to be 2 percent. An excerpt of the typical tables' format follows:

| | Upper Precision Limit at Occurrence Rate of | | |
Sample Size	*0.0*	*2.0*	*4.0*
200	1.5	4.5	7.1
250	1.2	4.2	6.7
300	1.0	3.9	6.4

Given the expectation of 2 percent and the upper precision limit of 4 percent, a sample size of 300 would be drawn. (One could interpolate downward from 3.9 to 4.0 to yield a sample size between 250 and 300, but a conservative typical practice is to take the largest of the two sample sizes between which the specified upper precision limit lies.)

Sample Selection. Random selection is possible by using a random number generator. Generate 300 numbers from one to 30,000 and count through the tape. A less efficient approach would be the randomization of the computer tape itself through use of a utility program, and then applying systematic sampling to the newly generated computer tape by selecting every "*i*th" balance. Since the population is 30,000 and the sample size is 300, every 100th balance would be selected for testing.

In this setting, the auditor felt the scrambling of order was important, since controls could be related to the timing of purchases. For example, more sales occur during the holiday season, and controls might be differentially applied. An "*i*th" sample applied to the tape formed by sorting and copying from chronologically ordered tapes of the subsidiary ledger might not serve as an effective random sample. If the auditor wanted to increase the randomization even more, he or she could take three random starts through the file, using the "every 300th" sampling interval. Obviously, the more expedient and effective approach would be the application of a random number generator.

Interpretation of Findings. During the tests, five deviations were found. One of these deviations was contested by the auditee, because files showed that a credit check had been performed, in spite of the omission of the actual credit report from available documentation. However, since the auditor had specified deviations as *any* flaw in (1) performing the check or (2) having complete documentation of such a check on file, this "missing" report constituted a deviation.

The five deviations had no apparent connection. One has already been described. The other four approvals without checks were made by different authorized personnel within the credit department at different points in time throughout the year. The amounts involved in the deviations ranged from $1,000 to $2,000, suggesting that greater care seemed to have been taken with very large balances.

The same table used for planning is also applied for evaluation. The five deviations out of 300 sampling units results in an error rate of 1.7 percent. For a sample size of 300, the occurrence rate of less than 2.0 implies an upper precision limit of better than 3.9 percent. This result lies within the desired 4 percent range. The conclusion can be stated as follows: there is a 95 percent chance that the true error rate is 3.9 percent or less. Note that the true error rate is unknown, but only a 5 percent statistical risk exists that it exceeds 3.9 percent.

Appropriate Inferences. The sample results support the credit department's compliance with prescribed procedures for balances of $1,000 or more.

Alternative Means of Responding to Findings. Had the computed upper precision limit exceeded the desired limit, the sample size could be expanded. This would assume that the original sample was unrepresentative and that the testing of additional units would result in a sufficiently lower error rate, so that the combination of results would be acceptable. Typically this is not a cost-beneficial strategy, since the likelihood is that extended sampling will merely reconfirm what the auditor had already concluded.

The conclusion of noncompliance would constitute a deficiency finding which may have implications for other facets of the control system or accounting records. Of course, in this example, the observed deviations are within the acceptable range. Other than reviewing the deviations for qualitative patterns, no further work need be done.

Variables Sampling   As described earlier, variables sampling is the term applied to those sampling techniques which result in a measurement of the value of an account balance or an estimate of some other amount. As an example, suppose an auditor wants to estimate the dollar value of construction in progress on 1,000 homes.

Audit Objective. The objective is to assess the reasonableness of recorded construction in progress.

Sampling Plan. Components of the sampling plan, following Exhibit 14-1, include:

- Population Definition: The 1,000 homes in various stages of construction.
- Sampling Unit Specification: Each home being constructed.
- Nature of Errors to Be Identified: Misstatement of construction in progress.
- Method of Selection: Random.
- Sampling Risk: 10 percent, or 90 percent confidence level.
- Sample Size: 286 (see details that follow).
- Evaluation Phase: Project the sample's estimation of construction work in progress.
- Interpretation of Sample Results: Compare the sample projection to the recorded value and assess whether they are significantly different.

Sampling Unit. Each home that is part of the total recorded value of construction in progress is a sampling unit. Each home was assigned a number and then a random number table was utilized for selection.

Sample Size Determination. For this type of variables application, the formula is identical to that reported earlier in the chapter, when mean-per-unit estimation was described. Assuming a desired reliability of 90 percent; desired precision of \$247,500; and an estimated population standard deviation, based on a presample of 40 homes, of \$3,000, unrestricted random sampling with replacement would require a sample size of:

$$n = \left(\frac{(1.65 \times 3{,}000 \times 1{,}000)}{247{,}500}\right)^2 = 400$$

Note that sampling without replacement (i.e., no sampling unit could be selected more than once to derive a sample estimate) would result in a lower required sample size. When sample size exceeds 10 percent of the population, a finite correction factor which takes into account the finite population should be considered in determining sample size. The finite population correction factor can be estimated by:

$$\frac{n}{1 + \frac{n}{N}}$$

Therefore, the revised sample size would be:

$$\frac{400}{1 + \frac{400}{1000}} = 286$$

Sample Selection. Note how large the sample size is in mean-per-unit estimation. This is due largely to the magnitude of the standard deviation. Note also that this sample size might very well be reduced by stratifying the population based on percentage of completion. This could be particularly useful in gaining audit coverage of most of the dollars recorded in the construction-in-progress account.

Interpretation of Findings. Assume that the actual standard deviation is essentially the same as that estimated from the pilot sample of 40 homes. The sample's average value is computed to be $22,000; hence, the population projection is derived by multiplying this sample value by the number of homes (1,000). Thus, $22,000,000 is the estimated inventory value. The precision interval can be calculated as:

$$\frac{N \times U_r \times S_x}{\sqrt{n}}$$

utilizing the same symbols applied earlier in the chapter, or:

$$\frac{1,000 \times 1.65 \times 3,000}{\sqrt{286}} = \$291,176$$

Since the sample size exceeds 10 percent of the population, the finite correction factor (taking into account the finite population) is appropriate. This simply means that the amount computed above should be multiplied by:

$$\sqrt{\frac{N - n}{N}}$$

or

$$\sqrt{\frac{1,000 - 400}{1,000}} = .77$$

The result of these formulas is 291,176 times .77, or $224,205. Hence, the 90 percent confidence interval is $22,000,000 plus and minus $224,205, or a range from $21,775,795 to $22,224,205.

Appropriate Inferences. The recorded book value is $24,000,000, which obviously exceeds the confidence interval formed from the sample results. The appropriate inference would be that recorded construction in progress is overstated at a 90 percent confidence level. Note that if the recorded amount were available, difference or ratio estimation would be more efficient than the mean-per-unit approach.

Alternative Means of Responding to Findings. The auditor in such a setting should evaluate the likelihood that some errors were made in forming the sample estimate. The reliability of the mean-per-unit estimation method can be substantially affected by a population's skewness (i.e., the lack of symmetry around its mean or average value). Furthermore, the efficiency of the estimation method is poor whenever population items are of widely diverse sizes.

While the standard deviation is not excessive in this application, its effects on sample size could be diminished further through stratification of the population. One possible basis for stratification would be the percentage of completion of the homes. Software is available to compute sample sizes for stratified sampling, to allocate the sample to the various strata, and to formulate a confidence interval for the population. The objective of stratification is to reduce standard deviations within each stratum, thereby reducing the total required sample size. A reduction in required sample sizes can be anticipated from forming up to 20 strata; beyond 20 strata, the effects on sample size become minor.

Dollar Unit Sampling

As described earlier, dollar unit sampling applies attributes sampling to individual dollars to form quantitative estimates, such as those typically formulated by variables sampling. Dollar unit sampling is often applied in the accounts receivable. Assume that an auditee has 20,000 accounts receivable that total $5,600,000. The internal auditor wants to "circularize" receivables (described below).

Audit Objective. The objective is to assess whether recorded receivables are overstated.

Sampling Plan. Following the outline in Exhibit 14-1, sampling plan components include:

- Population Definition: All recorded receivables.
- Sampling Unit Specification: Each recorded balance's individual dollars constitute a sampling unit which, in turn, "hooks" a receivable balance for circularization. For this reason, a $30,000 balance has twice the likelihood of selection as a $15,000 balance.
- Nature of Errors to Be Identified: Any exceptions noted by customers will require follow-up, but overstatement of receivables is the primary concern.
- Method of Selection: A systematic selection procedure is typical in a dollar unit sample application.
- Sampling Risk: 5 percent, or 95 percent confidence level.
- Sample Size: 112 (see details that follow).
- Evaluation Phase: The upper error limit is $352,800.

- Interpretation of Sample Results: The maximum error limit acceptable to the auditor was $150,000; hence, the account balances are deemed to be materially overstated.

Sampling Unit. By definition, dollar unit sampling always uses individual dollar bills as the sampling unit. This means that neither zero balances nor negative balances have any chance of selection.

Sample Size Determination. The average sampling interval is calculated by dividing the upper error limit in dollars by the appropriate upper error limit factor. For instance, if the auditor uses a tolerable basic precision of $150,000, an error size limit assumption of 100 percent, and a desired confidence level of 95 percent, the required average sampling interval would be:

$$\frac{\$150,000}{3 \times 100\%} = \$50,000$$

This implies a sample size of $5,600,000 minus $50,000, or 112. As should be apparent, sample size for dollar unit sampling is a direct function of the number of dollars in the population.

Sample Selection. Exhibit 14-5 illustrates the selection technique. This exhibit lists the first 20 account balances on the auditee's records, with a cumulative running total along the side. Using the $50,000 sample interval, the cumulative balance is used to flag the dollar bills of interest — $50,000, then $100,000, then $150,000, then $200,000, and so on. That dollar bill identifies the account balances selected.

Interpretation of Findings. Assume two exceptions were noted. That would result in an upper error limit of 6.30, at 95 percent confidence, based on readily available tables. Hence, the population value of $5,600,000 multiplied by .063 produces a $352,800 upper error bound, if the two errors were 100 percent overstated (i.e., had 100 percent tainting). This upper bound would have to be compared to desired precision to reach a conclusion. For example, if the maximum allowable error is deemed to be $150,000, the population would not be accepted.

Appropriate Inferences. Note that dollar unit sampling provides an overstatement assessment and is most efficient in low error environments. It would be inappropriate to draw inferences to zero or credit balances in accounts receivable. Such balances would require testing through an alternative sampling approach.

Exhibit 14-5
Dollar Unit Sample Selection

Account Number	Dollar Amount of Account	Cumulative Balance	Selected Account
1	$30,000	$ 30,000	
2	18,000	48,000	
3	4,000	52,000	X
4	70,000	122,000	X
5	10,000	132,000	
6	1,200	133,200	
7	15,000	148,200	
8	40,000	188,200	X
9	20,000	208,200	X
10	5,000	213,200	
11	2,000	215,200	
12	17,000	232,200	
13	25,000	257,200	X
14	14,000	271,200	
15	8,000	279,200	
16	500	279,700	
17	32,000	311,700	X
18	12,000	323,700	
19	9,500	333,200	
20	25,000	358,200	X

Nonstatistical Sampling

A nonstatistical sampling approach may be selected for a variety of reasons. If it is used because a cost/benefit assessment has indicated that the expense of selection through a statistical approach is excessive, a common methodology is "haphazard" sampling. While the name is a bit unfortunate, possibly implying a careless sampling approach, it actually is intended to represent one fact: that no pattern exists in the selection process. The selection is done haphazardly in the hopes that it will result in a representative sample that effectively parallels a random sample. When such a plan is applied, auditors frequently will try to determine sample size and interpret findings through analogy to statistical sampling plans. This means that the variation in the population, acceptable sampling risk, tolerable error, and expected error would need to be considered in selecting a sample size. An auditor should consider the need to select a larger number of items than is specified in sampling tables if there is a risk that the sample is not representative.

The relationship between a nonstatistical sampling plan and a statistical approach may be spurious. This could be due to a haphazard sample yielding unrepresentative sample units or due to any similar flaw in the sampling approach. It is more likely to result from intent; in other words, *the auditor often selects nonstatistical sampling due to his or her knowledge of the population of interest.*

Rather than drawing a random sample, the auditor may choose to draw a so-called Bayesian sample. The term Bayesian means that statistical concepts are applied to integrate sampling evidence (statistical or nonstatistical) with individuals' judgments. These judgments typically relate to the decision maker's experience with the auditee or the type of transactions under review.

For example, the auditor may know that operations are highly seasonal, resulting in peak pressures on the accounting department during the months of May and June. He or she may assess that the key risk of error in capturing accounting information exists in those two months, and therefore the auditor may choose to sample primarily from May and June transactions. Smaller sample sizes make sense if an auditor has a means of drawing those items with the greatest likelihood of error based on prior knowledge of operations, controls, and recent events likely to affect error rates (such as turnover in key management positions).

Cost/Benefit Considerations

Statistical sampling frequently is cited as expensive because of the necessity of training auditors in statistical techniques, and because of the costs that may arise in designing and selecting sample items if documents are not maintained in an organized manner. However, with available statistical tables and computer software, little knowledge is needed by the auditor using statistical sampling that is not similarly required to perform an adequate nonstatistical sample. As previously discussed, the same factors are considered in both methods of sampling.

The cost of applying statistical sampling due to a lack of prenumbered documents, the nesting of sampling units of interest within some larger population of little if any relevance, or other problems linked to file organization is likely to be exaggerated by an auditor without field experience using sampling methodology. Numerous adaptive techniques can be applied, including interval sampling tied to "inches of file space," sampling from a larger population and discarding irrelevant items drawn, stratifying a population to reflect the organization of files, or redefining either the population or the sampling unit to facilitate an efficient sampling plan.

The shortcoming of a nonstatistical approach is its inability to objectively quantify sampling risk. Unknowingly, bias may be introduced in specifying sample size, selection approaches, or in evaluating the findings. Often, this problem of nonstatistical sampling is understated, just as practical problems with statistical sampling are overstated. The result is that a lower level of statistical sampling occurs in audit work than would be optimal if these problems were viewed more realistically.

It is particularly important that the auditor begin to view Bayesian and statistical sampling as compatible techniques. A directed sample could merely mean defining a population that is expected to have a higher incidence of error and then statistically sampling from that population. In the example of the seasonal operations, this would mean that the population of interest could be defined as "all transactions booked in May and June."

Similarly, judgment may suggest the wisdom of a 100 percent audit of transactions exceeding a given dollar amount and be reflected in a stratified sampling plan with ease. Judgment does not necessarily dictate a nonstatistical approach, despite misconceptions to the contrary. Creative statistical planning can ensure that judgment and experience are integrated with statistical theory that quantifies sampling risk.

Directed Sampling

Auditors frequently are concerned about specific questions or problems where statistical sampling of an entire population, as discussed in this chapter, is not appropriate. Often they may use a method called "directed sampling," which is discussed in the next chapter.

Appendix

STATISTICAL TABLES

To assist you in applying the various statistical procedures introduced in this chapter, a set of tables has been compiled with a brief example of how each table can be used in planning or evaluating a statistical sample. The tables presented include:

1. Exhibit 14-A: Excerpts from a Table of Random Numbers
2. Exhibit 14-B: Cumulative Probabilities of the Standard Normal Distribution
3. Exhibit 14-C: Factors Required to Achieve Given Confidence Levels
4. Exhibits 14-D and 14-E: Sample Sizes for Attributes Sampling
5. Exhibit 14-F: Attributes Sample Evaluation Table
6. Exhibit 14-G: Sample Sizes for Discovery Sampling
7. Exhibits 14-H and 14-I: Sample Sizes for Stop-or-Go Sampling
8. Exhibit 14-J: Probability-Proportional-to-Size Sampling Table

Exhibit 14-A
Table of Random Numbers

	1	2	3	4	5	6	7	8	9
1	28421	19536	53416	54372	73856	28615	20700	16252	68585
2	54911	59323	50557	77755	84369	23111	58515	02165	14715
3	63100	53705	15932	99669	71654	16630	03003	18553	09789
4	46541	86218	40032	61434	29290	42725	48752	58421	39937
5	99458	03617	19903	98882	02453	96452	49989	00259	53730
6	79818	37331	31337	09522	32702	00410	01708	33560	32859
7	22275	00966	99204	04547	18495	03670	34143	10387	82045
8	40310	01425	56131	48921	53050	10564	77063	28178	54979
9	52480	74786	40199	11627	52012	73161	06900	63501	31758
10	62126	37642	08387	81002	98160	54599	62161	23456	30140
11	01330	16874	77593	19334	78293	14846	03300	22287	49084
12	57530	28608	05350	61101	67890	50261	59590	24436	25044
13	01849	84858	92705	89919	83278	11730	89591	40686	45319
14	30094	24828	36689	22976	93136	43401	29661	11442	65458
15	51692	40936	78378	84085	64331	23446	06276	01123	15499
16	27217	58636	76792	78431	87139	63739	91618	36888	51753
17	09737	46502	52303	71797	44822	19431	70412	67275	76229
18	47588	11067	91785	61811	03594	85004	12867	87941	34642
19	81332	27116	27504	33280	69446	28807	71697	08570	59169
20	50795	29431	26400	62834	96415	88036	87683	03073	81166
21	29071	13194	10054	02895	92934	03798	51933	59254	86074
22	44823	42245	31176	24518	23321	68006	51107	07477	26966
23	82269	74761	14787	93349	04880	75140	21922	78412	75183
24	77567	26333	12764	00444	54485	78876	14654	43704	98771
25	14057	28319	94858	94322	72854	56482	68676	02650	11886
26	55738	73524	84238	92630	63579	94545	73428	44497	25812
27	35047	25559	95459	93113	59825	55122	64030	55484	84212
28	83696	06300	83331	52563	16380	11814	43953	49950	65497
29	42026	62153	90812	40326	05076	93758	28305	21579	60650
30	80765	28101	39409	48668	56882	50403	73678	35544	72214
31	83897	95241	71783	05835	75423	66995	54650	35000	99083
32	23445	89672	29754	08566	47533	44710	41672	16418	63491
33	90366	55498	44019	64446	20472	72420	86011	93552	46393
34	93738	32930	97381	58921	73671	95789	70337	51494	10055
35	76371	08824	98489	41679	26965	93940	82349	21024	43312
36	21437	63280	31121	34506	97683	85287	15322	13587	20410
37	12282	88691	52602	62957	88013	99810	45860	80799	13590
38	11696	25139	59072	36320	70634	70601	19876	43628	31642
39	61159	08093	55810	09316	08048	74463	11360	22835	15340
40	74688	38618	03844	11178	03287	07514	35976	93450	80974
41	55120	94773	33677	14312	78798	56745	82835	46357	90662
42	46315	22908	17095	27126	89408	07869	52375	07274	42432
43	37878	00120	33822	65398	10433	32544	30387	07931	92211
44	33146	08854	76918	55383	87203	60556	54556	22112	94550
45	65045	35530	61016	23356	10178	52087	79336	23674	17293
46	55750	54542	19512	65206	24426	49163	98160	06790	63643
47	52549	15538	71874	70696	93357	36305	50239	30416	66474
48	27493	48414	11337	18147	24396	14077	31008	33072	87478
49	21770	59189	67181	69056	13691	27690	69883	08479	89323
50	15600	39508	74592	37635	78656	55703	74206	05610	91507
51	32538	45334	96852	71615	36052	53943	94033	53542	10016
52	12978	98892	82388	53640	42389	83592	95112	94987	88935
53	47130	58498	03842	24500	70593	32506	87770	41671	64983
54	27769	15158	65336	05371	25979	08921	99049	45132	31913
55	54691	24904	04007	25851	67200	75679	23741	85129	58609

	1	2	3	4	5	6	7	8	9
56	97998	85049	43598	52551	25255	79671	57697	87618	79050
57	31232	47948	54059	17902	58705	84566	07427	51966	76188
58	85975	02926	42521	22762	98955	94218	04975	16177	29190
59	40433	34130	24118	90941	65119	70469	46797	44634	10916
60	26208	04624	91057	33665	89853	24706	90978	79731	28042
61	19925	78883	90273	03382	54341	39612	76223	27066	88678
62	16640	07711	65004	99634	20737	61695	16210	66773	07784
63	71557	82213	20738	94462	22377	46238	46550	80601	35683
64	80884	35733	46900	87393	03096	81015	96802	02713	95120
65	07358	11255	71734	10254	33066	85111	29493	82093	54722
66	13921	44221	56051	49705	99863	57562	61894	90026	45573
67	20480	46038	61258	04600	68623	82369	80279	57265	80903
68	80320	05600	80658	65007	08970	34019	81518	13627	55902
69	77361	60767	75141	39591	13032	78418	82492	94034	02160
70	87641	84023	44421	69067	06707	20018	92551	35811	97574
71	88687	30780	05562	19877	45369	03220	88550	29035	78670
72	32966	64353	87268	07323	34080	74249	56253	41483	27097
73	37404	40157	52241	76790	84637	47825	93079	70958	03515
74	42852	17038	58973	88518	50297	33326	68843	90047	88787
75	47147	21552	55991	96765	26466	61397	59640	21620	39490
76	21105	07666	40467	06594	40461	21932	81315	10451	57200
77	88884	13374	08120	88918	70273	75250	88833	24744	68940
78	09789	21241	45533	43452	74300	33845	91322	65295	94935
79	72408	94799	12409	33938	78050	99545	92796	38554	29800
80	81782	91956	40321	95351	94394	37900	73497	33781	51961
81	77496	81391	93950	75558	57888	79321	52382	16074	06744
82	42968	34321	74785	05085	90877	61761	39962	46439	29838
83	72173	58221	76076	31912	51677	59411	04070	11851	26429
84	53754	85932	73654	55953	20001	64589	95016	72183	03361
85	67422	18416	07952	41940	52139	17593	58681	40449	95232
86	08176	21038	09919	16759	71185	52277	92198	35191	58186
87	94051	87946	46113	46834	04413	06910	18479	15554	41775
88	59198	02207	06115	44577	06344	40852	42843	50400	90857
89	83104	77228	98284	63067	86863	26666	58001	23960	09649
90	76094	30034	02797	79076	11273	60000	88238	37179	52447
91	11287	31742	52287	57154	39634	41966	92251	60927	13427
92	88949	52739	24627	23430	36799	34356	57176	25737	23647
93	62349	82429	61666	07621	42637	18932	98362	97583	47918
94	41320	33848	87386	27609	92117	10283	12383	35355	12666
95	79170	46966	67878	61943	62277	61873	08895	92036	51991
96	59990	71862	48990	94897	09443	35313	67802	02297	92688
97	64503	30312	31433	90379	13152	54723	81172	18740	98994
98	85524	45883	39212	46932	52545	71272	59111	93492	67903
99	55923	42057	46377	29594	42285	46905	92838	00472	40872
100	13963	50628	31367	31405	17201	55278	97099	84665	01251
101	77462	14129	48799	21898	64178	08595	43821	08861	97515
102	03504	08078	69563	64747	93797	40409	52694	33499	78071
103	81763	90269	25752	15675	80018	36961	84416	77958	81755
104	25445	26239	62411	94729	56515	74785	38433	64804	42712
105	67251	93506	11079	24210	28854	48499	62976	75733	08547
106	10868	43031	23230	69820	34490	39126	89057	3032C	54901
107	09945	84443	44053	68660	67361	67957	19917	25611	79545
108	88743	70307	02784	38513	33279	83555	28687	35888	94389
109	13944	26741	90606	81284	83046	46602	72332	89355	86151
110	52121	64326	48492	97508	34705	09508	68667	68159	20807

Source: *Sampling for Modern Auditors* (Altamonte Springs, Florida: The Institute of Internal Auditors, 1977), pp. 6-16 and 6-17.

Example of Use of Random Number Tables

The decision maker should arbitrarily select a point on the table to start; for example, close your eyes and point or use a dollar bill's serial number to select the column and the line number from which to begin. Assume you selected column 3, row 85, or the random number 07952. Now, define a systematic pattern that you will use as you move through the table. For example, you may decide to go down one column at a time, systematically returning to the top of the next column on that page. Alternatively, you could move across each row. The important point is that the movement through the table must be in a set, systematic pattern.

Assume you decide to move down the columns. To apply the table, you must have some concept of the population of interest. Assume that you are interested in selecting a sample from a population of 7,200 invoices. You define the last four digits to be relevant. This would mean that you would not select 7952 or 9919 because they exceed 7,200. However, 6113, 6115, 2797, 2287, 4627, and so on would be selected.

Exhibit 14-B
Cumulative Probabilities of the
Standard Normal Distribution

Entry is area A under the standard normal curve from $-\infty$ to $z(A)$

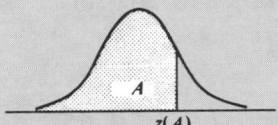

z	.00	.01	.02	.03	.04	.05	.06	.07	.08	.09
.0	.5000	.5040	.5080	.5120	.5160	.5199	.5239	.5279	.5319	.5359
.1	.5398	.5438	.5478	.5517	.5557	.5596	.5636	.5675	.5714	.5753
.2	.5793	.5832	.5871	.5910	.5948	.5987	.6026	.6064	.6103	.6141
.3	.6179	.6217	.6255	.6293	.6331	.6368	.6406	.6443	.6480	.6517
.4	.6554	.6591	.6628	.6664	.6700	.6736	.6772	.6808	.6844	.6879
.5	.6915	.6950	.6985	.7019	.7054	.7088	.7123	.7157	.7190	.7224
.6	.7257	.7291	.7324	.7357	.7389	.7422	.7454	.7486	.7517	.7549
.7	.7580	.7611	.7642	.7673	.7704	.7734	.7764	.7794	.7823	.7852
.8	.7881	.7910	.7939	.7967	.7995	.8023	.8051	.8078	.8106	.8133
.9	.8159	.8186	.8212	.8238	.8264	.8289	.8315	.8340	.8365	.8389
1.0	.8413	.8438	.8461	.8485	.8508	.8531	.8554	.8577	.8599	.8621
1.1	.8643	.8665	.8686	.8708	.8729	.8749	.8770	.8790	.8810	.8830
1.2	.8849	.8869	.8888	.8907	.8925	.8944	.8962	.8980	.8997	.9015
1.3	.9032	.9049	.9066	.9082	.9099	.9115	.9131	.9147	.9162	.9177
1.4	.9192	.9207	.9222	.9236	.9251	.9265	.9279	.9292	.9306	.9319
1.5	.9332	.9345	.9357	.9370	.9382	.9394	.9406	.9418	.9429	.9441
1.6	.9452	.9463	.9474	.9484	.9495	.9505	.9515	.9525	.9535	.9545
1.7	.9554	.9564	.9573	.9582	.9591	.9599	.9608	.9616	.9625	.9633
1.8	.9641	.9649	.9656	.9664	.9671	.9678	.9686	.9693	.9699	.9706
1.9	.9713	.9719	.9726	.9732	.9738	.9744	.9750	.9756	.9761	.9767
2.0	.9772	.9778	.9783	.9788	.9793	.9798	.9803	.9808	.9812	.9817
2.1	.9821	.9826	.9830	.9834	.9838	.9842	.9846	.9850	.9854	.9857
2.2	.9861	.9864	.9868	.9871	.9875	.9878	.9881	.9884	.9887	.9890
2.3	.9893	.9896	.9898	.9901	.9904	.9906	.9909	.9911	.9913	.9916
2.4	.9918	.9920	.9922	.9925	.9927	.9929	.9931	.9932	.9934	.9936
2.5	.9938	.9940	.9941	.9943	.9945	.9946	.9948	.9949	.9951	.9952
2.6	.9953	.9955	.9956	.9957	.9959	.9960	.9961	.9962	.9963	.9964
2.7	.9965	.9966	.9967	.9968	.9969	.9970	.9971	.9972	.9973	.9974
2.8	.9974	.9975	.9976	.9977	.9977	.9978	.9979	.9979	.9980	.9981
2.9	.9981	.9982	.9982	.9983	.9984	.9984	.9985	.9985	.9986	.9986
3.0	.9987	.9987	.9987	.9988	.9988	.9989	.9989	.9989	.9990	.9990
3.1	.9990	.9991	.9991	.9991	.9992	.9992	.9992	.9992	.9993	.9993
3.2	.9993	.9993	.9994	.9994	.9994	.9994	.9994	.9995	.9995	.9995
3.3	.9995	.9995	.9995	.9996	.9996	.9996	.9996	.9996	.9996	.9997
3.4	.9997	.9997	.9997	.9997	.9997	.9997	.9997	.9997	.9997	.9998

Selected Percentiles							
Cumulative probability A:	.90	.95	.975	.98	.99	.995	.999
$z(A)$:	1.282	1.645	1.960	2.054	2.326	2.576	3.090

Source: John Neter, William Wasserman, and Michael H. Kutner, *Applied Linear Statistical Models,* Second Edition (Homewood, Illinois: Richard D. Irwin, Inc., 1985), Table A-1.

Exhibit 14-C
Factors Required to Achieve
Given Confidence Levels

(Confidence levels in percentages converted to standard deviation units, based on the normal distribution curve.)

CONFIDENCE LEVEL	FACTOR
99.9	3.2905
99.7	3.0000
99.5	2.8070
99.0	2.5758
98.0	2.3263
95.5	2.0000
95.0	1.9600
90.0	1.6449
85.0	1.4395
80.0	1.2816
75.0	1.1503
70.0	1.0364
68.3	1.0000
60.0	0.8416
50.0	0.6745
40.0	0.5244
30.0	0.3853
20.0	0.2534
10.0	0.1257

Source: *Sampling for Modern Auditors* (Altamonte Springs, Florida: The Institute of Internal Auditors, 1977), p. 2-36.

Example of Use of the Normal Distribution Tables

Assume that you are doing a one-sided test of receivables; i.e., you want to determine whether they are overstated. You would like to achieve a 95 percent level of confidence in the results. The confidence levels are reflected on the inside of the table. The figure .9505 is the closest value. Because the auditor is always conservative when applying tables, .9505 would always be preferred to the .9495 value, assuming no interpolation is to be performed.

Once the confidence level is identified, you read first horizontally and then vertically to obtain the appropriate z-score. This results in 1.65 as the z-factor for a one-sided 95 percent confidence level.

If, instead, you wanted a two-sided test for both over- and understatements, the table would need to be adjusted. Explicitly, rather than having .05 in one tail, you wanted to have .05 divided by 2 or .025 in each tail. This translates to a 1.00 minus .025 or a .975 confidence level. The .975 in the table translates to a 1.96 factor for a two-sided 95 percent confidence level. These z-factors (reliability factors) are required to calculate variables sample sizes.

Exhibit 14-D
Sample Sizes for Attributes Sampling

EXPECTED ERROR RATE NOT OVER 5%

CONFIDENCE LEVEL 90%

POPULATION SIZE	SAMPLE SIZE FOR PRECISION PERCENTAGE OF PLUS OR MINUS						
	1.00	1.50	2.00	2.50	3.00	3.50	4.00
50	48	45	43	40	37	33	30
100	92	85	76	67	58	51	44
150	134	118	102	86	73	61	52
200	173	148	123	101	83	68	57
250	209	173	140	112	90	73	60
300	243	196	155	122	96	77	63
350	275	217	167	129	101	80	65
400	305	235	178	135	105	83	66
450	333	251	187	141	108	85	68
500	359	266	195	145	111	86	69
550	385	280	202	149	113	88	70
600	409	292	209	153	115	89	70
650	431	304	215	156	117	90	71
700	453	314	220	158	118	91	72
750	473	324	224	161	119	92	72
800	493	333	229	163	121	92	73
850	511	341	233	165	122	93	73
900	529	349	236	167	123	93	73
950	546	356	240	169	124	94	74
1000	562	363	243	170	124	94	74
1100	592	376	248	173	126	95	74
1200	620	387	253	175	127	96	75
1300	646	396	257	177	128	97	75
1400	670	405	261	179	129	97	75
1500	692	413	264	180	130	98	76
1600	712	420	267	182	131	98	76
1700	731	427	270	183	131	98	76
1800	749	433	272	184	132	99	76
1900	766	439	274	185	132	99	77
2000	782	444	276	186	133	99	77
2250	818	455	281	188	134	100	77
2500	848	465	284	190	135	100	77
2750	875	473	287	191	135	101	78
3000	899	479	290	192	136	101	78
3250	921	485	292	193	136	101	78
3500	940	491	294	194	137	101	78
3750	957	495	295	194	137	102	78
4000	972	499	297	195	137	102	78
4250	986	503	298	196	138	102	78
4500	999	506	299	196	138	102	78
4750	1011	509	300	197	138	102	78
5000	1022	512	301	197	138	102	79
5500	1041	517	303	198	139	102	79
6000	1058	521	305	198	139	103	79
6500	1073	525	306	199	139	103	79
7000	1085	528	307	199	139	103	79
7500	1097	530	308	200	140	103	79
8000	1107	533	308	200	140	103	79
8500	1116	535	309	200	140	103	79
9000	1124	537	310	201	140	103	79

EXPECTED ERROR RATE NOT OVER 5%

CONFIDENCE LEVEL 90%

POPULATION SIZE	SAMPLE SIZE FOR PRECISION PERCENTAGE OF PLUS OR MINUS						
	1.00	1.50	2.00	2.50	3.00	3.50	4.00
9500	1132	538	310	201	140	103	79
10000	1138	540	311	201	140	103	79
11000	1150	543	312	201	140	103	79
12000	1161	545	312	202	141	104	79
13000	1169	547	313	202	141	104	79
14000	1177	548	314	202	141	104	79
15000	1183	550	314	202	141	104	79
16000	1189	551	315	203	141	104	79
17000	1195	552	315	203	141	104	79
18000	1199	553	315	203	141	104	79
19000	1203	554	315	203	141	104	79
20000	1207	555	316	203	141	104	80
22500	1215	557	316	203	141	104	80
25000	1222	558	317	203	142	104	80
27500	1227	559	317	204	142	104	80
30000	1232	560	317	204	142	104	80
32500	1236	561	318	204	142	104	80
35000	1239	562	318	204	142	104	80
37500	1242	562	318	204	142	104	80
40000	1245	563	318	204	142	104	80
42500	1247	563	318	204	142	104	80
45000	1249	564	319	204	142	104	80
47500	1251	564	319	204	142	104	80
50000	1253	564	319	204	142	104	80
55000	1256	565	319	204	142	104	80
60000	1258	565	319	204	142	104	80
65000	1260	566	319	205	142	104	80
70000	1262	566	319	205	142	104	80
75000	1263	566	319	205	142	104	80
80000	1265	567	320	205	142	104	80
85000	1266	567	320	205	142	104	80
90000	1267	567	320	205	142	104	80
95000	1268	567	320	205	142	104	80
100000	1269	568	320	205	142	104	80
110000	1270	568	320	205	142	104	80
120000	1271	568	320	205	142	104	80
130000	1272	568	320	205	142	104	80
140000	1273	568	320	205	142	104	80
150000	1274	569	320	205	142	104	80
160000	1275	569	320	205	142	104	80
170000	1275	569	320	205	142	104	80
180000	1276	569	320	205	142	104	80
190000	1276	569	320	205	142	104	80
200000	1277	569	320	205	142	104	80
250000	1278	569	320	205	142	104	80
300000	1279	570	320	205	142	104	80
350000	1280	570	321	205	142	104	80
400000	1281	570	321	205	142	104	80
450000	1281	570	321	205	142	104	80
500000	1282	570	321	205	142	104	80

Source: *Sampling for Modern Auditors* (Altamonte Springs, Florida: The Institute of Internal Auditors, 1977), pp. 2-26 and 2-27.

Exhibit 14-E
Sample Sizes for Attributes Sampling

EXPECTED ERROR RATE NOT OVER 5%

CONFIDENCE LEVEL 95%

POPULATION SIZE	SAMPLE SIZE FOR PRECISION PERCENTAGE OF PLUS OR MINUS						
	1.00	1.50	2.00	2.50	3.00	3.50	4.00
50	48	47	45	42	40	37	34
100	94	89	82	74	66	59	53
150	138	126	112	99	86	74	64
200	180	160	139	118	100	85	72
250	219	191	161	134	111	93	78
300	257	218	180	147	120	99	82
350	293	244	198	159	128	104	86
400	328	267	213	168	134	108	88
450	360	289	226	177	139	111	90
500	392	309	238	184	144	114	92
550	422	327	249	190	148	117	94
600	451	344	259	196	151	119	95
650	479	360	268	201	154	121	97
700	505	375	276	206	157	122	98
750	531	389	283	210	159	124	98
800	556	402	290	213	161	125	99
850	579	415	296	217	163	126	100
900	602	426	302	220	165	127	101
950	624	437	308	223	167	128	101
1000	645	447	313	225	168	129	102
1100	686	466	322	230	171	131	103
1200	723	483	330	234	173	132	104
1300	759	499	337	238	175	133	104
1400	792	513	344	241	177	134	105
1500	823	526	349	244	178	135	105
1600	852	538	354	246	179	136	106
1700	880	549	359	249	181	136	106
1800	906	559	363	251	182	137	107
1900	930	568	367	253	183	138	107
2000	954	577	371	254	184	138	107
2250	1007	596	379	258	185	139	108
2500	1054	612	385	261	187	140	109
2750	1096	626	391	263	188	141	109
3000	1134	638	395	266	189	141	109
3250	1168	649	400	267	190	142	110
3500	1199	658	403	269	191	142	110
3750	1227	666	406	270	192	143	110
4000	1253	674	409	272	192	143	110
4250	1276	681	411	273	193	143	111
4500	1298	687	414	274	194	144	111
4750	1318	692	416	275	194	144	111
5000	1336	697	418	275	194	144	111
5500	1370	706	421	277	195	145	111
6000	1399	714	423	278	196	145	111
6500	1424	721	426	279	196	145	112
7000	1447	726	428	280	197	145	112
7500	1467	731	430	281	197	146	112
8000	1485	736	431	281	197	146	112
8500	1502	740	432	282	198	146	112
9000	1517	743	434	282	198	146	112

EXPECTED ERROR RATE NOT OVER 5%

CONFIDENCE LEVEL 95%

POPULATION SIZE	SAMPLE SIZE FOR PRECISION PERCENTAGE OF PLUS OR MINUS						
	1.00	1.50	2.00	2.50	3.00	3.50	4.00
9500	1530	747	435	283	198	146	112
10000	1543	750	436	283	198	146	112
11000	1565	755	438	284	199	146	112
12000	1583	759	439	285	199	147	112
13000	1600	763	440	285	199	147	113
14000	1614	766	441	285	199	147	113
15000	1626	769	442	286	200	147	113
16000	1637	771	443	286	200	147	113
17000	1647	774	444	287	200	147	113
18000	1656	776	444	287	200	147	113
19000	1664	777	445	287	200	147	113
20000	1672	779	446	287	200	147	113
22500	1687	782	447	288	200	147	113
25000	1700	785	448	288	201	148	113
27500	1711	787	448	288	201	148	113
30000	1720	789	449	289	201	148	113
32500	1727	791	449	289	201	148	113
35000	1734	792	450	289	201	148	113
37500	1740	793	450	289	201	148	113
40000	1745	794	451	289	201	148	113
42500	1749	795	451	289	201	148	113
45000	1753	796	451	290	201	148	113
47500	1757	797	451	290	201	148	113
50000	1760	798	452	290	201	148	113
55000	1766	799	452	290	202	148	113
60000	1770	800	452	290	202	148	113
65000	1774	801	453	290	202	148	113
70000	1778	801	453	290	202	148	113
75000	1781	802	453	290	202	148	113
80000	1784	802	453	290	202	148	113
85000	1786	803	453	290	202	148	113
90000	1788	803	453	291	202	148	113
95000	1790	804	454	291	202	148	113
100000	1792	804	454	291	202	148	113
110000	1794	805	454	291	202	148	113
120000	1797	805	454	291	202	148	113
130000	1799	805	454	291	202	148	113
140000	1801	806	454	291	202	148	113
150000	1802	806	454	291	202	148	113
160000	1804	806	454	291	202	148	113
170000	1805	807	454	291	202	148	113
180000	1806	807	455	291	202	148	113
190000	1807	807	455	291	202	148	113
200000	1808	807	455	291	202	148	113
250000	1811	808	455	291	202	148	113
300000	1813	808	455	291	202	148	114
350000	1815	809	455	291	202	148	114
400000	1816	809	455	291	202	148	114
450000	1817	809	455	291	202	148	114
500000	1818	809	455	291	202	148	114

Source: *Sampling for Modern Auditors* (Altamonte Springs, Florida: The Institute of Internal Auditors, 1977), pp. 2-28 and 2-29.

Example of How to Use Sample Size Tables for Attributes Sampling

The first step is to identify the appropriate table based on your expected error rate and desired confidence level. The table shown in Exhibit 14-D relates to a 90 percent confidence level, and the one shown in Exhibit 14-E relates to a 95 percent confidence level. Both tables apply to error rates not exceeding 5 percent. Assume that you expect the error rate not to exceed 5 percent and that you want to have 95 percent confidence. That would mean that Exhibit 14-E is appropriate. The population size of interest is 9,000 shipping documents. You actually want precision to be 3 percent. The sample size, based on Exhibit 14-E, is read from the inside of the table as 198 sampling units. Note that an expected precision of 4 percent would require only 112 sampling units.

Shifting the level of confidence to 90 percent and holding the population size at a level of 9,000, assume that you set the precision at 3 percent. Your sample size could then be taken from Exhibit 14-D and would be 140 units. If only 4 percent precision were required, a sample of 79 would be drawn.

This example bears out the idea that greater confidence and looser precision result in smaller sample sizes.

Exhibit 14-F
Attributes Sample Evaluation Table

REVISED PRECISION LIMITS
BASED ON ERROR RATE FOUND IN SAMPLE

SAMPLE ERROR RATE 5%

Universe Size of

Sample Size	500 Lower limit	500 Upper limit	1,000 Lower limit	1,000 Upper limit	2,000 Lower limit	2,000 Upper limit	10,000 Lower limit	10,000 Upper limit	50,000+ Lower limit	50,000+ Upper limit
				Confidence Level 90%						
80	2.0%	10.6%	1.8%	10.9%	1.8%	11.0%	1.7%	11.1%	1.7%	11.1%
90	2.2	10.1	2.0	10.4	1.9	10.5	1.9	10.6	1.9	10.7
100	2.3	9.7	2.1	10.0	2.1	10.1	2.0	10.3	2.0	10.3
120	2.6	9.1	2.4	9.4	2.3	9.5	2.2	9.6	2.2	9.7
140	2.8	8.7	2.6	9.0	2.5	9.2	2.4	9.3	2.4	9.3
150	2.9	8.4	2.7	8.7	2.6	8.9	2.5	9.0	2.5	9.0
160	3.0	8.2	2.7	8.5	2.6	8.7	2.5	8.8	2.5	8.9
180	3.1	7.9	2.9	8.3	2.8	8.4	2.7	8.6	2.7	8.6
200	3.3	7.6	3.0	8.0	2.9	8.2	2.8	8.3	2.8	8.4
250	3.6	7.1	3.3	7.5	3.1	7.7	3.0	7.9	3.0	7.9
300			3.4	7.2	3.3	7.4	3.2	7.6	3.2	7.6
400			3.7	6.7	3.5	7.0	3.4	7.2	3.4	7.2
500			4.0	6.4	3.7	6.7	3.6	6.9	3.5	6.9
600					3.9	6.4	3.7	6.7	3.7	6.7
700					4.0	6.3	3.8	6.5	3.8	6.6
800					4.1	6.1	3.9	6.4	3.8	6.5
900					4.2	6.0	3.9	6.3	3.9	6.4
1,000					4.2	5.9	4.0	6.2	3.9	6.3
				Confidence Level 95%						
80	1.7%	11.7%	1.5%	12.0%	1.5%	12.2%	1.4%	12.3%	1.4%	12.3%
90	1.8	11.1	1.7	11.4	1.6	11.6	1.5	11.7	1.5	11.7
100	2.0	10.6	1.8	11.0	1.7	11.1	1.7	11.3	1.6	11.3
120	2.3	9.8	2.1	10.2	2.0	10.4	1.9	10.5	1.9	10.6
140	2.5	9.4	2.3	9.8	2.2	10.0	2.1	10.1	2.1	10.1
150	2.6	9.0	2.3	9.4	2.2	9.6	2.1	9.8	2.1	9.8
160	2.7	8.8	2.4	9.2	2.3	9.4	2.2	9.6	2.2	9.6
180	2.8	8.4	2.6	8.9	2.4	9.1	2.3	9.2	2.3	9.3
200	3.0	8.1	2.7	8.6	2.6	8.8	2.5	9.0	2.4	9.0
250	3.3	7.5	3.0	8.0	2.8	8.3	2.7	8.4	2.7	8.5
300			3.2	7.6	3.0	7.9	2.9	8.1	2.8	8.1
400			3.5	7.0	3.3	7.3	3.1	7.6	3.1	7.6
500					3.5	7.0	3.3	7.2	3.3	7.3
600					3.7	6.7	3.4	7.0	3.4	7.0
700					3.8	6.5	3.6	6.8	3.5	6.9
800					3.9	6.4	3.7	6.7	3.6	6.7
900					4.0	6.2	3.7	6.6	3.7	6.6
1,000							3.8	6.5	3.8	6.5

Source: *Sampling for Modern Auditors* (Altamonte Springs, Florida: The Institute of Internal Auditors, 1977), pp. 2-32.

Example of How to Use the Attributes Sample Evaluation Table

Assume that you drew a sample of 200. The population had 10,000 units, and the desired confidence level is 95 percent. You found an error rate in the sample of 5 percent (i.e., you found 10 errors and 10 divided by 200 yields 5 percent). You would use the lower half of the table. Read across from the sample size of 200 and down from the columns labeled 10,000 universe size, and find precision limits to be 2.5 to 9.0. This is interpreted to mean that if you took repeated samples, you would expect them to estimate a true population error (for the 10,000 universe) which lay within the interval from 2.5 percent to 9.0 percent, 95 percent of the time. If you could not accept an error rate exceeding 7 percent, you would assess this error rate as unacceptable, whereas a tolerable rate of 10 percent would have been met by the sample results.

Exhibit 14-G
Sample Sizes for Discovery Sampling

PROBABILITY IN PERCENT OF FINDING ONE ERROR IF
TOTAL NUMBER OF ERRORS IN UNIVERSE IS AS INDICATED

Sample Size	Population of 500 Number of Errors				Population of 1,000 Number of Errors			
	2	5	10	20	5	10	20	30
55				90.7				
65				94.2				
75				96.4				90.7
85				97.8				93.3
100				99.0				96.0
125			94.5	99.7			93.3	98.3
150			97.3	99.9			96.3	99.3
200		92.3	99.4				98.9	99.9
250		96.9	99.9			94.5	99.7	
300		99.0				97.2	99.9	
350	91.0	99.8				98.7		
400	96.0				92.3	99.4		
450	99.0				95.0	99.8		
500					96.9	99.9		
550					98.2			

Sample Size	Population of 2,000 Number of Errors				Population of 5,000 Number of Errors			
	10	20	30	50	25	50	75	100
90				90.3				
100				92.6				
125				96.2				92.3
150			90.5	98.1			90.0	95.4
200			95.9	99.5			95.4	98.4
250		93.2	98.2	99.9		92.4	97.9	99.4
300		96.2	99.3			95.5	99.1	99.8
350		97.9	99.7			97.4	99.6	99.9
400		98.9	99.9			98.5	99.8	
450	92.2	99.4			90.6	99.1	99.9	
500	94.4	99.7			92.9	99.5		
550	96.0	99.8			94.6	99.7		
600	97.2	99.9			95.9	99.8		
650	98.1				97.0	99.9		
700	98.7				97.7	99.9		

PROBABILITY IN PERCENT OF FINDING ONE ERROR IF TOTAL NUMBER OF ERRORS IN UNIVERSE IS AS INDICATED

Sample Size	Population of 10,000 Number of Errors				Population of 15,000 Number of Errors			
	50	75	100	200	50	75	100	200
125				92.1				
150				95.3				
200				98.3				93.3
250			92.1	99.4				96.6
300			95.3	99.8				98.3
350		93.2	97.2	99.9			90.6	99.1
400		95.4	98.3				93.4	99.6
450	90.1	96.9	99.0				95.3	99.8
500	92.4	97.9	99.4			92.2	96.7	99.9
550	94.1	98.6	99.7			94.0	97.6	99.9
600	95.5	99.1	99.8			95.4	98.3	
700	97.4	99.6	99.9		90.9	97.2	99.2	
800	98.5	99.8			93.6	98.4	99.6	
900	99.1	99.9			95.5	99.0	99.8	
1000	99.5				96.8	99.4	99.9	

Sample Size	Population of 20,000 Number of Errors				Population of 25,000 Number of Errors			
	50	75	100	200	50	75	100	200
250				92.0				
300				95.2				91.1
350				97.1				94.1
400				98.3				96.1
450				99.0				97.4
500			92.1	99.4				98.3
600			95.3	99.8			91.2	99.2
700		93.1	97.2	99.9			94.2	99.7
800		95.3	98.3			91.3	96.2	99.9
900	90.0	96.9	99.0			93.6	97.5	99.9
1000	92.3	97.9	99.4			95.3	98.3	
1200	95.5	99.0	99.8		91.5	97.5	99.3	
1400	97.4	99.6	99.9		94.4	98.7	99.7	
1600	98.5	99.8			96.3	99.3	99.9	
1800	99.1	99.9			97.6	99.6	99.9	

PROBABILITY IN PERCENT OF FINDING ONE ERROR IF TOTAL NUMBER OF ERRORS IN UNIVERSE IS AS INDICATED

Sample Size	Population of 35,000 Number of Errors				Population of 50,000 Number of Errors			
	50	75	100	200	75	100	200	300
400				90.0				91.1
450				92.5				93.4
500				94.4				95.1
600				96.9			91.1	97.4
700				98.3			94.1	98.6
800			90.1	99.0			96.1	99.2
900			92.6	99.5			97.4	99.6
1000			94.5	99.7			98.3	99.8
1100		90.9	95.9	99.8			98.8	99.9
1200		92.7	97.0	99.9		91.2	99.2	99.9
1300		94.2	97.7	99.9		92.8	99.5	
1400		95.3	98.3			94.2	99.7	
1600	90.4	97.0	99.1		91.3	96.1	99.9	
1800	92.9	98.1	99.5		93.6	97.5	99.9	
2000	94.7	98.8	99.7		95.3	98.3		

Sample Size	Population of 100,000 Number of Errors				Population of 200,000 Number of Errors			
	200	300	500	1000	300	500	1000	2000
250				91.9				91.9
300				95.1				95.1
350				97.1				97.0
400				98.2				98.2
500			91.9	99.4			91.9	99.3
600			95.1	99.8			95.1	99.8
700			97.0	99.9			97.0	99.9
800		91.0	98.2				98.2	
900		93.4	98.9				98.9	
1000		95.1	99.4			91.9	99.3	
1200	91.1	97.3	99.8			95.1	99.8	
1400	94.1	98.6	99.9			97.0	99.9	
1600	96.0	99.2			91.0	98.2		
1800	97.4	99.6			93.4	98.9		
2000	98.2	99.8			95.1	99.3		

Source: *Sampling for Modern Auditors* (Altamonte Springs, Florida: The Institute of Internal Auditors, 1977), pp. 5-14 through 5-16.

Example of How to Use the Sample Size Table for Discovery Sampling

Sample size tables for discovery sampling are similar to attribute tables in that they tie to population size, confidence level, and the number of expected errors.

Assume a population of 20,000, an expectation of 1 percent error, and a desire for 95 percent confidence. This would direct you to the second page of Exhibit 14-G. The 1 percent expected error translates to .01 times 20,000 or 200. Reading down the column, you would stop at 95.2, then read across to the left to determine the sample size. In this case, a sample size of 200 is indicated. If the auditor selects 300 and finds no errors, the discovery sampling results would be acceptable.

Exhibit 14-H
Sample Sizes for Stop-or-Go Sampling

PROBABILITY THAT ERROR RATE IN UNIVERSE SIZE OF 200 IS LESS THAN:

Size of Sample Examined	No. of Errors Found	1%	2%	3%	4%	5%	6%	7%	8%	9%	10%
40	0	36.08	59.35	74.28	83.82	89.87	93.70	96.10	97.60	98.53	99.11
	1				49.97	63.04	73.39	81.24	87.01	91.14	94.05
	2							55.78	65.78	74.13	80.84
	3									50.35	59.78
50	0	43.84	68.68	82.65	90.46	94.79	97.18	98.48	99.19	99.57	99.77
	1				63.77	76.32	84.99	90.72	94.39	96.67	98.06
	2						61.53	72.82	81.42	87.65	92.00
	3								60.21	70.55	78.88
	4										59.32
60	0	51.11	76.30	88.62	94.58	97.44	98.81	99.45	99.75	99.89	99.95
	1			58.26	75.02	85.74	92.15	95.80	97.81	98.88	99.44
	2					62.20	75.52	84.86	91.00	94.82	97.10
	3						50.99	65.20	76.48	84.77	90.50
	4								55.47	67.71	77.59
	5										59.08
70	0	57.86	82.44	92.76	97.05	98.81	99.53	99.81	99.93	99.97	99.99
	1			68.45	83.63	91.95	96.20	98.26	99.23	99.67	99.86
	2				57.49	74.48	85.66	92.36	96.11	98.09	99.09
	3						65.93	78.88	87.64	93.12	96.33
	4							58.18	72.02	82.35	89.42
	5								51.23	65.34	76.74
	6										58.98
80	0	64.12	87.30	95.57	98.47	99.48	99.83	99.94	99.98	99.99	100.00
	1		52.57	77.07	89.84	95.76	98.31	99.35	99.76	99.91	99.97
	2				68.89	83.93	92.30	96.53	98.51	99.39	99.76
	3					62.16	78.24	88.44	94.25	97.30	98.79
	4						56.48	72.88	84.40	91.61	95.75
	5							51.58	67.90	80.30	88.70
	6									63.28	76.23
	7										58.99
90	0	69.87	91.07	97.40	99.26	99.79	99.94	99.98	100.00	100.00	100.00
	1		61.05	84.03	94.06	97.93	99.31	99.78	99.93	99.98	99.99
	2			55.98	78.49	90.62	96.24	98.59	99.50	99.83	99.94
	3				52.39	73.97	87.31	94.34	97.66	99.09	99.66
	4					49.59	70.17	84.19	92.34	96.57	98.56
	5							66.89	81.27	90.31	95.36
	6								64.00	78.54	88.27
	7									61.43	75.99
	8										59.09
100	0	75.13	93.94	98.55	99.66	99.92	99.98	100.00	100.00	100.00	100.00
	1		68.94	89.42	96.76	99.08	99.75	99.94	99.98	100.00	100.00
	2			65.86	86.05	94.97	98.35	99.50	99.85	99.96	99.99
	3				63.95	83.44	93.31	97.55	99.18	99.74	99.92
	4					62.62	81.36	91.80	96.74	98.81	99.60
	5						61.63	79.66	90.44	95.93	98.41
	6							60.86	78.24	89.21	95.15
	7								60.24	77.03	88.10
	8									59.72	75.98
	9										59.29

Source: *Sampling for Modern Auditors* (Altamonte Springs, Florida: The Institute of Internal Auditors, 1977), pp. 3-21.

Exhibit 14-I
Sample Sizes for Stop-or-Go Sampling

PROBABILITY THAT ERROR RATE IN UNIVERSE SIZE OF 2,000 IS LESS THAN:

Size of Sample Examined	No. of Errors Found	1%	2%	3%	4%	5%	6%	7%	8%	9%	10%
50	0	39.50	63.58	78.19	87.01	92.31	95.47	97.34	98.45	99.10	99.49
	1				59.95	72.06	81.00	87.35	91.73	94.68	96.62
	2						58.38	68.92	77.40	83.95	88.83
	3								57.47	66.97	74.97
	4										56.88
70	0	50.52	75.69	88.14	94.26	97.24	98.69	99.38	99.71	99.86	99.94
	1			62.47	77.51	87.03	92.81	96.10	97.93	98.92	99.45
	2				53.44	68.63	79.87	87.59	92.60	95.72	97.58
	3						61.15	73.07	82.10	88.53	92.88
	4							54.77	66.80	76.61	84.12
	5									61.06	71.28
	6										55.82
100	0	63.40	86.74	95.25	98.31	99.41	99.80	99.93	99.98	99.99	100.00
	1		59.67	80.54	91.28	96.29	98.48	99.40	99.77	99.91	99.97
	2			58.02	76.79	88.17	94.34	97.42	98.87	99.52	99.81
	3				57.05	74.22	85.70	92.56	96.33	98.27	99.22
	4					56.40	72.32	83.68	90.97	95.26	97.63
	5						55.93	70.86	82.01	89.55	94.24
	6							55.57	69.68	80.60	88.28
	7								55.29	68.72	79.40
	8									55.06	67.91
	9										54.87
120	0	70.06	91.15	97.41	99.25	99.79	99.94	99.98	100.00	100.00	100.00
	1		69.46	87.82	95.53	98.45	99.48	99.83	99.95	99.98	100.00
	2			70.16	86.28	94.25	97.75	99.17	99.71	99.90	99.97
	3				71.13	85.56	93.40	97.19	98.87	99.60	99.84
	4				52.67	72.18	85.27	92.83	96.75	98.61	99.44
	5					55.85	73.23	85.23	92.47	96.42	98.40
	6						58.50	74.26	85.35	92.26	96.18
	7							60.81	75.25	85.57	92.16
	8								62.85	76.21	85.86
	9									64.70	77.14
	10									52.06	66.39
	11										54.45
150	0	77.86	95.17	98.96	99.78	99.95	99.99	100.00	100.00	100.00	100.00
	1		80.39	94.15	98.41	99.60	99.90	99.98	100.00	100.00	100.00
	2		57.91	83.07	94.16	98.19	99.48	99.86	99.96	99.99	100.00
	3			66.16	85.42	94.52	98.14	99.42	99.83	99.95	99.99
	4				72.04	87.44	95.01	98.20	99.40	99.81	99.95
	5				55.76	76.56	89.17	95.52	98.31	99.41	99.81
	6					62.71	80.16	90.66	96.03	98.45	99.44
	7						68.34	83.12	91.94	96.50	98.60
	8						54.84	72.98	85.58	93.04	96.93
	9							60.93	76.85	87.65	94.00
	10								66.16	80.13	89.40
	11								54.32	70.66	82.91
	12									59.82	74.55
	13										64.70
	14										53.98
180	0	83.62	97.37	99.58	99.94	99.99	100.00	100.00	100.00	100.00	100.00
	1	53.84	87.69	97.27	99.45	99.90	99.98	100.00	100.00	100.00	100.00
	2		70.01	90.86	97.65	99.46	99.89	99.98	100.00	100.00	100.00
	3			79.10	93.20	98.10	99.52	99.89	99.98	100.00	100.00
	4			63.01	84.99	94.93	98.50	99.60	99.90	99.98	100.00
	5				72.95	89.05	96.21	98.84	99.68	99.92	99.98
	6				58.32	80.02	91.93	97.16	99.11	99.75	99.93
	7					68.21	85.15	94.03	97.88	99.32	99.80
	8					54.77	75.79	88.92	95.57	98.42	99.49
	9						64.37	81.58	91.72	96.70	98.82
	10						51.90	72.13	86.00	93.81	97.55
	11							61.13	78.32	89.38	95.37
	12								68.91	83.21	91.96
	13								58.33	75.33	87.06
	14									66.03	80.57
	15									55.86	72.59
	16										63.44
	17										53.63

PROBABILITY THAT ERROR RATE IN UNIVERSE SIZE OF 2,000 IS LESS THAN:

Size of Sample Examined	No. of Errors Found	1%	2%	3%	4%	5%	6%	7%	8%	9%	10%
220	0	89.04	98.83	99.88	99.99	100.00	100.00	100.00	100.00	100.00	100.00
	1	64.69	93.55	99.04	99.87	99.98	100.00	100.00	100.00	100.00	100.00
	2		81.77	96.21	99.35	99.90	99.99	100.00	100.00	100.00	100.00
	3		64.30	89.84	97.75	99.58	99.93	99.99	100.00	100.00	100.00
	4			79.15	94.15	98.66	99.74	99.95	99.99	100.00	100.00
	5			64.88	87.67	96.58	99.21	99.84	99.97	99.99	100.00
	6				77.99	92.66	97.99	99.53	99.90	99.98	100.00
	7				65.67	86.34	95.61	98.81	99.72	99.94	99.99
	8				51.99	77.48	91.57	97.38	99.30	99.83	99.97
	9					66.51	85.50	94.83	98.43	99.59	99.90
	10					54.32	77.32	90.79	96.85	99.07	99.76
	11						67.35	84.98	94.21	98.09	99.45
	12						56.27	77.36	90.22	96.40	98.85
	13							68.19	84.67	93.72	97.78
	14							57.98	77.53	89.82	96.02
	15								69.00	84.51	93.35
	16								59.50	77.78	89.54
	17									69.80	84.46
	18									60.89	78.09
	19									51.53	70.57
	20										62.17
	21										53.29
240	0	91.04	99.22	99.93	99.99	100.00	100.00	100.00	100.00	100.00	100.00
	1	69.31	95.38	99.44	99.94	99.99	100.00	100.00	100.00	100.00	100.00
	2		86.01	97.60	99.66	99.96	99.99	100.00	100.00	100.00	100.00
	3		70.85	93.10	98.75	99.81	99.97	100.00	100.00	100.00	100.00
	4		52.52	84.85	96.49	99.34	99.90	99.99	100.00	100.00	100.00
	5			72.81	90.04	98.19	99.66	99.94	99.99	100.00	100.00
	6			58.23	84.79	95.80	99.06	99.82	99.97	99.99	100.00
	7				74.69	91.60	97.78	99.51	99.91	99.98	100.00
	8				62.44	85.16	95.40	98.83	99.74	99.95	99.99
	9					76.43	91.49	97.50	99.38	99.87	99.98
	10					65.82	85.73	95.20	98.65	99.68	99.93
	11					54.14	78.04	91.58	97.33	99.28	99.83
	12						68.67	86.38	95.14	98.53	99.62
	13						58.17	79.51	91.79	97.24	99.20
	14							71.13	87.07	95.16	98.46
	15							61.63	80.88	92.07	97.21
	16							51.57	73.32	87.76	95.25
	17								64.65	82.15	92.39
	18								55.32	75.28	88.45
	19									67.34	83.33
	20									58.66	77.06
	21										69.75
	22										61.66
	23										53.15
260	0	92.67	99.48	99.96	100.00	100.00	100.00	100.00	100.00	100.00	100.00
	1	73.42	96.70	99.67	99.97	100.00	100.00	100.00	100.00	100.00	100.00
	2		89.36	98.50	99.83	99.98	100.00	100.00	100.00	100.00	100.00
	3		76.48	95.39	99.31	99.91	99.99	100.00	100.00	100.00	100.00
	4		59.59	89.20	97.93	99.68	99.96	99.99	100.00	100.00	100.00
	5			79.39	94.99	99.06	99.86	99.98	100.00	100.00	100.00
	6			66.51	89.79	97.67	99.57	99.93	99.99	100.00	100.00
	7			52.05	81.92	95.02	98.92	99.81	99.97	100.00	100.00
	8				71.54	90.60	97.60	99.50	99.91	99.99	100.00
	9				59.44	84.09	95.24	98.86	99.77	99.96	99.99
	10					75.49	91.46	97.64	99.46	99.89	99.98
	11					65.21	85.98	95.55	98.85	99.75	99.95
	12					53.97	78.72	92.30	97.74	99.44	99.88
	13						69.88	87.63	95.90	98.87	99.74
	14						59.92	81.42	93.09	97.88	99.45
	15							73.76	89.07	96.26	98.93
	16							64.94	83.73	93.82	98.04
	17							55.40	77.05	90.35	96.62
	18								69.22	85.71	94.49
	19								60.54	79.87	91.47
	20								51.45	72.91	87.44
	21									65.05	82.31
	22									56.60	76.12
	23										69.01
	24										61.21
	25										53.02

Source: *Sampling for Modern Auditors* (Altamonte Springs, Florida: The Institute of Internal Auditors, 1977), pp. 3-29 and 3-30.]

Example of How to Use Sample Size Tables for Stop-or-Go Sampling

Note that two separate tables are shown: one for a universe of less than 200 (Exhibit 14-H) and one for a universe of less than 2,000 (Exhibit 14-I). Assume that you are interested in a population of 1,500 receiving reports and that you believe that the error rate is fairly low. You want to reach a 95 percent confidence level as you apply stop-or-go sampling. This suggests that if you examined 50 sampling units and found no errors, you would have reached 97.18 percent confidence that the error rate was less than 6 percent. However, if you found one error, it would be necessary to find no additional errors in the next 30 items examined (i.e., a total sample size of 80 would be required) to reach a 96.20 percent level of confidence.

Exhibits 14-H and 14-I must be matched to the appropriate universe size; otherwise, the tables are identical in their application.

Exhibit 14-J
Probability-Proportional-to-Size
Sampling Table

Reliability Factors for Errors of Overstatement

Number of Overstatement Errors	Risk of Incorrect Acceptance								
	1%	5%	10%	15%	20%	25%	30%	37%	50%
0	4.61	3.00	2.31	1.90	1.61	1.39	1.21	1.00	.70
1	6.64	4.75	3.89	3.38	3.00	2.70	2.44	2.14	1.68
2	8.41	6.30	5.33	4.72	4.28	3.93	3.62	3.25	2.68
3	10.05	7.76	6.69	6.02	5.52	5.11	4.77	4.34	3.68
4	11.61	9.16	8.00	7.27	6.73	6.28	5.90	5.43	4.68
5	13.11	10.52	9.28	8.50	7.91	7.43	7.01	6.49	5.68
6	14.57	11.85	10.54	9.71	9.08	8.56	8.12	7.56	6.67
7	16.00	13.15	11.78	10.90	10.24	9.69	9.21	8.63	7.67
8	17.41	14.44	13.00	12.08	11.38	10.81	10.31	9.68	8.67
9	18.79	15.71	14.21	13.25	12.52	11.92	11.39	10.74	9.67
10	20.15	16.97	15.41	14.42	13.66	13.02	12.47	11.79	10.67
11	21.49	18.21	16.60	15.57	14.78	14.13	13.55	12.84	11.67
12	22.83	19.45	17.79	16.72	15.90	15.22	14.63	13.89	12.67
13	24.14	20.67	18.96	17.86	17.02	16.32	15.70	14.93	13.67
14	25.45	21.89	20.13	19.00	18.13	17.40	16.77	15.97	14.67
15	26.75	23.10	21.30	20.13	19.24	18.49	17.84	17.02	15.67
16	28.03	24.31	22.46	21.26	20.34	19.58	18.90	18.06	16.67
17	29.31	25.50	23.61	22.39	21.44	20.66	19.97	19.10	17.67
18	30.59	26.70	24.76	23.51	22.54	21.74	21.03	20.14	18.67
19	31.85	27.88	25.91	24.63	23.64	22.81	22.09	21.18	19.67
20	33.11	29.07	27.05	25.74	24.73	23.89	23.15	22.22	20.67

Source: *Audit Sampling* (New York: American Institute of Certified Public Accountants, 1983), p. 117.

Using the Probability-Proportional-to-Size Sampling Table

Assume a tolerable error, already adjusted for expected errors, of $77,600 for a population of $2,000,000. You want to have a 95 percent confidence level, otherwise referred to as a 5 percent (1.00 minus .95) risk of incorrect acceptance. You expect to find three errors. Exhibit 14-J indicates a 7.76 reliability factor for three errors for a 5 percent risk level. The sampling interval would be $77,600 divided by 7.76 or $10,000. This interval translates to a sample size of $2,000,000 divided by $10,000, or 200 units.

QUESTIONS

1. Distinguish between nonstatistical and statistical sampling. What are the advantages of a statistical sampling approach?

2. What types of sampling approaches are commonly used in compliance testing? In substantive testing? Describe the circumstances in which each approach is likely to be preferred.

3. Describe the relevant population and sampling unit for testing in order to fulfill the following audit objectives:
   a. To determine whether all purchases are properly authorized; controls require written authorization of purchases in excess of $2,000, with lesser dollar purchases ordered verbally directly from suppliers.
   b. To estimate year-end inventory balances.
   c. To test whether recorded receivables are overstated.
   d. To gain assurance that all sales are recorded.

4. What type of sampling procedure is likely to be used when the documents to be tested are not prenumbered? Why?

5. Are the sample characteristics resulting from the use of a random number table, a random number generator, systematic selection, and cluster sampling expected to be the same? Explain your response.

6. Why is stratified sampling used?

7. Describe how sample size relates to:
   a. Population size.
   b. The variability of the population.
   c. Expected error rate.
   d. Desired precision.
   e. Reliability.
   f. Risk.

8. What is accomplished by using the ratio or differencing approach, rather than mean-per-unit estimation? What conditions must exist for these methods to be applied?

9. What is the purpose of a pilot sample? Can a pilot sample be merged into a sampling plan for evaluation purposes?

10. When are upper precision limits utilized rather than dollar precision measures? How does precision relate to reliability?

11. Distinguish between confidence limits and bounds.

12. Which risk tends to be of paramount importance to the auditor — alpha risk or beta risk? Why?

13. If an auditor were to apply discovery sampling and find two compliance deviations, what would be the conclusion drawn from the sample?

14. When a sample produces unacceptable results, what are the auditor's alternative means of responding to that sampling evidence?

15. What is the sampling unit when applying PPS? Define tainting. Under what conditions may PPS be applied?

16.   Comment on the proficiency requirements of an auditor in applying statistical sampling techniques. Compare these requirements to those needed to apply nonstatistical sampling.

17.   How might the nature of accounting populations affect sampling techniques?

18.   Multiple-stage sampling is a term sometimes applied to stop-or-go sampling and more often related to a layered approach to sampling. Describe the types of settings in which multiple-stage sampling is likely to arise.

19.   You are an internal auditor for a retail operation with 250 similar stores located across the United States. What special problems are likely to arise in designing a sampling plan?

EXERCISES

E-1

Multiple Choice: Select a single answer which best completes the statement or answers the question:

1.   To determine the sample size in an attribute-sampling survey, what must be specified?
    a.   Population mean, expected error rate, precision.
    b.   Precision, reliability, standard deviation.
    c.   Precision, reliability, expected error rate.
    d.   Population mean, standard deviation, precision.

2.   When would difference estimation or ratio estimation sampling methods be inappropriate?
    a.   If differences between the book values and audit values of a population are rare.
    b.   If the average difference between the audit value and book value of a population is small.
    c.   If differences between the book value and audit value of a population are numerous.
    d.   If the average difference between the audit value and book value of a population is large.

The following information is to be used in answering #3 and #4, below:

An internal auditor has been assigned to conduct a dollar-unit sample of a population of vouchers in the purchasing department having a total book value of $300,000. The internal auditor feels that a maximum error of $900 is acceptable and would like a 95 percent confidence-level factor in his results. (The reliability factor at 95 percent and 0 errors is 3.00.)

Table of First 10 Vouchers in the Population

Voucher No.	Balance	Cumulative Balance
1	$100	$ 100
2	$150	$ 250
3	$ 40	$ 290
4	$200	$ 490
5	$ 10	$ 500
6	$290	$ 790
7	$ 50	$ 840
8	$190	$1,030
9	$ 20	$1,050
10	$180	$1,230

3. Given (1) a random start of $50 as the first dollar amount and (2) the table above of the first 10 vouchers in the population, determine the number of the fourth voucher that will be selected (assuming that the sample size will be 1,000).
    a. 4
    b. 6
    c. 7
    d. 8

4. In examining the sample, one overstatement error was detected, causing an extension of $270 to the maximum tolerable error. Assuming (1) a sample size of 1,000 and (2) that the maximum dollar amount of overstatement at zero was established to be $900 before the sampling analysis, what conclusion can the auditor now make from the sampling evidence?
    a. He is 95 percent confident that the dollar amount of overstatement in the population of vouchers is between $900 and $1,170.
    b. He is 95 percent confident that the dollar amount of overstatement in the population of vouchers exceeds $1,170.
    c. He is 95 percent confident that the dollar amount of overstatement in the population of vouchers is less than $1,170.
    d. An insufficient number of errors were detected to warrant a conclusion.

5. What is the chief advantage of stop-or-go sampling?
    a. The error rate in the population can be projected to within certain precision limits.
    b. It may reduce the size of the sample that needs to be taken from a population, thus reducing sampling costs.
    c. It allows sampling analysis to be performed on nonhomogeneous populations.
    d. It allows the sampler to increase the confidence limits of the analysis without sacrificing precision.

6. Which of the following is *not* a criterion for a successful stratified random-sampling plan?
   a. Every item must belong to one and only one stratum.
   b. The original population of items must be normally distributed.
   c. There must be an identifiable means of subdividing a heterogeneous population into groups with more homogeneous characteristics.
   d. The number of items in each group must be known or determinable.

   (CIA Exam Adapted)

E-2

Multiple Choice: Select a single answer which best completes the statement or answers the question:

1. An auditor's finding was stated as follows: "Twenty of 100 randomly selected items tested revealed that $200.00 in cash discounts on purchases were lost." This variable sampling finding is deficient because:
   a. The recommendation specifies no action.
   b. The sampling methodology is not defined.
   c. The amount is not material.
   d. The probable effect on the entire population is not provided.

2. The risk of concluding from the sample evidence that the book value is not correctly stated, when in fact it is correctly stated, is referred to as alpha risk. The risk of incorrect rejection can be decreased by:
   a. Using a higher statistical reliability level.
   b. Using a lower statistical reliability level.
   c. Reducing the sample size.
   d. Using monetary unit sampling, thereby reducing the population standard deviation.

3. Company policy calls for stores personnel to release specific materials only upon written request from authorized parties. To ascertain that only authorized request forms are being filled, the auditor should select a statistical sample of:
   a. Authorized request forms and examine them for authorized signatures.
   b. Perpetual inventory credits and trace them to properly authorized request forms.
   c. Inventory release forms and trace them to the perpetual inventory records.
   d. Authorized request forms and trace them to cost accumulation records.

4. An attributes sampling plan would be useful in determining an estimate of:
   a. The percentage of customers more than 30 days late in making payments.
   b. The frequency of late payments and their aggregate dollar amount.
   c. The audit value of inventory.
   d. The total purchases from subsidiaries.

5. A bank auditor wishes to confirm liability demand deposits. The bank has excellent internal control. The auditor might efficiently use all of the following sampling techniques in confirming demand deposits *except*:
   a. Discovery sampling.
   b. Monetary unit sampling (probability-proportional-to-size).
   c. Cluster sampling.
   d. Stratified mean-per-unit (variables estimation) sampling.

6. An auditor used the following information in a discovery sampling situation:
   - Population size: 1,000
   - Sample size: 200
   - Estimated number of errors in population: 5
   - Probability of finding at least one error if the actual number of errors is 0.5%: 67%

   If the auditor found no errors in the sample, what would be the most appropriate audit determination?
   a. The auditor is 67 percent confident that the error rate is zero.
   b. The auditor is 67 percent confident that the error rate does not exceed 1 percent.
   c. The auditor is 67 percent confident that the error rate is less than 0.5 percent.
   d. The auditor is 95 percent confident that there are not more than 5 errors in the population.

7. An internal auditor is using variables estimation as the statistical sampling technique to estimate the monetary value of a large inventory of parts. Given a sample standard deviation of $400, a sample size of 400, and a 95 percent two-tail confidence level, what precision can the auditor assign to his estimate of the mean dollar value of a part?
   a. ±$39
   b. ±$2
   c. ±$52
   d. ±$4
   e. ±$20

8. A test of 200 invoices randomly selected by the internal auditor revealed 35 which had not been approved for payment. At the 95 percent confidence level, what precision can be assigned?
   a. 6.9 percent
   b. 5.3 percent
   c. 9.1 percent
   d. 3.5 percent
   e. 1.7 percent

9. An internal auditor plans to sample an insurance claims settlement file to ascertain evidence of fraudulent claims. The auditor draws a sample of claims for auditing which will provide a specified confidence level of detecting at least one fraudulent claim if

a certain rate of fraudulent claims actually exists in the population. This type of sampling plan is known as:
a. Acceptance sampling.
b. Stratified sampling.
c. Discovery sampling.
d. Chi-square sampling.
e. Variables sampling.

10. An auditor's statistical sample drawn from a population of invoices indicates a mean value of $150 and a sampling precision of ±$30 at a 95 percent confidence level. Which of the following statements is a correct interpretation of this sample data?
a. There is a 95 percent probability that the true population mean is $150.
b. There is a 95 percent probability that the true population mean falls in the range of $135 to $165.
c. In repeated sampling, about 95 percent of the intervals with precision of ±$30 around the sample mean will contain the true population mean.
d. In repeated sampling, the true population mean will fall in the precision range of $120 to $180 about 95 percent of the time.
e. In repeated sampling, the point estimate of the true population mean will be $150 about 95 percent of the time.

11. An internal auditor determines that a sample size of 250 units is appropriate. There is then an observed sample standard deviation of $386, and a 99 percent confidence interval using a two-tailed test. The sampling precision is ±63. What sampling precision would be achieved with a 95 percent, two-sided confidence interval?
a. ±40.3
b. ±63.0
c. ±34.5
d. ±83.7
e. ±47.8

(CIA Exam Adapted)

E-3

Multiple Choice: Select a single answer which best completes the statement or answers the question:

1. The concept of standard deviation is significant in statistical sampling in auditing because:
a. The central limit theorem states that repeated samples from a population will produce sample standard deviations that cluster around the actual standard deviation of the population.
b. The calculation of sample sizes for variables estimation is directly related to the magnitude of the population standard deviation.
c. The magnitude of the finite population correction factor is directly related to the magnitude of the standard deviation of the population.

    d. Statistical sampling techniques are inappropriate if the standard deviation of a population is very small relative to the mean of the population.

    e. The choice between attributes sampling and variables sampling is related to the magnitude of the population standard deviation.

2. An auditor wants to statistically sample a large population of open orders to determine the proportion of back orders on file due to a lack of stock. This proportion is expected to be 20 percent; accordingly, the auditor draws a sample of 246 open orders which yields 95 percent confidence with a precision of ±5 percent. If the auditor wants to change the precision to ±2.5 percent, the required sample size is:

    a. 174

    b. 492

    c. 697

    d. 945

    e. 984

3. Sample selection using dollar unit sampling for inventory valuation will most likely result in selection of a sample with characteristics roughly equivalent to one provided by:

    a. Judgment (nonstatistical) sampling plans.

    b. Variables sampling plan with substantial stratification by dollar amount.

    c. Selection of inventory records using a random starting point for the record selection.

    d. Difference or ratio estimation plans on an unstratified basis.

    e. Mean-per-unit or direct extension unstratified sampling plans.

4. Which of the following would be an improper technique when using dollar-unit statistical sampling in an audit of accounts receivable?

    a. Combining negative and positive dollar-error item amounts in the appraisal of a sample.

    b. Using a sample technique in which the same account balance could be selected more than once.

    c. Selecting a random starting point and then sampling every "*i*th" dollar unit (systematic sampling).

    d. Defining the sampling unit in the population as an individual dollar and not as an individual account balance.

    e. All of the above.

5. Statistical sampling enables the internal auditor to:

    a. Perform the audit with much less effort.

    b. Determine the exact value of a population parameter.

    c. Limit the scope of the audit examination.

    d. Quantify the risks associated with estimating population parameters.

    e. Reduce the need for analyzing the audit situation.

6. Increasing the size of a statistical sample used in an internal audit will:
   a. Increase the confidence level if the precision is held constant.
   b. Decrease the confidence level if the precision is held constant.
   c. Widen the precision range if the confidence level is held constant.
   d. Narrow the precision range if the confidence level is held constant.
   e. (a) and (b) above.

7. Separate statistical samples of invoice payments in each of 15 branch offices of your company show a number of errors. In determining whether the quality of performance among the 15 offices is significantly different, which of the following statistical distributions should you assume to be most applicable?
   a. Poisson.
   b. Chi-square.
   c. Student's t.
   d. Hypergeometric.
   e. Binomial.

8. An internal auditor is using statistical sampling to estimate the monetary value of an inventory. Which of the following statistical sampling techniques is *not* appropriate for estimating the monetary value where perpetual inventory records are maintained?
   a. Ratio.
   b. Acceptance.
   c. Stratification.
   d. Difference.
   e. Regression.

9. The internal auditor's statistical sample of 100 sampling units indicates an average inventory understatement of $200, with a sampling error of ±$40 at the 95 percent confidence level. To reduce the sampling error to ±$20 at the 95 percent confidence level for the same population would require a statistical sample size in units of about:
   a. 700
   b. 200
   c. 1,200
   d. 400
   e. 800

10. In an audit of a population of 100,000 invoices using a sample size of 625, with an average sample unit value of $200 and a sample standard deviation of $100, the lower confidence limit at the 95 percent confidence level for the average sampling unit would be about:
    a. $180
    b. $192
    c. $198
    d. $171
    e. $163

11. For a population of 25,000 items, an estimated error rate not to exceed 5 percent, a confidence level of 95 percent, and a precision of ±3 percent, the required sample size is 201. Using the same criteria, the required sample size for a population of 100,000 items would be:
    a. 202
    b. 302
    c. 402
    d. 502
    e. 602

12. The auditor can change the standard deviation of the mean for a statistical sample by:
    a. Stratifying the population.
    b. Increasing the size of the sample.
    c. Decreasing the size of the sample.
    d. All of the above.
    e. (a) and (b) above.

13. One measure of the variability among values in a given population is the:
    a. Arithmetic mean.
    b. Median.
    c. Range.
    d. Mode.
    e. Harmonic mean.   (CIA Exam Adapted)

E-4

Identify the factual error in each of the following three statements:

1. In any normal distribution of population values, the mean of the distribution plus or minus one standard deviation includes 25 percent of the area under the normal curve.
2. To avoid bias in the selection of a sample, every item must have a systematic (every "*i*th" item) chance of selection.
3. Assuming the same population size, sample size, and estimated error rate, an increase in the confidence level will result in a narrowing of the range of precision.

                                                               (CIA Exam Adapted)

E-5

Assume a random number table is used to select a sample from a subsidiary ledger which contains 420 pages with 40 lines per page. Which sampling units would be selected if the following column of numbers appeared in the relevant section of the random number table?

                                    41938
                                    00342
                                    00218
                                    20931
                                    31608

E-6

A payroll run is printed according to the job classification of each employee, with top management printed first. Can systematic sampling be applied to such a run? Why or why not?

E-7

Assume a desired reliability of 90 percent (1.65 is the related factor), desired precision of $8,000,000, an estimated population standard deviation of $20,000, and a population size of 2,000. What would be the required sample size if unrestricted random sampling with replacement were to be applied?

PROBLEMS

P-1

An audit of inventory records disclosed that the population comprises 20,000 items of inventory. Units within the items vary from 30 to 750. The values of the units vary from $20 to $1,500. The auditor had estimated the error rate at not over 5 percent, and since a confidence level of 95 percent and a precision of ±3 percent was desired, the tables showed a sample of 200 items. The selection was made from the north end of the storeroom, picking items having 100 or more units.

In the test, 40 instances were found in which the number of units in stock varied by one or more units from the number shown on the inventory records.

The report to management states that the auditor is 95 percent confident that the number of records in the population which are in error is somewhere between 970 and 1030.

Required:
Describe five errors in the auditor's technique.

(CIA Exam Adapted)

P-2

Listed below are five situations for which you plan to use statistical sampling:

1. You will observe an annual physical verification of a perpetual inventory. A statistical sample of the inventory will be counted under the observation of the internal auditors.
2. You suspect that prices were deliberately raised on some of the perpetual inventory line items to cover inventory shrinkage caused by thefts.
3. A large number of errors are occurring in the keypunch operation. You recommend the installation of a continuous statistical sample.
4. Your audit program calls for examination of purchase orders to see if they were issued within the prescribed time limits. You plan to use minimum audit effort for this test. Your audit objective will be satisfied with a 95 percent probability that not more than 2 percent of the purchase orders were issued late.
5. You find that material issue documents for the period under audit are stored in a records warehouse in serial number order in boxes containing 1,000 documents each. There are 900 boxes of documents.

Required:

For each of the situations described above:

a. Identify the sampling plan or selection technique that would be most appropriate.
b. State why the particular plan or technique should be used.

(CIA Exam Adapted)

15 Quantitative Methods for Auditors

Numerous quantitative methods are available to the internal auditor. These tools are means of gaining a thorough understanding of operations, drawing conclusions about varied populations, analyzing both the effectiveness and the efficiency of operations, performing cost-effective audits, and preparing operational recommendations for auditees and top management. This chapter introduces basic terminology and describes the potential usefulness of various quantitative tools in an internal auditing context. As the techniques and computational rules for applying them are reviewed, keep in mind that EDP resources are available to assist internal auditors in the use of these quantitative methods. Numerous software packages are available for computing statistics, drawing samples, performing tests, and estimating various models and relationships.

Both statistical and nonstatistical sampling procedures are described in the previous chapter. Statistical sampling techniques focus on random sampling approaches which are intended to give every item within a population an equal chance of selection. Random sampling presumes that items in the population are homogeneous and that no rationale exists for selecting one particular item instead of another. When reasons do exist for focusing greater audit attention on specific transactions or sets of transactions, the auditor often will use nonstatistical sampling techniques to ensure that the sample is properly "directed" to those areas or items of special concern. For this reason, such techniques are often termed "directed sampling." Of course, statistical sampling procedures can be applied to a narrower population, defined as a "directed" area of interest, such as "all related-party transactions."

Means of Directed Sampling

The term *directed sampling* implies that sampling is being directed by auditors' knowledge of which transactions are of particular interest for sample selection. Such direction often stems from auditors' understanding of operations and from other audit tests that have suggested transaction types or periods of time that are more likely to contain error. The focus of this chapter is upon means of gaining the knowledge with which to direct a sampling plan.

Analytical Review Techniques

In particular, analytical review techniques, or reasonableness tests, commonly direct the auditor's attention to unreasonable account balances or to unexpected and unexplained changes in account balances or operating statistics.

Fluctuation Analysis. "Unreasonable" often is defined relative to a prior period. If the current period's operations vary more than 5 percent to 10 percent from past experiences, investigation often will be required, with sampling directed toward those operations and time periods most out of line. For example, if total advertising expense had grown by 40 percent on an annual basis, current monthly expenditures might be compared to the prior year's to identify which months should be investigated.

Ratio Analysis. Fluctuations tend to focus upon one piece of information at two points in time, whereas ratio analysis can consider account interrelationships across time. For example, rather than merely comparing inventory balances, inventory turnover statistics, number of days' sales of inventory on hand, and current ratio statistics can be reviewed to assess the reasonableness of an entity's investment in inventory. Not only can ratios be compared against historical experience, they can also be compared to the industry's experiences. This procedure has the advantage of external validation of "reasonableness" and helps quantify the effects of general economic and industry events across similar companies.

Actual-to-Budget Comparisons. Another meaningful benchmark for assessing reasonableness is expectations, as formalized in budgets and standards. Typically, comparisons of such expectations to actual performance are part of the routine controls over operations. If so, analyses can be the starting point of the internal auditors' evaluation. Of course, in order to utilize management reports, the internal auditor must understand how to perform and interpret the figures reported in typical comparisons of expected and actual operations.

Variance Analysis. Comparisons of production standards to actual performance have been structured into the key relationships reported in Exhibit 15-1. Notice that the analysis distinguishes between variations in costs or rates and variations in use. Costs exceeding standards flag unfavorable variances, while costs below standards flag favorable variances.

Exhibit 15-1
Variance Analysis: An Example in a Manufacturing Setting

PRODUCTION STANDARDS	ACTUAL PRODUCTION
Raw materials: 2 pounds per unit of output at $ .30 per pound	10,000 units of output; 23,000 pounds of material purchased and used
Direct labor: 15 minutes per unit of output at $16 per hour	$ .25 per pound cost of material
Overhead: $2 per direct-labor hour	2,400 hours of labor at a total cost of $52,800; overhead cost of $3,500

Raw Material Price Variance

(Actual Price – Standard Price) $\times$ Number of Pounds Purchased

($ .25 – $ .30) $\times$ 23,000 = $1,150   Favorable

Raw Material Use Variance

(Actual Pounds Used – Standard Use) $\times$ Standard Price

(23,000 – 20,000) $\times$ $ .30 = $900   Unfavorable

Direct Labor Rate Variance

(Actual Rate – Standard Rate) $\times$ Number of Direct-Labor Hours Worked

($16 – $22) $\times$ 2,400 = $14,400   Unfavorable

Direct Labor Efficiency Variance

(Actual Hours Worked – Standard Hours) $\times$ Standard Rate

(2,400 – 2,500) $\times$ $16 = $1,600   Favorable

Overhead Spending Variance

Actual Overhead Costs – (Standard Overhead Rate $\times$ Actual Direct-Labor Hours)

$3,500 – ($2 $\times$ 2,400) = $1,300   Favorable

Overhead Efficiency Variance

(Actual Direct-Labor Hours – Standard Direct-Labor Hours) $\times$ Standard Overhead Rate

(2,400 – 2,500) $\times$ $2 = $200   Favorable

The control of volume changes apart from price changes permits the likely cause of the deviation to be flagged — for example, has purchasing exceeded its spending standard, have labor negotiations led to higher pay than expected, or has efficiency in production led to losses or cost savings? Of course, the mere classification of variances does not clearly set responsibility. For example, a favorable material price variance coupled with an unfavorable material use variance may indicate that lower-quality materials were purchased, causing waste and inefficiencies on the production line. If this occurred, responsibility for the unfavorable variance would be centered in the purchasing department rather than in production, where the classification scheme might lead the auditor.

The usefulness of variance analyses in directing internal auditors' work should be obvious. The likely source of problems is highlighted, as well as the magnitude of unexpected variations. Normal control procedures typically require follow-up of variations in excess of certain amounts, so that explanations of exceptions should be available for the auditor's review. By reviewing these control reports, the auditor can be more efficient in directing tests toward unexplained fluctuations in operations.

The Role of Flexible Budgeting. One difficulty with any comparison of budget-to-actual is that the budget may have been formulated with an operating level in mind that differs from the subsequent actual operating level. A so-called static comparison of budget-to-actual may very well lack meaning since all variances could be traceable to a difference in the unit of measure (i.e., the assumption of 10,000 units of output for the budget versus 20,000 units of actual output). Therefore, flexible budgeting is the widely accepted means of adapting budgeted data to actual operating levels. In Exhibit 15-2, the standards presented in Exhibit 15-1 are translated into three alternative flexible budget levels, facilitating comparisons to actual operations at those levels of production.

The High-Low Method. Examination of Exhibit 15-2 bears out the assumption of an entirely variable relationship between costs and output. In actuality, many costs are mixed, demonstrating (1) some fixed or constant level regardless of the quantity of output, and (2) some variable component that does move in direct proportion to production. This fact implies a need to develop flexible budget formulas that reflect cost behavior. One tool for doing so is the high-low method. This approach uses past experience to identify total costs at the lowest and at the highest levels of output recently experienced.

Exhibit 15-2
An Example of Flexible Budgeting

Production Standards

Raw materials: 2 pounds per unit of output at $ .30 per pound
Direct labor: 15 minutes per unit of output at $16 per hour
Overhead: $2 per direct-labor hour

10,000 units of output:

Raw materials	$ 6,000[1]
Direct labor	40,000[2]
Overhead	5,000[3]

15,000 units of output:

Raw materials	$ 9,000
Direct labor	60,000
Overhead	7,500

20,000 units of output:

Raw materials	$12,000
Direct labor	80,000
Overhead	10,000

---

[1](2 pounds × 10,000 units) × $ .30
[2](1/4 hour × 10,000 units) × $16
[3](1/4 hour × 10,000 units) × $2

It is presumed that those costs fluctuating with the difference in the number of units of output at these two levels are variable costs, whereas those remaining constant are fixed costs. Such a computation appears in Exhibit 15-3, which focuses on actual overhead costs as they are related to direct labor hours. The estimated relationship is then applied to three different levels of direct labor hours, demonstrating the use of this more sophisticated flexible budgeting approach that reflects cost behavior.

Exhibit 15-3
The High–Low Method:
An Example Involving Overhead Costs

	Low	High
Actual Overhead Costs	$6,000	$6,600
Total Direct-Labor Hours	3,000	4,000

$$\frac{\$6,600 - 6,000}{4,000 - 3,000} = \frac{600}{1,000} = \$ .60 \text{ per hour variable-cost component}$$

$6,000 – ($ .60 × 3,000) = $6,000 – 1,800 = $4,200 fixed-cost component

Test of formula: $ .60 (4,000) + $4,200 = $6,600

Alternate activity levels:

3,200 direct-labor hours	$ .60 (3,200) + $4,200 = $6,120
3,500 direct-labor hours	$ .60 (3,500) + $4,200 = $6,300
3,800 direct-labor hours	$ .60 (3,800) + $4,200 = $6,480

<u>Summary of Flexible Budget Formula:</u>

$ .60 (Direct-Labor Hours) + $4,200 = Total Overhead Costs

Variable Component   Fixed Component

Once cost behavior is analyzed and quantified, a useful planning tool is cost-volume-profit analysis, or breakeven analysis. In its simplist form, the breakeven point is calculated as fixed costs divided by contribution margin (selling price minus variable cost).

Trend Analysis. Beyond comparisons of one year to another, analyses of trends over longer periods can serve as useful benchmarks in assessing the reasonableness of observed fluctuations over time. This is particularly true of cyclical operations. Consider the information content of a year-to-year comparison versus a long-term trend evaluation based on the graph depicted in Exhibit 15-4. In volatile climates, internal auditors often find it useful to compute three- to five-year averages for comparison of financial and operating performance statistics during the current period to those of past periods, as well as for ratio analysis.

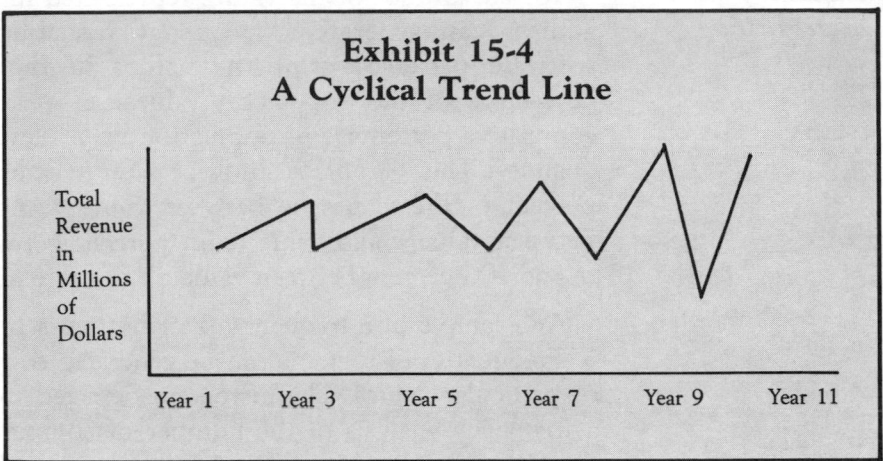

Exhibit 15-4
A Cyclical Trend Line

Model Building. The high-low method captures cost behavior but uses only two data points for estimating such behavior. Trend analysis uses numerous data points but focuses on only one variable, such as revenue across time (as reflected in Exhibit 15-4). Model building is a means of considering a set of data points for a set of variables that relate to some item of interest, such as total revenue. In particular, regression analysis can be used to quantify expectations of revenue based on economic, industry, nonfinancial, and financial data which, in turn, can be compared with recorded values to identify unusual deviations. Sampling can then be directed to such deviations. The topic of regression analysis will be explored further later in this chapter.

The Bayesian Approach

Any time that judgment is merged with classical sampling, a Bayesian approach is in use. Judgment, based on past experience with the auditee, other audit tests, and expertise in the area, is referred to as the auditor's "priors." Generally accepted approaches are available for eliciting and quantifying these priors and for combining them with sampling evidence. While details on how this is done are beyond the scope of this book, the internal auditor should be aware that such an approach exists and is generally familiar to individuals trained in quantitative methods.

Data Analysis — the Use of Descriptive Statistics

To gain familiarity with data sets, various data analysis tools are available to the internal auditor. The basic approach to describing a population so that it can be compared to other data sets is to compute descriptive statistics.

**Frequency
Distributions**

To gain an idea of the values represented in a data set, an internal auditor can generate a frequency distribution. Most statistical software packages print the values in the population set, the percentage of the population values set at that quantity, and the cumulative percentage of population values less than or equal to that quantity. This permits a study of interquartile distributions, i.e., 25 percent of the values lie between value *a* and value *b*, 50 percent between value *a* and value *c*, 75 percent between value *a* and value *d*, and 100 percent between value *a* and value *e*.

An example of a frequency distribution is provided in Exhibit 15-5. Frequently, histograms can be generated to illustrate the incidence of particular values. The histogram depicted in Exhibit 15-5 reports a frequency analysis of the number of competitive bids solicited on various orders by the purchasing department. The dominant practice clearly is to solicit three competitive bids per order. A summary histogram and frequency analysis will raise questions as to why no competitive bids were solicited on certain orders and why as many as five bids were solicited on others — i.e., what criteria are utilized to determine the number of competitive bids to be solicited?

The drawback of a frequency distribution becomes apparent when one considers a population in which few, if any, items have exactly the same value. For example, an analysis of 2,000 purchases would likely generate close to 2,000 different values, resulting in a large amount of output which would be cumbersome to review. In this setting, a histogram would be almost flat, depicting one occurrence per value. Often, class intervals are specified to overcome this problem, e.g., purchases ranging from $1 to $500 and those from $501 to $1,000, etc. In lieu of such a detailed breakdown summary, statistics for data analysis are useful.

Range

The range of a distribution refers to the difference between the lowest value and the highest value. Hence, if the lowest dollar purchase was $13.50 and the highest dollar purchase was $78,760.10, the reported range would be the difference between these two values, or $78,746.60. Presumably, the internal auditor has some expectation as to how large purchase orders can be, and this range statistic permits him or her to check the accuracy of those expectations.

Mean

The mean or average value of a data set is computed as the sum of all values, divided by the number of data points. For example, if three measurements are made by the quality control department of the weight of packages produced — 11 ounces, 16 ounces, and

Exhibit 15-5
A Frequency Distribution for
Competitive Bidding Practices

Number of Bids	Incidence	Percentage	Cumulative Percentage
0	5	.5	.5
1	20	2.0	2.5
2	200	20.0	22.5
3	400	40.0	62.5
4	300	30.0	92.5
5	50	5.0	97.5
6	25	2.5	100.0

Histogram

15 ounces — then the average weight would be $(11 + 16 + 15) \div 3$, or 14 ounces. The internal auditor frequently would find it useful to compare sampling means to averages computed during normal control and processing activities.

Standard Deviation

To evaluate the meaning of average statistics, standard deviations need to be reviewed. Standard deviations measure dispersion around the mean, thereby providing an indication of how accurately the mean estimate represents items in a data set. Utilizing the three weights measured by the quality control department, the standard deviation can be calculated as the square root of the average of squared deviations from the mean:

$$11 - 14 = (-3)^2 = 9$$
$$16 - 14 = (2)^2 = 4$$
$$15 - 14 = (1)^2 = \underline{1}$$
$$14$$
$$14 \div 3 = 4.67$$
$$\sqrt{4.67} = \underline{2.16}$$

This measure indicates that the dispersion of the three measures is not extreme. This suggests that the mean estimate is likely to be a fairly precise descriptive statistic for each of the three weighings.

Median

When a sample has some extreme values, means can be somewhat misleading. A far more useful measure in such a setting is the median. The median is the value at the 50 percent mark or midpoint of the sample's values when they are ranked from highest to lowest. For the three weights, the rank order would be 16, 15, and 11 ounces, and the median value would be 15.

Mode

Another useful statistic is the mode, which is the most frequently occurring value within a data set. Hence, if six weighings were performed, yielding 16, 15, 15, 11, 14, and 12, the mode would be 15. If inferences were to be drawn as to the weight most commonly put into a package by the production line, the mode would be a useful measure.

Skewness

The skewness of a distribution refers to its propensity not to be symmetrical. A perfectly symmetrical distribution such as a normal bell curve (depicted in Exhibit 15-6) has a skewness of zero. In contrast, a distribution with most observations to the right of the mean is said to be negatively skewed, and a distribution with most observations to the left of the mean is said to be positively skewed. These types of distributions are similarly depicted in Exhibit 15-6. Many accounting populations are skewed. In fact, most are probably positively skewed. For example, most customer balances may be small dollar amounts, with five or six large-dollar customers that skew the distribution (similar to the positively skewed diagram in Exhibit 15-6).

The computation of skewness takes the deviations from the mean, divides them by the standard deviation, and raises them to the third power; these figures are then added together and divided by the number of data points. Returning to the three weights taken by the quality control department, skewness would be computed as follows:

Exhibit 15-6
Illustrations of Skewness

Zero Skewness (symmetrical curve)

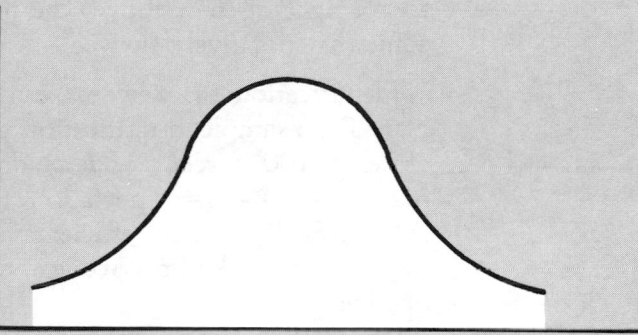

Negative Skewness

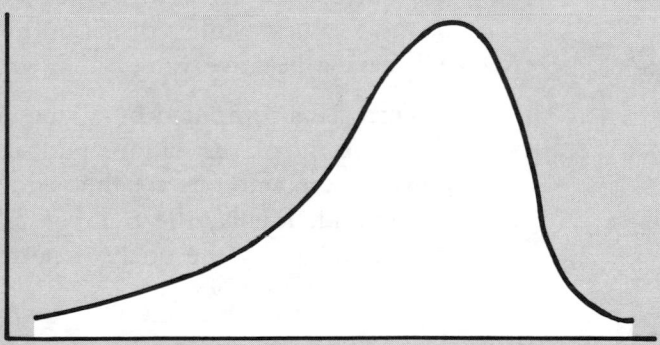

Positive Skewness

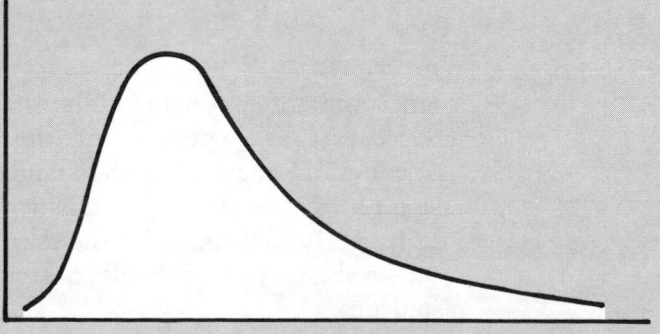

$$11 - 14 = (-3/2.16)^3 \rightarrow -2.68$$
$$16 - 14 = (\ 2/2.16)^3 \rightarrow \ \ .79$$
$$15 - 14 = (\ 1/2.16)^3 \rightarrow \ \underline{\ .10}$$

$$\frac{-1.79}{3} = -.60$$

A positive value indicates a clustering of data points to the left of (i.e., below) the mean, while a negative value indicates a clustering to the right of (i.e., above) the mean. The weight measurements are somewhat negatively skewed.

Identification of skewness can lead to a more efficient sampling plan. For example, stratification of the "tail of the distribution" for close to 100 percent of large-dollar customers could substantially reduce the standard deviation for the remaining population and thereby facilitate more efficient sampling through smaller sample size requirements. Audit coverage of higher dollar amounts is also obtained.

Kurtosis

The term "kurtosis" refers to the relative flatness or peakedness of a curve. A normal bell-shaped curve, as shown in Exhibit 15-6, has kurtosis of zero. More peaked or narrower distributions have positive values, while a distribution that is flatter than a normal curve will have a negative value.

Kurtosis is computed by taking deviations from the mean, dividing by the standard deviation, and raising these values to the fourth power; these amounts are then added, divided by the number of data points and, finally, the number 3 is subtracted. Utilizing the three weights taken by the quality control department, kurtosis would be computed as follows:

$$11 - 14 = (-3/2.16)^4 \rightarrow 3.72$$
$$16 - 14 = (\ 2/2.16)^4 \rightarrow \ .73$$
$$15 - 14 = (\ 1/2.16)^4 \rightarrow \ \underline{.05}$$

$$\frac{4.50}{3} - 3 = -1.5$$

Since the three weights differ from one another, this measure of flatness is as expected for the small data set. The flatter the distribution, the higher the standard deviation tends to be and the less informative the mean statistic. Hence, it is important for auditors to have a visual image of the data base being described so that they can evaluate the probable descriptive power of various summary statistics.

Distributional
Assumptions

The mean, standard deviation, skewness, and kurtosis measures are referred to as the first, second, third, and fourth moments of a distribution. They tend to be evaluated in relation to the normal distribution, which is totally described by the first and second moments (since the third and fourth moments assume zero values). Variables statistical sampling requires a normal sampling distribution. Many of the statistical tests routinely used to analyze samples are parametric tests which assume a normal distribution for the data base. If a distributional assumption is thought not to apply to a particular data set — for example, if the data set is highly skewed — then nonparametric tests usually should be applied. These statistical tools make no assumptions about underlying distributions of the data under analysis. Examples of both types of tests follow.

t-tests

The term *t-tests* refers to a parametric statistical analysis of whether the mean or average value of two different samples or populations are statistically equivalent. If an internal auditor wanted to test whether there had been a perceptible shift in the efficiency of a production process, he or she could estimate the average time taken to produce a product prior to the expected shift and the average time taken to produce a product following the shift. A paired-sample t-test can then be performed to determine if the two averages are significantly different (i.e., due to a cause rather than just random variations).

In a similar setting, assume you wish to evaluate the efficiency of two different plants. You can estimate the average time required to produce one unit of output at plant A and plant B and then perform a t-test between the two groups to determine if these average times are the same, statistically speaking.

The t-test for independent samples is computed by taking the difference in average values per sample and dividing by the standard deviation for the difference of sample means. The degrees of freedom (i.e., data points available for estimation) are the combined sample sizes used to estimate each average, minus 2 (since two data points were used up when the average values were estimated). If the standard deviations are different for the two samples, separate standard deviations (instead of a pooled measure) are used in the denominator. Paired-sample t-tests take the difference in the two paired-sample values, compute the mean difference, and divide through by a standard deviation for the differences.

To demonstrate the calculation of a comparison of means of independent samples with similar standard deviations, assume that plant A had an average production-time value of four minutes with a standard deviation of 2, while plant B had an average production-time value of six minutes with a standard deviation of 2.5. The averages were based on samples of 20 and 30 units of output, respectively. The resulting t-test would be computed as follows:

$$\frac{(4 - 6)}{\sqrt{2^2/20 + 2.5^2/30}} = 3.13$$

with 20 + 30 – 2, or 48, degrees of freedom.

Readily available tables indicate that in order to represent a significant difference in mean values at a 95 percent level of confidence, the t-value would have had to be 2.021. Clearly, plants A and B have statistically different levels of efficiency as measured by the average time required to produce one unit of output. Formulas for samples with unequal standard deviations and for paired-sample analyses are reported in most basic statistics books. Due to the general availability of software to make such calculations, further computations for t-test analyses are not illustrated here.

Chi-Square Tests

Chi-square analyses are nonparametric tests capable of analyzing relationships between qualitative data. For example, do operating units in the South have particular patterns of operation different from those in the North? In this setting, the qualitative characteristic of interest would be geographical region. Note that data of interest to an internal auditor may be in any of the following forms:

1. *Nominal Data:* Classification data, such as plant A versus plant B.
2. *Ordinal Data:* Ranking data, such as quality A is better than quality B, which is better than quality C.
3. *Interval or Ratio Data:* Count data that have consistent proportional relationships and may be subjected to mathematical formulas; for example, the total number of units produced by plant A and plant B.

The t-test, as a parametric statistical tool, is intended to compare interval or ratio data and presumes underlying normal distributions. In contrast, chi-square tests can check for the independence of nominal classifications and ordinal data, and require no particular distributional pattern for the data.

To illustrate a chi-square statistic, assume an internal auditor wants to determine if any relationship exists between the proportion of managerial versus nonmanagerial positions and the presence or absence of a union. The relationship can be illustrated in a two-by-two matrix format:

	Managers	Non-Managers
Union Shop		
Non-Union Shop		

If these two dimensions (manager/nonmanager and union/nonunion) were totally independent, you would expect the values in each of the boxes or cells to be equal. On the other hand, if more managers were present in nonunion shops, the value in the lower left-hand box would be higher, as would the top right-hand box, than the other two cells. This finding would indicate a likely association. Statistically, the distribution of data points or actual cell frequencies is compared to what would be expected if no interrelationship exists. If these distributions are statistically different, then a relationship is indicated — the larger the chi-square statistic, the more likely a relationship. However, a chi-square statistic is unable to measure the strength of a relationship; it only verifies the existence of a relationship.

Again, due to the general availability of computer software that can generate chi-square tests, computations are not presented here.

Other Common Statistics

Measures of the strength of associations abound. Nonparametric statistics such as eta squared quantify the proportion of movement in one variable predicted by movements in another. Most software packages provide a diverse set of both parametric and nonparametric tests of statistical association — among them lambda, gamma, tau b, tau c, and eta — along with explanations of their underlying assumptions, applicability, and interpretation. An excellent means by which internal auditors can check their understanding of an auditee's operations and the interrelationship of various data sets is to calculate statistical measures of association, compare these measures to the expected results, and investigate unexpected deviations between actual and expected interrelationships.

Merging Sampling Approaches with Prior Audit Knowledge

It is imperative that the internal auditor recognize how prior audit knowledge about data sets can be merged with different sampling approaches to produce more efficient and effective audit evidence. (Sampling is discussed in Chapter 14.) As suggested earlier, very flat or skewed distributions are likely to be more efficiently sampled by stratifying such data sets. In fact, any time standard deviation is relatively high, stratification tends to improve sampling efficiency.

If t-tests have demonstrated substantial differences between operations at two plants, a multi-location sampling plan should consider the two plants as separate populations, rather than as one homogeneous population for which samples drawn from plant A would be assumed to apply at plant B.

Careful review of descriptive statistics can alert an auditor to peculiar characteristics of a data set that might affect the applicability or interpretability of a variety of analytical tools and sampling plans.

Ratio and Trend Analysis

Ratios can be extremely useful to an internal auditor in gaining an understanding of auditees' operations, identifying trouble spots, evaluating performance relative to other entities, and analyzing specific problems. Three levels of ratio analysis are commonly used:

1. General financial analysis which focuses on published financial data.
2. Specific financial ratios pertaining to specific product lines or other similar subsets of data that are more detailed than published financial statements.
3. An operational emphasis, in which operating data are aimed at the analysis of a specific problem that has been identified.

Ratios utilized in general financial analysis are classified according to the attribute they are intended to measure.

Liquidity

The ability of an entity to meet its short-term obligations is referred to as its liquidity, or solvency level. A common statistic used to measure liquidity is the current ratio, calculated as current assets divided by current liabilities. A general rule of thumb is that the current ratio should be at least 2.0. However, the most desirable range for the ratio will depend on the type of business in which the entity operates. For example, a grocery store needs to have far more liquid capital on hand than an operation that primarily sells on credit. While a higher current ratio generally means greater liquidity, an excessive current ratio can mean a greater loss of returns that could be earned on longer-term investments. Hence, a range of current ratio is preferred, as distinct from maximization of that ratio.

The acid test or quick ratio is a tougher test of solvency, since it considers only quick assets, i.e., cash, marketable securities, and receivables. Inventory balances are not quick assets, nor are prepaid items. The emphasis is placed on those assets most able to be converted into cash. The quick ratio is calculated as quick assets divided by current liabilities.

Another common measure used in evaluating liquidity, though not a ratio in form, is working capital. It is calculated as current assets minus current liabilities.

Activity

How effectively entities use resources is evaluated by means of activity ratios. The efficiency of an entity's inventory management practices can be assessed by computing the inventory turnover ratio: cost of goods sold divided by average inventory (i.e., beginning inventory plus ending inventory divided by 2). A one-to-one turnover ratio would imply that the entity had one year's worth of sales in inventory, which is an excessive inventory investment for most entities. Attendant inventory handling costs and obsolescence risk would represent operating inefficiencies.

The number of days of inventory on hand often is computed as another means of interpreting efficiency; it is calculated by dividing the number of days in a year by the inventory turnover. The number of days can be set at 300 business days, 360 banking days, or 365 days, as deemed appropriate. Once again, the preferred quantity of this statistic depends heavily upon the industry in which an entity operates. For example, an entity selling perishable goods would need to maintain a high inventory ratio, with only a few days' sales in stock.

The efficiency of an entity's collection practices can be assessed by computing the accounts receivable turnover ratio: net credit sales divided by average accounts receivable. The number of days of receivables represented in the balance is calculated as the number of days in a year divided by the accounts receivable turnover ratio. Too high a turnover suggests that credit policies may be too stringent, and too low a turnover may indicate that such policies are lax or that collection activities are insufficient.

The level of productive assets is monitored by computing the fixed asset turnover ratio: sales divided by net fixed assets. Alternatively, the level of capital investment relative to revenue can be measured by the asset turnover ratio: sales divided by total assets. In each case, the focus is upon the capital investment required to sustain current operations, as measured by revenue. One problematic aspect of ratios is that they can move in what appears to be a desirable direction for undesirable reasons. As an example, if a company is lax in replacing assets on a timely basis, the fixed asset turnover ratio would be higher. One might erroneously infer more efficiency due to a smaller capital base being required to support current revenue. In fact, a short-term tradeoff with potentially critical long-term implications has been made.

Profitability

The earnings capability of an entity can be evaluated by several return measures which compare net income to a variety of bases. Common profitability ratios include:

$$\text{Return on Sales:} \quad \frac{\text{Net Income}}{\text{Sales}}$$

$$\text{Return on Assets:} \quad \frac{\text{Net Income}}{\text{Assets}}$$

$$\text{Return on Stockholders' Equity:} \quad \frac{\text{Net Income}}{\text{Stockholders' Equity}}$$

While net income maximization is often thought of as a desirable goal, short-term and long-term considerations may indicate otherwise. Following through on the earlier discussion, if return on assets is sacrificed over the short term to improve capital facilities, the long-term payback could be substantial.

Capital Structure

The source of the capital base is of interest in analyzing an operation. Leverage is a term defined as "the use of other people's money;" favorable leverage suggests that the return on that money exceeds its cost. To use leverage, a corporation must incur some debt. The extent to which financing is obtained via debt (as opposed to stock issuances and related stockholders' investments) is often referred to as the debt ratio. This ratio is calculated as total liabilities divided by total assets, and it essentially measures the proportion of assets on which creditors have claims. A rule of thumb is that it is desirable to have a debt ratio of less than 50 percent. However, if favorable leverage is expected and an entity considers the risk of failure low, then higher debt ratios may be desirable. Alternative measures that assess the same basic attribute include:

$$\text{Debt to Equity Ratio:} \quad \frac{\text{Total Liabilities}}{\text{Common Stockholders' Equity}}$$

$$\text{Equity Ratio:} \quad \frac{\text{Total Stockholders' Equity}}{\text{Total Assets}}$$

A joint measure of the extent of debt and solvency is referred to as times interest earned, which measures cost-of-debt coverage. It is calculated as follows:

$$\frac{\text{Net Income} + \text{Interest Expense} + \text{Income Tax Expense}}{\text{Interest Expense}}$$

A higher margin of safety over fixed interest charges indicates less risk. Some risk is desirable, however, because of possible positive returns from using leverage.

Other Common Analyses

These ratios are often analyzed by assessing their interrelationship. Such an approach tends to bear out the reason for changes in the ratios' values. In particular, operating performance (as measured by return on net sales) multiplied by asset turnover and the capital structure measure of average total assets, divided by average stockholders' equity, equals return on stockholders' equity.

Auditors analyzing statements also find the use of per-share statistics to be helpful in their evaluation. Simply stated, earnings per share is net income divided by the average number of common shares outstanding. This statistic is a popular profitability indicator. In actuality, this ratio is adjusted in accordance with generally accepted accounting principles for the potentially dilutive effects of certain securities (e.g., options, warrants, and convertible bonds). The ratio is presented in two forms: primary and fully diluted. This calculation is discussed in detail in intermediate accounting textbooks.

Other per-share analyses that are commonly performed are measures of book value per share: net assets available to common stockholders divided by the number of shares of common stock outstanding. Yield, pertaining to the payout of dividends, is computed as dividends per share divided by market value per share.

To facilitate comparisons of account balances, common-sized financial statements in which all accounts are re-expressed as percentages of total sales or total assets have been computed. These statements are sometimes referred to as vertical analyses. Horizontal analyses emphasize percentage changes over time and can similarly be useful in evaluating the significance of fluctuations.

Static vs. Trend Analysis

Rather than concentrating exclusively on percentage change from last year to this year, the internal auditor may want to evaluate trends. Three- to five-year trends are more likely to imply a norm than is any static analysis or period-to-period calculation.

Of course, trend analyses assume that ratios are comparable across time. If there have been substantial changes in operations, changes in the accounting treatment of similar operations, or severe fluctuations in price indices, adjustment of the raw data for trend comparisons is needed.

Intra- vs. Inter-Company Comparisons

Although across-time comparisons and across-account calculations within a company can be enlightening, a key benchmark is inter-company comparability of ratios. Have competitors experienced similar ratios, and if not, why not? Inter-company comparisons can be made based on widely available information sources, such as Dun & Bradstreet, Moody's, Standard & Poor's, and Value Line. Regulatory agencies like the Federal Trade Commission and the Securities and Exchange Commission (SEC) also retain information on competitors' performance which often can be integrated in the evaluation process. Generally, information is reported by broad industrial categories.

Industry averages tend to be broad, sometimes making it difficult to draw conclusions regarding relative performance. For that reason, auditors often look to information on specific competitors, sometimes designing their own "average industry statistics" over a relatively small and homogeneous set of competing companies.

Complications

The complications of inter-company comparisons are similar to problems in intra-company analyses, except that they tend to be more problematic. For example, companies within an industry tend to adopt varying accounting practices, are of different age, may have diverse product lines, and may be differentially affected by inflation and other economic factors. It is helpful to read financial statement footnotes carefully to provide a basis for adjusting companies' accounts before computing various ratios for comparison across time and across companies.

Use of Line-of-Business Disclosures. One means of addressing the problem of diverse product lines is to utilize line-of-business disclosures for the computation of financial ratios. In this manner even conglomerates can be evaluated.

Limitations of the Ratio Technique

The ratio technique is limited by the available information set, extreme differences in measurements over time and/or across entities, and the presumptions underlying the ratio computation itself. Regarding this last point, any ratio presumes a change in that same proportion as the numerator and denominator fluctuate. However, if the behavior of the components of the ratio is mixed (i.e., there is both fixed and variable movement), that presumption is in error and may result in erroneous projections about the values of various ratios.

The biggest limitation is that changes in any ratio may be due to changes in either the numerator or the denominator. The source of changes is not always evident; moreover, changes in one aspect of the ratio could be favorable (e.g., increased income), whereas changes in the other aspect of the ratio could be unfavorable (e.g., smaller asset base). Hence, the internal auditor should be careful when interpreting ratios.

Correlation Analysis

The measurement of the association of one variable with another is known as correlation analysis. Two variables are said to be correlated when they move systematically in a discernible pattern. A positive or direct correlation is said to exist when both variables increase or decrease together. For example, one would expect sales to increase as the number of customers increases; this indicates a positive correlation. A negative or inverse correlation is said to exist when one variable decreases as the other increases. For example, if an entity monitored the number of customers lost, sales would be expected to decrease as the number of lost customers increased.

Exhibit 15-7 shows the calculation for the Pearson product-moment correlation statistic for a fairly small data set, notes the range of such statistics, and describes the inferences that can be drawn. This is a parametric correlation measure that is commonly generated by software packages. Nonparametric correlation measures are also widely available, including the Spearman and Kendall rank-order correlation values.

Correlation analysis can be of use to internal auditors in model building to identify key factors that move in systematic patterns with one another. A simpler application, with substantial potential as an audit tool, is to use correlation statistics to check the reasonableness of recorded values and nonfinancial statistics. Price lists can be correlated to industry price data; output can be correlated to direct labor hours, units shipped, and recorded sales; and economic data can be correlated to entity factors expected to fluctuate in relation to such data. Problems with how these statistics are computed, shortcomings in the internal auditor's understanding of auditees' operations, or real inefficiencies or misstatements can be pinpointed through correlation analysis.

Exhibit 15-7
An Illustration of
Bivariate Correlation Analysis

Data Set

Total Revenue	Number of Customers
$100,000	10,000
$130,000	11,000
$170,000	15,000
$200,000	16,500
$210,000	17,500

First Step: Compute the average value per variable.

Second Step: Compute deviations from the mean per variable, multiply these deviations, and add them together.

Third Step: Compute the sum of the squared deviations per variable, multiply them, and take the square root of the product.

Fourth Step: Divide the results of step 2 by step 3.

First:

Average total revenue = 162,000

Average number of customers = 14,000

Second:

	Revenue Deviations			Customer Deviations
100,000 – 162,000 =	–62,000	10,000 – 14,000 =	–4,000
130,000 – 162,000 =	–32,000	11,000 – 14,000 =	–3,000
170,000 – 162,000 =	8,000	15,000 – 14,000 =	1,000
200,000 – 162,000 =	38,000	16,500 – 14,000 =	2,500
210,000 – 162,000 =	48,000	17,500 – 14,000 =	3,500

Product of Deviations	Sum of Products
240,000,000	607,000,000
96,000,000	
8,000,000	
95,000,000	
168,000,000	

Third:

Sum of Squared Deviations

Revenue	Customers
3,844,000,000	16,000,000
1,024,000,000	9,000,000
64,000,000	1,000,000
1,440,000,000	6,250,000
2,304,000,000	12,250,000
8,676,000,000	44,500,000

Product of Sums = 386,082,000,000,000,000

Square Root of Product = 621,354,971

Fourth: $\dfrac{607,000,000}{621,354,971} = .98$

Note: Correlation statistics can range from minus one to plus one. A zero value means no correlation. Negative values are inverse relationships, and positive values are direct relationships. The closer the correlation is to an absolute value of one, the stronger the relationship.

Inference: As the number of customers increases, revenue is observed to increase. This systematic pattern of movement is a very strong association as reflected by the .98 value. This might be interpreted to mean that 98 percent of the upward movement in number of customers is associated with proportional upward movement in revenue.

Correlation Trend Analysis

Correlation analysis is a summary statistic of how data points are related. These data could relate to different points in time or to different operating units. If a correlation statistic is less than expected, one question to be addressed is whether this unexpected result is due to one or two very atypical data points. To determine the plausibility of unexpected effects stemming from a limited number of extreme data points, an illustration of the data set can be very useful.

Graphical Analysis. The term *scatter diagram* is applied to any graph of data points. The more systematic a discernible pattern in the graph, the more likely one variable can be utilized to predict the other's value. Exhibit 15-8 depicts three possible scatter diagrams. The first is a random set of data points, suggesting no relationship between variables *x* and *y*. Such a graph is often described as looking like pellets from a shotgun — scattered, with no systematic pattern. The correlation value for this plot would be expected to be close to zero.

The second graph illustrates a strong positive correlation, similar to that computed in Exhibit 15-7. Whenever a cigar-shaped pattern is present in the data, either with a positive or a negative slope, correlation values can be expected to approach an absolute value of 1.

The third graph offers one possible explanation of why a correlation statistic is less than expected. Correlation values measure linear patterns. This nonlinear pattern would not be evident in a correlation statistic, in spite of the usefulness of *x* values in predicting *y* values. Another explanation for a correlation value being less than expected would be the presence of a single data point like (*) in the middle plot of Exhibit 15-8. This is often referred to as an "outlier," since it lies apart from the central data set's pattern.

Graphical analyses can be useful to the internal auditor in identifying data errors, interrelationships, and atypical operations.

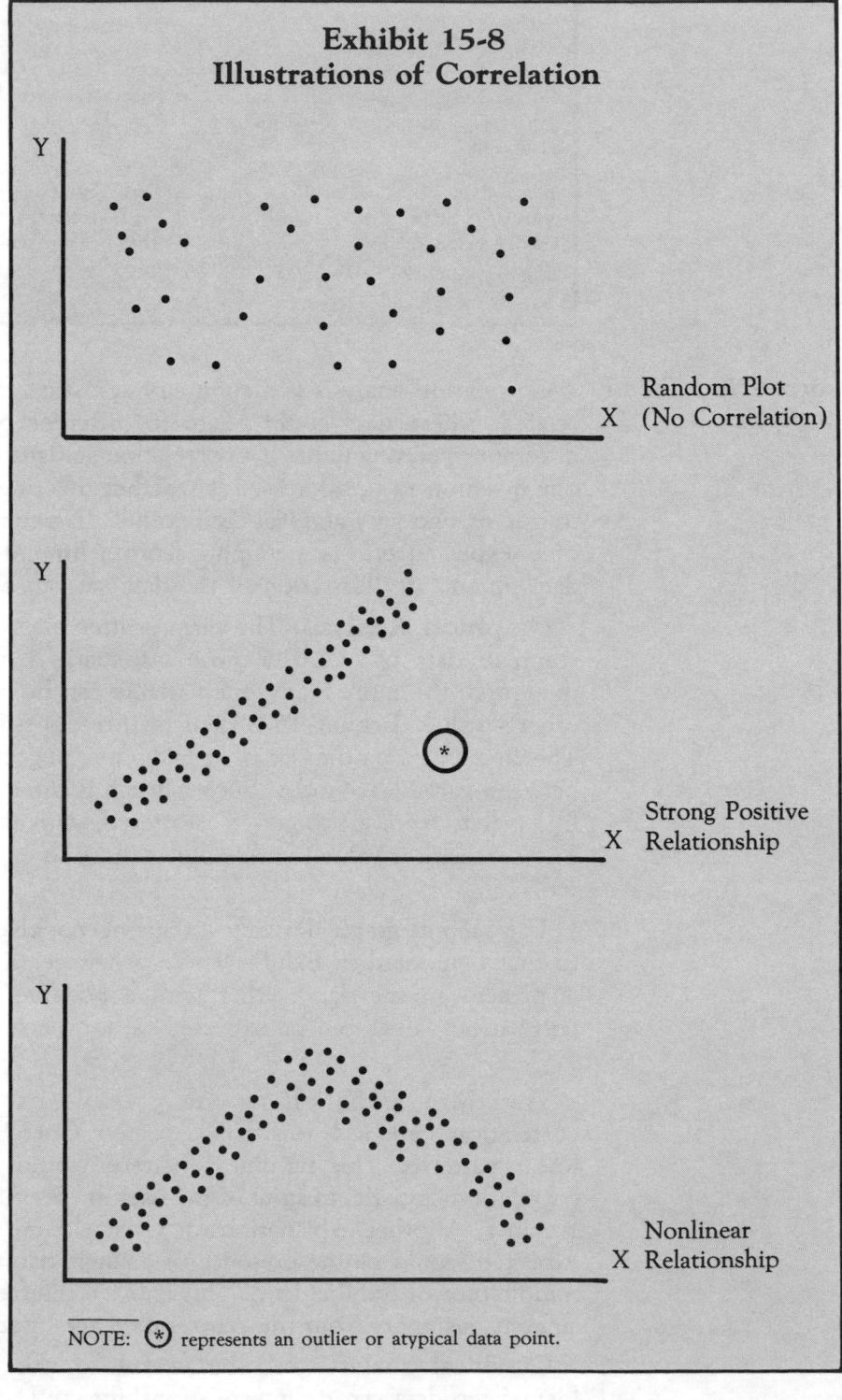

Exhibit 15-8
Illustrations of Correlation

Random Plot
(No Correlation)

Strong Positive
Relationship

Nonlinear
Relationship

NOTE: ✱ represents an outlier or atypical data point.

Trendline Projections and Growth Curves. Software packages commonly offer extrapolation techniques which extend trend lines into the future.

Equal-weight forecasting applies equal importance to every observation in a data set, often using only time as a descriptor variable — i.e., how has this variable changed over time? Moving-average techniques are available which can use unweighted series or apply weightings through generally accepted smoothing approaches.

Growth-rate analysis computes an annual growth rate for each time interval specified and then assumes this constant growth rate over time. The formula typically used is:

$$Y_t = Y_O (1 + r)^t$$

where Y_O = value of the data series in the base year
Y_t = value of the data series t years later
r = annual growth rate as a fraction.

Both average rates and a continuous growth rate can be calculated (the continuous relationship is $Y_t = Ae^{Bt}$ where $A = Y_O$ and $e^B = r$). Growth curve analyses can be extremely useful for short-term projections; however, long-term projections tend to be unreliable because of the infrequency with which entities maintain a constant growth curve.

Exponential Smoothing. One common method of calculating moving averages is the exponential-smoothing forecasting approach. Smoothing methods tend to place greater weight on the more recent data, thereby stressing the latest trends in the data of interest. An unweighted average forecast would be the mean of a data set. A p-period moving average would calculate means for various time periods within a data set. A weighted moving average merely assigns weights to each observation; these weights add up to 100 percent. The basic equation of exponential smoothing is:

$S1_t = ax_t + (1 - a)S1_t - 1$

where t = 1, 2, 3, . . . n

a = smoothing constant greater than zero and less than one

$S1_t$ is the exponentially smoothed average through time t.

The weights age data exponentially so that the weight given the data p periods ago should be $a(1 - a)^P$. Once again, these calculations can be easily performed through available software. The important point for the internal auditor to assess is the reasonableness of expecting increased accuracy by weighting later observations more than older observations when generating forecasts.

All of the trend analysis techniques would be useful in the auditor's performance of analytical review procedures intended to evaluate auditees' activities relative to expectations.

Model Building

Ratio analysis compares two numbers and assumes a set proportional relationship between the numerator and denominator. Mixed behavior (as distinct from purely variable behavior) can be estimated through simple regression analysis. For example, a model of accounts receivable as a function of sales could estimate the tendency for the two to move in direct relationship with one another, as well as some constant level of receivables which tends to exist without proportional variations in sales. Simple regression models are summarized in the form: $y = a + bx$, with a referred to as the constant term and b as the regression coefficient (the slope coefficient). This relationship takes the same form as the flexible budgeting formula described earlier in this chapter (i.e., based on the high-low method). Regression analysis is an extension of the concepts of correlation analysis. It focuses on interrelationships between data sets, quantifies these associations, and thereby permits projections/predictions to be formed on new data points.

Simple Regression Analysis

A simple regression analysis can be illustrated graphically. Assume that an internal auditor wants to analyze the relationship between salary costs (y) and direct labor hours (x). Because of the nature of certain benefit plans and tax calculations, some mixed relationship is expected, although a dominantly variable association is anticipated. Assume the availability of the following data set:

y = Payroll	x = Direct Labor Hours
$20,000	3,500
$22,000	3,600
$17,000	3,000
$25,000	4,000
$18,000	3,200

A scatter diagram could be prepared and the data summarized by trying to "fit" a line to the data set. However, each individual's ability to "eyeball" such a fit will rest with their analytical capability. An objective means of deriving the best fit of a line is through the use of ordinary least squares, or regression analysis.

This algorithm searches for that line which will produce the least sum of squared deviations for the set of actual data points from the regression line that is estimated. The computation of a simple regression model can be algebraically derived from the following formulas:

b = <u>sum of the product of deviations from the mean for x and y</u>
       sum of squared deviations from the mean for x

a = mean of y minus the product of b and the mean of x

The computations are illustrated in Exhibit 15-9. Then actual direct labor hours are "plugged into" the regression model, and regression estimates are generated. The regression line is plotted, with the deviations of its estimates from actual data points quantified (e.g., 20,000 − 20,729.60 = −729.60 as a deviation). The regression algorithm minimizes the sum of squared deviations. Negative quantities such as −729.60 must be squared since distance measures that do not "net out" are desired (i.e., negative values should not be offset by positive values, but the minimum vertical distance from the set of data points needs to be measured). As Exhibit 15-9 indicates, the sum of squared deviations for the regression line is 972,979.2, and this is the minimum quantity obtainable by fitting a linear model to the data set. While the meaning of this number is not very intuitive, adjustment by the degrees of freedom of n − 2 (in this example, 5 − 2, or 3) and conversion to square root, or 569.50, relates to precision and is in the same unit of measure as the y value. Had 30 points been utilized for estimation, this quantity would be precise at about a 67 percent level of confidence. Since only five data points were used in this example, achieved confidence would be far lower. This value is referred to as the standard error of the model.

An important phase of model building is interpreting the reasonableness of the regression model. The regression coefficient of a simple regression model is interpreted as the change in y per unit change in x. This means that payroll would increase by $8.24 per each additional direct labor hour. However, the constant term adjusts this downward slightly (i.e., by −8,110.40). This negative constant term makes sense, particularly when one considers the ceiling on unemployment taxes and FICA contributions once salary goes beyond a certain level. Both the direction and magnitude of regression coefficients should be evaluated for reasonableness. Software reports the standard error and t-value per coefficient (based on the same

Exhibit 15-9
Illustration of Simple Regression Analysis

μ of Payroll = \$20,400 μ of Direct-Labor Hours = 3,460

Deviations from Mean

		Product
20,000 – 20,400 = –400	3,500 – 3,460 = 40	–16,000
22,000 – 20,400 = 1,600	3,600 – 3,460 = 140	224,000
17,000 – 20,400 = –3,400	3,000 – 3,460 = –460	1,564,000
25,000 – 20,400 = 4,600	4,000 – 3,460 = 540	2,484,000
18,000 – 20,400 = –2,400	3,200 – 3,460 = –260	624,000
		4,880,000

Squared Deviations from Mean for Direct-Labor Hours

$(40)^2 = $ 1,600   b = 4,880,000/592,000

$(140)^2 = $ 19,600

$(-460)^2 = $ 211,600

$(540)^2 = $ 291,600   b = 8.2432432

$(-260)^2 = $ 67,600

            592,000   a = 20,400 – 8.24 (3,460)

                                     a = 20,400 – 28,510.4

                                     a = –8,110.40

Regression Model

Y = –8,110.40 + 8.24 (Direct-Labor Hours)

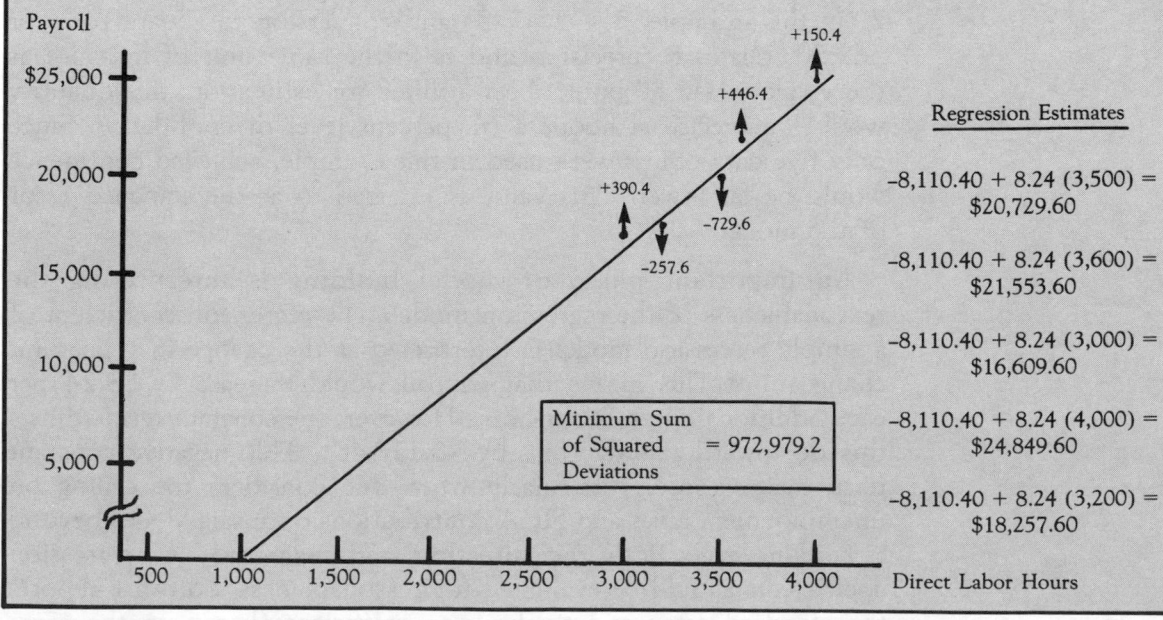

Regression Estimates

–8,110.40 + 8.24 (3,500) = \$20,729.60

–8,110.40 + 8.24 (3,600) = \$21,553.60

–8,110.40 + 8.24 (3,000) = \$16,609.60

–8,110.40 + 8.24 (4,000) = \$24,849.60

–8,110.40 + 8.24 (3,200) = \$18,257.60

Minimum Sum of Squared Deviations = 972,979.2

distributional theory as t-tests, described earlier) so that model builders can evaluate the statistical significance of the coefficient. Generally, a t-value in excess of an absolute value of 2.0 (assuming at least 30 data points for estimation) is statistically significant. The t-value assumes the same sign as the regression coefficient.

To assess the goodness of fit of a regression relationship, many model builders use the R^2 measure. It quantifies that proportion of variation in the y variable that is accounted for by the x variable. It is calculated as the total sum of squared deviations from the mean of the y variable minus the sum of squared deviations from the line, divided by the total sum of squared deviations from the mean of the y variable. In the example, the sum of squared deviations from the mean of y would be $(-400)^2 + (1,600)^2 + (-3,400)^2 + (4,600)^2 + (-2,400)^2$, or 41,200,000. Hence, R^2 equals $(41,200,000 - 972,979) \div 41,200,000$, or .9764. R^2 values range from zero to one, with the former indicating no relationship and the latter indicating a perfect relation. In this example, the internal auditor can state that 97.6 percent of the variability of payroll costs is explained by variability in direct labor hours.

It should be evident that regression analysis can assist the auditor in understanding and quantifying data interrelationships. In addition, it can flag unusual fluctuations for follow-up. In the example illustrated in Exhibit 15-9, the largest deviation is −729.60, resulting when direct labor hours were 3,500 and recorded payroll costs were $20,000. The regression model estimated $20,729.60. This difference between expectations and recorded values warrants investigation. The recorded data could be in error, the direct labor hour statistic could be wrong, or some event not accounted for by the regression model could explain the lower-than-expected costs.

Multiple Regression Analysis

Because of the tendency for more than one factor to be related to the attribute which the model builder is attempting to explain, multiple regression analysis is a popular analytical tool. Its intuitive approach is identical to simple regression, although matrix algebra is required for the computations. The interpretation of regression coefficients changes slightly. They represent the change in y per unit change in x, holding all other variables in the model constant. As multiple variables are selected in modeling, net relationships (as opposed to gross relationships) are estimated. While the latter are pure one-to-one comparisons, the former net out other attributes in the model, quantifying that variable's marginal contribution.

For this reason, the model builder should consider the intercorrelation between descriptor (independent) variables. If, for example, two variables have a correlation of .97, it is unlikely that both will be important net explanatory variables within a multiple regression model. They most likely have redundant information, and if both were included within the model, interpretation of the regression coefficients would be difficult. This model-building consideration is termed multicollinearity.

Generally, the higher the correlation to the variable being explained (the dependent variable), the greater the explanatory power. However, it does not hold that a low correlation means little association in a multiple regression model. This is due to the concurrent adjustment of other factors in a model in order to estimate net relationships, which can be very strong despite low gross relationships.

Potential Applications. Whenever the auditor wants to compare interrelationships between variable sets, regression modeling techniques can be applied. If the benchmark of interest is historical experience, a time-series analysis will be performed, whereby past data are used to project current and future operations. If the benchmark is other operations, a cross-sectional analysis would be appropriate. For example, an internal auditor for a bank might want to compare branch banks' operations. Data pertaining to interest income per branch might be collected and described by such factors as the type of loans made, their volume, and local economic factors relating to each branch's operations.

As with most statistical tools, regression analysis has a set of underlying assumptions that must be met for its use and interpretations to be valid. Simply stated, the key assumptions relate to residuals (the differences in actual values and regression estimates):

- The average value of residuals is assumed to be zero (i.e., unbiased estimates will result).
- Residual values are assumed to be independent of one another.
- Residual values are assumed to have a common standard error in their estimation.
- Residual values are assumed to be independent of the descriptor variables included in the regression model.

Statistical tests of these assumptions are well defined. The most problematic assumption in time-series models has to do with the independence of residuals. Since general economic factors tend to relate to the various financial and nonfinancial measures being evaluated in regression models estimated over time, patterns often arise in the residuals. However, first differencing of data (i.e., subtracting February from January, March from February, and so on), or the application of an estimation tool known as the Cochrane-Orcutt approach, can be effective in eliminating such patterns. These adjustments, as well as statistical tests of residuals, are beyond the scope of this text. However, be assured that numerous transformations are available for achieving compliance with key regression assumptions; software packages are also available to perform these transformations and to test the residual values of regression models.

Discriminant Analysis

A variation of regression analysis known as discriminant analysis can be a useful internal audit tool when the question being asked is a classification variable. For example, the internal auditor may ask whether a particular set of variables discriminates between those operations that are capital intensive and those that are labor intensive. Discriminant analysis has been applied in attempts to predict bankruptcy or troubled operations. Discriminant models are based on comparisons of troubled entities to matched but untroubled entities. These models are then applied to current and future operations to infer the likelihood of an entity having economic trouble. Discriminant models are also available in numerous software packages.

Statistical Control Charts

Regression analysis is applied by engineers in evaluating the effectiveness with which operations are controlled. Statistical control charts can be generated showing operations planned, the tolerable range of cost components, and actual performance.

Learning Curves

Assume that an internal auditor is asked to evaluate the efficiency with which a new production process has been put into place by several plants. It is expected that a learning curve would be observable in the implementation phase. In other words, production would become more efficient, with a faster rate of output, as employees gained experience with the new process. During the early implementation phase, the length of time to produce units was expected to become progressively shorter.

Most production studies of learning curves have observed curves between 60 and 80 percent. An 80 percent curve means that the time required per unit of output is reduced by 20 percent each time that the cumulative production level is doubled. This type of curve is the most common.

Assume the internal auditor had statistics from the first day of implementation indicating that at 150 units of output, production time averaged five minutes per unit. By applying learning curve theory based on these statistics, a set of benchmarks can be calculated, against which actual experience can be evaluated. Specifically, these benchmarks would be projected as follows:

Cumulative Units of Output	Average Time per Unit
150	5
300	4 (5 × 80%)
600	3.2 (4 × 80%)
1,200	2.56 (3.2 × 80%)

These figures indicate that by the time output reaches 300 units, the average time required per unit will have fallen from five minutes to four minutes. Obviously, such increases in efficiency would only be expected in the initial phases of implementation. Later, the average time per unit would be expected to stabilize.

Linear Programming

A tool that is commonly applied whenever scarce resources are being allocated or when optimal blends of raw materials are being determined is linear programming. It is an operations research tool in which the constraints applicable to the decision setting and the objective function or goal to be optimized are formalized into equations. The decision variables in the model are then analyzed to identify that solution which optimizes the objective function, yet meets each of the constraints. If the number of variables equals the number of equations, a finite solution exists; if the number of variables exceeds the number of equations, an infinite number of possible solutions exists.

To illustrate the specification of a linear programming model, assume that production scheduling is reviewed and that the following statistics are available for two product lines:

Product	Selling Price	Variable Cost	Labor Hours Required for Production
X	$5.00	3.50	2.5
Y	$3.00	1.00	.5

Only 250 total labor hours are available for production in the time period being scheduled. Market demand would warrant the production of no more than 200 units of product Y. The objective function for the entity is to maximize gross profit (GP), which can be formalized as follows:

$$(5 - 3.50)X + (3 - 1)Y = GP$$

or

$$1.50X + 2Y = GP$$

The key constraint in this setting is labor time, which can be formalized as follows:

$$2.5X + .5Y < 250$$

In addition, the output of Y should be no more than 100 of these hours because of the sales constraint: $.5Y < 100$. Linear programming maximizes the objective function, subject to resource constraints. Solution methods include:

1. Graphical identification of the areas that meet the constraints, then focusing on where constraints intersect to find that point which maximizes the objective function. This technique is useful only in simple problems.
2. Algebraic trial-and-error derivation, until no improvement in the objective function results.
3. The simplex method, which is an iterative technique that moves toward an optimum solution.

In evaluating the linear programming problem described, specify that $X > 0$ and $Y > 0$, since negative production is impossible. A graphical solution is depicted in Exhibit 15-10. First, the constraints are drawn to outline the feasible range, then the objective function is calculated for each corner and the maximum profit combination is identified.

The algebraic and simplex methods are described in more detail in cost-accounting textbooks and operations-research reference books. Internal auditors often have colleagues trained in the use of these tools, and as long as the maximization and constraint equations can be defined by the internal auditor, software is available to solve the problem.

Internal auditors need to develop the ability to recognize the circumstances in which particular analytical tools are likely to be of use. Specific examples of business applications of linear programming include the determination of optimum:

- Product mix.
- Machine utilization.
- Manpower allocation.

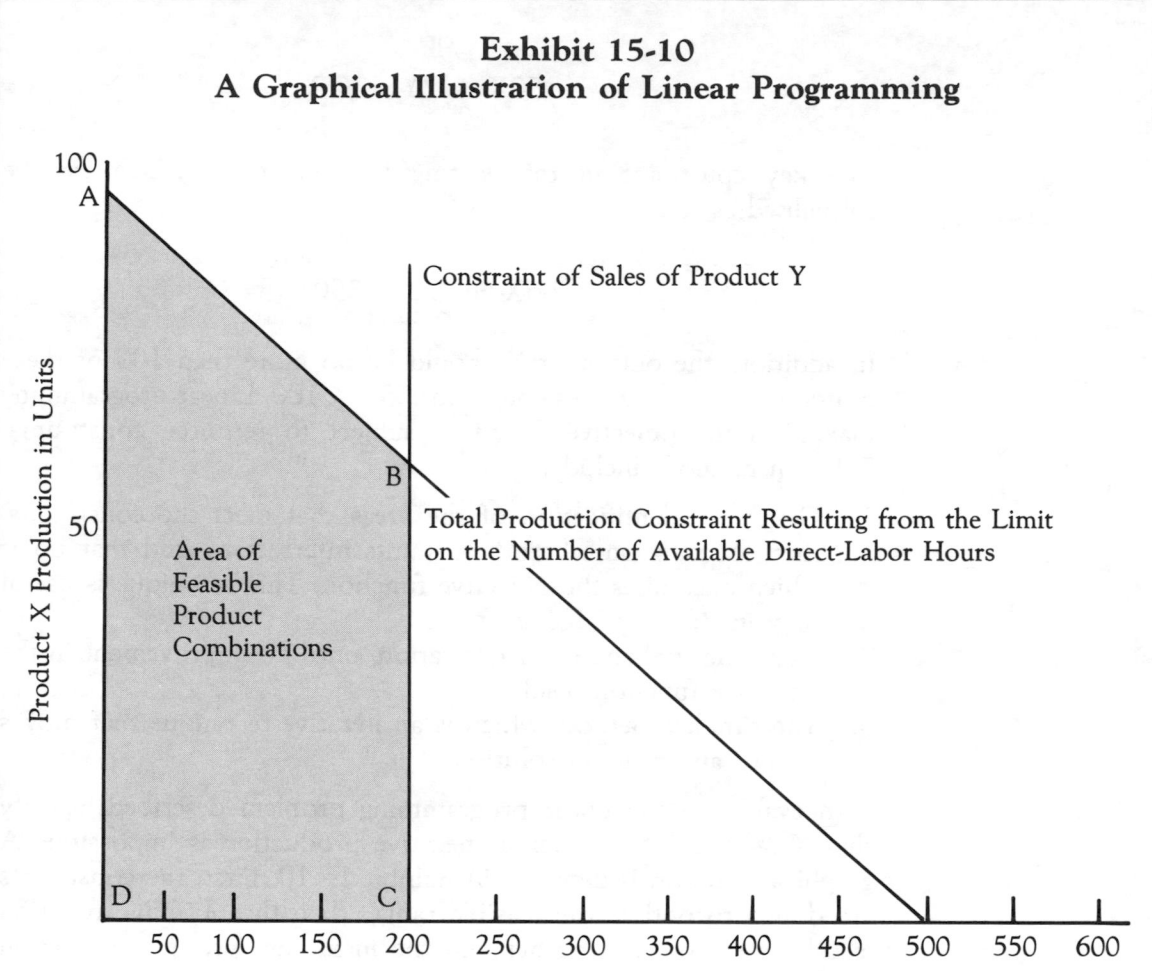

Exhibit 15-10
A Graphical Illustration of Linear Programming

Check GP at the corners of the feasible range:

$1.50X + 2Y = GP$
$1.50(0) + 2(200) = 400$
$1.50(100) + 2(0) = 150$
$1.50(60) + 2(200) = 490$

The optimal corner is (200, 60), since this combination produces the maximum gross profit. Note that Y contributes $4 per productive hour, the scarce factor, whereas X contributes only $ .60 per hour. Therefore, Y's production would always be preferable to X as long as output can be sold.

- Material mix.
- Transportation arrangements.
- Storage space allocation.
- Shipping facilities.

In each case, the internal auditor must determine the objectives sought, basic relationships, constraints, available feasible situations and, finally, the optimum solution.

**Project
Scheduling
Techniques**

Several scheduling techniques are commonly used in organizing construction projects. These techniques are in fact applicable to any type of project, and in particular may be of assistance to internal auditors in planning audit engagements.

**Program
Evaluation Review
Technique (PERT)**

To control large-scale projects, PERT diagrams are drawn to summarize:

- The key tasks involved in the project (referred to as activities that require resources and take time to accomplish).
- The starting point and ending point of an activity (referred to as events, consuming no resources).
- The critical path for the project (i.e., that path along which delays in an activity will delay the entire project). Note that at least one, and sometimes more than one, critical path exists and that any paths which are not critical are said to have "slack time."

An example of a PERT network diagram is presented in Exhibit 15-11. While only one activity time is noted on the diagram, the time could be estimated with associated probabilities to reflect optimistic, pessimistic, and most likely activity times. Computer software is available to calculate critical paths.

**Critical Path
Method (CPM)**

The critical path method (CPM) is a scheduling tool that was developed independently of PERT but effectively utilizes the same sort of diagram as that depicted in Exhibit 15-11. However, activity-time estimates are made for both normal effort and for "crash" effort. The latter quantifies the time required for completion if all available resources were committed to that task. The time estimates are then augmented by cost estimates which are similarly quantified for normal and crash efforts. Two critical paths are then identified: one for normal times and one for the crash effort assumption. The calculation of the minimum cost of completing the project in minimum time is referred to as "crashing the network." With CPM it is common to update charts as work progresses.

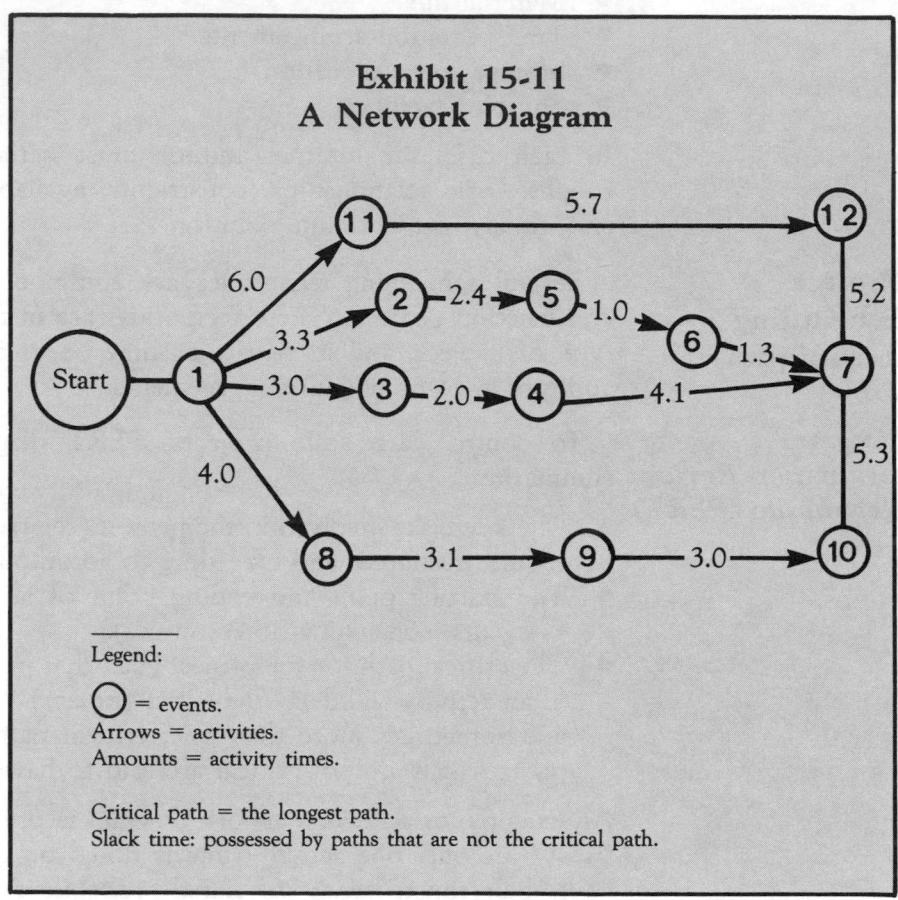

Exhibit 15-11
A Network Diagram

Legend:

⬭ = events.
Arrows = activities.
Amounts = activity times.

Critical path = the longest path.
Slack time: possessed by paths that are not the critical path.

Gantt or Bar Charts

A simpler planning tool that requires no mathematical calculations is the Gantt chart. Such a chart is displayed in Exhibit 15-12. The left margin outlines the tasks or activities and the horizontal lower margin marks off time. The chart illustrates activities over the life of the project with actual and projected times contrasted. It can be a useful tool in organizing work and monitoring progress through the various stages of a project. Of course, the interrelationships of activities are not apparent as they would be in PERT or CPM analyses, so care must be taken in applying this technique.

Typical types of projects that might require scheduling tools include research and development projects, special task forces to consider new products, the feasibility of certain plans or proposals, merger analyses, construction projects, and audit engagements. Internal auditing departments frequently have several projects on line simultaneously; bar charts detailing such projects, with the starting

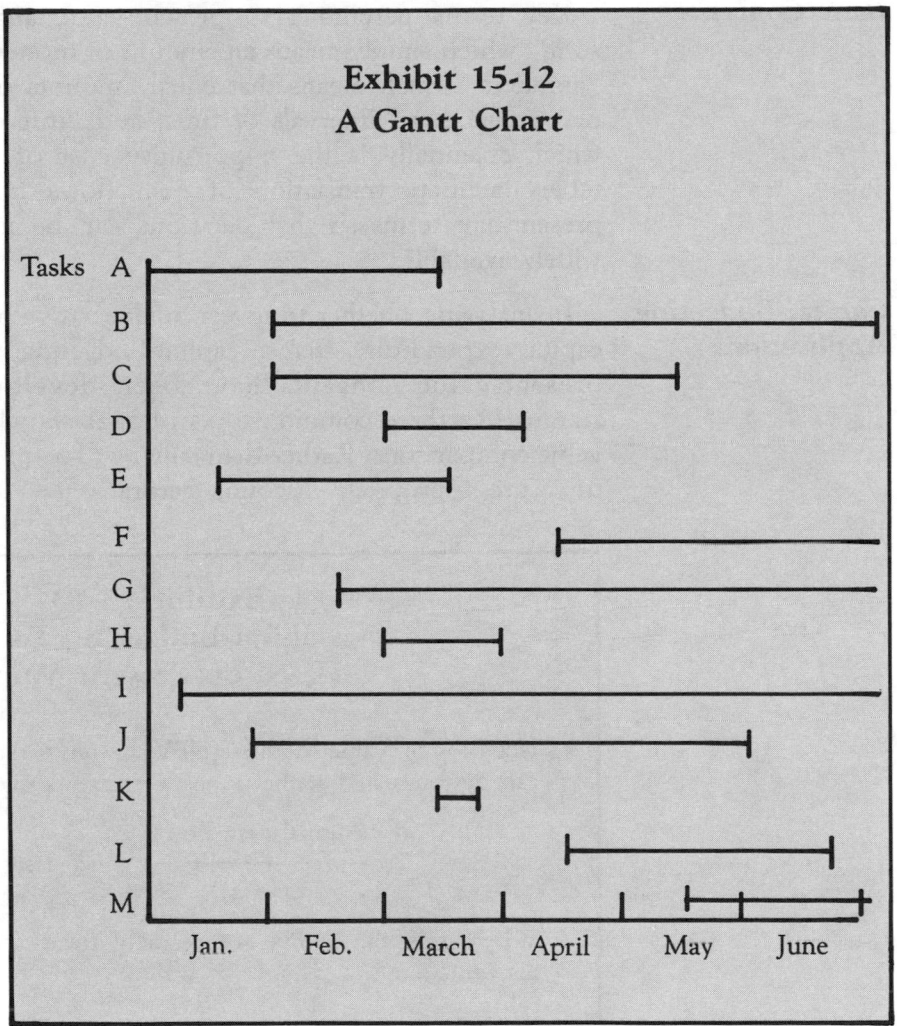

**Exhibit 15-12
A Gantt Chart**

and completion dates of each, can be valuable planning tools. If internal auditors are requested to review task-force efficiency, comparison of approaches taken on projects to the inferences drawn from PERT or CPM can provide a basis for evaluation.

Present Value

It is well recognized that a dollar received today is worth more than a promise to receive a dollar a year from now, even if receipt is guaranteed. This is because the dollar received today can be used during the interim period to earn interest. The time value of money makes it imperative that like units of measure expressed in present-value terms be utilized when comparing projects.

Basic Concepts

Key terms pertaining to present-value analyses include "lump sum," which simply means an amount of money at one point in time; "annuity," which means that equal amounts of money are received or paid at equal intervals of time; and "interest or discount rate," which essentially is the opportunity cost of money. Present-value tables facilitate translation of cash flows in future periods into present-day terms so that decisions can be made. Such tables are widely available.

Capital-Budgeting Applications

In analyzing whether to invest in alternative plant facilities or other capital expenditure items, capital-budgeting techniques based on present-value concepts have been developed. Exhibit 15-13 summarizes three common tools of analysis which generate present-value comparisons. Rather than solving $(1 + r)^i$, tables can be utilized to secure appropriate discount factors.

Exhibit 15-13
Capital-Budgeting Tools
Based on Present Value

- Net Present Value Method (NPV) assumes that cash flows generated can be reinvested at the project's cost of capital or discount rate:

$$NPV = \sum_{i=1}^{n} \frac{\text{Annual cash flows}}{(1 + r)^i} - \text{net cash investment}$$

Where n = the number of years of future cash flows and r = the discount rate

- Internal Rate of Return (IRR) assumes that cash flows generated are reinvested at the internal rate of return (r):

Future Cash Flows (r) = Cost of Investment

Where r = the rate that equalizes the equation

- Profitability Index: $\dfrac{\text{PV of Future Net Cash Flows}}{\text{Net Cash Invested}}$

The topic of present value and capital budgeting is treated in considerable depth in management-accounting, cost-accounting, and finance texts. Again, the emphasis here is upon the internal auditor's recognition that such tools are available for use in analysis.

Relationship to Accounting Estimates and Valuation. When an internal auditor is asked to assess the reasonableness of a reserve for obsolescence, insurance claims, warranty costs, or similar expenditures, the effect of present value on those accounts should be evaluated. If payout of warranty expenses is to be in dollars three years from today, those dollars are in some sense cheaper than current dollars.

Probability

The chance of an event happening is referred to as its probability. Most statistical tests and modeling approaches rely on probability measures to quantify the likelihood that associations noted between variables are statistically significant. Similarly, probabilities are an intrinsic facet of all sampling plans. Statistical probability theory permits objective determination of how likely it is that particular events will happen.

As with most analytical tools, there are several specialized terms typically used in applying probability theory, including:

- *Mutually exclusive events* — events that cannot occur at the same point in time, i.e., either this event or that event will happen, but not both.
- *Independent events* — the occurrence of one event has no effect on another event's likelihood of occurring.
- *Dependent events* — the occurrence of one event does affect another event's likelihood of occurring.
- *Joint probability* — the likelihood that both events will occur (for independent events, this would be the product of the probability of each event occurring).
- *Conditional probability* — the likelihood that one event will occur, given that another event has happened.

To exemplify circumstances in which probabilities would be used by the auditor, consider a setting in which a sample has been drawn and the auditor wants to evaluate its representativeness. Assume that 70 percent of the inventory is known to be within the $10 to $25 cost-per-unit category, and one-tenth of the units in this category are expected to be obsolete. In the sample drawn, there is one obsolete item in that category, and the auditor wants to know the likelihood of that selection. The joint probability of the item would be (1) the probability of the item being in that category and (2) the probability of the item being obsolete, given that category: 70% × 10%, or 7%.

Expected Value

Probabilities are closely tied to the topic of expected value. Whenever alternatives are to be selected in a risky or uncertain decision process, they can be evaluated by using expected-value techniques. By multiplying each alternative by the probability of its occurrence and then summing the resulting products, expected value can be calculated. The highest expected value would signal the best alternative in quantitative terms.

Applications to Inventory Purchase Decisions

Payoff tables based on expected-value calculations are commonly used in making inventory purchase decisions. Assume that you are an internal auditor for an entity that owns concession rights at the local stadium, and you want to evaluate how efficiently the concession operations have been run. In particular, you want to evaluate the entity's purchasing practices with respect to perishable load items. Consider the payoff table illustrated in Exhibit 15-14. The expected value calculations indicate that ordering 3,000 units is the preferred strategy.

Exhibit 15-14
An Example of Analyzing Expected Value

Units Ordered	Events: Sales		
	k – 1,000	2,000	3,000
Alternatives	Probability: .2	.3	.5
1,000	$2,000	$2,000	$2,000
2,000	$1,750	$4,000	$4,000
3,000	$1,500	$3,750	$6,000

Net revenue per unit = $2
Cost per unit over ordered = $ .25

Expected value of:
    Ordering 1,000 $2,000
    Ordering 2,000 $(.2 \times 1,750) + .8(4,000) = $3,550$
    Ordering 3,000 $(.2 \times 1,500) + (.3 \times 3,750) + .5(6,000) =$
                     $4,425

Expected value of perfect information:
$(.2 \times 2,000) + (.3 \times 4,000) + (.5 \times 6,000) =$
$400 + 1,200 + 3,000 = \underline{$4,600}$

Expected Value of Perfect Information

A related question is, how much better off would the entity be if it could somehow forecast sales accurately? This would mean a return equal to the expected value of perfect information (EVPI), which is calculated as the diagonal of a payoff table as shown in Exhibit 15-14. This implies that the entity would be willing to pay $4,600 – $4,425, or $175, for perfect information on sales. Thus, if the entity is expending $175 or more for imperfect forecasting data, then resources are not being used efficiently.

Application to Accounting Estimates

It should be evident that expected-value calculations can be useful in formulating accounting estimates such as warranty expenses and other contingent liabilities. Various levels of costs are possible, with related probabilities of occurrence; the most likely outcome should be reflected as the accounting balance. Of course, accounting for contingencies permits the lowest point of an estimated range to be recorded in the accounts, yet that range should be commensurate with expected-value calculations.

Decision-Tree Analysis

One of the more difficult aspects of decision making is recognizing the plausible alternatives and outcomes. A tool which can effectively summarize such detail is decision-tree analysis. Assume that an auditor wants to evaluate the effectiveness of compliance tests performed. He or she might summarize the decision tree as shown in Exhibit 15-15. This analysis recognizes the auditor's perceptions as to the likely states of nature, the effectiveness of particular compliance tests in correctly identifying the state of nature, and the overall likelihood of reaching correct conclusions based purely on compliance test results.

Sensitivity Analysis

Because there is uncertainty in decision making, tools have evolved for evaluating the sensitivity of outcomes and decisions to such uncertainty. For example, assume that a purchase decision regarding new plant facilities is based in part on expected cash-flow projections about which there is some uncertainty. A simulation study can evaluate how the purchase decision would be affected by changes in the cash-flow projections.

Monte Carlo Simulations

A sophisticated simulation approach is referred to as the Monte Carlo Method. It uses the computer to simulate uncertainty via random behavior and then estimates specified models several times to determine average performance. For example, if management felt that there was a 30 percent chance of cash flows being lower than projected, the computer would determine this likelihood for each simulation via random numbers to evaluate its effects on the decision model. The problem with simulations is that they can be costly to develop and a chance always exists that the forecasts generated will be in error.

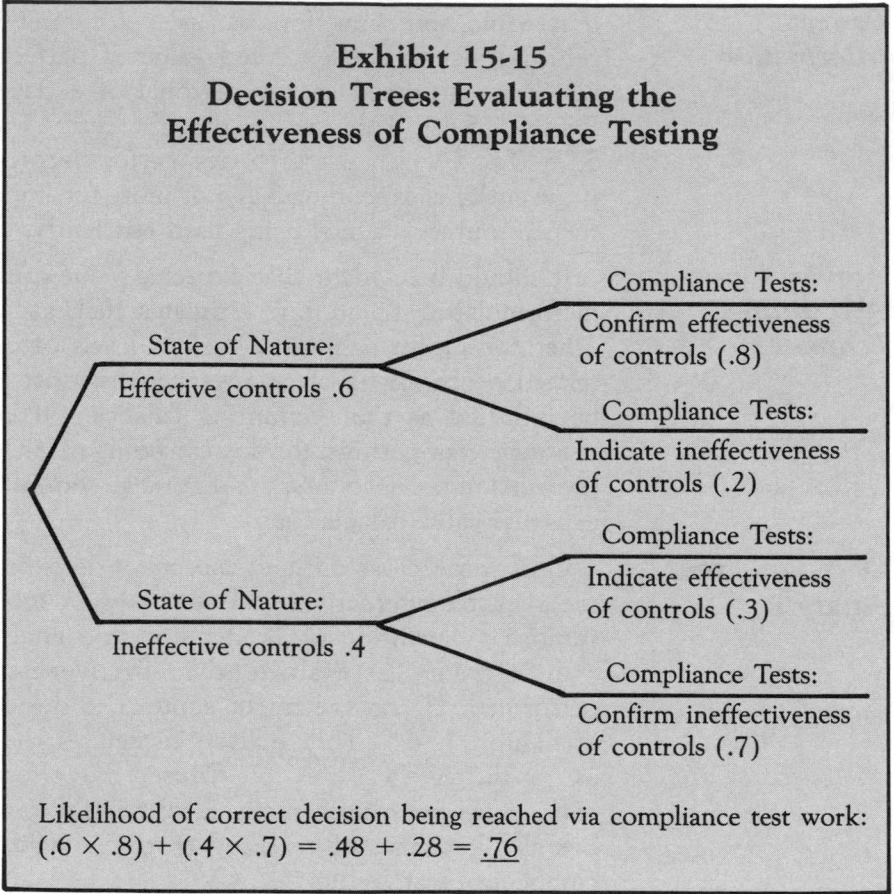

**Exhibit 15-15
Decision Trees: Evaluating the
Effectiveness of Compliance Testing**

State of Nature:
Effective controls .6

Compliance Tests:
Confirm effectiveness
of controls (.8)

Compliance Tests:
Indicate ineffectiveness
of controls (.2)

State of Nature:
Ineffective controls .4

Compliance Tests:
Indicate effectiveness
of controls (.3)

Compliance Tests:
Confirm ineffectiveness
of controls (.7)

Likelihood of correct decision being reached via compliance test work:
$(.6 \times .8) + (.4 \times .7) = .48 + .28 = \underline{.76}$

The types of settings in which Monte Carlo simulation is commonly applied include:

- Corporate planning.
- Financial planning.
- Research and development projections, particularly with respect to new product lines.
- Inventory control.

***"What If"
Analyses***

Less sophisticated than Monte Carlo techniques, "what if" analyses merely substitute alternative possibilities into the decision model to determine when the decision outcome would be altered. This can be done by hand or with the aid of the computer. Numerous financial-planning interactive programs are available which, for example, will compute various breakeven points given a diverse set of possible selling prices and cost levels. These "what if" summaries can be very useful to decision makers, particularly in evaluating risk.

Internal auditors can assess risk levels and the care exercised in decision making by applying "what if" analysis tools to auditees' major decisions and forecasts.

Game Theory

The term "game theory" refers to mathematical models of optimal strategies under various incentive schemes and in negotiation settings. A zero-sum game is said to exist when a payoff simply transfers from a loser to a winner. If, instead, profit is generated in which it is possible for both participants to share, a non-zero-sum game is being played. While beyond the scope of this text, game theory can assist an internal auditor in understanding various parties' incentives to pursue particular strategies, as well as the effectiveness of parties in negotiation sessions.

Queuing Theory

Businesses often have waiting lines to service customers and have to decide how many waiting lines should be provided. Queuing theory provides mathematical models to minimize the total cost for a given rate of customer arrivals; the minimized cost includes both service costs (facility and operating costs) and waiting costs (the idle resources of customers waiting in line or having paid employees waiting to serve). A simple queuing system can be algebraically solved, whereas simulation is needed for more complex systems. Queuing theory is clearly applicable to checkout lines at grocery stores and teller lines at banks, as well as any type of service facility where the key costs for consideration are operating and waiting costs.

As an example of the application of waiting-line models, assume that an internal auditor is evaluating the efficiency with which a shipping dock operates. As many as five trucks per hour may arrive for pickup, although in some hours no trucks arrive. In other words, the arrivals have a random pattern. On average, 32 trucks arrive per eight-hour day, or four trucks per hour. The probability of three trucks arriving in one hour can be calculated by applying the formula:

$\dfrac{\lambda^X}{X!}e^{-\lambda}$ where X = the number of trucks for which the probability is being computed;

$e \cong 2.71818$;

λ = average or expected number of arrivals for a set time period.

$$\frac{4^3 e^{-4}}{3!} = \frac{64 e^{-4}}{1 \cdot 2 \cdot 3} = \frac{64\ (1/54.598002)}{6} = .195$$

Hence, the arrival of three trucks per hour would be expected 19.5 percent of the time.

Now assume that shipping-dock workers are capable of servicing an average of four trucks per hour. We can compute the probability that service will be completed within a certain time. For example, what is the probability of unloading one truck in 15 minutes? The formula is:

$$1 - e^{-mt}$$ where mt = the average number of units that can be handled during a specified time period.

Hence, $1 - e^{-4(.25)} = 1 - e^{-.1} = .6321$. In other words, the likelihood of unloading one truck in a quarter of an hour is .6321.

An internal auditor's ability to evaluate timeliness of service and arrivals of customers clearly can be helpful in evaluating the performance of service facilities.

Economic Order Quantity (EOQ)

Inventory control can be enhanced by applying quantitative models to control the costs of ordering and storing inventory as well as costs related to inventory shortages (i.e., stockout costs). The basic economic order quantity (EOQ) model minimizes ordering and carrying costs. It is calculated as the square root of twice the annual demand, multiplied by the order cost, and divided by the unit holding cost. For example, if an entity had uniform annual demand of 500,000 units, incurred a cost of $10 per order to place orders, and estimated that one unit in inventory for a year cost $5, then:

$$EOQ = \sqrt{\frac{2 \times \$10 \times 500,000}{\$5}}$$

$$= \sqrt{\frac{\$10,000,000}{\$5}}$$

$$= 1,414.21$$

The average level of inventory would be $1,414.21 \div 2$, or 707.10 units. Note that the EOQ increases as demand and costs of ordering increase, but decreases as holding costs climb. Proportionately, if demand quadruples, EOQ only doubles. The number of orders per year is the annual demand divided by the EOQ; hence, in the example, 500,000 ÷ 1,414.21, or 353.55, orders would be placed. The timing of orders would need to be adjusted for the lead time required for delivery.

Internal auditors can use EOQ or variations thereof to evaluate the efficiency of inventory ordering practices and the economic preferability of maintaining current inventory levels.

Risk Analysis

The analysis of risk can be performed using analytical tools to quantify possibilities, probabilities, and likely consequences. Risk analysis will guide the audit planning process and can be a particularly useful tool in prioritizing audit projects. Capital-budgeting tools frequently are altered slightly to reflect risk-adjusted discount rates. Sensitivity analyses as well as simulation analyses are useful tools for assessing risk and quantifying how much the discount rate should be adjusted.

Cost/Benefit Studies

Almost all performance audits entail cost/benefit analysis of alternatives and should include some adjustment for risk. Each of the tools described in this chapter is likely to be relevant to such analyses. Audit risk assessments may be (1) judgmentally evaluated, (2) key to dollars of assets involved in various aspects of operations, and (3) emphasize cyclical rotations to ensure 100 percent coverage over some reasonable time frame.

Dynamic Programming

Quality control packages are available for analyzing control risks. In most analyses, decision-makers must identify key risks, possible losses, and associated probability statistics; then the available analytical tools provide summary risk profiles, figuring cost trade-offs across various control and operating configurations.

Dynamic programming is a maximization theory that can be utilized to calculate the benefits of expending large amounts of resources on controls over the short term in anticipation of key efficiency savings over the long term. By specifying a series of conditions, each of which results in an action or decision dependent on the preceding condition, this approach helps in analyzing period-by-period consequences of decision-making and overall risk assessments.

QUESTIONS

1. Describe how directed sampling differs from random sampling. How can analytical review be used to direct sampling?
2. How does the high-low method differ from trend analysis?
3. What is meant by a Bayesian approach?
4. An internal auditor wants to describe a data set collected during an operational audit related to a time and motion study of control procedures. The procedural testing resulted in the following time estimates: 7 minutes, 15 minutes, 9 minutes, 9 minutes, and 12 minutes. Compute the various descriptive statistics that are available for providing a profile of such data sets.

   In another plant, similar studies produced the following estimates: 8 minutes, 10 minutes, 9 minutes, 11 minutes, and 11 minutes. Are the two plants comparable with respect to the efficiency with which control procedures are being performed? Quantify your response.
5. How do parametric tests differ from nonparametric tests? Which type of test is a chi-square analysis?
6. How do activity ratios differ from profitability measures? How are such ratios incorporated into general versus specific financial analysis?
7. What problems commonly arise in making inter-company comparisons of ratios?
8. Would you expect positive or negative correlations between the following sets of variables?
   a. Number of units produced and pounds of raw materials used in production.
   b. Age of retail stores in operation and the book value of the stores' capital facilities.
   c. Number of loans extended and interest income.
   d. Advertising expense and sales dollars.
9. Are growth curves more likely to be effective in forming short-term or long-term forecasts? Why?
10. How do exponential smoothing techniques differ from unweighted moving-average techniques?
11. Distinguish between time-series and cross-sectional regression analyses. Describe how cross-sectional regression might be applied to a retailer.
12. If a new production process is expected to have a 70 percent learning-curve effect and the first 300 units required 10 minutes per unit to produce, prepare the learning-curve effect that might be anticipated through a production level of 9,600 units.
13. For what types of business applications might linear programming techniques be useful?
14. Define the meaning of "critical path" and "crashing."
15. How does the net present-value approach differ from the internal rate of return approach to evaluating capital-budgeting projects?
16. Distinguish between independent and dependent events with respect to probability analysis.
17. What is meant by EVPI?
18. What is the key purpose of sensitivity analysis?

19. What types of problems can be addressed by queuing theory?
20. If an entity has an annual demand for 100,000 units of product, incurs $3 per order to place an order, and estimates the cost of carrying one unit in inventory for a year to be $7, what is the EOQ? How does the EOQ relate to the number of orders which should be placed per year?

EXERCISES
E-1
A manufacturer has set the following standards for production:

- 3 pounds of material per unit at a cost of $1 per pound.
- 15 minutes of direct labor time at a cost of $10 per hour.
- Overhead costs of $4 per direct labor hour.

Actual production statistics follow:

- 20,000 units were produced.
- 56,000 pounds of material were purchased and used.
- $55,000 were spent on these materials.
- 4,900 hours of direct labor were used at a cost of $52,000.
- $20,000 in overhead costs were incurred.

Required:
Perform a variance analysis.

E-2
The auditor for a bank believes that its customer base has remained rather stable over time and that interest expense should parallel prevailing interest rates. The auditor decides to apply time-series regression analyses to the following data set:

INTEREST RATES	INTEREST EXPENSE
8%	$ 75,000
9%	$ 86,000
11%	$113,000
12%	$118,000
10%	$101,000

Required:
a. Compute the regression relationship of interest.
b. How "good" is the regression model's explanatory power?
c. What are the underlying assumptions of the regression tool?
d. How might this application be improved?

E-3

An auditee produces two product lines: Zebo and Zabo. Zebo takes one hour to produce at a cost of $7 per unit and can be sold for $20 per unit. Zabo takes one-half hour to produce at a cost of $15 per unit and retails for $22 per unit. Only 10,000 units of Zebo can be sold on the market because of stiff competition. Production facilities can provide 8,000 total hours.

Required:

a. Formalize this linear programming problem to evaluate the auditee's production plans.
b. Use the graphical approach to solve the problem.

E-4

An auditee is planning the introduction of a new product line. Alternative production schedules have been narrowed down to three possibilities: 10,000 units, 20,000 units, or 30,000 units. Production costs total $3 per unit and retail value is $5 per unit. The probability distribution for sales is as follows: a 10 percent likelihood of sales of 10,000 units, a 60 percent likelihood of sales of 20,000 units, and a 30 percent likelihood of sales of 30,000 units.

Required:

a. Construct a payoff table from this data.
b. Compute the expected value of each of the alternative production schedules.
c. Which schedule should be selected?
d. What amount should the entity be willing to spend for market studies that could improve the estimate of market demand? Support your response.

E-5

Examine the income statement and balance sheet shown on the next page.

Required:

Perform a complete financial statement analysis for this entity. Explain how each ratio is to be interpreted. What additional data would you request to improve your analysis?

E-6

Multiple Choice: Select a single answer which best completes the statement or answers the question:

1. EOQ formulas, ABC analysis, and two-bin systems are commonly used elements of the control cycle for the stores process. These controls primarily relate to what part of the cycle?
   a. Determination of need.
   b. Acceptance of materials.
   c. Storage of materials.
   d. Release of materials.

INCOME STATEMENT FOR THE YEAR
            ENDED 1987   BALANCE SHEET

			12/31/87	12/31/86
Sales	$2,900,000	Cash	$ 10,000	$ 8,000
Cost of Goods Sold	1,500,000	Marketable Securities	20,000	15,000
Gross Profit	$1,400,000	Accounts Receivable	100,000	90,000
		Inventory	200,000	180,000
Administrative Expenses	400,000	Prepaid Expenses	6,000	5,000
Interest	20,000	TOTAL CURRENT		
		ASSETS	$336,000	$298,000
Income Before Taxes	$ 980,000	Net Plant, Property, &		
		Equipment	420,000	440,000
Taxes	400,000	Intangible Assets	80,000	60,000
NET INCOME	$ 580,000	TOTAL ASSETS	$836,000	$ 78,000
		Current Liabilities		
		Accounts Payable	$120,000	$100,000
		Notes Payable	100,000	95,000
		TOTAL CURRENT		
		LIABILITIES	$220,000	$195,000
		Bonds Payable	150,000	140,000
		Common Stock ($1 par)	100,000	100,000
		Paid in Capital in Excess		
		of Par	200,000	200,000
		Retained Earnings	160,000	163,000
		TOTAL EQUITIES	$836,000	$798,000

2. A soft-drink bottling company is opening a new bottling plant and wants to project future production costs. If the company expects the production costs as they relate to volume to be similar to its current operations at several other bottling plants, it should consider applying:
   a. Cross-sectional regression analysis.
   b. Time-series regression analysis.
   c. Learning-curve analysis.
   d. Simulation analysis.

3. The numerical process that would be most helpful to an auditor in evaluating projected general and administrative expense rates for a division under review is:
   a. Game theory.
   b. Linear programming.
   c. Probability theory.
   d. Regression analysis.

4. A bakery developed the payoff or conditional profit table shown on the next page for their daily production of cakes sold.

	10	15	20	25	Number Sold
	.2	.3	.3	.2	Probability
Bake: 10	50	50	50	50	
15	15	75	75	75	
20	-20	40	100	100	
25	-55	5	65	125	

Based on this table, the number of cakes they should bake to maximize expected profit is:
a. 10
b. 15
c. 20
d. 25

5. A maker of one-pound cans of mixed nuts assembled the following information:

NUT	COST/POUND	CONTENT BY WEIGHT
Cashew	$1.50	20% to 40%
Pecan	$1.20	10% to 30%
Peanut	$0.70	40% to 60%

The optimal mix can be found using linear programming with an objective function of:
a. Maximize: 0.2 Cashew + 0.1 Pecan + 0.4 Peanut
b. Minimize: 1.5 Cashew + 1.2 Pecan + 0.7 Peanut
c. Minimize: 0.3 Cashew + 0.12 Pecan + 0.28 Peanut
d. None of the above

6. The major advantage of Monte Carlo simulation is that it permits:
a. Low-cost employee training.
b. Assessment of an individual's managerial skills.
c. Experimentation using models.
d. Evaluation of alternative competitive strategies.

7. Which of the following items would most likely be included in the calculation of economic order quantity?
a. Price.
b. Cost.
c. Demand.
d. Supply.

8. Because of limited capacity, a manufacturer must choose only one of two possible new products to introduce. Based on the decision tree below, they should introduce:

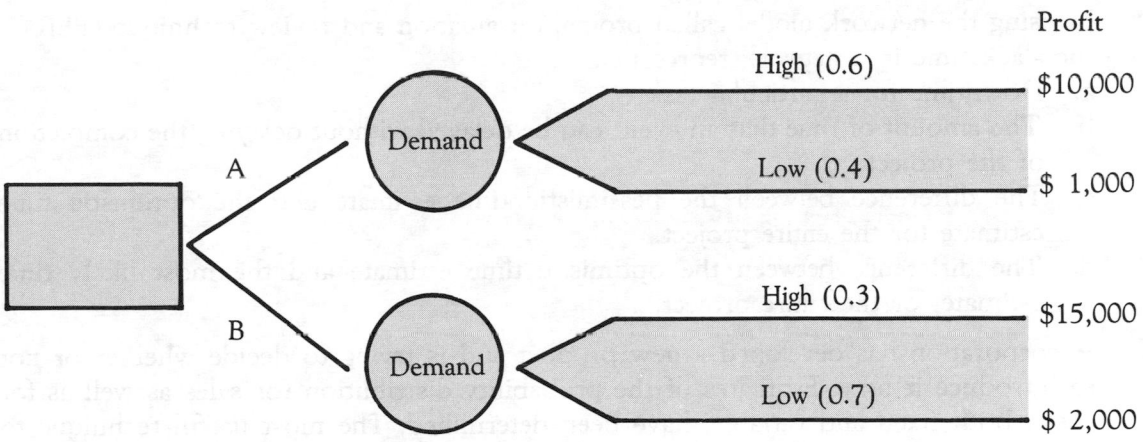

Profit

High (0.6) — $10,000

Low (0.4) — $ 1,000

High (0.3) — $15,000

Low (0.7) — $ 2,000

a. Product A with expected profit of $5,500.
b. Product B with expected profit of $8,500.
c. Product C with expected profit of $5,900.
d. Product D with expected profit of $6,400.

9. A producer of small executive jet aircraft found labor hours for a new model to be as follows:

PLANE	LABOR HOURS PER PLANE
1	2,000
2	1,400
3	1,137
4	980
5	874
6	796
7	735

Given that the data show a 70 percent learning-curve effect, the labor hours needed to build plane number 8 would be closest to:

a. 500
b. 700
c. 800
d. 1,050

(CIA Exam Adapted)

E-7

Multiple Choice: Select a single answer which best completes the statement or answers the question:

1. In using the network model called program evaluation and review technique (PERT), the slack time in a network represents:
    a. Downtime for a particular task.
    b. The amount of time that an event can be delayed without delaying the completion of the project.
    c. The difference between the pessimistic time estimate and the optimistic time estimate for the entire project.
    d. The difference between the optimistic time estimate and the most likely time estimate for the entire project.

2. A corporation has developed a new product and is trying to decide whether or not to introduce it now. Estimates of the probability distribution for sales as well as for costs, both fixed and variable, have been determined. The most useful technique to aid the corporation's decision-makers is:
    a. Market research.
    b. Decision-tree analysis.
    c. Distribution logistics.
    d. Linear programming.

3. A corporation faces a decision on increased plant capacity to keep up with rapid growth. The decision is complicated by several different forecasts of future product demand and three different expansion plans, each with several location alternatives. A useful device for analyzing this situation is:
    a. Simulation analysis.
    b. Integer programming.
    c. Network analysis.
    d. Queuing theory.

4. The value of ratio analysis stems from its capability to:
    a. Effectively describe a mixed relationship (i.e., fixed and variable components of a relationship).
    b. Isolate the single cause of a change in operations.
    c. Simultaneously consider two or more variables affecting operations.
    d. Provide a measure that can be effectively compared to those of similar companies within an industry.

5. The controller of a company wants to develop a regression model to forecast overhead costs. Based on past data, the controller prepares the correlation coefficient matrix shown on the following page.

Labor Hours

	Overhead($)	Regular	Overtime	Sales ($)	Depreciation
Overhead	1.000	0.915	0.117	0.834	0.050
Regular	0.915	1.000	0.348	0.384	0.070
Overtime	0.117	0.348	1.000	0.953	0.100
Sales	0.834	0.384	0.953	1.000	0.430
Depreciation	0.050	0.070	0.100	0.430	1.000

If the model-builder wanted to include only two variables in the model, which variables should be selected?
a. Sales and regular labor hours.
b. Overtime labor hours and depreciation.
c. Overtime and regular labor hours.
d. Sales and depreciation.

6. Assume that your company develops regression models for sales in its various lines of business. One of the models developed was:

$$Y = 10,000 + 2,000X$$

Where Y = Sales
$\quad$ X = Number of customers making purchases

To which product line is this model likely to relate?
a. Used cars.
b. Cosmetics.
c. Shoes.
d. Electrical Appliances.

7. A battery manufacturer warrants its automobile batteries to perform satisfactorily for as long as the owner keeps the car. Auto industry data shows that only 20 percent of car buyers retain their car for three years or more. Historical data suggests:

Number of Years Owned	Probability of Battery Failure	Battery Exchange Costs	Percentage of Failed Batteries Returned
Less than 3 years	0.2	$50	75
3 years or more	0.6	$20	50

If sales for 1982 were 50,000 batteries, what would be the estimated warranty cost for these sales?
a. $375,000
b. $435,000
c. $500,000
d. $620,000

8. If a manufacturer has a high inventory-turnover ratio, which of the following is the most likely cause?
   a. Unreliable suppliers.
   b. Obsolescence.
   c. Stockouts.
   d. Highly seasonal operations.

9. The president of a conglomerate is to receive a $100,000 lump-sum pension payment at the end of five years. The conglomerate originally calculated its annual payments to fund this pension commitment at 16 percent interest, but, because of a decline in interest rates before the first payment was made, a more conservative figure of 8 percent will be used. Given that the future value of a $1 annuity after five years is $5.867 at 8 percent and $6.878 at 16 percent, what calculation would yield the change in required annual payments?
   a. (100,000/6.878) — (100,000/5.867)
   b. (100,000/6.878) — (100,000 × 5.867)
   c. (100,000 × 5.867) — (100,000 × 6.878)
   d. (100,000/5.867) — (100,000/6.878)

10. A decision tree has been formulated for the possible outcomes of introducing a new product line:

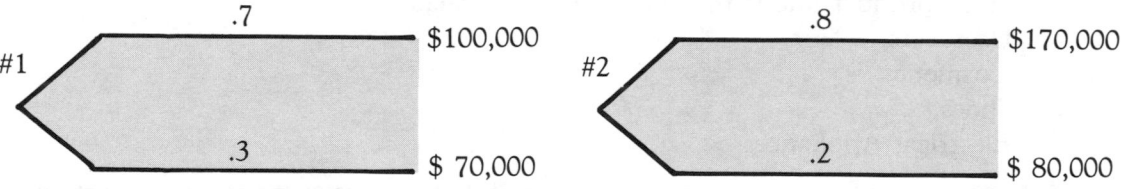

   Branches related to alternative #1 reflect the possible payoffs from introducing the product without an advertising campaign, while the branches for alternative #2 reflect the possible payoffs from introducing the product with an advertising campaign. The campaign costs $40,000. The expected values of alternatives #1 and #2, respectively, are:
   a. #1: (.7 × $100,000) + (.3 × $70,000)
      #2: (.8 × $170,000) + (.2 × $80,000)
   b. #1: (.7 × $100,000) + (.3 × $70,000)
      #2: (.8 × $130,000) + (.2 × $40,000)
   c. #1: (.7 × $100,000) + (.3 × $70,000)
      #2: (.8 × $170,000) + (.2 × $80,000) — $40,000
   d. #1: (.7 × $100,000) + (.3 × $70,000) — $40,000
      #2: (.8 × $170,000) + (.2 × $80,000) — $40,000

   (CIA Exam Adapted)

E-8

Multiple Choice: Select a single answer which best completes the statement or answers the question.

1. The economic order quantity (EOQ) model can be used to determine the optimum size of a purchase. The objective of the EOQ model is to minimize:
   a. The cost of placing an order.
   b. The number of orders placed in a specified period of time.
   c. The cost of carrying the units of inventory.
   d. The sum of the cost of placing an order and the cost of carrying the units in inventory.
   e. The sum of the cost of the products purchased and the cost of carrying these units in inventory.

2. In multiple linear regression analysis, the coefficient of determination (R^2) indicates:
   a. The relationship between the independent variables.
   b. The percentage of the total variation in the dependent variable that is explained by the regression equation.
   c. The percentage change in the dependent variable for a given change in the independent variables.
   d. Whether there is a linear relationship between the independent variables and the dependent variable.
   e. The slope of the regression line.

3. A company's break-even point in sales dollars may be affected by an increase in both selling price and variable cost per unit by an equal percentage (assuming all other factors are equal within the relevant range). The equal percentage changes in selling price and variable cost per unit will cause the break-even point in sales dollars to:
   a. Decrease by less than the percentage increase in the selling price.
   b. Decrease by more than the percentage increase in the selling price.
   c. Increase by less than the percentage increase in the selling price.
   d. Increase by more than the percentage increase in the selling price.
   e. Remain unchanged.

4. Given the following events and their associated probabilities of outcome, determine the probability of events A and C occurring simultaneously.

Events and Probability

Events	A	B	C	A or C	A or B
Probability	1/3	1/4	1/2	5/6	5/12

a. 5/6
b. 1/2
c. 1/6
d. 1/24
e. 0

5. When making predictions of gross sales, an internal auditor would most likely use:
   a. Regression analysis.
   b. Linear programming.
   c. Sensitivity analysis.
   d. Monte Carlo method.
   e. Stochastic methods.

6. Clerks A, B, and C process 50 percent, 20 percent, and 30 percent of the sales orders, respectively. The percentage of errors made in processing a sales order by clerks A, B, and C are 2 percent, 5 percent, and 10 percent, respectively. A sales order is audited and found to be in error. What is the probability that this invoice was processed by clerk C?
   a. .30
   b. .60
   c. .10
   d. .03
   e. None of the above.

7. An internal auditor is reviewing the budget of a manufacturing division. The division has estimated its expected profit for next year on the basis of the probability-rated profit forecast shown below:

Volume (Units)	Probability	Profit or (Loss)
10,000	15%	$(20,000)
20,000	24%	(5,000)
30,000	42%	10,000
40,000	14%	25,000
50,000	5%	40,000
	100%	

What is the expected profit for the division based on the above data?
   a. $10,000
   b. $27,000
   c. $13,900
   d. $5,500
   e. $50,000

(CIA Exam Adapted)

8. A company has developed a learning (improvement) curve for one of its newer processes from its accounting and production records. Management asked internal audit to review the curve. Which of the following events would tend to mitigate the effects of the learning curve?
   a. Labor costs incurred for overtime hours and charged to an overhead account.
   b. The number of pre-assembled purchased parts used exceeded the plan.
   c. The number of skilled, higher-paid workers used in production exceeded the plan.
   d. Newly developed processing equipment with improved operating characteristics is used.
   e. All of the above.

9. An internal auditor developed the data below for a linear programming model for its southern plant.

	Product		
	X_1	X_2	X_3
Selling price	35	90	20
Costs:			
Material	15	30	10
Labor	15	30	3
Variable overhead	2	5	1
Fixed overhead*	5	10	1
Profit/(loss) per unit	(2)	15	5

*Allocated to products on the basis of labor hours.

Based on the data above, which of the following should the internal auditor select as the correct function to maximize profit from that plant?
   a. $35X_1 + 90X_2 + 20X_3$
   b. $-2X_1 + 15X_2 + 5X_3$
   c. $15X_2 + 5X_3$
   d. $3X_1 + 25X_2 + 6X_3$
   e. $5X_1 + 30X_2 + 7X_3$

10. A linear-programming model produces a unique solution by:
    a. Ignoring resource constraints.
    b. Minimizing production costs.
    c. Minimizing both variable production costs and labor costs.
    d. Maximizing the objective function subject to resource constraints.
    e. Finding the point at which various resource constraints intersect.

(CIA Exam Adapted)

E-9

Shown on the following page is a regression diagram prepared by an internal auditor setting forth the line of best fit for overhead and wages.

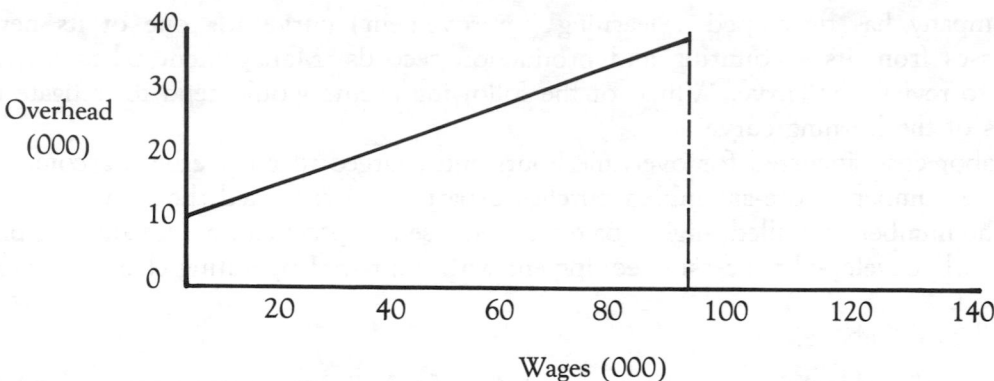

The line of best fit in this diagram is described by the formula y = a + bx.

Required:

a. What is the slope of the line of best fit in numeric terms?
b. When wages amount to $176,251, how much is the estimated overhead (rounded to the nearest dollar)?

(CIA Exam Adapted)

E-10

The internal auditors of Arnold's, Inc. are considering conducting an audit of Zappo, a newly acquired subsidiary. Past experience suggests there is a 60 percent likelihood that Zappo's internal controls are adequate. If they are not adequate, estimated losses of $70,000 due to theft and waste will be incurred. The auditors can perform (1) a full audit at a cost of $60,000, (2) a limited review at a cost of $20,000, or (3) no examination. A full examination can be expected to result in the elimination of the losses due to theft and waste. A limited review can be expected to result in the elimination of 50 percent of these losses. A decision table presenting this information is diagrammed as follows:

Possible Audit Actions	Expected Control States	
	Adequate (60%)	Inadequate (40%)
No Examination	$ 0	-$70,000
Limited Review	-$20,000	-$55,000
Full Audit	-$60,000	$10,000

Required:

a. Calculate the expected value of each possible audit action.
b. Considering only the expected value of the various actions the auditors have identified, what audit action should Arnold's auditors take?
c. What audit action should Arnold's auditors take if Zappo's internal controls are known to be inadequate?

(CIA Exam Adapted)

PROBLEMS

P-1

The auditor general of a large state government has recently decided to audit the state's highway construction and maintenance operation for the last year. The audit will relate to highways in selected counties in the state and will cover land procurement, construction, purchasing, maintenance, and administration. The audit manager in charge formed a steering committee consisting of senior members of several different audit units to oversee this complex project.

At the first meeting of the committee, the committee chairman (named by the audit manager in charge) proposed that the audit schedule be controlled by the use of Gantt chart techniques. While several members of the committee agreed with this proposal, the audit manager in charge suggested that the complexity of the project required a more sophisticated project-control technique such as PERT (Program Evaluation and Review Technique). As many members of the committee were not familiar with PERT, a decision was postponed until the next meeting when the audit manager in charge would make a presentation of the PERT technique and its applicability to audit scheduling and control.

Required:

a.   Specify in outline form the key elements of PERT that the director should stress at the next meeting of the steering committee.
b.   Identify three ways in which PERT is superior to Gantt chart techniques in this circumstance.
c.   Discuss how PERT would be used in planning the above audit.

(CIA Exam Adapted)

P-2

The internal auditing staff of Green Lake, Inc. uses regression analysis to analytically review each period's sales expense. Based on data collected over a long period, the following statistical regression equation was developed:

Sales expense ($thousands) = 34.5 + .04 company sales ($thousands) + .2 shipping costs ($thousands) + .01 industry sales ($millions).

The following statistical report was generated by a standard computer program:

	Coefficient	Standard Error	t-Statistic
Constant	34.50	.6100	56.60
Company sales	.04	.0026	15.40
Shipping costs	.20	.0150	13.30
Industry sales	.01	.2500	.04
Standard error of regression	10.20		
R^2	70.00		

Required:
a. Identify the dependent and the independent variables in the regression equation.
b. Assume that, for the current period, the company incurred sales expenses of $400,000 and shipping costs of $800,000 to generate sales of $5,000,000. Industry sales for the period are estimated to be $2 billion. Based on this information, what point estimate of this period's sales expense would the regression model provide?
c. Indicate how a 95 percent confidence interval for the current period's sales expense point estimate would be constructed. Assume that sales expense is normally distributed.
d. Which variables, if any, in the equation could be eliminated without seriously reducing the explanatory power of the regression model?

(CIA Exam Adapted)

P-3
Multiple Choice: Select the letter corresponding to the best answer:

1. Microtech, Ltd. uses statistical tests to indicate the reasonableness of sales representatives' monthly expense reports. The relationship between sales revenue and sales representatives' expenses was plotted on the scattergram shown below:

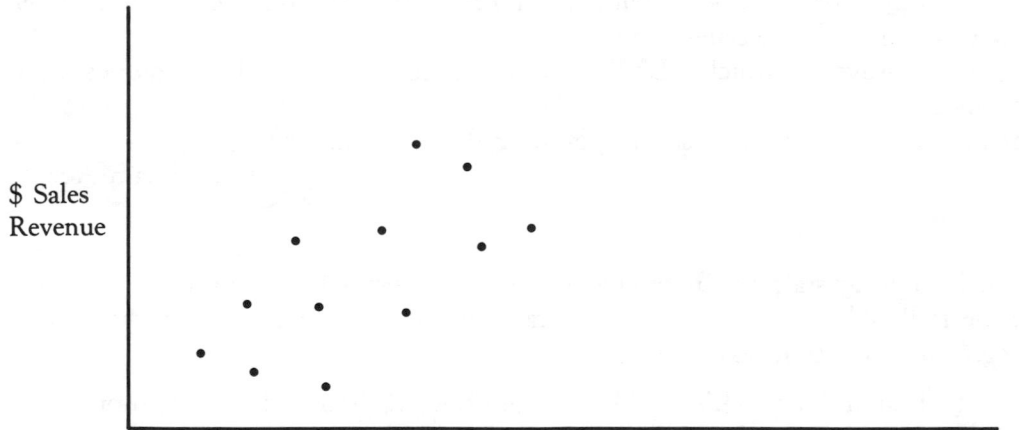

Monthly Sales
Representatives' Expense

Which of the following statements about this scattergram is correct?
a. Since no association apparently exists, a regression model would not be meaningful.
b. Since an association apparently exists, a regression model would not be meaningful to assess the reasonableness of a sales representative's expense report.
c. Since an association apparently exists, a regression model can be used to assess the reasonableness of a sales representative's expense report.
d. Since this scattergram is based on past data, it would not be useful in estimating the reasonableness of current and future relationships.

e. Since there are several regression equations which may explain the relationship between sales representatives' expenses and sales revenues, a regression model should not be used.

(CIA Exam Adapted)

2. Concerning the appropriate measure of central tendency for the frequency distribution of loss experience shown below, which of the following statements is correct?

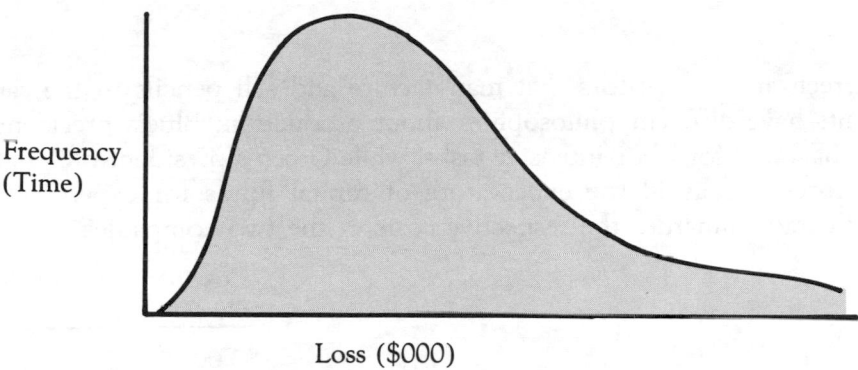

a. The mean should be used since it represents the dollar loss which has occurred most frequently in the past.
b. The mean, median, and mode are equal because the distribution is symmetrical.
c. The mode is the most appropriate measure because it considers the dollar amount of the extreme losses.
d. The median is the most appropriate measure because it is not affected by the extreme losses.
e. The mean is the best measure of central tendency because it always lies between the median and mode.

(CIA Exam Adapted)

P-4

The data shown below were gathered while planning a special project.

Activity	Duration (days)	Predecessor
A	10	None
B	8	None
C	30	None
D	12	A
E	15	A
F	14	B
G	15	D
H	20	E, F
I	5	C

Required:
Show your work for the items below:
a. Draw a network diagram for this project.
b. Identify any critical path.
c. What is the earliest project completion time?
d. Find the slack time for each activity.
e. Discuss possible courses of action if the project must be completed within 40 days.

(CIA Exam Adapted)

P-5

Blue and Green are competitors that manufacture and sell pencils in the same market. Their presidents have different philosophies about production: Blue's president prefers to use robotized machines for labor-intensive tasks, while Green's president prefers to maintain a large work force and avoid the expenditure of capital funds for expensive equipment. The following data summarizes the respective costs of the two companies.

	Cost per Gross of Pencils	
	Blue	Green
Materials	$3.00	$3.00
Labor	$1.50	$6.00
Variable manufacturing overhead	$ .50	$1.00

1. Fixed costs for Blue are $1,500,000 per year, and for Green, $870,000 per year.
2. The selling price for a gross of pencils is expected to remain at the present level of $20.
3. Normal output and sales for both companies is 200,000 gross of pencils per year.

Required:
a. Compute the expected results for both companies at the normal level of output and explain why one company outperformed the other.
b. Assume that the sales outlook for next year is bleak and each company will produce and sell only 90,000 gross of pencils. Compute their respective profits or losses; if one company would outperform the other, explain why.
c. At what level of production would both companies have the same results?
d. Which company's president would most likely be willing to reduce the sales price to obtain a larger volume of sales? Why?

(CIA Exam Adapted)

P-6

A recently prepared staff report recommends changes in certain operating procedures. Implementation of the recommendations is being considered. The process of implementation would require review by a number of departments. The estimated network for review is shown on the next page. All times are shown in days.

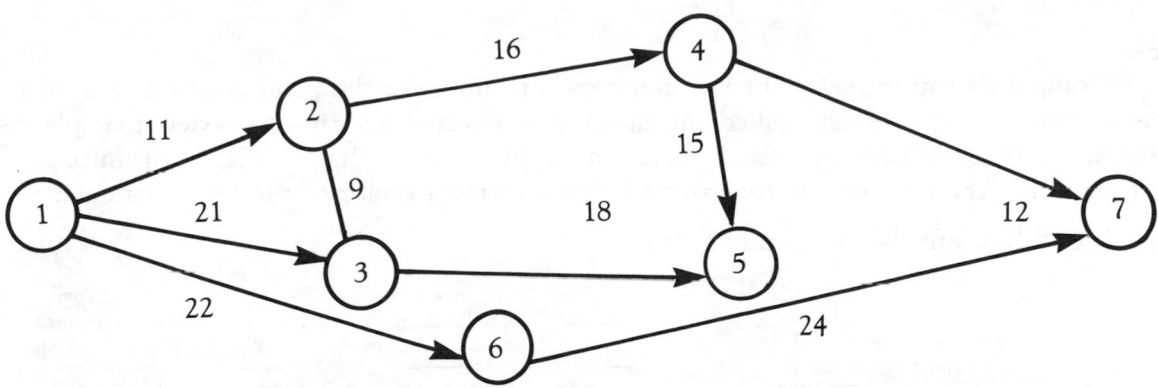

Required:
a. Identify the critical path.
b. For each activity, specify the earliest time it can begin, the earliest time it can be completed, and the slack time.

(CIA Exam Adapted)

P-7

The expected-value technique represents a methodology to choose among investment opportunities. Below are two investment opportunities where information is available to use the expected-value technique in choosing among investments. You may assume that both alternatives require the same outlay of resources and have the same investment life.

	Probability of Outcome	Outcome*
Investment A	.9	15%
	.1	20%
Investment B	.4	0%
	.5	40%
	.1	60%

*Expected annual rate of return on investment.

Required:
a. Which investment should be chosen if you use the expected value approach? Support your answer with appropriate calculations.
b. The expected value approach forces managers to consider some things that would not otherwise be considered using a "best estimate" approach. What are these additional factors introduced for consideration by the expected value approach?
c. Considering the two investments above, what basic assumptions underlie the expected value approach that might deter a division manager from using only the results from the expected value technique in making the investment decision?

(CIA Exam Adapted)

P-8

A company's top management is seeking ways to improve the profitability of one of its newer plants. The president asked the director of internal auditing to review that plant's product-mix decisions to assist management in meeting its objective of improved profitability. The internal auditor assigned to the review developed the following data:

1. Monthly profit data by product line:

	X_1	Product X_2	X_3	Total Hours Available
Sales	$3,750	$3,000	$6,000	
Variable costs	$1,200	$1,350	$2,250	
Fixed costs	$2,625	$1,050	$3,675	
Operating profit	$ (75)	$ 600	$ 75	
Monthly production (units)	150	50	150	
Unit selling price	$ 25	$ 60	$ 40	
Unit variable cost	$ 8	$ 27	$ 15	
Net contribution per unit	$ 17	$ 33	$ 25	
Labor hours per unit:				
Department 1	2	5	3	1,000
Department 2	3	1	4	1,360

2. Demand for each of the plant's three products is so great that the plant can easily sell whatever quantity of each product it produces. The internal auditor constructed the following LP (linear programming) model of the plant's operation:

$$\text{Maximize } z = \$17\, x_1 + \$33\, x_2 + \$25\, x_3$$

$$\text{Subject to:} \quad 2\, x_1 + 5\, x_2 + 3\, x_3 \leq 1000$$
$$3\, x_1 + 1\, x_2 + 4\, x_3 \leq 1360$$
$$x_1 \geq 0$$
$$x_2 \geq 0$$
$$x_3 \geq 0$$

3. Slack variables x_4 and x_5 were added to constraints 1 and 2, respectively, and the optimal tableau shown on the next page was generated by a computer program:

Required:

Analyze the information given and provide answers to the following questions:

a. How many units of x_1 and x_3 should be produced, and what would be their total contribution margin?

b. How many units of x_2 should be produced? Explain your answer.

c. Why is linear programming the appropriate technique to employ in the situation above?

(CIA Exam Adapted)

<u>Variables</u>

c_j x_o		17 x_1	33 x_2	25 x_3	0 x_4	0 x_5
25	x_3 280 units	0	13	1	3	-2
17	x_1 80 units	1	-17	0	-4	3
$z_j - c_j$	$8,360	$0	$3	$0	$7	$1

SECTION IV

TYPES OF AUDIT APPLICATIONS

16 Audit Applications

The steps in the audit process usually are similar, regardless of the type of audit. The differences among various types of audits relate primarily to the objectives and scope of examination, which may result in different kinds of audit tests. This chapter examines some of the different types of audit applications:

- Operational auditing.
- Performance auditing.
- Compliance auditing.
- Auditing of financial controls.
- Auditing of financial statements.

Operational Auditing

Operational audits examine and evaluate systems of internal control and the quality of performance in carrying out assigned responsibilities with respect to an organization's operating functions. Auditors examine and evaluate a variety of activities related to such functions as marketing, facilities management, production, inventory management, security, electronic data processing, personnel management, financial management, and accounting.

The key to understanding operational auditing is to understand internal controls (discussed in Chapter 3). Most internal auditors agree that the objectives, types, and methods of internal control encompass all operations of an organization.

Exhibit 16-1 illustrates relationships among the general methods, types, and objectives of internal control. The exhibit also gives a few examples of specific control methods employed by management and examples of audit tests that may be used to examine those methods.

Specific applications of controls and audit methods differ among organizations. As you study Exhibit 16-1, however, notice the comprehensive nature of audit interests and how the audit activity ties directly to operations. For example, one important organizational control is the establishment of specified lines of authority, whereby only certain people are authorized to approve certain decisions. The specific application of this control generally requires approval

Exhibit 16-1
Illustrations of Internal Control and Audit Tests

CONTROL METHODS	PRIMARY TYPE	PRIMARY CONTROL OBJECTIVES	EXAMPLES OF CONTROL METHODS	EXAMPLE AUDIT TESTS
Organizational:				
Establishment of purpose, authority, and scope of responsibility for entity	Preventive	Achievement of organizational objectives and goals	Formal statement by management and by the board setting forth organizational purpose, authority, and responsibility	Examination and verification of statement
Establishment of organizational structure and lines of authority and responsibility	Preventive	Achievement of organizational objectives and goals	Formalized organization chart	Examination of organization chart for appropriate lines of individual authority and responsibility
Establishment of authorization procedures for key decisions	Preventive	Compliance with policies, plans, procedures, laws, and regulations	Requirement for management's signature on purchase orders	Examination of documents bearing authorization signatures
Preparation of job descriptions and separation of related duties	Preventive	(1) Compliance with policies, plans, procedures, laws, and regulations and (2) safeguarding assets	(1) Written job descriptions and (2) job orientation and training	(1) Examination of written job descriptions and (2) interviews with management and labor
Operational:				
Planning	Preventive	(1) Compliance with policies, plans, procedures, laws, and regulations and (2) achievement of organizational objectives and goals	Planning meetings	Examination of minutes of planning meetings
Budgeting	Preventive	(1) Economy and efficiency of operations and programs and (2) achievement of organizational objectives and goals	(1) Formal budget preparation and (2) approved budget	(1) Documentation of budget process and (2) examination of approved budget for consistency with organizational objectives

CONTROL METHODS	PRIMARY TYPE	PRIMARY CONTROL OBJECTIVES	EXAMPLES OF CONTROL METHODS	EXAMPLE AUDIT TESTS
Accounting and information systems	Detective	(1) Reliability and integrity of information, (2) economy and efficiency of operations and programs, and (3) achievement of organizational objectives and goals	Production reports	Testing production reports and comparing actual performance results with budgeted performance
Documentation of activities	Preventive and detective	(1) Compliance with policies, plans, procedures, laws, and regulations and (2) safeguarding assets	Purchase orders, checks, invoices, production reports, minutes of meetings, etc.	Flowcharting activities with document preparation, walk-through, and testing of documents
Authorization of decisions and activities	Preventive	All five objectives	Required approval to begin project	Examination of documentation for authorization signatures
Written policies and procedures	Preventive, detective, and corrective	Compliance with policies, plans, procedures, laws, and regulations	Production quality-control checks with rejected production reworked to meet production standards	Examine and evaluate policies and procedures; test compliance with established policies and procedures
Personnel:				
Recruiting and selecting suitable personnel	Preventive	All five objectives	Background checks on new job applicants	Verify performance and documentation of background checks of job applicants
Training and development	Preventive	All five objectives	Training and development programs made available to employees	Verify appropriate training and development programs available to employees and employee participation in such programs
Supervision	Preventive, detective, and corrective	Compliance with policies, plans, procedures, laws, and regulations	Appropriate instructions given to employees and periodic monitoring of performance with appropriate measures to make needed improvements	Observe supervision process; examine documents recording the supervision process

CONTROL METHODS	PRIMARY TYPE	PRIMARY CONTROL OBJECTIVES	EXAMPLES OF CONTROL METHODS	EXAMPLE AUDIT TESTS
Review:				
Internal review of each employee	Detective and corrective	Compliance with policies, plans, procedures, laws, and regulations	Semiannual performance evaluation of employees	Interview employees to confirm such reviews; examine documentation recording the review
Internal review: system, operations, and programs	Detective and corrective	(1) Compliance with policies, plans, procedures, laws, and regulations; (2) economy and efficiency of operations and programs; and (3) achievement of organizational objectives and goals	Internal auditing	Verify the performance of internal audits by examining previous audit reports
External review	Detective and corrective	(1) Reliability and integrity of information; (2) safeguarding assets; (3) compliance with policies, plans, procedures, laws, and regulations	CPA audits	Examine audit opinion on financial statements; examine CPA's management letter relating to control weaknesses in accounting system
Facilities and equipment:				
On-site security measures	Preventive	Safeguarding assets	Fences, door locks, computer passwords, well-lighted buildings, and physical restraints on valuable equipment	Examination and testing of facilities and equipment

signatures or initials by the designated individuals. To examine and evaluate the effectiveness of this control, internal auditors (1) determine that authorization procedures, including approval signatures/initials, have been established, and (2) examine relevant documents for the required approvals.

Likewise, all operational audit tests generally are linked directly to some aspect of organizational operations.

Operational auditing, however, is a generic term. Many people use it synonymously with "internal auditing." For them, everything the internal auditor does is operational auditing. Other people subclassify internal auditing into either operational or financial auditing. Still others subclassify this work into other categories, such as "management auditing," "performance auditing," and "compliance auditing." Obviously, there is no standardized use of these terms, but some differentiation among them is helpful — especially when it is important to clarify audit objectives.

"Management auditing" typically means the auditing of management controls. Management auditing often is considered the same as operational auditing in general, since (1) management permeates the entire organization and all of its operations; (2) internal controls are established, maintained, and monitored by management; and (3) management should be subject to the established internal control systems. Some internal auditors, however, reserve the term "management auditing" for audits of specific management activity, such as planning, budgeting, supervising, and reviewing. The inconsistent use of this term almost always requires a definition to clarify what is meant in specific situations.

In contrast to the brief explanation of management auditing, "performance auditing," "compliance auditing," the auditing of financial controls, and the auditing of financial statements are given more extensive treatment in the following sections.

Performance Auditing

Performance audits generally focus on efficiency and effectiveness and require that operating standards be established. These audits depend upon the availability of a set of accepted objectives and goals against which performance can be evaluated.

Effectiveness and Efficiency as Performance Measures

The internal auditor's examination and evaluation of effectiveness and efficiency does not substitute for management's performance evaluations. Rather, internal auditing provides one source of information to assist management in its evaluation. A number of factors may influence management's judgments, many of which may be largely subjective. Internal auditors, however, require objective measures to conduct performance audits. Objectives need to be well defined in terms of measurable goals which can be compared to actual results. Similarly, efficiency is defined in terms of operating standards against which to compare actual performance.

Also, some auditors contend that performance audits relate almost exclusively to effectiveness, with far less emphasis on efficiency. Others believe that because efficiency is so closely related to effectiveness, internal auditors are able to anticipate many performance problems by identifying key inefficiencies before overall effectiveness is threatened.

Determining Effectiveness and Efficiency

Effectiveness refers to the accomplishment of objectives. Efficiency refers to the resources consumed in achieving those objectives. Generally speaking, the consumption of fewer resources means greater efficiency.

Internal auditing sometimes is criticized as lacking clear criteria, second-guessing management, and placing auditors in judgment roles that exceed the support of available audit evidence. However, to set internal auditing aside because of its difficulty would suggest that the effectiveness of organizations cannot be evaluated. Yet performance evaluation programs, incentive packages, and market share studies have all developed under the presumption that effectiveness can be monitored and periodically assessed.

Auditors need only to be given a set of criteria by which effectiveness is to be judged in order for them to obtain objective evidence capable of supporting audit conclusions. A common approach to evaluating effectiveness is to compare costs and benefits prior to certain activities to costs and benefits after these activities. The presumption is that any changes in costs or benefits are attributable to the introduction of these activities. Such changes thereby help in measuring program or operating effectiveness.

Another approach is to compare performance to other similar operating units.

For years, the efficiency of routine jobs, such as keypunching or piecework on production lines, has been evaluated through time and motion studies using engineering techniques. Business analysis tools are available for evaluating capital-budgeting decisions, make-or-buy decisions, and return on investment (ROI). To effectively evaluate efficiency, the primary requirement is that information be collected on the costs and benefits of selected approaches, budgeted expectations, and available alternatives. In this manner, benchmarks are available for assessing efficiency. Productivity measures such as cost-per-unit and revenues-per-unit are often emphasized in making efficiency assessments.

Examples of
Effectiveness

An example of an internal performance audit would be an assignment to assess whether a particular governmental agency has effectively met its assigned objective of achieving elevator safety.

Well-Defined Objectives. For the internal auditor to reach a conclusion about the agency's effectiveness, objectives need to be defined at an appropriate level of detail. For example, is the objective to see that all elevators in the city are inspected at least once a year? Is the objective to ensure that no fatalities occur as a result of elevator breakdowns, or that no breakdowns occur? The availability of detailed objectives provides criteria about which evidence can be collected for evaluation.

Control Over Operations and the Implementation of Objectives. Assuming that the objective is to ensure that annual inspections are made of all elevators, the auditor must first assess the control setting and the means by which the agency attempts to implement the objective. Information would need to be maintained about the location of all elevators; which are in operation; when and by whom they were last inspected; whether each elevator passed inspection, and if not, whether corrective actions were taken. In addition, inspectors would have to be trained. They would need to file timely reports and should be responsible for follow-up to ensure that exceptions are responded to appropriately.

To ensure that these activities take place, adequate internal controls would be essential. In other words, competent employees who are aware of the role of control procedures as well as operating procedures, and who document operations in a responsible, thorough, and accurate manner, are essential to effective performance.

Achievement of Desired Objectives. The internal auditor can gather objective evidence that the operating objective was met. A sample of elevators can be drawn, evidence can be collected as to when they were last inspected, and an inference can be drawn to all of the elevators in the city. In addition, blueprints of city buildings can be examined and elevator locations traced to the agency's list to ensure completeness. Additional tests on newly constructed buildings would be appropriate to assess the timeliness with which the central listing is updated.

Less objective data may be available on inspectors' qualifications or the propriety of past inspections; however, a review of resumes, training programs, competency exams, and performance reports, as well as reperformance of the inspection procedures for a sample of elevators, would provide corroborating evidence of inconsistencies in reported and actual conditions.

Again, more intensive testing should be done on those elevators thought to be problematic (e.g., older elevators) and on those for which follow-up reports were filed after exceptions were to have been corrected. The auditors also may investigate accident reports to determine the circumstances and what corrective measures were taken.

Collection of evidence may require a trained and independent elevator inspector. Hence, performance audits may occasionally require expert judgment beyond that of the auditor's in reaching conclusions.

In conducting a performance audit, the auditor should investigate several questions, as summarized in Exhibit 16-2. Auditors sometimes do not express an opinion on performance audits other than noting exactly what was examined and the number of instances in which the predefined criteria were or were not met.

Exhibit 16-2
Key Questions Relevant to Performance Audits

1. Is the activity being conducted as intended by top management?
2. Are prescribed policies being followed?
3. Is the function being performed necessary?
4. Are administrative and financial controls effective?
5. Are the costs of such controls in line with the function's effectiveness and the risk involved in the activity?

Adapted from Dan M. Guy, "Inclusion of Performance Auditing Concepts in the Auditing Course," *The Internal Auditor,* March/April 1975, pp. 68-72.

Examples of Inefficiency

Efficiency measures relate to resource use. Many efficiency problems are detectable by gaining an understanding of how day-to-day activities are performed.

No Unwarranted Duplication of Efforts. One common flaw is the duplication of efforts that may result from overlooking simple time-saving tools. As an example, multi-copy forms can expedite authorization, shipping, receiving, and accounting functions by permitting some concurrent processing of documents. Data base management systems in an EDP environment can help avoid some undesirable duplicate generation and maintenance of computerized data files.

Another type of duplication occurs in what are called "shadow systems." These systems are created informally by employees when the formal information system they are supposed to be using fails to meet their needs. The employees then create their own information, documents, logs, journals, reports, etc., and keep them separate from the formal system. The work required for the formal system is thereby often duplicated with the work performed on the informal system. The need for shadow systems can be eliminated in a variety of ways, depending upon the system. Sometimes training on the formal system can help the employee learn to utilize the system better. Sometimes the formal system can be changed to accommodate the employee's needs. Sometimes the employee may not understand his or her needs. Occasionally the employee's system is better than the formal system, in which case it should replace the formal system.

Proper Staffing. A well-designed operation can perform inefficiently if it is improperly staffed. Too few employees, too many, or the lack of qualified personnel are all common reasons for inefficiencies.

Authorized Use of Assets. Another factor that may contribute to inefficiency is the absence of appropriate authorization requirements for the use of assets. The absence of an approval process means that the location of equipment may be unknown and its use less than optimal. For example, assume that a company has one forklift and one truck, and an employee takes the forklift to do work which could have been done by the truck. In the meantime, the loading dock's activities come to a halt until the forklift is returned. Clearly, the wasted loading time is inefficient and directly attributable to the absence of a formal authorization procedure.

By reviewing findings related to efficiency and economy, one can sense the types of issues about which evidence might be gathered. To illustrate, Exhibit 16-3 summarizes some efficiency and economy findings by the New York state comptroller's office when auditing state and city agencies.

Exhibit 16-3
Examples of Efficiency and Economy Findings

Inadequate Personnel Utilization:

Item   The city's public assistance case load contained an intolerable number of people who were ineligible for such assistance. A quality control system designed to measure the level of ineligibility and to highlight procedural weaknesses contributing to the problem was experiencing inordinate delays. Our audit showed that a major cause of this delay was poor supervision and the absence of work standards for the quality-control employees. Thus, the failure to efficiently implement a key managerial control was contributing to the continued waste of program funds.

Item   An audit of the Tax Department showed that, despite increasing backlogs of work, vacant tax-auditor positions were not being filled. Many of the filled positions were "on loan" to less productive units. We concluded that the department was being "penny-wise and pound-foolish," since every dollar spent on tax enforcement produced many additional dollars of tax revenue and since the potential for collecting delinquent taxes tended to decrease with the passage of time.

Item   An audit of the junior high schools showed that many teachers had an unusually high number of "administrative hours," performing nonteaching clerical tasks. There was a potential for using the teachers by reducing class sizes (presumably increasing the effectiveness of the teaching program), or by replacing a portion of the teaching staff with lower-paid clerical personnel.

Item   An audit of employee attendance and activities at various unannounced times during the day, evening, night, and weekend shifts disclosed many instances of employees sleeping on the job, congregating in offices, arriving late for work, and leaving early. This condition was a major factor in the poor level of patient care at a state hospital.

Basic Managerial Weaknesses:

Item   Our comparative analysis of state and private schools for
              the treatment of juvenile offenders showed significant vari-
              ations in the portions of the schools' budgets spent for ed-
              ucation, treatment, and administration. Private schools
              were spending more funds on program activities such as
              education and psychiatric services, whereas the state
              schools were spending more on administrative costs.
              Agency management should have obtained such compara-
              tive data and evaluated their implications.

Item   Drug addicts were treated at numerous facilities through-
              out the state. Our audit showed that per diem costs
              ranged from $23 to $47. There was a need for manage-
              ment to evaluate the program implications of this wide
              disparity in costs among the various facilities to maximize
              program accomplishment and minimize the costs.

Consolidations of Activities and "Make-or-Buy" Analyses:

Item   A separate hospital with its own administrative staff occu-
              pied three buildings on the grounds of another state hospi-
              tal. Our audit showed that the limited workload of admi-
              nistrative activities at this separate hospital, as well as its
              proximity to the offices of the main hospital, would per-
              mit consolidation of the administrative functions of the
              two hospitals at a savings of $145,000 a year.

Item   A local school district exercised control over 29 facilities.
              Our audit showed that the unused classroom facilities
              amounted to about 28 percent (the equivalent of eight
              schools) and that enrollment was continuing to decline.
              We recommended consolidating and closing facilities to
              the extent feasible. Such action would not only reduce
              costs but also provide greater flexibility in class sizes and
              course offerings.

Inadequate Management of Assets:

Item   The outstanding accounts receivable at a teaching hospital
              increased from $7 million to $11 million during a two-
              year period. An audit showed that this situation was
              caused in part by a lack of aggressive follow-up action, in-
              sufficient supervision, and insufficient staff to keep up
              with an increasing workload.

Item   More than $6 million in available federal funds were being lost each year because of the failure to bill certain outpatient services. An audit showed that the problem was caused by the inability of the state and local officials to agree upon a billing format.

Source: Martin Ives, "Auditing for Efficiency and Economy," *The Internal Auditor,* January/ February 1985, pp. 79-80.

Compliance Auditing

Internal auditors frequently perform "compliance audits." The objective of these audits is to determine whether, and to what degree, an organization conforms to certain specific requirements of policy, procedures, standards, or laws and governmental regulations. The nature of compliance auditing is more objective than other internal auditing applications, especially management auditing.

To perform a compliance audit, the auditor must know precisely what policies, procedures, standards, etc., are required. Such requirements almost always are documented, as are the activities they govern. For example, job qualifications usually are specified for particular positions, especially for key positions in the organization. These qualifications usually are outlined in job descriptions. To determine if the organization's employees conform to these requirements, auditors can check the backgrounds and qualifications of employees. Information on each employee should be contained in his or her personnel file, including job application form, resume, and references.

Usually, compliance audits require relatively little initial survey work or review of internal controls, except to outline precisely what requirements are being audited. The audit focuses almost exclusively upon detailed testing of conditions. The audit report usually outlines the degree of compliance observed and indicates the number of items conforming to requirements and the number of exceptions. The internal audit report also may indicate reasons for noncompliance.

Compliance Audits of Laws and Governmental Regulations

Federal, state, county, and city governments have many laws, ordinances, and regulations to govern the activities of organizations. These governmental requirements affect almost every aspect of an organization's operations.

Internal auditors are only one group of important players in this environment. Others also play important roles with respect to legal compliance. Organizations employ legal staffs for counsel on many issues of legal compliance, including real estate purchases, equal employment opportunity for minorities, pension provisions, environmental codes, and operating safety. CPA firms specialize in financial reporting and in auditing for compliance with governmental reporting requirements, such as for the Securities and Exchange Commission (SEC) and the Internal Revenue Service. Various governments consider some legal requirements so important that they employ their own auditors and inspectors to check compliance by individual organizations.

In most cases, internal auditors examine areas of legal compliance first, so that they can inform management early of potential problems. It is usually less expensive for the internal auditors to find the problems and for management to correct them early than for outside examiners to find them. If outside legal counsel, CPAs, or governmental auditors discover problems, they almost always investigate further than they would otherwise, taking more time at the organization's expense. Early detection and correction can also help avoid legal sanctions, penalties, and fines.

If internal auditors have already audited the activities, and management has taken action to correct observed problems, the outside examiners and auditors often can use documentation from the internal audit and management follow-up, which can help decrease costs.

Compliance Auditing as a Profession

Compliance auditing has evolved into an important part of today's economy. Many auditors, especially those employed by the government, specialize in auditing for compliance. These auditors are trained extensively, often in highly technical, detailed areas. They must know and understand large bodies of information and precisely how organizations should operate with respect to specific criteria and standards. They are skilled in specific audit techniques and how to work with management to encourage and motivate proper compliance, even when management may feel inconvenienced and imposed upon.

Auditing of Financial Controls

Internal auditors examine two aspects of financial internal controls: (1) controls over funds and (2) controls over the accounting for funds. Audits of the management of the acquisition and use of the organization's funds usually are considered operational or management audits. Audits of specific controls over the flow of funds and the accounting function are generally considered financial audits. In this section we shall examine financial control concepts, specific financial control systems, and the auditing of financial statements.

Financial Control Concepts

Financial controls are primarily designed to accomplish three internal control objectives: (1) the safeguarding of the organization's financial assets, (2) the reliability and integrity of financial information, and (3) compliance with generally accepted accounting principles (GAAP) as established by the Financial Accounting Standards Board and other recognized entities, such as the Government Accounting Standards Board, the Cost Accounting Standards Board, and governmental taxing authorities.

Safeguarding relates to the potential risk of loss of an organization's funds and other assets. The emphasis of controls over safeguarding is placed primarily on preventive controls. These controls are designed to help ensure:

- That the organization receives all of the funds to which it is entitled.
- That the funds are adequately secured and maintained.
- That the funds are appropriately spent for authorized purposes.

The emphasis of controls over the reliability and integrity of financial information is primarily on detective and corrective controls. Financial data provides management with accurate information pertaining to the acquisition, security, maintenance, and expenditure of financial resources. This information alerts management to problems arising in the funds-flow process, thereby assisting management in correcting those problems and avoiding or minimizing any losses.

Detective and corrective controls are primarily used to help ensure compliance with prescribed accounting procedures and guidelines.

While particular controls related to these three internal control objectives may emphasize different types and methods of establishing internal control, notice the integrative nature of not only the objectives, but the controls themselves. Preventive, detective, and corrective controls are coordinated within the organization's financial management function to ensure that the funds-flow process is operating properly. Because of the integration of these different controls, auditors frequently encounter compensating controls — i.e., controls aimed at one objective that fulfill another objective as well.

There also may be directive controls related to financial management, but these relate primarily to decisions on how funds are to be acquired and used. For example, management's decision to invest in certificates of deposit rather than bonds represents a type of directive measure to achieve certain income objectives and goals. These directive controls would be covered primarily as an operational issue. Realistically, of course, auditors are likely to examine operational issues and financial control issues in the same audit of an organization's financial management function.

Financial Control Systems

An organization's financial management function includes a number of integrated yet identifiable subfunctions. These subfunctions might include cash receipts, cash disbursements, cash management, accounts receivable, accounts payable, long-term investments, long-term payables, capital acquisition, and payroll.

Specific controls are designed into these different subsystems. Exhibit 16-4 outlines some of the more common controls over cash receipts and cash disbursements. These controls are categorized by specific objectives. The exhibit also outlines common audit tests used to examine these various controls.

A variety of books and subscription services outline specific control measures for specific financial activities. While these sources also may outline audit procedures to examine and test these controls, it is up to the individual internal auditor to determine the most appropriate audit procedures for a particular circumstance.

Auditing Financial Statements

Financial audits are directed at assessing the reasonableness of recorded balances on an organization's financial statements. A good example of a financial statement audit is a setting in which an insurance company's investment group owns shopping centers that are leased on a percentage of sales plus a fixed rate basis. Obviously, the company is very interested in collecting adequate rental revenue, which depends largely on the accuracy of revenue reported by tenants. Such leasing contracts commonly have a clause that permits the company to audit reported sales. Clearly, these audits are a service to management that can be evaluated in cost/benefit terms to assess whether they produce a net profit for the company — i.e., how does additional rent revenue compare to the cost of utilizing the internal auditors in such an engagement in lieu of allocating their time to other audit projects?

The Objective of Audits of Financial Statements

Audits of financial statements focus on the accuracy of financial reports pertaining to financial conditions and operating performance. These audits appropriately emphasize the auditor's concern for financial measures. They are most often associated with the external

Exhibit 16-4
Typical Cash Controls and Audit Procedures

CONTROL OBJECTIVES	SPECIFIC CONTROL METHOD OR PROCEDURE	TYPICAL AUDIT PROCEDURES
I. General Cash		
A. Appropriate safeguards are in place to protect cash	1. Segregation of duties related to handling and record keeping	1. Review organizational structure, functional responsibilities, and job descriptions
	2. Protection of unused checks	2. Verify existence and describe protection procedures for unused checks; examine unused checks, including security measures
	3. Maintenance of petty cash system	3. Review petty cash controls and count cash on hand
B. The amount of cash is accurately and appropriately recorded and reported on financial statements	1. Regular bank reconciliations	1. Examine bank reconciliations, footing totals and comparing cash account balances; confirm bank balances; investigate overdrafts and checks more than 30 days outstanding; verify cut-off of receipts and disbursements; obtain a cut-off bank statement
	2. Authorized movement of cash among cash and investment accounts	2. Examine documentation of authorization for cash movement and trace all bank transfers immediately before and after the end of the reporting period
	3. Generally accepted accounting principles for reporting cash	3. Evaluate the reporting of cash on financial statements
II. Cash Receipts		
A. All cash due is received	1. Collect cash at specified locations	1. Verify the existence of appropriate procedures and facilities; observation
	2. Customer receives written receipt and acknowledges the totals	2. Observation

CONTROL OBJECTIVES	SPECIFIC CONTROL METHOD OR PROCEDURE	TYPICAL AUDIT PROCEDURES
	3. Cash register displays total	3. Observation
	4. Vigorous efforts to collect past-due accounts	4. Review collection procedures and perform an analytical review of accounts receivable; confirm balances of accounts receivable
	5. LOCKBOX systems whereby banks collect mailed cash receipts from organizations' security boxes at the post office; monies are deposited directly to the organizations' accounts and remittance advices are sent to the companies	5. Review contracts and charges, observe system, and test bank documentation to remittances received
B. Safeguarding cash receipts	1. Each day's cash receipts are deposited together	1. Compare cash receipt lists to the receipts journal and bank deposit slips
	2. Cash register locks in copies of written receipts and sales totals	2. Observation
	3. Mailed cash receipts are opened in the mail room	3. Review the segregation of duties, observe, and test cash receipt lists
	4. Lists are prepared of all mailed cash receipts and are sent to the controller	4. Verify cash receipt lists
	5. Mailed cash receipts of remittance advices are sent to the cashier	5. Describe cash receipt procedures and verify performance
C. Cash receipts are promptly recorded	1. Written receipts are prepared immediately upon receiving cash	1. Test and compare written receipts to cash receipt journal and cash register transactions
D. Cash receipts are properly and accurately recorded	1. Controller's staff reconciles remittance advices to list of mailed receipts	1. Vouch a sample of cash receipts to the general ledger
	2. Accounts receivable clerk posts credits to customers' accounts from the remittance advices	
E. Cash receipts are appropriately reported on financial statements	1. Generally accepted accounting principles for cash receipts	1. Evaluate reporting of cash receipts

CONTROL OBJECTIVES	SPECIFIC CONTROL METHOD OR PROCEDURE	TYPICAL AUDIT PROCEDURES
III. Cash Disbursements		
A. Propriety of expenditures	1. All expenditures are reviewed and authorized by an appropriate official	1. Test expenditure documentation for the appropriate supervisor's signature of approval; scan disbursement journal for checks payable to cash bearer for unusual amounts and to related parties; investigate
B. Safeguarding cash for expenditures	1. Regular bank reconciliations by employee not involved in disbursements, authorization of expenditures, or handling cash	1. Examine bank reconciliations, including a review of separation of duties
C. The correct amounts are disbursed	1. Voided checks are marked and filed	1. Examine voided checks
	2. Computer or check-writing machine prints the check amounts	2. Observation and examination of current and cancelled checks
	3. Supporting documents for expenditures are stamped or perforated to prevent reuse	3. Test supporting documents for appropriate stamp or perforation
	4. Use of supporting documentation to prepare checks	4. Test check amounts by supporting documentation
D. Expenditures are authorized	1. Payments by check only except for petty cash items	1. Verify disbursement policies and scan cash disbursement journal for unusual cash transactions; investigate
	2. Prenumbered checks	2. Examine checks
	3. Check-signers review documentation for payment	3. Examine documentation of supervisor's signature of approval
	4. Until mailed, check-signer maintains custody of checks; signed checks are not returned to the preparer	4. Review disbursement procedures for processing checks
	5. Facsimile signature plates may be used on check-signing machine: (a) check-signing machine counts signed checks; (b) checks are	5. Review the check-signing procedures and verify controls

CONTROL OBJECTIVES	SPECIFIC CONTROL METHOD OR PROCEDURE	TYPICAL AUDIT PROCEDURES
	locked inside machine to prevent unauthorized removal; (c) signature plates are removed when not in use; and (d) an additional authorized signature by an official may help prevent some abuses	
	6. Use of a voucher system	6. Review controls for cash-disbursement documentation
E. Disbursements are promptly recorded	1. Immediate, dated journal entries of expenditures by using supporting documentation	1. Test journal entries by comparing dates with supporting documents
F. Disbursements are properly and accurately recorded	1. Documented supervisory review of journal vouchers (supervisor initials the supporting documentation indicating a review)	1. Test journal vouchers for supervisor's approval signature; vouch a sample of disbursement transactions
G. Appropriate reporting of cash disbursements	1. Generally accepted accounting principles for cash disbursements	1. Evaluate the reporting of cash disbursements

audit function, since certified public accountants (CPAs) are perceived to be independent attestors whose primary function is to provide the public with assurance that entities' financial statements are fairly presented. "Fairly" does not imply exact accuracy, but it does suggest that material error is not present.

The Fairness of Financial Statement Representations

One might wonder why internal auditors would be concerned about the fairness of financial statements, given that external auditors are usually responsible for expressing an opinion on them. In fact, external auditors are liable should they fail to discover material errors that would have been revealed if generally accepted auditing standards had been followed, as prescribed by the American Institute of Certified Public Accountants (AICPA). Given that internal auditors are employees of an entity, they are unlikely to be perceived as independent by third-party users of the financial statements. Therefore, an internal auditor's attention to financial audits is unlikely to substitute for external auditors' work. Nor is it the case that regulations such as the provisions of the SEC would permit such one-for-one substitution.

However, internal auditors are interested in the entity's control system capabilities with respect to producing a set of reasonable financial statements. The entity views its control system as a set of alternative resources that can be combined into an almost endless variety of configurations. Alternative resources include the allocation of internal auditors' time, the hiring of external auditors, investments in security systems, establishment of specific control procedures, and similar control measures related to the control environment, such as hiring and training practices which enhance the competency of employees. Increased use of any single resource is expected to decrease the required use of alternatives, and the entity must reach a decision as to the optimum "mix" of resources.

The Interface with the External Auditor

Statement on Auditing Standards (SAS) No. 9, set forth by the AICPA, recognizes the role of internal auditors as a dimension of an entity's control system which merits some reliance in the course of conducting an external audit. Although mere substitution of work is not permitted, the external auditor can test internal auditors' working papers and then rely on them in lieu of repeating all test work. The emphasis of *SAS No. 9* is on the external auditors' evaluation of the internal auditors' independence, objectivity, and overall quality of performance. This evaluation is used as the basis for determining the extent of the interface between external and internal auditors. It is common for internal auditors to:

1. Coordinate their audit plans with those of the external auditors.
2. Do some test work on behalf of the external auditors.
3. Assist in identifying explanations for unexpected fluctuations in account balances.
4. Assign staff members to temporarily work under the direction of the external auditors.

This latter step is helpful because internal auditors have an in-depth knowledge of operations. Approaches to selecting sampling units, access to records, interpretation of acronyms and jargon used by employees, and optimal execution of audit plans can be improved upon by involving internal auditors in the external auditors' examination. The result is more efficient auditing by CPAs and, very likely, lower audit fees for the entity being examined.

The internal auditor's relationship with external auditors is the subject of *Statement on Internal Auditing Standards No. 5,* which is included as an appendix at the end of this chapter.

A Critical Role Regarding Interim Financial Statements

In addition to the interest of third parties in the reasonableness of financial statements, managers have a keen interest in the fairness of financial records. This interest is at least three-pronged. Managers base their decisions on information drawn from the accounting system; if that information is in error, pricing decisions, investment decisions, and all critical day-to-day evaluations could also be in error, creating both short-term and long-term operating problems.

A second concern stems from management's interest in the entity's reputation in financial markets. Integrity is a trait valued by businesses both in promoting products and services and in attracting investors and creditors. When financial information is disseminated to the public, management wants to send a reasonably fair signal of operations. In spite of external auditors' participation in providing the market with certain assurances along these lines, the auditors' report clearly states that the financial statements presented are those of management. Not only might errors in such statements tarnish the reputation of an entity, but they may very well lead to litigation against both the external auditor and management. Hence, financial penalties are tied to financial statement misrepresentations, providing added incentive for managers to invest in controls, including the involvement of internal auditors in financial audits.

A third concern may be paramount in certain circumstances where external auditors may not be examining an entity's operations or may be involved in only a limited review capacity. If management wants to obtain audit satisfaction for a particular period of interest —

especially for an interim period such as the first quarter of operations — the sole source of such assurance may be the internal auditors. The scope of management's interest and the level of detail of management's concerns may differ from external auditors' risk and may have led to certain one-sided audit tests. For example, external auditors may test for the understatement of expenses, when the entity has an equal interest in the overstatement of expenses. If an external auditor performs only a limited review, typically only analytical review procedures are applied. If audit coverage is desired for management's use, internal auditors may be the logical party to provide such coverage.

Finally, the presence of either external auditors' examination or review reports cannot be taken for granted. Entities in many sectors of the economy still have a choice as to whether to undergo an audit. If an entity is closely held, for example, financial audits by internal audit staff may be sufficient to meet management's needs.

Interim financial statements issued on a quarterly basis are often used to project year-end performance. Management may desire added assurance that such statements are reasonably accurate and can be used for planning and forecasting. Since interim statements often are made public and often are required as a basis for obtaining credit or for issuing securities, care is taken to ensure that they are fairly stated for all of the aforementioned reasons. Internal audits can serve an extremely important role in this regard.

Envision a scenario in which an entity is considering an acquisition at mid-year. The acquisition candidate has last year's audited financial statements but presents unaudited interim statements. Management might very well request that the internal auditors perform some financial auditing procedures in key account areas. These procedures can provide assurance that the merger decision will be based on an adequate set of information for that interim period.

The "Continuous Audit" Advantage

Since internal auditors are employees of a single entity, they have a very real advantage over external auditors. Rather than coming onto the entity's premises a few times each year to perform interim work and to complete the year-end audit, as the external auditors do, the internal auditors are continuously on the entity's premises. Since internal auditors observe the operations throughout the year, they are unlikely to be misled about the overall quality of controls. It has been pointed out that the possibility of "duping" an external auditor may exist; employees might comply with controls only while the "unknown periodic observer" — easily identified as the external auditor — was watching. In contrast, as the adage says, it is difficult to "fool all of the people all of the time." The internal auditors' continuous access to operations can be expected to enhance audit effectiveness.

Note that sampling procedures from the population of transactions are intended to give some assurance that external auditors are provided with a more complete picture of operations than would be provided by a single point in time. Nevertheless, the whole story is not always evident from such procedures. To give a classic example, imagine that an entity experiences a computer crash which does substantial damage to on-line files. The entity strives to recreate such files from the available audit trail, and when the external auditor tests the available audit trail at year-end, things look fine. However, when the comparison to prior years is performed, the item of interest is found to be a far lower percentage of expenditure in prior years. Only then does the external auditor through inquiry procedures eventually uncover the facts that a crash had occurred and that files were irretrievably "lost." With the benefit of hindsight, the external auditors probably would have proposed a different audit approach — i.e., one intended to find "missing" transactions rather than testing retrieved transactions. Through the "continuous audit" advantage, the internal auditors probably would have already been aware of the computer crash and its likely consequences.

The computerized on-line environment is a setting in which continuous monitoring has special advantages. The very nature of computers means that a single programming error will occur over and over again, potentially creating material misstatements. Timely recognition of problems through the application of financial auditing techniques can be important to both efficiency and audit effectiveness. Another critical element of an EDP system evaluation is assessing the likelihood that the appropriate program was in use at various points in time throughout the year, as claimed within the EDP system documentation. The internal auditors could more easily conduct surprise or unannounced audits of EDP and other facets of operations, since they have continuous access to such operating systems.

The Governmental Setting   Internal auditors within the governmental sector sometimes assume primary financial audit responsibilities. For example, the General Accounting Office (GAO) is sometimes requested to report on the financial accountability of the federal government's operations. Similarly, many state, county, and city auditors perform financial audits of state and local entities' financial statements and express opinions thereon. The AICPA was asked to acknowledge that such auditors were sufficiently "independent" to qualify as external auditors for regulatory purposes. In other words, the question can be asked: Since the GAO has its salaries paid by Congress, can the GAO be independent in auditing governmental operations? Similarly, would state auditors meet the auditing requirements set forth by Federal Revenue Sharing Legislation or other mandatory audit provisions? Although we might tend to view such auditors as a part of the internal audit environment, the AICPA did acknowledge that state governmental auditors were sufficiently "independent" to express audit opinions that were acceptable by the federal government in meeting mandatory audit requirements for the purpose of qualifying for revenue sharing funds. Hence, it is not at all uncommon for state auditors to express an opinion on the fairness of municipalities' financial statements.

Planning for Audit Coverage

As we have suggested, internal auditors often address a different scope or time frame than external auditors would commonly apply.

The Role of Materiality. Materiality is a term that communicates the importance of a particular piece of information in forming a decision. Any information that affects a decision is considered material. For example, if users of a report would be affected by knowing some additional fact or detail, such data is deemed to be material. The magnitude of materiality depends on the entity being audited. For example, if the entity is a conglomerate, entire subsidiaries may be immaterial, whereas for separate opinions on such subsidiaries, the materiality level might be set at 3 percent to 5 percent of just one given subsidiary's net income. External auditors look to court decisions and regulators, in part, to signal the expected level of materiality to which CPAs are expected to audit. These signals are consistent with considering the entity involved, the account under audit, the type of transaction recorded, the total dollars involved, and the users of financial statements. The SEC has indicated that more than a 3 percent change in earnings per share has a likelihood of being material. Many external auditors use 5 percent to 10 percent of earnings before taxes as a general guideline.

Internal auditors do consider the above aspects, but are likely to place greater emphasis on cost/benefit choices as they evaluate materiality. This is due in large part to the intended user group. Internal auditors most often perform financial audits on behalf of management. The question of materiality should be addressed in the initial plan for audit coverage within the context of users' interests.

For example, if management is interested in a single branch operation, the nature of that interest should be used to guide the scope and depth of the internal auditor's examination. One critical problem is that a standard for materiality does not exist, since entities are defined in a variety of ways and the concerns of management may vary greatly from a pure investor's perspective. As an example, assume that a branch manager is being evaluated for promotion. The sole concern of management is whether the recorded sales revenue for that branch is reasonable. The amount management deems to be material can be requested as part of the audit project specifications. The "materiality definition" can then guide audit planning and allow the internal auditors to draw a conclusion about the reasonableness of recorded sales with the desired precision and level of confidence.

Risk Considerations. Just as materiality guidelines can be elicited from the key user group of management, risk considerations can be delineated for the internal auditors' use in planning for audit coverage. For example, revenue could be overstated or understated due to:

1. Clerical error.
2. Intentional error.
3. Temporary postponement of returns and allowances.
4. One-time orders for longer future periods by key customers.
5. Other atypical revenue variations which may relate to nonrecurring items.

The auditor's approach to a financial audit would be influenced by the relative risk of each alternative as perceived by management. If fraud is suspected, the entire nature of the audit would shift to a so-called fraud audit (discussed in depth in Chapter 18). If clerical errors are feared because of programming problems in past years or a high staff turnover, there are specific implications for the approach to audit testing that is likely to be effective. If the risk of concern is the possibility that sales are improperly matched to returns or are nonrecurring in nature, then testing should center on the contra-account or on attributes of orders, rather than merely on balances. The latter would move toward an operational, rather than a financial, auditing goal.

Whenever audit coverage is being planned, cost/benefit evaluations are the basis for selecting the level, extent, and nature of testing. The cost assessment is based on the total combined cost of the planned audit procedures and the risks of not detecting problems that might exist. The benefits are the discovery of problems, the production of reliable information, and the explicit control of risks. Many of the materiality and risk dimensions of such an evaluation are tied to the key objectives of any financial audit.

Key Objectives   When forming a conclusion about a financial balance, five key representations of the auditee are relevant to audit planning.

Existence. The most obvious representation is that the assets reflected on the books are in fact in existence, as are the claims of creditors and investors: inventory is not bogus, receivables are from valid sales, credit claims can be explicitly tied to legitimate contracted commitments, investors have made real investments, and so forth. This existence claim is most commonly evaluated through observation, inspection, and confirmation procedures, although some detailed testing can be usefully applied. For example, inspection of cash receipts subsequent to a balance sheet date can provide evidence that receivables did in fact exist.

Completeness. Once assurance is gained that representations relate to real transactions, the second concern centers on how complete the representations are. Were all sales recorded? Have commitments been made, yet left unrecorded? Completeness is addressed by tracing source documents to the records to ensure that they are reflected in the account totals. In addition, confirmations are mailed to known creditors and legal counsel to inquire about outstanding obligations.

Valuation. Once records are tested for the completeness of entries, consideration should be given to the corresponding values recorded per transaction. Valuation can be tested by referring to similar market exchange values, by examining detailed documentation supporting exchanges of assets and commitments, by testing for the involvement of related parties, and by utilizing appraisers to analyze the reasonableness of recorded values. Observation procedures may uncover damaged or obsolete assets which have not been written down, just as inquiry procedures can bring problems to an auditor's attention.

Presentation and Disclosure. Entities commonly include the phrase "footnotes are an integral part of these financial statements" when reporting on their financial position. This phrase emphasizes the necessity of viewing presentations in the context of related disclosures. For example, inventory balances clearly have different interpretations if an entity uses LIFO versus FIFO valuation and has a rather slow inventory turnover in a market of erratic price changes. Presentation and disclosure practices in a financial audit setting that parallels an external audit examination would be expected to be in accordance with generally accepted accounting principles. Underlying all of the detailed disclosure requirements is the overall objective of effectively communicating financial position or financial performance over some specified time period. While these same guidelines are available to the internal auditor, alternative presentations and disclosures may be preferred for the specified user group — particularly for management. Certain disclosures may be superfluous to the issue at hand or assumed to be known by all of the financial report users. On the other hand, more extensive disclosures may be essential to managers as they attempt to analyze such areas as accounts receivable or the type of contract underlying revenue.

Compliance. Many financial representations relate to contracts or transactions. Compliance questions can arise in these areas which can lead to distortions in reported numbers. For example, debt contracts typically have debt covenants which require such attributes as minimum working capital levels and limited dividend payouts. If an auditee were not in compliance with such restrictions, the debt could be called. This situation could create potentially severe liquidity and solvency problems. The auditor addresses compliance issues by first identifying existing restrictions and then comparing reported transactions to those provisions to ensure that they have been met. If they have not, formal approval of such noncompliance with loan covenant provisions will be sought from the trustee.

Risk of Misstatement

The auditor must assess the risk of misstatements and the dollar amount of materiality represented by each account regarding each objective. For example, the risk of valuation problems would appear greater in the presence of related-party transactions involving assets that are thinly traded (i.e., only a limited number of transactions occur regularly, in contrast to an active market such as a stock exchange). On the other hand, if inventory is widely traded and has easily identified characteristics for which market values exist, little valuation risk would seem to be present. If an entity's assets comprised only 5 percent of resources, little audit coverage might be required. However, if the assets comprised 40 percent of the resources, an audit plan for substantial audit coverage would evolve in reaction to this high-risk setting.

Distinguishing Internal Audit from External Audit Objectives

External audit objectives are a joint function of generally accepted auditing standards and the intended financial statement users. In contrast, internal audit objectives may very well veer from the direction of those standards, since internal audit objectives by definition focus on the objectives of management. Financial materiality will often be set on a subunit basis, rather than for the total entity's operations. Certain transfer pricing and intercompany transactions that would be eliminated in consolidated financial statements, and would therefore be of very limited interest to the external auditor, may be of primary interest in a financial audit performed on management's behalf.

Obviously, if the internal auditors' work is being planned to assist the external auditors, the objectives driving the audit work would be aligned. Similarly, if external auditors were requested to perform a special financial audit engagement on behalf of management, their objectives would be more aligned with those of an internal auditor (i.e., focused on the intended users).

Coordinating the Planning Stage with External Auditors and the Board of Directors or Audit Committee

Because of the potential cost savings in external audit fees, most internal audit directors will be encouraged to coordinate their planning activities with the external auditors. Similarly, because of potential benefits from serving special audit requests by management, the director will be asked to coordinate planning with the board of directors or audit committee. Given that the audit committee is entrusted with oversight responsibilities for the external and internal audit functions, a three-way planning interaction can be effective in providing assurance of optimum audit coverage.

The internal auditors should solicit input from management, auditees, and the external auditors to coordinate planning. The internal auditors should be encouraged to make requests for audit projects, to document the perceived costs and benefits of particular proposed projects, and to prioritize their requests. External auditors should be requested to quantify the extent to which various internal auditing activities are expected to influence their work and the corresponding fee for the audit engagement. One approach to obtaining this information is to request that the auditor propose various fee arrangements — for example, if internal audit provides X hours of assistance, then the audit fee would be Y dollars. If the timing of the internal auditors' assistance is particularly important, such details should be communicated. By providing a copy of the tentative audit plans to the external auditors, they often can give feedback about adjustments which might generate a "payback" or savings in audit fees. More importantly, the external auditors can plan their work to coordinate with that of the internal auditors. For example, by supervising or observing certain aspects of the internal audit work, the external auditors can place far more reliance on the internal audit function.

The internal audit plan for the year, the degree to which it responds to the requests of auditees, management, and external auditors, and the basis for setting priorities all should be clearly documented and communicated to the board. Typically, this detail is reviewed, adjusted as deemed necessary, and approved, directing the department to proceed in its varied audit projects. Exhibit 16-5 provides an example of a worksheet that might be useful in coordinating audit activities.

Exhibit 16-5
Worksheet for Coordination of Audit Activities

TYPE OF INTERNAL AUDIT ACTIVITY	TOTAL INTERNAL AUDIT MAN-HOURS	INTENDED SUBSTITUTION OF EXTERNAL AUDIT HOURS	EXPLICIT INTERFACE WITH EXTERNAL AUDITORS
Operational audit	400	50	Test of working papers
Field visit: Tests of controls	50	25	Coordination of sites with external auditors
Limited-scope Data Center review	120	70	Supervision by external auditors
Confirmation of receivables	40	40	Internal auditor assigned during interim work to external audit staff

---

Overall Audit Coverage

The main purpose of the coordination phase is to optimize overall audit coverage. Through explicit coordination of external and internal auditors' work, it is possible to obtain almost 100 percent audit coverage of assets, as well as revenue and expense cycles over at least a three- to five-year period. A common example of the coordination of activities is in the planning of field visits for multi-location entities. If, for example, internal auditors visit 20 of 100 locations, external auditors will often select the units they plan to visit from the remaining 80 locations. In this manner the audit coverage can be maximized.

The Audit Process Applied to Auditing Financial Statements

As we have said, the basic differences between operational auditing and financial auditing are in (1) the objectives and scope of the audit and (2) the specific audit tests applied.

The overall process is essentially the same. Exhibit 16-6 outlines six of the steps in the audit process as they may be applied in auditing financial statements.

Exhibit 16-6
The Audit Process Applied to Financial Auditing

Audit Preparation	Similar to preparation for an operational audit, except that (1) the objectives are primarily to examine and test account balances on the financial statements and (2) the scope probably is the accounting information system.
Initial Survey	Similar to that for an operational audit, with adjustments for more limited scope and objectives.
Review of Internal Controls	Similar to that for an operational audit, with adjustments for objectives and scope.
Expanded Testing	Primarily tests of compliance with integral accounting controls and substantive tests* of transactions and account balances.
Development of Findings	Similar to that for operational auditing with regard to internal controls. Determination of acceptability of account balances and presentation of financial statements for financial reporting purposes.
Reporting the Audit	Expression of a standardized auditor's opinion in accordance with generally accepted auditing standards. This report is prepared by the external auditor. A "management letter" addressing significant control weaknesses (similar to an internal auditor's report) usually accompanies the auditor's opinion and is prepared by the external auditors.

---

*Substantive testing in accordance with generally accepted auditing standards as set forth by the American Institute of Certified Public Accountants (AICPA) is discussed in detail in financial auditing textbooks. The main objective of substantive tests is to examine and verify account balances in the general ledger and on the financial statements.

Professional Standards Bulletin 83-8 states that auditors generally do not need to perform substantive tests to ascertain the adequacy and effectiveness of an internal control system. However, internal auditors may occasionally encounter circumstances in which substantive tests are helpful. The auditors should refer to a financial auditing textbook for guidance, although in many cases the particular test necessary to determine an account balance will be evident.

Complete textbooks are available for the study of financial auditing as practiced by independent CPAs. The point of this discussion is not to try to condense all of that information into a small space, but rather to show the similarity of audit processes for financial auditing and operational auditing, as well as to indicate the internal auditor's role in the financial auditing process. Notice that the main differences between financial auditing and operational auditing lie in the objectives and scope of the audit, in the more narrow selection of auditing procedures for financial auditing, and in the types of reporting.

Appendix

STATEMENT ON INTERNAL AUDITING STANDARDS NO. 5
Internal Auditors' Relationships with Independent Outside Auditors

Foreword

The Institute of Internal Auditors issued the *Standards for the Professional Practice of Internal Auditing* in 1978 "to serve the entire profession in all types of business, in various levels of government, and in all other organizations where internal auditors are found . . . to represent the practice of internal auditing as it should be . . . ." The *Standards* have been widely accepted and remain current despite continuing changes in business, society, and the profession of internal auditing.

This statement interprets Standard 500, External Auditors, and establishes additional elements of guidelines for internal auditors regarding their relationship with independent outside auditors. Specific focus is on guidelines 550.01 and 550.02. The term "independent outside auditors" as used in the statement refers to those professionals who perform independent annual audits of an entity's financial statements. The term has been used in place of "external auditors" (the term used in Standard 500) because "independent outside auditors" is less likely to suggest external auditors other than those professionals who perform the independent annual audit of an entity's financial statements.

Summary

A summary of the practices outlined in this statement follows:

- To the extent that professional and organizational reporting responsibilities allow, internal auditors should conduct examinations in a manner that allows for maximum audit coordination and efficiency.
- The director of internal auditing should make regular evaluations of the coordination between internal and independent outside auditors.
- A sufficient number of meetings should be scheduled to discuss audit activities planned by both internal and independent outside auditors to assure appropriate coordination of audit work; that duplicate efforts are kept to a minimum; that audit activities are efficient and timely; and that the scope of planned audit work is appropriate.
- Internal auditors need reasonable access to the programs, working papers, audit reports, and management letters of independent outside auditors and conversely should provide the independent outside auditors reasonable access to internal audit programs, working papers, and audit reports.
- The director of internal auditing should ensure that the independent outside auditors' techniques, methods, and terminology are sufficiently understood by the internal auditors, and conversely he/she should provide sufficient information to enable the independent outside auditors to understand the internal auditors' techniques, methods, and terminology.

Background

The scope and objectives of the work of internal auditors differ from the scope and objectives of the work of independent outside auditors, but their auditing activities can overlap unnecessarily if not coordinated properly. Coordination of internal and independent outside auditors' work is essential to ensure adequate audit coverage and to minimize duplicate efforts, and because each should have a good understanding of the work of the other.

Interpretations of Existing Guidelines
Guideline 550.01

Guideline 550.01 states that the internal and independent outside audit work should be coordinated to ensure adequate audit coverage and to minimize duplicate efforts.

.1 The scope of internal audit work encompasses both financial and operational objectives and activities. The scope of internal audit work is covered by Standard 300. On the other hand, the independent outside auditors' ordinary examination is designed to obtain sufficient evidential matter to support an opinion on the overall fairness of the annual financial statements. The scope of the work of independent outside auditors is determined by their professional standards, and they are responsible for judging the adequacy of procedures performed and evidence obtained for purposes of expressing their opinion on the annual financial statements.

.2 Oversight of the work of the independent outside auditor, including coordination with internal auditing, is generally the responsibility of the audit committee or its equivalent. Actual coordination should be the responsibility of the director of internal auditing. The director of internal auditing will require the support of the audit committee or its equivalent to achieve effective coordination of audit work.

.3 In coordinating the work of internal auditors with the work of independent outside auditors, the director of internal auditing should ensure that work to be performed by internal auditors in fulfillment of Standard 300 does not duplicate the work of the independent outside auditors which can be relied on for purposes of internal audit coverage. To the extent that professional and organizational reporting responsibilities allow, internal auditors should conduct examinations in a manner that allows for maximum audit coordination and efficiency.

.4 Internal auditing may agree to perform work for the independent outside auditors in connection with their annual audit of the financial statements. Work performed by internal auditing to assist the independent outside auditors in fulfilling their responsibility is subject to all relevant provisions of the *Standards for the Professional Practice of Internal Auditing.*

.5 The director of internal auditing should make regular evaluations of the coordination between internal and independent outside auditors. These evaluations may also include assessments of overall efficiency of internal and independent outside auditing, including aggregate audit cost.

.6   In exercising its oversight role, the audit committee or its equivalent may ask the director of internal auditing to assess the performance of the independent outside auditor. Any assessment provided by the director of internal auditing should be based on sufficient evidence of the efficiency and effectiveness of the work of the independent outside auditor.

Guideline 550.02

Guideline 550.02 states that coordination of audit effort involves:

.1   Periodic meetings to discuss matters of mutual interest.
.2   Access to each other's audit programs and working papers.
.3   Exchange of audit reports and management letters.
.4   Common understanding of audit techniques, methods, and terminology.

Each of these points is repeated and expanded upon as follows:

.1   Periodic meetings to discuss matters of mutual interest.

    .11   Planned audit activities of internal and independent outside auditors should be discussed to assure that audit coverage is coordinated and duplicate efforts are minimized. Sufficient meetings should be scheduled during the audit process to assure coordination of audit work and efficient and timely completion of audit activities, and to determine whether findings from work performed to date require that the scope of planned work be adjusted.

.2   Access to the independent outside auditors' programs and working papers may be important in order for the internal auditor to be satisfied as to the propriety for internal audit purposes of relying on the independent outside auditors' work. Such access carries with it the responsibility for internal auditing to respect the confidentiality of those programs and working papers. Similarly, access to the internal auditors' programs and working papers should be given to the independent outside auditors in order for the independent outside auditors to be satisfied as to the propriety, for external audit purposes, of relying on the internal auditors' work.

.3   Exchange of audit reports and management letters.

    .31   Internal audit reports, managements' responses to those reports, and subsequent internal audit follow-up reviews should be made available to the independent outside auditors. These reports assist the independent outside auditors in determining and adjusting the scope of work.

    .32   Internal auditors need access to independent outside auditors' management letters. Matters discussed in management letters assist internal auditing in planning the areas to emphasize in future internal audit work. After review of the management letter and initiation of any needed corrective action by appropriate members of management and the board of directors, the director of internal auditing should ensure that appropriate follow-up and corrective action have been taken.

.4   Common understanding of audit techniques, methods, and terminology.

.41   The director of internal auditing should understand the scope of work planned by the independent outside auditors and should be satisfied that the independent outside auditors' planned work, in conjunction with internal auditing's planned work, satisfies the requirements of Standard 300, Scope of Work. Such satisfaction requires an understanding of 1) the level of materiality used by the independent outside auditors for planning, and 2) the nature and extent of the independent outside auditors' planned procedures.

.42   The director of internal auditing should ensure that the independent outside auditors' techniques, methods, and terminology are sufficiently understood by internal auditors to enable the director of internal auditing to 1) coordinate internal and independent outside audit work, 2) evaluate, for purposes of reliance, the independent outside auditors' work, and 3) ensure that internal auditors who are to perform work to fulfill independent outside audit objectives can communicate effectively with the independent outside auditors.

.43   The director of internal auditing should provide sufficient information to enable the independent outside auditors to understand the internal auditors' techniques, methods, and terminology to facilitate reliance by the independent outside auditors on work performed using such techniques, methods, and terminology.

.44   It may be more efficient for internal and independent outside auditors to use similar techniques, methods, and terminology to effectively coordinate their work and to rely on the work of one another.

QUESTIONS

1. What is the main factor that differentiates various audit applications?
2. What is operational auditing?
3. What is the difference between operational and financial auditing?
4. What is the difference between operational auditing and internal auditing?
5. What are the two different types of financial auditing as discussed in the chapter?
6. Define the following terms: performance audits, compliance audits, and management audits.
7. When internal auditors conduct a performance audit, what are the two dimensions of an organization's operations that are usually of primary interest?
8. How would you characterize effectiveness? Efficiency?
9. How do auditors measure effectiveness and efficiency?
10. What are some ways in which inefficiency may occur in an organization?
11. How does a compliance audit restrict the objectives and scope of an internal audit, compared to other types of internal audits? Why should auditors perform compliance audits?
12. What is the internal auditor's role in compliance auditing with respect to laws, ordinances, and regulations?
13. What are the three primary objectives of financial internal controls?
14. Why are preventive controls important to the safeguarding of financial resources?
15. Financial information provides what primary types of control to assist management?
16. What primary types of controls help ensure compliance with accounting policies, procedures, and guidelines?
17. How does the integration of various controls give rise to compensating controls? Why would auditors combine in a single audit the examination of operational and financial controls?
18. Identify at least one general cash control objective, one control objective for cash receipts, and one control objective for cash disbursements. For each control objective, identify a specific internal control and an audit procedure to examine the control.
19. What is the objective of audits of financial statements?
20. What does it mean that financial statements are "fairly presented"? What are the respective concerns of external and internal auditors with respect to the "fairness" of financial statements?
21. Describe the relationship of internal auditors to an organization's external auditors from a CPA firm. Specify the *Statement on Auditing Standards (SAS),* as established by the American Institute of Certified Public Accountants, that dictates to what extent an internal auditor's work may be used by outside CPAs. What criteria does the CPA firm use in deciding the extent to which internal auditors' work may be used?
22. What is the significance of interim reporting to the relationship between internal and external auditors?
23. What is the "continuous audit" advantage?
24. Who are government's "independent" auditors?
25. What is "materiality"? What effect does it have upon the conduct of audits of financial statements?

26. Discuss the following statement: What "materiality" is to external auditors, "risk" is to internal auditors.
27. Outline five key objectives of audit tests for financial statements.
28. How do the audit objectives of internal and external audits differ?
29. Why and how might internal auditors coordinate their work with external auditors?
30. Outline the audit process as it might be applied to audits of financial statements.

EXERCISES

Note to the Student: These exercises and problems go beyond the specific chapter material. They offer the student an opportunity to exercise his or her audit judgment and skills acquired in the study of previous chapters, but within operational and financial audit settings.

E-1

An internal auditor is testing internal controls over the recording of payables for a manufacturing organization. The internal auditor has examined 60 unpaid vouchers entered in the voucher register during the week following the fiscal year-end. Five material items were found that should have been recorded as of year-end. This finding led the internal auditor to the tentative conclusion that the system was not recording material accounts payable in the appropriate year.

Required:

List additional audit procedures for the internal auditor to follow in determining if the system is recording material accounts payable in the appropriate year.

(CIA Exam Adapted)

E-2

Jodam Manufacturing Company has approximately 1,000 production employees who are paid hourly wages. The internal auditors examined records maintained by the personnel department to determine the basis of deductions from payroll. They found that no system existed for the maintenance of current and proper payroll deduction authorizations in personnel files. In their sample of 50 employees, the auditors found six instances in which personnel files failed to contain proper payroll deduction authorizations signed by employees. The internal auditors promptly reported their findings. In response, the personnel manager had the six employees sign appropriate authorization forms for payroll deductions. He then reported to the internal auditors that he had thereby corrected the deficient condition.

Required:

a. Discuss the extent to which internal auditors are responsible for follow-up to determine that appropriate corrective action is taken by management on reported audit findings.
b. What criteria should the internal auditor consider in judging the propriety of corrective action?
c. Assess the adequacy of the personnel manager's remedial actions according to the specified criteria. (Your discussion need not focus on specific control procedures.)

(CIA Exam Adapted)

E-3

Five financial control objectives which should be achieved relative to the acquisition of goods and services are listed below:

1. The expenditure bears a reasonable relationship to the requirements of the business.
2. Quantities or volumes purchased are reasonable and consistent with needs.
3. Prices and terms of the purchase are consistent with written agreements.
4. Goods or services are received.
5. Proper documentary evidence backs up the transaction.

Required:

For each of the financial control objectives listed above, describe two control techniques which can be used to achieve the objective.

(CIA Exam Adapted)

E-4

Imagine that you are the internal auditor of an organization that produces and distributes energy. You are assigned to audit the cost and budget function. The following six audit steps are included in your audit program:

1. Determine whether sales forecasts are approved by senior marketing management.
2. Compare sales and production, by producing units, with total plant forecasts.
3. Appraise the propriety of the bases used for distribution of the fixed and semifixed expenses.
4. Determine the usefulness of performance reports by interviews with the various levels of line management and by examining the correspondence initiated by those interviewed.
5. Verify the accuracy of monthly budget reports and determine the adequacy of explanations given for budget variances.
6. Review major inventory adjustments written off to profit or loss.

Required:

Briefly explain the audit objective of each of the audit steps above.

(CIA Exam Adapted)

E-5

Multiple Choice: Select a single answer which best completes the statement or answers the question.

1. During an audit of the Third National Bank, the internal auditor found several serious deficiencies in the commercial loan files. After the internal auditor informed the bank's chief loan officer of this situation, the commercial loan department attempted to remedy the deficiencies. Which would be the appropriate follow-up procedure for the internal auditor to undertake?
   a. Review the corrections during next year's audit.
   b. Ask the chief loan officer to send a letter within 60 days to the internal auditor indicating that the corrections have been made.

c. Ask the chief loan officer to send a letter within 60 days to the chief executive officer indicating that the corrections have been made.

d. Stop by the loan department to ask if the corrections were properly made.

e. Conduct a follow-up audit within a short period of time.

(CIA Exam Adapted)

2. In determining that purchase requisitions were authorized by appropriate personnel, the internal auditor should review:

a. Procedures for selecting individuals to approve purchase requisitions.

b. Evidence of approval by an official having authority for the type of purchase.

c. The matching of requisitions with the corresponding purchase orders.

d. Control over the security of the requisition process.

e. Items a and b above.

(CIA Exam Adapted)

3. When auditing the purchasing activities of a manufacturing organization in a computer system environment, which of the following should be included in the permanent file portion of the audit working papers?

a. Copies (or details relating thereto) of the computer program documentation.

b. Printouts using auditor-prepared programs and test decks.

c. The prior year's working papers, revised to reflect changes taking place during the current year.

d. Information concerning administrative controls over the computer operations at each location.

e. Printouts resulting from the use of compliance test procedures.

(CIA Exam Adapted)

4. Flowcharting a disbursements/payments cycle would require information on the use of the following documents and records: purchase requisition, purchase order, receiving report, voucher, and:

a. Bill of materials.

b. Vendor's invoice.

c. Cancelled check.

d. Economic order quantity document.

e. Bidder's list.

(CIA Exam Adapted)

5. Which of the following is the most important internal control procedure for acquisitions of property, plant, and equipment?

a. Establishing a written company policy to distinguish between capital and revenue expenditures.

b. Using a budget to plan, authorize, and control acquisitions.

c. Analyzing monthly variances between authorized expenditures and actual costs.

d. Establishing a property ledger.

e. Requiring approval of capital expenditures by the chief financial officer.

(CIA Exam Adapted)

6. Which of the following is an internal control for disbursements by check?
   a. Checks are signed by the controller.
   b. Checks are prenumbered and independently accounted for.
   c. Supporting documents are marked "Paid" immediately after the cancelled checks are returned by the bank.
   d. Checks are mailed by the employee who prepares the documents that authorize the check preparation.
   e. The bank statements and the checks are sent directly by the bank to the accounts payable department.

   (CIA Exam Adapted)

7. A surprise observation by an internal auditor of the distribution of paychecks is primarily designed to verify that:
   a. Individuals paid present proper employee identification.
   b. Gross pay amounts are accurately reflected on paychecks.
   c. Names shown on the payroll are those of current employees.
   d. The paymaster is not involved in the distribution of paychecks.
   e. All unclaimed paychecks are returned to the cashier.

   (CIA Exam Adapted)

8. In evaluating the procedures of the claims payment department of a casualty insurance company, the audit step least likely to be included in the audit program is:
   a. Determine that the payment was within the terms of coverage.
   b. Review the claims documentation.
   c. Inspect the site to substantiate the extent of the loss claims.
   d. Determine that the claimants' payments on their policies are current.
   e. Confirm receipt of the claims payment with the policyholder.

   (CIA Exam Adapted)

9. A procedure for an internal auditor to ascertain whether retail inventory thefts are occurring is to:
   a. Review the year-end cutoff of purchases and sales transactions.
   b. Observe the taking of physical inventory and make test counts.
   c. Test the pricing of merchandise inventory.
   d. Investigate significant differences between physical inventory results and retail inventory estimates.
   e. Inquire of knowledgeable personnel.

   (CIA Exam Adapted)

10. When auditing the controls over raw material quality, it would not be useful to review and evaluate:
    a. The fire protection arrangements of the materials storage area.
    b. The receiving procedures.
    c. The purchasing procedures.
    d. The procedures for handling materials.
    e. Policies for recognizing and disposing of damaged and obsolete materials.

    (CIA Exam Adapted)

11. An auditor made several recommendations to improve utilization of plant personnel in a large manufacturing company. Which of the following recommendations would probably have the opposite effect of that intended?
    a. Use applicable time and motion study data to specify the cost/job relationship.
    b. Eliminate supervision of line personnel.
    c. Rotate job responsibilities for repetitious tasks.
    d. Develop detailed job performance standards.
    e. Use a time clock to document the hours worked by employees.

    (CIA Exam Adapted)

12. During the 1987 audit of an organization, an internal auditor found that 1986 audit deficiency findings had not been acted upon with respect to receiving department procedures. What would be the most appropriate action for the auditor to take?
    a. Instruct the head of the receiving department to adopt new receiving procedures.
    b. Direct the plant manager to adopt new receiving procedures.
    c. Ignore the situation since it had been commented on last year.
    d. Repeat the comment in the 1987 audit report and indicate that no changes have been made despite the inclusion of the comment in the 1986 report.
    e. Report the finding immediately to the vice president of manufacturing.

    (CIA Exam Adapted)

13. During the 1986 audit of the local county's purchasing department, the state auditor's office found and reported to the county commissioners a lack of documentation for purchases. During the 1987 audit, the state auditor's office wished to determine if steps were taken to rectify the documentation deficiency. Identify which of the following audit procedures is most likely to disclose the failure to correct the deficiency:
    a. Review the purchasing procedures manual maintained in the purchasing department.
    b. Examine receiving department records to be sure that prenumbered receiving reports are issued for goods and services received.
    c. Ask departments requesting goods and services if they are receiving ordered items.
    d. Review a sample of requisitions to determine if appropriate purchase approvals were entered.
    e. Review a sample of disbursement vouchers to see if there are corresponding purchase requisitions, purchase orders, and reports.

    (CIA Exam Adapted)

PROBLEMS

P-1

Imagine that you are an internal auditor and you have completed an audit of activities within the purchasing department of your company. The department employs 30 buyers, seven supervisors, a manager, and clerical personnel. Purchases total about $500 million per year. Your audit disclosed the following conditions:

1. The company has no formal rules on conflicts of interest. Your analysis produced evidence that one of the buyers owns a substantial interest in a major supplier and that he procures supplies averaging $50,000 a year from that supplier. The prices charged by the supplier are competitive.
2. Buyers select proposed sources without submitting the lists of bidders for review. Your test disclosed no evidence that higher costs were incurred as a result of that practice.
3. Buyers who originate written requests for quotations from suppliers receive the suppliers' bids directly from the mail room. In your test of 100 purchases based on competitive bids, you found that the low bidders were awarded the purchase orders in 75 of the 100 cases.
4. Requests to purchase (requisitions) received in the purchasing department from other departments in the company must be signed by an authorized person. Your examination of 200 such requests disclosed that three requisitions, all for small amounts, were not properly signed. The buyer who had issued all three orders honored the requests because he misunderstood the applicable procedure. The clerical personnel charged with reviewing such requests had given them to the buyer in error.

Required:

For each of these four conditions, state:

a. The risk, if any, which is incurred if the condition is permitted to continue.
b. The control, if any, that you would recommend to prevent continuation of the condition.

(CIA Exam Adapted)

P-2

You are auditing the inventory management function of a large maintenance operation for city-owned vehicles. At this point in your audit, the following information has been discovered:

1. Vehicle maintenance records indicate that the number of inoperative trucks waiting for spare parts is increasing, even though the total number of trucks is decreasing.
2. Stockroom employees have been unable to find some parts, even though the perpetual inventory system shows that the parts are on hand.
3. The investment in spare-parts inventory has remained at about the same level since the last audit three years ago.
4. Many of the spare parts can be used for passenger cars.
5. The perpetual inventory is maintained on inventory record cards by a clerk in the parts warehouse office.

Required:

Prepare two audit steps to be included in the audit program for each of the five items above.

(CIA Exam Adapted)

P-3

A senior auditor completed a preliminary survey of certain marketing activities of a company. The following situations were disclosed:

1. Billings from the advertising agency for insertions in magazines and newspapers are approved for payment without adequate review by advertising department personnel.
2. Purchases of advertising materials and artwork are made by one employee of the advertising department.
3. Company-owned materials such as artwork, furniture, company products, and other items used for photographic sets are retained by the advertising agency.

Required:

For each of the three situations, prepare four audit steps to be included in the audit program.

(CIA Exam Adapted)

P-4

A preliminary survey of a maintenance service operation for office machines and equipment produced the following information:

1. The manager of the maintenance service operation stated that, in his opinion, the objective of the organization was to respond to calls for service in a minimum amount of time.
2. When a backlog of service calls accumulated, a contract was issued to a local repair organization to assist in covering the overload.
3. The manager assured the auditor that the maintenance service operation was very efficient.
4. More experienced repairmen were used to respond to second calls when the original repairs were not effective.
5. A comprehensive perpetual inventory system was maintained for all repair parts and supplies.

Required:

For each of the five items above, list two key questions that the auditor would attempt to answer in performing the audit.

(CIA Exam Adapted)

17   EDP Audits

Electronic data processing (EDP) is proliferating as a business tool, influencing the nature and form of the audit trail, how operating activities are performed and monitored, the capabilities for applying sophisticated decision models, and the overall control environment. An EDP audit may be directed at a variety of dimensions of EDP use, ranging from initial conversion to EDP to particular applications of available software. This chapter describes key criteria to be considered in performing EDP audits and some computer audit tools likely to be useful in their performance.

Assessing EDP's Effect upon the Control Environment

The use of EDP can have substantial effects upon the overall control environment, as it influences the possibility of a well-controlled data base and the continuous accountability for assets. The role of EDP may be primarily automation (e.g., the mere transition from a manual to an automated accounting system), or it may be progressive integration throughout operations (e.g., automation of inventory purchases and use as an analytical review tool by management).

How EDP is utilized may be the primary determinant of its effect on the control environment. For example, management sometimes may regard computers merely as a sophisticated mechanization process and fail to realize the computer's valuable potential as a management tool. As a result, lower levels of EDP expertise often are made available to the company, and any specialization that does occur tends to be within EDP rather than outside, making it unlikely that broad use of and familiarity with EDP will evolve. In such a setting, an emphasis on manual controls over EDP is common. This condition can have adverse control implications since competence may be at issue, segregation of duties can be problematic, and controls may be less effective.

Three typical EDP configurations are described in Exhibit 17-1, with a brief reference to the differences in control emphasis per setting. The varied means of organizing EDP facilities are outlined. Once the role of EDP and related control implications are considered, the auditor may find it an effective evaluation approach to treat EDP as though the function were a single individual. This approach can clarify the scope of EDP operations, which frequently is quite broad. For example, if EDP processes payroll records and prints payroll checks, accounting and custody responsibilities are improperly segregated. An effective control environment over EDP can be maintained only when an independent third party observes the printing of the checks, maintains a count of the printed checks, and retains control of the facsimile signature plate when it is not in use.

The formality with which responsibilities are assigned and the documentation of control procedures are key aspects of a control environment in which EDP is prevalent. Turnover can cause expensive downtime, and the lack of formal delegation of responsibilities can lead to inadequate record-keeping and even unintentional destruction of data. Detailed assessment of the effect of EDP on the control environment is explored through considering alternative types of audit assignments.

Selecting the Type(s) of Audit of Primary Interest

Numerous aspects of the EDP environment may be the subject of an internal audit project. The potential topics can be categorized into two key types of EDP audits: *data integrity* and *security*. These two general objectives can be focused upon stages of EDP development, alternative processors of EDP records, and components of EDP systems.

Systems Development Process

As with most capital expenditure items, enhancements to EDP are often cheaper if acquired at the initial point of converting to EDP, rather than "adding on" enhancements at a later date. However, this generalization is highly dependent upon the organization's readiness to use EDP and upon technological advancements. Improvements in EDP may relate to service capabilities or to control over EDP operations. The latter is the primary concern that creates a demand for the involvement of internal auditors in the systems development process.

Several common stages have been recognized as a part of the system development life cycle, as diagrammed in Exhibit 17-2. The cycle is illustrated in chronological order from left to right. The idea of establishing formal plans and follow-up is to avoid inefficiencies, ineffectiveness, and uncontrolled EDP operations. Lines of communication with users are critical to system development. One means of obtaining users' input is to circulate a questionnaire. Exhibit 17-3 provides an example of such a survey form.

Exhibit 17-1
Common EDP Configurations

COMPLEXITY OF CONFIGURATION	CONTROL EMPHASIS
Minicomputers with little networking or larger mainframe tie-ins	Establishment of edit, verification, and balancing controls over data entry and controls over the access and use of data files
Batch systems*	Reconciliation of control totals to batch controls with rejected data carefully followed through to correction
Data base systems (DBS)* — a central information file allowing direct access on a shared basis by data systems, eliminating duplication	Control over access to the data base and emphasis on recovery from a system breakdown

ORGANIZATION	DEFINITION
Centralized	One computer configuration with remote terminals for input
Decentralized	Multiple independent computer centers with separate staff and no telecommunication among or between the independent computer centers
Distributed	Combines centralized and decentralized data processing, linking processing units and permitting the exchange of essential data

*Minicomputers can be used both in batch systems and in DBS systems.

Exhibit 17-2
Stages in a System Development Life Cycle

(1) | SYSTEMS ANALYSIS |

a. What is the status quo?
b. What does this suggest should be the system design?
c. Detail specifications, requirements, costs, and feasibility.
d. Adequately document the analysis.

(4) | TEST THE SYSTEM'S COMPLETENESS |

a. Is it in line with users' requirements?
b. Is output accurate?
c. Are test files available for future use?

(6) | MAINTAIN OPERATION |

a. Control all program changes.
b. Periodically review system.
c. Check adequacy of documentation.

(1)   (4)   (6)
_____
(2)   (3)   (5)   (7)

(2) | PROJECT DEFINITION |

a. What do users desire?
b. What applications are planned?
c. Who should have input as to future facilities?
d. What cost/benefit trade-offs are apparent?

(3) | DETAILED DEVELOPMENT |

a. Write programs.
b. Monitor correspondence of actions to system design and explain deviations.
c. Acquire equipment and organize documentation guidelines and practices.

(5) | PLACE EDP SYSTEM IN OPERATION |

(7) | AFTER IMPLEMENTATION |

a. Evaluate whether objectives were met.
b. Consider system improvements.
c. Continually develop the system's capabilities.

Exhibit 17-3
Evaluation Form for Information Systems Users

Completed by: _____ Date: _____

EVALUATION CRITERIA

SCALE: 1 is low; 8 is high
(Please circle your rating.)

1. Rate the quality of the reports
   presently prepared by Information Systems according to these
   criteria:

a. Timeliness.	1	2	3	4	5	6	7	8
b. Completeness.	1	2	3	4	5	6	7	8
c. Accuracy/reliability.	1	2	3	4	5	6	7	8
d. Usefulness (value of information).	1	2	3	4	5	6	7	8
e. Readability.	1	2	3	4	5	6	7	8
f. Distribution (are reports distributed accurately).	1	2	3	4	5	6	7	8

2. Rate Information Systems' responsiveness to meeting your requests for program or system
   changes.   1   2   3   4   5   6   7   8

3. Rate their responsiveness to meeting your requests for new pro-
   gram or system development.   1   2   3   4   5   6   7   8

4. Evaluate the extent of your department's involvement during:

   a. The definition of a new
      system (planning stage).   1   2   3   4   5   6   7   8
   b. Its implementation (testing
      and conversion).   1   2   3   4   5   6   7   8
   c. The implementation of needed
      changes.   1   2   3   4   5   6   7   8

5. Rate the quality of support offered by Information Systems
   during and after implementation
   of a new system (such as users'
   manuals and on-site DP help dur-
   ing the early operational stages).   1   2   3   4   5   6   7   8

6. Evaluate the overall performance
   of the Information Systems Department in satisfying your infor-
   mation needs.*   1   2   3   4   5   6   7   8

COMMENTS

If you circled a "poor" rating (1 or 2) for any of the above criteria, please comment on the back by citing particular instances that support your evaluation.

*Please comment on the back about anything that you feel will help Information Systems better satisfy your information needs.

———————

Source: A.D. Burger, "EDP Audit: Don't Forget the User," *The Internal Auditor,* February 1978, p. 25.

During a systems development audit, primary concerns are the adequacy of the planning process and documentation of objectives, costs, benefits, responsibilities, and communication lines. Monitoring progress throughout the development stages and adequate testing before implementing the EDP system also are crucial to ensuring effective EDP operations.

Systems Design

In auditing systems design, specific procedures are performed on existing EDP operations and on the plans for those operations. Internal auditors must understand the intended role for EDP if they are to evaluate systems design.

Exhibit 17-4 outlines the key audit procedures performed in design-phase audits. Alertness to behavioral problems, poor allocation of available EDP time, wasteful use of resources, and obsolescence can facilitate a thorough basis for reporting on whether typical EDP problems are present and how adequately the overall design of the system is meeting current and anticipated needs.

Hardware Considerations

The proliferation of computer hardware led to the installation of more than three million data communication terminals by 1980, 12 times the reported number of terminals installed as of 1970. Those terminals are so diverse that old jargon distinguishing microcomputers from minicomputers from mainframes has started to blend together. The power of both micro and mini systems is increasing so rapidly that many have capabilities analogous to old mainframe systems. One of the most significant results of technological developments is that decentralized processing (often referred to as distributed data processing) is far more common than centralized EDP operations. This means that all problems related to hardware selection, maintenance, and control are multiple problems that must be dealt with by each processing facility.

Exhibit 17-4
Key Audit Procedures Commonly Performed in Design-Phase Audits

Review Existing Controls and Formulate Recommendations Directed at Control Design

Test Controls. Evaluate the Probable Cause and Attendant Risks of the Types of Errors Observed and Control Inadequacies Detected

Review Documentation for Completeness. Direct Particular Attention to System Design and Users' Manuals

Assess the Adequacy of Security. Investigate Apparent Security Problems and Formulate Recommendations

Review the Cost/Benefit Analysis Prepared during Planning:
- Is it reasonable?
- Are dollar and man-hour estimates of costs and benefits reasonable?
- Was consideration of risks comprehensive in scope?

Appraise the Appropriateness of Planned EDP Applications

Test the Auditee's Compliance with Described Procedures with Respect to Design Activities

Compare Actual Costs and Benefits to Estimates

Compare Operations to Stated Objectives by Emphasizing:
- Timeliness of output
- Comprehensiveness of output
- Completeness and effectiveness of edit and logic checks
- Demand for EDP
- Operating efficiency
- Fulfillment of user's needs
- Adequacy of personnel

Physical Setting. One of the initial hardware-related questions has to do with the physical setting established for EDP use. Is the setting conducive to efficient, secure operation? The internal auditor should examine the adequacy of:

- Space.
- Air conditioning.
- Power lines and backup power services.
- Anti-static floor covering.
- Housekeeping (whether the environment is clean).
- Location.
- Fire detectors.
- Maintenance practices.

Facilities should be located away from the main traffic flow and be physically secure.

Hardware Selection. The next issue focuses upon the hardware selected. Do hardware devices operate efficiently? Do they appear optimal for their intended use? A hardware monitor should be available, and the nature and level of use should be compatible with the equipment's design. A key question is whether the use of particular software programming or certain types of data base structures, which might be desirable from an operating efficiency perspective, are precluded by the type of hardware selected. For example, purchasers of microcomputers (or any other type of computer, for that matter) are commonly advised by management consultants to first identify intended applications, then software requirements, and finally the hardware which is compatible with the software packages to be used.

Processing Bottlenecks. Internal auditors should be alert to bottlenecks in processing. The central processing unit (CPU), which directs and coordinates the operations called for in a program, must have adequate working storage for handling operations. Multiprocessing, whereby more than one set of processing circuitry within a single computer operates simultaneously, is common. This capability enhances efficient EDP operations. The medium used for storage also should be evaluated for its compatibility with efficient processing.

For example, those files which need to have small subsets of their data updated on a regular basis may be best suited to direct access storage on disk. In contrast, if direct access isn't needed because of the routine updating of almost all records, the cheaper storage medium of magnetic tapes is more appropriate.

Tape drives, which handle magnetic tape by (1) reading data stored on the tape for input to the processing unit and (2) recording output onto tape, must be sufficient to service users' needs. Some operations still use card punch for input, and card readers are capable of handling input at high speed. However, CRT terminals permit key verified data entry with fast visual response, and they have become far more commonplace.

Hardware Reliability. The reliability of hardware can be evaluated based on past experience and industry data. Records of all equipment failures should be maintained, with documentation of the time, date, and apparent reason for the failure. The maintenance of computer services depends heavily upon hardware. Care should be taken in adequately training employees to operate the computer equipment to ensure against unintentional damage. Regular preventive maintenance should be performed on all computer systems. The effectiveness and maintenance of hardware configurations can be evaluated, in part, by tracking statistics on:

- Equipment use.
- EDP personnel's time.
- Cost of EDP operations.
- System failures.
- Software reliability.
- Program productivity.

Problems may flag a need to improve physical settings or change hardware devices. To help address restart needs, checkpoints should be set up, whereby during processing a record is made of the status of all of the contents of the computer registers and main storage. The checkpoints can minimize restart efforts should a failure occur.

Hardware Controls. Hardware controls are another area for audit review, as shortcomings recommend adjustments to existing or future acquisition policies. Hardware should be equipped with automatic error detection features, with documentation provided by the vendor as to how operators should respond to hardware errors or breakdowns. An example of hardware controls are echo checks, which basically transmit and "echo" back to the originator of messages received to confirm their accuracy. This is a means of ensuring that the communications equipment and lines are operating appropriately.

Security. A final consideration in evaluating hardware is security. Locks, alarms, guards, and identification badges should limit access to physical facilities. Logs should be maintained to monitor and control access to EDP. Because of the sensitivity of equipment and the speed with which destruction is possible, care must be taken to avoid heat damage or damage from natural disasters, to the extent possible (e.g., facilities should not be constructed in a flood zone). An important control policy is not to allow access to equipment or files to EDP personnel who have been terminated. Similarly, service personnel and visitors should be accompanied whenever they are around EDP facilities. Intentional (or unintentional) destruction of either equipment or software can be extremely expensive.

Software Considerations

The overall objective of an audit of software is to determine if the software systems are operating effectively and efficiently to meet the auditee's needs. Throughput, or useful work performed by a computer system during a period of time, is one measure of system performance. Technical questions, such as whether the programming languages in use are compatible with the programming applications, should be addressed. For example, FORTRAN may be necessary for higher-level mathematical applications, but COBOL is more appropriate in basic business applications. If obsolete programming languages are in use, obtaining software compatibility with the EDP system in place may be expensive.

Software Revision. Software often undergoes revision, which creates room for programming errors or delays in the routine application of certain software. An explicit decision process that weighs potential efficiencies from revision against the ease of making these programming changes should be in place.

Software Monitors. Just as auditees are expected to maintain hardware monitors, they should similarly establish software monitors. Specifically, the auditor should review the level and nature of applications and determine their consistency with the cost of acquiring and maintaining software. The auditee's use of software to simulate alternative EDP work allocations for possible cost-saving opportunities should be encouraged, as should the use of software that eases programming, testing, and documentation procedures (e.g., flowchart generators and test-data generators).

Software Reliability. The auditee should be encouraged to document software reliability to serve as a basis for evaluating operations. Similarly, usage logs should be maintained to track access to software and use of the operating system. To prevent unauthorized modifications to software, user approval should be required for all changes in production programs. Access to these programs and data files also should be controlled. Source codes for programs can be protected by establishing "read only" locks on programs and using compiled programs for day-to-day processing. Program library activity logs should be used, protecting operators' overrides or alterations of programs. (Library routines are standard sets of program instructions maintained in on-line storage that may be called in and processed by other programs.) Password protection of both programs and data files should also be established.

Testing of Software. One of the most critical control elements with respect to software is ensuring that software is correct before being placed into live use in monitoring operations. This requires that standards be set specifying that test files, not live files, are to be used in debugging programs. New programs should be run in parallel with current versions for a minimum of one processing cycle in order to gain assurance that results are comparable.

Changing Software. The second most problematic aspect of operations related to software has to do with controlling changes to programs. An entity must always know which version of a program is in use at what point in time. Beyond the controls already discussed, any changes to programs should be carefully documented as to the:

- Date of change.
- Nature of change.
- Purpose of change and source of program change requests, and testing procedures with respect to the changes made to programs.

Software standards should be established, particularly with respect to required documentation and testing procedures. Structured programming techniques should be used to the fullest extent possible to help maintain effective control over development and maintenance of software.

Default Options. Software can be designed to input default values in a manner that reduces the cost of data entry. A default option is the automatic utilization of a predetermined value in situations where input transactions have certain values left blank. As an example, consider an auditee that uniformly offers a specified discount to certain types of customers. The default option would preclude the need for separate entry of such a discount rate.

Controls

The types of audits described thus far all suggest important control procedures. In addition to those already noted, controls should focus upon users' needs, the segregation of duties, input and processing controls, the adequacy of audit trails, and report distribution controls.

User Controls. Numerous user controls are important to effective and efficient EDP operations. Users should maintain cumulative totals of master file balances and compare them to master file balances to achieve a balancing control. Computer-generated reports, including exception reports generated by EDP, should be reviewed by users for overall reasonableness. Initiation of data entry and all corrections should be the responsibility of the users.

Segregation of Duties. EDP operations should be designed to maintain the segregation of duties across the:

- Authorization of transactions.
- Accounting for transactions.
- Custody of assets.

Control can be achieved by requiring that someone external to the accounting and EDP departments authorize transactions and that some other third party exercise physical control over assets passing through EDP. In considering control over assets, both direct and indirect access to assets must be considered — e.g., shipping orders for inventory can provide constructive control over inventory assets.

Certain types of duties need to be segregated within centralized EDP departments. For example, it is advisable to segregate the activities of operators, programmers, and system designers, considering these three positions as analogous to custody, accounting, and authorization responsibilities, respectively. A librarian function should be used to restrict operators' access to programs and data files. In a data base system, the data base administrator's responsibilities include controlling access to various files, changes in programs, and availability of source code details to individuals, focusing on "as needed" conditions. If an automated data file is used, available output should be reviewed by installation management.

Overall enhancement of the effectiveness with which duties are segregated will result from:

- Rotating operators periodically.
- Requiring vacations of at least five consecutive calendar days.
- Setting policies such that no one other than the operator is allowed to be in the computer room when certain programs are run, and having users who are segregated from EDP exercise controls over input and output.
- Assigning responsibility for the adequacy of documentation to a party outside EDP.

Controlled Access. Input can be controlled, in part, by controlling access to input devices through locks and passwords. All passwords should be changed periodically, and employees should be educated as to the importance of maintaining the secrecy of passwords. Levels of passwords, directed at certain files or at certain capabilities (e.g., "read only" access versus "write" access) should be in use.

Data Entry. The completeness and accuracy of data entry will be enhanced by using a standard format for data entry and prompting users for missing data. On-line computer editing of data codings against authorized codings, numeric or alphabetic characters against those expected, and magnitudes against plausible ranges (i.e., limit checks) can improve the quality of data entered onto the system. An answer-back feature built into software can encourage users' verification of data entry.

Control of Data Processing Facilities. In controlling the processing of data, control needs to be maintained over facilities and over the data base. Important audit trails include maintenance of a console log by the operators to keep track of what jobs were processed, and creation of a magnetic file reflecting the entry and termination of each job processed. These records of system activity should be reviewed by the operator's supervisor as key controls over the use of EDP.

Processing Control of Data. To maintain data integrity, batch totals should be created and transaction log files generated, to which output totals are compared. A master file control record of opening and closing balances of records processed per shift should be created and periodically balanced to totals to facilitate the identification of errors. Validity checks and check digits are useful means of ensuring accurate processing. A validity check matches codings to a "valid master file set of codings" to be certain that accounts being charged or credited actually exist and are authorized to have particular types of transactions affecting their balances. Check digits take advantage of formulas which can be applied to certain types of codings to ensure that they are valid numbers or have been transmitted in their entirety. For example, multiplying, adding, and dividing numbers of account codes may be expected to be a multiple of 9; this digit can be computed and checked.

Processing Control of Files. To ensure that appropriate files are being processed, internal labels should be used on all applications. At a minimum, external labels such as color-coded disk covers should be used. Internal labels typically report the program file's name, the numbers of records and blocks, the date, and the retention period for the file. Supervisory approval of overrides of internal labels and a log of all such overrides should be maintained.

Processing Control of Documentation. The adequacy of the audit trail will depend upon the console log's use throughout systems testing and all nonroutine processing activities. Similarly, special controls should be set over utility programs which are capable of changing programs and data without creating any audit trail. When computers generate accounting transactions automatically, a transaction log file and master file record should be maintained.

Output Controls. Finally, controls need to be created over the distribution of EDP-generated reports. Limits should be set as to the number of copies of each report, and a distribution list should be maintained. The frequency with which reports are to be generated should be cost/benefit-based. Output logs can record the actual distribution of all output reports and documents.

Efficiency and Effectiveness of Use

As described elsewhere in this text, effectiveness is evaluated relative to the objectives of auditees and managers. If objectives are met, presumably operations have been carried out effectively. The economy with which such effectiveness is achieved can be termed efficiency. The use of EDP has both an effectiveness and an efficiency dimension, as do all operations. The complete and accurate processing of information is likely to be the key basis of assessing effectiveness, while the cost and timeliness of that processing relate to efficiency.

Users' Feedback on EDP — Are Expectations Being Met? Since users' service is the key focus of any EDP operation, one means of evaluating effectiveness and efficiency is to obtain users' feedback. Are users' expectations being met?

- Is turnaround time adequate?
- Are reports and system interfaces user friendly?
- Is the cost of EDP deemed to be reasonable?
- Are any perverse incentive effects evident which stem from the organization or pricing of EDP operations and services?
- Are any changes to EDP requested?

Recall the survey form provided in Exhibit 17-3. That type of questionnaire can help in the evaluation of an auditee's EDP facilities and day-to-day activities.

Does the Scheduling of Services and the Assignment of Priorities Indicate that Formal Control Exists? Certain established procedures can be expected to be present if an EDP operation has formalized controls. For example, EDP services can be expected to be scheduled, with priorities given to certain services to ensure expedient processing of priority reports. All requests should not automatically be filled. Instead, a justification process should be established whereby the rationale for resource expenditures must be provided and approved. After an expedient review process, requests accepted should be processed efficiently.

One means of ensuring appropriate use of EDP services is to charge for such services. Yet too high a charge will deter use, resulting in idle capacity or expansion to unnecessary facilities. For example, one university had such a high transfer price on its computer services that each college within the university raised money to acquire its own computer — a very inefficient global result from the overall university's perspective. Of course, it is also common to walk through university settings and see numerous computer "pictures" and "greetings" because computer services are treated as virtually a "free good." Some happy medium is necessary. Charging more for services during peak times or for disk versus magnetic tape storage can help to align incentives with efficient use of facilities.

Is the EDP Configuration Suitable for the Entity's Needs? The information needs of an auditee should be matched to an appropriate EDP configuration. Decentralized access to terminals and output, communication lines between users, hook-ups to the mainframe and desired data banks, and sufficient disk and CPU space to store and process data are examples of users' needs that should influence the EDP configuration.

Often, mismatches of hardware, software, and users' needs are obvious and lead to both inefficient and ineffective EDP operations. As an example, a totally centralized EDP operation may force manual input forms, whereas dummy terminals on site would permit direct automated input of data. Similarly, the unavailability of desired software for the EDP facilities would signal a mismatch.

Compliance Objectives

The emphasis in the chapter thus far has been placed on systems design and use considerations. A different type of audit focuses on the compliance of EDP operations with specified policies and procedures. These practices may be legalistic in nature — such as being assured that the terms of the agreements with various software vendors have been met — or related to operating control guidelines. As with any compliance audit, the auditor will assess whether or not an auditee is complying with prescribed policy. The auditor may suggest ways of encouraging compliance or preferred approaches to meeting the objectives of various guidelines through some change in operations.

The distinction between compliance with the *form* of policies and compliance with the *substance* of policies is particularly important. For example, in form, a requirement may exist that an activity log is to be maintained. Yet the substance of this policy implies that the log be routinely received and unusual items be investigated. If the latter does not occur, compliance is lacking.

Documentation

At times, internal auditors may be requested to review EDP operations solely to assess the adequacy of documentation. This is a critical operating control, since turnover and expansion of the EDP staff occurs. In either setting, documentation is essential for training purposes and smooth operations.

The documentation underlying EDP should describe data flows and processing steps throughout the system. Instructions on converting data, transmitting data, handling files, and controlling operations are essential. Input/output descriptions with examples should be prepared, illustrating forms, formats, and card layouts. Program flowcharts, source listings, specifications, summary descriptions, and dates of changes or authorizations for normal use should be available as support for EDP operations. Operating instructions should include the sequence of operations to start, run, and terminate, as well as the required computer switch settings to make progress compatible with the computer. Operating notes should be prepared that report program messages, halts, and actions required to signal the end of jobs. Should an emergency arise, the operator should have appropriate instructions, including advice on recovery and restart procedures. Special features for error detection routines, program switches, and similar concerns should be documented.

System users will need documentation of the EDP control group's procedures and who is responsible for which controls. Review procedures need to be delineated, as do procedures for correcting errors. Retention policies should be prescribed for all report forms. To ensure efficient use of services, approval processes should be documented, as should the purpose for each of the varied operations.

Recall that Exhibit 17-2 cited a stage in the system development life cycle of testing the system's completeness. It is imperative that these tests and tests of any system changes (including software revisions) be well documented. Obviously, test applications should be performed, documented, and reviewed before new systems or changes are put on line.

Contingency Plans   Contingency plans are an integral part of any effective EDP system. They provide for alternative means of responding to disasters so that business interruption is minimized and operations are not crippled. In reviewing contingency plans, an internal auditor should confirm that formal arrangements have been made for access to computer facilities that are compatible with normal operating systems, should an emergency arise. The types of specific issues to be addressed in formal contingency plans are outlined in Exhibit 17-5.

Exhibit 17-5
Key Considerations in Evaluating the Adequacy of Formal Contingency Plans

- Has the new site been checked to determine its adequacy with respect to (a) EDP equipment; (b) supportive office equipment such as typewriters, calculators, and copying facilities; and (c) environmental compatibility such as air conditioning and power supply?
- Is the site convenient?
- Has a means of notifying employees expediently as to changes in sites been designed and tested?
- Has an inventory of personnel skills been taken to facilitate substitution of positions, if needed, under disaster conditions?
- Are contingency operating plans sufficiently documented to guide employees' performance of day-to-day duties?
- Have separate storage facilities been arranged to ensure the availability of operating documentation, software, and data files for the alternate or backup facility should it be put in use?
- Are employees aware of the disaster plan; has the plan been tested; and are changes to the plan adequately documented?

Amazingly, many entities have no contingency plans. Other entities may have "plans" but have made no formal tests of those plans to ensure that they are workable in an emergency situation. In fact, it may be the case that no formal assurance is given by "backup facilities" that they will be available when needed or that they will be adequate to meet the full processing needs of the entity.

Service Center   At times, part of the EDP operations of an auditee will be carried out by an independent service center. An auditor should review contracts with such service centers to be certain that data ownership and confidentiality concerns have been addressed. Liability for errors or delays, loss of records, or termination of service should be explicitly defined. A contingency plan should exist for emergency situations affecting the service center's operations, as well as explicit arrangements for EDP services should the center terminate or relocate. The issue of whether the auditee can gain access to key programs should a need arise must be addressed.

Controls over input and output are critical whenever service centers are in use. Auditees should focus on user controls that check for the completeness and accuracy of data flows. Batch controls should be established over data and reports between the entity and its service center. Users should reconcile such controls on a routine basis and should review reports for overall reasonableness.

At times, internal auditors may be able to perform compliance testing of controls at the service center. However, since numerous clients of a service center share similar concern over controls, many centers undergo third-party reviews by an external auditor whom they engage to review controls on their customers' behalf. Most of the time only limited testing is performed by such an auditor. If an internal auditor is placed in a position that requires him or her to rely on a report by a third-party auditor, he or she should obtain satisfaction that the auditor is both independent and has a professional reputation. Preferably, the objectives of the audit engagement can be defined by the users of the service center. This ensures that the scope is commensurate with the internal auditors' needs to evaluate controls over the service center, as well as the reasonableness of the cost of such service.

Planning for EDP Audits

In planning an EDP audit, the internal auditor has to make many decisions pertaining to the audit's scope. The auditor must also take several steps to coordinate audit activities with EDP to facilitate an effective and efficient audit.

The Materiality of EDP

The first important scope decision relates to the materiality of EDP. How much of the accounting system and day-to-day operations is automated? The greater the proportion of the information system that is automated, the more material EDP is to an auditee's operations. Obviously, the greater the materiality of EDP, the more in-depth the review process for EDP. In evaluating EDP's materiality, a cost/benefit framework can be applied. What would be the consequences of poorly controlled EDP operations? What are the benefits of gaining assurance that EDP is well controlled? What would be the costs of reviewing EDP? What level of assurance would appear to be attainable in a manner that would be cost effective?

The Hardware Configuration

Once the importance of EDP has been assessed, the hardware layout needs to be reviewed to determine (1) the types of questions relevant to reviewing controls and (2) the plausibility of using particular types of generalized audit software in the audit process. In particular, if hardware is decentralized and located in users' departments, different control issues arise than would be the case if EDP were centralized. Similarly, certain types of equipment may not be compatible with particular software packages. For example, SAS, a widely used statistical analysis package, is not available for CDC equipment.

Coordinating with EDP Personnel

Once the hardware configuration is considered in a control context, the next issue is how to gain access to the hardware to carry out the audit process. Coordination with EDP personnel is essential. Documentation of EDP, access to hardware for testing, and availability of computer time for performing audit tests are all likely to be within the control of EDP personnel.

Professional Standards on the Internal Auditor's Involvement in Systems Design

Internal auditors must refrain from actually participating in designing the EDP system, but they should make suggestions during the development of EDP. It is very advantageous for internal auditors to suggest controls and audit trails to be built into an EDP system. Neither objectivity nor independence would be compromised by making recommendations. Yet internal auditors must take care to remain independent of any system that subsequently will be audited. This means that internal auditors may establish a rapport with EDP, but must refrain from actually designing or approving a system.

A communication link should be established through which control requirements are itemized and testing plans are reviewed. Suggestions regarding documentation practices should be provided, as well as means by which the development process can be effectively controlled. During the implementation phase, the internal auditor can review testing results, documentation, and the conversion process. A post-installation audit should also be performed.

The Preliminary Survey

The first step of an EDP audit, integrated with the planning stage, is the preliminary survey. This survey will collect the types of information already described in the context of the various types of EDP audits.

Security Controls

Information as to which security controls have been established would be collected through a preliminary survey. Inquiry procedures can be applied to gain an understanding of the rationale for including or not including particular controls, as well as the perceived role and effectiveness of the controls. As an example, certain security controls would be impractical if EDP facilities were decentralized. Certain apparent controls will lack substance, such as the use of combination locks to which everyone knows the combination.

Safeguard Review Controls

Highly related to security controls are safeguard controls. The former tries to limit access to sensitive materials, while the latter tries to protect assets. Safeguarding incorporates protection from natural disasters like floods or tornadoes. The safeguarding process will include the purchase of insurance coverage so that the asset base can be kept intact.

Physical Document Control

In the preliminary survey, documentation standards should be reviewed, and the batch control system used to ensure complete processing of documents should be reviewed and tested. In becoming familiar with physical documents, protection needs to be provided against both lost documents and the inclusion of bogus documents. The accounting for numerical sequences of preprinted forms is the most common means of establishing control over physical documents.

Controls Over Design Specifications

In the preliminary survey, the internal auditor should collect information as to what controls exist over design specifications. Who participates in the design process? Who has final decision power? What approvals are required? Presumably, care is taken to get input from users, to make new equipment compatible with present systems and employees' expertise, and to obtain the most cost-beneficial EDP support system.

Risk Analysis Controls

An ongoing dimension of EDP systems is a set of risk analysis controls. It is imperative that the design phase, post-implementation audit, and subsequent testing of EDP facilities and operations all consider risk exposure.

Monitoring Activities. Periodic testing for compliance with prescribed control procedures and review of reports on usage, priorities, turnaround, and overall adequacy of service are two monitoring activities that should exist and be reviewed by internal auditors to detect problems or opportunities for improvement. Risk exposure can shift over time due to excessive use of facilities, aging equipment, turnover of staff, or a breakdown in compliance with established documentation and control procedures. Timely detection of shifts in risk facilitates timely reaction.

Facility Controls. The controls over the use of facilities include security controls, accessibility, user turnaround, and maintenance issues. The risks of postponing maintenance, increasing accessibility, decreasing operating hours, or similar facility-related actions need to be evaluated in a cost/benefit context. Change of locations or equipment can pose user difficulties that lead to underutilization of facilities and higher risk in terms of the timeliness and adequacy of management's information system.

System Risk. The integrity of the EDP system underlies the entire decision-making process of management whenever EDP operations are material. Risks of computer system failure, systematic program errors, unauthorized alteration of EDP operating and processing systems, and any flaws in general controls over EDP — such as a lack of properly segregated duties — must be continually monitored and evaluated for necessary follow-up actions.

Hardware and Systems Software Controls

The presumption of the internal auditor that typical hardware and software controls are in operation has to be verified in the preliminary survey phase of the audit. Are echo checks, run-to-run totals, "read only," and similar controls present? Do controls exist to prevent circumvention of the operating system's logs or routine control checks? Problems in both the design of, and compliance with, such controls are of critical interest.

Access Controls

Controls over access overlap with security, safeguard, and physical document controls. However, it is helpful during the preliminary survey phase to consider the issue of accessibility as a unique control and performance issue. A balance has to be obtained between user accessibility and control, as these are often conflicting objectives. Frequently terminals are intended to be portable, which raises control considerations such as: who has which terminal, for how long, and where? Beyond hardware access is the question of software and data file access. A librarian function can restrict and track access, and passwords within the data base can restrict access or user capabilities (such as "read only" versus "read and write" accessibility).

Procedural Controls

An EDP operation should have a procedures manual with established means of monitoring compliance. Duties should be clearly defined and control-related procedures should be taken seriously in day-to-day operations. Both formal documentation and informal inquiries will serve to acquaint internal auditors with the procedural controls that are present and attitudes regarding such controls.

Application Controls

Application controls is a term applied to specific controls in an EDP environment. Such controls are intended to ensure proper recording, processing, and reporting of data.

Input. As described earlier, control over input is established to ensure that the data base is complete, accurate, and properly authorized. Examples of input controls are provided in Exhibit 17-6. Input to an EDP system frequently requires conversion of manually prepared data to machine-readable form. Controls are essential to achieve conversion of the entire data base in accurate form.

Exhibit 17-6
Input Controls in an EDP Environment

Authorizations
- Program an internal check that validates that an individual is authorized to both operate the terminal and enter the type of transaction that is requested.
- Use fingerprint-checking devices.
- Require review and approval of input documents.

Edit Checks
- Programmed edit checks should include checking the (a) validity of alphabetic versus numeric input, (b) field size for propriety (e.g., if an account number is expected to have nine digits, confirm that nine are entered), (c) field sign to ensure that impossible values like negative sales balances are not computed, and (d) accuracy via check digits.
- Programmed logic checks such as if/then commands to ensure that if a sales entry is entered, the relevant pricing and discount data are also input.

Data Conversion
- Tie original record counts into batch controls.
- Verify input (e.g., through key verification).
- Program limit checks (e.g., no payroll check is expected to exceed a specified dollar amount) and generate exception reports.

Processing. Once data are input to EDP, prescribed processing is to be done on all authorized transactions. To ensure this, various specific processing controls are commonly used. Examples of these controls are reported in Exhibit 17-7. Of course, the most critical control is to follow through on all detected errors to ensure that they are resolved and that the error correction process is well controlled.

Exhibit 17-7
Processing Controls in an EDP Environment

Totals
- Balance input totals to processing totals: run-to-run totals with exception reporting of out-of-balance numbers.
- Use batch controls as documents are transmitted from one processing phase to another.

Correct Processing
- Verify external labels, internal labels, and file identification before processing.
- Use program boundary protection to restrict which files can be accessed, read, or written during particular program runs.

Access
- Review operator's console log.
- Review recovery journals.
- Generate control report listing.

Hardware
- Use parity controls that are intended to detect electronic failures in the transmission of binary-coded data.
- Insert overflow checks that do a limit check on memory capacity.

Logic
- Use edit checks cited in Exhibit 17-6 during processing.
- Match codings to master files for propriety.

Output. The output of an EDP system can serve as a check on the accuracy of both the input and processing activities. Review of reports (especially exception reports) by users, maintenance of error source statistics, and periodic audits of EDP-generated data are all key output controls. A distinct dimension of control over output relates to ensuring only authorized access to computer reports. A distribution list of authorized users, set data retention policies, and standards for ensuring confidentiality are all desirable output controls.

Users' Controls

In many ways, users' controls can be viewed as input and output controls. However, such controls expand to incorporate authorization issues and error correction responsibilities. Because the EDP operation is accounting in nature, authorization and custody responsibilities should be separated from the information orientation of EDP, to the extent possible. This is most easily done by having users authorize transactions, authorize error corrections, and oversee processing activities such as the printing and signing of checks. Analytical review of all EDP reports and feedback about their effectiveness are key user controls that can lead to both useful and efficient EDP support services.

The Audit Program

The audit program over EDP operations evolves in three major phases:

1. Control review and evaluation.
2. Tests of controls.
3. Tests of data.

The chapter discussion thus far has focused on those controls expected to be present and the various purposes of each control procedure. Both the testing of controls and the testing of data will often involve the use of generalized audit software and/or various computer audit techniques.

Generalized Audit Software

Generalized audit software is primarily directed at testing data. However, it sometimes can be used to replicate processing control procedures as a check on whether the EDP system is operating as expected. Exhibit 17-8 introduces the common terms for generalized audit software capabilities, with an example of the type of audit procedure which could be performed with such functions.

Generalized audit software is easy to use with limited computer knowledge. Some packages require virtually no programming expertise. Of course, should the auditor wish to perform a tailored function similar to those capabilities presented in Exhibit 17-8, the special-purpose programmed routines necessary would require programming knowledge and test procedures.

Computer Audit Techniques

Rather than focusing on data, computer audit techniques test the system that processes information, as well as specific application controls.

In considering EDP audits, critical differences in approaches are discernible. For example, some approaches focus on the process itself, while others focus on results. Similarly, certain procedures are continuous monitoring approaches, while others are noncontinuous.

Exhibit 17-8
Generalized Audit Software Capabilities

FUNCTION	EXAMPLE OF ITS USE
Sort	Place purchase orders from highest to lowest amount so that the auditor can check compliance with the requirement that all purchases over a certain amount undergo a competitive bidding process.
Matching	Compare all credit sales to the authorized customer master file to ensure that credit checks have been performed.
Merge	Combine part A's inventory file with part B's so that a random sample of items for testing can be generated.
Update	Add discount terms applicable to each customer for reference in testing billing procedures.
Generate and Save	Copy the sample of loans to be confirmed so that it is available for second requests.
Summarize Function	Aggregate all sales of a particular part number and prepare a summary record with the total of all of these sales.
Mathematical Functions	Recalculate and subtotal balances for comparison to current and expected numbers.
Extract	Extract all related-party transactions and subtotal them for review.
Conditional Operations	Select only those repairs exceeding a set dollar amount for testing purposes.
Sampling	Random, interval, and various sampling plans proportional to size are commonly available for such procedures as confirmation work.
Report Writing	Generate an aging of inventory to assess obsolescence.
Data Management	Edit check-input data.
Statistical Routines	Compute sample sizes or estimate various analytical review models.

Internal auditors have a comparative advantage over external auditors because of their ability to perform more continuous testing.

For example, assurance that the appropriate program is in use at various points in time can be gained by applying varied computer audit tools on a surprise basis throughout the year. We will now briefly describe the available computer audit techniques and their relative strengths and weaknesses when compared to one another. These techniques should be viewed as a "tool bag" which is available for EDP auditing and can help to gain assurance of effective and efficient EDP operations.

Test Data. One way to check whether an EDP system is operating as expected is to develop test data intended to trigger various logic routines. In the past the use of test data was referred to as "test deck applications." However, the commonality with which data are now entered by key directly into terminals makes "test data" a more descriptive term. The test data will include both normal and atypical data intended to provide evidence that controls are in effect.

The results from processing the test data will be compared to expectations, based on the system evaluator's understanding of the system design. For example, if certain data fall outside limit checks, an exception report would be expected. Similarly, if codings cannot be matched to an approved file of customer codings, an exception report would again be expected.

The difficulty with the test data approach is that it only checks those controls thought about by the auditor. Other data combinations and controls may in fact be present but go untested. Another shortcoming of test data is that no absolute assurance exists that the program which processes the test data is the same program which has been used by the auditee over a period of time. Different programs could generate output comparable to that expected, yet contain malicious codes that go undetected. ("Malicious code" is the term applied to unauthorized programming that intentionally misstates accounting records and/or extracts assets.) Considerations for using test data are outlined in Exhibit 17-9.

Parallel Simulation. Since malicious code may camouflage problems, an alternative approach to testing an EDP system is via parallel simulation. In this approach, the auditor creates a set of application programs intended to simulate the auditee's processing function. The data set analyzed may be test data which are run on both the auditee's system and the auditor's system. Or it may be actual data that have been run through the auditee's system in the past and are now run through the parallel simulation so that results can be compared.

Exhibit 17-9
Auditor's Considerations When Using Test Data
to Audit EDP Systems

- Decide where the test data are to be entered (i.e., the exact point in the EDP system).
- Determine the types of transactions to include in the test data.
- Obtain the master records to process against the test transactions so that predetermined results can be computed for comparison to the test-processing output.
- Consider the effects of the processing of the test transactions on the results of the system produced under normal operating conditions.
- Obtain the auditee's regular processing programs and gain assurance that the program is used to process the test data.
- Make necessary arrangements to get the test data prepared and processed and the output generated in the desired format.

Adapted from W. Thomas Porter, "Evaluating Internal Controls in EDP Systems," *Journal of Accountancy,* August 1964, p. 36.

The shortcomings of parallel simulation are similar to the limitations of test decks. The comparability of output only holds for the data that are processed. Furthermore, the mere comparability of output does not mean that actual processing logic is comparable.

Controlled Processing or Reprocessing. Obviously, parallel simulation can be quite expensive, since the auditor essentially has to create application programs. A less expensive, widely applied audit tool is controlled processing or reprocessing. This technique involves processing data initially or reprocessing data that had been processed earlier by the auditee on the auditee's EDP system. This approach precludes the need for creating programs. It requires only that the auditor control the auditee's EDP operations during the processing of the selected data set. The limitations of this technique are the same as those faced by parallel simulation, except that the required computer expertise is far less.

Integrated Test Facility (ITF). To address the shortcomings of the EDP audit techniques described so far, integrated test facilities

(ITFs) were developed. These facilities are sometimes referred to as "dummy companies," because dummy test data are processed concurrently with live data by the auditee's system. This approach permits the system's performance to be tested on a continuous basis, thereby providing greater assurance that the program being tested is in fact the program that was in use throughout the period. However, there is a drawback to the ITF approach. The auditee's real transaction data may be unintentionally destroyed or contaminated as the auditor tries to reverse the bogus data from the summarized accounting records.

Tagging and Tracing. A compromise that can avoid such contamination is to tag certain data or classes of transactions and have this tagging instigate the creation of an audit data file. That file will document the processing of and control checks on the tagged transactions. This file can then be used to audit the EDP system. In tracing tagged transactions through the system, the risk exists that major logic points in the program may be missed due to inadequacies in the tagging of transactions. In addition, the risk exists that the mode of tagging transactions will be detectable by the auditee, which could lead to circumvention of the audit test. The tagging technique requires imbedded program routines and hence some computer expertise.

Mapping and Program Analysis. An alternative audit technique is known as mapping. In this approach, the auditor identifies the logical paths of a program, emphasizing the paths that have and have not been crossed in a specific programming application. Mapping requires substantial programming expertise. Controlled processing or reprocessing is used hand-in-hand with mapping so that actual data processing output can be compared to expectations. The major shortcoming is that any exceptions noted will likely be limited to those which the auditor expects.

Program code analysis, as the name suggests, includes detailed analysis of process codes. Again, programming expertise is essential. This approach tends to be slow and costly, and human limitations may make it difficult to obtain the thorough, line-by-line review of program code required.

Other Techniques. Many audit techniques that merge audit software with computer audit tools are available for EDP environments. Flowchart verification is a term applied to reviewing programs, and it is frequently facilitated by using a software routine to generate a logic flowchart for review. In all cases, the audit plan should consider the auditor's skills, the level of risk, and the effectiveness of the various tools for the particular context under review.

Innovative Means of Evaluating Data Base Systems

A data base management system poses unique risks of data access and destruction. It is more difficult to back up, since the normal grandfather-father-son tapes are not applicable. Similarly, tagging and tracing through EDP activities is complicated by the joint use of a single data file by several user groups within an organization. By necessity, the auditor must focus on the data base administrator's responsibilities and abilities in order to evaluate control and perform an effective EDP audit. Innovative means of evaluating data base systems often call for a creative attitude of "trying to beat the system," i.e., trying to discover if means are available to gain unauthorized access or to make inappropriate changes in data files.

Selection of the Audit Team

The selection of an audit team will be a function of the materiality of EDP, the planned audit tools, and the sophistication of the system design. For example, plans for mapping would dictate programming expertise, while reliance on generalized audit software may require little EDP expertise. Of course, the availability of expertise is also an issue to be addressed.

Today it is essential that auditors have some familiarity with EDP auditing requirements, but not every member of the internal audit staff needs to be a specialist. The critical training should ensure that auditors can recognize those conditions in which EDP specialists need to be involved in the audit process.

Supervising the Audit

The order of the audit process should evolve in a manner that first calls for the investigation of general controls, and then permits the auditor to coordinate the results of the general control evaluation with the examination of specific controls. The absence of certain general controls will make particular specific controls meaningless. Hence, the testing of some specific controls can virtually be precluded by the general control evaluation.

Occasions also will arise when two or three specific controls serve similar purposes, but only one needs to be operative to provide the desired level of assurance for an audit judgment to be formulated. The supervision process should call for the identification of such occasions and the review of the professional staff's assessment of what should be done in the audit process. This commonly will result in the examination of fewer specific controls to reach an audit conclusion at the desired level of confidence.

Working Paper Documentation

The virtual invisibility of much of an EDP audit trail increases the importance of working paper documentation procedures. Some special reports may have to be prepared to appropriately support the adequacy of the audit process. Care should be taken to note what is and is not typically available for review and which reports were generated solely for auditing purposes.

In a minicomputer or microcomputer environment, working paper documentation will need to relate to locations performing the analysis, number and scope of services to users, and available software for applications. Special considerations as to the adequacy with which duties are segregated, the availability of expertise when needed, and access to the system as required suggest that special care is needed in documenting EDP audits.

Common flowcharting symbols were introduced in an earlier chapter. These symbols vary to indicate the type of EDP medium in use — for example, magnetic tape versus punched cards. The primary symbol relevant to an EDP environment signifies program modification: $\square\!\!\rangle$. This symbol can denote an instruction or group of instructions that would change a program.

Another point of working paper documentation relates to the service center operations discussed earlier in this chapter. If such an EDP center hires a third-party auditor, that auditor's report will become an integral part of the EDP audit process.

Establishing Rapport with the Auditee

In any audit setting, auditors must exert their energies to establish a rapport with auditees. In an EDP environment, this is a particularly challenging task due to the specialized jargon of EDP operations and the specialist nature of the processes being tested. It is imperative that the auditee be cultivated as an assistant in sorting out intended system design from actual system design.

Financial, Operational, and Management Audit By-Products of EDP Audits

As EDP is reviewed and tested, evidence may be obtained as to the propriety of financial balances, the effectiveness and efficiency of particular operations, and overall performance levels. These are essentially by-products of the primary focus on EDP. The influence of EDP on audit trails will affect the audit plans beyond the EDP audit setting.

As one example, consider an internal auditor's review of the handling of electronic funds transfer (EFT) systems. To ensure proper authorization and accounting, an audit trail needs to be created documenting all transactions. This facilitates follow-up should problems arise.

Another EDP audit concern which affects all other operations is the confidentiality issue. Is the data base sufficiently secure so that sensitive data or information regulated under various privacy acts is not accessible to unauthorized individuals? Obviously, liability exposure as well as competitive harm could arise from data base security shortcomings. These in turn could affect financial, operational, and management audit findings.

The Communication Link

All EDP audit findings should be discussed with auditees to avoid misunderstandings and ensure the accuracy of the eventual report. The key steps in drafting an audit report (described in earlier chapters) should be followed. Report users should be kept in mind and specialist jargon avoided to the extent possible.

Auditees should be given an opportunity for formal feedback on the EDP audit report and encouraged to take any corrective action deemed necessary.

Finally, the internal auditor should follow up on determining the extent of corrective action taken and prepare a report addressing any remaining problems.

Appendix

MICROCOMPUTER-ASSISTED AUDITING

Computers have changed the environment in which auditors work, as well as the sources of some auditing information. This new age of computer technology, especially the miniaturization of equipment and an explosive growth in software, also is providing auditors some valuable new auditing tools.

Almost all internal auditing departments utilize computer technology to some extent in the performance of their work, some departments moreso than others. This appendix outlines the ways in which some readily available and relatively inexpensive electronic data processing tools can be used to facilitate the audit process.

Before discussing the specifics, however, it will help to mention briefly why, after more than 40 years of commercially available computer systems, internal auditors are just now beginning to enjoy this technology in a direct way to assist the general audit process.

The answer is basically simple. The tremendous advantage of computers is that they can process large amounts of data very quickly. The disadvantages are:

1. They have been expensive.
2. Although they have been used in a variety of settings for a variety of purposes, each separate application has required extensive time and effort to develop and implement.
3. Because of their size, computer installations have been relatively immobile.
4. The people operating the EDP systems have required extensive training.

The advent of microprocessor technology has effectively eliminated all of the above disadvantages. Powerful computer systems are becoming more affordable by even the smallest of organizations. New generalized software has greatly increased the flexibility and adaptability of EDP use. Miniaturization has greatly increased portability and decreased the need for specially constructed facilities. And such systems are becoming more "user friendly."

Auditors, among many others, are becoming increasingly attracted to this powerful new tool. Admittedly, use of computer-assisted auditing techniques is still in the development stage, but even with currently available equipment and software, auditors can work more efficiently and effectively in each step of the audit process.

Our purpose here is not to present state-of-the-art information about computer-assisted auditing and its latest developments. Our purpose is to show how a simple, inexpensive system with only a few software packages may be used effectively by internal auditors. We will discuss hardware, software, and audit applications.

Hardware for Computer—Assisted Auditing

Two types of computers are particularly well suited for the auditor. First is the desktop micro-business computer system, or the "personal computer," as it has come to be known. This system typically includes the processing unit, disk drives, sometimes a disk for data storage, a monitor, a keyboard, and a printer. The system may be used independently, several may be used in a local area network, or such systems may be used as smart terminals linked to a larger mainframe computer. It is safe to say that most auditing departments now utilize at least one of these systems. A few departments now provide a machine for each auditor on the staff.

The second type of machine of special interest to auditors is the portable computer. A variety of portable computers are available, but all have a common purpose: to allow the user to conveniently transport the computer from site to site. Some systems are small enough to fit into a briefcase-sized carrying case. The system usually includes a processing unit, disk drives, a keyboard, and a monitor.

A growing number of internal auditing departments are making use of these small machines. Auditors take them into the field, perform their audit tests, do their analyses, prepare their working papers, and enter their findings on the computer, storing the information on disks.

Software for Computer-Assisted Auditing

There are so many software packages available to the auditor that it is impossible to discuss all of them in this space. In addition to literally hundreds of commercially available programs, in-house programmers for many companies produce special customized packages for specific audit applications. We shall limit discussion here to eight general-purpose, commercially sold programs. These include:

1. Word processing.
2. Spreadsheet programs.
3. Data base management and file maintenance.
4. Sampling.

5. Graphics analysis.
6. Flowcharting.
7. Quantitative analysis.
8. "Downloading" programs.

Word Processing

The greatest use of small computers so far has been in the preparation of text. Word processing packages essentially have replaced the typewriter as the standard technology for preparing business documents — letters, reports, memoranda, and so forth. Word processors, by use of a standard typewriter keyboard, allow the operator to type textual matter into the computer, after which the text may be edited on the monitor screen. Words, sentences, paragraphs, or even pages may be moved, rearranged, and otherwise changed to suit the writer. Most popular word processing systems include spelling dictionaries that search an entire document for spelling errors and list those words not matching words contained in the dictionary. The operator then can make any needed corrections.

A complete document may be drafted, revised, edited, and reviewed on the screen before it is actually printed.

Spreadsheet Programs

Generalized spreadsheet programs offer a row and column format for use in a variety of applications. The individual cells in spreadsheets may be varied in width and length and may contain either text or numerical entries. One great time-saving feature of these computerized spreadsheets is the ability to automatically compute and enter row and column totals and subtotals as changes are made in numerical entries.

Data Base Management and File Maintenance Programs

Almost all organizations have large amounts of several types of information. Examples include customer billings, vendor listings, inventory records, purchase orders, and client files. Such records may be stored in computerized data bases designed to provide convenient access to this information.

For example, an accounts receivable clerk may need a listing of all customers (with addresses) whose accounts are more than 90 days past due. A data base management program can quickly provide this listing without the clerk having to examine each customer's payment record.

Sampling Programs

Sampling programs are used to select statistical samples from populations. Each member of the population is assigned a number, and the program then makes a selection of numbers according to a predetermined sampling plan. Chapter 14 describes sampling plans in detail. Sampling programs may range from the basic (e.g., selecting simple random samples) to the relatively sophisticated (e.g., selecting stratified, clustered, and dollar-unit samples).

Graphics Analysis Programs

Graphics provide an additional form of analytical perspective on many problems. Graphics encompass a variety of techniques, including bar charts, pie charts, vector analysis, diagramming, and many others. The aim is to create a visual representation of the analysis with an illustration. Graphics programs actually allow the user to create such pictorial illustrations using a variety of methods, including the keyboard, light pens, or a "mouse."

Flowcharting Programs

A specific type of graphics analysis is the flowchart. Flowcharting may actually be a part of a more general graphics program. Flowcharting applications are different enough from other types of graphics, and important enough, to be considered separately. Flowcharting programs may be utilized for both vertical and horizontal flowcharts, with some textual material and identification of key control points.

Quantitative Analysis Programs

Quantitative techniques include probability and statistical analysis as well as the use of deterministic models such as linear programming. Network and scheduling analysis also fall into this category. Several software packages are available for these types of analysis. Various quantitative techniques have been in use for many years, but since computers have become available, these techniques are being applied to more and more problems. Microcomputer applications are now making these tools available to even the smallest organizations; as few as 15 years ago, only relatively large computer installations had such tools.

"Downloading" Programs

Large organizations typically retain large volumes of data in files stored on large computer systems. Users of the much smaller microcomputer systems may gain access to these files by "downloading" them to the small systems. Special programs allow the microcomputer to use and manipulate data contained on the larger system. Auditors have found this ability to access data in the auditee's computer systems quite useful.

Applications for Internal Auditors

Exhibit 17-A outlines how microcomputer systems may be applied in the nine steps of the audit process. The exhibit is not definitive, since different auditing organizations use microcomputers in different ways. The information shown does, however, outline the ways in which a modern auditing organization might choose to employ microcomputer technology. It is evident that the microcomputer can have a significant effect on how auditors perform their work.

Exhibit 17-A
The Use of Microcomputer Systems
in the Audit Process

AUDIT STEP	AUDIT ACTIVITY	HARDWARE	POSSIBLE SOFTWARE
Selecting auditee	Risk analysis	Desktop microcomputer	Spreadsheet program
Audit preparation	Develop purpose and scope of audit		
	Review of audit files and background material; selection of audit team and audit resources	Desktop microcomputer	Downloading programs, spreadsheet, data management programs, sampling program, graphics, and quantitative analysis programs for study of background material
	Preparation of preliminary audit program	Desktop microcomputer	Word processing or spreadsheet
	Preliminary communication; approval of audit work plan	Desktop microcomputer	Word processing for memos and letters
Initial survey	Opening conference	Desktop microcomputer or portable computer system	Word processing for preparing agenda
	On-site tour; study of documents	Desktop computer	Downloading, spreadsheet, data management, sampling, graphics, and quantitative analysis programs for study of computerized information.
	Written description of auditee	Desktop or portable computer	Word processing, graphics analysis, and flowcharting

AUDIT STEP	AUDIT ACTIVITY	HARDWARE	POSSIBLE SOFTWARE
Review of controls	Description and analysis, preliminary evaluation, reassessment of risk	Desktop or portable computer	Word processing, spreadsheet, and flowcharting
Expanded testing	A variety of audit tests	Desktop or portable computer	All software packages may be used, depending on the tests employed
Development of audit findings	Summary of results of audit tests	Desktop or portable computer	Word processing
Reporting	Preparing written report	Desktop computer	Word processing and graphics analysis
Follow-up	A variety of audit follow-up tests	Desktop or portable computer	All software packages may be used, depending on the tests employed
Evaluation	Evaluation of audit and of audit team members		

QUESTIONS

1. Describe the most common EDP environments.
2. Outline the common stages of a system development life cycle.
3. How can users' evaluations of EDP be obtained? Describe your approach in depth.
4. How can an auditor evaluate hardware reliability?
5. Give an example of a hardware control.
6. What are the key concerns in a software audit?
7. How should segregation of duties be evaluated in an EDP setting?
8. How are the completeness and accuracy of data entry and processing maintained in an EDP setting?
9. Distinguish between effectiveness and efficiency concerns in EDP auditing.
10. What basis can be used to schedule EDP services and to allocate available resources?
11. Provide two examples of circumstances in which an EDP configuration would probably be unsuitable for an auditee's needs.
12. What would be the compliance objectives in an EDP audit?
13. Prepare a checklist of desired documentation in an EDP environment.
14. What are contingency plans? Be specific.
15. What unique concerns face an auditor when a service center is being used to provide EDP support?
16. What is meant by the materiality of EDP?
17. Why is coordination with the auditee particularly important in an EDP setting?
18. What do the professional standards prescribe with respect to internal auditors' involvement in systems design?
19. What are the key questions to raise in the preliminary survey phase of an EDP audit?
20. List three input, processing, and output controls.
21. What are the major phases of an EDP audit program?
22. Describe the capabilities of generalized audit software.
23. Describe the common computer audit techniques available to systems testing. Elaborate on their relative advantages and disadvantages.
24. What is meant by $\triangleright$?
25. What are the advantages of electronic data processing in businesses? What have been the disadvantages, especially for auditors?
26. How have microcomputers overcome the disadvantages of computers?
27. What two types of hardware have been helpful to internal auditors?
28. Outline and briefly discuss the types of audit software that may be useful and readily available for the internal auditor. How do these differ in purpose and application from the computer audit tools discussed earlier in the chapter?

EXERCISES

E-1

Multiple Choice: Select a single answer that best completes the statement or answers the question.

1. Modern data processing configurations often consist of networks of minicomputers which replace or supplement large mainframe systems. When evaluating such a system in the preliminary survey, the internal auditor should recognize that security may be a concern because:
   a. It is possible for networks to be modified, expanded, and rearranged by users.
   b. Minicomputers cannot have sign-on protection.
   c. It is not possible to limit or restrict file access in a typical minicomputer network.
   d. Minicomputers require specialized electrical power sources and climate control for their operations.

2. An audit procedure involving the creation of simulated transactions that are processed through a system to generate results for comparison with predetermined results is:
   a. Desk checking.
   b. Use of a test deck.
   c. Completing outstanding jobs.
   d. Parallel simulation.

3. The role of the internal auditor in computerized system development and conversion should be to:
   a. Evaluate the development and cost-effectiveness of the controls provided.
   b. Participate in the work of the development team under the authority of the project leader.
   c. Develop adequate processing and procedural controls.
   d. Avoid participation until the system development phase is complete.

4. If management desires to maintain adequate segregation of duties, which of the following internal positions in the EDP department should be made responsible for working with the user department to reduce input errors?
   a. Data entry operator.
   b. EDP manager.
   c. Data control supervisor.
   d. Computer operator.

5. In auditing a computerized system, how would reviewing the record layout assist the auditor?
   a. It would show the predetermined arrangement of data in a record.
   b. It would present a graphical representation of a sequence of operations.
   c. The auditor could trace back to the previous good record should the data base need reconstruction.
   d. Files could be identified by name, serial number, and creation date.

6. The internal auditor must be able to distinguish between different types of data processing controls to evaluate their applicability and effectiveness in a given situation. Which of the following is the best procedural detective control?
   a. Use of data encryption techniques.
   b. Review of machine utilization logs.
   c. Policy requiring password security.
   d. Backup and recovery procedure.

7. In a small system using minicomputers, generalized software often contains access controls which associate authorized users to terminal locations and allowable functions. The internal auditor should recognize that the effectiveness of these controls is seriously weakened if:
   a. The user can gain access to generalized utility programs.
   b. The terminals are not kept secured under the control of the information systems department.
   c. The environment does not provide the organizational structure for formally segregating duties.
   d. System developers use tools which generate documentation as a by-product of the development process.

8. Which of the following statements are advantages of standard system development methodologies?
   1. Programmers rarely need to learn new programming techniques.
   2. Managers, analysts, and programmers can communicate with each other in a common nomenclature.
   3. Management has a common base for measuring performance.
   4. Analysts and programmers need not review the work of their predecessors.
   a. 1 and 2
   b. 1 and 4
   c. 2 and 3
   d. 2 and 4

9. In evaluating internal control, the internal auditor must be alert for situations which affect more than one location. In a multi-site distributed data processing (DDP) environment, which of the following should be a goal of compliance testing?
   a. Consistency of programs.
   b. Centralized password control.
   c. Detailed testing of randomly selected transactions.
   d. Policy prohibiting multi-location master files.

10. In a distributed data base (DDB) environment, compliance tests for access control administration can be designed which focus on:
    a. Reconciliation of batch control totals.
    b. Examination of logged activity.
    c. Prohibition of random access.
    d. Analysis of system-generated core dumps.   (CIA Exam Adapted)

E-2

Multiple Choice: Select a single answer which best completes the statement or answers the question.

1. A control ensuring that the output file received for printing or processing is then transmitted to the appropriate site is:
   a. Comparison of batch totals with header record contents.
   b. Review of output by data control personnel.
   c. Control over access to job and output spool files.
   d. Creation and transmission of a confirmation message to the sending site.

2. Of the following, the greatest advantage of a data base management system is:
   a. Programs access data according to predefined subschema.
   b. Conversion to a data base management system is inexpensive and can be accomplished quickly.
   c. Multiple occurrences of data items are useful for consistency checking.
   d. Backup and recovery procedures are minimized.

3. Which of the following are effective techniques for managing resources in a time-sharing system?
   1. Require computer operator intervention to permit sign-on of each user.
   2. Allocate and control the amount of CPU time available to each user.
   3. Allocate to each user the CPU time needed to complete that user's current request or command.
   4. Allocate pages of virtual memory to each user.
   a. 1 and 2
   b. 1 and 3
   c. 2 and 3
   d. 2 and 4

4. All of the staff members of a merger and acquisitions department in an investment banking firm use spreadsheet programs on microcomputers to analyze potential client matches. The data is highly confidential. An appropriate control over the department's use of microcomputers is:
   a. Prohibit departmental staff from programming their own applications.
   b. Keep the program and data diskettes in a secure location when they are not in use by departmental staff.
   c. Require departmental staff to use the spreadsheet applications only through custom-designed menus.
   d. Divide duties among the departmental staff so that some only prepare the application templates and others only run the applications.

5. Water damage caused a computer to fail while running an on-line transaction processing program updating a customer data base. Once the computer is again operable, the best procedure for restarting the processing program is:

    a. Process the backup copy of the data base with the log of changes and prompt data entry operators to verify their last transactions.

    b. Prompt data entry operators to reenter their last transactions.

    c. Reinitialize the disconnected teleprocessing lines and process the last transactions from data entry operators using those lines.

    d. Prompt data entry operators to verify their last transactions.

6. Effective access control requires that passwords be changed when:

    1. Test programs are installed in production libraries.

    2. Personnel changes occur.

    3. A security violation has occurred.

    4. A new version of an on-line system is installed.

    a. 1 and 3

    b. 1 and 4

    c. 2 and 3

    d. 2 and 4

7. The number of terminals that can be used in a computer system will be constrained by:

    a. The availability of lockwords and passwords.

    b. Any batch control requirements in the system.

    c. The line protocol.

    d. The number of channels and ports included in the configuration.

8. The greatest advantage of programming standards is that they:

    a. Reduce the effects of technological change.

    b. Minimize the effects of personnel turnover.

    c. Impose consistent data names and definitions across applications.

    d. Facilitate subsequent maintenance of existing programs and creation of new programs.

9. The program design principle with the greatest potential for yielding efficiencies in system development is:

    a. Structured programming.

    b. Decision trees.

    c. Feedforward.

    d. Bottom-up.

10. A distributed processing system:

    a. Achieves economies of scale.

    b. Allocates computing resources to locations consistent with local processing demands.

    c. Maintains data independence across applications and processing sites.

    d. Requires interaction among neighboring sites to coordinate processing.

(CIA Exam Adapted)

E-3

Multiple Choice: Select a single answer which best completes the statement or answers the question.

1. A control used by the management of a computer center to minimize the likelihood that output includes unauthorized data would be:
   a. Department controls over report distribution.
   b. Restricted access to terminals.
   c. Detailed scheduling for input, processing, and delivery of output.
   d. Monitoring of terminal response time.

2. The ability to restore a data base in the event of a computer malfunction would rely most on:
   a. A dual data processing function.
   b. Parity checks.
   c. A continuous log of all transactions affecting the data base.
   d. Field edits.

3. A major new objective for an audit of the EDP systems development process is to evaluate the adequacy of controls designed for a new application. Given this objective, which of the following conditions would most likely result in an adverse finding?
   a. The process calls for heavy user involvement throughout the development phases.
   b. A new system was brought on-line after running parallel to the old system for a substantial period of time.
   c. Neither a feasibility study nor a cost/benefit evaluation was performed early in the EDP systems development process.
   d. Users are not required to sign off as to the adequacy of appropriate controls.

4. In an internal auditor's review of the input, processing, and output controls of the company's EDP system, which of the following is typically termed a processing control?
   a. Reasonableness.
   b. Validation.
   c. Edit check.
   d. Checkpoint/restart.

5. You have been assigned to evaluate production variances as part of the internal audit department's periodic audit of production activities. You would be likely to use a generalized audit software package to substantiate:
   a. Footings, extensions, and summations of production costs incurred and variances recorded.
   b. Overhead account classifications.
   c. The appropriateness of the application formula used in assigning overhead cost to production.
   d. Data entries from terminals located in the production department.

6. Two individuals in a payroll department have been assigned the same password and user identification for use in updating payroll files stored on the computer. The primary control weakness on which the internal auditor's report should focus is:
   a. Passwords are used to access payroll files.
   b. Transactions lack accountability.
   c. Computer files can be accessed by more than one person.
   d. Payroll's employees are able to update computerized payroll files.

7. Auditing through the computer must be used when:
   a. Input transactions are batched and system logic is straightforward.
   b. Processing primarily consists of sorting the input data and updating the master file sequentially.
   c. Processing is primarily on-line and updating is real-time.
   d. Generalized audit software is not available.

8. An internal auditor is reviewing the data base administration function in a manufacturing organization to ascertain whether adequate provision has been made for controlling data (a corporate asset). The internal auditor should determine that:
   a. The responsibilities of the function are well defined.
   b. The function reports to data processing operations.
   c. The data base administrator is a competent systems programmer.
   d. The audit software has the capability of efficiently accessing the data base.

9. The primary reason an internal auditor often recommends establishment of control standards for a company is because:
   a. They present criteria by which both existing and newly developed controls can be evaluated.
   b. They facilitate the development of internal control questionnaires.
   c. They are necessary to comply with the *Standards for the Professional Practice of Internal Auditing.*
   d. They are an important prerequisite to the use of generalized audit software.

10. The technique that provides the capability of reviewing the contents of a specific portion of computer memory as transactions are processed through the program is called:
    a. Sequencing.
    b. Tracing.
    c. Snapshot.
    d. Logic point.

11. Which of the following input controls in a computerized accounts receivable application should detect a customer account number entered in the wrong field or omitted?
    a. Check digits on the customer account number.
    b. Validity or completeness edit checks on the field for customer account numbers.
    c. Limit tests on the field for customer account numbers.
    d. Record counts of transactions processed.

12. The computer console log usually provides information on the:
    a. Jobs processed.
    b. Appropriate operation of limit checks.
    c. Computation of run-to-run totals.
    d. Proper detection and investigation of application errors.

13. If a company utilizes a computer service center, which of the company's in-house controls becomes most important?
    a. Check digits.
    b. File labels.
    c. Edit criteria.
    d. Reconciliation of inputs and outputs.

14. Data base privacy should be considered by a company in designing systems. Which of the following is most likely to reflect a company's attempt to comply with such privacy considerations?
    a. Record counts.
    b. Dedicated communication links.
    c. Multi-level authorizations.
    d. Data-manipulation language.   (CIA Exam Adapted)

E-4

Automated program library systems are major software systems often purchased for use in medium- to large-scale data processing installations.

Required:
a. Distinguish between "source" code and "object" code program libraries.
b. Briefly define and describe "automated program libraries." What are they and what do they do?
c. Briefly describe the major features that one might find in an automated program library that should interest both data processing management and internal auditors.
                                                                      (CIA Exam Adapted)

E-5

Multiple Choice: Select a single answer which best completes the statement or answers the question.

1. A probable advantage to an organization that uses outside data processing services rather than its own internal data processing department is that:
    a. Data are more secure because data are handled by fewer organizational personnel.
    b. Processing priorities can be established and enforced internally.
    c. More direct control can be exercised over computer operations.
    d. The using organization pays only for the amount of computer operations.
    e. There is greater user involvement because of the need to better communicate user needs.

2. Many people believe that a data processing department ought to have a long-range plan. Which of the following is not likely to appear in a long-range plan?
   a. Organizational goals and objectives.
   b. Detailed flowcharts for each computer program that will be developed.
   c. Schedule of the development of each project.
   d. Identification of the hardware, personnel, and financial resources that will be required.
   e. Forecast of future hardware developments.

3. Restart and recovery procedures used with computer systems:
   a. Are limited to data base management systems.
   b. Require the use of magnetic tape storage to hold the backup data.
   c. Can be used only in computers that have virtual storage.
   d. Increase the efficiency of computer operations since restart eliminates the need to rerun the complete program.
   e. Reduce the need for off-site data storage.

4. Many organizations are considering microcomputers for business use. In comparison with large-scale computers, microcomputers:
   a. Are generally more reliable because there is less hardware to malfunction.
   b. Use only compiler-based languages, such as COBOL or FORTRAN.
   c. Cannot be connected to large-scale computers.
   d. Have faster processor functions due to the increased density or core design.
   e. None of the above.

5. A potential advantage of fixed-length computer records (compared to variable-length computer records) is that:
   a. They are better suited for use with magnetic tape than on disk.
   b. They use disk space more efficiently.
   c. They are easier to block, thus facilitating access to stored data.
   d. They are better suited for data transmissions because they require less space.
   e. They are more compatible with internal computer storage which contains fixed-length registers.

6. The key verification process associated with keypunching computer cards for input to the computer system is:
   a. Effectively used to detect the erroneous recording of data on source documents.
   b. Inexpensive and therefore widely used.
   c. Used to detect errors introduced by the keying process.
   d. Used generally with a computer program written to check the data.
   e. Most effective when control totals are utilized.

7. Who is primarily responsible for seeing that cost-effective controls are implemented in an electronic data processing system?
   a. Internal audit department director.
   b. Electronic data processing audit manager.

    c. Audit committee of the board of directors.

    d. Control group in the EDP department.

    e. Operating management.

8. A data security system developed for the data base environment should provide assurance that:

    a. Access is limited to authorized portions of the data base.

    b. Operations performed on the data are limited to authorized activities.

    c. Access to the data base is authorized through the data dictionary.

    d. Accesses are recorded and reviewed by the EDP auditor.

    e. Both (a) and (b) above.

9. Data base elements should be defined by:

    a. Application programmers.

    b. Systems analysts.

    c. Data base administrator.

    d. Systems programmer.

    e. Security specialists.

10. Which of the following procedures constitutes a sound segregation of duties with respect to computer operations?

    a. The programming group authorizes program corrections.

    b. Operations personnel make needed changes in the source code.

    c. The programming group initiates a request for program enhancement.

    d. Operations personnel control the movement of programs from test program libraries to production libraries.

    e. Console operators schedule production.

11. Which of the following represents the most effective control over the data dictionary in a data processing environment?

    a. Changes to existing data elements or additions of new elements are approved by those responsible for the data.

    b. Users provide assurance that data does not duplicate or conflict with existing data.

    c. Changes are approved by each user of the data.

    d. Data administrator establishes duplicate data elements in the data dictionary when different attributes are necessary for the same data element.

    e. Each user establishes data element and name standards for the data they will use.

12. The internal auditor's primary concern with an auditee's programmer writing a program to age inventory would be:

    a. The auditor's programming expertise.

    b. Loss of independence.

    c. Saving valuable audit time.

    d. Limited use of the program.

    e. Programmer's access to confidential information.

(CIA Exam Adapted)

E-6

Listed below are eight procedural controls often found in an electronic data processing function. Following this list is another list of definitions and/or explanations of various types of procedural controls.

Required:

Place the numbers 1 through 8 on your answer sheet. Next to each number, write the letter of the definition/explanation which corresponds to the named procedural control. Each procedural control will have only one definition/explanation.

Procedural Controls

1. Default option.
2. Hash total.
3. Completeness check.
4. Read back.
5. Keystroke verification.
6. Drum card (or program card).
7. Trailer record.
8. Validity check.

Definitions/Explanations of Procedural Controls

a. Rekeying data to verify the accuracy of prior entries.
b. A test of specified-amount fields against stipulated high or low limits of acceptability.
c. A test of characters in a coded field against an acceptable set of values, patterns, formats, subcodes, or character values.
d. A test to determine that data entries are made in fields which cannot be processed in a blank state.
e. A device that permits automatic spacing and format shifting of data fields on a keypunch machine.
f. The automatic utilization of a predetermined value in situations where input transactions have certain values left blank.
g. Internally initiated processing in a predetermined manner, unless specific input transactions are received that specify processing with different values or in a different manner.
h. The immediate return of input information to the sender for comparison and approval.
i. Provides a control total for comparison with accumulated counts or values of records processed.
j. A meaningless but useful value developed from the accumulated numerical amounts of nonmonetary information.
k. Any type of control total or count applied to a specific number of transaction documents or to the transaction documents that arrive within a specified period of time.

(CIA Exam Adapted)

E-7

Steering committees composed of high-level personnel are increasingly being used in many organizations for making key decisions about data processing.

Required:
a. List four responsibilities of a steering committee for data processing.
b. Give two reasons why it is desirable for a steering committee, rather than the manager of data processing, to perform these responsibilities.

(CIA Exam Adapted)

E-8

Software may be purchased or developed in-house.

a. State three possible advantages of purchasing available software instead of developing it in-house.
b. State three possible disadvantages of purchasing available software instead of developing it in-house.

(CIA Exam Adapted)

E-9

Common problems in small computer departments are that (1) employees have easy access to master files and object code and (2) programming personnel operate the computer.

Required:
What compensating control is likely to be critical in such a setting?

PROBLEMS

P-1

An article in *The Wall Street Journal** on computer fraud cases cited the example of Mr. Slyngstad, a programmer for the state of Washington, who wrote vocational rehabilitation checks to himself in the name of Mr. *Lyngstad.* He reportedly had no problem cashing the checks. The bank tellers simply assumed that the computer had made an error and dropped the *S* from his name.

Required:
a. In what sense would generalized audit software be incapable of detecting this defalcation?
b. How could generalized audit software be adjusted to facilitate detection of this defalcation?

---

*Erik Larson, "Crook's Tool: Computers Turn Out to Be Valuable Aid in Employee Crime," *The Wall Street Journal,* January 14, 1985, p. 1.

P-2

Describe plausible solutions to each of the following control problems common in an EDP environment:

a. Operations personnel are not rotated between shifts or applications. This permits an individual to have continual access to the same processing activity.
b. Control attention is being directed primarily to the correction of errors in the output of the entity's service bureau.
c. The use of terminals is not well controlled.
d. In the event of extended computer downtime, the EDP department has an informal arrangement that data processing will be performed by an outside service bureau.

Adapted from: Wanda A. Wallace, *Handbook of Internal Accounting Controls* (Englewood Cliffs: Prentice-Hall), 1984.

18   Fraud Audits

The Narrow Objective of Fraud Audits

A fraud audit has the narrow objective of uncovering the presence, scope, and means of intentional misstatement of records and/or misappropriation of assets. Such an audit engagement is atypical, as fraud is an unusual occurrence. A fraud audit tends to be more detailed in approach, since it must uncover that which has been intentionally hidden. Flows of accounting numbers, as well as assets, may have to be reconstructed without an audit trail.

Obviously, a fraud audit approach would not be cost-effective for the typical audit engagement, as some reliance on controls and management's information system is commonly warranted. The ability to recognize that setting in which a fraud audit is required is a skill which auditors must work hard to develop. The term *fraud* indicates some sort of deceptive act which harms another party. It is this deception which makes the discovery of fraud far more difficult than the discovery of errors.

The Impetus for Fraud Audits

An auditor must be alert to clues which suggest possible irregularities. In fact, alertness and healthy skepticism may well be two of the auditor's most important skills. Critical inquiry as to what irregularities are possible should be followed by an assessment of their likelihood, given controls, supervisory practices, and the overall control environment. Of course, anything detected as questionable should be followed through. Most often, the impetus for a fraud audit is some telltale sign of an unusual transaction or a missing record.

One reason for internal auditors' attention to the possibility of fraud is that management expects internal auditing activities to reduce the risk of undetected defalcations. In fact, internal auditors are likely to face higher expectations than are external auditors. Some ideas as to why this might be true are presented in Exhibit 18-1.

The Qualitative Materiality of Fraud

No matter what the dollar magnitude involved, a fraud is considered to be qualitatively material. The reasons for this definition are that (1) frauds, by their very nature, can balloon quickly if not deterred; (2) the existence of fraud in and of itself indicates a weakness in controls; and (3) frauds imply integrity issues that may have far-reaching consequences. For example, if management made illegal payments, the company and the individual executives involved could face legal consequences and highly adverse publicity.

Exhibit 18-1
Possible Explanations for Managers' Expectations That Internal Auditors Will Detect Irregularities

- Internal auditors issue no explicit disclaimer that they do not look for fraud; i.e., COMMUNICATION GAP.

- Managers perceive that internal audits are of sufficient scope and depth to detect irregularities; i.e., PERCEIVED GAP BETWEEN EXTERNAL AND INTERNAL AUDIT ACTIVITIES.

- Managers perceive internal auditors to be more familiar with operations and controls than external auditors; i.e., HIGHER EXPECTATIONS.

- Internal auditors' primary focus is on controls; i.e., CONTROLS EXPECTED TO DETER FRAUD.

The Cost Profile of Fraud Audits

It is far too costly to test every transaction. Moreover, if transactions are unrecorded, such tests would still lack completeness. A special problem arises in a fraud setting because the auditor has no real legal ability to encourage thoughtful responses. Nor can an auditor commonly use records "on the other side of the transactions" as a basis for reconstructing fraud-related transactions. All of these aspects increase the relative cost of fraud audits and help to explain why no guarantee of fraud detection exists and why estimates of the scope of a fraud or total losses are always subject to error.

Two important cost dimensions of fraud audits that go beyond direct audit costs are legal problems and bad publicity. Both of these topics will be explored later in this chapter. The point is that management must analyze the entire cost/benefit picture in determining the extent of the audit and the actions to be taken to prevent future frauds.

The Scope of the Problem

Frauds have been a problem throughout time. In fiscal year 1950, accountants with the Federal Bureau of Investigation reportedly handled 674 bank defalcations totaling $4 million. (Source: Lee R. Pennington, "How FBI Accountants Trap Criminals," *The Journal of Accountancy,* April 1982, pp. 456-463.)

From 1975 through mid-1978, over 400 U.S. corporations disclosed illegal political contributions, bribes, kickbacks, and similar improprieties. An investigation by the Internal Revenue Service uncovered 480 cases alleging illegal slush funds. (Source: S. Thomas Moser, "Meeting the Challenge of the 'Corporate Watergate' Phenomenon," *The Internal Auditor,* April 1978, pp. 19-25.)

White-collar crime is likely to be far greater than these statistics suggest. Although fraud articles frequently appear in *The Wall Street Journal* (with frauds in the United States estimated at more than $2 billion annually), there are many reasons that entities choose not to "go public" when fraud is discovered. Corporate embarrassment, management pride, negative publicity, an inferior image, fear of reprisals, and concern for the perpetrator's family all work against public disclosure of discovered frauds. Imagine the possible customer reaction to news that a bank lost $2 million due to an employee's extraction of depositors' funds through malicious coding of computer programs. Most entities would prefer not to risk such a potential loss of confidence by their customers.

Fraud problems are not confined to the corporate sector. Many of the published cases of computer fraud involve financial services in the private sector, and many computer frauds have occurred in governmental computer installations. For example, one state's social services agency had $1.5 million in "extra" payroll checks taken under fictitious employee names. (Source: Michael J. Berkery and Irwin T. David, "Computer Control and Audit in the Public Sector," *Government Finance,* August 1977, pp. 34-40.) Similar cases abound of fraud involving food stamp programs, governmental loan programs, and sweetheart deals with contractors. The problem is not merely domestic. A 1980 study by the Centro Investmenti Sociali found that Italian civil servants are heavily engaged in conflicting interests:

Problem	Percentage of Sample Involved
• Moonlighting and second jobs	54%
• Frequent personal absences from work to take part in events	45%

- Took twice their normal   33%
  vacation

- Took on occasional private   27%
  work

- Seldom report for work at all   19%

Such actions suggest attitudes which may increase exposure to frauds in government and breakdowns in control systems.

Sensitive Information

Given the scope and pervasiveness of fraud, entities are effectively forced to set policies to deter and detect such activities. The sensitive nature of fraudulent activities or suspicions of such activities suggest a need for formal guidelines on reporting and investigation practices.

Reporting Links

An internal auditor must take care to distinguish suspicions from fact. Furthermore, the evidence must be sufficient to support whatever judgments are reported. Many entities may encourage the establishment of reporting links to communicate mere suspicions. The purpose of such reporting is to enable management to determine how it wishes to proceed.

Professional Standards Bulletin 83-5 states that when internal auditors suspect wrongdoing, they "should determine the possible effects . . . , discuss the matter with the appropriate level of management who (management or the internal auditor) should investigate or otherwise follow up the suspicion. When wrongdoing is suspected, the auditor's responsibility extends to the appropriate level of management within the organization."

Internal Audit Referrals to Internal Security Investigations

For highly sensitive detective work, many entities will establish internal security departments. Internal auditing will be instructed to make referrals to the internal security group so that it can make investigations. The basis for suspicions by internal auditing, as well as any available evidence and ideas on how the security group might proceed, should be communicated by internal audit to the security department. The *Standards* explicitly states that when fraud is suspected or is evident, "the appropriate authorities" inside the organization are to be notified. Often these authorities will be the security department.

The Role of Security Departments

Security departments can be expected to know the legal implications of and evidential requirements in a fraud setting. Security personnel often have police or detective training and experience and can play a unique investigative role that is quite distinct from the service provided by internal auditors. Surveillance activities and procedures, such as collecting fingerprints or planting "bait" for a suspected defrauder, are the unique responsibilities of the security department. Such activities may be critical in eliminating or confirming suspicions.

Joint Internal Audit/Security Investigations

In forming a "case" against a defrauder, there are certain steps that may be performed more effectively by the internal auditors. For example, if the suspected defrauder is responsible for a certain aspect of purchasing, the auditors may be asked to perform extensive tests of those transactions handled by that individual, with the intent of uncovering both the mode of fraud and its scope. Any aspect of the possible defalcation which relates to accounting records can be more efficiently handled though a joint internal audit/security investigation.

Circumstances may arise in which referrals will need to be made to criminal investigators, due to either the nature of the case or the lack of in-house expertise. In such a setting, special care must be taken to preserve confidentiality.

Unique Audit Approaches

In approaching fraud audits, a *threat analysis* — i.e., an analysis of exposure to fraud — should be performed. What assets are held? How could they be taken? The concept behind this analysis is to "outsmart the crooks." A threat analysis can help to direct the audit plan and, in particular, to highlight the most vulnerable assets when assessing the likelihood of fraud. As an example, if an entity stocked small tools, the exposure to pilferage would be far greater than if the entity stocked only large, cumbersome items. To minimize the risk of loss in a cost-effective manner, physical access to the small tools should be controlled and appropriate documentation required whenever inventory is taken from stock. Guards could examine any briefcases or lunchboxes carried by employees or others as they leave the company's premises. The auditor would evaluate the threat of stolen inventory in light of such controls.

Integrity-Development Projects: Review Priorities

Hand-in-hand with fraud detection is the promotion of integrity within the organization. Internal auditors are often requested to perform integrity-development projects, in which the priorities of top management are reviewed with all personnel. Ethics, the desirability of avoiding conflicts of interest, the preference to avoid management override, and the encouragement of whistle-blowing are all topics which might be stressed in an integrity-development project.

"Red Flag" Indicators

However, no matter how many resources are allocated to promoting integrity, the risk remains that a defalcation might occur. The question then becomes how to assess the likelihood of such a problem arising. An entire body of literature has evolved, commonly referred to as the "red flag" literature, which suggests conditions under which fraud is more likely to occur. The indicators suggested by this literature were inferred from studies of past frauds. In other words, red flags are those common characteristics or conditions observed in past frauds which appear to indicate a higher likelihood of fraud whenever they are present elsewhere.

Exhibit 18-2 summarizes some of the red flags which have been suggested. These flags are rather general and often may exist when no fraud is present. Hence, while they do provide some insight on the likelihood of fraud, their information value is somewhat limited.

Creating Errors

One means of assessing control weaknesses and vulnerability to fraud is to actually create errors and see if they pass through the control system. As an example, an internal auditor might take a blank check and make it payable to a fictitious payee. Then, to see if controls are easily circumvented, a note could be attached stating that "supporting documents will follow; please process this immediately." Should this check get through the check-signing operation, it would suggest that payments may be made for goods not received and duplicate payments may have been processed. While this audit approach can be very effective in detecting fraud exposure, the auditor must be careful to trace such erroneous transactions and remove them from the information system. This step is necessary to prevent misstatements in the accounting records.

The advantage of creating errors and observing how they are processed is that specific information regarding the entity's probable exposure to fraud is thereby obtainable. In contrast, the "red flag" approach is very general in form.

The Preliminary Survey

If an internal audit department is directed to proceed in a suspected fraud audit, a key phase of the survey is to apply threat analysis in conjunction with control evaluation as a basis for formulating the audit program. It is helpful to recognize the types of problems that can arise during this phase.

Possible Integrity Breaches

The key types of irregularities that may arise include embezzlement, extortion, bribery, fraud in disclosure practices, conflicts of interest, and misuse of authority. While these irregularities are fairly general, it is possible to pinpoint the most common methods of embezzlement that have been observed across time. The likely risk exposure can also be inferred from past experience; in certain settings, the very nature of the assets involved suggests the likely magnitude of the possible loss. Exhibit 18-3 summarizes some of the common forms of fraud and their likely magnitude.

Exhibit 18-2
Examples of "Red Flags"

1. Personal situation creating undue pressure:
   a. Indebtedness.
   b. Serious illnesses.
   c. Gambling problems.
   d. Alcohol problems.
   e. Resentment, frustration, or perceptions of inequity that encourage revengeful actions.
   f. Lack of personal ethics.

2. Company setting creating undue pressure:
   a. Economic hardship.
   b. Dependency on a limited number of customers or suppliers.
   c. Excessive leverage.
   d. Rapid growth.
   e. Tight credit.
   f. Increased competition.
   g. Restrictive loan provisions.
   h. A large number of adjusting audit entries.
   i. Poorly controlled operations.

3. Specific control risks:
   a. One person handles all portions of an important transaction.
   b. Poor supervision.
   c. No clear assignment of responsibility and accountability.
   d. No required vacations; when employees are on vacation, there is no covering of their work.
   e. No rotating of workers or cross-training of employees.
   f. Conflicts of interest are apparent in assigned duties.

See *Management Fraud: Detection and Deterrence* for further development of, and literature citations on, red flags. [Robert K. Elliott and John J. Willingham, *Management Fraud: Detection and Deterrence* (New York: Petrocelli Books, 1980).]

Exhibit 18-3
Common Methods of Embezzlement
and Likely Risk Exposure

LIKELY MAGNITUDE			COMMON FORMS OF FRAUD
LRG	MED	SML	
		X	1. Removing small amounts from cash on hand.
	X	X	2. Failing to record sales of inventory and pocketing the cash.
	X	X	3. Creating overages in cash funds and registers by underrecording transactions on the books.
	X	X	4. Overloading expense accounts or diverting advances to personal use.
	X	X	5. Lapping collections on customers' accounts.
	X	X	6. Pocketing payments on customers' accounts and issuing receipts on scraps of paper or in self-designed receipt books, or not giving receipts at all.
	X	X	7. Collecting an account, pocketing the money, and writing it off; collecting write-offs and then not reporting the collections.
	X	X	8. Misstating sales returns and allowances to customers or recording unauthorized discounts, particularly cash discounts.
	X	X	9. Failing to make bank deposits daily or depositing only part of the money.
	X	X	10. Altering dates on deposit slips to cover up stealing.
	X	X	11. Carrying fictitious extra help on payrolls, increasing pay rates or hours worked per books, carrying employees on the payroll beyond severance dates, falsifying additions to payrolls, or withholding unclaimed wages.
	X	X	12. Transferring cash across accounts to cover cash collections taken.

LIKELY MAGNITUDE			COMMON FORMS OF FRAUD
LRG	MED	SML	
	X	X	13. Destroying, altering, or voiding cash-sales tickets and pocketing the cash.
	X	X	14. Using personal expenditure receipts to support false paid-out items.
	X	X	15. Using carbon copies of previously used original vouchers or using a properly approved voucher of a prior period by changing the date.
X	X	X	16. Paying false invoices, either self-prepared or obtained through collusion with suppliers or other third parties.
X	X	X	17. Increasing the amounts of suppliers' invoices through collusion or misstating discounts provided.
	X	X	18. Charging personal purchases to the company through the misuse of purchase orders.
	X	X	19. Billing stolen merchandise to fictitious accounts.
X	X	X	20. Falsifying inventories to cover thefts or delinquencies using such creative approaches as stacking empty boxes.
	X	X	21. Increasing canceled bank checks to agree with fictitious entries or otherwise adjusting the bank reconciliation.
X	X	X	22. Inserting fictitious ledger sheets.
	X	X	23. Misfooting or misposting cash receipts and disbursements books or other key ledgers and subsidiary ledgers.
	X	X	24. Selling waste and scrap and pocketing the proceeds.
	X	X	25. Selling door keys or combinations to safes or vaults.
	X	X	26. Falsifying bills of lading and splitting the revenue with the carrier.
	X	X	27. Obtaining unprotected blank checks and forging the signature. Other blank documents can similarly be abused.

| LIKELY MAGNITUDE | | | COMMON FORMS OF FRAUD |
LRG	MED	SML	
X	X	X	28. Permitting special prices or privileges to customers or granting business to favored suppliers for kickbacks.
	X	X	29. Investment schemes involving the public.
X	X	X	30. Outright stealing of inventory, equipment, or other assets.

Adapted from Roy C. Taylor, "Methods of Embezzlement and Protective Measures," *N.A.C.A. Bulletin,* February 1953, pp. 747-754.

Past Occurrences

Beyond considering the possible methods of fraud, a key indicator of the more likely types of exposure faced by an auditee is the auditee's past experience. Past occurrences of fraud have implications about management's attitudes and integrity. In addition, such occurrences can serve as a signal to employees as to what type of reaction can be expected if they are discovered to be involved in an impropriety. In other words, a lack of corrective and/or disciplinary actions in the past can actually encourage future problems.

The Control System's Ability to Deter or Prevent Fraud

On the other hand, corrective action taken to improve controls so that fraudulent activities in the past were either prevented or detected on a timely basis would be a positive indicator of management's concern and ability to follow through. In the threat analysis, control review and evaluation is the key means for evaluating the likelihood of irregularities.

Inherent Limitations of Control Systems

However, even if no material weaknesses exist in designed controls, there is no such thing as a perfect system. Controls can be overridden or circumvented, given sufficient human ingenuity. Furthermore, fatigue and carelessness can lead to perfunctory, error-prone performance of duties, which can make designed controls ineffectual.

**The Audit
Program**

A fraud audit program should evolve from the preliminary survey in a manner that follows company policy, responds to the highest risk areas, and tests those means which appear to be the most likely mode by which the entity might be defrauded. For example, if collusion is suspected, the number of individuals involved can be a clue to the size of the defalcation and can often lead to deteriorating documentation over time. Awareness of such clues can facilitate more effective audit plans. Telltale signs of trouble include frequent management override of controls, use of copies of documentation in lieu of originals, tendency for a manager to get involved in areas of operations which otherwise would be deemed incompatible, assumption of others' duties, and repeated lateness of reports.

The nature of fraud commonly involves lapping, kiting, or outright theft. *Lapping* means that when receipts are obtained from a customer, they are pocketed until the next customer pays. This customer in turn provides the funds for recording the first customer's payment. In other words, by lapping chronological payments so that each customer's payment is credited to another customer's account which was due earlier, the defrauder can extract funds periodically, as long as no one account becomes delinquent. This type of fraud is often referred to as "robbing Peter to pay Paul."

Kiting means that a transfer is made between two bank accounts, with the deposit recorded but the withdrawal intentionally omitted from the books. It commonly is a device for covering up cash shortages.

If lapping is suspected, the audit program should call for a comparison of the name, the date, and the dollar amount on remittance advices with cash receipts, their related journal entries, and the corresponding deposit slips.

If kiting is suspected, a transfer schedule should be prepared. All bank transfers around year-end would be traced to the accounting and banking records, and a proof of cash bank reconciliation would be used.

Outright theft will center on more liquid assets via creating fictitious payees, converting services like corporate perquisites to personal use, or colluding with other employees or outside parties. To avoid detection of duplications, the defrauders may reuse original documentation, create fictitious journal entries, and misfoot journals and ledgers. By recognizing these tendencies, the auditor can more easily identify control weaknesses that could lead to an increased exposure to frauds.

General Risk Areas

In any operation, there is a set of general types of irregularities which relate to the operating cycles. With respect to the revenue cycle, reported numbers can be overstated by fictitious sales. Similarly, in the cost-of-production cycle, the recognition of total costs might be delayed until some date after the revenue was realized, thereby distorting profitability. The general types of irregularities that may occur are outlined in Exhibit 18-4. The concern of the auditor is how to detect such irregularities, should they be present.

Exhibit 18-4 also demonstrates the actual types of audit steps justified by various risks of irregularities. While these risk areas and audit responses are tailored to a municipality's internal audit setting, the ideas carry across easily to the corporate environment.

Liability Concerns

In gathering evidence, the legal ramifications of fraud audit work must be considered. To facilitate appropriate evaluation of such issues, let's review some relevant legal jargon.

The Legal Issues

The concern facing the internal auditor is that fraud suspects not be treated unjustly. To that end, attention must be given to several legal dimensions of an investigation. The relevant legal jargon is outlined and discussed in Exhibit 18-5. In essence, to avoid legal exposure to suspects, means of soliciting information and reporting findings should adapt to these various legal exposure areas.

As frauds are investigated, inquiry can prove to be a key audit tool. When talking with someone who may be involved in a defalcation, the internal auditor should strive to "hold his cards close to his chest," so to speak. Asking questions to which one already knows the answer is a good start; this method can help reveal the interviewee's truthfulness and attitude toward cooperation. As additional questions are asked, the auditor should be alert to anxious movements or replies that might suggest a problem.

One reason that an interview technique is so valued in a fraud setting is that most fraud discovery comes from an informant's tip. A study performed in the United Kingdom estimated that only 19 percent of frauds were uncovered by auditors, while 51 percent were uncovered by accident. Only 10 percent were uncovered by management controls, and over 20 percent were tips from disgruntled associates or outsiders. Of course, conscience did lead to some confessions.

This type of experience is one reason why some companies are encouraging employees to "blow the whistle" on both fraud and waste. Ironically, legal issues can arise for the whistle-blowers

Exhibit 18-4
Internal Auditing Responses
to Potential Accounting Abuses

POTENTIAL ACCOUNTING RISK AREAS	POTENTIAL AUDIT RESPONSES

Revenue-Related Errors and Irregularities:

1. Gross revenues estimate

    1. Confirm receivables
    2. Vouch any material past charge-offs to reveal prior years' padding of revenue
    3. Vouch subsequent collections
    4. Assess propriety of property included in tax base
    5. Vouch revenue items to source to isolate improper recognition of transfers, loans, etc.

2. Collectibility estimates

    1. Consider effect of economy on taxpayer's ability to pay
    2. Aging receivables
    3. Examine payment histories
    4. Obtain credit information for large taxpayers
    5. Perform reasonableness tests for collectibility based on past performance, considering present environment and future prospects

3. Timing and recognition

    1. Perform cutoff tests (proof of revenue)
    2. Examine subsequent period events
    3. Tests of proper accrual

POTENTIAL ACCOUNTING RISK AREAS	POTENTIAL AUDIT RESPONSES
Expenditure-Related Errors and Irregularities:	
1. Improper application of definitional criteria	1. Search for unrecorded liabilities 2. Evaluate treatment for accounting and disclosure of contingencies 3. Search for improper payment sources: capital fund payment of general fund liabilities, etc.
2. Timing of expenditure and recognition	1. Perform cutoff tests 2. Assess expenditure accruals and deferrals 3. Observe and value material inventories

Source: William W. Holder, "The Role of the Internal Auditor in Responding to Crises in Local Government," *The Internal Auditor,* December 1977, p. 81.

Exhibit 18-5
Relevant Legal Jargon

CAUSE OF ACTION

Libel and slander are two forms of personal injury for defamation of character. A written or printed defamation is libel. A spoken defamation is slander. The elements of both are the same. The three elements that are necessary to give rise to a cause of action are:

1. Defamatory nature. (The words must be injurious to the person's character or reputation or hold him up to ridicule.)
2. Publication. (The utterance or showing of those words to someone other than the injured person by or on behalf of the person accused of being libelous or slanderous.)
3. Actual damages. (The defamatory communication must actually damage the person claiming injury as a proximate result of the defamatory publication.)

Obviously, care must be taken by internal auditors to avoid acts of libel and slander.

DAMAGES

With respect to the element of actual damages, certain words or phrases are considered inherently defamatory and actual damages are conclusively presumed to have occurred without further proof.

Inherently defamatory words, if communicated orally, are called slander, per se; if communicated in writing, they are called libel, per se. For example, saying an employee committed a crime is slander, per se.

The amount of recovery for defamation of character depends upon the facts. Once some actual damages are shown or a libel or slander per se is shown to have occurred, punitive damages are recoverable. Punitive damages are damages which are awarded, as the phrase implies, to punish the wrongdoer. They are awarded to deprive him of more than is necessary to redress the wrong he has done. Malicious or willful and wanton conduct will be grounds for punitive damages. Libel and slander lawsuits, when successfully prosecuted, frequently result in awards of punitive damages. Irresponsible accusations of criminal conduct are undoubtedly vulnerable to punitive damage awards. When punitive damages are awarded in a libel or slander case, they may amount to 50 or 100 times as much as the actual damage caused.

Accusations must not be made without sufficient evidence of wrongdoing; the risk exposure to punitive damage claims can be substantial.

PRIVILEGED COMMUNICATIONS

Even if the truth cannot be proven, an action for slander or libel may not lie against the internal auditor or his employer if the written report or discussions come within the scope of the privileged communications rule.

With respect to libel or slander, privileged communications are, generally speaking, communications that are justified or necessary under the circumstances for the performance of legitimate duties by the person communicating the defamatory words. The prudent internal auditor will not discuss his suspicions of fraud with more employees than are necessary. Common sense would seem to dictate a minimum of communication of these matters for employee morale and corporate publicity purposes, if nothing else. The action of libel or slander will exist, however, if the communication of suspicion or imputation of a crime goes beyond that justified for investigation or notification to management.

Concerns as to causes of action and damages do not preclude communication of suspicions, provided that communication can be defined as privileged.

FALSE IMPRISONMENT

False imprisonment is another costly error that can be committed by an employer or his internal auditor. Specifically, false imprisonment is the confinement, without legal justification, of a person within boundaries fixed by the imprisoner by an act or the breach of a duty with intent to confine.

False imprisonment, sometimes called false arrest, is the restraint of free movement. The term "imprisonment" may originally have meant stone walls and iron bars. It is now no longer necessary to lock the individual up in an impregnable fortress to commit false imprisonment. Locking a store employee in the store was quite sufficient according to a New York court in 1940. It isn't even necessary to lock doors on a building of any kind. All of you are familiar with the classic detective story dialogue with the officer saying to the suspect, "I am not taking you in, but don't try to leave town." In one extreme case, when confinement was to an entire city, false imprisonment was found to exist. This case shows how elastic the term "imprisonment" is legally.

The rule of law is that anyone who participates in an unlawful arrest or procures it or instigates it will be liable for the consequences. Internal auditors must take care not to unlawfully detain a suspect or witness.

COMPOUNDING A FELONY

Under American law, the right to punish or forgive a criminal act is reserved to the state. The employer who has been defrauded has no right to forgive or punish the criminal. In fact, agreeing for a consideration not to prosecute a criminal is itself a crime. This crime is called "compounding a felony" and can result in punishment to the employer or his auditor. The elements of the crime of compounding a felony are:

a. A crime actually committed by one person.
b. Receipt of something of value by another.
c. Under an agreement not to prosecute for such a crime or to limit or handicap such prosecution.

An employer may lawfully accept restoration equal to the loss suffered through employee fraud, but it is illegal for him to bargain for restoration by agreeing the defrauding employee shall not be prosecuted. Internal auditors should not make "deals" in an attempt to gain restitution.

CONFESSIONS

Contrary to popular misconception, confessions are not considered the most trustworthy form of evidence of guilt. Three important types of untrustworthy confession exist:

1. Those given by mistake; e.g., the accused is so confused, so frightened, or so bewildered by the surge of events that he mistakenly acknowledges guilt simply to get away from his tormentors.
2. Those given under hallucination; e.g., the accused is a classical psychotic or is suffering from some other mental defect so that he confesses to most anything that his disturbed mind fancies. In this connection, it might be pointed out that people in this category are genuinely convinced of their guilt and can most often fabricate cogent and detailed stories of their chimerical guilt.
3. Those given under coercion; e.g., the accused is subjected to brutality, prolonged and intensive questioning, starvation, threats, or intimidation of whatever sort in order to extort a confession. This is the type of untrustworthy confession we read about most often.

Confessions are rarely a sufficient basis for supporting accusations. Other evidence should be gathered.

Source: W.D. Courtney, "Employee Fraud Investigation: A Lawyer's View," *The Internal Auditor*, Spring 1965, pp. 13-24.

themselves. This is one reason that tips are often provided anonymously. Internal auditors, in conjunction with the security department, should thoroughly investigate every allegation or rumor of wrongdoing, as deemed appropriate.

A Key Distinction between Fraud Audits and Other Engagements: Objectives

The typical audit can be viewed as a *diagnostic* venture. In such engagements, the internal auditor:

- Looks for signs or symptoms of problems.
- Looks for weaknesses in the system, including its vulnerability to problems.
- Advises how to be more efficient.
- Provides comfort to management.
- Emphasizes compliance with established practices, designed controls, and improvements therein.

In contrast, a fraud audit is a *discovery* venture. The fraud auditor:

- Looks for evidence of specific irregularities.
- Determines the details of the defalcation.
- Quantifies the loss and/or scope of the problem, including timing, mode, and perpetrator.
- Serves as the information-gatherer (i.e., not the prosecutor).

Although system vulnerabilities and efficiency issues receive some attention by the fraud auditor, in a sense the fraud audit goes a step beyond the diagnostic phase and focuses on what has actually happened.

Selection of an Audit Team

It is suggested that seasoned auditors be used on a fraud audit team. There are many reasons for this bias. Perhaps foremost, the audit trail often is nonexistent. Records often are destroyed, inadequate in coverage, misstated, or intentionally altered. Expertise is required to perform the more complicated fraud audit process. In addition, it is likely that members of a fraud audit team will be interviewing many individuals, including those implicated. The auditors must have well-developed skills in discovery and testimonial interviews and in documenting such discussions. The auditors themselves may be required to testify, in which case experience is highly desirable. Similarly, working papers are likely to be introduced as evidence and to be very carefully inspected. Impeccable working papers are more likely to be produced by an experienced professional.

One practical staffing consideration is that fraud audits cannot be forecasted or budgeted in advance, because they are "discovered" and require follow-up quickly. A call from management might ask, "Can you get a heads-up person down here fast?" It tends to be easier to reassign more seasoned people on short notice.

Consideration must also be given to the other people who frequently become a part of fraud investigation teams:

- Staff from the corporate controller's office.
- Staff from the divisional controller's office.
- An attorney from the corporate legal staff.

In all cases, this team should strive to be objective, to avoid accusations, to double-check testimony, to gather copies of incriminating evidence, to emphasize confidentiality, and to act professionally at all times.

Working Paper Documentation

The security of working papers is of acute concern in a fraud setting. Because of the many legal concerns (outlined in Exhibit 18-5), special care should be given to controlling access to working papers. If interviews are held, written transcripts or comments should be included in the working papers with the interviewee's signature of approval. This will prevent claims that the evidence is inadequate or inaccurate and help to ensure the content's security against later cross-examination. All incriminating evidence should be copied into the working papers. Testimonies should be double-checked to provide a sufficient basis for reaching a judgment about the occurrence of fraud.

Because of the sensitive nature of working papers and their litigation potential, retention policies for such working papers need to be set apart from normal retention policies. This procedure helps to ensure that the sufficiency of evidence supporting the audit report can, in fact, be produced.

Drafting an Audit Report

Because of the sensitive nature of fraud audits, access to the audit report should be restricted to a "need to know" basis. The report should carefully distinguish between findings and remaining points to be investigated. As fraud audit reports are drafted, legalities should be considered, as well as the overall quality and sufficiency of the evidence. Corrective action by management is frequently recommended in fraud audit reports.

Pros and Cons of Possible Corrective Actions

The types of corrective action that might be recommended are illustrated in Exhibit 18-6. Some companies have even adopted polygraph tests upon hiring. However, there are legal, ethical, and effectiveness questions about this procedure that merit investigation before adopting it as a standard procedure. Similarly, enforcement actions and publicity decisions have pros and cons. While rumors and erroneous tales can be squelched, individuals can be unnecessarily harmed and legal problems can arise from mass announcements of problems.

The incentive effects of apparent inaction or publicity policies require evaluation in selecting appropriate corrective actions. Similarly, the morale effects of using detective agencies or other hiring screening devices warrant attention.

As management considers corrective action, one thought should be kept in mind: learn to prepare for fraud because fraud itself is one of the most planned of all crimes. It may also be helpful to remember that trust puts one at risk. Fraud can be viewed as misplaced trust — one generally cannot be defrauded by someone he or she doesn't trust.

Feedback

The typical feedback loop to and from auditees differs somewhat in a fraud audit setting. Legal considerations, the sensitive nature of the engagement, and the typical confidential policies regarding such audits all result in limited communication. Hostile feedback would be anticipated and very often would be totally unproductive. Hence, follow-up activities will tend to be conducted by managers who are at least one level above those auditees involved in any defalcation that was discovered.

Professional Standards

The Institute of Internal Auditors has issued a *Statement on Internal Auditing Standards* concerning fraud, which is included in the following appendix.

Exhibit 18-6
Management Actions That Can Minimize
Conflict-of-Interest Problems and Losses

1. Adopt a conflict-of-interest policy addressing:
    a. The acceptance of money, gifts, or services from any person or entity with whom an employee does business.
    b. The use of company information for private purposes.
    c. The use of company time or facilities for private interest.
    d. Participation in management (directly or indirectly) of any private company.
    e. Loaning or borrowing money from other employees.
    f. Publishing articles on trade or company matters.
    g. Ensuring that patents and copyright privileges are clearly spelled out.
    h. Addressing part-time-paid work rights.

Note: All these are usually prohibited without first informing a manager in writing.

2. Require review of such a policy at time of hiring — signature.
3. Require annual review — signature.
4. Authorize job-sensitivity audits; i.e., identify the jobs that offer the most to be gained from conflicting interest before a problem arises.
5. Adopt prudent pre-employment screening procedures.
6. If suspicious, use covert investigations.
7. Seek legal remedies.
8. Purchase fidelity insurance.

Appendix

STATEMENT ON INTERNAL AUDITING STANDARDS NO. 3
Deterrence, Detection, Investigation, and Reporting of Fraud

Foreword

The Institute of Internal Auditors issued the *Standards for the Professional Practice of Internal Auditing* in 1978 "to serve the entire profession in all types of business, in various levels of government, and in all other organizations where internal auditors are found . . . to represent the practice of internal auditing as it should be . . . ."

The IIA's standards have been widely accepted and remain current despite continuous changes in business, society, and the profession of internal auditing. Promoted widely in management texts and used extensively in professional and technical symposia, such increasing acceptance and use demonstrate the credibility of the principles established by the *Standards for the Professional Practice of Internal Auditing*.

Fraud is a significant and sensitive management concern. This concern has grown in recent years owing to a substantial increase in the number and the size of the frauds disclosed. The tremendous expansion in the use of computers and the size of and publicity accorded computer-related frauds intensify this concern.

The internal auditor's responsibilities for deterring, detecting, investigating, and reporting of fraud have been a matter of much debate and controversy. Some of the controversy can be attributed to the differences in internal auditing's charter from country to country and from organization to organization. Another cause of the controversy may be unrealistic expectations of the internal auditor's ability to deter and detect fraud.

While several standards and guidelines directly or indirectly address the issue of internal auditors' responsibilities in cases of fraud, the following directly address these responsibilities:

Standard 280 — Due Professional Care
Internal auditors should exercise due professional care in performing internal audits.

280.01   In exercising due professional care, internal auditors should be alert to the possibility of wrongdoing, errors and omissions, inefficiency, waste, ineffectiveness, and conflicts of interest. They should also be alert to those conditions and activities where irregularities are most likely to occur.

280.02   The possibility of material irregularities or noncompliance should be considered whenever the internal auditor undertakes an internal auditing assignment.

280.03   When an internal auditor suspects wrongdoing, the appropriate authorities within the organization should be informed. The internal auditor may recommend whatever investigation is considered necessary in the circumstances. Thereafter, the auditor should follow up to see that the internal auditing department's responsibilities have been met.

Standard 300 — Scope of Work

The scope of the internal audit should encompass the examination and the evaluation of the adequacy and the effectiveness of the organization's system of internal control and the quality of performance in carrying out assigned responsibilities.

330.01   Internal auditors should review the means used to safeguard assets from various types of losses such as those resulting from theft, fire, improper or illegal activities, and exposure to the elements.

Summary

This statement interprets the *Standards* and establishes guidelines for internal auditors regarding their responsibility for deterring, detecting, investigating, and reporting of fraud. It does not provide guidance on specific audit procedures used in performing audits; rather, it establishes guidelines by which internal auditors conform their activities with the stated concepts of due professional care.

Major conclusions of this statement are:

DETERRENCE OF FRAUD

Deterrence of fraud is the responsibility of management. Internal auditors are responsible for examining and evaluating the adequacy and the effectiveness of actions taken by management to fulfill this obligation.

DETECTION OF FRAUD

Internal auditors should have sufficient knowledge of fraud to be able to identify indicators that fraud might have been committed.

If significant control weaknesses are detected, additional tests conducted by internal auditors should include tests directed toward identification of other indicators of fraud.

Internal auditors are not expected to have knowledge equivalent to that of a person whose primary responsibility is to detect and investigate fraud. Also, audit procedures alone, even when carried out with due professional care, do not guarantee that fraud will be detected.

INVESTIGATION OF FRAUD

Fraud investigations may be conducted by or involve participation of internal auditors, lawyers, investigators, security personnel, and other specialists from inside or outside the organization.

Internal auditing should assess the facts known relative to all fraud investigations in order to:

- Determine if controls need to be implemented or strengthened.
- Design audit tests to help disclose the existence of similar frauds in the future.
- Help meet the internal auditor's responsibility to maintain sufficient knowledge of fraud.

REPORTING OF FRAUD

A written report should be issued at the conclusion of the investigation phase. It should include all findings, conclusions, recommendations, and corrective action taken.

Characteristics of Fraud

.1 Fraud encompasses an array of irregularities and illegal acts characterized by intentional deception. It can be perpetrated for the benefit of or to the detriment of the organization and by persons outside as well as inside the organization.

.2 Fraud designed to benefit the organization generally produces such benefit by exploiting an unfair or dishonest advantage that also may deceive an outside party. Perpetrators of such frauds usually benefit indirectly, since personal benefit usually accrues when the organization is aided by the act. Some examples are:

   a. Sale or assignment of fictitious or misrepresented assets.
   b. Improper payments such as illegal political contributions, bribes, kickbacks, and payoffs to government officials, intermediaries of government officials, customers, or suppliers.
   c. Intentional, improper representation or valuation of transactions, assets, liabilities, or income.
   d. Intentional, improper transfer pricing (e.g., valuation of goods exchanged between related entities). By purposely structuring pricing techniques improperly, management can improve the operating results of an organization involved in the transaction to the detriment of the other organization.
   e. Intentional, improper related-party transactions in which one party receives some benefit not obtainable in an arm's-length transaction.
   f. Intentional failure to record or disclose significant information to improve the financial picture of the organization to outside parties.
   g. Prohibited business activities such as those which violate government statutes, rules, regulations, or contracts.
   h. Tax fraud.

.3 Fraud perpetrated to the detriment of the organization generally is for the direct or indirect benefit of an employee, outside individual, or another firm. Some examples are:

   a. Acceptance of bribes or kickbacks.
   b. Diversion to an employee or outsider of a potentially profitable transaction that would normally generate profits for the organization.

Note: As used in this statement, the term "management" includes anyone in an organization with responsibilities for setting and/or achieving objectives.

   c. Embezzlement, as typified by the misappropriation of money or property, and falsification of financial records to cover up the act, thus making detection difficult.

   d. Intentional concealment or misrepresentation of events or data.

   e. Claims submitted for services or goods not actually provided to the organization.

Deterrence of Fraud

.4 Deterrence consists of those actions taken to discourage the perpetration of fraud and limit the exposure if fraud does occur. The principal mechanism for deterring fraud is control. Primary responsibility for establishing and maintaining control rests with management (see *SIAS No. 1,* Control: Concepts and Responsibilities).

Internal Auditing's Responsibilities

.5 Internal auditing is responsible for assisting in the deterrence of fraud by examining and evaluating the adequacy and the effectiveness of control, commensurate with the extent of the potential exposure/risk in the various segments of the entity's operations. In carrying out this responsibility, internal auditing should, for example, determine whether:

   a. The organizational environment fosters control consciousness.

   b. Realistic organizational goals and objectives are set.

   c. Written corporate policies (e.g., code of conduct) exist that describe prohibited activities and the action required whenever violations are discovered.

   d. Appropriate authorization policies for transactions are established and maintained.

   e. Policies, practices, procedures, reports, and other mechanisms are developed to monitor activities and safeguard assets, particularly in high-risk areas.

   f. Communication channels provide management with adequate and reliable information.

   g. Recommendations need to be made for the establishment or enhancement of cost-effective controls to help deter fraud.

Detection of Fraud

.6 Detection consists of identifying indicators of fraud sufficient to warrant recommending an investigation. These indicators may arise as a result of controls established by management, tests conducted by auditors, and other sources both within and outside the organization.

Internal Auditing's Responsibilities

.7 In conducting audit assignments, the internal auditor's responsibilities for detecting fraud are to:

   a. Have sufficient knowledge of fraud to be able to identify indicators that fraud might have been committed. This knowledge includes the need to know the characteristics of fraud, the techniques used to commit fraud, and the types of frauds associated with the activities audited.

b. Be alert to opportunities, such as control weaknesses, that could allow fraud. If significant control weaknesses are detected, additional tests conducted by internal auditors should include tests directed toward identification of other indicators of fraud. Some examples of indicators are unauthorized transactions, override of controls, unexplained pricing exceptions, and unusually large product losses. Internal auditors should recognize that the presence of more than one indicator at any one time increases the probability that fraud might have occurred.

c. Evaluate the indicators that fraud might have been committed and decide whether any further action is necessary or whether an investigation should be recommended.

d. Notify the appropriate authorities within the organization if a determination is made that there are sufficient indicators of the commission of a fraud to recommend an investigation.

.8 Internal auditors are not expected to have knowledge equivalent to that of a person whose primary responsibility is detecting and investigating fraud. Also, audit procedures alone, even when carried out with due professional care, do not guarantee that fraud will be detected.

Investigation of Fraud

.9 Investigation consists of performing extended procedures necessary to determine whether fraud, as suggested by the indicators, has occurred. It includes gathering sufficient evidential matter about the specific details of a discovered fraud. Internal auditors, lawyers, investigators, security personnel, and other specialists from inside or outside the organization are the parties that usually conduct or participate in fraud investigations.

Internal Auditing's Responsibilities

.10 When conducting fraud investigations, internal auditing should:

a. Assess the probable level and the extent of complicity in the fraud within the organization. This can be critical to ensuring that the internal auditor avoids providing information to or obtaining misleading information from persons who may be involved.

b. Determine the knowledge, skills, and disciplines needed to effectively carry out the investigation. Assess the qualifications and the skills of the internal auditors and of the specialists available to participate in the investigation to ensure that it is conducted by individuals having the appropriate type and level of technical expertise. This should include assurances on such matters as professional certifications, licenses, reputation, and that there is no relationship to those being investigated or to any of the employees or management of the organization.

c. Design procedures to follow in attempting to identify the perpetrators, extent of the fraud, techniques used, and cause of the fraud.

d. Coordinate activities with management personnel, legal counsel, and other specialists as appropriate throughout the course of the investigation.

e. Be cognizant of the rights of alleged perpetrators and personnel within the scope of the investigation and the reputation of the organization itself.

.11 Once a fraud investigation is concluded, internal audit should assess the facts known in order to:

a. Determine if controls need to be implemented or strengthened to reduce future vulnerability.

b. Design audit tests to help disclose the existence of similar frauds in the future.

c. Help meet the internal auditor's responsibility to maintain sufficient knowledge of fraud and thereby be able to identify future indicators of fraud.

Reporting of Fraud

.12 Reporting consists of the various oral or written, interim or final communications to management regarding the status and results of fraud investigations.

Internal Auditing's Responsibilities

.13 A preliminary or final report may be desirable at the conclusion of the detection phase. The report should include the internal auditor's conclusion as to whether sufficient information exists to conduct an investigation. It should also summarize findings that serve as the basis for such a decision.

.14 *SIAS No. 2,* Communicating Results, which expands on Specific Standard 430 and provides interpretations, is applicable to internal audit reports issued as a result of fraud investigations. Additional interpretive guidelines on reporting of fraud are as follows:

a. When the incidence of significant fraud has been established to a reasonable certainty, management or the board should be notified immediately.

b. The results of a fraud investigation may indicate that fraud has had a previously undiscovered materially adverse effect on the financial position and results of operations of an organization for one or more years on which financial statements have already been issued. Internal audit should inform appropriate management and the audit committee of the board of directors of such a discovery.

c. A written report should be issued at the conclusion of the investigation phase. It should include all findings, conclusions, recommendations, and corrective action taken.

d. A draft of the proposed report on fraud should be submitted to legal counsel for review. In those cases in which the auditor wants to invoke client privilege, consideration should be given to addressing the report to legal counsel.

QUESTIONS

1. Why does management expect internal auditors to be more effective at detecting fraud than external auditors?
2. How would you describe the materiality of fraud?
3. Why would an entity have both a security department and an internal audit department? Most likely, what would be their respective roles in dealing with frauds?
4. What are "red flags"? Give six examples.
5. What is meant by creating errors? Critique the advantages and disadvantages of such an audit approach.
6. What is threat analysis?
7. Define lapping and kiting.
8. Outline the key legal problems facing internal auditors as they approach a fraud audit.
9. How do the objectives of fraud audits differ from typical audit engagements?
10. What criteria would you utilize in selecting a fraud audit team, and why?
11. Why is care in working paper preparation and control particularly important in a fraud auditing situation?
12. What recommendations would you offer to management in addressing circumstances which have made frauds possible in past years? Explain the rationale for your recommendations.

EXERCISES

E-1

The "red flag" literature has been criticized for its generality. It is difficult to make general measures of problems operational. For example, a lack of management integrity has been cited as a "red flag," yet how does one assess such a factor?

Required:

Prepare a response to such criticisms by identifying how you would operationalize the red flags introduced in this chapter.

E-2

Related parties are generally cited as indicators of a higher risk of fraud existing for an auditee. The idea is that arm's-length transactions in and of themselves exercise control over the propriety of transactions, whereas a related-party transaction is much more vulnerable to manipulation, because of the joint interest of those who are negotiating the exchange.

Required:

How would you proceed to identify related parties, as well as related-party transactions?

E-3

You are auditing petty cash and discover that a friend of yours, who is in charge of the petty cash funds, has forged some petty cash vouchers amounting to $100 over the last five months. He "explains" that he was just short of cash a few times and did not think that the small amount withdrawn would be a problem, since he intended to repay it by year-end. He pleads with you not to report him, assuring you that he will stop the practice and reimburse the fund on the very next payday.

Required:

How should you proceed? Explain the rationale for your response.

E-4

While testing a bank reconciliation, you observe that part of the payee line on certain checks has been "whited out" (i.e., erased or covered up), as has the endorsement on the back of cancelled checks. It appears that the payee line had indicated the supplier's name or some other name, now removed from the checks. When you ask the check-preparer about the "white-out," he immediately confesses to having embezzled some funds and asks you not to report him. You tell him that you have to report him, and he immediately yells, "I'll deny any accusation."

Required:

What can you do with the preparer's initial confession in either an evidential or a legal sense? How would you proceed?

E-5

Multiple Choice: Select a single answer which best completes the statement or answers the question.

1. When an auditor suspects wrongdoing and informs the appropriate authorities in the organization, the next action the auditor should take is to:
   a. Make a separate report to the audit committee.
   b. Obtain a signed statement from management acknowledging their acceptance of responsibility.
   c. Report the matter to appropriate governmental authorities.
   d. Follow up to see that appropriate action is taken.

2. Fraudulent use of corporate credit cards would be minimized by which of the following internal control procedures?
   a. Establishing a corporate policy on the issuance of credit cards to authorized employees.
   b. Reviewing the validity of credit card need at executive and operating levels on a periodic basis.
   c. Reconciling the monthly statement from the credit card company with the submitted copies of the cardholders' charge slips.
   d. Subjecting credit card charges to the same expense controls as those used on regular company expense forms.

3. A procedure for an internal auditor to ascertain whether retail inventory thefts are occurring is to:
   a. Review the year-end cutoff of purchases and sales transactions.
   b. Observe the taking of physical inventory and make test counts.

   c.   Test the pricing of merchandise inventory.

   d.   Investigate significant differences between physical inventory results and retail inventory estimates.

4.   An internal auditor would be more likely to detect duplicate vendor payments in a high-exposure environment with certain internal control weaknesses by using which of the following audit tools?

   a.   Trend analysis.

   b.   Dollar validity.

   c.   Proportional analysis.

   d.   Substantive testing.

5.   After reviewing audit work which indicated possible fraudulent activity, the internal auditor-in-charge should:

   a.   Continue the investigation alone until sufficient evidence has been gathered to present the findings to senior management.

   b.   Discuss the findings privately with the auditee management to determine if the facts have been correctly interpreted.

   c.   Corroborate the validity and completeness of the audit findings and present the information to the audit manager.

   d.   Organize a fraud investigative unit after receiving clearance from corporate counsel.

6.   An internal auditor is testing purchase orders to detect possible instances of fraudulent activity by an employee. Believing the occurrence rate of the fraudulent purchase orders to be quite low, the internal auditor would like to specify the probability of observing at least one irregularity if its true rate of occurrence is greater than expected. The most appropriate sampling technique for this situation is:

   a.   Stop-or-go sampling.

   b.   Cluster sampling.

   c.   Dollar-unit sampling.

   d.   Discovery sampling.   (CIA Exam Adapted)

E-6

Multiple Choice: Select a single answer which best completes the statement or answers the question.

1.   The internal auditor would consider embezzlement a likely possibility when:

   a.   Employees in the finance department are working overtime regularly.

   b.   Production reports are found to contain inaccurate descriptions of work completed.

   c.   Vacations are not taken by employees in the accounting and cashiering functions.

   d.   Allowances for doubtful accounts are found to be inadequate.

2.   To strengthen internal control, you have recommended that quantities be omitted from the copy of the purchase order going to the receiving department. Your recommendation is primarily intended to:

   a. Ensure that the receiving department clerks make physical counts.
   b. Improve the reliability of the perpetual inventory records.
   c. Discourage theft in those cases when a supplier ships more than the quantity ordered.
   d. Make the receiving department more effective.
   e. Ensure the quality of the material received.

3. When an internal auditor suspects wrongdoing, the *Standards for the Professional Practice of Internal Auditing* explicitly requires the auditor to:
   a. Interrogate the suspected employees.
   b. Notify the appropriate law-enforcement agency.
   c. Perform an investigation of the activity involved.
   d. Inform the appropriate authorities within the organization.
   e. Evaluate the internal controls that should have prevented the wrongdoing.

4. A procedure for an internal auditor to ascertain whether retail inventory thefts are occurring is to:
   a. Review the year-end cutoff of purchases and sales transactions.
   b. Observe the taking of physical inventory and make test counts.
   c. Test the pricing of merchandise inventory.
   d. Investigate significant differences between physical inventory results and retain inventory estimates.
   e. Inquire of knowledgeable personnel.

5. Of the procedures listed, which is the most likely to detect kiting?
   a. Compare the detail of cash receipts (log listings) to the cash receipts journal, accounts receivable postings, and deposit slips.
   b. Investigate checks that have been outstanding for long periods.
   c. Account for bank transfers made during a few days before and after selected dates.
   d. Confirm accounts receivable balances as of a cutoff date.
   e. Count cash on hand.   (CIA Exam Adapted)

E-7
   A study of past computer frauds indicates that some of the most common means of manipulating transactions are to:
1. Add unauthorized transactions such as phony purchase orders.
2. Alter transactions (for example, by posting debits to another account).
3. Not process transactions (for example, interest income).

Required:
   What audit procedures are likely to uncover each of these manipulations?

Adapted from: Brandt Allen, "The Biggest Computer Frauds: Lessons for CPAs," *Journal of Accountancy*, May 1977, pp. 52-62.

E-8

A company transfers products for intracompany and intercompany sales at prices above costs. Its internal auditors are concerned that recorded gross profit is not the net of unrealized profits for financial statements.

Required:

What audit approach can address this concern?

E-9

Untimely cutoffs of sales or cash recipts can occur due to delays in shipping, mishandling of consigned goods shipped as sales, retroactive posting of cash received after the year-end, or "holding open" the cash book.

Required:

How can such cutoff misstatements be deleted?

E-10

Due to particularly poor operating performance, managers have increased incentives to present financial statements in a more favorable light than is appropriate. As an internal auditor, you believe that there is increased likelihood of unrecorded liabilities.

Required:

How can you search for such unrecorded liabilities?

E-11

A secretary to the vice president of personnel regularly processes travel and entertainment expenses twice for the various managers for whom she works. She has discovered that by allowing a two-week lapse of time, reports are not compared with each other by the cash disbursements department. Since the secretary receives the checks for reimbursement, there is no problem extracting the second check when it arrives. She has perpetrated this fraud during the past six months.

Required:

As the internal auditor, how could you:

a. Detect the fraud?
b. Recommend controls to deter such a defalcation in the future?

PROBLEMS

P-1

An internal auditor with more than 20 years of experience was asked to comment on the most important points an auditor should keep in mind when performing an audit expected to detect fraud. He commented that internal auditors had to "leave the office" and investigate in order to be effective. He then offered an example of a purchasing agent who set up his own dummy company, bought letterhead and invoices, and proceeded to "purchase" goods and services from this authorized vendor. This defalcation was discovered by going to the address of the vendor and discovering a "store-front operation" which merely picked up its mail. Further inquiry connected the purchasing agent to this operation and the magnitude of the fraud began to unfold.

"No amount of detailed testing of invoices or internal documentation would have uncovered this fraud, which was obvious with just a little bit of leg work," commented the internal auditor.

Required:

Explain how the advice provided would help an internal auditor discover the following types of fraud:

a. Fictitious employees receiving payroll checks.
b. Sweetheart deals with certain contractors.
c. Receipts being embezzled and covered up by writing off "bad debts."
d. Theft of inventory received as "overshipments," avoiding accountability by merely reporting that goods ordered were received.
e. Falsifying inventories to cover thefts by stacking empty boxes.

P-2

Put yourself in the shoes of a new controller of a company who discovers that the inventory on the books is overstated by a material amount. While you want the inventory balance to be correctly stated, you do not want that magnitude of an adjustment across several years. You decide that your optimal strategy would be to charge a small proportion of the overstatement against income, and thus prevent discovery of the misstatement. The alternative would seem to be bleak, particularly since this is your first year as controller.

Required:

a. As controller, how would you proceed to implement your "strategy"?
b. What problems do you anticipate in implementing your "strategy"?
c. Now put yourself in the shoes of an internal auditor. How could you uncover the misstated books and the attempted coverup?

P-3

An internal auditor has drafted the following report on a recently completed fraud investigation and has submitted it to you, the internal audit director, for review:

Report

The internal audit department, upon analysis of cost components, suspected that excessive amounts were being expended for materials. Upon investigation, we discovered that low competitive bids were being discarded to ensure the use of a single supplier who made kickbacks to purchasing agents. Mr. Jopnes, the manager of the purchasing agent, has confessed the collusive activities and has indicated the involvement of Mr. Thomas, Mr. Lee, and Ms. Cox.

We recommend that these employees be fired and that legal action be taken so that future defalcations can be effectively deterred.

The internal audit evidence collected by directly soliciting competitive bids proves that the purchasing agents are guilty.

Distribution: Normal recipients of such reports.

Required:
Summarize your review points.

P-4

As internal auditor for a retailer, you notice a large increase in the inventory shrinkage account. You decide to have a new staff member go "undercover" as a retail clerk to see if he can uncover the nature of the shrinkage problem. It is expected to be an internal pilferage problem, involving employees, but the means by which the assets are being extracted cannot be pinpointed.

The "undercover" work pays off. The new staff member posing as a retail clerk is approached by a fellow employee and told that he can "order" any piece of merchandise at about 20 percent of cost. The merchandise would be made a part of a window display, after which it would be delivered to the employee's address. The payment had to be in advance, since it covered handling costs and, of course, a profit to the window display employees who had discovered the "hole" in controls which facilitated the fraud. No monitoring device was present over inventory after it had been checked out for a window display.

Required:
a.   What do you think of such an "undercover" approach to fraud detection?
b.   What recommendations would you make as to future control procedures?
c.   Assume that you discover that this fraud has been perpetrated for two years and that 30 percent of retail clerks were involved in "buying" merchandise from display windows. Management asks for your input as to how the employees should be disciplined. What would you recommend?
d.   Assume that top management chooses to merely establish new controls and "let bygones be bygones." What implications would such a choice have for the internal auditor?

APPENDICES

Appendix I
Internal Control Systems

Chapter 3 discusses the principles of internal control, and other chapters in the text discuss individual applications of those principles. In addition to this information, many internal auditing students desire a reference for internal controls related to specific systems or operations. This appendix contains lists of common internal controls for marketing and sales, accounts and notes receivable, purchasing and receiving, inventory management, personnel and payroll, production and cost accounting, and fixed assets. Cash controls are discussed and illustrated in Chapter 16, and EDP controls are discussed in Chapter 17.

In addition to specific internal controls, this appendix outlines typical sources of audit evidence related to each control.

Sources of internal control information contained in these lists include James A. Cashin, *Handbook for Auditors,* McGraw-Hill Book Co., 1971; Victor Z. Brink and Herbert Witt, *Modern Internal Auditing,* John Wiley & Sons, 1982; and Jack C. Robertson and Frederick G. Davis, *Auditing,* 3rd Edition, Business Publications, Inc., 1982.

Marketing and Sales*

Internal Controls

1. Marketing objectives and overall strategy are documented and consistent with organizational objectives. Marketing objectives and strategy are approved by the board of directors.

Sources of Audit Evidence

a. Documentation of marketing objectives and strategy.

b. Organizational objectives.

c. Minutes of board of directors' meeting approving marketing objectives and overall strategy.

d. Interviews with marketing and executive management.

---

*Internal controls for cash collections from sales are illustrated in Chapter 16.

Internal Controls

2. The following activities are segregated as shown:

a. Receipt of customer orders and preparation of inventory requisitions or production orders. *Responsibility:* Sales department.

b. Customer credit approval and collection activities. *Responsibility:* Credit and collections department, as a function of the overall financial responsibility.

c. Preparation of shipping documents and shipment of goods. *Responsibility:* Billing department, as a function of the overall financial responsibility.

d. Maintenance of accounts receivable records. *Responsibility:* Accounts receivable section, as a function of the overall financial responsibility. May be combined with credit and collection function; however, record keeping should be separate from cash handling.

e. Write-offs of uncollectible accounts and authorization of returns and allowances. *Responsibility:* Accounts receivable section, after approval by manager who is not responsible for any of the above functions.

f. Receipt, deposit, and initial listing of customer payments. *Responsibility:* Cashier, as a function of the overall financial responsibility. (Preferably, at least two individuals open the mail and prepare the initial listing of receipts.)

Sources of Audit Evidence

a. Organization chart, for separation of functions.

b. Job descriptions.

c. Documentation of each activity.

Internal Controls	*Sources of Audit Evidence*

Internal Controls

3. Marketing and sales policies and procedures are written and approved by an appropriate level of executive management.

4. The marketing/sales department projects sales, which are budgeted and help guide the coordination of production and inventory management.

5. Actual sales are regularly reported to management in comparison with budgeted sales. These reports are meaningfully categorized in enough detail for management's use.

6. Printed price lists are provided for marketing, sales, and accounting personnel.

7. Changes in established prices receive proper management approval and documentation.

8. Price adjustments beyond approved, established price ranges are approved in writing by management.

9. The credit and collections department authorizes all customer orders for processing.

10. All shipments of goods are cleared through the shipping department.

Sources of Audit Evidence

a. Marketing and sales policies and procedures.

b. Approval signatures for the policies and procedures.

a. Marketing/sales policies and procedures.

b. Organization budget policies and procedures.

c. Organization budgets.

d. Interviews with marketing, executive management, and the controller or chief budget officer.

a. Accounting policies and procedures.

b. Management financial reports, including budget-to-actual comparisons.

c. Interviews with marketing and executive management.

a. Printed price.

b. Price list locations.

a. Pricing policies and procedures.

b. Documentation of price changes.

c. Approval signatures for price changes.

a. Pricing policies and procedures.

b. Documentation of individual price adjustments.

c. Signatures approving price adjustments.

a. Sales policies and procedures.

b. Approval signatures/initials on customer orders or other appropriate documents.

a. Sales and shipping policies and procedures.

Internal Controls

Sources of Audit Evidence

b. Documentation of individual sales (approved customer orders and sales invoices) and shipping documents (logs and individual shipping orders).

11. All shipments are authorized by a shipping supervisor after reviewing supporting documentation.

a. Shipping policies and procedures.

b. Documentation for individual shipments, especially sales invoices.

c. Approval signatures/initials for individual shipments.

12. Shipping orders are pre-numbered, controlled, and periodically reconciled.

a. Used and unused shipping orders.

b. Policies and procedures for shipping orders.

c. Reconciliations of prenumbered shipping orders.

d. Storage facilities for shipping orders.

13. Sales invoices are prenumbered, secured, and periodically reconciled.

a. Billing policies and procedures.

b. Used and unused sales invoices.

c. Reconciliations of prenumbered sales invoices.

d. Storage facilities for sales invoices.

14. The details of completed invoices are checked prior to issuance, including products, salesman, prices, extensions, totals, and postings. The reviewer initials and dates the approved invoice.

a. Billing policies and procedures.

b. Approved invoices.

c. Approval initials.

15. Receiving reports are prepared in the receiving department for returned goods.

a. Policies and procedures for receiving department and for sales returns.

b. Journal vouchers or credit memoranda for returned goods compared with relevant receiving reports.

16. Sales of products other than those regularly sold are approved by management and all relevant information is documented. Examples include used office furniture, automobiles, computers, or other equipment.

a. Sales policies and procedures.

b. Documentation of such sales.

c. Journal entries for such sales.

d. Inventory listings of assets showing disposals and changes from previous listings.

Internal Controls

17. Sales quantities from accounting records are reconciled periodically with inventory records.

18. Shipping carriers are selected by formal bidding procedures and contracts are negotiated. (Where an intra-organizational transportation function is employed, controls are established similarly to other functions.)

19. Scrap sales are recorded.

20. A customer service department is established in the marketing/sales function.

21. Product planning and development activities are coordinated with sales, market and product research, advertising, finance, and production functions.

22. Contracted advertising and promotion services are periodically reviewed for (a) adequacy of contracts, (b) propriety of billings from the advertising and promotion agencies to the organization, and (c) adequacy of liaison activities with the agencies.

23. Marketing and sales personnel are provided adequate orientation, training, and professional development.

Sources of Audit Evidence

a. Accounting policies and procedures.

b. Accounting sales records.

c. Inventory records.

a. Shipping policies and procedures.

b. Formal bids submitted by competing carriers.

c. Contracts with carriers.

d. Shipping and accounting documents for comparison to contracts' provisions.

a. Sales policies and procedures.

b. Scrap inventory records.

c. Scrap sales receipts and invoices.

a. Organization chart and job descriptions.

b. Interviews with customer service and other sales management.

a. Product planning and development policies and procedures.

b. Product development and market introduction records.

c. Interviews with product, sales, research, advertising, finance, and production managers.

a. Marketing policies and procedures.

b. Contracts with agencies.

c. Billings from agencies.

d. Interviews with marketing management and advertising agency officials.

a. Marketing department policies and procedures.

b. Orientation, training, and professional development facilities, materials, and instructors.

Internal Controls	Sources of Audit Evidence
	c. Interviews with sales supervisors, marketing and sales management, trainers, and marketing and sales employees.
	d. Regional and product sales records.

Accounts and Notes Receivable

Internal Controls	Sources of Audit Evidence
1. Cashier and subsidiary receivables ledger responsibilities are functionally separated.	Organization chart.
2. Cashier does not have access to accounts and notes receivable records.	a. Policies and procedures for accounts and notes receivable.
	b. Interviews with subsidiary ledger accountants and accounting management.
3. Customer accounts in subsidiary ledger are reconciled regularly (preferably monthly) with general ledger control account.	a. Accounting policies and procedures.
	b. Reconciliations.
4. Customer statements are mailed monthly by personnel independent of accounts receivable bookkeepers and billing clerks.	a. Billing policies and procedures.
	b. Customer accounts.
	c. Copies of monthly bills and billing register.
	d. Job descriptions and organization chart.
5. Mailing of monthly statements is controlled by the accounts receivable department.	a. Billing policies and procedures.
	b. Observation of monthly mailing.
	c. Interviews with accounting management and accounts receivable personnel.
6. Differences in statements and customer claims are handled and documented by the credit and collections department.	a. Billing policies and procedures.
	b. Job descriptions and organization chart.
	c. Documentation of customer claims and disposition of individual items.

Internal Controls

7. Accounts receivable are periodically aged by the credit and collections department. Delinquent accounts are listed for and reviewed by management.

8. Accounts that have been written off are kept in a memorandum ledger or credit report file for reference.

9. Credit memoranda are prenumbered, secured, and periodically reconciled.

10. Noncash credits, exceptions to discount policies, and credits for returned merchandise are approved by management and documented.

11. Returned goods are properly recorded in the receiving department and accounted for.

12. Accounts and notes receivable are confirmed periodically, and the confirmations are sent by the accounting department and received by an independent party such as the internal auditing department or the external auditors.

Sources of Audit Evidence

7.
a. Accounting policies and procedures.
b. Aging documents.
c. Lists of delinquent accounts.
d. Documents recording disposition of delinquent accounts.
e. Approvals of decisions with respect to delinquent accounts.

8.
a. Accounting policies and procedures.
b. Subsidiary ledger for customer accounts.
c. Memo ledger or credit report file.

9.
a. Accounting policies and procedures.
b. Credit memoranda.
c. Storage facilities.
d. Reconciliations.

10.
a. Sales and accounting policies and procedures.
b. Documentation of such transactions.
c. Approval signatures/initials.

11.
a. Receiving policies and procedures.
b. Accounting policies and procedures.
c. Receiving reports for returned goods.
d. Journal vouchers and entries for returned goods.
e. Customer accounts in the accounts receivable subsidiary ledger.

12.
a. Accounting policies and procedures.
b. Confirmations.
c. Subsidiary ledger of accounts and notes receivable.

Internal Controls

13. All notes are documented, authorized in writing by responsible officers of the organization, and signed by borrowers.

14. Large loans or advances to employees or related parties are documented, signed by the borrower, and approved in writing by the board of directors.

15. Someone other than the cashier or accounts receivable bookkeeper is responsible for notes receivable.

16. Negotiable collateral on notes is under the custody of someone other than those handling cash or keeping records.

Sources of Audit Evidence

a. Financial policies and procedures.

b. Copies of the notes.

c. Signatures of borrowers and organizational officials approving notes.

a. Financial policies and procedures.

b. Loan contracts.

c. Approval signatures by the borrowers and directors.

a. Organization chart and job descriptions.

b. Location and storage of notes receivable.

a. Organization chart, job descriptions, financial policies and procedures.

b. Titles and other documentation of collateral.

c. Observation and inspection of receipt, recording, storage, and disposition of collateral merchandise.

d. Accounting records of receipt, recording, storage, and disposition of collateral.

Purchasing and Receiving Systems

Internal Controls

1. The purchasing department is separate from the treasury, accounting, and receiving and shipping departments.

2. Competitive bids are requested from approved vendors for the purchase of large-ticket items.

Sources of Audit Evidence

Organization chart.

a. Policies and procedures requiring competitive bids.

b. Approved vendor lists.

c. Filed copies of competitive bids submitted by vendors.

Internal Controls	*Sources of Audit Evidence*
3. Approved purchase requisitions from requesting departments are required for all purchases.	a. Policy requiring use of purchase requisitions and prescribed procedures for processing them. b. Filed purchase requisitions supporting specific purchases. c. Approval signatures on purchase requisitions.
4. All purchases are made by a purchasing department.	Organization chart.
5. Purchase prices are reviewed and approved by a purchasing officer.	Purchase officer's approval signature on filed copies of purchase orders.
6. Approved purchase orders (or contracts, where applicable) are required for all purchases.	a. Filed purchase orders. b. Documentation of cash disbursement for purchases for which no purchase order was prepared. c. Approval signatures on purchase orders.
7. Purchase order forms are prenumbered and are properly secured for authorized access only.	a. Blank purchase order forms. b. Storage equipment for purchase orders. c. Procedures for processing purchase orders.
8. Purchased goods are received by a receiving department separate from the purchasing, accounting, or treasury departments.	Organization chart.
9. Goods are inspected in the receiving department for quantity and quality at the time of receipt. Receiving information is documented at that time.	a. Procedures for processing goods received. b. Receiving documents.
10. Receiving documents are prenumbered and secured against unauthorized access.	a. Blank, unused receiving forms. b. Completed, filed receiving documents. c. Storage facilities for receiving documents.

Internal Controls

11. Copies of receiving reports are sent to inventory, purchasing, and accounting departments.

12. Partial deliveries on purchase orders are properly recorded and subsequently monitored.

13. Goods rejected by the receiving department are documented and transferred to the shipping department for return to vendors. Returned goods are processed and documented in the shipping department, and copies of the rejection and shipping documents are sent to accounts payable.

14. Vendors' invoices recorded immediately upon receipt and matched by the purchasing department against purchase orders and receiving reports.

15. Quantities, prices, and terms on vendors' invoices are matched in the accounting department against purchase orders and receiving reports.

16. The accounts payable subsidiary ledger (or the voucher register) is balanced regularly with accounts payable in the general ledger control account.

Sources of Audit Evidence

a. Policies and procedures governing receipt of goods and services.

b. Filed copies of receiving reports in each location.

a. Policies and procedures for recording goods received.

b. Records documenting partial deliveries.

c. Unfilled purchase orders.

a. Documents prepared for returned goods.

b. Journal entries for returned goods.

c. Procedures required for handling rejected goods.

a. Paid and unpaid vendors' invoices.

b. Documentation of invoices received.

c. Purchase orders.

d. Receiving reports.

e. Policies and procedures for processing vendors' invoices.

a. Policies and procedures for processing vendors' invoices.

b. Vendors' invoices.

c. Signatures/initials of accounting personnel performing the tests.

d. Purchase orders.

e. Receiving reports.

a. Policies and procedures manual specifying what accounting reconciliation procedures are required.

b. Worksheets prepared by accounting employees at the time of reconciliation and then filed.

Internal Controls	*Sources of Audit Evidence*
17. Vendors' invoices are matched against accounts payable or unpaid vouchers.	a. Paid and unpaid vendors' invoices.
	b. Accounts payable or vouchers unpaid at the time the invoices were received.
	c. Policies and procedures for processing vendors' invoices.
18. Unmatched invoices are checked frequently with the receiving department to monitor arrival of goods.	a. Unmatched invoices.
	b. Purchase orders.
	c. Receiving documents.
	d. Procedures for controlling receipt and payment of goods.
19. Unmatched receiving reports are reviewed frequently for investigation.	a. Policies and procedures for unmatched receiving reports.
	b. Unmatched receiving reports.
20. Distribution of invoice charges to general ledger accounts is prepared and approved in the accounting department.	a. Filed journal vouchers prepared for disbursement for goods and services.
	b. Vendor invoices supporting journal vouchers.
	c. Approval signatures/initials on journal vouchers.
21. Purchases for employees are documented, approved by an appropriate official, and recorded in a separate general ledger account.	a. Purchase orders prepared for employees.
	b. Approval signatures/initials on purchase orders.
	c. Journal vouchers to record employee purchases.
	d. General ledger entries.
	e. Policies for purchases on behalf of employees.
22. All purchases of goods and services are processed through the accounting department, rather than directly through cash disbursements. Even when the original entry is made by cash disbursements, a journal voucher is prepared and filed.	a. Accounting policies and procedures for purchases.
	b. Cash disbursements journal.
	c. Journal vouchers.

Inventory Systems

Internal Controls

1. Inventory management is coordinated with production and/or sales schedules and forecasts.

2. Inventory levels are planned and managed to optimize purchase, holding, and stockout costs.

3. Employees who keep perpetual inventory records are separate from purchasing, storekeeping, and shipping.

4. Perpetual inventory records are kept for all inventories (except those considered to be immaterial in amount) and support general ledger control accounts.

5. Inventory records are computerized.

6. Perpetual inventory records show quantities and prices.

7. Perpetual inventory records are kept up to date.

8. Perpetual inventory records are maintained by someone other than the inventory custodian.

Sources of Audit Evidence

a. Sales, production, and inventory budgets.

b. Sales, production, and perpetual inventory records.

c. Interviews with sales, production, and inventory management personnel.

a. Calculations of economic order quantities for comparisons.

b. Policies on inventory management.

c. Interviews with inventory and executive management.

d. Cost accounting records.

Organization chart.

a. Inventory policies and procedures.

b. Inventory records.

c. General ledger inventory control accounts.

a. Computer hardware and software.

b. Inventory system documentation.

c. Computerized inventory records.

Inventory records.

a. Inventory records.

b. Purchase orders, receiving reports, journal vouchers, and production records.

a. Inventory policies and procedures.

b. Organization chart.

c. Location of inventory records.

d. Preparer's signature/initials on inventory records.

Internal Controls

9. Inventory storage facilities are suitably located, designed, and maintained to adequately organize and manage inventory and to protect it from the elements, unnecessary deterioration, and unauthorized access.

10. Inventory custodians are assigned responsibility for designated categories of inventories.

11. Inventory custodians document and notify the accounting department of all additions to or issues from their respective inventories.

12. Inventory custodians issue items only on the authority of approved requisitions, sales invoice, shipping notices, bills of lading, etc.

13. Inventory requisitions, sales invoices, shipping notices, bills of lading, etc., are prenumbered, controlled, and accounted for.

14. Overstocked, obsolete, and slow-moving items are periodically identified for appropriate disposition and documentation.

15. Inventory valuation adjustments are made to account for changes in inventory due to deterioration, obsolescence, etc.

Sources of Audit Evidence

a. Storage facilities.

b. Interviews with inventory and executive management.

c. Inventories.

Organization chart.

a. Policies and procedures for the accounting of inventories.

b. Perpetual inventory accounting records.

c. Custodian advises of changes in inventory.

a. Inventory custodian advises.

b. Perpetual inventory records.

c. Inventory requisitions, sales invoices, shipping notices, bills of lading, etc.

a. Copies of each of the documents.

b. Storage facilities and control procedures for each of the documents.

c. Periodic reconciliations of the documents.

a. Policies and procedures for inventory management.

b. Documentation of periodic reviews of such items.

c. Documentation of disposition of these items.

a. Documentation of periodic reviews for changes in inventory values.

b. Journal vouchers for such changes.

c. Accounting entries.

Internal Controls

16. Periodic physical inventory counts are conducted, particularly at year-end, by personnel separate from inventory custodians. Physical count sheets are prepared and reviewed for accuracy.

17. Accounting adjustments are prepared, approved, and made to record discrepancies between perpetual inventory records and physical count records.

Sources of Audit Evidence

a. Auditor observation of physical count.

b. Physical count sheets.

c. Reviewers' signatures on physical count sheets.

d. Policies and procedures for inventory management and evaluation.

a. Physical count sheets.

b. Journal vouchers to record changes.

c. Accounting policies for recording changes in inventory valuation.

Personnel and Payroll Systems

Internal Controls

1. The personnel function is centralized, at least within organizational units.

2. Manpower planning is coordinated with other organizational activities.

3. The budgeting process includes detailed personnel and payroll provisions.

4. Recruiting is coordinated with the various departments.

Sources of Audit Evidence

Organization chart.

a. Policies and procedures for management planning.

b. Planning documents.

c. Quantitative analysis of planning coordination.

a. Budgeting policies and procedures.

b. Budget documents.

a. Recruiting policies and procedures.

b. Interviews with personnel department managers and managers from other departments.

c. Filed memoranda between other departments and the personnel department.

d. Personnel department records showing the opening and filling of positions.

Internal Controls

5. Formal job analysis and evaluation is performed for all key positions.

6. Appropriate training and development opportunities are available for all personnel. Documentation of training and development activities in individual personnel files.

7. Appropriate compensation packages are provided for employees.

8. Management conducts regular, periodic performance evaluations for individual employees, and performance evaluations are documented and placed in each employee's personnel file.

9. Promotions, transfers, and terminations are approved and documented in employee and departmental records.

10. Personnel records are adequately maintained and stored against accidental damage or loss and against unauthorized access.

Sources of Audit Evidence

a. Personnel policies and procedures.

b. Job analysis and evaluation committee members.

c. Documentation of job analysis and evaluation.

a. Personnel policies and procedures.

b. Interviews with management and individual personnel.

c. Documentation of training provided for employees in individual personnel files.

a. Organizational compensation policies.

b. Individual employee records.

c. Descriptions of approved benefits packages.

d. Economic and industry comparative statistics on employee compensation. This information is available from a number of governmental and private sources.

a. Personnel policies and procedures.

b. Performance evaluation forms in employee files.

c. Interviews with management and individual personnel.

a. Personnel policies and procedures.

b. Personnel files.

c. Departmental personnel.

a. Facilities to house, process, file, and store personnel records.

b. Policies for processing and maintaining personnel files and records.

c. Computer software for processing employee records and payroll.

d. Personnel records and files.

Internal Controls

11. Legal obligations to pension funds, government agencies, insurance companies, etc., are reviewed regularly by management, external auditors, and legal counsel for needed changes and compliance.

12. Management and legal counsel review employee contracts periodically for compliance and update contracts as needed.

13. Appropriate provisions are made for hearing and acting upon employee grievances.

14. Changes in employee compensation status, including new hires, are reported to the payroll department following proper review and approval.

15. The payroll master file is periodically compared by the payroll and personnel departments to personnel files.

Sources of Audit Evidence

a. Personnel and payroll policies and procedures.

b. Laws and regulations.

c. Contractual agreements with financial institutions, insurance companies, etc.

d. Interviews with legal counsel, management, and external auditors.

e. Documentation of compliance reports and reviews.

a. Interviews with legal counsel and management.

b. Employee contracts.

c. Minutes of selected meetings.

d. Personnel policies and procedures.

a. Personnel policies and procedures.

b. Minutes of meetings held for such review.

c. Documentation of employee grievances.

a. Personnel department and payroll policies and procedures.

b. Documentation in personnel and payroll files of such changes.

c. Approval signatures on documents.

a. Personnel and payroll policies and procedures.

b. Interviews with personnel and payroll management.

c. Signatures/initials on payroll master file and personnel documents indicating completion of such reviews.

d. Payroll master files.

e. Personnel listings and file documents.

Internal Controls	*Sources of Audit Evidence*
16. All salaries and wages are determined by contract or policy and are approved by appropriate officials.	a. Personnel policies and procedures. b. Individual employee agreements. c. Payroll master file.
17. Employees authorize their own payroll deductions by signed statements kept in their individual files.	a. Personnel policies and procedures. b. Signed employee authorization statements.
18. The payroll schedule or register preferably is prepared by a computerized payroll system; otherwise it is prepared by a payroll clerk. The payroll schedule or register is compared with the master payroll file, reviewed for completeness, and approved by a payroll supervisor, who also reviews and approves payroll input documents received from personnel.	a. Payroll policies and procedures. b. Payroll software. c. Input documents. d. Payroll register. e. Individual personnel files. f. Payroll master file.
19. All employees are paid by prenumbered check (although in many places outside the United States, especially in less affluent countries and countries with exceptionally high rates of inflation, employees will accept only cash payment).	a. Payroll policies and procedures. b. Observation of payroll. c. Disbursements journal. d. Reconciliations of bank accounts. e. Storage facilities for blank payroll checks. f. Reconciliations of unused check numbers.
20. If payroll payments are made in cash, an independent security agent should be used for delivery of the cash payroll.	a. Payroll policies and procedures. b. Contracts with the independent agent. c. Observation of payroll distribution procedures.
21. Where payroll is distributed by cash, employees placing currency in pay envelopes do not prepare payroll schedules, registers, or advices. Currency is counted by two employees. The counts must agree before the cash is placed in the envelopes.	a. Payroll policies and procedures. b. Observation of payroll preparation. c. Signatures/initials of the employees preparing the pay envelopes, indicating compliance with preparation procedures and agreement between scheduled amounts on the payroll register and counted amounts.

Internal Controls

22. Signed receipts are obtained from employees for payroll envelopes or checks.

23. A special payroll bank account is used that fills and empties with each payroll distribution.

24. Payroll checks are signed by persons other than those preparing the checks, who do not have accounting or cash management responsibilities. Even when signature plates are used and these plates bear the signatures of appropriate persons, custody of the plates should be with an independent person, and they should be strictly controlled at all times.

25. Payroll checks are distributed by someone other than the employee's immediate supervisor.

26. Unclaimed wages are deposited in a special bank account or secured by an assigned official outside the payroll department. Short-term security necessitated by a brief illness or business trip may be provided in the employee's department or in the personnel department.

27. Where applicable, timekeeping departments are separate from the payroll department.

28. Timekeeping records and cost-accounting records for payroll are reconciled regularly with payroll department calculations of wages and salaries.

Sources of Audit Evidence

a. Payroll policies and procedures.

b. Observation of payroll distribution.

c. Signed receipts from employees for each payroll distribution.

a. Payroll policies and procedures.

b. Payroll account reconciliations by someone who does not prepare payrolls and does not sign or distribute checks.

a. Payroll policies and procedures.

b. Interviews with payroll management and those authorized to sign payroll checks or those who apply the approved signatures via the plates.

c. Observation of payroll procedures.

d. Security/storage facilities for signature plates.

a. Payroll policies and procedures.

b. Observation of payroll distribution.

c. Interviews with management and employees.

a. Payroll policies and procedures.

b. Observation of payroll distribution.

c. Reconciliations of unclaimed wages.

d. Short-term storage facilities.

e. Interviews with employees receiving wages after payroll distribution.

Organization chart.

a. Payroll policies and procedures.

b. Timekeeping records.

c. Cost-accounting reports for payroll.

Internal Controls

29. Time cards or piecework sheets are prepared by the individual worker and approved by a supervisor.

30. Payroll department duties are rotated among employees periodically.

31. Payroll personnel are required to take vacations for a given number of consecutive days.

32. Payroll personnel are covered by fidelity bond insurance.

Sources of Audit Evidence

d. Payroll register.

e. Reconciliations.

a. Payroll policies and procedures.

b. Time cards.

c. Piecework sheets.

d. Employee and supervisor signatures.

a. Payroll department policies and procedures.

b. Job assignment records in payroll department files or in employee files.

a. Payroll department policies and procedures.

b. Employee vacation records.

a. Payroll department policies and procedures.

b. Employee fidelity bond insurance policies.

Production and Cost Accounting

Internal Controls

1. Production is planned, budgeted, and scheduled in coordination with sales and inventory management.

2. A production quality control function organized separately from the production department.

3. Adequate maintenance and prompt repair is performed on production facilities and equipment.

Sources of Audit Evidence

a. Production policies and procedures.

b. Production planning, budgeting, and scheduling documents.

c. Sales and inventory planning, budgeting, and scheduling documents.

d. Interviews with executive management and the management of each of the related functions.

a. Organization chart.

b. Quality control reports.

a. Maintenance and repair schedules and records.

Internal Controls

Sources of Audit Evidence

b. Manufacturer/vendor maintenance and repair manuals and guidelines.

c. Interviews with production management and equipment operators.

d. Interviews with purchasing and accounting management personnel.

4. Appropriate input, processing, and output controls should be in place. Of course, these may vary depending upon the specific application, but the principle is the same whether the business is a service (such as law, accounting, or insurance), retailing, or industrial production.

a. Input, processing, and output procedures.

b. Observation of the operations.

c. Documentation of input resources, processing activities, and outputs.

5. The employment of appropriate technology and neither too much nor too little production capacity.

a. Manufacturer equipment specifications.

b. Interviews with production management and equipment operators.

c. Production schedules and records.

d. Sales records documenting the history of particular orders.

e. Customer service records.

f. Inventory schedules and sales forecasts.

g. Comparative information published by and about competitors, and information published by industry and trade associations.

6. Appropriate layout of facilities and design of the production/operations flow and process.

a. Observation of facilities and operations.

b. Layout charts and flowcharts.

c. Industrial engineering literature and interviews with industrial engineers.

d. Interviews with production management and personnel.

e. Production records for inputs, key processing transition points, outputs, and inventories.

Internal Controls	Sources of Audit Evidence
7. Adequate documentation is prepared and retained for production.	a. Policies and procedures for documentation of production activities.
	b. Production records.
8. Regular, accurate, and timely production and cost reports are prepared for management at an appropriate level of detail.	a. Internal reporting policies and procedures.
	b. Management production reports.
	c. Interviews with production and executive management.
	d. Reporting system software.
	e. Reporting schedules.
	f. Production budget information.
9. Production reports are prepared and approved by authorized production personnel. Cost reports are prepared and approved by the production/cost accounting function.	a. Production and accounting policies and procedures.
	b. Production and cost reports.
	c. Preparer and reviewer signatures.
10. Production orders are prenumbered, adequately secured, and periodically reconciled.	a. Production policies and procedures.
	b. Blank production orders.
	c. Storage facilities for production orders.
	d. Filed production orders.
	e. Reconciliations.
11. Only authorized persons prepare and approve production orders.	a. Production policies and procedures.
	b. Filed production orders.
	c. Authorized signatures on production orders.
12. Bills of materials and manpower schedules are prepared and approved by authorized production personnel on prenumbered forms and are properly secured.	a. Production policies and procedures.
	b. Bills of materials and manpower schedules.
	c. Preparation and approval signatures.
	d. Storage facilities for forms.
13. Materials requisitions and job time tickets are prepared by a plant or job foreman and are reviewed by a production supervisor.	a. Production policies and procedures.
	b. Materials and job time tickets.
	c. Foremen's and supervisors' signatures.

Internal Controls

14. Material requisitions and job time tickets are prenumbered and appropriately secured, with restricted access to the forms.

15. Cost clerks account for the numerical order of inventory issue slips, which are compared to materials used and recorded on production reports. Differences are reported to the accounting supervisor. The accounting supervisor includes material differences in an accounting report to management.

16. Differences between job time tickets and labor hours on production reports are calculated by the cost accounting function and reported to the accounting supervisor. Material differences are reported to management.

17. Standard costs are used where appropriate and are reviewed and revised periodically, as needed.

18. A cost accounting clerk calculates the differences between the reported production units completed and the reported units received in finished goods. The accounting supervisor reports material differences to management.

19. Cost accounting personnel prepare summary production journal entries which are approved by a cost accounting supervisor.

Sources of Audit Evidence

a. Production policies and procedures.

b. Materials requisitions and job time ticket forms.

c. Storage facilities.

d. Periodic reconciliations accounting for the forms.

a. Cost accounting policies and procedures.

b. Inventory issue slips.

c. Production reports including materials used.

d. Reconciliations for numerical sequence of issue slips.

e. Exception reports to management.

a. Accounting policies and procedures.

b. Job time tickets.

c. Production reports including labor information.

d. Exception reports to management.

a. Accounting policies and procedures.

b. Cost reports.

a. Accounting policies and procedures.

b. Copies of the reconciliations.

c. Exception reports to management.

a. Cost accounting policies and procedures.

b. Journal vouchers.

c. Approval signatures on journal voucher.

Facilities and Equipment

Internal Controls	*Sources of Audit Evidence*
1. Detailed property records are maintained for individual real estate, facilities, and equipment.	a. Policies and procedures for fixed assets. b. Property records and files.
2. Major capital expenditures and leases are reviewed and approved by the board of directors. Other expenditures are reviewed and approved by designated levels of management.	a. Policies and procedures related to capital acquisitions. b. Board minutes. c. Contract approval signatures.
3. Expenditures for capital acquisitions are approved in advance by designated levels of management.	a. Policies and procedures for capital acquisitions. b. Documentation of approvals, with appropriate signatures, prior to actual expenditure.
4. Adequate maintenance and prompt repair is performed on facilities.	a. Policies and procedures for maintenance and repair. b. Preventive maintenance schedules. c. Maintenance and repair logs. d. Manufacturer/vendor maintenance and repair manuals and guidelines. e. Interviews with management and equipment operators.
5. The board of directors, or some other designated authority, reviews capital acquisition expenditures that materially exceed previously authorized amounts.	a. Policies and procedures for capital acquisitions. b. Authorization documents. c. Check register. d. Cancelled checks.
6. Physical assets are periodically inspected and inventoried.	a. Policies and procedures for inspection and inventorying of fixed assets. b. Documentation (logs/diaries/journals, inventory listings, and completed forms) of these activities.

Internal Controls	*Sources of Audit Evidence*
7. Physical assets are covered by appropriate insurance, the types and amounts of which are supported by periodic appraisals.	a. Policies and procedures on insurance coverage. b. Appraisals. c. Insurance policies.
8. Periodic property taxes are reviewed for compliance and possible capital budgeting implications.	a. Policies and procedures on property tax review. b. Documentation of reviews by management and possibly legal counsel and external auditors.
9. Accounting policy distinguishes capital expenditures from repairs and maintenance expenses.	a. Accounting policy. b. Journal vouchers. c. Posted entries into the general ledger. d. Trial balance of general ledger accounts.
10. Capital and operating leases are clearly differentiated in the accounting records.	a. Accounting policies. b. Applicable Financial Accounting Standards Board provisions. c. Journal vouchers. d. Posted entries into the general ledger. e. Memorandum entries for operating leases. f. Trial balance of general ledger accounts.
11. Disposal or idling of physical assets is approved by the board of directors or a designated officer. Similar approvals are required for termination of leases and major rentals.	a. Policies and procedures for physical assets. b. Documentation related to disposals and/or idling of productive assets. c. Approval signatures.
12. Accounting entries for new physical assets trigger procedures to determine whether there are any associated disposals or replacements of old assets.	a. Accounting policies and procedures. b. Documentation of the application of these procedures for specific accounting entries.

Internal Controls	*Sources of Audit Evidence*
13. Procedures are in place to notify the accounting department of disposals of assets when no replacement occurs.	a. Accounting and departmental policies and procedures for such disposals.
	b. Documentation of such disposals.
	c. Inventories of physical assets compared with recorded assets.
14. Appropriate policies and procedures are in place to properly calculate and record depreciation on physical assets.	a. Depreciation policies and procedures.
	b. Depreciation schedules.
	c. Journal vouchers.
	d. Posted entries into the general ledger.
	e. Trial balance of general ledger accounts.

Appendix II
Professional Standards Bulletins

These bulletins are prepared for information only by the standards information service subcommittee of The Institute of Internal Auditors' Professional Standards Committee. They are not official pronouncements of The IIA. For official guidance, readers should refer to the Standards for the Professional Practice of Internal Auditing.

81-1   Independence — Bank Reconciliations

Question: *Can internal auditors routinely prepare bank reconciliations and still be in compliance with the* Standards?

Answer: Internal auditors should not prepare bank reconciliations as an operating responsibility. However, this activity does not necessarily preclude overall compliance with the *Standards.*

The director of internal auditing should avoid preparing bank reconciliations as an operating responsibility. If management requires the internal audit department to perform bank reconciliations, the director of internal auditing should inform management and the company's public accountants that this activity is not an internal audit activity; and, therefore, audit-related conclusions should not be drawn. In addition, while operating responsibilities are assigned to the internal audit department, special attention must be given to ensure objectivity whenever an internal audit in the cash area is undertaken. These facts should also be mentioned when reporting the results of an audit of the bank-reconciliation process.

81-2   Scope of Work — Effectiveness

Question: *Is a system of internal control which is functioning as intended necessarily effective as implied in Section 300.03 of the* Standards?

Answer: The effectiveness of an organization's system of internal control is evaluated on the basis of whether it is functioning as intended. However, the system, though it functions as intended, may not be adequate to meet the organization's requirements.

The scope of work in evaluating the effectiveness of an organization's system of internal control should be set to determine whether individual controls taken together provide the necessary level of control. This overall evaluation is necessary because complex operations often involve trading off controls between certain areas to achieve efficiency. A system of internal control which is functioning as intended should compensate for weakly controlled areas by providing strong controls at critical points within the operating system. The internal auditor's final assessment is of the overall system of internal control to determine whether it is functioning as intended and whether the system is sufficient to meet the organization's requirements.

81-3   Independence — Operating Responsibilities

Question: *What is a reasonable period of time to allow before sending someone to audit those activities he or she previously performed?*

Answer: Assigning personnel to audit the activities for which they previously had authority or responsibility should be delayed until their successors have had the time and opportunity to influence the system of control for the activity. Such work should never involve making audit judgments about the accuracy or integrity of data which the internal auditor generated while employed in the audit area.

An internal auditor's knowledge of an activity which he or she previously performed may greatly reduce the time necessary for the familiarization stage of an audit. This knowledge and scheduling efficiency must be carefully weighed against the presumption that the auditor will lack objectivity in performing the audit. Even though objectivity could be preserved by carefully scheduling steps in the audit program, the director of internal auditing must consider whether those members of the organization who read the final report will accept the results if the auditor previously had operating responsibility or authority within the audit area.

81-4   Scope of Work — Compliance with Laws

Question: *How can internal auditors determine whether the activities audited are complying with local laws and regulations?*

Answer: Internal auditors are not responsible for ensuring compliance with local laws and regulations. Management is responsible for designing and establishing systems for this purpose.

Internal auditors should inquire and test whether management has provided the systems necessary to ensure compliance with local laws and regulations. Criteria applicable to specific laws in the pension, payroll, and income tax area may, for instance, be included in the audit program. However, legal counsel and opinion may be necessary to provide sufficient assurance that all applicable laws and regulations have been considered at the audit location.

81-5   Scope of Work — Quality of Performance

Question: *Why is the purpose of a review for quality of performance in carrying out assigned responsibilities limited to ascertaining whether the organization's goals and objectives have been achieved?*

Answer: Assigning responsibilities within an organization is directly related to carrying out essential business activities and achieving the goals and objectives of the organization. The quality of performance in carrying out assigned responsibilities is, therefore, most directly related to the organization's goals and objectives.

Quality of performance is sometimes related to how well an individual performed or the level of performance which an individual achieved. The *Standards* sought to emphasize the concept that internal auditing does, directly or indirectly, comment on the success of individual managers in their role in the organization. This success is measured against the goals and objectives of the organization in order to utilize the most objective criteria available for such an assessment.

82-1   Performance — Report Signing
Question: *Who should sign the final internal audit report?*

Answer: The *Standards* does not specify which individual in the internal audit department should sign the final audit report. The size of the internal audit department should be assessed in relation to the many factors in the organization which determine the most appropriate level of authorization for issuing the final internal audit report.

Current practice in the industry has the auditor-in-charge, supervisor, or lead auditor sign the report. The director of internal auditing or designee should approve the report before it is issued, but the approval does not have to be evidenced by a signature on the report itself.

82-2   Scope of Work — Adequacy
Question: *What is the primary concern of the internal auditor when performing an examination and evaluation of the "adequacy" of an organization's system of internal control?*

Answer: The auditor's primary concern when reviewing adequacy is whether key controls are designed into the system to prevent, detect, or correct material errors and irregularities and to assure that the organization's objectives and goals will be met.

Through observation, inquiry, questionnaires, flowcharts, and other procedures, the auditor obtains and documents the flow of transactions and related activities. Based on these data, the auditor is able to determine whether key controls exist within the system as currently designed. For example, the auditor would identify whether transactions are properly authorized or duties are properly segregated. From this evaluation, the auditor may conclude whether the organization's system of internal control is adequate.

82-3   Scope of Work — Effectiveness
Question: *What do internal auditors mean when they state that an organization's system of internal control is "effective"?*

Answer: By "effective," internal auditors mean that the degree of compliance with key control procedures within the system is satisfactory.

The internal auditor renders an opinion on effectiveness after determining that the system is adequate and after performing compliance tests on the key controls. Therefore, an effective system is one which, in the auditor's opinion, is functioning in accordance with management's intentions.

82-4   Scope of Work — Internal Control

Question: *How does the external auditor's study and evaluation of an organization's system of internal control differ from that of the internal auditor's?*

Answer: The external auditors' primary role is to express opinions on financial statements. They study and evaluate internal control, primarily internal accounting control, to determine the nature, extent, and timing of audit tests.

The internal auditors' primary concern is reporting on the adequacy and effectiveness of an organization's system of internal control. They also determine whether the system of internal control is sufficient to meet management's needs.

External and internal auditors are both interested in reliance on an organization's system of internal control. In many areas, their methods and procedures for examining and evaluating internal control are similar. Internal auditors generally perform more detailed testing than external auditors. This is because internal auditors are apt to thoroughly review certain business activities such as service or program activities which are not the primary interest of external auditors. Internal auditors require more precision in certain areas which affect their evaluation of whether key controls are sufficient to minimize the risk of loss and maximize the likelihood of achieving management's goals and objectives.

82-5   Independence — Objectivity

Question: *Can internal auditors be objective when performing an audit of an area that they have audited several times in succession?*

Answer: Objectivity is an independent mental attitude which internal auditors should maintain in performing audits. Auditing the same area several times in succession might result in personal relations with the auditee that could impair objectivity. For example, internal auditors may not continue to use professional skepticism in reviewing areas with which they are familiar. Accordingly, it is a prudent policy to rotate auditors periodically from assignment to assignment.

An internal auditing department's professional development program for staff should include, among other things, methods to assure that auditors receive well-rounded audit experience. This should include proper job rotation that will allow professional growth and will assure that audits are performed objectively.

82-6   Performance — Statistical Sampling

Question: *Is the internal auditor required to use statistical sampling when examining and evaluating the effectiveness of the organization's system of internal control?*

Answer: Statistical sampling is *not* required when performing audit procedures. Nevertheless, sampling (statistical or judgmental) is inherent in the auditing process. Sampling involves estimating the rate of occurrence of a particular characteristic or estimating population totals by examining less than all of the items in a population. Internal auditors are constantly faced with the assignment of drawing conclusions about entire populations based on the examination of only a portion of the items in the population. The decision to use statistical or judgmental sampling to select items for examination is based on the professional judgment of the auditor. Statistical sampling is useful for quantifying the judgment of the auditor.

In some circumstances statistical sampling is more appropriate than judgmental sampling. Before deciding whether to use statistical or judgmental sampling, the auditor must determine the audit objectives; identify the population characteristics of interest; and state the degree of risk that is acceptable. After making those determinations, it may be advisable to use statistical sampling if the auditor has a well-defined population and can easily access the necessary documentation.

82-7   Management of an Internal Audit Department — Small Staff Compliance
Question: *Would a small staff of internal auditors or a single internal auditor be able to comply with the* Standards?

Answer: The general *Standards* are worded in such a way as to enable compliance by small staffs or a single internal auditor in an organization.

Many organizations are not large enough to allocate resources for an internal auditing department which utilizes all the specific standards and guidelines. However, any personnel assigned internal audit responsibilities should seek the best available professionals to successfully carry out the duties within their organization. Internal auditing should be a continuous, full-time, independent appraisal activity.

82-8   Management of an Internal Audit Department — External Reviews
Question: *Would a review of an internal auditing department that is performed by individuals of another department within the same organization satisfy the external review requirements of the* Standards?

Answer: External reviews are conducted by individuals or a team of individuals who are not part of the internal auditing department or the corporate entity to which the internal auditing department belongs. Reviews conducted by individuals who are in another department of the entity (for example, by individuals in the legal or controller's departments), although organizationally independent of the internal auditing function, are not considered independent for purposes of an external review. Also such individuals would have a real or apparent conflict of interest. Thus, such reviews would not satisfy the external review requirements of the *Standards.*

External reviews should be performed by qualified individuals who are independent of the corporate entity and who do not have a real or apparent conflict of interest. Review groups could include internal auditors from outside the organization, outside consultants, or external auditors.

82-9   Performance — Working Papers

Question: *Should audit working papers be made available to the auditees?*

Answer: Audit working papers are organized and accumulated to achieve audit objectives. They primarily serve to record the information obtained during the course of an audit and support the findings and recommendations. They may be necessary to substantiate or explain a finding or recommendation, and they may be made available to auditees for this purpose.

Management may sometimes request audit working papers for other purposes. They may, for instance, want to utilize the systems documentation. This by-product of certain audits often provides a ready-made source of current documentation. The internal audit department management should determine and evaluate the intended use by auditee personnel of specific audit working paper documentation. In this respect, however, the *Standards* does not discourage making audit working papers available to auditees on a selective basis.

82-10   Performance — Report on Economy and Efficiency

Question: *May the internal auditing department issue its report on the subject of economy and efficiency within the audit area in a separate memorandum from the audit report?*

Answer: The final report should present the results of the work performed including work done to appraise the economy and efficiency of operations. Presenting these results under separate cover such as a memorandum may suggest that the findings are not provided objectively or that reporting on the economical and efficient use of resources is not within the scope of internal audit activity in the organization.

The *Standards* includes a specific standard which states, "Internal auditors should appraise the economy and efficiency with which resources are employed." Communicating the results of audit procedures directed toward this specific standard should be viewed in conjunction with the results of the other control objectives pursued during the course of the audit. The director of internal auditing may choose to excerpt portions of the final audit report in a separate memorandum to emphasize economy and efficiency, but the results of the audit process should be initially reported along with other findings and recommendations from the audit process.

82-11   Independence — Objectivity in Systems Development

Question: *What tasks can the internal auditor perform in the system development life cycle which do not impair audit objectivity?*

Answer: Reviewing and documenting systems are necessary parts of performing an audit. Familiarity with the process of documenting systems and integrating recommendations into systems of control are skills which management requires for day-to-day operations. The proscription against performing these operating responsibilities serves to maintain internal auditors' objectivity while allowing comment and participation in the standards of control for systems or procedures before they are implemented.

Internal auditor objectivity would not be impaired when performing such tasks as:

1. Reviewing the adequacy of internal controls.
2. Assisting in identifying and defining control objectives and responsibilities.
3. Testing compliance with systems development process standards.
4. Reviewing the adequacy of systems and programming standards.
5. Testing compliance with systems and programming standards.
6. Advising on control techniques.
7. Evaluating performance.

82-12   Scope of Work — Efficiency Expert

Question: *Because internal auditors are concerned with "the efficient use of resources," could they be considered "efficiency experts"?*

Answer: Internal auditors are not efficiency experts. Nevertheless, because of their experience and expertise in auditing the system of internal control, they develop an objective attitude toward the efficient use of an organization's resources. Additionally, they are aware of methods and procedures that can be used to establish and maintain efficient internal controls.

Internal auditors appraise the efficiency of resources during the course of their audit. Their appraisal is by no means based on a comprehensive study specifically designed to improve the use of resources. Instead, their appraisal is based on the results of their overall examination, which is primarily designed to determine the adequacy and effectiveness of the organization's system of internal control and the quality of performance in carrying out assigned responsibilities.

82-13   Performance — Standard Reports

Question: *When reporting to management about the examination and evaluation of the organization's system of internal control and the quality of performance in carrying out assigned responsibilities, should internal auditing departments use standard reports?*

Answer: While not required, standard reports are recommended when reporting to management on the adequacy and effectiveness of the organization's system of internal control and the quality of performance in carrying out assigned responsibilities. Standard reports generally include two paragraphs that use standard wording to describe the scope of the audit and the internal auditor's opinion. Standard reports allow management to easily distinguish an "unqualified" opinion from a "qualified" opinion. In organizations that use standard reports, when management receives other than the standard report, they are immediately put on notice that the auditors have taken exception to the adequacy or effectiveness of the organization's system of internal control and quality of performance in carrying out assigned responsibilities.

Standard reports allow auditing departments to be consistent in their reporting. Often members of management receive several audit reports on different systems under their responsibility. Although the auditor may have arrived at the same conclusion about each system, without a report with standard wording, it is sometimes difficult for the reader to know this. Standard reports help to promote audit efficiency by eliminating the need to continually re-word audit reports.

82-14   Scope of Work — Responsibility for Determining Scope and Activities Audited

Question: *Should the director of internal auditing decide the scope and the activities to be audited?*

Answer: It is the responsibility of the director of internal auditing to decide the scope and the activities to be audited. This decision should be based on professional judgment and should be made objectively.

The director of internal auditing should be open to suggestions and other input.

The concern expressed most frequently is that management and the board decide the activities to be audited; the director of internal auditing influences only the scope. In practice, this concern may be valid where authority and responsibility for directing the activities of the internal auditing department have not been adequately described in the charter or effectively carried out in the audit planning process. The director of internal auditing should seek to establish or maintain discretion in deciding the scope and the activities to be audited as a foundation for objectivity and independence within the internal auditing function.

82-15   Management of the Internal Auditing Department — Charter

Question: *Must the charter for the internal auditing department be in writing for compliance with the* Standards?

Answer: The charter or statement of purpose, authority, and responsibility for the internal auditing department should be in writing. A written statement provides formal communication for review and approval of management and for acceptance by the board.

Providing a formal, written document containing the charter of the internal auditing department is necessary in managing the audit function within the organization. The purpose, authority and responsibility should be defined and communicated to establish the role of the department and to provide a basis for management and the board to use in evaluating the operations of the department. If a question should arise, the charter also provides a formal, written agreement with management and the board about the role and responsibilities of the department within the organization.

82-16   Scope of Work — Internal Control Objectives

Question: *Should every internal audit assignment include all five of the internal control objectives listed in Section 300.05 of the* Standards?

Answer: The primary objectives of internal control listed in Section 300.05 provide fundamental guidance for the review of an audit area. As such, they should be used in assessing the scope of work and constructing the program for each audit activity.

Internal control objectives selected for audit activity may derive from those listed in 300.05 and they may be constructed from control objectives which are not specifically cited in the *Standards*. The director of internal auditing should select the internal control objectives which are most suitable for the purpose and scope of the audit activity and the area under review.

83-1   Scope of Work — Operations
Question: *What are "operations" as used in Section 350 of the* Standards?

Answer: "Operations" as used in Section 350 relate primarily to the ongoing activities of an enterprise. Results from operations are measured against its objectives and goals usually in the form of a budget or operating plan.

Section 350 indicates that management is responsible for establishing operating goals and objectives, developing and implementing control procedures, and accomplishing desired results from operations. Internal auditors can provide assistance to managers who are developing operating goals, objectives, and systems by determining whether underlying assumptions are appropriate, information is current and relevant, and suitable controls are incorporated into the operations in question. Internal auditors should ascertain whether such objectives and goals conform with those of the enterprise and whether they are being met.

83-2   Scope of Work — Programs
Question: *What are "programs" as used in Section 350 of the* Standards?

Answer: "Programs" as used in Section 350 are primarily single-purpose activities. Results from a program are measured against the program's stated objectives and goals.

Section 350 states that management is responsible for establishing program objectives and goals, developing and implementing control procedures, and accomplishing desired program results. Internal auditors should ascertain whether the program's objectives and goals conform with those of the organization and whether they are being met. The term *program* as used in Section 350 relates primarily to government programs but could also relate to nongovernmental organizations.

83-3   Professional Proficiency — Staffing Plans
Question: *What criteria should be considered by the director of internal auditing when establishing staffing plans?*

Answer: When establishing staffing plans, the director of internal auditing should consider the department's goals and audit work schedules designed to achieve those goals.

The goals of the internal auditing department should be capable of being accomplished within specified operating plans and budgets and, to the extent possible, should be measurable. Staffing plans — including the number of auditors, knowledge, skills, and disciplines required to perform their work — should be determined from the audit work schedules, administration activities, education and training requirements, and audit research and development efforts.

83-4   Independence — Budget Restrictions

Question: *Do budgeting restrictions impact the auditor's independence to carry out work freely and objectively?*

Answer: Budget restrictions, in and of themselves, do not impact independence. Independence permits internal auditors to render the impartial judgments essential to the proper conduct of audits. Independence is achieved through organizational status and objectivity.

Financial restrictions impact the scope of the audit work schedule, not the audit independence required to carry out scheduled audits. Annually, the director of internal auditing should submit to management for approval and to the board for its information a summary of the department's work schedule and financial budget. Management and the board should be informed of the scope of internal auditing work and any limitations placed on that scope.

83-5   Professional Proficiency — Suspected Wrongdoing

Question: *Does an internal auditor have a responsibility to notify outside authorities of suspected wrongdoing?*

Answer: When an internal auditor's procedures lead to suspicion of some kind of wrongdoing, the auditor should determine the possible effects of the wrongdoing, discuss the matter with the appropriate level of management who (management or the internal auditor) should investigate or otherwise follow up the suspicion. When wrongdoing is suspected, the auditor's responsibility extends to the appropriate level of management within the organization.

83-6   Performance of Audit Work — Reperformance Tests

Question: *Should internal auditors perform key control procedures (such as adding columns of financial information, matching order, receipt, and payment documentation, etc.) when collecting, analyzing, interpreting, and documenting information to support audit results about the effectiveness of an organization's system of internal controls?*

Answer: When examining an organization's system of internal controls, internal auditors generally find it necessary to reperform or redo key internal control procedures so that they obtain a detailed, hands-on understanding of the flow of documents and activities. The reperformance is generally part of the auditors' "walk through" which confirms what the auditor has learned as a result of observations and interviews with auditees. Such reperformance activity usually is needed to aid in determination of whether the system is adequate. When determining the effectiveness of a system, the auditor performs tests to determine whether key internal control procedures are functioning as prescribed (i.e., tests of compliance). These tests may or may not include reperformance.

83-7   Scope of Work — Testing for Effectiveness

Question: *Can the internal auditor determine the effectiveness of the system of internal controls without performing audit testing procedures?*

Answer: The internal auditor must perform audit testing procedures to determine whether a system of internal controls is effective. The internal auditor determines effectiveness by performing tests designed to provide reasonable assurance that controls are being applied as prescribed. The internal auditor cannot determine the effectiveness of controls without applying audit testing procedures to a representative sample of transactions. The type of testing may differ due to the internal auditors' judgment and the circumstances. In any event, testing must be performed before a conclusion can be reached about effectiveness.

A liberal interpretation of Section 300.03 could lead auditors to believe that the "review" required therein does not require any testing. This is not the intention of that section. An auditor cannot ascertain whether a system is functioning as intended by performing a "review" that does not include testing of the controls identified as key procedures.

83-8   Scope of Work — Verification Test of Balances
Question: *Is it necessary, to comply with Section 300 of the* Standards, *for the internal auditor to perform verification tests of balances during the examination and evaluation of an organization's system of internal controls?*

Answer: Although internal auditors may utilize techniques that verify the results of processing, such procedures are seldom used for substantiating financial reports.

Generally, verification tests of balances are used in connection with examination of financial information, particularly financial statements. Such tests are designed to substantiate amounts in accounts. Often they are referred to as substantive tests. Internal auditors in some organizations are called upon to give management comfort about the amounts that are generated by the systems of internal controls. In such cases, the internal auditor finds it necessary to perform substantive tests (such as confirmation procedures to verify financial amounts).

The internal auditor who intends to design the scope of his audit to comply with Section 300 need not be concerned with performing tests to verify balances. Such tests are beyond the intended scope of work addressed in that standard. The standard requires that the internal auditors design their audits to determine the adequacy and effectiveness of the system. Generally, this requires identification of key control procedures, determination of whether such control procedures are adequate to achieve management's objectives, and tests of the effectiveness of key control procedures. Verification tests of balances would be needed in such an audit only if the system were deemed to be inadequate or adequate but ineffective, since in such circumstances financial amounts generated by the system could not be relied upon. If the system were adequate and effective, verification tests would not be needed.

83-9   Performance of Audit Work — Confirmation Procedures
Question: *Should internal auditors consider the use of audit confirmation procedures when examining and evaluating an organization's system of internal controls?*

Answer: Confirmation procedures generally provide evidence about the genuineness of a financial amount at a particular point in time. They are used to verify whether an account balance (particularly a receivable) is bona fide and accurate. Confirmation procedures provide little if any evidence about the adequacy and effectiveness of a system of internal controls, and accordingly should not be used on such engagements.

Internal auditors can use confirmation procedures to verify amounts if the organization's system of internal controls cannot be relied upon to generate reasonably accurate financial information. Additionally, some audit departments have a few regularly scheduled financial examinations that are designed to prove balances. These audits usually involve extensive use of confirmation procedures.

Internal auditors must be responsible to the desires of management and boards of directors and to the special needs of their own companies.

83-10 Management of the Internal Auditing Department — Formal Plan
Question: *Should a formal written plan to carry out responsibilities of an internal auditing department be developed and, if so, what should be included in the plan?*

Answer: A formal audit plan should be in effect and well documented. The plan should be consistent with the internal auditing department's charter and with the goals of the organization and should include answers to these related questions:

- What overall objectives should be achieved by the audit function?
- Which of the functions and activities of the organization should be audited?

Thus, to be effective, the internal auditing function should undertake the following interrelated planning steps:

- Development of a comprehensive long-range, strategic plan which outlines the overall objectives to be achieved by the auditing department.
- Identification of all functions and activities which the auditing department is responsible for auditing.
- Determination of which of those functions and activities should be audited and why, through evaluation of the risk associated with each function and activity.

The complete planning process should include goals, audit work schedules, staffing plans, financial budgets, and activity reports.

Goals and objectives should be long- and short-term. The long-term objectives should generally include those authorized within the internal auditing department's charter. In addition, they should include organizational development objectives such as to make the auditing organization a leader in the profession, to expand the service to management, to help the individual auditor to achieve greater dimension and stature, to increase the level of professional competency, and to improve the audit approach.

The short-term goals should include emphasis on specific objectives such as increasing the staff's computer and quantitative skills via both in-house and external training programs and to expand the coverage of operational audits.

The audit work schedules should include those audits that are to be done and the scope and purpose of those audits. This schedule should generally include such information as project number and report date, the last time the particular audit was performed, identification number of applicable permanent or master program files, area of coverage, evaluation of audit priority and risk, frequency with which the audit should be made, years in which the audit should be made, and number of audit days allotted to each project. This schedule is then used in developing staffing plans and financial budgets.

After individual audit arrangements are established, an overall plan should be discussed with the board or audit committee. A monitoring mechanism should be put in place to assure actual activity is progressing in accordance with the plan.

83-11   Performance of Audit Work — Reporting Key Controls
Question: *Should key controls be mentioned in an internal auditor's opinion about the system of internal controls?*

Answer: Key controls within a system of internal control should not be mentioned in the auditor's opinion unless management must be apprised of the significance of such controls. The auditor's communication should emphasize the entire system of internal control whenever possible to focus on the collective nature of controls rather than specific controls within the system.

The positive aspect of including key controls in the auditor's report is that it draws attention to the accomplishments of management and identifies specifically things such as policies, procedures, and activities which establish good control and which must be preserved. The negative aspects of including key controls in the auditor's report must also be weighed. Management may be influenced to think that only the key controls mentioned in the report need to be monitored. Also, a system of internal control involves key controls which may be inseparable and, therefore, it is not appropriate to list them individually. Therefore, the internal auditor is usually best served to refer to the *system* of internal control when writing the opinion section of the report.

83-12   Performance of Audit Work — Follow-up
Question: *How should follow-up activity be scheduled?*

Answer: Follow-up activity is part of the internal audit process and should therefore be scheduled along with the other steps necessary to perform the audit. Since specific follow-up activity is dependent upon results of the audit, it may be scheduled at the closing conference or as a separate activity within the internal auditing department.

Scheduling can begin when corrective action is confirmed by acceptance of an audit recommendation or when management elects to accept the risk of not implementing the recommendation. Based on the risk and exposure involved, as well as the degree of difficulty in achieving the recommended action, follow-up activity should be scheduled to monitor the situation or confirm completion of the changes which were planned. These same factors establish whether a simple phone call would suffice or whether further audit procedures would be required. Many internal audit departments schedule follow-up as a separate activity because it is dependent upon the nature and significance of the audit findings.

83-13   Scope of Work — Objectives and Goals

Question: *What does Section 350.01 require when stating that "Internal auditors should ascertain whether . . . objectives and goals conform with those of the organization"?*

Answer: Section 350 is written and directed toward program auditing within a governmental setting, but it applies as well to other industries. The objectives and goals of the function(s) or unit(s) under review should be compatible and conform with those of the company and organization.

Objectives and goals in nongovernmental operations are typically written into planning statements and budget documentation. Reviewing this information may provide the basis for a particular emphasis or expenditure within the operation under review which is not supported in corporate or organizational statements. It then provides appropriate background for on-site audit procedures. The internal auditor should be aware of local as well as company-wide or organizational objectives and goals to assess compatibility as part of the audit process.

83-14   Performance of Audit Work — Audit Findings

Question: *Does failure to agree with operating management on appropriate standards or criteria affect the internal auditor's position on whether to report an audit finding?*

Answer: Failing agreement with operating management, the internal auditor should state the standards or criteria used in evaluating the situation and report the audit finding. Higher levels of management need this information to evaluate the auditee's response and to decide whether appropriate controls have been implemented.

When operating standards or criteria are vague or do not exist, auditors should seek agreement with auditees on appropriate standards or criteria used in evaluating audit observations. Such criteria should take the form of operating procedures or other published statements which provide what management has designed and installed as performance standards. In the absence of such published statements, the internal auditor should evaluate the situation on the basis of similar operations in the organization or other authoritative sources which may include prudent business practices or the internal auditor's own knowledge of sound internal control procedures.

83-15   Independence — Effect of Promotion on Objectivity

Question: *Is it appropriate to continue on an audit assignment of a division or department for which the auditor will soon be responsible as the result of promotion?*

Answer: An internal auditor who will soon be responsible for a division should not be assigned to the audit or should not continue on the audit of that activity. The *Standards* explain that internal auditors are not to be placed in situations in which they feel unable to make objective professional judgments.

Objectivity is presumed to be impaired when an auditor performs such functions as 1) assuming operating responsibilities, or 2) auditing any activity for which the auditor has had or will have authority or responsibility. The question does not specify if the auditor has knowledge of the pending promotion. Since auditors would be implementing their own recommendations or may be perceived as making it easier on themselves by not disclosing certain findings, it should be determined whether the auditor's promotion creates a situation in which the auditor would feel unable to make objective professional judgments.

83-16   Performance of Audit Work — Reporting Auditee/Auditor Irreconcilable Disagreement

Question: *What course of action should the internal auditor take when an irreconcilable disagreement between the auditor and auditee management results from an audit finding?*

Answer: Discussion of conclusions and recommendations is usually accomplished during the course of the audit and/or at post-audit meetings (exit interviews). These discussions help ensure that there have been no misunderstandings or misinterpretations of fact. When such discussions do not provide the auditor or auditee with sufficient information for change and there continues to be an honest disagreement on significant control weaknesses or audit conclusions, the auditee's views should be included in the report and the auditee given the opportunity to read the added material to avoid misquoting. The director of internal auditing also has the option of determining the significance of the finding in question and, if appropriate, deleting the finding to ensure the report meets its objectives in a positive manner.

The auditor and auditee should avoid using the written report as a forum for debate through rebuttal techniques. However, sufficient information should be available from the text to describe each of the views expressed so third-party readers can understand the situation.

83-17   Performance of Audit Work — Additional Follow-up Responsibility

Question: *What further responsibility, if any, does the internal auditor have when management has assumed the risk of not taking corrective action on reported audit findings?*

Answer: Implicit in the definition of internal auditing is the responsibility to identify actual and potential risks to the organization. Internal auditors who are aware of such risks are required to report them to the appropriate levels within the organization.

Section 440 of the *Standards* states that the auditor should follow up to determine that appropriate action is taken on reported findings. Appropriate action would be either correction of the deficiency or assumption of the risk of not taking corrective action by management or the board. The *Standards* place no further responsibility on the auditor when management or the board elects to accept this risk.

The auditor should keep in mind, however, that the *Standards* do require the auditor to comply with professional standards of conduct such as The Institute of Internal Auditors' *Code of Ethics* which states that a member shall not knowingly be a party to any illegal or improper activity.

83-18   Performance of Audit Work — Interim Reporting

Question: *How can the time between audit completion and report distribution be minimized without sacrificing quality-control review?*

Answer: Audit work should be based on a definitive audit plan. To ensure timely reporting of audit findings, interim reporting should be considered.

The internal auditor should discuss the interim reports with appropriate levels of management during conduct of the field work. Copies of the interim reports and auditee responses should be reviewed by the director of internal auditing before the final report is prepared.

Quality-control review should be an ongoing process through all phases of an audit. Review comments relating to interim findings and recommendations can be resolved during the audit before the final report is prepared. This should minimize the time between audit completion and report distribution without sacrificing quality-control review.

83-19   Management of the Internal Auditing Department — Assessing the Adequacy of Scope of Work

Question: *How can an internal auditing organization assess the adequacy of its "scope of audit work" within its company?*

Answer: Major considerations used in assessing the adequacy of the internal auditing organization's scope of audit work are:

- General direction provided by management and the board of directors.
- A formal audit plan.
- A quality-assurance program.

Management and the board of directors provide general direction as to the scope of the work and the activities to be audited. The purpose, authority, and responsibility of the internal auditing department should be defined in a formal written document (charter). The director of internal auditing is responsible for establishing formal plans including audit work schedules. A formal audit plan should include the following planning steps:

- Development of a comprehensive long-range, strategic plan which outlines the overall objectives to be achieved by the auditing department.
- Identification of all functions and activities which the auditing department is responsible for auditing.
- Determination of which of those functions and activities should be audited and why, through evaluation of the risk associated with each function.

The audit work schedules should include those audits that are to be done and the scope and purpose of those audits. This schedule should generally include the last time the particular audit was performed, the area of coverage, the evaluation of audit priority and risk, frequency with which the audit should be made, years in which the audit should be made, and number of audit days allotted to each project. This schedule is then used in developing staffing plans and financial budgets.

After individual audit arrangements are established, an overall plan should be discussed with the board or audit committee. A monitoring mechanism should be put in place to assure actual audit activity is progressing in accordance with the plan.

The director should establish and maintain a quality-assurance program to evaluate the operations of the internal auditing department. A quality-assurance program may include supervision, internal, and external reviews.

Through regular meetings with management and the board and implementation of a quality-assurance program, the director of internal auditing should be able to assess the adequacy of the department's scope of work.

83-20   Professional Proficiency — Effect of Annual Bonus on Objectivity
Question: *Does an annual bonus included in the director of internal auditing's compensation package impair the director's objectivity?*

Answer: If bonuses and/or incentive compensation packages are an integral part of the organization's compensation program, internal auditing should not be precluded from such benefits. Such compensation programs generally do not impair audit objectivity.

Salary packages for the directors of internal auditing are normally administered by the organization's salary administration committee and are based on regional and industry standards for similar positions and similar experience. Under most circumstances, such packages do not impair objectivity.

The director of internal auditing's objectivity should not be impaired where:

- The bonus and/or incentive package is part of a comprehensive compensation program administered by the board of directors or its salary administration committee, especially where outside board members are members of the committee.
- The director does not report to an auditee which directly affects the director's bonus and/or incentive package.
- The scope of internal auditing's work is primarily directed to reviewing control rather than reviewing account balances.

On the other hand, the director of internal auditing's objectivity may be impaired where:

- The bonus and/or incentive package is not part of a comprehensive organization compensation program.
- The bonus and/or incentive package is primarily determined by the director's supervisor.
- The bonus and/or incentive package is based on operating results or dollar recoveries and recommended future savings as a result of audit activities.
- The scope of internal auditing's work is primarily directed to reviewing account balances rather than reviewing control.

It is, therefore, critical that internal auditing be given an independent organizational status to carry out its audit responsibilities. An independent relationship and the use of a board compensation committee provide additional environmental factors which enhance the director of internal auditing's independence and objectivity.

84-1   Management of the Internal Auditing Department — Audit Committee Communication

Question: *What information should the director of internal auditing periodically communicate to the audit committee?*

Answer: Audit committees generally perform an oversight and advisory role for the board of directors or other such designated governing bodies. Their role includes a review and appraisal of the overall audit resources available, objectives, scope, and audit results of both the external and internal auditors.

Audit committees provide the board of directors with their evaluation and recommendations of the internal auditing department's operation and activities. This may include a review of the internal auditing charter, qualifications, organization structure, financial budgets, long- and short-range plans, audit work schedules, activity reports and the report on external review of the internal auditing department.

The director of internal auditing should provide the audit committee with:

- A copy of the formal plan.
- Staff makeup.
- Activity reports highlighting significant findings and recommendations.
- Major variances against department goals, work schedules, and financial budgets.
- Any other information requested by the audit committee and considered appropriate by the director of internal auditing.

It is not normally necessary for the director to provide detailed individual audit reports to the audit committee unless specifically requested.

A written copy of the formal plan should be presented annually by the director of internal auditing to the audit committee. The formal plan should include, among other relevant matters, internal auditing's overall objectives, audit work schedules, staffing requirements, financial budgets, and a description of any limitations placed on internal auditing's scope of work.

84-2   Management of the Internal Auditing Department — Distinction Between Standards and Guidelines

Question: *What materials contained within the* Standards for the Professional Practice of Internal Auditing *are considered standards?*

Answer: The *Standards* booklet includes a foreword and introduction, a summary of general and specific standards, the five general standards, 25 specific standards, and related guidelines sequentially organized within the general standard captions. The foreword and introduction to the *Standards* were not considered to be part of the official authoritative material, that is, part of the standards. However, they explain the role of the *Standards,* especially when they go beyond the coverage in the official *Standards* and the supporting guidelines. The introduction to the *Standards,* for example, was based in part on *The Statement of Responsibilities.* This section includes material which is not in the *Standards,* such as the nature and objectives of internal auditing.

The introduction also specifically delineated three levels within the *Standards* and supporting materials. The term *standards* applies only to the general and specific standards. The term *guidelines* was used to describe a suitable means of meeting the standards. A further distinction was made by stating the words, "the standards and accompanying guidelines," which further support the position that the *Standards* refers only to the general and specific standards.

In summary, the general and specific standards are the goals that all internal auditing departments should strive to achieve. The guidelines are suggested as an acceptable means to reach these goals, but they are not necessarily the only means. There may be alternatives which are equally as acceptable.

84-3   Independence — Responsibility for Detecting All Irregularities
Question: *Is the internal auditor responsible for detecting all irregularities in the audit?*

Answer: Audit tests are not designed to make detailed examinations and verifications of all transactions. Internal auditors have the basic responsibility to use due professional care in the application of audit skills, tests, and conclusions based on the appropriate complexities of the audit being performed. The responsibility of internal auditors is also extended to adequate planning and supervisory review.

Internal auditors cannot give absolute assurance that irregularities do not exist. The possibility of material irregularities should be considered by internal auditors when undertaking an internal audit assignment.

84-4   Performance of Audit Work — Correction of Error in Final Report
Question: *Should an error in a final audit report be corrected?*

Answer: Audit reports are summaries for high-level management which describe areas for improvement in internal control systems. Reports normally include the identification of the inefficient use of resources. Internal auditors base their recommendations for improvement on reported findings. Management relies on the audit report's information being correct and then implements its plan for corrective action based on the information reported.

When it is determined that the substantive information published in a final audit report is incorrect, the director of internal auditing should issue an amended audit report which clearly highlights the information being corrected. The substantive information errors may have an effect on auditors' recommendations, management's action, or both. The amended audit report should be distributed to all individuals who received the audit report being corrected.

84-5   Independence — Receipt of Gifts or Fees: Effects on Objectivity

Question: *Is it appropriate for an internal auditor to receive items, services, or information of value from any area within the company or a company employee when an audit is not being made in the applicable area?*

Answer: The *Standards* state that internal auditors should be objective in performing an audit. Accepting a fee or gift may imply that the auditor's objectivity has been impaired.

The IIA *Code of Ethics* prohibits internal auditors from accepting a fee or gift from an employee, a client, a customer, or a business associate of their employer without the knowledge of senior management. No consideration should be given to the audit status as justification for receiving fees or gifts.

The receipt of promotional items (such as pens, calendars, or samples) which are available to the general public and have minimal value should not hinder internal auditors' professional judgments.

Internal auditors should report the offer of all material fees or gifts immediately to their immediate supervisors.

84-6   Independence — Regular Communication with the Board

Question: *What is meant by "regular communication" with the board and how does this help "assure independence," especially if senior management receives copies of all reports before they are distributed to audit committee members?*

Answer: Even though senior management receives copies of all reports issued to the audit committee, it should be implicit in the audit department charter that the director also has a direct line of communication with the board. If senior management is represented at audit committee meetings, the committee often meets only with the director of internal auditing, in an "executive session."

Guideline 110.01.2 states that "regular communication with the board helps assure independence and provides a means for the board and the director to keep each other informed on matters of mutual interest."

In this context, "regular" includes formally scheduled meetings. Although senior management may receive copies of planned reports and agendas, most audit committee agendas stipulate at least one private meeting with the audit director on an annual basis. As a result, a framework is established for direct communication.

The actual number of meetings required may vary by organization due to complexity and size. Normally, the director is expected to meet with the board at regular intervals during the year. Other meetings may be scheduled by the audit committee or by the director of internal auditing as the need arises. An important element of communication is established when the director has the confidence to discuss major concerns directly with the board. The submission of reports through senior management to the board may not in itself establish "regular communication."

84-7   Independence — Conflicts of Interest

Question: *How should a director of an internal audit department obtain information concerning potential or actual conflicts of interest?*

Answer: The underlying philosophy of a policy dealing with conflict of interest is to ensure that all concerned employees avoid situations which might be interpreted as a conflict between their personal interests and those of the organization. It is impossible to enumerate every circumstance which could give rise to a question concerning a conflict of interest.

Ordinarily, a person in the exercise of good judgment will know whether or not a particular activity involves an actual or potential conflict of interest. Many organizations have developed a conflict of interest policy which requires certain employees to read and confirm (in writing) that the employee is familiar with the policy and has no knowledge of any violation of the policy. The internal audit department should have unrestricted access to such information.

If the organization does not have a conflict of interest policy, the auditor may recommend that one be developed. In the absence of a written policy, audit programs may be designed to examine conflict of interest situations. Within the internal audit department, one way to obtain conflict of interest information would be to request each auditor to complete and sign a statement each year regarding the department's activities to disclose any potential or actual conflicts of interest, including relationships with potential auditees.

84-8   Management of the Internal Audit Department — Revisions to the Audit Plan

Question: *Under what circumstances and by whom should subsequent revisions to the audit plan be reviewed and approved?*

Answer: The term "audit plan" is defined several ways in current auditing literature and practice. It is commonly used to refer to the overall planning for the internal auditing department or the planning of an individual audit assignment.

The *overall or total plan* for the audit department is usually for a one-year period but may possibly be longer, or for full coverage of the "audit universe" (all systems, processes, operations, functions, and activities of the organization which are subject to review by the internal audit department). The steps toward the plan's review and approval often parallel the strategic-planning processes for other departments within the organization. Such a framework normally contains provisions for altering the original plan. The plan itself should be flexible enough to accommodate minor, unexpected changes.

Significant changes to this audit work schedule should be reviewed and approved by members of the same management level that reviewed and approved the original plan. According to Guideline 110.01.5, a summary of the department's audit work schedule, staffing plans, and financial budget should be submitted annually to management for approval and to the board for its information. Any significant interim changes should also be submitted for approval and information.

The *individual audit assignment or project plan* is the plan of activity to accomplish a specific objective within a particular operating area. The *Standards* refers to this plan as the "audit work plan" (Guideline 410.01.8). It includes the planning elements for an individual audit assignment. These may include the purpose of the audit, the processes to be evaluated, the evaluation criteria, the audit-procedure steps to accomplish the audit objectives, the resources to be utilized, the audit project, time-budget schedule, and any other information necessary for planning the individual audit assignment. The steps toward the review and approval of the audit work plan are similar to other tactical-planning processes within the organization.

Changing conditions may require revisions to the audit work plan. For example, the preliminary survey results may indicate less risk than previously assumed or the auditee organization or process may have changed since the preliminary survey. As a result, the scope of the examination may be expanded or reduced.

Significant changes to the audit work plan should be reviewed and approved by members of the supervisory level that reviewed and approved the original plan. This will help ensure that the audit work fulfills the overall plan for the department. In addition, auditee management should be advised of all significant changes to the audit work plan.

84-9   Performance of Audit Work — Discussion of Conclusions and Recommendations with Appropriate Levels of Management

Question: *What is meant by the phrase "appropriate levels of management" as it relates to the auditee audience for discussion of conclusions and recommendations before the issuance of final audit reports?*

Answer: Guideline 430.2 specifies that "the internal auditor should discuss conclusions and recommendations at appropriate levels of management before issuing final written reports." These discussions give auditee management the opportunity to review the facts expressed in audit findings and to state their views about audit conclusions and recommendations.

Statement on Internal Auditing Standards No. 2, "Communicating Results," in interpreting Guideline 430.02 of the *Standards,* states, "Although the level of participants in the discussions and reviews may vary by organization and by the nature of the report, they will generally include those individuals who are knowledgeable about detailed operations and those who can authorize the implementation of corrective action."

85-1   Performance of Audit Work — Appropriate Corrective Action Taken

Question: *How does the director of internal auditing ensure appropriate action on audit recommendations?*

Answer: It is the director's responsibility to ensure that audit reports are distributed to those members of management who are in a position to ensure that audit results are given appropriate consideration.

The director of internal auditing can ensure appropriate action on audit recommendations by instituting a follow-up routine which includes a time frame within which a response is required, an evaluation of the response (when appropriate), a follow-up audit, and a reporting mechanism that escalates unsatisfactory responses to an appropriate level of management. Of course, one of the most expedient ways to ensure appropriate action is to direct audit commentary to that level of management that is responsible for taking appropriate action.

Some organizations require certification from appropriate members of senior management that all findings in the audit report have been satisfactorily resolved by operating management.

If audit findings were especially significant, the director of internal auditing should consider performing a follow-up audit to ensure that appropriate action was taken on audit recommendations. Otherwise, follow-up on audit findings can be made by correspondence or as part of the next regularly scheduled audit.

85-2   Performance of Audit Work — Recommendations
Question: *Can an auditor make a recommendation for improvement which is not related to an audit finding?*

Answer: *Statement on Internal Auditing Standards No. 2,* "Communicating Results," specifies that "recommendations are based on the internal auditor's findings . . . ."

Findings are statements of fact which emerge from the process of comparing actual conditions with expected results.

Based on these definitions, an audit recommendation must always be the result of an audit finding. A recommendation is the call for action or the suggestion for improvement when the auditor finds a difference between actual conditions and expected results.

However, if we are talking about advice and assistance to management outside the audit process, the answer is quite different. The introduction to the *Standards for the Professional Practice of Internal Auditing* states the objective of internal auditing "is to assist members of the organization in the effective discharge of their responsibilities." As the company experts on control, auditors can be called upon to give opinions concerning an operational situation that may not be the subject of an audit. As such, auditors can, within the contexts of the *Standards,* provide members of the organization with analyses, appraisals, recommendations, and counsel concerning the organization's activities.

85-3   Scope of Work — Appropriateness of Objectives and Goals
Question: *Should internal auditors comment upon the appropriateness of management's objectives and goals?*

Answer: According to Specific Standard 350 of the *Standards for the Professional Practice of Internal Auditing*, internal auditors should assess established objectives and goals and provide assistance to managers as they develop them. The IIA's *Statement on Internal*

Auditing Standards No. 1, "Control: Concepts and Responsibilities," defines criteria for evaluating objectives and goals in its interpretive Guidelines 300.02.1 and 300.02.2, while Guideline 300.08.2 requires determination that reasonable assurance exists that objectives and goals are being achieved.

The introduction to the *Standards* states that the objective of internal auditing is to assist members of the organization in the effective discharge of their responsibilities. Auditors may be asked to provide advice and assistance to managers in the process of setting objectives and goals. As a consultant, the auditor should determine if underlying assumptions are appropriate; if accurate, current, and relevant information is being used; and if goals under development support organizational objectives. It is clearly management's responsibility to develop objectives and goals. However, internal auditing may review the development process.

85-4   Performance of Audit Work — Materiality

Question: *What significance does the term "materiality" have to the practice of internal auditing?*

Answer: The term "materiality" is widely discussed within the external and internal auditing professions. The American Institute of Certified Public Accountants' (AICPA) *Statement on Auditing Standards No. 47,* "Audit Risk and Materiality in Conducting an Audit" discusses materiality of errors in relation to the impact on the financial statements being audited. Materiality is used primarily in relation to the potential impact an identified error may have on the organization's financial statements. In this context, it was developed and defined by the AICPA to serve as a guide in conducting audits for the purpose of certifying financial statements.

The term has a different significance to the practice of internal auditing. The IIA's *Statement on Internal Auditing Standards No. 1,* "Control: Concepts and Responsibilities" (Guideline 300.02.5), states that reasonable assurance that objectives and goals are met efficiently and economically:

> . . . is provided when cost-effective actions are taken to restrict deviations to a tolerable level. This implies, for example, that material errors and improper or illegal acts will be prevented or detected and corrected within a timely period by employees in the normal course of performing their assigned duties.

The cost–benefit relationship is taken into consideration by management when deciding to correct weaknesses in the overall system of control since the ultimate responsibility for the control system lies with them.

From the internal auditor's perspective, all errors should be corrected where it is economically feasible to do so. Equally important are economic considerations related to preventive controls — guarding against the same error happening again. On the other hand, detective controls may be the most economical alternative. The auditor should consider the costs and benefits associated with any enhancements to controls before making recommendations for improvement.

85-5   Professional Proficiency — Continuing Education

Question: *Is continuing formal education the only means for internal auditors to maintain technical competence?*

Answer: Formal education is not the only means of maintaining technical competence. According to Section 270 of the *Standards for the Professional Practice of Internal Auditing*, internal auditors should maintain their technical competence through continuing education.

Continuing education can be defined as an educational program designed to update the knowledge and skills of its participants, while the term *technical competence* indicates an individual having special skills and the requisite ability or qualifications to use them. Continuing education — whether through a formal, academic program conducted at an institution of higher learning, through specialized courses offered by the company or outside consultants, or through research efforts — is necessary to ensure an individual's competence in a specialized field.

Continuing education should encompass the discipline of auditing, as well as the areas and processes subject to audits. While having the necessary skills and knowledge of auditing is a prerequisite, having knowledge in the area being audited and maintaining the trust of the client are also integral parts of the job. This enables auditors to perform the audit function in a knowledgeable, timely fashion, causing the least disruption of activities to the client by being able to converse in and understand the language being spoken. Thus, we provide both a service to our clients and a favorable impression of the internal auditing group.

The educational program internal auditors pursue is usually a formalized program of academic study. Auditors' educational preferences may also be more informal, utilizing in-house training sessions, workshop participation, reading of periodicals and journals, on-the-job training, and self-education. Many of these informal means qualify for continuing professional development (CPD) credits in The Institute of Internal Auditors' CPD Program for Certified Internal Auditors.

Whatever avenue auditors choose, they must remain proficient and competent in the discipline of auditing and continually pursue technical competence.

85-6   Independence — Independence of Internal Auditors vs. External Auditors

Question: *Are internal auditors less "independent" than external auditors?*

Answer: Both internal and external auditors operate under standards requiring independence. In the *Standards*, Standard 100 requires that "internal auditors should be independent of the activities they audit."

For external auditors, the second general standard is "in all matters relating to the assignment, an independence in mental attitude is to be maintained by the auditor or auditors." No less independence should be implied or assigned to internal auditors than to external auditors based on their respective professional standards.

The greatest single issue concerning the independence of internal auditors is that they are "inside looking in." Some contrast this to the external auditors' role because they are hired or replaced at the discretion of the management on whose representations they are expected to report. Primarily, internal auditors rely on audit administration and quality assurance to ensure proper mental attitudes and performance; the external auditors have helped create a body of law and practice to assist in meeting their objectives. The key, however, is the level of independence which auditors are allowed and able to achieve. Practical independence is defined as independence in relation to actual audit practices and procedures. All auditors, when in compliance with their standards, are equally independent; therefore, all internal and external auditing organizations strive to maximize management's knowledge of, understanding of, and agreement with the standards governing their efforts. In this way, practical independence is enhanced.

As long as the internal auditors subscribe and adhere to the standards and do not have line responsibility or accountability for operations subject to review, they may be as independent as any other entity providing appraisal services to an organization.

85-7   Professional Proficiency — Minimum Qualifications
Question: *Are there minimum qualifications needed to be an internal auditor?*

Answer: All internal auditors should possess the technical and practical qualifications which are essential to the performance of their duties. Due to the variety of audit assignments, the qualifications needed by auditors vary among industries and also within specific audit departments themselves.

The level and type of technical and practical expertise required for each position within the internal auditing department of the organization should be determined by the director of internal auditing and documented in the position descriptions or in the audit policy manual.

Entry-level internal auditors should possess the academic and experience background required for their specific positions within the organization; and should obtain the additional training necessary to assure their ability to employ due professional care — including data gathering, sound analysis, proficient communications, and appropriate documentation.

Senior-level internal auditors should have accumulated pertinent audit experience and actively pursued further training and knowledge directed toward achieving professional designation and/or recognition as deemed appropriate by their organization. They should be capable of preparing audit programs, preparing cost/benefit analyses, directing the activities of audit team members, conducting opening and closing conferences with auditees, preparing audit reports, and handling such other assignments as deemed appropriate by audit management in the organization served.

Individual internal auditors should recognize those situations whereby their knowledge, skills, training, and experience have not fully prepared them for a specific situation encountered; and should seek appropriate counsel and advice from audit management before proceeding with the assignment.

85-8   Professional Proficiency — Reporting Underbilling to Contractors

Question: *Is the internal auditor ethically required to report findings to an operator or contractor when an outside audit is performed (e.g., joint-venture or contractor audit) and exceptions are found which would create additional costs for the internal auditor's company?*

Answer: If the amount of the exception is immaterial and/or especially clear-cut, the auditor is advised to review these findings with internal audit management and then report these findings to the third-party operator/contractor.

However, if the exception is a complex issue, or a particularly significant amount, the preferable action would be to advise internal audit management and the company's operating employees responsible for the contract/service. It would then be appropriate for the responsible operating personnel to examine the information supplied by the internal auditor. If management reaches the same conclusion, then it is their responsibility to resolve the underbilling with the outside firm.

There could be underlying issues or historical events, with which the internal auditors are unfamiliar, that will bear on the eventual settlement. This is the reason that the auditors are advised to notify operating management of unusually large or complex audit findings prior to informing third parties.

85-9   Performance of Audit Work — Interim Findings in the Final Report

Question: *If an interim audit report is issued and corrective action taken prior to issuance of a final report, is it necessary to reiterate the interim finding in the final report?*

Answer: Standard 430 of the *Standards* states that audit results should be reported and include the purpose, scope, and results of the audit; and, where appropriate, reports should contain an expression of the auditor's opinion.

Inclusion of an interim finding again in a final report depends upon the significance of the finding and management's response. If management's response has been immediate and complete and the finding is not material to the operation being audited, then it would not accomplish anything to include the item in the final report.

If, however, the finding has importance in the auditee's operation, then it should be included again in the final report. The final report should include a description of the auditee's response and progress in addressing the finding.

It should be recognized that the use of interim reports does not diminish or eliminate the need for a final report on the results of the audit work.

85-10   Management of the Internal Auditing Department — Reduction of External Audit Fees

Question: *Should internal audit resources be devoted to the reduction of external audit fees?*

Answer: Standard 520 of the *Standards for the Professional Practice of Internal Auditing* states that the director of internal auditing should establish plans to carry out the responsibilities of the internal auditing department.

The question of devoting resources to reducing the external auditor's fees is a resource-allocation problem. Whether we allocate resources to assist the external auditors or for an audit of a specific activity, the choice is a cost/benefit decision. If our payback in terms of monitoring control, assessing risks, and improving organizational economy, efficiency, and effectiveness through cost saving and revenue enhancing recommendations exceeds reduction of external audit fees, then obviously we should allocate internal audit resources to these higher payback areas.

The director of internal auditing has the responsibility to determine if such work is consistent with the internal auditing department's charter and goals and is in the best interest of the organization. The director's determination should be in keeping with his/her overall responsibility to minimize duplicate efforts and equate audit coverage with risk.

85-11   Independence — Task Force Participation

Question: *Does participation in a task force compromise an internal auditor's objectivity or independence?*

Answer: Guideline 120.03 of the *Standards for the Professional Practice of Internal Auditing* states that "the internal auditor's objectivity is not adversely affected when the auditor recommends standards of control for systems or review procedures before they are implemented. Designing, installing, and operating systems are not audit functions. Also, the drafting of procedures for systems is not an audit function. Performing such activities is presumed to impair audit objectivity."

Mere participation in a task force should not impair an auditor's independence or objectivity. In fact, due to previous audit work, the auditor may possess a unique understanding of a process, control, or system which would enhance an ultimate recommendation made by the task force.

Task-force work which includes designing or installing operating systems or drafting detailed control procedures clearly are not audit functions. Doing so may, in fact, compromise objectivity, depending on the circumstances involved. Audit management should weigh the benefits of having auditors participate in a task force against the risk of losing objectivity.

86-1   Management of the Internal Auditing Department — Assessing Professional Proficiency

Question: *Much has been written about auditors' effective communication with auditees, but less written about auditees' perceptions about the quality, timeliness, and value of an audit. What tools are available to assist the director in assessing the professional proficiency of the audit staff?*

Answer: Standard 560 of the *Standards for the Professional Practice of Internal Auditing* states that "The director of internal auditing should establish and maintain a quality assurance program to evaluate the operations of the internal auditing department."

In assessing the professional proficiency of the audit staff, the director has three primary tools for making an objective assessment. Auditee questionnaires, addressed to the primary auditees, are frequently used by audit directors at the conclusion of each audit. These questionnaires, which can be written or oral, should elicit frank and constructive feedback about the quality, timeliness, and usefulness of an audit. Both recurring positive and negative comments can be covered in training sessions with staff.

Secondly, an internal review of the internal audit department, as defined in Guideline 560.03 and conducted by a supervisory or management member of the audit staff, can give the internal audit director observations about the professional proficiency of the staff.

Finally, an external review can give the audit department its most objective and thorough feedback regarding the strengths and weaknesses of the staff's proficiency.

86-2   Performance of Audit Work — Negotiating Settlement for Contract/Joint-Venture Audits

Question: *Who is responsible for negotiating settlements of audit findings from third-party contract/joint-venture audits?*

Answer: It is the responsibility of management to determine a satisfactory settlement amount and conduct settlement negotiations with third parties. The internal auditor will need to promptly inform management of the findings, make available all necessary working papers and adequately brief management about the nature of the findings. It may be necessary for the auditor, or a member of audit management, to attend settlement meetings to elaborate upon the audit findings and assist in negotiation.

Delegating settlement of audit findings exclusively to the audit department places audit staff in a position of management and presumes awareness of all related issues which could affect the final settlement amount. Such delegation is not properly an audit function and could preclude independent audit activity of financial or operational aspects of the joint venture.

86-3   Independence — Reviewing Contract Drafts

Question: *Our company plans to include internal audit in the review cycle of contracts prior to execution. Is the auditor's independence/objectivity impaired by review and comment on contract drafts?*

Answer: No, an internal auditor's objectivity and independence are not impaired by this activity. This is a good example of preemptive auditing, and is an opportunity to evaluate the adequacy of controls and audit trails. In reviewing contract drafts, the internal audit department generally confines its comments to items such as inclusion of an adequate audit clause, appropriateness of billing provisions, clarity of definitions and formulas, documentation and recordkeeping requirements and factual provisions of the contract about which it is knowledgeable. These clearly are within the expertise of the department, and weaknesses identified in drafts and subsequently corrected will improve the auditability of the contract.

86-4   Performance of Audit Work — Reporting Fraud Investigations to Outside Authorities

Question: *Should the internal auditor voluntarily report the results of a fraud investigation to outside authorities?*

Answer: The determination as to whether external reporting is desirable and/or required depends upon the nature and magnitude of the fraud, the industry within which the organization operates, the organization's policy, and, in the absence of a legal requirement, the decision of senior management. In general, internal auditors are responsible to management of their organizations, not to outside agencies.

SIAS No. 3 states that internal auditors should report the incidence of significant fraud to management or the board when its existence has been established to a reasonable certainty. Additionally, a full report should be made at the conclusion of the investigation phase.

PSB 83-17 postulated that appropriate action on an audit report by management or by the board could take the form of either correction of reported deficiencies or assumption of the risk of not taking corrective action. *PSB 83-17* further emphasized that the *Standards* placed no further responsibility on the auditor when management or the board elected to assume the risk of no action.

While *SIAS No. 3* applies to the professional practice of internal auditing, statutory and other official considerations may require other forms of compliance which may either vary with or supplement its guidelines. Examples are bank auditors who report pursuant to established banking law and regulation; federal auditors whose activities are governed by the GAO *Standards for Audit of Governmental Organizations, Programs, Activities, and Functions*; as well as state and municipal government auditors who examine and report pursuant to relevant governmental auditing standards and applicable law.

Depending upon the materiality or nature of the alleged fraudulent event, statutory filings with regulatory agencies may be required. The internal auditor should consult with the organization's legal counsel on mandated compliance versus other considerations of confidentiality and privilege. Where statutory compliance is mandated, the internal auditor should immediately inform an appropriate level of senior management, not believed to be a party to or otherwise implicated in the event. In some organizations, auditors should report to internal investigative or security officers when fraud is suspected.

Oral or written "early warning" reports to interested or affected parties may be desirable and/or required. An example of an interested or affected party is the organization's fidelity bonding company. As a condition for honoring claims, fidelity insurance carriers (bonding companies) customarily require notification of loss within time limitation terms, and other conditions stated in the bonding contract.

Internal auditors should be aware that outside agencies, organizations, or individuals may have an interest in their findings, reports, and possibly the underlying audit working papers and company records. Such interest may develop when management moves to file an indictment-seeking complaint with a prosecuting agency, or when the organization's rights subrogate to a bonding company against which a claim for loss is filed. In either event, the agency would expect a copy of the auditor's report to be provided voluntarily.

In some instances, internal auditors may expect enforcement agencies to be interested in their work. Either voluntarily, or via subpoena if necessary, such agencies may seek to examine the methodology and the evidence which corroborate audit findings. Internal auditors should be cognizant of the ramifications of the findings disclosed in their reports, the contents of audit workpapers, and, with the assistance of the organization's legal counsel, be prepared to furnish information to and cooperate with the enforcement agencies.

In conclusion, there are many factors which affect the reporting of a fraud incident. The internal audit department should obtain appropriate professional guidance to determine whether the company is in compliance with appropriate and necessary reporting.

86-5   Independence — Political Action Committee

Question: *Are objectivity and independence impaired when the director of an internal auditing department is also the head of the company's political action committee (PAC) and, as such, solicits contributions from all levels of management? (The internal audit department, under the director's control, audits PAC activities.)*

Answer: Guidelines for Standard 120 state that "Internal auditors should not assume operating responsibilities. But if on occasion management directs internal auditors to perform nonaudit work, it should be understood that they are not functioning as internal auditors. Moreover, objectivity is presumed to be impaired when internal auditors audit any activity for which they had authority or responsibility. This impairment should be considered when reporting audit results."

Guideline 120.02.6 states, "The results of internal auditing work should be reviewed before the related audit report is released to provide reasonable assurance that the work was performed objectively."

This question implies considerable depth of involvement by the audit director. This involvement in the decision-making and management processes could affect the director's objectivity not only relative to the PAC operation but also relative to officials who supported or did not support the PAC effort. It is important not only that auditors be independent and objective, but also that knowledgeable third parties perceive them to be so. These circumstances present at least an appearance of a conflict of interest and the audit director should avoid such situations whenever possible — particularly if the audit staff is small.

If there is no other alternative, and the audit director serves as chairperson of the PAC, the PAC audit should be performed and supervised by other members of the audit staff, and special steps should be taken to disassociate the audit director from the audit. Additionally, details of the circumstances, special provisions taken, and possible impairment should be included when reporting the audit results.

86-6   Management of the Internal Audit Department — IIA *Standards* Division

Question: *Does The IIA plan to revise the* Standards *for the Professional Practice of Internal Auditing?*

Answer: The *Standards* was issued in 1978 after extensive research and review. The intent was that the *Standards* would set forth a strong base of principles which would guide the practice of internal auditing. The five general standards represent generally accepted internal auditing standards. The 25 specific standards represent elements which must be present to meet the general standards. The guidelines describe suitable methods to meet the *Standards*.

The Institute has assigned responsibility for monitoring and updating the *Standards* to its Professional Standards and Responsibilities (PS&R) Committee. Within this committee, several subcommittees are responsible for individual sections of the *Standards*, and these subcommittees constantly monitor the status and need for authoritative interpretations of and/or changes to these sections.

The *Standards* is a living document, and as such may need revision to adapt to changes taking place in business, industry, and government. While it is unlikely that changes will occur in the general standards, specific standards and guidelines may and do change. As significant issues face the profession, they are researched, studied, and receive public exposure, and any changes to or expansions of the *Standards* initially are issued as a *Statement on Internal Auditing Standards (SIAS)*. Currently there are three* *SIAS*s:

- Control: Concepts and Responsibilities.
- Communicating Results.
- Deterrence, Detection, Investigation, and Reporting of Fraud.

When enough *SIAS*s are issued to warrant a revision of the *Standards,* the PS&R Committee will initiate the revision.

86-7   Professional Proficiency — Continuing Professional Development

Question: *Is continuing professional development necessary to maintain the CIA designation?*

Answer: *Standard 250* of the *Standards for the Professional Practice of Internal Auditing* states that internal auditors should possess the skills and disciplines essential to the performance of internal audits. Standard 270 states that internal auditors should maintain their technical competence through continuing education.

An underlying theme throughout the *Standards* is the professionalism with which auditors must perform their duties. As in similar specialized fields, one means of demonstrating an internal auditor's professionalism is the certified internal auditor (CIA) designation.

---

*Three additional *Statements on Internal Auditing Standards* have since been issued: *SIAS No. 4,* "Quality Assurance;" *SIAS No. 5,* "Internal Auditors' Relationships with Independent Outside Auditors;" and *SIAS No. 6,* "Audit Working Papers."

Once the CIA designation has been attained, it is the CIA's responsibility to remain current with state-of-the-art developments and all applicable standards. This is achieved through continuing education. Presently, ongoing efforts on the part of CIAs to enhance and maintain their skills and disciplines need to be reported only on a voluntary basis. The reporting of these continuing professional development (CPD) activities is not required for maintenance of certified status.

Finally, the profession is growing and changing. In order to maintain state-of-the-art qualifications, all internal auditors must pursue varied means of continuing their education. Internal auditors and, more specifically, certified internal auditors, should pursue CPD activities as set forth in the *Standards*. Like those in similar professions, CIAs should document and report CPD to The Institute in order to promote the continued professionalism of CIAs. Although the possession of a CIA designation alone cannot be considered a sole measure of qualification under the audit standards, it is a strong presumption for such a status.

86-8   Performance of Audit Work — Contract Audit Clause

Question: *What items should be addressed in a contract audit clause?*

Answer: An audit clause is incorporated into a contract to afford companies an opportunity to examine the outside parties' books and records which support billed costs. In some cases, terms and conditions of contracts are specific and require neither audits nor audit clauses.

Frequently, it is necessary for a company to have more than one standard audit clause. Several versions may be used due to the variety of contractual terms and arrangements (i.e., fixed-cost/cost-plus contracts or the use of subcontractors). In all cases, the organization's legal department should review the proposed audit clause for sufficiency.

Items which are typically included in audit clauses are as follows:

- Parties authorized to perform the audits (i.e., internal and/or external auditors).
- Length of advance notice required before initiation of the audit.
- Duration of audit rights (this should be a length of time that will permit examination of all costs if the contract is for an extended period).
- Communication of audit findings to the audited organization.
- Items that are auditable (i.e., all costs, payments, settlement or supporting documentation which result from the agreement).
- Items that will be furnished by the contractor (i.e., books, records, reports or other items of supporting documentation which result from the agreement or are in support of billed costs).
- Length of time supporting documentation must be retained by the audited organization.
- Statement that the audit will be conducted in accordance with generally accepted auditing standards or other appropriate guidelines.
- Statement that the audited organization will cooperate in the conduct of the audit which will facilitate a timely completion.

- Settlement process for audit exceptions.
- Interest provisions for monetary audit exceptions which are agreed upon by the parties.
- Statement whether an audit clause should be inserted in subcontractors' contracts to give the auditing organization access to all costs and records.

Without an adequate audit clause, the audit organization may be unable to perform a thorough audit, thus precluding assurance to management about the results of contractual arrangements. It therefore behooves the initiator of the contract, the legal, purchasing, and internal audit organizations to jointly develop and support the use of audit clauses in all contracts requiring audit.

86-9   Management of the Internal Audit Function — Deferring Audit Requests

Question: *Is it appropriate for the audit organization to defer an audit based upon a request by the auditee (e.g., request due to staffing vacancies, filing deadlines, special projects)?*

Answer: Guidelines of Standards 110, 120, and 410 state that, ". . . the charter should authorize access to records, personnel, and physical properties relevant to the performance of audits;" "Internal auditors are not to subordinate their judgment on audit matters to that of others;" and lastly, planning involves ". . . communicating with all who need to know about the audit."

In scheduling audits, the audit organization should normally consider workload requirements of auditees to ensure that auditees will have the necessary resources to devote to the audit; it should also consider the presence of other audit activity in the auditee organization and the cyclical nature of the auditee's activity.

The audit organization should notify auditees sufficiently in advance of most audits to provide time for their preparation and to ensure that there are no impediments to the conduct of the audit. The amount of advance time needed depends upon the scope of the audit; two or three weeks would generally provide adequate time for a routine audit, while several months' notice may be required for audit of remote locations or contract audits.

The audit organization should schedule audits so that a representative sample of activity is observed. This can be negated if auditees unjustifiably alter audit activity or schedules.

If an auditee requests rescheduling of the audit, internal audit management should discuss the reasons for this request with the appropriate level of auditee management. If it is determined that no adverse audit impact would occur, then a deferral, with a rescheduled date, could be agreed upon. This, however, should be viewed as an infrequent occurrence.

86-10   Professional Proficiency — Compliance with IIA *Code of Ethics*

Question: *How does The IIA determine compliance with The IIA's Code of Ethics?*

Answer: Guideline 240.01 of the *Standards* states that maintaining the standards of professional conduct set forth in the *Code of Ethics* is a responsibility incumbent upon all members of The IIA. Primarily, the *Code* addresses internal auditors' responsibilities to their employers.

The IIA Board of Directors oversees compliance with The IIA's *Code of Ethics* through Board Policy Statements included in the Board Policy Manual. When a member commits an act judged to be contrary to the spirit of the *Code*, and thus discreditable to the profession of internal auditing, a formal complaint should be prepared by the person making the judgment.

Complaints are referred to The IIA Professional Standards and Responsibilities (PS&R) Committee which is responsible for receiving, interpreting, investigating, and hearing complaints on behalf of The IIA's Board of Directors. The PS&R Committee makes recommendations to the Board on action to be taken. Disciplinary actions may include censure or suspension/expulsion from membership. A person shall be suspended from membership without a hearing upon receipt by the Board of Directors of proper notice that a judgment of conviction has been imposed on the member for a felony, and expelled upon receipt that a final felony conviction has been entered against the member. Notice of disciplinary actions taken against members are printed in a membership periodical.

Similar procedures are used to monitor compliance with *The Certified Internal Auditor Code of Ethics.* Disciplinary action in this situation may be censure or suspension/forfeiture of the CIA designation. The same procedures as described in the previous paragraph apply to a CIA who has been convicted of a felony.

86-11   Management of the Internal Auditing Department — External Review Conflict of Interest

Question: *Is there a conflict of interest if the independent accounting firm that examines and reports on an entity's financial statements also performs an "external review" of the internal audit organization?*

Answer: Guideline 560.04 states in part that "External reviews of the internal auditing department should be performed to appraise the quality of the department's operations. These reviews should be performed by qualified persons who are independent of the organization and who do not have either a real or an apparent conflict of interest."

One of the factors most critical to a successful external review is obtaining personnel who are both independent and qualified. If the entity's independent accounting firm is proposed as the external reviewer, consideration should be given to a conflict of interest which it might be perceived to have, due to the firm's past reliance on the work of the internal auditing organization or other relationships with the entity. One method for partially overcoming these concerns is to staff the review with members of the independent accounting firm who have not been associated with the audit engagement.

These concerns should be balanced with the potential advantages of using the company's independent accounting firm. These include familiarity with the internal audit organization, knowledge about needs of senior management and the audit committee, and the likelihood of needing less time to perform the external review.

In conclusion, appointment of the entity's independent accounting firm to conduct an external review might be perceived to be a conflict of interest. The best way to overcome that perceived conflict would be to retain a firm that is not now, nor has been in the recent past, the independent accountants of the company. If the independent accounting firm is selected as the external reviewer, discussions should be held with the firm and all possible steps should be taken to mitigate the apparent lack of independence.

86-12   Management of the Internal Auditing Department — Internal Review Objectivity

Question: *Is objectivity impaired when an internal audit organization conducts an "internal review" of itself?*

Answer: Guideline 560.03 states that "Internal reviews should be performed periodically by members of the internal auditing staff to appraise the quality of the audit work performed. These reviews should be performed in the same manner as any other internal audit."

The purpose of an internal review is to give the director of internal audit timely assurance that the audit organization is in compliance with the *Standards* and that it complies with departmental and applicable company policies. The primary beneficiary of an internal review is the internal audit director, although reporting the results of the review to others outside the audit organization may be beneficial.

While complete objectivity of staff members is difficult to achieve, the audit director should emphasize the need for an independent and objective frame of mind. The director should also assure that the team or individual reviewer i) has been given full authority to conduct the review; ii) possesses the necessary technical and specialized knowledge; and iii) is given adequate time and staff to perform a thorough review.

Internal review fieldwork may exclude testing those areas in which the director is closely involved and has personal knowledge about their effectiveness (e.g., Standards 110 and 510–560). If the director has influenced the scope of review, these actions should be noted in the final report, stating the director's reasons for the scope limitations.

An *internal review* will not accomplish all the objectives of an external review. Its purpose is primarily a self-assessment for the internal audit director. An *external review*, on the other hand, provides both the real and apparent objectivity that persons outside the department can rely upon to assess the department's effectiveness.

The Institute's *Quality Assurance Review Manual* provides guidance, including suggested questionnaires and review steps, for conducting internal reviews.

86-13   Management of the Internal Auditing Department — External Review by Qualified Persons

Question: *Guideline 560.04 states that external reviews should be performed by "qualified persons." How does The IIA define "qualified persons"?*

Answer: As stated in *Statement on Internal Auditing Standards No. 4*, "Quality Assurance," 560.04.3: " ' Qualified individuals' are persons with the technical proficiency and educational background appropriate for the audit activities to be reviewed and could include internal auditors from outside the organization, outside consultants, or independent outside auditors."

Although the designation "Certified Internal Auditor" or other appropriate IIA professional qualification outside North America should evidence an individual's knowledge of the *Standards for the Practice of Internal Auditing*, there are additional considerations which influence the selection of an external reviewer. These include experience in the conduct of internal audits, knowledge of the industry or company desiring an external review, educational background, and the independence and objectivity that the external reviewer can bring to the engagement. (*SIAS No. 4* discusses independence and objectivity in greater detail.) Therefore, independent accountants who have performed only financial statement audits should not be regarded as having adequate experience; nor would consultants with experience in only specialized areas of auditing (i.e., contract, joint venture, EDP, etc.).

Ideally, external review team members would have experience at the level of internal audit manager or director, and the external review team leader's experience should be comparable to that of the audit executive responsible for the department under review.

In conclusion, the value of an external review is directly tied to the caliber of personnel on the external review team. The two factors which most directly affect the qualifications of the external review team are a thorough knowledge of the *Standards* and their application, and the external review team members' prior internal audit experience.

87-1   Professional Proficiency — Computer Proficiency

Question: *I know a lot about internal auditing interview and record-review techniques. How much do I really need to know about computers?*

Answer: Specific Standard 250 states that "Internal auditors should possess the knowledge, skills, and disciplines essential to the performance of internal audits." Guidelines of Specific Standard 280 on due care cover the added responsibilities for the application of skill expected of a competent auditor and professional care which is appropriate to the complexities of the audit.

Today in our fast-changing work environment, a better understanding of computerized information systems is needed than what was necessary at the time Guideline 250.01.4 was issued in 1978. It states, "An appreciation is required of the fundamentals of such subjects as . . . computerized information systems." In many businesses and industries, the computer is becoming commonplace. It processes and records transactions and provides data for decision making. The computer as an audit tool is also becoming commonplace. It is used daily for data management and comparisons, statistical analysis, and extracting information for test purposes. In these situations, a greater knowledge and understanding of computers by the auditor is necessary. In the terminology of the guidelines to Specific Standard 250, the knowledge level needed by auditors today would most likely be between "proficiency" and "understanding."

As technology and other factors impacting the workplace change, the internal auditor's knowledge, skills, and disciplines also must change in order to respond adequately to management's needs. Presently, in most companies and businesses, this means the knowledge of EDP techniques and the ability to apply them to situations likely to be encountered, to recognize significant problems, and to carry out the research necessary to arrive at reasonable solutions.

87-2 Professional Proficiency — Evidence of Supervision

Question: *What is meant by the term* appropriate evidence of supervision *used in Guideline 230.03?*

Answer: In the area of professional proficiency, Specific Standard 230 is devoted to a discussion of internal audit supervision. Guideline 230.03 states that "Appropriate evidence of supervision should be documented and retained."

Evidence of supervision would include items such as the following, most of which would become part of the workpaper package:

- Issuance of an audit initiation letter to the auditee, signed by audit management, outlining the scope of the audit and authorizing its conduct.
- Signatures on audit programs which evidence approval of the audit scope and audit steps.
- Use of a time budget to establish audit resources allocated to the project.
- Initialling of workpapers, preparation of formal review notes, or other evidence of workpaper review by audit management.
- Evidence of audit management review and approval of interim memos, draft reports, final reports, and other written communication with auditees.
- Use of questionnaires to auditees at the conclusion of audits which solicit their comments about the conduct of specific audits.
- Performance of more traditional supervisory functions such as performance evaluation, disciplinary actions, training, time control, approval of travel expense, and schedules of staff assignments.

In the area of retention, auditors should consult with corporate records and/or legal personnel to identify retention requirements for audit work.

87-3 Coordination of Internal/External Audit Effort

Question: *The internal auditing profession has changed substantially in the 10 years since the American Institute of Certified Public Accountants (AICPA) issued* Statement on Auditing Standards No. 9, *"The Effect of an Internal Audit Function on the Scope of the Independent Auditor's Examination." What is The Institute of Internal Auditors (IIA) doing to encourage revision of SAS No. 9 to reflect a more current perspective?*

Answer: The IIA's standard dealing with external auditors is Standard 550 which states, "The director of internal auditing should coordinate internal and external audit efforts."

The IIA is working toward a broader framework of internal/external auditors' relationships, including a possible recommendation for AICPA reconsideration of *SAS No. 9*, better implementation of IIA Standard 550 on coordination of internal and external audit efforts, and other related matters. Meetings have been held with the AICPA Auditing Standards Board representatives to discuss these and other items of mutual interest, and further meetings will be held. The IIA's interest is not limited to *SAS No. 9* in the United States, but also extends to similar standards for external auditors in other countries.

SAS No. 9, issued in 1976, begins with the statement, "The work of internal auditors cannot be substituted for the work of the independent auditor . . . . " It focuses on "the internal audit function as it relates to the independent auditor's study and evaluation of internal control . . . ." *SAS No. 9* naturally emphasizes areas and functions of internal audit which are pertinent to the independent outside auditor's specific scope; thus from an internal audit viewpoint, more weight is attributed to these somewhat limited functions. In contrast to *SAS No. 9*, Auditing Guideline 408 of the Institute of Chartered Accountants in England and Wales, "Reliance on Internal Audit Work" (November 1984), goes further toward recognition and acceptance of internal auditors' work by focusing on internal auditors' professional status and capabilities. That Guideline discusses criteria for making "an assessment of the likely effectiveness and relevance of the internal audit function" as a basis for a decision to place reliance on that function. In practice, both documents permit the external auditor to make use of internal auditors' work after a review of the competence and objectivity of the internal auditors and an evaluation of their work on a test basis.

Points under review by The IIA in connection with internal/external auditors' relationships, and also relevant to the present wording of *SAS No. 9*, include the following internal auditing developments and events which occurred during recent years:

- Changes in the professional qualifications and competence of auditing personnel.
- Increased independence, status, and authority for the internal auditing function within the organization.
- Increased audit committee and senior management support.
- The development of *Standards for the Professional Practice of Internal Auditing* and their increasing application in internal auditing functions.
- The IIA's issuance of a *Code of Ethics* and a *Statement of Responsibilities.*
- Improvement in the resources available to internal auditing.
- Improved tools and techniques for development of the audit universe, assessing risks, planning and performing audits.
- Increased expectations of shareholders, and the public generally, about services provided by internal auditing.

An important objective of The IIA is not only to remove any perception of a limited or subordinated role by internal auditing in connection with the overall audit, but also to foster a "single audit concept" and achieve fully the coordination of internal and external audit efforts as suggested by Standard 550.

87-4   Professional Proficiency — Expert Witness Testimony

Question: *In communicating the results of audit work, as described in Standard 430, it is possible that an auditor would be requested to testify in court as an expert witness. Please provide some suggestions about how an auditor should prepare for testifying as an expert witness.*

Answer: Testifying in court as an expert witness can involve communicating results as discussed in Specific Standard 430, but also involves issues such as due professional care (Specific Standard 280) and an auditor's knowledge, skills, and disciplines (Specific Standard 250).

Before appearing as a witness, it is advisable to consult with an attorney who can inform the auditor as to what the nature, scope, and strategy of the trial are and how the expert testimony provided by the internal auditor fits into the resolution of the matter before the court. In addition, internal auditors need to inform the appropriate members of their organizations' management about court appearances. Adequate preparatory work should be done prior to appearing as a witness; this includes studying prior briefs, testimony, decisions, and documentation. The following suggestions are provided as additional guidance.

- *Anticipate questions and attorneys' lines of reasoning.* It is advisable to formulate answers in advance for questions that you expect will be asked. A mock trial exercise can also be helpful in identifying weak areas of testimony.
- *Provide counsel with information to develop your testimony.* Specific questions should be developed in advance to ensure that your testimony is as useful as possible.
- *Review workpapers or exhibits.* Study exhibits and other documents presented to you as long as necessary to understand them. Do not jump to conclusions because the documents may not be what they appear to be. As audit workpapers are prepared, it is equally important that they fully support the conclusions reached.
- *Understand questions before answering.* Witnesses are not required to, nor should they, answer any question that is not fully understood. Request rephrasing or clarification until the question is understood. Do not be led into saying something that isn't meant. Avoid quick answers to leading or overly simplistic questions.
- *Do not guess.* It is acceptable for the witness to state "I don't know." Do not speculate in order to answer the question.
- *Answer only the question asked.* Do not volunteer information or elaborate on answers. Answers should stay well within the scope of the question.
- *When asked if you agree with statements from previous witnesses, be specific.* If you agree or disagree in part and the attorney will not allow you to explain, state that you can't answer the question.
- *Do not denigrate opposing witnesses.* When disagreeing, attempt to cite authoritative support.
- *Correct errors in testimony.* If you become aware of errors in previous testimony given by you, correct it as soon as possible. This can be accomplished by stating that an item, which was discussed previously, needs to be corrected. Correct it, and explain at that time why the mistake occurred.

- *Listen to lawyers' objections.* If a lawyer objects to a question, do not answer it until the lawyer has completed the objection. In a deposition, follow the advice of your attorney. At trial, wait to answer until the judge rules on the objection. If in doubt, ask the judge.
- *Tell the truth.* The value of an expert witness is the knowledge and experience that can be provided to solve the dispute at hand. Speak loudly and clearly in delivering answers.
- *Present facts versus feelings or unsupported opinions.* It is not the witness's responsibility to advocate a party's position in a lawsuit. Testimony should be given in a manner which is free of bias or the appearance of favoritism. Don't quibble or be evasive.
- *Be yourself.* Do not play a role. Being yourself will make it easier to think and answer questions. An expert witness should avoid the appearance of arrogance as this will diminish the value of his or her testimony in the opinion of the judge or jury.
- *Dress conservatively.* An expert witness's testimony will be more believable if the person is dressed neatly and professionally.
- *Avoid joking or sarcastic remarks.* Be courteous and polite to everyone in the courtroom. Jokes and sarcasm rely on eye contact and facial gestures to convey their meaning, and these are missing from written depositions and court transcripts.
- *Do not lose your temper or become argumentative.* Each answer should be given only after careful reflection of the question. Avoid anger or fatigue by requesting a short break.
- *Avoid the use of jargon or technical terms which may confuse the jury or judge.* Take extra care to present testimony that is understandable to the layman. Become familiar with courtroom facilities which will be needed if more than oral testimony is used (e.g., blackboard, slides).
- *Do not look at your lawyer.* This can be mistaken as direction from your attorney. Short answers should be directed to the lawyer asking the question; longer answers should be directed to the jury, particularly members who appear receptive. Do not force eye contact on a member of the jury who avoids it.
- *Do not talk with members of the jury.* It is inappropriate for a witness to converse with a member of the jury. If this occurs, politely state that the court has instructed you not to converse with them. If this action persists, inform the lawyer who arranged for your appearance. Be very cautious in discussing the status or strategy of the trial outside the courtroom since conversations can be overheard in even the most unsuspecting places.

87-5   Professional Proficiency — Handling a Management Impropriety

Question: Statement on Internal Auditing Standards No. 3, *"Deterrence, Detection, Investigation, and Reporting of Fraud," includes some general guidance on this subject matter. Specifically though, how should an auditor handle an alleged impropriety at a very high management level?*

Answer: Allegations, of the seriousness outlined above, will generally be communicated by an individual outside the audit department to the director of internal auditing. If another member of the audit staff becomes aware of such information, it should immediately be brought to the attention of the director.

The director, or designee, should obtain as much information about the alleged impropriety as quickly as possible. This will better ensure that the appropriate interviews or documents are obtained before more people become aware of the allegation. Depending on the severity of the situation, this action may require that the director involve a superior of the employee (not involved in the allegation), legal or security staffs, or outside consultants.

One of the first concerns of the director is when to inform the senior-management employee of the allegation. Generally, it would be preferable that the audit director inform the individual before it would be heard from a nonaudit source. This will minimize the possibility of jeopardizing their future working relationship should the allegation prove groundless, and ensure that the facts are communicated as clearly as possible rather than through rumor.

At this initial meeting, the director should endeavor to involve the employee's superior and suggest that all three meet to discuss a mutual item of interest. Whenever possible, the audit director should have a third party present when discussions are held with the employee in question.

Another concern of the director is if and when the audit committee should be told of the allegation. This determination should be made by the director after evaluating the severity of the charge and the audit committee's past directives about their involvement in these situations. *SIAS No. 3* states that a written report should be issued at the conclusion of the investigation phase and a draft report be reviewed by legal counsel prior to issuance.

In all cases, the audit director should ensure that the allegation is handled with utmost confidentiality and that nothing is said or done which would defame the senior-management employee.

87-6   Professional Proficiency — Handling Tip-offs or Complaints

Question: *How should an auditor handle a confidential "tip-off," or oral or written complaints from employees or others that could have a significant exposure for the organization?*

Answer: Anonymous tips and other forms of complaint are becoming more commonplace, especially in organizations which have developed a formal communication line to foster such reporting. Frequently, such tips, rather than the results of more traditional auditing techniques, initiate an auditor's fraud-detection investigation.

When an auditor is contacted by someone wishing to pass along a tip/complaint, the auditor should caution the caller that a serious charge is being made and that it may have unfavorable consequences for the caller, the employee or situation being targeted, and perhaps the organization itself. The caller should be encouraged to consider the implications of the allegations that are about to be made before proceeding further. The auditor should explain that the normal policy is to make every effort not to reveal sources but that no guarantees can be provided, and if this makes the person uncomfortable, it would be desirable for them to write an anonymous letter.

Having considered these cautions, and electing to continue, the informant should be asked for details and evidence which would prove the accuracy of the allegations. With this initial information, the auditor, after consultation with appropriate members of audit management, should undertake the necessary audit tests to determine whether the allegations have merit and what further action or investigative work is appropriate.

In undertaking audit work to evaluate the allegations, auditors may need to inform other members of the organization such as attorneys and security staffs. As stated in *Statement on Internal Auditing Standards No. 3*, the level of management to be contacted should only be decided after an analysis of who could be involved in the situation. Auditors should not investigate allegations without keeping a member of audit management informed of the investigation's status at all times.

When reporting on the audit results of an informant's allegations, the report should follow guidelines contained in *SIAS No. 2*, "Communicating Results," and *SIAS No. 3*, "Deterrence, Detection, Investigation, and Reporting of Fraud."

87-7   Professional Proficiency — Documenting Work Performed

Question: *What action should be taken when evidence is found that an auditor has not actually performed audit work denoted by tick marks or other notations of audit tests in the audit working papers?*

Answer: Specific Standard 280 states that "Internal auditors should exercise due professional care in performing internal audits," and Specific Standard 420 states that "Internal auditors should collect, analyze, interpret, and document information to support audit results."

This question raises serious concerns about the due professional care exercised by auditors and the adequacy of audit supervision. Audit supervisors and managers are not always a party to the result of every audit interview and observation; neither can they always review the accuracy of all audit work. This is why the integrity and professional care exercised by auditors is so critical. Careless audit techniques could have a damaging effect on the operations of the organization and the credibility of the entire audit department.

Audit working paper preparation standards should be addressed in training sessions with the audit staff. In these sessions, supervisors and managers of the audit department should make clear to auditors their policy concerning warnings, disciplinary action, and the possibility of termination should auditors falsify audit working papers. Auditors should understand the purpose of each audit program step before it is executed. Any audit tests which were not or could not be performed as outlined in the audit program should be explained.

Auditors should take care in the placement of tick marks and not use them until the test defined by the tick mark has been completed. Additionally, the definition of tick marks and the purpose and conclusion of audit working papers should be stated clearly so that misunderstandings will not develop from their use or review.

87-8   Independence — Conflicts Arising from Incentive Compensation

Question: *Our firm is considering extending bonus/incentive compensation to internal audit managers. (The bonus would be tied to the profitability of the subsidiary they audited along with accomplishment of subsidiary goals.) The audit committee has expressed concern that this may place audit managers in a conflict-of-interest situation where the auditors' personal compensation could be affected by the results of audit work. Please provide some opinion about this practice.*

Answer: One of the cornerstones of auditing is that auditors must be independent and objective in performing their work. *Professional Standards Bulletin 83-20* states that generally, bonus/incentive compensation programs which are an integral part of the organization's compensation program and administered by the board or its salary administration committee would not impair audit objectivity. However, it states that such programs which are based on operating results may impair audit objectivity.

From the description provided, it does appear that the proposed bonus/incentive plan *could* impair audit objectivity. It is possible that an audit manager may fail to report the results of audit work completely or release the results of audit work with timing favorable to the bonus/incentive computation. Extra care needs to be taken in designing a bonus/ incentive plan for auditors due to the unique reporting responsibilities they have in the organization.

87-9   Performance of Audit Work — Follow-up Techniques

Question: *What are some of the techniques the internal auditor can use to follow up on audit recommendations and ensure appropriate action is taken?*

Answer: Specific Standard 440 states that "Internal auditors should follow up to ascertain that appropriate action is taken on reported audit findings." Adequate and timely audit follow-up is critical; without follow-up to close the audit cycle, the value of audits may be seriously diminished.

Effective follow-up begins at the time the audit report is issued. One commonly used technique is to address the report to a level of management that is responsible for taking action. It is their job to specify how the audit recommendations will be addressed by providing a written reply within a reasonable time period after the report is issued. Some audit departments carry this process a step further and assign audit recommendations to specific employees (by job title or name) after conferring with the auditee's organization as to how the audit recommendation will be addressed. Regardless of which method is used, it is best to include in the final report the intended action, or a specific time frame for resolution, so auditors can schedule follow-up accordingly.

Other follow-up techniques to encourage management to move in the direction of implementation are: use of a department "tickler" file which is used to remind auditors to follow up at predesignated dates or fixed intervals depending upon the auditee's targeted completion date; personal computer (PC) applications to summarize each audit recommendation as it is issued with an audit staff member responsible for updating the PC file after conferring with the audit staff; and postaudits at interim points if there have been extremely significant findings to deterimine that appropriate action has been taken promptly. On future audits, auditors should compare the action taken on prior audit recommendations with action that was oulined in the auditee's response to evaluate the responsiveness to future audit recommendations.

At the end of each year, management may appreciate receiving a recap of the year's significant recommendations and their status (opened or closed) along with any audit recommendations which still remain open.

87-10   Professional Proficiency — Working Paper Review Notes

Question: *Should the audit supervisor's/manager's review notes be retained once those notes have been properly cleared?*

Answer: Standard 420 states that "Internal auditors should collect, analyze, interpret, and document information to support audit results." Guideline 420.01.5 states that "Working papers that document the audit should be prepared by the auditor and reviewed by management of the internal auditing department. These papers should record the information obtained and the analyses made and should support the bases for the findings and recommendations to be reported." These two statements indicate the need for adequate documentation of the audit process, as well as the importance of supervisory review.

It is common practice for reviewers of working papers to make a written record ("review notes") of questions arising from the review process and of instructions as to how certain audit points should be resolved. Two acceptable alternatives, with respect to disposition of such review notes, are as follows:

1. Retain the review notes as a record of the points raised by the reviewer and the steps taken in their resolution. Care should be taken to ensure that such notes and the information provided to resolve them are complete and are adequately referenced to the underlying working papers.
2. Discard the review notes after amending the underlying working papers to provide the additional information requested.

Appendix III
Case Studies

Case 1
The Happy Dragon Hotel and Casino

The Happy Dragon* is a small, high-quality hotel and casino located in downtown Las Vegas. An animated, 12-foot-high, fire-spitting dragon greets customers at the entrance to the hotel lobby and casino, called the "Dragon's Den." The casino area is decorated to resemble the inside of a cave. The likeness of the dragon is featured throughout the casino's decor, and all employee uniforms and costumes display a small dragon on the left chest pocket. When a customer wins one of the various jackpots in the casino, the dragon at the entrance roars and spits fire and smoke. The building complex has 300 hotel rooms; an Oriental restaurant that also serves a limited menu of steaks, sandwiches, and specialty desserts; a gift shop; a bar; a health club featuring a weight-training center and oriental baths; and a parking area for patrons.

The hotel/casino operation is owned and managed by a small group of Las Vegas businessmen through a closely held corporation. The Happy Dragon caters to a select regional clientele, although because of its location, creative decor, and reputation for outstanding food, the casino also attracts a significant amount of business from passing tourists and local residents of Las Vegas.

Exhibits I and II on the following page show a balance sheet and income statement, respectively, for The Happy Dragon Hotel and Casino Complex. These financial statements were filed with the Nevada State Gaming Control Board for the fiscal year ended June 30, 1986.

At the last executive committee meeting, the top management of The Happy Dragon established a set of objectives for the coming year's operations:

1. 15 percent net profit on total revenue.
2. 85 percent average occupancy rate for the hotel rooms; no less than 50 percent occupancy during the Christmas season, traditionally the low point during the year; and 100 percent occupancy during the months of May, June, September, and October, as well as during holiday weekends other than Christmas.
3. 10 percent growth in total revenue.

---

*The authors appreciate the assistance of the Riviera Hotel in Las Vegas, Nevada in the preparation of these case materials.

Exhibit I
The Happy Dragon, Inc.
Balance Sheet as of June 30, 1986

Assets	
Current	$ 1,070,870
Fixed	4,432,040
Other	687,090
Total Assets	$ 6,190,000
Liabilities and Stockholders' Equity	
Current Liabilities	$ 1,176,100
Long-Term Liabilities	3,720,190
Other Liabilities	129,990
Total Liabilities	$ 5,026,280
Common Stock	500,000
Retained Earnings	663,720
Total Stockholders' Equity	$ 1,163,720
Total Liabilities and Stockholders' Equity	$ 6,190,000

Exhibit II
The Happy Dragon, Inc.
Income Statement for the Period Ended June 30, 1986

Revenue	
Casino	$ 7,720,218
Hotel Rooms	1,715,604
Restaurant	1,598,631
Bar	1,013,766
Other	844,805
Total Revenue	$ 12,893,024
Expenses	
Cost of Sales	$ 974,775
Direct Expenses	8,918,249
General and Administrative Expenses	3,367,761
Total Expenses	$ 13,260,785
Net Income	$ (367,761)

In addition to these overall objectives for the year, management intends to improve the cash controls in the casino operations. The Nevada State Gaming Control Board has requested from management an updated version of the document explaining the casino's internal control system. Each gaming establishment in the state of Nevada is required to file such a document with the Gaming Control Board. The board's review team examined The Happy Dragon's operations during the spring of last year, and the team's report expressed concern about the control of cash in the casino, specifically that the opportunity for "skimming" seemed too great. ("Skimming" occurs when employees or management take — i.e., "skim" — cash from the operations so that the income is never recorded and, therefore, not missed.) As a result of that review, management is studying casino operations, specifically cash controls, with the intention of making necessary adjustments in the cash control procedures and documenting those adjustments in the organization's internal control description to be filed with the Gaming Control Board. Of all of management's concerns, those related to cash controls in the casino are perhaps the most pressing, since the company's gaming license can be cancelled if the Gaming Control Board rejects the proposed internal control system.

Casino Operations. As customers enter the Dragon's Den, they can find the hotel registration area and hotel cashier's counter against the right wall. Bellhops stay along the front wall near the hotel registration and checkout area. The rest of the Dragon's Den is devoted to casino games. Three hundred slot machines are spread out along sections of the front, side, and back walls as well as in an area covering approximately one-fourth of the casino floor space toward the right as customers come in the entrance. The table games are located directly in front and to the left of the entrance. This area, called "the pit," includes 12 "21" (blackjack) tables, two craps (dice) tables, and one roulette table. A keno game is located in the rear of the casino, although customers throughout the casino and in the adjacent bar, restaurant, and gift shop can play keno with the assistance of "runners" to help them place and collect bets. The "cage" is located in the rear corner of the casino floor. This area is where the casino safe is located and where the casino chips and money are kept before being distributed to and after being collected from the gaming areas.

A description of how each of the casino games is played will help you better understand these operations:

Slot machines. Of all casino games of chance, the slots seem to be the most popular. Each machine accommodates one person at a time. The player places a coin in a slot on the front of the machine and then pulls a handle on the side, which causes several wheels inside the machine to spin. Positions on the wheels are marked with various designs, such as fruits or numbers. When all of the wheels stop spinning, the player can see which combinations of positions appear in a window on the front of the machine. The player may lose the bet or win various amounts of money, depending upon the particular combinations appearing in the window. The casino has nickle, quarter, and dollar slots, which can be programmed to pay out to customers certain percentages of the total revenue. These machines are not programmed to pay particular players, but rather to pay certain percentages over the course of many bets. Player winnings come out the front of the slot machines into metal pans so that players can enjoy both the sight and the sound of their winnings. The slot machines are emptied periodically, and the coins are kept in the casino safe until they are transported by armored car to the bank for deposit.

"21" (Blackjack). In this game, a dealer employed by the casino deals two cards to each player and two cards to himself or herself. Both of the players' cards are face down, while the first of the dealer's cards is face up. The object of the game is for each player to get as close to a total of 21 points on the cards as possible without going over 21, and at the same time totalling more points than the dealer. After the first two cards are dealt to each player, he or she may choose for the dealer to deal additional cards to his or her hand. After all players have received all of their desired cards, the dealer then chooses whether to deal additional cards to the "house" (the dealer's hand). When the dealer is finished, all of the hands are then compared.

All face cards (Jack, Queen, and King) count 10 points, the Ace counts either one point or 11 points as the player or dealer prefers, and all other numbered cards are counted at their face values. Those players whose totals are greater than the dealer's, but 21 or below, win. Those players whose totals are below the dealer's lose. If the player's total equals the dealer's, nobody wins. When the player's hand totals more than 21, the hand goes "bust" and the dealer wins, unless, of course, the dealer's hand also totals more than 21, in which case both hands "bust" and nobody wins.

Players have two chances to place bets in this game. The first bet is made before any cards are dealt; the second bet may be placed after all players and the dealer have received their first two cards, but before additional cards are distributed. To make their bets, players place the desired amount of chips on the table directly in front of them. Players do not play the table games with cash. Instead, players buy chips corresponding to different dollar denominations, such as $5, $10, $25, $50, $100, etc. Players bet their chips, and when they are finished playing, they cash in their chips.

Craps. Craps is an extremely popular game in which bets may be placed not only by the player throwing the dice (called the "shooter"), but also by other players who bet on possible outcomes of the throws. Bets are made by placing the desired amount of chips on various positions on the craps board.

An illustration of the craps board appears on the following page. The circled letters A through J indicate areas on the board where different bets may be made:

A   "Pass Line." A bet on "pass line" pays even money, i.e., the same amount the player bet. A player wins on 7 or 11 and loses on 2, 3, or 12 on the first throw of the dice. If any other number comes up, that number is the player's "point." If the same number is thrown again before a 7 is thrown, the player wins. Otherwise, the player loses. The bet is made before the first throw.

B   "Don't Pass Bar." The opposite of A. The player loses on 7 or 11 and wins on 2 or 3 on the first throw. A 12 on the first throw is a stand-off and nobody wins. The player also loses if the "point" number is thrown before a 7. Again, the bet is made before the first throw.

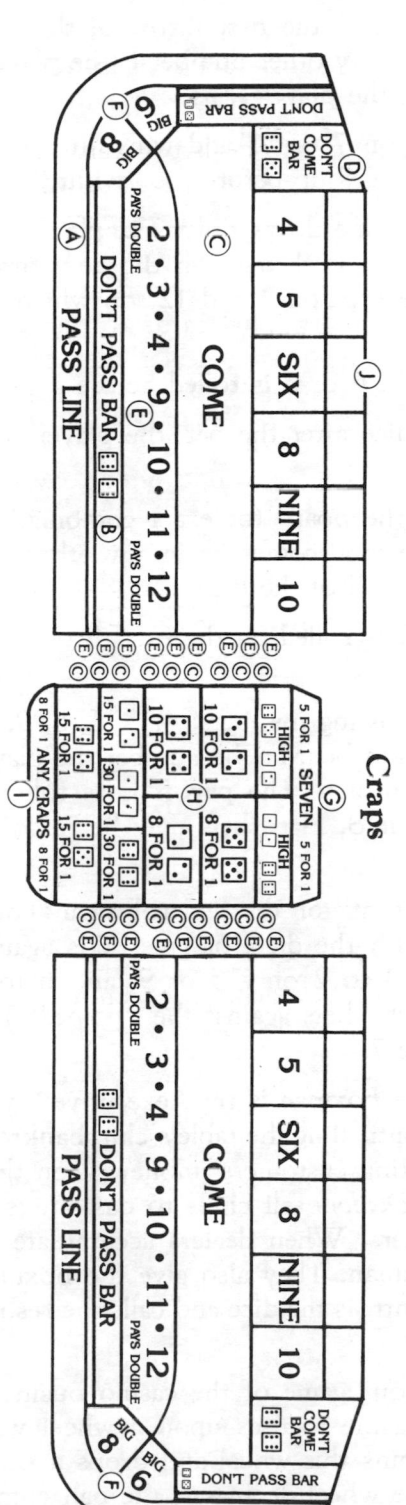

Craps

Roulette

C   "Come." A "come" bet may be made at any time after the first throw of the dice. The player wins on 7 or 11 and loses on 2, 3, or 12. Any other number is the player's "point," and if that number occurs again before a 7, the player wins.

D   "Don't Come." The reverse of C. The player loses on 7 or 11 and wins on 2 or 3. A throw of 12 is a stand-off. The player wins if 7 comes up before the "point."

E   "Field." This area of the table is reserved for bets for one throw only. The player bets on 2, 3, 4, 9, 10, 11, or 12. If any of these numbers is thrown on the next throw after the bet is made, the player wins even money, except on 2 and 12, on which the player wins 2 to 1.

F   "Big 6" and "Big 8." The player wins even money if a 6 or 8 is rolled before a 7.

G   "Any 7." If a 7 is thrown on the first roll of the dice after the bet, the player wins 5 to 1.

H   "Hard Ways." The player wins at odds quoted on the board for exact combinations of numbers on the dice. The player loses if the same total comes up in any other way or if a 7 comes up. These bets are made for a single roll of the dice.

I   "Any Craps." The player wins 8 to 1 if a 2, 3, or 12 is rolled on the first throw after the bet is made.

J   "Place Bets." Players may make place bets on the following numbers: 4, 5, 6, 8, 9, or 10. You can see these numbers along the top of the craps board. The number the player places must be rolled by the shooter before a 7 is thrown. The payoff is as follows: 9 to 5 on 4 or 10; 7 to 5 on 5 or 9; 7 to 6 on 6 or 8. Place bets may be removed at any time before a roll.

Also, once a "point" is established (either a "shooter's point" on the first roll or a "come point" on a succeeding roll), the player can get odds with the dice, or give odds against the dice. The player gets 2 to 1 on a roll of 10 or 4; 3 to 2 on a 5 or 9; and 6 to 5 on 8 or 6. The player lays the same odds when he or she bets against the "point." The payoff is made on whether the "point" occurs before the 7.

Three types of employees work at the craps table. The *boxman* is the "executive" who supervises the table. This person also is responsible for controlling the table's chip bankroll, making sure the dice are not changed or damaged, counting customers' money when they buy chips, and handling customer disputes and claims. *Dealers* sell chips to customers at the table, collect bets from the table, and pay the winners. When dealers accumulate an excess number of chips, they give the excess to the boxman. They also give the boxman the cash collected from the sale of chips. The *stickman* controls the dice and calls the results of each throw by the shooter.

Roulette. Roulette often is considered to be the glamour game of the casino business, with the continental atmosphere of Monte Carlo. The game focuses upon a wheel with colored numbers marked on its perimeter. The dealer spins this wheel and drops a small white ball onto the wheel as it spins. As the speed of the wheel decreases, the ball comes to rest in a small slot corresponding to one of the colored numbers.

The game offers a wide variety of bets, where players bet on a single number, color (red or black), odd or even, or they may make combination bets where they split bets in a combination of adjoining numbers on the table. Bets are made by positioning the amount of chips to be bet on various areas of the table. A number of typical bets are indicated by means of letters A through I circled on the roulette layout shown on page 883. The black numbers are indicated by black areas containing white numbers, and the red numbers are indicated by white areas containing black numbers. The 0 and 00 are neither black nor red, and are indicated in the illustration by grey shaded areas.

Bets can be made on any corresponding combinations of numbers. For example: bet "F" — the same placement on number "28" would pay off 28, 29, and 30. The same principle applies to all other combination bets. The winning odds for each bet illustrated are as follows:

Straight Bets

A   Odds: 35 to 1. A *straight-up* bet is made on a particular number, including all red and black numbers as well as 0 and 00.

B   Odds: 2 to 1. *Column bets* are made on one of the three columns of numbers. Bets pay off if the ball comes to rest on any number in the column for which a bet is made.

C   Odds: 2 to 1. A "*1st dozen*" bet pays off on any number 1 through 12. Of course, bets also may be placed for the "2nd dozen" or "3rd dozen," as the positions on the table indicate.

D   Odds: even. A bet on this position pays off for any number 1 through 18.

Combination Bets

E   Odds: 17 to 1. Positioning chips on the line between two numbers (such as the 11 and 12) indicates a *split* bet, and if the ball comes to rest on the number on either side of the line, the player wins.

F   Odds: 11 to 1. Positioning chips on the edge of a row, such as shown in the illustration, results in a payoff for any of the three numbers in the row. In this case, a 13, 14, or 15 would win.

G   Odds: 8 to 1. By placing the chips on a corner of four adjacent numbers, the player wins on any one of the four numbers. In this case, the player would win on a 17, 18, 20, or 21.

H   Odds: 6 to 1. This particular positioning of a bet between the top two rows pays off on 0, 00, 1, 2, and 3.

I   Odds: 5 to 1. Similarly, positioning a bet on the interior boundary of the number table and between two rows pays off on any number in the two rows. In this example, the bet is made on the five numbers 22, 23, 24, 25, and 26. If the ball comes to rest on any of these numbers, the player wins.

The roulette dealer is responsible for selling chips, taking all bets on each game, operating the wheel, paying the winners, and collecting the losing wagers.

Keno. Keno is a numbers guessing game. A player gets a card numbered from 1 through 80. The player selects 10 of the numbers that he or she thinks may come up in the game. The player gives a copy of the card to the Keno dealer or one of several "runners" who collect bets from various locations in the casino, restaurant, bar, and gift shop. The player gets and keeps a copy of the card with the selected numbers.

The Keno dealer chooses 10 balls from a large metal basket containing 80 balls numbered 1 through 80. The numbers from the 10 balls are flashed on Keno boards located throughout the casino and adjacent areas. Players know immediately whether or not they have won. A typical payoff schedule for a $1.20 bet is outlined below:

Number Chosen Correctly	Amount of Winnings
5	$ 2.40
6	24.00
7	180.00
8	1,320.00
9	4,800.00
10	25,000.00

The player collects his or her winnings in chips from the Keno dealer or one of the Keno "runners," after which the chips may be cashed in.

Other Considerations for Casino Management. In order for the casino to maximize its profits, it is important for each of the games to operate quickly, but not so quickly that customers become discouraged or think that they are being cheated. Human relations become an important part of casino management, especially since many of the customers may become somewhat irrational when they have consumed too much alcohol. Also, many people continue playing for long hours and become very tired mentally, which also may interfere with their better judgment.

The casino cash flow system may be diagrammed as shown on the following page.

Required:
Suppose that you are given the responsibility of establishing effective internal controls for the cash management of The Dragon's Den.

1. Flowchart the play of each of the casino games, being sure to identify cash flows.
2. Identify key control points in each game.
3. Recommend control policies and procedures that you think are important to an effective internal cash control system for each of the games.
4. Are there any more general concerns over cash management, other than those specific to the particular games, that you think are important to the control system? Identify them and suggest possible internal control measures addressing these additional concerns.

5.   How could skimming be done in the casino operation if management were trying to avoid taxation by diverting cash away from the accounting system? What controls would help avoid this problem?

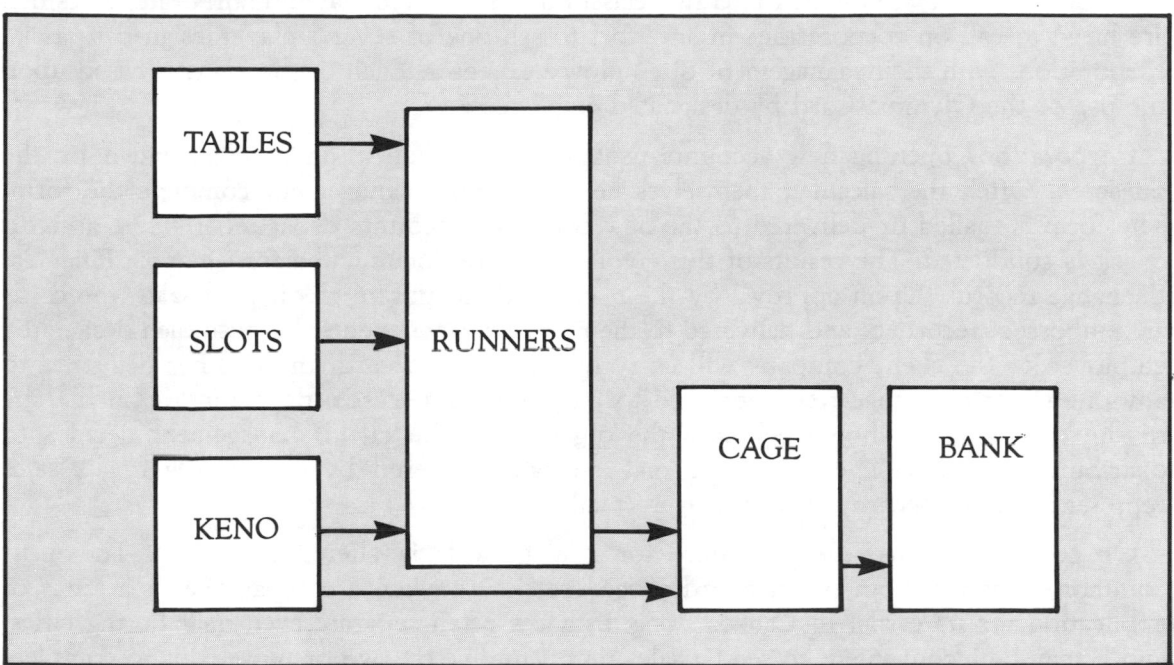

Case 2
Olympia Financial Exchange Corporation

The Olympia Financial Exchange Corporation* is a multinational company with three branches of activity — an internal credit card business, traveler's checks, and travel insurance. The company was founded in 1947 with its traveler's checks operations. Travel insurance was added five years later, and the credit card operations followed in 1954. The company has marketed itself worldwide as a prestigious institution and has developed an exclusive upper-class clientele. In fact, persons carrying an "Olympia Card" often are given VIP treatment in many establishments simply because the card itself identifies its owner as a wealthy member of the international set. Companies have come to value the card because of the prestige it gives their employees and also because of the excellent service Olympia Financial Exchange provides. While the traveler's checks and travel insurance are marketed to a broader clientele, these products also are highly regarded for their excellent service and reasonable cost. Olympia Financial Exchange has successfully developed a reputation as a well-managed, profitable, and quality-oriented company.

*The authors appreciate the assistance of American Express Corporation in the preparation of these case materials.

The Eastern Continental Region auditors for Olympia Financial Exchange examined the corporate credit card sales operations in Montreal. This audit was requested by the director of credit card operations of the Montreal office.

Credit card sales are divided into two classifications — personal and corporate. Salesmen are hired to call on corporations in an effort to sell one of several plans designed to assist corporations with their management of employee expenses. Each of the plans is based upon the use of the Olympia Card by designated employees.

Corporations opening new accounts usually file an application form provided by the salesmen. Often the salesmen themselves help corporate management complete the form. The form is mailed or delivered to the new corporate accounts department where a credit check is conducted. The results of this credit check are documented for Olympia Financial Exchange records. Upon approval by the manager of corporate credit card sales, the cards are embossed, recorded, and delivered to the new corporate clients. Because each designated employee of the client company will carry his or her own card, the number delivered to any one client can range from one card to more than 100 cards, depending upon the size of the company and how deep into the organization the client management decides to distribute the cards. The new cards may be hand-delivered by one of Olympia's sales representatives or sent by special-delivery mail.

On some occasions, the procedure for issuing cards is altered somewhat. The most common deviation from the standard procedure occurs when a company sends a letter of application for its cards. In Canada, long distances often separate even neighboring cities, and it may be inconvenient to send a sales representative on two or more trips to complete the usual application process. Also, since Olympia Financial Exchange likes to give its customers as much personal service as possible, Olympia management has decided that it is better to do a credit check on a company, and if this check is good, then to go ahead and issue the cards prior to the signing of a formal contract. The formal application may be delivered by a sales representative at the same time of delivery of the cards. The application, which serves as a binding contract, may be completed and signed at that time.

Upon receipt of the cards with the signing of the application contract, the client companies then distribute cards to the designated employees. The employees use the cards at various places throughout the world. The places of business where the cards are used then send the credit slips to the nearest regional operations center of Olympia Financial Exchange, which then reroutes the slips to the Canadian Regional Operations Center in Montreal. A computer tape with records of all transactions is sent with the slips. Interestingly, the accounting records for the Montreal office are not held or managed in Montreal, but in Miami, Florida.

All of Olympia's offices worldwide are on a computerized communication network. As the Montreal Regional Operations Center collects the sales slips for its customers, the records of these credit purchases are sent via the computer network to Miami, where the accounting records are updated. A record of each customer's account is updated in a large data base format. Each month the customer's bill is printed in Montreal from the records in Miami and mailed with all sales slips received during the month to the client company. In some cases the client companies want their employees billed directly, with a summary report sent to the company reporting the use of each outstanding card. The employees then pay their own bills and request reimbursement from their employers. All payments for bills issued from the Montreal office are received at that office, and records of the payments are transmitted to the Miami office. The Miami office performs an aging analysis report monthly on all of the Montreal accounts and then transmits this report to the Montreal management so that appropriate action may be taken on those accounts that are past due.

There are four types of documentation created for sales to client companies:

1. The applicant company's letter of application.
2. The formal application contract.
3. Monthly computerized reports containing:
   a. All of the companies using the credit card program.
   b. New companies added during the month.
   c. Companies dropping the service during the month.
   d. The number of cards issued to each of the companies listed in the report.
   e. The number of cards cancelled during the month.
   f. The total cards outstanding.
   g. The month's billing amount for each company with totals for the year-to-date.
   h. A combined total billing amount for all companies during the month with a year-to-date total.
4. A manual, local office report summarizing and comparing the performance during the month and the year-to-date sales of each sales representative in the office.

Of course, not all companies will generate all four types of documentation. Some of these sales will be recorded only in an application contract, the monthly computerized report, and the manual office report. Only those companies that initiate the sale in writing will have a letter of application.

Olympia Financial Exchange offers an incentive plan for sales representatives to promote the corporate credit card program among the large companies of the region. The regular compensation for a sales representative is $2,000 per month with an additional $100 commission on each corporate sale. If the corporate account results in between 25 and 59 cards being issued to the account, an additional $250 bonus is paid. If the number of cards is between 60 and 99, the bonus is $500 in addition to the $100 commission for the sale. If the sale results in 100 or more cards issued to the company, the bonus is $750. Olympia Financial Exchange has a policy that if a client company decides at any time after the original application that it wants to decrease the number of outstanding cards issued on its account, a written request for the cancellation of the desired number of cards must be submitted. In order to simplify the bonus plan and maintain the incentive plan, Olympia Financial Exchange does not alter the bonuses if cards are cancelled by a client company, even if the cancellation means that the client company's number of cards places it in a lower bonus category. Even if the company changes its mind on the day the cards are issued, the original bonus holds for the sales representative. There are 10 sales representatives working out of the Montreal Regional Operations Center.

A six-month summary of corporate sales is shown below:

Month	Corporate Sales (Total)	Less than 25 Cards	25-59 Cards	60-99 Cards	100 or More Cards
January	205	125	40	25	15
February	215	155	45	5	10
March	160	105	50	5	0
April	260	171	30	32	27
May	270	170	40	36	24
June	220	157	31	20	12

The director of credit card operations in the Montreal office had requested the audit because of some suspicious information that had come to his attention. He had been transferred to the Montreal office from the company's San Francisco office only a month before requesting the audit, and during that month he had reviewed all of the various documentation related to credit card operations. The number of duplicate names being issued to companies was of particular concern to him. That is, many of the companies would receive a number of cards issued to the same person within the company. He also became concerned when he noticed what appeared to be an inordinant number of card cancellations.

The director of credit card operations asked the manager of corporate card sales about these concerns. The manager of corporate card sales explained that the duplicate names could occur in one of two ways. First, many corporations order a number of cards in addition to the ones that they already have designated for particular employees. These additional cards are kept by the companies for additional employees who might later be designated as card holders. Also, sometimes the companies would let some employees use the additional cards on a temporary basis. The additional cards usually were issued with the company presidents' names on them.

The second way duplicate cards might be issued relates to the Olympia "Hospitality Card" program. Some companies may wish to offer a gift of an Olympia Card to executives of some of their prized clients. A special program was designed to accommodate these gifts. Olympia Financial Exchange allows individual cardholders to apply for temporary cards which may be given as gifts. The cards appear just like regular Olympia Cards, but are embossed across the bottom with the message, "Hospitality Card." The cards also may be issued with short-term expiration dates. Again, these cards usually were printed in the name of the giver, who was already an Olympia Card holder. All of the bills for the card are charged to the one account number of the original card. Consequently, duplicate cards are issued, and all may be active at the same time.

The manager also explained that the cancellation policy had existed ever since Olympia Financial Exchange began a separate corporate sales operation. He noticed that the number of cancellations had seemed to increase during the past two years, shortly after the current sales incentive program had gone into operation, but corporate card sales also had increased significantly during this same period.

The director of credit card operations still wasn't satisfied. The situation just didn't feel right. He wanted the auditors to examine the corporate sales operations.

Required:
1. Flowchart the corporate card transaction cycle, from the initial application for the corporate cards through billing.
2. Locate likely key control points in this cycle.
3. What current dangers seem to exist in the sales operations, especially with respect to how the sales representatives handle the corporate sales?
4. Write an audit program stating your audit objectives, specific audit procedures, and the evidence you would expect from these audit procedures.
5. What corrective measures might be taken to minimize the dangers you outlined in #3, above?

Case 3
CASI Energy Company Golf Course

CASI Energy Company* is a medium-sized fossil-fuel production and energy research company, with headquarters located in Houston, Texas. The company offers its employees a variety of recreational facilities. The company owns the CASI Club, a complex comprising a restaurant, fitness center, and tennis courts. It also owns a nine-hole golf course. The use of these facilities is available for nominal fees to all CASI employees and their guests.

CASI's internal auditors examined the records and operations of these facilities in addition to those of the business functions of the company. Christine Kelly, a senior auditor, and Jonathan Berkley, an intern from a nearby university, were assigned to audit the company golf course. The materials in this case represent their working paper file, including a copy of the audit report and a letter of transmittal from David Jackson, the director of internal auditing. You will notice the initials "AR" designating the person reviewing the auditors' working papers. The "AR" stands for Al Reynolds, an audit supervisor for the company. You also will notice that these working papers are computer generated. Auditors for CASI are issued portable microcomputers, with appropriate auditing software, for all of their assignments.

Required:
Critique the working papers, including the audit report and the letter of transmittal. You should evaluate the performance, documentation, and reporting of this audit in general. You also should critique the form, style, and content of the working papers specifically, noting which working papers are faulty and how they might be improved. In your analysis you should be alert to such problems as incorrect terminology, poor formatting, unsubstantiated findings, illogical recommendations, improperly reviewed working papers, missing working

---

*The authors appreciate the assistance of Randy Van Dyke and Richard Mitchell, director of internal auditing and audit manager for the University of Utah, respectively, in the preparation of these case materials.

papers, weak evidence, strong evidence of problems that were unreported, suspicious evidence needing further investigation, improper indexing, and numerical or other logical inconsistencies. Although all of these (and possibly other) problems may or may not be present in these papers, the point is to be as thorough as you would expect a professional auditor to be in such a review.

Remember that there may not be one "best" solution to this case. It is important to keep in mind, however, that certain objectives should be satisfied when performing, documenting, and reporting an audit. You should be prepared to defend your solution in terms of how it meets these objectives.

GOLF COURSE

Summary Workpaper Index

100   Indexed audit report

200   Findings and recommendations

300   Audit Program

400   Preliminary survey (see section index)

500   Administrative (see section index)

Page Index No.:

```
                    INTERNAL AUDITING DEPARTMENT


             OPERATIONAL REVIEW OF CASI GOLF COURSE



                         May 18, 1984






Distribution:

     Paul E. Gardner, President of CASI Energy Co.
     C. G. Morris, Director of Employee Relations
     David Jackson, Director of Internal Auditing




                                        Audit No. 4.034
```

```
Page Index No.:
```

(logo here)   Internal Auditing Department
                                                   9876 Childress Blvd.
                                                   Houston, Texas 75641

                                                   713-654-8630

                                                   May 18, 1984

President Paul E. Gardner
CASI Energy Co.
9870 Childress Blvd. Suite A
Houston, Texas 75641

Dear President Gardner:

     We have completed an operational review of the CASI Golf Course.
The general objectives of our review were to determine the
effectiveness of controls over financial and physical assets and to
evaluate the business operation of the golf course.

     Based on our review, we have concluded that the CASI Golf Course
is a well-managed auxiliary service which serves a useful purpose to
the company and its employees. However, we have made several audit
recommendations which we believe will further strengthen management
control over golf course funds.

     Background information concerning the company golf course, along
with our specific audit objectives, findings and recommendations are
summarized on the following pages. Within six months of the date of
this report, the Internal Auditing Department will conduct a compliance
review of the golf course.

     We wish to express our appreciation for the cooperation and
positive attitudes demonstrated by the golf course employees during the
conduct of the audit.

Respectfully,

David Jackson
Director of Internal Auditing

Page Index No.:

BACKGROUND

CASI Energy Co. operates a nine-hole, 3,457-yard golf course for the use of company employees and their guests. The golf course is classified as an auxiliary service and as such receives limited support from company operational funds. Nominal green fees are charged, which, along with golf instruction fees and the sale and rental of clothing and equipment, cover most of the cost of operating the course, including maintenance of the golf shop, equipment shed, fairways, and putting greens.

The golf course employees a full-time golf professional, who also manages the course and facilities, and who hires other part-time personnel on a seasonal basis.

Revenues, expenditures, and income of the course for recent years were as follows:

	1981	1982	1983
REVENUE			
Green Fees	36,655	40,950	31,959
Merchandise Sales/Rentals	15,891	11,286	5,720
Transfer of Company Funds	20,000	21,000	26,000
GolfInstruction	1,295	3,269	500
Total Revenues	73,841	76,505	64,179
EXPENSES			
Salaries and Wages	35,226	38,485	20,818
Repairs and Maintenance	25,000	25,620	26,000
Allocated Overhead	970	1,033	749
Supplies	1,184	2,286	742
Telephone	258	329	266
Cost of Goods Sold	7,554	6,675	4,671
Rental Equipment	367	428	52
Other	701	651	270
Total Expenses	71,260	75,507	63,568
INCOME	2,581	998	611

AUDIT OBJECTIVES

After a preliminary survey of the operations and financial records of the company golf course, we determined the specific objectives of this review to be as follows:

1. To evaluate the accuracy and completeness of financial records and to determine whether expenditures are adequately documented, prudent, and in compliance with company policy.

   The company golf course has a 1984 budget of $75,000 and projected revenues of $75,600. Approximately 53% of the budget is to be expended for salaries and wages and 35% percent for repairs and maintenance. Approximately 9% is budgeted for cost of goods to be sold during the year. Green fees are again expected to be the chief source of revenues during the year, providing a budgeted $41,500, or 55% of the budgeted revenues. The next highest source of revenue is expected to be transfers from company funds, a budgeted $20,000. The golf course management expresses the hope that should actual earned revenues fall short of expectations, the company will continue to provide adequate funds to adequately maintain the course for play.

2. To determine whether internal controls over cash and other assets are reasonable and adequate.

   Golf course revenue is derived primarily from cash sales (annual passes or daily green fees), sale of merchandise, rental of equipment, sale of golfing instruction. Strong internal controls are normally required in the sale of such merchandise and services.

3. To determine whether the gold course is meeting the objective of providing a quality recreation facility at a reasonable cost to officers and employees of the company.

4. A fee schedule covering daily, quarterly, and annual passes has been prepared and is designed to recover the cost of operating the course. During 1983 approximately 52 season passes were sold, 194 complimentary passes were issued to visiting officials, and $41,000 in green fees was collected for individual play. Approximately 23,700 rounds were played on the course during the year.

RECOMMENDATIONS

I. Internal Control

   A. Cash Receipts Reconciliations

     We noted that daily cash receipts are not reconciled to amounts
     shown on the "starter" sheets. All golfers are required to sign
     in and record amount paid for green fees on the "starter" sheet.
     These amounts should agree with applicable cash register totals.
     We also noted that no sign-in record is maintained for golf
     lessons.

     We recommend that golf lesson sign-up sheets be maintained to
     record all lessons sold. We also recommend that daily sales
     reports prepared by the golf course management include totals from
     starter sheets and from lesson sign-up sheets to reconcile with
     cash register totals.

   B. Undeposited Receipts

     The golf course change fund and current days receipts are
     sometimes taken home by the golf pro, because the golf shop is not
     considered secure. We believe that transporting and retaining
     overnight custody of these funds results in undue risk to a
     company employee.

     We recommend that the golf pro consider installing a small safe in
     the golf shop. Also, arrangements could be made to have daily
     receipts delivered to the company's cashier if the receipts exceed
     a designated amount. The change fund and evening receipts would
     then be secured in the golf shop safe overnight.

   C. Golf Passes

     Season and quarterly golf passes are sold at the golf shop and
     through the company cashier's office. There is no listing
     maintained of individuals who buy passes against which a
     reconciliation can be made of passes originally issued, sold, or
     which remain unsold.

     We recommend that a listing be maintained showing name, date,
     amount, and pass number for each pass sold. Periodic
     reconciliations should be made to ensure positive control over
     passes.

II. Policies and Procedures

   Reports of Property Damage or Injury

     There is no clear policy or instruction to be followed by golf
     course employees concerning property damage or personal injury to
     passers-by resulting from golf course play. Correct actions or
     statements by company employees could minimize the company's
     liability in case of such occurrences.

     We recommend that the Employee Relations Dept. and the golf pro
     outline a set of instructions concerning appropriate actions when
     damage or injury complaints are received. A set of these
     instructions should be kept at the golf shop at all times.

RESPONSE

I. Internal Control

   A. Cash Receipts Reconciliations

      Recommendation:

      Internal Audit recommends that a golf lesson sign-up record should
      be maintained to record all lessons sold. They also recommend
      that daily sales reports prepared by the golf pro include totals
      from starter sheets and from lesson sign-up sheets to reconcile
      with cash register records.

      Response:

      Agree with the recommendation. We are currently working on forms,
      which will be used by the golf course management, which will
      include the above information.

   B. Undeposited Receipts

      Recommendation:

      Internal Audit recommends that the golf pro consider installing a
      small safe in the golf shop. Also, arrangements could be made to
      have daily receipts delivered to the cashier's office each
      afternoon if the receipts exceed a designated amount. The change
      fund and evening receipts would then be secured in the golf shop
      safe overnight.

      Response:

      Disagree with this recommendation. We feel that the golf pro can
      drop off the day's receipts at the night depository of the
      Commercial Bank, where golf course accounts are kept. We would
      not want to leave money in the golf shop due to its history of
      break-ins and its isolated location. Although a safe would
      probably prevent theft, it would probably be damaged by a would-be
      thief.

   C. Golf Passes

      Recommendation:

      Internal Audit recommends that a listing be maintained showing
      name, date, amount collected and pass number for each golf pass
      sold. Periodic reconciliation should be made to ensure positive
      control over passes.

      Response:

      Agree with the recommendation. We have this system in operation
      at this time, using a ledger book at both the cashier's office and
      the golf shop.

II. Policies and Procedures

    Reports of Property Damage or Injury

    Internal Audit recommends that the Employee Relations Dept. and
    the golf pro work together to outline appropriate actions when
    damage or injury complaints are received.

    Response:

    Agree with the recommendation. A written procedure statement is
    currently being formulated. Copies will be sent to the Internal
    Auditing Department.

Recommendation #1

Auditor _CK_ Date _5-16-84_

Finding: The change fund and current days rerceipts are usually taken home in the evening by the folf course manager because the golf course office is not considered secure. The amount of funds sometimes exceeds several hundred dollars. We believe that this practice exposes a company employee to unnecessary exposure to possible robbery and harm.

Recommendation: We recommend that some arrangement be made to either have daily deposits secured in the company offices, such as the cashier's office, each evening or that a floor safe be installed in the golf shop and cash be secured there each evening.

Discussion: This condition came to light through discussion of cash handling procedures with the golf pro. He indicateda concern for securing the funds and had assumed the responsibility by taking the cash home without regard for the personal risk. We believe that the company should take necessary action to ensure employee and asset security. The matter was discussed with the company Employees Relations Director and the assistant controller, both of whom agree with the finding and agree to take appropriate action.

Workpaper Reference: 403, 404

Report Reference: Audit Report, p. 4

Page Index No.: 200

RECOMMENDATION #2

Auditor <u>CK</u> Date <u>5-16-84</u>

<u>Finding</u>: Season and quarterly passes are sold at the company cashier's office and the golf shop. There is no on-going record maintained, by pass number, or passes sold and passes remaining. There is no reconciliation made to ensure accountability for passes.

<u>Recommendation</u>: We recommend that at each location where passes are sold, a continuous listing be maintained showing pass number, purchaser, amount of payment, and date of purchase. We recommend that a periodic check be made to reconcile cash collected and unsold passes on hand.

<u>Discussion</u>: The practice of poor control over passes was discovered when we attempted to determine how many passes had been sold and how many were being held in unsold inventory. We discossed the problem with the golf pro, who agreed to address the problem.

<u>Workpaper Reference</u>: 403,404

<u>Report Reference</u>: Audit Report, p. 4

```
                    RECOMMENDATION #3

              Auditor  CK  Date 5-16-84


Finding: There is no reconciliation of golf customer sign-in sheets or
golf lesson sales sheets to daily sales recorded on the cash register.
All golfers are required to sign in for play (but not for lessons) and
indicate payment the amount of payment made.  Cash received for play
and lessons is rung up on the cash register.  These two records are not
compared.  Tests indicated regular overages and shortages. (See 502.1)

Recommendation: We recommend that sign-up sheets be maintained for both
lessons and play and that a daily reconciliation be made between cash
receipts and sign-up sheets.

Discussion: We discussed this situation with the golf pro who offered
some resistence to the recommendation, saying that the sign-up sheet
wasnot intended as an accounting record, but to control play.  We are
convinced that it should serve both purposes.

Workpaper Reference: 502, 501, 404, 403

Report Reference:  Audit Report, p. 4
```

```
Page Index No.: 202
```

RECOMMENDATION #4

Auditor _CK_ Date _5-16-84_

Finding: There is no written policy or instruction tobe followed by golf course personnel concerning property damage or personal injury resulting from golf course play. Two public-use roads cross the course with a moderately heavy traffic flow. Correct actions or statements by golf course employees in the event of accidents could serve tominimize the company's liability.

Recommendation: We recommend that golf course employees be provided written instructions concerning appropriate actions to be taken in dealing with injury or damage complaints. Perhaps these instructions might be drawn up by the golf pro and the director of employee relations.

Discussion: We discussed this situation with the company director of employee relations and with the company risk manager, both of whom agreed that such a policy document would be desirable.

Workpaper Reference: 403

Report Reference: _Audit Report, p. 5_

Preparer _CK_ Date 4-20-84

Reviewer_____Date____

GOLF COURSE
Audit Program

Done By   Index

Planning and Preliminary

1. Confer with the Director of Auditing
   to determine the scope of the
   assignment, audit objectives, and
   areas of special attention.   ✓

2. Prepare and send a letter to the golf   ✓   601
   pro and the director of employee
   relations informing them of the audit.

3. Review applicable background information
   relevant to the area under review.

   a. Previous audit reports and working   ✓
      papers.
   b. Company policies and procedures   ✓
      manual.   ✓
   c. Audit correspondence files.

4. Arrange and conduct an opening   ✓   602
   conference.

5. Interview key employees.   ✓   403-404

Page Index No.: 300

```
                                              Preparer_____Date_____

                                              Reviewer_____Date_____

     GOLF COURSE
     Preliminary Survey
     Workpaper Index


     Index

     401 Review of Financial Data

     402 Review of Other Operating Statistics

     403 Interview--Golf Pro

     404 Interview--Assistant Cashier
```

```
Page Index No.: 400
```

Preparer _CK_ Date _4-29-84_

Reviewer _AK_ Date _4/30_

GOLF COURSE
Review of Financial Data

	1981	1982	1983
REVENUE			
Green fees	36,655	40,950	31,959
Merchandise sales/rentals	15,891	11,286	5,720
Transfer of company funds	20,000	20,000	26,000
Golf Instruction	1,295	3,269	500
Total Revenue	73,841	76,505	64,179
EXPENSES			
Salaries and wages	35,226	38,485	30,818
Repair and maintenance	25,000	25,620	26,000
Allocated overhead	970	1,033	749
Supplies	1,184	2,286	742
Telephone	258	329	266
Cost of goods sold	7,544	6,675	4,671
Rental equipment	367	428	52
Other	701	651	270
Total Expenditures	71,260	75,507	63,568
OPERATING INCOME	2,581	998	611

Page Index No.: 401

Preparer _JB_ Date _5/3/84_
Reviewer _AK_ Date _5/5_

GOLF COURSE
Usage Schedule (from green fee starter sheets)

	Employees	Guests	Comps (free)	Total
Fall '82	3,034	1,177	1,257	5,468
Winter '82	519	157	136	812
Spring '82	4,219	2,422	2,291	8,932
Summer '82	4,195	2,620	1,537	8,352
Total Rounds	11,967	6,376	5,221	23,564
% of Total	51%	27%	22%	100%
Green Fees	$2.00/9 hls	$3.00/9 hls		
Revenue	$23,934	$19,128		$43,092

COMMENT: We totalled the data on the daily starter sheets for green
fees and determined that most of the usage is by company personnel,
second by employee guests. There do, however, appear to be a rather
large number of free passes given.

Page Index No.: 402

Preparer _C. K._ Date 5-10-84

Reviewer _AK_ Date 5/14

GOLF COURSE
Interview with golf pro

Date of interview: May 5, 1984
Location: Golf shop
Present: Christine Kelly, lead auditor
         Jonathan Berkley, intern
         Kenneth (Ken) Larsen, golf pro

Ref.

Synopsis of Items Discussed

1. Discussed the general policies of the golf course operation,
including starting times, special groups, playing lessons, regular
lessons, etc. Also procedures for signing up and controlling
play. No problems noted.

2. Discussed maintenance responsibilities for golf course,
facilities and equipment. Spring and summer employees include one
full-time greens keeper, four part-time maintenance personnel, and
one golf shop assistant. During the fall only two part-time
maintenance personnel are employed, and during winter months the
golf pro employs the green keeper full-time and the golf shop
assistant part-time.

3. Discussed golf lessons. Lessons are scheduled by the golf pro,
but there is no sign-up sheet. Cost is $20 per hour, which is
rung up at the time of payment, but there is no record against
which this transaction can be reconciled. PROBLEM: This current
procedure results in a loss of control, because of the involvement
of only one employee and no cross-check possibility.

4. Discussed green fee procedures. Players sign starter sheet and
record amount paid. Employee rings up sale on cash register.
Normally no receipt is issued. Amounts on starter sheet are not
reconciled with cash amount. PROBLEM: The possibility for a
counter-check is available but not used.

5. Discussed the risks involved in having two public roads with
moderate traffic passing over them during playing hours. There
have been several instances of vehicles being struck by errant
golf balls. Golf course personnel have not instructions on what
to do or say in these cases when confronted by the drivers of the
vehicles. There is no provision at present for complaints to be
referred beyond the golf pro, who no authority to act on behalf of
the company in issues of company liability. PROBLEM: The company
could be held liable if serious accident occurs and situation is
mishandled by golf course personnel.

6. Discussed cash handling procedures. A change fund is
maintained and each evening the golf pro takes the day's receipts
plus the change fund home with him and deposits the money the
following morning at Commercial Bank, where the golf course
accounts are held. PROBLEM: The golf pro is exposed to the danger
of being robbed if it were discovered that he is transporting and
keeping these funds overnight.

Page Index No.: 403

Preparer _CK_ Date _5-10-84_
Reviewer _AK_ Date _5/14_

GOLF COURSE
Interview with assistant controller

Date of interview: May 6, 1984
Location: Accounting Dept. Conference Room
Present: Christine Kelly, lead auditor
        Jonathan Berkley, intern
        Maud Griggs, assistant controller

Q. Please explain how revenue from the company golf course is handled.

A. Ken brings to the cashier's office the previous day's cash register tapes and the bank deposit slips for the day's deposit. The cashier's office then delivers the tapes and deposit slips to the assistant contrtoller's office, at which time one of the bookkeeping clerks enters the information in the company's books.

Q. Does Ken bring the sign-in sheets?

A. No.

Q. How do you know all green fees are rung up?

A. Can's be sure. There is no check. We do check the cash register tapes with the deposit slips, which almost always reconcile to the penny.

Q. What about golf lessons? Is there any kind of reconciliation of information regarding the number of lessons and the fees collected?

A. Same situation. We assume things are all right there.

Q. Who receives complimentary memberships?

A. This past year we don't know. Public relations gives them out. We asked for a list of the recipients, but they have given us the list yet.

Q. Are the membership cards, the complimentary ones, numbered?

A. Yes. They are preprinted with numbers.

Page Index No.: 404

```
                                              Preparer_____Date_____

                                              Reviewer_____Date_____
       GOLF COURSE
       Detailed Tests and Analysis
       Workpaper Index


       Index

       501   Internal control review--cash and negotiable items

       502   Cash receipts test

       503   Surprise cash count

       504   Review and analysis of complimentary passes

       505  Operating expenditures test
```

```
       Page Index No.: 500
```

Preparer ___ Date 5/7
Reviewer ___ Date 5/14

GOLF COURSE
Internal controls review--cash and negotiable items

Objective: To determine whether control over cash and negotiable items
by golf course personnel is adequate.

Procedures: Review proceduresd with personnel concerned, observe
transactions and review documents and records involved to learn
procedures followed in handling cash and negotiable assets.

Results: We observed that the cash collection procedures were weak in
that no cash register receipt was issued when a customer paid a green
fee or a lesson fee, or for merchandise purchased or rented. Also, no
reconciliation between the green fee sign-up sheet and the green fees
collected. It would be possible for an employee to accept payment and
ring up a no-sale on the cash register and direct the cash to other
purposes.

Reference: workpapers 403, 404

Page Index No.: 501

Preparer _C K_ Date _5-7-84_

Reviewer _AK_ Date _5/17_

GOLF COURSE
Cash receipts test

Objective: Evaluate the accuracy of recorded green fee revenue by
comparing documentation of deposits with the underlying "starter
sheets" that indicate how many rounds of golf were played each day.

Sample Selection: 21 days during peak activity periods were
judgmentally selected for testing.

Results: There is an averagedaily overage of $5.79. While the amount
is not too significant, this is an indication of loose control in
either cash-handling, record-keeping, or both.

Conclusion: Daily reconciliations of the deposits with the starter
sheets should be performed. This would help ensure that all fees are
rung through the cash register, that all golfers sign the starter
sheet, and that discrepancies are identified and resolved on a timely
basis.

Page Index No.: 502

Preparer __CK__ Date __5-7__

Reviewer __AK__ Date __5/14__

GOLF COURSE
Cash receipts test

Date	Deposit Amounts	Starter-Sheet Totals	Overages (Shortages)
4/28/83	$360.25	$355.25	$ 5.00
5/04/83	202.75	199.75	3.00
5/15/83	476.25	443.00	33.25
6/03/83	247.50	242.50	5.00
6/07/83	302.25	291.25	11.00
6/13/83	137.00	144.00	(7.00)
6/25/83	167.75	155.75	12.00
6/30/83	223.75	230.25	(6.50)
7/09/83	428.25	406.00	22.25
7/22/83	195.50	187.00	8.50
8/10/83	195.50	187.00	8.50
8/12/83	223.00	225.25	(2.25)
8/18/83	188.50	165.75	22.75
8/20/83	168.25	167.75	0.50
8/24/83	190.00	176.25	13.75
8/26/83	137.50	130.25	7.25
8/28/83	326.00	329.00	(3.00)
9/06/83	480.00	494.50	(14.50)
9/12/83	44.00	43.00	1.00
10/04/83	105.75	100.00	5.75
10/09/83	89.00	93.25	(4.25)
Totals	$4,888.25	$4,762.25	$125.50

Reference: 201

Page Index No.: 502.1

Preparer _JB_ Date _5/7_
Reviewer _AK_ Date _5/14_

GOLF COURSE
Surprise cash count

Objective: Verify the balance of the imprest change fund ($600) for golf course operatiions on an unannounced basis. /also, observe and evaluate general security over cash and negotiable items.

Date of count: 5/8/84   3:00 p.m.

Results: The following items were noted:

1. The cash register contained an IOU representing funds informally borrowed by an employee. This practice is against company policy.

2. The cash register is also used for petty cash transactions. A separate petty cash fund should be considered.

3. There was a shortage of $3.25 at the time of the count. The auditors received recorded overagesshortages for the prioir three weeks. While they occurred quite frequently, there does not appear to be a consistent pattern and the amounts have been small.

4. Physical security over the funds on hand appeared adequate.

Conclusion: The items noted are not significant enugh to be included in the formal audit report. They should, however, bementioned to supervisory personnel during the exit conference.

Page Index No.: 503

```
Surprise cash count--page 2


Contents of Cash Register:

    Checks from customer                          229.60
    Currency
      Ones                                         23.00
      Fives                                         25.00
      Tens                                          30.00
      Twenty's                                      80.00
    Coin
      Pennies                                        0.06
      Nickels                                        0.35
      Dimes                                          1.20
      Quarters                                       3.50
    Petty cash voucher to buy postage stamps        3.00
    IOU from employee (part-time mower)            10.00

    Total                                         405.71


    Imprest change fund balance                   200.00
    Cash register total--5/8 sales                202.46
    Unidentified shortage                           3.25
      Total                                       405.71


    physically verified
```

Page Index No.: 503.1

Preparer __JB__ Date __5/8__
Reviewer __AK__ Date __5/14__

GOLF COURSE
Complimentary golf pass analysis

	1981	1982	1983
Company officers and family	60	73	91
Employees	58	69	50
Clients	198	230	916
Legislators and family	29	40	110
Totals	345	612	1,162

COMMENT: Analysis of complimentary season golf passes revealed the above data. Until 1983 (through 1982) golf passes were issued through the Employee Relations Department and at the golf shop, with special request being made company executives. Starting on January 1, 1983, all passes are issued by the Public Relations Department.

Page Index No.: 504

Preparer __CK__ Date __5-3__

Reviewer __AK__ Date __5/14__

GOLF COURSE
Test of expenditures

<u>Objective</u>: To determine whether expenditures made from golf course
accounts were reasonable, authorized, properly classified, and properly
receipted.

<u>Procedure</u>: Selected 16 expenditures amounting to $3,639.18 and tested
for attributes listed in the stated objective.

<u>Results</u>: All expenditures except one were satisfactory in all areas.
The one expenditure listed as a business luncheon was not documented.

(See detailed test at __505.b__

Page Index No.: __505__

Preparer _C K_ Date _5-8_

Reviewer _AK_ Date _5/14_

```
GOLF COURSE
Detailed test of expenditures
```

Date	Doc. No.	Description	Amount	Auth	Rec't	Am't	Class
1/15/83	R9578	Equipment	279.10	✓	✓	✓	✓
1/25/83	R39859	Goods for sale	330.00	✓	✓	✓	✓
3/20/83	R59881	Maintenance--sod	500.00	✓	✓	✓	✓
4/06/83	R39858	Battery	234.00	✓	✓	✓	✓
4/13/83	C51972	Promotional Ad	152.00	✓	✓	✓	✓
4/21/83	C145907	Electrical repairs	16.50	✓	✓	✓	✓
5/24/83	C145897	Greens Maintenance	617.00	✓	✓	✓	✓
5/31/83	C145900	Printing of Passes	74.48	✓	✓	✓	✓
6/14/83	C145904	Score Cards--Print	338.04	✓	✓	✓	✓
7/05/83	C151396	Promotional Ad	45.00	✓	✓	✓	✓
7/06/83	V475837	Repair Windshield	245.21	✓	✓	✓	✓
7/15/83	V431068	Golf Tees	184.35	✓	✓	✓	✓
8/02/83	V430710	Repair Push Cart	27.10	✓	✓	✓	✓
3/06/83	V438175	Golf Balls	112.20	✓	✓	✓	✓
9/15/83	V598927	Business Luncheon	159.60	X	X	X	X
10/23/83	V398620	Replace Flags	324.60	✓	✓	✓	✓
		Total Tested	3,639.18				

```
__✓__Reviewed, okay

__X__No authorization, documentation does not support


Auth = Properly Authorized
Rec't = Evidence of proper rerceipt
Am't = Amount reasonable
Class = Properly classified
```

Page Index No.: 505.1

```
                                              Preparer_____Date_____

                                              Reviewer_____Date_____
     GOLD COURSE
     Administrative workpapers
     Workpaper index


     Index

     601 Notice of audit intent
     602 Notes from opening conference
     603 Time budget and summary
     604 Notes from exit conference
     605 Close-out checklist
```

MEMORANDUM

Internal Auditing Department   Date: April 1, 1984

From: David Jackson, Director of Internal Auditing

To: Kenneth Larsen, golf professional

Subject: Operational review of CASI Golf Course

The CASI Golf Course is scheduled for an operational review by the
Internal Auditing Department this year. Christine Kelly, one of our
auditors, will call you within the next week to schedule an initial
meeting. To acquaint you with the scope of our reviews, I have
enclosed a copy of the Company Internal Auditing Policy. The policy
contains a concise description of the general procedures for conducting
audits.

It would expedite our planning if you could assemble an organization
chart, departmental policies and procedures, and any other documents
that would help familiarize our auditors with the golf course
operations. Also, I have attached a summary of golf course financial
operating results for recent years. We would like to briefly review
this information with you during the opening conference.

If you have questions about this upcoming review, please feel free to
call either Mrs. Kelly or me at Extention 8360.

_____

Enclosures

Preparer _CK_ Date _5-10_

Reviewer _MK_ Date _5/14_

GOLF COURSE
Opening Conference

Date of Meeting: May 1, 1984
Location: Golf shop
Present: Christine Kelly, Senior Staff Auditor
        Jonathan Berkley, Audit Intern
        C. G. Morris, Director of Employee Relations
        Kenneth Larsen, Golf Professional and golf course manager
        Maud Griggs, assistant controller

Synopsis of Items Discussed

1. Auditors presented the tentative scope, objectives, and timetable
for the audit. Also, reviewed the final report distribution and
company policies regarding formal response by the auditee to each
finding and recommendation.

2. Reviewed briefly the organization structure of the golf course and
the Employee Relations Dept., along with financial operating results of
recent years.

3. In response to the auditors' inquiry, the Mrs. Griggs indicated that
there were no ares of special attention she would like the audit to
include. Mr. Larsen indicated that he was somewhat concerned about the
reliability of reported revenues for the golf course. Considering the
current rate schedule and the level of course utilization, he felt that
reported revenues were low for 1983 and the current year. He was
unable to be more specific, and appeared unfamiliar with accounting
data. Mrs. Griggs promised to review the prior-year cutoff for any
problems that could possibly distort the reported revenues for 1983 and
this year.

4. Mr. Morris, Mr. Larsen, and Mrs. Griggs acknowledged the value of
periodic audits and expressed an attitude of cooperation.

Page Index No.: 602

Preparer _CK_ Date _4-29_

Reviewer _AK_ Date _4/30_

GOLF COURSE
Time and budget summary

Activity	Time Budget Auditor	Intern	Actual Hours Auditor	Intern
1. Review of background information, opening conference	4	2	6	2
2. Discussion with key employees	10	2	12	1
3. Audit program preparation	2	1	2	
4. Internal control review	4	1	2	4
5. Detailed tests Cash receipts	4	2	3	3
Surprise cash count		1		1
Complimentary passes	2	1	6	1
Operating expenditures	1	4	1	6
6. Report preparation	10	5	8	4
Subtotals	37	19	40	22
		37		40
Combined subtotals		56		62
Manager Review		5		2
				64
Total		61		

AK

Page Index No.: 603

Preparer _CK_ Date _5-15_
Reviewer _AK_ Date _5/16_

GOLF COURSE
Exit conference

Date of meeting: May 14, 1984
Location: Golf shop
Present: Christine Kelly, Senior Staff Auditor
        Jonathan Berkley, Audit Intern
        Ken Larsen, Golf professional and golf course manager
        Maud Griggs, assistant controller

Report recommendations discussed

1. Cash receipt reconciliations. Mr. Larsen and Mrs. Griggs indicated
their agreement with the recommendation. The will implement the
recommendation shortly.

2. Undeposited receipts. Mr. Larsen questioned whether the risks of
loss justified the added expense of purchasing a safe. He also
indicated that because of the remote location of the golf shop, the
danger of burglary would increase if a safe were installed, and while
the burglars may not be able to break into the safe, they likely would
cause significant damage to the golf shop, merchandise, and equipment
stored there. He suggested taking each day's deposits to the company
cashier's office instead, and if it is after hours for that office, he
just make a direct deposit to Commercial Bank. Mr Larsen said he would
include this alternative proposal in his formal written response this
week.

3. Golf passes. Mr. Larsen and Mrs. Griggs agreed with this
recommendation and said they will implement it shortly. Mrs. Griggs
said she will be primarily responsible for maintaining the new records.

4. Reports of property damage or injury. Mr. Larsen agreed with the
need for written directions, and said he feels that he would be able to
develop such a document with someone from the Employee Relations Dept.

Other items discussed:

1. Mr. Larsen and Mrs. Griggs both expressed the opinion that operating
results for 1984 will be much improved over 1983. They are considering
the purchase and rental of electric golf carts as a possible additional
revenue source.

2. Mr. Larsen and Mrs. Griggs both expressed the feeling that the audit
recommendations will result in greater internal control and will be
beneficial to the golf course operations.

Page Index No.: 604

Preparer _MB_ Date _5/16_

Reviewer _AK_ Date _5/16_

```
GOLF COURSE
Close-out checklist
```

Done By   Index

Final report review

1. Proofread audit report carefully for
typographical and grammatical errors
and clerical accuracy where applicable.

✓ 5/18

2. Check agreement of all important
factual statements or assertions made
in the audit report to underlying
workpapers. This check includes:

   a. financial or operating statistics
   b. stated audit objectives
   c. findings and recommendations

✓ 5/18

Final workpaper review

1. Determine whether the form and content
of all workpapers meet department standards
for clarity, completeness, and relevance.

✓ 5/17

2. Evaluate whether the audit procedures
employed and the results obtained were
appropriate. Identify any items requiring
additional follow-up or an additional audit
at a later date.

✓ 5/17   606

3. Ensure that all review notes and follow-
up questions have been satisfactorily resolved.

✓ 5/17

```
Page Index No.:  605
```

Preparer __CK__ Date __5-16__
Reviewer __AK__ Date __5/17__

GOLF COURSE
Follow-up reviews

Memo to file

1. A follow-up review to ascertain compliance with audit
recommendations will be scheduled within six months of the date of the
audit report.

2. An additional review should be considered to analyze in detail the
relative costs and benefits of the purchase and rental of electric golf
carts. It is not likely that employee relations personnel will be able
to perform an in-depth analysis. Alternatively, it may be appropriate
to simply offer assistance from the Internal Auditing Department to the
director of employee relations regarding this decision.

Page Index No.: 606

Case 4
Tobie Industries, Inc.

The internal auditors for Tobie Industries, Inc. are examining the financial internal controls for the organization's expenditures. One of the staff auditors has been assigned to assess the effectiveness of the organization's voucher system as a control device. The supervising auditor has stated that the staff auditor should be alert to six types of problems in this examination. These problems are:

1. Losses of discounts on purchases.
2. Missing verification of information contained in vouchers.
3. Incorrect check amounts.
4. Missing approval signatures.
5. Missing vouchers.
6. Nonpayment of vouchers.

Tobie Industries has separate departments for purchasing, receiving, accounting, and disbursing. The company's voucher system uses vouchers, a voucher register, a file for paid vouchers, and a check register. Paid invoices also are filed, but separately from the vouchers. The check register and voucher register are contained in the company's computerized accounting system.

The supervising auditor is concerned that if the voucher system is not operating effectively, other important aspects of Tobie's financial management also may be weak.

The staff auditor is provided with the following information for the examination:

1. Thirty vouchers randomly selected from 4,000 contained in the paid vouchers file for the three-month period of June 1 through August 31, 1986.
2. Information from the voucher register on each of the sampled vouchers.
3. Information from the check register on each of the sampled vouchers.

The supervising auditor also stated that the auditor should consider that any possible discounts on invoices paid more than 10 days after the invoice date are lost because most companies providing discounts usually set their terms at 2/10, net 30, thereby limiting the discount period to 10 days.

Required:
1. State the objectives of this examination of the voucher system.
2. Define the statistical population of interest in the staff auditor's assignment.
3. Define the sampling unit.

4. Define the attributes of interest in the audit test. Explain why they are relevant to the auditor's work.

5. Examine and evaluate the sampled vouchers with the related information from the voucher register and the check register, and evaluate the company's voucher system. Use your own judgment with regard to confidence levels, acceptable error rates, etc.

6. What do you think of the supervising auditor's grasp of the voucher system? Explain your position and outline any problems that you think are evident in addition to those listed by the supervising auditor. Also, does the supervisor understand the potential problems he listed?

7. Is there any additional evidence you would like to check that has not been provided in the case materials?

TOBIE INDUSTRIES, INC.
Check Register Information for 30 Audited Vouchers

Check Number	Date	Payee	Voucher Number	Amount
4630	06/02/86	Allis-Chalmers	0003	$71,050.00
4650	06/02/86	All States Whlsl Dist	0023	17,228.40
4703	06/02/86	Kelly Co	0076	120.50
4710	06/04/86	Bennet Paint Co	0083	432.50
4800	06/02/86	Texaco	0173	175.80
4843	06/01/86	Baum & Adamson	0216	1,971.76
4858	06/11/86	Firestone & Rubber	0231	6,350.40
4880	06/16/86	Brown-Ferris Ind	0353	45.00
5156	06/26/86	Newspaper Agency Corp	0629	171.50
5499	06/26/86	Chris and Dicks Lumber	0972	124.70
7860	08/11/86	B.F. Goodrich Tires	1112	3,351.60
6050	07/08/86	Brand L Electric	1520	450.00
6394	07/14/86	Peterson Tractor	1864	694.50
6473	07/14/86	Benson & Benson	1943	210.00
6586	07/21/86	Kelly Springfield	2056	5,750.00
6594	07/23/86	Petersen Tractor	2064	3,475.00
6871	07/28/86	Farmers Ins Group	2341	560.00
6930	07/30/86	Caterpiller Equip	2400	742.84
7039	08/04/86	Massey-Ferguson Equip	2509	964.91
7345	08/03/86	Mathew K. Davis	2815	22,680.00
7458	08/06/86	Roper Tractors	2928	827.33
7956	08/11/86	Kubeta Tractor & Imp	3426	522.42
7992	08/11/86	Intermountain Fleet	1204	2,618.56
7993	08/18/86	Nelson Equipment Co	3463	589.18
0013	08/18/86	Massey-Ferguson	3483	132,400.00
0036	08/28/86	Bonham Star Co	3506	1,332.20
0400	08/28/86	Century Equipment Co	3870	6,553.26
0430	08/29/86	ADP Dealer Services	3900	6,811.00
0449	09/05/86	All States Whlsl Dist	3919	714.33
0492	09/05/86	Roper Tractors	3960	36,456.00

TOBIE INDUSTRIES, INC.
Voucher Register Information for 30 Audited Vouchers

Sampled Voucher Number	Date	Payee	Date Paid	Check Number	Amount
0003	05/30/86	Allis-Chalmers	06/02/86	4630	$71,050.00
0023	05/30/86	All States Whlsl Dist	06/02/86	4650	17,228.40
0076	06/02/86	Kelly Co.	06/04/86	4703	120.50
0083	06/02/86	Bennet Paint Co	06/04/86	4710	432.50
0173	06/09/86	Texaco	06/10/86	4800	175.80
0216	06/09/86	Baum & Adamson	06/11/86	4843	1,971.76
0231	06/09/86	Firestone Tire & Rubb	06/11/86	4858	6,480.00
0353	06/16/86	Daisy-Ferris Indust	06/16/86	4880	45.00
0629	06/23/86	Newspaper Agency Corp	06/26/86	5156	171.50
0572	06/23/86	Chrys and Dix Lumber	06/26/86	5499	124.70
1112	06/30/86	B.F. Goodrich Tire	08/11/86	7843	3,351.60
1204	06/30/86	Intermountain Fleet	08/11/86	7844	2,618.56
1520	07/07/86	Brandle Electric	07/08/86	6050	450.00
1864	07/08/86	Petersen Tractor	07/14/86	6394	694.50
1943	07/12/86	Benson & Benson	07/14/86	6473	210.00
2056	07/25/86	Kelly Springfield	07/21/86	6586	5,750.00
2064	07/25/86	Mountain West Whlsl Tire	07/23/86	6594	3,475.00
2341	07/25/86	Farmers Insurance Grp	07/28/86	6871	560.00
2400	07/28/86	Caterpiller Equip	07/30/86	6930	758.00
2509	08/01/86	Massy Ferguson	08/04/86	7039	984.60
2815	08/04/86	Mustang Tires	08/05/86	7345	2,680.00
2978	08/04/86	Roper Tractors	08/06/86	7458	810.78
3426	08/08/86	Kubeta Tractor & Imp	08/11/86	7956	522.42
3463	08/11/86	Nelson Equipm. Co.	08/18/86	7993	589.18
3483	08/11/86	Massey-Furgesen Equipm	08/18/86	0013	132,400.00
3506	08/22/86	Bonham Stan-Co.	08/28/86	0036	1,332.20
3870	08/22/86	Century Equip Co.	08/28/86	0400	6,553.26
3900	08/27/86	ADP Dealer Services	08/29/86	0043	6,811.00
3919	08/29/86	All States Whlsl Dist.	09/05/86	0449	714.33
3960	08/29/86	Roper Tractors	09/05/86	0492	36,456.00

TOBIE INDUSTRIES, INC.
Salt Lake City, Utah

Voucher No. _____0003_____

Date _____5/30/86_____

PAY TO ____Allis-Chalmers_____

_____Chicago, Illinois_____

_____

Date of Invoice _____5/29/86_____

Invoice No. _____A460-372-11_____

Date Due _____7/29/86_____

Invoice Amount _____72,500.00

Discount _____1,450.00

Net Amount _____71,050.00

Verification:
    Extensions and footing   *clr*
    Credit terms   *clr*
    Prices per purchase order   *clr*
    Quantities per receiving report   *clr*
    Distribution to accounts   *cry*

Approved _____*ap*_____

ACCOUNT DISTRIBUTION

Account Debited	Amount
Purchases	72,500 / 00
	/
	/
	/
	/
	/
	/
	/
	/

Payment

Date _____6/2/86_____

Check No. ____4630_____

Amount ____71,050.00_____

Credit Vouchers Payable ____72,500 / 00____

TOBIE INDUSTRIES, INC.
Salt Lake City, Utah

PAY TO _____ All States Wholesale Dist. _____

_____ Grand Junction, Col. _____

_____

Date of Invoice _____ 5/29/86 _____

Invoice No. _____ 077-0215 _____

Date Due _____ 6/29/86 _____

Verification:
    Extensions and footing
    Credit terms
    Prices per purchase order
    Quantities per receiving report
    Distribution to accounts

ACCOUNT DISTRIBUTION

Account Debited	Amount	
Purchases	17,580	00
		/
		/
		/
		/
		/
		/
		/
		/

Credit Vouchers Payable _____ 13,080 / 00

Voucher No. _____ 0023 _____

Date _____ 5/30/86 _____

Invoice Amount _____ 13,080.00

Discount _____ 351.60

Net Amount _____ 12,728.40

Approved _____

Payment

Date _____ 6/2/86 _____

Check No. _____ 4650 _____

Amount _____ 17,228.40

TOBIE INDUSTRIES, INC.
Salt Lake City, Utah

Voucher No. _____ 0076 _____

Date _____ 6/2/86 _____

PAY TO ___ Kelly Co. _____

_____ SLC _____

_____

Date of Invoice _____ 5/23/86 _____

Invoice No. _____ 330 _____

Date Due _____ 6/23/86 _____

Invoice Amount _____ 120.50

Discount _____

Net Amount _____ 120.50

Verification:
    Extensions and footing
    Credit terms
    Prices per purchase order
    Quantities per receiving report
    Distribution to accounts

Approved _____ *AP* _____

ACCOUNT DISTRIBUTION

Account Debited	Amount
Office Supplies	120 / 50
	/
	/
	/
	/
	/
	/
	/
	/

Payment

Date _____ 6/4/86 _____

Check No. _____ 4703 _____

Amount _____ 120.50 _____

Credit Vouchers Payable _____ 120 / 50

TOBIE INDUSTRIES, INC.
Salt Lake City, Utah

Voucher No. _____0083_____

Date _____6/2/86_____

PAY TO ___Bennet Paint___

___Salt Lake City___

_____

Date of Invoice _____5/30/86_____

Invoice No. _____280-B_____

Date Due _____6/30/86_____

Invoice Amount _____432.50_____

Discount _____

Net Amount _____432.50_____

Verification:
    Extensions and footing   *ch*
    Credit terms   *ch*
    Prices per purchase order   *ch*
    Quantities per receiving report   *ch*
    Distribution to accounts   *cly*

Approved _____*AP*_____

ACCOUNT DISTRIBUTION

Account Debited	Amount
Repairs Expense	432 / 50
	/
	/
	/
	/
	/
	/
	/
	/

Payment

Date _____6/4/86_____

Check No. _____4710_____

Amount _____432.50_____

Credit Vouchers Payable _____432 / 50_____

TOBIE INDUSTRIES, INC.
Salt Lake City, Utah

Voucher No. _____ 0173 _____

Date _____ 6/9/86 _____

PAY TO _____ Texaco _____

_____ Houston, Texas _____

_____

Date of Invoice _____ 6/2/86 _____

Invoice No. _____ 90472 _____

Date Due _____ 7/2/86 _____

Invoice Amount _____ 175.80

Discount _____

Net Amount _____ 175.80

Verification:
    Extensions and footing
    Credit terms
    Prices per purchase order
    Quantities per receiving report
    Distribution to accounts

Approved _____

ACCOUNT DISTRIBUTION

Account Debited	Amount
Co. Auditor Expense	175 / 80
	/
	/
	/
	/
	/
	/
	/
	/

Payment

Date _____ 6/10/86 _____

Check No. _____ 4800 _____

Amount _____ 175.80

Credit Vouchers Payable _____ 175 / 80

TOBIE INDUSTRIES, INC.
Salt Lake City, Utah

Voucher No. _____ 0216 _____

Date _____ 6/9/86 _____

PAY TO _____ Baum and Adamson _____

_____ Salt Lake City _____

_____

Date of Invoice _____ 6/2/86 _____

Invoice No. _____ A 607-921 _____

Date Due _____ 7/2/86 _____

Invoice Amount _____ 2,012.00

Discount _____ 40.24

Net Amount _____ 1,971.76

Verification:
    Extensions and footing
    Credit terms
    Prices per purchase order
    Quantities per receiving report
    Distribution to accounts

Approved _____

ACCOUNT DISTRIBUTION

Account Debited	Amount	
Purchases	2,012 / 00
	/
	/
	/
	/
	/
	/
	/

Payment

Date _____ 6/11/86 _____

Check No. _____ 4843 _____

Amount _____ 1,971.76

Credit Vouchers Payable _____ 2,012 / 00

TOBIE INDUSTRIES, INC.
Salt Lake City, Utah

Voucher No. _____ 0231 _____

Date _____ 6/9/86 _____

PAY TO ___ Firestone Tire and Rubber Co. _____

_____ Phoenix, Arizona _____

_____

Date of Invoice _____ 5/20/86 _____

Invoice No. _____ 370 A 217 _____

Date Due _____ 6/20/86 _____

Invoice Amount _____ 6,480.00 _____

Discount _____ 129.60 _____

Net Amount _____ 6,350.40 _____

Verification:
  Extensions and footing
  Credit terms
  Prices per purchase order
  Quantities per receiving report
  Distribution to accounts

Approved _____ AP _____

ACCOUNT DISTRIBUTION

Account Debited	Amount
Purchases	6,480 / 00
	/
	/
	/
	/
	/
	/
	/

Payment

Date _____ 6/11/86 _____

Check No. _____ 4858 _____

Amount _____ 6,350.40 _____

Credit Vouchers Payable _____ 6,480 / 00 _____

TOBIE INDUSTRIES, INC.
Salt Lake City, Utah

Voucher No. _____0353_____

Date _____6/16/86_____

PAY TO ___Brown-Ferris Industries___

___SLC___

_____

Date of Invoice ___6/11/86___

Invoice No. ___39062___

Date Due ___7/11/86___

Invoice Amount ___45.00___

Discount _____

Net Amount ___45.00___

Verification:
    Extensions and footing
    Credit terms
    Prices per purchase order
    Quantities per receiving report
    Distribution to accounts

Approved _____

ACCOUNT DISTRIBUTION

Account Debited	Amount
Operating Expense	45 / 00
	/
	/
	/
	/
	/
	/
	/
	/

Payment

Date ___6/16/86___

Check No. ___4880___

Amount ___45.00___

Credit Vouchers Payable ___45 / 00___

TOBIE INDUSTRIES, INC.
Salt Lake City, Utah

Voucher No. _____ 0629 _____

Date _____ 6/23/86 _____

PAY TO _____ Newspaper Agency Corp. _____

_____ Salt Lake City _____

_____

Date of Invoice _____ 6/13/86 _____	Invoice Amount _____ 175.00
Invoice No. _____ 4-11-3634 _____	Discount _____ 3.50
Date Due _____ 7/14/86 _____	Net Amount _____ 171.50

Verification:
    Extensions and footing
    Credit terms
    Prices per purchase order
    Quantities per receiving report
    Distribution to accounts

Approved _____

ACCOUNT DISTRIBUTION

Account Debited	Amount
Advertising	175 / 00
_____	/
_____	/
_____	/
_____	/
_____	/
_____	/
_____	/
_____	/

Payment

Date _____ 6/26/86 _____

Check No. _____ 5156 _____

Amount _____ 171.50 _____

Credit Vouchers Payable _____ 175 / 00

TOBIE INDUSTRIES, INC.
Salt Lake City, Utah

Voucher No. _____0972_____

Date _____6/23/86_____

PAY TO ___Chris and Dix Lumber___

___Salt Lake City___

_____

Date of Invoice ___6/20/86___

Invoice No. ___C-6091___

Date Due ___7/21/86___

Invoice Amount ___124.70___

Discount _____

Net Amount ___124.70___

Verification:
    Extensions and footing   *cr*
    Credit terms   *cr*
    Prices per purchase order   *cr*
    Quantities per receiving report   *cr*
    Distribution to accounts   *cr*

Approved ___ap___

ACCOUNT DISTRIBUTION

Account Debited	Amount
Repairs Expense	124 / 70
	/
	/
	/
	/
	/
	/
	/
	/

Payment

Date ___6/26/86___

Check No. ___5499___

Amount ___124.70___

Credit Vouchers Payable ___124 / 70___

TOBIE INDUSTRIES, INC.
Salt Lake City, Utah

Voucher No. _____ 1112 _____

Date _____ 6/30/86 _____

PAY TO ___ B.F. Goodrich Tires ___

___ SLC ___

_____

Date of Invoice _____ 6/16/86 _____	Invoice Amount _____ 3,420.00
Invoice No. _____ 02-460104 _____	Discount _____ 68.40
Date Due _____ 7/16/86 _____	Net Amount _____ 3,351.60

Verification:
    Extensions and footing
    Credit terms
    Prices per purchase order
    Quantities per receiving report
    Distribution to accounts

Approved ___ cls ___

ACCOUNT DISTRIBUTION

Account Debited	Amount
Purchases	3,420 / 00
	/
	/
	/
	/
	/
	/
	/
	/

Payment

Date _____ 8/11/86 _____

Check No. _____ 7860 _____

Amount _____ 3,351.60 _____

Credit Vouchers Payable _____ 3,420 / 00

TOBIE INDUSTRIES, INC.
Salt Lake City, Utah

Voucher No. _____ 1204 _____

Date _____ 6/30/86 _____

PAY TO _____ Intermountain Fleetwood Tire _____

Bountiful, Ut. _____

_____

Date of Invoice _____ 6/27/86 _____

Invoice No. _____ R-11-210 _____

Date Due _____ 7/28/86 _____

Invoice Amount _____ 2,672.00

Discount _____ 53.44

Net Amount _____ 2,618.56

Verification:
    Extensions and footing
    Credit terms
    Prices per purchase order
    Quantities per receiving report
    Distribution to accounts

Approved _____ Cls _____

ACCOUNT DISTRIBUTION

Account Debited	Amount
Purchases	2,672 / 00
	/
	/
	/
	/
	/
	/
	/
	/

Payment

Date _____ 8/11/86

Check No. _____ 7992

Amount _____ 2,618.56

Credit Vouchers Payable _____ 2,672 / 00

TOBIE INDUSTRIES, INC.
Salt Lake City, Utah

Voucher No. _____ 1520 _____

Date _____ 7/1/86 _____

PAY TO ___ Band L. Electric _____

_____ SLC _____

_____

Date of Invoice _____ 7/1/86 _____

Invoice No. _____ 042-6944 _____

Date Due _____ 7/15/86 _____

Invoice Amount _____ 450.00

Discount _____

Net Amount _____ 450.00

Verification:
    Extensions and footing
    Credit terms
    Prices per purchase order
    Quantities per receiving report
    Distribution to accounts

Approved _____

ACCOUNT DISTRIBUTION

Account Debited	Amount
Repairs Expense	450 / 00
	/
	/
	/
	/
	/
	/
	/
	/

Payment

Date _____ 7/8/86 _____

Check No. _____ 6050 _____

Amount _____ 450.00 _____

Credit Vouchers Payable _____ 450 / 00 _____

TOBIE INDUSTRIES, INC.
Salt Lake City, Utah

Voucher No. _____ 1864 _____

Date _____ 7/8/86 _____

PAY TO _____ Peterson Tractor and Implement _____

_____ Kansas City, Kansas _____

_____

Date of Invoice _____ 7/1/86 _____

Invoice No. _____ 720694 _____

Date Due _____ 8/1/86 _____

Invoice Amount _____ 694.50 _____

Discount _____ 13.89 _____

Net Amount _____ 680.61 _____

Verification:
    Extensions and footing
    Credit terms
    Prices per purchase order
    Quantities per receiving report
    Distribution to accounts

Approved _____

ACCOUNT DISTRIBUTION

Account Debited	Amount
Purchases	694 / 50
	/
	/
	/
	/
	/
	/
	/
	/

Credit Vouchers Payable _____ 694 / 50

Payment

Date _____ 7/14/86 _____

Check No. _____ 6394 _____

Amount _____ 694.50 _____

TOBIE INDUSTRIES, INC.
Salt Lake City, Utah

Voucher No. _____1943_____

Date _____7/12/86_____

PAY TO ____Benson and Benson____

_____SLC_____

_____

Date of Invoice _____7/10/86_____

Invoice No. _____

Date Due _____8/11/86_____

Invoice Amount _____210.00_____

Discount _____

Net Amount _____210.00_____

Verification:
    Extensions and footing
    Credit terms
    Prices per purchase order
    Quantities per receiving report
    Distribution to accounts

Approved _____

ACCOUNT DISTRIBUTION

Account Debited	Amount
Accounting Services	210 / 00
	/
	/
	/
	/
	/
	/
	/
	/

Payment

Date _____7/14/86_____

Check No. ____6473____

Amount _____210.00_____

Credit Vouchers Payable _____210 / 00_____

TOBIE INDUSTRIES, INC.
Salt Lake City, Utah

Voucher No. _____ 2056 _____

Date _____ 7/25/86 _____

PAY TO _____ Kelly Springfield Tires _____

_____ Woods Cross, Utah _____

_____

Date of Invoice _____ 6/25/86 _____

Invoice No. _____ 20-662 _____

Date Due _____ 7/25/86 _____

Invoice Amount _____ 5,750.00

Discount _____ 115.00

Net Amount _____ 5,635.00

Verification:
  Extensions and footing
  Credit terms
  Prices per purchase order
  Quantities per receiving report
  Distribution to accounts

Approved _____

ACCOUNT DISTRIBUTION

Account Debited	Amount
Purchases	5,750 / 00
_____	/
_____	/
_____	/
_____	/
_____	/
_____	/
_____	/
_____	/

Payment

Date _____ 7/21/86 _____

Check No. _____ 6586 _____

Amount _____ 5,750.00

Credit Vouchers Payable _____ 5,750 / 00

TOBIE INDUSTRIES, INC.
Salt Lake City, Utah

Voucher No. _____ 2064 _____

Date _____ 7/25/86 _____

PAY TO ___ Mountain West Whlsl Tire ___

_____ SLC _____

_____

Date of Invoice _____ 6/32/86 _____

Invoice No. _____ 1401-21 _____

Date Due _____ 7/22/86 _____

Invoice Amount _____ 3,475.00

Discount _____ 69.50

Net Amount _____ 3,405.50

Verification:
    Extensions and footing
    Credit terms
    Prices per purchase order
    Quantities per receiving report
    Distribution to accounts

Approved ___ _____

ACCOUNT DISTRIBUTION

Account Debited	Amount
Purchases	3,475 / 00
_____	/
_____	/
_____	/
_____	/
_____	/
_____	/
_____	/
_____	/

Payment

Date _____ 7/23/86 _____

Check No. _____ 6594 _____

Amount _____ 3,475.00 _____

Credit Vouchers Payable _____ 3,475 / 00

TOBIE INDUSTRIES, INC.
Salt Lake City, Utah

Voucher No. _____ 2341 _____

Date _____ 7/25/86 _____

PAY TO ___ Farmers Insurance Group ___

_____ Sandy, Utah _____

_____

Date of Invoice _____ 7/21/86 _____

Invoice No. _____

Date Due _____ 8/21/86 _____

Invoice Amount _____ 650.00

Discount _____

Net Amount _____ 650.00

Verification:
    Extensions and footing
    Credit terms
    Prices per purchase order
    Quantities per receiving report
    Distribution to accounts

Approved _____

ACCOUNT DISTRIBUTION

Account Debited	Amount
Insurance	560 / 00
	/
	/
	/
	/
	/
	/
	/
	/

Credit Vouchers Payable _____ 560 / 00

Payment

Date _____ 7/28/86

Check No. _____ 6871

Amount _____ 560.00

TOBIE INDUSTRIES, INC.
Salt Lake City, Utah

Voucher No. _____ 2400 _____

Date _____ 7/28/86 _____

PAY TO ___ Caterpiller Equipment ___

___ Denver, Colorado ___

_____

Date of Invoice _____ 7/24/86 _____

Invoice No. _____ 110684632 _____

Date Due _____ 8/25/86 _____

Invoice Amount _____ 758.00

Discount _____ 15.16

Net Amount _____ 742.84

Verification:
    Extensions and footing
    Credit terms
    Prices per purchase order
    Quantities per receiving report
    Distribution to accounts

Approved ___ *Cff* ___

ACCOUNT DISTRIBUTION

Account Debited	Amount
Purchases	758 / 00
	/
	/
	/
	/
	/
	/
	/
	/

Payment

Date _____ 7/30/86

Check No. _____ 6930

Amount _____ 742.84

Credit Vouchers Payable _____ 758 / 00

TOBIE INDUSTRIES, INC.
Salt Lake City, Utah

Voucher No. _____2509_____

Date _____8/1/86_____

PAY TO _____Massey-Fergusen Equipment_____

_____Salt Lake City_____

_____

Date of Invoice _____7/28/86_____

Invoice No. _____61-08261-86_____

Date Due _____8/28/86_____

Invoice Amount _____984.60_____

Discount _____19.69_____

Net Amount _____964.91_____

Verification:
    Extensions and footing   BW
    Credit terms   BW
    Prices per purchase order   BW
    Quantities per receiving report   BW
    Distribution to accounts   BW

Approved _____BW_____

ACCOUNT DISTRIBUTION

Account Debited	Amount
Purchases	984 / 60
	/
	/
	/
	/
	/
	/
	/
	/

Payment

Date _____8/4/86_____

Check No. _____7039_____

Amount _____964.91_____

Credit Vouchers Payable _____984 / 60_____

TOBIE INDUSTRIES, INC.
Salt Lake City, Utah

Voucher No. _____2978_____

Date _____8/4/86_____

PAY TO ___Roper Tractors_____

___Dallas, Texas_____

_____

Date of Invoice ____8/1/86_____

Invoice No. ____24-1693472_____

Date Due ____9/2/86_____

Invoice Amount _____827.33

Discount _____16.55

Net Amount _____810.78

Verification:
    Extensions and footing   *BW*
    Credit terms   *BW*
    Prices per purchase order   *BW*
    Quantities per receiving report   *BW*
    Distribution to accounts   *BW*

Approved ___*BW*_____

ACCOUNT DISTRIBUTION

Account Debited	Amount
Purchases	827 / 33
	/
	/
	/
	/
	/
	/
	/
	/

Payment

Date _____8/6/86_____

Check No. _____7458_____

Amount _____827.33_____

Credit Vouchers Payable ____827 / 33

TOBIE INDUSTRIES, INC.
Salt Lake City, Utah

Voucher No. _____3426_____

Date _____8/8/86_____

PAY TO ____Kubota Tractor & Implement____

Phoenix, Arizona _____

_____

Date of Invoice _____8/6/86_____

Invoice No. _____941406-2_____

Date Due _____9/8/86_____

Invoice Amount _____533.42_____

Discount _____10.67_____

Net Amount _____522.75_____

Verification:
    Extensions and footing   _BW_
    Credit terms   _BW_
    Prices per purchase order   _BW_
    Quantities per receiving report   _BW_
    Distribution to accounts   _BW_

Approved ____BW____

ACCOUNT DISTRIBUTION

Account Debited	Amount
Purchases	533 / 42
	/
	/
	/
	/
	/
	/
	/
	/

Payment

Date _____8/11/86_____

Check No. _____7956_____

Amount _____522.75_____

Credit Vouchers Payable _____533 / 42_____

TOBIE INDUSTRIES, INC.
Salt Lake City, Utah

Voucher No. _____ 3463 _____

Date _____ 8/11/86 _____

PAY TO ____ Nelson Equipment Co. ____

_____ Grand Junction, Colorado _____

_____

Date of Invoice _____ 8/8/86 _____

Invoice No. _____ 33907 _____

Date Due _____ 9/8/86 _____

Invoice Amount _____ 601.20

Discount _____ 12.02

Net Amount _____ 589.18

Verification:
    Extensions and footing .... *BW*
    Credit terms .... *BW*
    Prices per purchase order ...... *BW*
    Quantities per receiving report . *BW*
    Distribution to accounts .... *BW*

Approved _____ *BW* _____

ACCOUNT DISTRIBUTION

Account Debited	Amount
Purchases	601 / 20
	/
	/
	/
	/
	/
	/
	/
	/

Payment

Date _____ 8/18/86 _____

Check No. ____ 7993 ____

Amount _____ 589.18 _____

Credit Vouchers Payable ____ 601 / 20

TOBIE INDUSTRIES, INC.
Salt Lake City, Utah

Voucher No. _____3483_____

Date _____8/11/86_____

PAY TO ____Massey-Fergusen Equipment____

____Salt Lake City____

_____

Date of Invoice _____8/8/86_____

Invoice No. _____61-09433-86_____

Date Due _____9/8/86_____

Invoice Amount _____132,400.00_____

Discount _____

Net Amount _____132,400.00_____

Verification:
    Extensions and footing   _____
    Credit terms   _____
    Prices per purchase order   _____
    Quantities per receiving report   _____
    Distribution to accounts   _____

Approved ____BV____

ACCOUNT DISTRIBUTION

Account Debited	Amount
Repairs Expense	132,400 / 00
	/
	/
	/
	/
	/
	/
	/
	/

Payment

Date _____8/18/86_____

Check No. _____0013_____

Amount _____132,400.00_____

Credit Vouchers Payable _____132,400 / 00_____

TOBIE INDUSTRIES, INC.
Salt Lake City, Utah

Voucher No. _____3506_____

Date _____8/22/86_____

PAY TO ___Bonham Stan-Co._____

_____SLC_____

_____

Date of Invoice _____8/21/86_____

Invoice No. _____38-B-69_____

Date Due _____9/22/86_____

Invoice Amount _____1,360.00

Discount _____27.20

Net Amount _____1,332.80

Verification:
    Extensions and footing   _____
    Credit terms   _____
    Prices per purchase order   _____
    Quantities per receiving report   _____
    Distribution to accounts   _____

Approved _____

ACCOUNT DISTRIBUTION

Account Debited	Amount
Purchases	1,360 / 00
	/
	/
	/
	/
	/
	/
	/
	/

Payment

Date _____8/28/86_____

Check No. _____0036_____

Amount_____1,332.20_____

Credit Vouchers Payable _____1,360 / 00_____

TOBIE INDUSTRIES, INC.
Salt Lake City, Utah

Voucher No. _____ 3870 _____

Date _____ 8/22/86 _____

PAY TO ___ Century Equipment Co. ___

_____ Murray, Utah _____

_____

Date of Invoice _____ 8/22/86 _____

Invoice No. _____ 11462 _____

Date Due _____ 9/22/86 _____

Invoice Amount _____ 6,687.00

Discount _____ 133.74

Net Amount _____ 6,553.26

Verification:
    Extensions and footing   _____
    Credit terms   _____
    Prices per purchase order   _____
    Quantities per receiving report   _____
    Distribution to accounts   _____

Approved _____

ACCOUNT DISTRIBUTION

Account Debited	Amount
Purchases	6,687 / 00
	/
	/
	/
	/
	/
	/
	/
	/

Payment

Date _____ 8/28/86

Check No. _____ 0400

Amount _____ 6,553.26

Credit Vouchers Payable _____ 6,687 / 00

TOBIE INDUSTRIES, INC.
Salt Lake City, Utah

Voucher No. _____ 3900 _____

Date _____ 8/27/86 _____

PAY TO ___ ADP Dealer Services ___

___ SLC ___

_____

Date of Invoice _____ 8/20/86 _____

Invoice No. _____ 313-4 _____

Date Due _____ 9/2/86 _____

Invoice Amount _____ 6,950.00

Discount _____ 139.00

Net Amount _____ 6,811.00

Verification:
    Extensions and footing _____
    Credit terms _____
    Prices per purchase order _____
    Quantities per receiving report _____
    Distribution to accounts _____

Approved _____

ACCOUNT DISTRIBUTION

Account Debited	Amount
Computer Systems	6,950 / 00
	/
	/
	/
	/
	/
	/
	/
	/

Payment

Date _____ 8/29/86

Check No. _____ 0430

Amount _____ 6,811.00

Credit Vouchers Payable _____ 6,950 / 00

TOBIE INDUSTRIES, INC.
Salt Lake City, Utah

Voucher No. _____ 3919 _____

Date _____

PAY TO ____ All States Wholesale Dist. ____

_____

_____

Date of Invoice _____

Invoice No. _____

Date Due _____

Invoice Amount _____

Discount _____

Net Amount _____ 714.33 _____

Verification:
    Extensions and footing   _____
    Credit terms   _____
    Prices per purchase order   _____
    Quantities per receiving report   _____
    Distribution to accounts   _____

Approved _____

ACCOUNT DISTRIBUTION

Account Debited	Amount
_____	/
_____	/
_____	/
_____	/
_____	/
_____	/
_____	/
_____	/
_____	/

Payment

Date _____ 9/5/86 _____

Check No. _____

Amount _____ 714.33 _____

Credit Vouchers Payable _____ 728 / 91 _____

TOBIE INDUSTRIES, INC.
Salt Lake City, Utah

Voucher No. _____3960_____

Date _____8/29/86_____

PAY TO ___Roper Tractors_____

___Dallas, Texas_____

_____

Date of Invoice ____8/22/86_____

Invoice No. _____24-1786123_____

Date Due _____11/21/86_____

Invoice Amount _____36,456.00____

Discount _____

Net Amount _____36,456.00_____

Verification:
    Extensions and footing   _____
    Credit terms   _____
    Prices per purchase order   _____
    Quantities per receiving report   _____
    Distribution to accounts   _____

Approved _____

ACCOUNT DISTRIBUTION

Account Debited	Amount
Purchases	36,456 / 00
_____	/
_____	/
_____	/
_____	/
_____	/
_____	/
_____	/
_____	/

Payment

Date _____9/5/86_____

Check No. ____0492____

Amount ____36,456.00____

Credit Vouchers Payable _____/____

Case 5
Valley Junior College

Valley Junior College* is a two-year school affiliated with Summit University (a private four-year institution located 200 miles away). The University provides a variety of data processing (DP) services to the College.

As a Summit University internal auditor, you have been assigned to perform a brief review of the data processing system at Valley Junior College. The objectives of the review are to:

1. Determine (a) what University DP services are being used by the College and the level of satisfaction with those services, (b) the EDP equipment currently being used at the College's data service center, and (c) which business applications are running at each center.
2. Identify (a) the physical safeguards, systems backup, and other security measures being employed by the College's data service center and (b) areas of weakness in these security measures.
3. Review the College's computer center operating standards and procedures.
4. Render a judgment as to the reliability and effectiveness of the College's EDP-related operations.

Because of time constraints, you are advised that this engagement should be limited to conducting interviews and should not include actual testing or verification of potential control weaknesses. However, when possible, test procedures designed to verify such weaknesses should be noted to facilitate follow-up work scheduled later in the year.

You have conducted a series of interviews. The following material represents some of the information gathered in your interview notes:

Dr. Jay Thomas Walleford is the Vice President of Administration for Valley Junior College. He has full responsibility for all of the College's non-academic affairs. He and the vice president of academic affairs report to the College president. Dr. Walleford reports that all of the College's administrative DP needs are supplied by the University's DP Center (UDPC) and by the College's DP Center (CDPC). CDPC is responsible for managing the College's work funneled through UDPC. The director of CDPC is responsible for all of the College's administrative DP matters.

Dr. Walleford says that the College's DP objective is simply to provide efficient and effective data processing services to the College's administrative management at the lowest possible cost. He recited a history of failures in this regard until the current CDPC director was hired two years ago. Since then, he has been satisfied with the results.

---

*The authors appreciate the assistance of Erwin J. Haltinner in the preparation of these case materials.

Dr. Walleford uses his management staff as a steering committee to establish DP project priorities and review DP problems requiring management attention. The staff consists of the budget director, director of accounting, director of CDPC, registrar, director of physical facilities, director of administrative services, and director of security. Dr. Walleford is pleased with this advisory arrangement and feels there is no need to formalize a DP planning process. He indicates that the group meets monthly and the items discussed are recorded in minutes kept by his secretary. The group has no formal executive authority or written charter.

An examination of Dr. Walleford's steering committee minutes revealed the following:

- The first meeting was held two years ago, and a total of 10 meetings have been conducted since then.
- During the last year, only three meetings were held. The last meeting was held three months ago.
- Except for the first and third meetings, excused absences have kept the group from meeting as a whole.
- The minutes for the fifth meeting are missing.

The only ongoing DP-related problem reported by Dr. Walleford is that the College gets much better service from its in-house DP facility than from UDPC, and thus the College would like to move away from using UDPC. He believes the University board prefers to have the College utilize UDPC as much as possible because it helps the University to justify procurement of new hardware and software.

Dr. Walleford was unable to provide a current organization chart. He indicated that his new secretary is very busy learning her job and has not been able to keep it current.

Juanita Dean is the Manager of CDPC and reports to Dr. Walleford. She has a 15-year background in data processing with progressively increasing responsibilities. She responded to your questions with confidence and authority, and most answers were at the tip of her tongue. In those few cases where she didn't know the answers, she committed to providing a response within a day or two (although the information was never provided, even after one reminder).

Ms. Dean has a staff of six people reporting to her: an operations supervisor, four programmer/analysts, and a part-time student trainee. No job descriptions were available for these positions.

During the interview, Ms. Dean was interrupted by two telephone calls and by a staff programmer, all needing some urgent information concerning computer problems associated with month-end production processing. In one lengthy conversation, the questions centered on problems with a program recently designed and implemented by Ms. Dean.

You were provided with a current CDPC hardware configuration (see Attachment A). It shows a typical ABC System 30 Model 12 shop with two disk drives and one tape drive. The System 30 is used both for in-house processing and as a remote batch job entry (RJE) terminal to UDPC's mainframe computer. The General Ledger System and Student

Attachment A
Valley Junior College's Computer Hardware/Software

System 30 Model 12 (quantity: 1)
512K bytes of RAM memory
64K bytes of ROM memory

Model 30-5 disk storage drive (quantity: 2)
40 megabytes/drive

Model 30-20 tape drive (quantity: 1)
800 bits/inch
10.5 inches/second read/write speed

Model 30-30 line printer (quantity: 1)
300 lines/minute

Model 30-40 video terminal (quantity: 15)

Model 30-50 console terminal (quantity: 1)

RADIX model 2000 modem

Operating System software:
VM multitask DOS Level 3.2

Programming languages:
COBOL
BAL (Basic Assembler Language)
Easywriter (report writer)

Registration System are processed at UDPC. All other applications are run in-house. These applications include payroll, accounts payable, employee time reporting, library circulation, alumni mailing lists, student traffic violations, student transcript system, and a number of minor systems.

You are informed that user requirements for a new Student Registration System (SRS) are nearly completed, with design and programming expected to start within two months. Ms. Dean reports that the system will be implemented on the System 30, but she is worried that the application may overload the computer.

All planning functions are performed by Ms. Dean. She is concerned that she doesn't have enough time to "sell" her planning ideas to her manager because there never seems to be time for such discussion. Dr. Walleford is mostly interested in the status of various DP problems that have been reported by his other managers.

Ms. Dean agrees that there is presently no formal steering committee specifically chartered to address DP policy, planning, and operational issues. Within the constraints of her limited operating budget, she makes technical DP decisions pretty much autonomously. Major hardware acquisitions and major new application development projects are reviewed with Dr. Walleford, who eventually must present them for approval to the University's board of directors.

A discussion of DP operation and development standards indicated that Ms. Dean, after having long been a strong advocate of formally documented standards, was beginning to have second thoughts about whether such manuals would be cost-beneficial. She had produced a "Programming Standards Manual" 18 months ago. You judged the manual to be substantially incomplete and outdated. She stated that it was her intention to update and complete the manual, but that her other responsibilities have delayed completion of the task. (She now works an average of 50 hours per week.) In the absence of a manual, she has an informal understanding with each of the programmer/analysts that standards will be achieved by review of their work as it is completed.

Ms. Dean believes her users are generally satisfied with her performance. Ms. Dean reports that Dr. Walleford has two expectations of CDPC: (1) it should respond to administrative DP needs quickly, accurately, and in a cost-effective manner, and (2) it should move data processing away from UDPC as quickly as possible. Ms. Dean is not sure how to accomplish the latter because all major hardware expenditures must be approved by the University's board of directors. The board's actions of the past suggest that additional processing needs should be satisfied through greater utilization of UDPC. Furthermore, the College president has stated many times that "CDPC's objective should be to utilize the University's data processing center so as to more effectively serve at minimum cost the DP needs of all administrative departments of the College."

CDPC's total annual operating budget (salaries, supplies, terminals, maintenance, etc.) is $450,000, including $50,000 for UDPC services. CDPC typically underspends its budget by about 5 percent. Although the labor budget is typically underspent by about 15 percent, the "headcount" budget is filled. Ms. Dean says that Dr. Walleford "is death on staff expansion."

Ms. Dean teaches a computer fundamentals class three days a week for one hour each day. She doesn't believe her teaching presents any conflict and she quite enjoys it.

All operational and security matters are the responsibility of Harold Pinnegar, Operations Supervisor for CDPC. Ms. Dean is pleased with Mr. Pinnegar's work. Her only concern is that Mr. Pinnegar is often unavailable because he is the instructor for a laboratory session to train computer operators. He spends about 10 hours per week with his lab students operating production work on the System 30. Ms. Dean also wishes that Mr. Pinnegar had an assistant to fill in during times of vacation and illness. Presently, one of the programmer/ analysts must operate the computer when Mr. Pinnegar is absent.

Harold Pinnegar reports directly to Ms. Dean. He has been employed at CDPC for almost four years. He is about 25 years old and determined to make a career of supervising the operations. He boasted that he had been offered several opportunities for promotion to other departments, but declined them because of his love for the computer. In fact, he proudly states that except for a few hours here and there, he hasn't taken any vacation since he began employment at the College. He puts in considerable overtime in order to get all of the work done. He is assisted by three part-time students.

Computing Center hours are 7:00 a.m. to 8:00 p.m. The computer facility is housed in two adjacent rooms — the computer room, containing the computer and its peripherals, and the input/output (I/O) room, containing data entry terminals and an I/O counter, behind which is a safe where disk packs and magnetic data tapes are stored. You noticed that the door to the safe was open.

A bell button at the I/O counter is for users and programmers to signal the operator. The operator must leave the computer room to attend to their needs. The I/O room is otherwise not attended. Two programmers were in the computer room getting information from Printfast when you arrived for your interview. You noticed that the College payroll checks were being printed at the time.

Mr. Pinnegar acknowledged responsibility for all security matters. He carefully described the intrusion alarm connected to the Campus Security office, but stated that the facility did not have any automatic fire detection or suppression equipment. He is certain that all of the staff are well trained in emergency procedures, but there have been no emergency drills in the past two years.

Mr. Pinnegar is very unhappy with the services being provided by UDPC. That system is reported to be down frequently, and turnaround on remote job entry (RJE) jobs is unpredictable — typically four to six hours (occasionally less than two hours and sometimes as many as 24 hours). Users complain because month-end reports are rarely available on schedule.

Mr. Pinnegar has responsibility for maintenance of the operating system software for the System 30. Mostly he implements changes recommended by the vendor, but occasionally he programs small fixes needed to make the system operate better in the college environment. He also cycles backup copies of all system files (libraries, data, etc.) once every two weeks, keeping two generations of backups. He believes backups should be taken more frequently, but can't afford to keep the system down for the two hours it takes because of a slow and somewhat unreliable tape drive. He reports that UDPC automatically cycles four generations of all registration and ledger tapes through a secured vault located in the University's Administration Building. He further reports that UDPC maintains the control of those backup tapes and that he has nothing to do with them. He also informs you that the accounting department maintains control of scratching production ledger tapes.

During your interview, you noticed two hand-held fire extinguishers sitting on the floor behind the printer. You were advised that each programmer has a key to the computer center and can operate the machine at any time, day or night, providing it is not scheduled for production work. This is done to encourage working extra hours when it is convenient for the individual. There is no system usage log, problems log, or a log of preventive maintenance available for review.

Joanne Post also reports to Ms. Dean and is presently functioning as project manager for the new Student Registration System. She enjoys the technical challenge of designing and writing programs and has played an important role in the development of three systems currently in operation at CDPC. Ms. Post expressed some concerns about her job:

- Compensation is not competitive with similar jobs being offered by other companies in the community. At times Ms. Post feels financial pressures, and she has been doing some moonlighting to satisfy her financial commitments.
- The programming staff is too small to adequately support the existing workload — too much crisis pressure.
- Training opportunities are limited because of reported budget constraints. Ms. Post feels she is falling behind because the technology is advancing at such a rapid rate.
- Ms. Post is anxious to get experience on larger, more complex hardware and operating systems. The technology of the System 30 is 10 years old, and the vendor is no longer supporting much of the operating software.

On the positive side, Ms. Post reported:

- She likes the informal college atmosphere that allows her to work flexible hours.
- She appreciates the opportunity to occasionally take classes during the day.
- She likes the freedom of running the computer (hands-on operation).
- She likes working for Ms. Dean, because she is fair and not particularly strict concerning documentation, etc. However, she thinks Ms. Dean may leave the college because of problems associated with the use of UDPC services and the pressure being exerted by Dr. Walleford to justify getting more equipment for the college.

This is Ms. Post's first opportunity to work as a project manager, and she feels the responsibilities often are overwhelming. Concerns she has about the project include:

- Users are unable to reach agreement on several key policy issues that have an impact on system design.
- The System 30 may not be able to handle the additional processing load without a major impact on terminal response time.
- Project schedules are slipping because of constant interruptions that occur as she satisfies other user needs, including computer science students who frequently ask for help with their academic assignments.

While talking to Ms. Post, you make the following observations:

- Several program listings were on her desk that appeared unrelated to college business. A quick glance at the code reveals a reference to ACME Production Scheduling Report.
- Ms. Post received three phone calls requesting help on some programming problems.
- Several notes were taped to the terminal, displaying what appeared to be labor charge codes and file access passwords.
- She received a phone call from her stockbroker.

Mark Q. Goode is employed by UDPC as a technical support analyst. He is responsible for serving the CDPC's needs pertaining to work on the UDPC mainframe computers. He works hard answering operational and technical questions and resolving problems in behalf of CDPC.

He challenges CDPC's claim that UPDC provides poor service, asserting that turnaround is typically one to two hours on RJE jobs that don't require special handling, but he acknowledges that there have been "rare occasions" when turnaround has been as long as 20 hours. He was unable to produce any record of specific complaints from CDPC, nor did he have any record of problems he had resolved for them. Also, there was no log available that recorded turnaround time for CDPC computer jobs.

Mr. Goode reports that UDPC has a mechanism for automatically cycling backup tapes through the University's data storage vault, but it is the user's responsibility to specify backup parameters. CDPC has not made any such specifications and so no registration or ledger tapes are being cycled through the vault.

Mr. Goode further reports that on two occasions in the past 12 months, CDPC has ordered certain payroll tapes to be scratched well ahead of their normal scratch date. He provided a copy of the tape scratch list submitted by CDPC requesting the premature releases.

Mr. Goode doesn't understand why CDPC wants to move in the direction of expanding its own computer facility. He points out that it is in the University's best interest to maximize the utilization of the central facility so as to reduce the unit cost to all University users. Also, Mr. Goode feels that CDPC doesn't have a large enough staff to effectively handle its present processing commitments. He believes that increasing the workload on new, expanded hardware would ultimately have disastrous operational consequences.

Mr. Goode would like to spend more time helping CDPC resolve some of its problems, but his instructions, because of other responsibilities, are to spend approximately one day per week on college matters.

Required:

1. Construct an organization chart that reflects the reporting lines described. Where possible, include the position title and the individual's name.
2. Complete a report fulfilling the first two objectives of your review, as stated at the beginning of the case.
3. List tests you plan to conduct to verify the identified weaknesses.
4. List findings that indicate there may be problems in the following areas:
    a. EDP planning and the setting of project priorities.
    b. Conflict of interest.
    c. Staff morale.
    d. Organization.
    e. Meeting commitments.

Index

Y

Z